M000216949

The Rise of English

The Rise of English

Global Politics and the Power of Language

ROSEMARY SALOMONE

OXFORD
UNIVERSITY PRESS

OXFORD
UNIVERSITY PRESS

Oxford University Press is a department of the University of Oxford. It furthers
the University's objective of excellence in research, scholarship, and education
by publishing worldwide. Oxford is a registered trade mark of Oxford University
Press in the UK and certain other countries.

Published in the United States of America by Oxford University Press
198 Madison Avenue, New York, NY 10016, United States of America.

CIP data is on file at the Library of Congress
ISBN 978–0–19–062561–0

DOI: 10.1093/oso/9780190625610.001.0001

3 5 7 9 8 6 4

Printed by Integrated Books International, United States of America

In memory of my parents

CONTENTS

PART III   DEFYING THE MONOLINGUAL MINDSET

CONCLUSION

PREFACE

The metaphor of a journey is often used to describe the process of researching and writing a book. For me this book has been an especially long and winding expedition, taking me across four continents and through the parallel universe of a global pandemic that only science fiction writers could envision. It began in 2013 with several commentaries that I wrote involving legal disputes in Italy and France over the use of English to teach university courses. I soon realized that unpacking those debates meant delving into the impact of globalization, international education, and the knowledge economy as shaped by neoliberalism and the force of English as the dominant lingua franca. Once I set on that course, the bigger project began to take shape.

Along the way, I encountered the work of activists, political philosophers, jurists, economists, linguists, and literary icons, within and beyond the Western canon, who guided me through conflicts over the power of language in shaping the identity of nations and their people. A visit to Ravenna, Italy, to engage with one hundred *cittadini* (local citizens) reciting verses from Dante Alighieri's *La Divina Commedia* before the master of the vernacular's tomb, followed by a procession through the streets and a live performance of the *Inferno*, made palpable the enduring force of language in defining a community. I also carried with me personal experiences. I grew up in a community where multiple languages were spoken. As a young adult, I worked in the world of language learners—teaching French to elementary school children; developing French-Haitian, Italian, and Spanish bilingual programs across the grades; teaching English to international university students—before turning to the law and entering the legal academy.

My initial plan was to write a book on the value of language in the global economy, examining winners, losers, and resisters on both sides of the Atlantic. The deeper I dug into the research and the more world events evolved, the more I viewed the issues through a wider global lens and the clearer the connections to educational equity, identity, and democratic participation appeared. I also came to understand the role that France historically has played in pushing back on English dominance and Anglo-American influence, and the more recent competition from China in using the "soft power" of language, especially in Africa. Selecting other countries to explore beyond Europe and the United States grew organically from history, politics, and the disputed role that English has played over time in diverse settings.

Searching for distinctly relevant stories, I looked toward French-speaking Rwanda in resolving the genocide and Morocco in navigating its Arab roots, South Africa in its struggle to move beyond apartheid, and India in undoing the caste system against longstanding religious and linguistic conflicts. A court case in the Netherlands, where English has been widely embraced, gave more texture by way of contrast to the French and Italian debates on higher education. From there, the storm of global anxiety over English versus the calm of Anglophone satisfaction quickly took hold. Drawing on a vast store of interdisciplinary research, interviews, court decisions, political commentary, literature, and popular culture from around the globe and in multiple languages, I then faced the task of weaving together all that I had learned into a coherent discussion on English and its kaleidoscopic effects both past and present.

The book began with my sights on Europe and especially on Italy. And so it poignantly ended. In the final year of completing the manuscript, I watched with alarm as the global pandemic took a horrific toll initially on Italy and subsequently on countries, including my own, that I had spent these years closely exploring. Through that time, I touched base with many of my contacts in those settings and shared our common angst and fears. My deepest hope is that by the time the book goes to press, like Dante being led by his guide Virgil up and out of the *Inferno*, we too will have exited the darkness to see all that is beautiful in the heavens and "riveder le stelle" ("once again see the stars").[1]

ACKNOWLEDGMENTS

In the course of researching and writing this book, I came to know dozens of professors, university administrators, lawyers, and advocates—at conferences, in virtual meetings, and through email correspondence—who shared with me their scholarship and their historical understandings and views on debates within their own and related countries. I am especially grateful to Annette de Groot, Hans de Wit, Catherine Baylin Duryea, Mekki Ebdari, Christine Hélot, Kathleen Heugh, Francis Hult, Fabrice Jaumont, Anton Kok, Peter Kraus, Anik Nandi, Timothy Regan, Gregg Roberts, Arundhati Satkalmi, Robert Slater, Margaret Winters, Marie de Briey Wyatt, and Richard Wyatt for generously reading various chapters and for their incisive comments and corrections. My thanks also go to Peter Kwikkers and Gisela Langé who answered endless questions with patience and detail on the Netherlands and Italy, respectively. Video conferencing, email, or telephone correspondence with Rama Agnihotri, Mathilde Anquetil, Alana Bailey, Alessandro Balducci, Presley Bergen, Marina Cavallini, Sherry Spiegel-Coleman, Dan Davidson, Janneke Gerards, Hermann Giliomee, Michele Giovannini, François Grin, Kristina Hultgren, Felix Huygen, Mercy Kannemeyer, Ralph Mociket, Christine Musselin, Daniela Poli, Olivia Ramsey, Danie Rossouw, Emmanuel Saint-Martin, Ad Verbrugge, and Quentin Williams offered additional direction. Frederick Schaffer wisely suggested that I dust off my decades-old student copy of Dante's *Inferno* for clarity and hope. Weekly conversations with Natalie Nicolai throughout the early years of the project provided invaluable insights into French education, history, and contemporary culture while sharpening my French and uplifting my spirits. I am especially grateful to Emilio Matricciani for providing me with a wealth of court documents from the Milan Polytechnic Institute litigation, and to the professors, administrators, and students at the institute, including legal counsel Maria Agostina Cabiddu, who welcomed me into their classrooms and their world.

The arguments advanced here evolved over the course of seven years and several prior publications, portions of which I have incorporated into this work. Chapter 2, "Myth or Reality?" is a significant update and expansion of "Multilingualism and Multiculturalism: Transatlantic Discourse on Language, Identity, and Immigrant Schooling," previously published in *Notre Dame Law Review* 87, no. 5 (2012): 2031–62. Chapter 3, "A High Stakes Movement," and Chapter 4, "Shakespeare in the Crossfire," are revised and updated versions of "The Rise of English: Challenges for English-Medium Instruction and Language Rights," previously published in *Language Problems and Language Planning* 39, no. 3 (2015), 245–68. Symposia presentations at the University of Teramo, the University of Trento, the Université de Montréal, the Université Catholique de l'Oeust, Princeton University, and annual symposia sponsored by the Study Group on Language and the United Nations in New York provided opportunities to gather useful perspectives on the research as it evolved. I thank Humphrey Tonkin and his band of language advocates for welcoming me into the group and sharing their passion for linguistic diversity.

Throughout the writing, I benefited from a succession of dedicated and talented student research assistants from St. John's University School of Law, including Courtney Morgan ('14), Melissa Brown ('16), Marie-Alexis Valente ('16), Mackenzie Brennan ('18), Allison Cabibbo ('19), Mollie Galchus ('19), and Brent Bomkamp ('21). I thank Caroline Fish ('18) who used her semester in The Hague to help move the Netherlands research forward. I especially thank Eva-Maria Ghelardi ('21), whose multilingual skills proved invaluable, and Eric Zang ('21), who never failed at finding just the right data. Both of them diligently and cheerfully plowed through the manuscript text and notes despite all the uncertainty and upheaval of the COVID-19 pandemic beginning in spring 2020. I most especially thank the dean of St. John's University School of Law, Michael Simons, for his generous support through numerous summer research and travel grants and a sabbatical leave. I also thank Associate Dean and Director of the Law Library Courtney Selby and staff, particularly Christopher Anderson and Saadia Iqbal, for repeatedly finding the most obscure historical documents and news reports in multiple languages from the four corners of the world. No words can express my heartfelt thanks to Janet Ruiz-Kroll, who skillfully mastered translation software, however imperfect, providing me with a steady stream of articles and reports in seven languages and helped format the chapters and final manuscript. The depth of the research owes much to her work. My thanks go to Hallie Stebbins, who originally offered me the opportunity to publish the book with Oxford University Press, to my editor Meredith Keffer for steadfastly seeing the project through to completion, to Macey Fairchild and Helen Nicholson who smoothed the way to production, and to my publicist Gretchen Crary for launching the book on to the world with great care and thought. On a personal note, I thank my friends and family members who indulged my distraction and never ceased to ask how the book was coming along.

Most importantly, I owe a deep debt of gratitude to my husband Joseph Viteritti, who read and commented on individual chapters and, most of all, withstood the many evenings, weekends, and summers when I was buried in this project. I likewise owe immeasurable thanks to my son, Andrew Viteritti, who initially planted the seed in my head that there was a book to be written on the rise of English. Over these years, I have benefited greatly from his keen understanding of the world economy and politics and his tirelessly sharing that with me. Finally, I dedicate the book to my parents, Louise Sansone Salomone and Albert Salomone, who each nurtured my love of language.

INTRODUCTION

The English Divide

In 1794, while hiding from the Jacobins during the French Revolution, the Marquis de Condorcet wrote his landmark work, *The Progress of the Human Mind*.[1] Condorcet, an advocate of educational reform and equal rights, believed that the key to social equality was equality in the use and learning of language. Condorcet's concern was that Latin had held a monopoly over claims to truth until vernacular languages made the sciences "more popular" and widely available. If Latin had continued, he said, it "would have divided men into two classes, would have perpetuated in the people prejudices and errors, [and] would have placed an insurmountable impediment to true equality . . . to an equal knowledge of necessary truths."[2] Condorcet's thoughts on language echoed those expressed several centuries earlier by Dante Alighieri, the Italian poet and moral philosopher, whose epic poem, *La Divina Commedia*, set aside the elitism of Latin to create an Italian vernacular more accessible to "the people."[3]

Inasmuch as Condorcet endorsed vernacular languages, he also believed that "politics in the vernacular" was merely a "transitional phase." Universal education ultimately would lay the ground for "cosmopolitan democracy" in a very simplified universal language that all could read, like the language of algebra, with "similar facility" as the language of one's own country. Condorcet obviously underestimated the inability or reluctance that many people have in learning another language. He also could not foresee the nineteenth-century rise of nation-states and the link between language and national identity.[4]

Leap forward to 2001 when an article in *Bloomberg Businessweek* put a twenty-first-century turn on Condorcet's cautionary words. The title of the article, "The Great Divide: In Europe, Speaking the Lingua Franca Separates the Haves and the Have-Nots," is as evocative now as it was in 2001, and as it would have been back in 1794. The accompanying illustration is even more so. It depicts three men in business suits. Two are large, broad-shouldered, and powerful-looking figures, smiling at each other as they forcefully stride ahead apparently on a cloud. One with his arm on the back of the other asks, "Speak English?" The other responds, "Of course!" The third man, a small figure (about a third of their size) is frantically running after them on the ground. He holds an open book in his right hand and clutches another closed book under his left arm. Other books are falling from his grasp. The books have words, pictures, or titles that represent learning English. In the background is a church with a steeple, representing a European town or city. The message is clear. English is the sine qua non of happiness and power ("Of course!"). It gives you entrée to a world of colleagues with a similar state of mind and professional stature. Without it, you're left behind. You're insignificant. You're desperately trying to catch up.

With a string of examples, the article goes on to explain that English had become "firmly entrenched nearly everywhere as the international language of business, finance, and technology." Even more so, it was becoming the "binding agent for Europe." English had already become "Europe's language." It was an "imperative." Though British and American managers working in Europe would be wise to develop bilingual skills, "new forces," including the internet, were "pushing Europe toward a common language." The article warned that while speaking English was bringing Europe together in some ways, it also was dividing the continent into "haves" and "have-nots." Only 29 percent of Europeans were able to carry on a conversation in English.[5] That was two decades ago. By 2012, the last date of an official European language survey, a majority of EU citizens (56 percent) spoke English as a first or second language.[6] Setting aside the loss of first language speakers since the United Kingdom's departure from the European Union, and not considering levels of fluency, the figure on second language speakers especially among young people is presumably higher today but certainly nowhere near universal.

In the intervening years, English has become not just the "language of Europe;" it has become the dominant lingua franca of the world. It is an official language of the United Nations, the World Trade Organization, the International Criminal Court, and NATO. Yet just as in Europe, English divides the world population in complex ways and creates cultural strains across the globe. As we will see, the ongoing impact in any setting has much to do with history, politics, and economics, which shape decisions over language choices and policies, most notably in education from primary school through the university. Those decisions, in turn, determine "opportunities and access" that socially include or exclude certain groups.[7] English governs the books young people read, the films and television programs they watch, the cultural values they absorb, and their career options. As that reality has intensified in recent years, it has spawned loosely connected debates with decidedly common themes that continue to engage scholars, educators, policymakers, and the courts across continents.

In the postcolonial world, despite distinct histories, the debate typically revolves around the place of local and regional languages in the schools, the unequal allocation of English, and overlapping justifications for officially adopting English—from economic mobility in India and Morocco to the added push toward redress and transformation in South Africa and, to some extent, in Rwanda. In Europe, aside from the growing use of English in European Union institutions, it generally centers on educational quality and access in higher education, the burdens on students and faculty, and the preservation of national languages and identity, with an occasional reference to less privileged students, many of whom are immigrants. The Nordic countries and the Netherlands, which have long embraced English, now question whether they have gone too far, especially in higher education. That rethinking affirms concerns within other European countries including France and Italy. France, above all, resolutely strives to preserve its national language and its international status, particularly in Africa, where English is weakening France's grip. China has jumped onto the African bandwagon and into the fray of Anglo-French rivalries, assertively using its language to gain an economic foothold on the continent. At the same time, language advocates in the United States and the United Kingdom argue that the unstoppable spread of English is not a win-win for anglophone countries. It's isolating them in a way that harms their economic and political interests. It's also denying their children essential linguistic skills and intercultural understandings.

Lingua Franca Old and New

In confronting the rise of English it's tempting to compare English to Latin, the most prominent though not the only lingua franca of another era. Certainly Greek, Arabic, and even Phoenician had their day. Whether and when English eventually will meet the fate of Latin in particular is the subject of much speculation. Like Latin as both Condorcet and Dante viewed it, English holds a monopoly on knowledge, especially in the sciences. In some cases, it can be an obstacle to democratic participation, particularly for less privileged classes. Yet beyond those unsettling commonalities, the comparison between the two languages breaks down on a number of counts. Latin did not threaten clearly formed national identities tied to a common national language, neither of which then existed. Spoken languages, though related to Latin in different ways, were also fluid and diverse. Writing in the early 1400s, Dante described in his *De Vulgari Eloquentia* at least fourteen regional Italian vernaculars and perhaps one thousand sub-varieties.[8] And though Latin remained the language of science long after the fall of the Roman Empire in the fifth century, the invention of the printing press in the 1500s made scientific knowledge and literature more widely accessible to the educated classes. At that point, vernacular languages, most prominently French and German, slowly began to replace Latin. English has operated in the reverse, marginalizing those same vernacular languages and overtaking others.

Latin did not have modern technology, and particularly the internet, nor high-speed air travel to more widely spread and solidify its status as a common means of communication. For the Romans to cross over the Alps by foot or by beast was an arduous endeavor, while communicating through live messengers was time consuming beyond current imagination. And so Latin could not encompass the globe and fuel a world economy as English has done. It was rather confined geographically to the Roman Empire, extensive though it was, with Greek dominating its eastern end. Nor did Latin have compulsory education and a system of government schools to calibrate its influence, either promoting or resisting it.

It remains to be seen whether English will be the "last lingua franca," as Nicholas Ostler predicted a decade ago.[9] Even so, it is still not likely to follow the trajectory of Latin into the realm of a "dead" language anytime soon. With mounting urbanization, a growing middle class, and the increase in multinational business, English simply has too much social and economic force behind it to inadvertently lead us back to the Babel of mutually unintelligible languages. Of course, national loyalties will continue to deter countries from adapting English as their "mother tongue" and justifiably so.[10] English may further lose its gloss over time as other languages become globally or regionally more significant. The extent of that loss depends on the vicissitudes of global politics and especially on the direction the United States takes for the short and long term to preserve its dominance and redeem its reputation on the world stage.

All that being said, the term lingua franca itself is not neutral. English is not the "universal" language that Condorcet may have envisioned or an artificial language like Esperanto. Nor is it simply a recent geopolitical phenomenon. It still bears the imprint of its colonial past and its modern-day clout tied to anglophone countries, particularly the United Kingdom and the United States. Its global spread began with the British Empire, which at its height extended over a quarter of the world. English was a powerful sorting mechanism that detached the colonized from their familiar frames of reference. A core strategy of colonialism was to control language, which became a means of establishing "truth," "order," and "reality."[11] Devaluing local languages and knowledge preserved the colonial myth that these languages lacked depth and complexity to function beyond everyday life. The system of government, education, and worldview that English, like other colonial languages, carried left a lasting linguistic and cultural legacy in countries from Asia, to Africa, to the Caribbean, not to forget North America, Australia, and New Zealand. At the point of independence, despite high levels of multilingualism, many of these countries retained English as a national or official language. Accepting the western European notion of one nation, one language, yet politically unable or unwilling to choose among many indigenous languages, the English-speaking elite cast the deciding vote to protect their own status.

The rise of the United States as a world leader in the mid-twentieth century, just when the British Empire was unraveling and Europe was struggling to recover from the ravages of war, gave the global weight of English a new and more expansive life. With the seeds that Britain had sown with its military might, the United States was able to further grow the appeal and importance of English through political, economic, and cultural influence. For many years, multinational corporations and international development organizations helped drive the spread of English in the postcolonial world. The International Monetary Fund, the World Bank, the British Department for International Development, the British Overseas Development Association, the British Council, and the United States Agency for International Development all imposed a pro-English agenda that effectively suppressed native languages and cultures. In different degrees they promoted English through scholarships, training, textbooks, curricular experts, program designers, and research reports. With the rationale of bringing countries into the anglophone arena, the aim was to increase social advancement but also to open trade opportunities for mutual benefit. UNESCO stood alone in steadfastly producing studies and reports to advance mother tongue instruction notably in the early years of schooling.[12] More recently the World Bank and the British Council have come around to recognize that a "second language is learned best when a first language is learned well.[13]

That being said, relying solely on English to the exclusion of indigenous languages has been a dangerous blind spot in the developing world. As a 2018 report revealed, languages have generally low priority in development work—few NGOs have language policies, and they typically lack staff speaking the languages of the communities they serve. The report found, moreover, that the UK Department for International Development (DfID), the government agency leading the United Kingdom's work to end poverty, only accepted funding proposals submitted in English. The inevitable result was that many communities and groups were unable to participate fully in project design and were foreclosed from seeking funding in the first place. Even where they could hire someone to write the application, they could not check the quality of the application or understand the reasons why it might have been rejected.[14]

To fully comprehend the rise of English over the past half century is to recognize it as both the product and the engine of three interrelated forces: *globalization*, basically the flow of people, goods, capital, and services shaped by an integrated world economy and information technology; *internationalization*, that is, policies and programs used in response to globalization; and a *knowledge-based economy*, in which the production and use of knowledge (rather than goods or services) are primary and in which language and languages have become "strategic economic assets" in themselves.[15] Tying these forces together are market-driven *neoliberal principles* promoting individual competition and outputs at the expense of equalizing opportunities through government intervention. Though the terms themselves are somewhat ambiguous and intellectually overworked, the trends they describe have had profound consequences for language and education.

Each of these factors has generated scholarship and commentary, mostly critical and far too vast for this discussion.[16] Suffice it to say that the backlash against globalization and its homogenizing effects on language and culture, its negative impact on domestic industries and jobs, and its role in heightening economic inequalities have been credited with a rise in populist nationalism that works against international mobility and academic cooperation directly related to English as a lingua franca. Meanwhile, neoliberalism is critiqued for having distorted the values underlying education for democratic citizenship and for human flourishing. It specifically has fostered the false belief that one's ancestral identity and home language impede personal advancement and should be set aside in favor of a more economically valuable and "neutral" language like English.[17]

In recent years, the demands of the knowledge-based economy along with political unrest, economic turmoil, and advances in technology have triggered an unprecedented migration worldwide. Though the effects on the nation-state have not been as fatal as predicted, together these forces have blurred national borders, allegiances, and ideas of citizenship, transforming the social construction of language into a less fixed idea. Non-dominant language speakers—whether regional, immigrant, or indigenous—have further weakened the link between language and nationalism with increased calls for legal recognition. Weaving through these developments is the seemingly unstoppable force of English, which complicates even well-intentioned attempts to establish workable policy solutions within and across countries. These factors overall not only highlight the stresses of linguistic pluralism; they also focus attention on the intrinsic and extrinsic value of language, tied to education, for individuals and for communities.

Dominance and Appeal

English is no longer solely a language for ethnic or national identification as languages are conventionally considered. For better or for worse, it is an economic skill, a marketable commodity, and a form of cultural capital. English is the most marketable language in today's globalized economy. It is more sought-after than any conventional commodity traded in the market, pervading the entire range of social and business relations in which it is used and discussed.[18] It implicates accent, register, and levels of native fluency, which all carry economic value as markers of social class and educational background. It is the language of global communication, both driving the knowledge economy and gaining from it. It is the language in which the Brazilians speak to the Dutch and the Japanese speak to the Italians. There are now more nonnative speakers of English in the world than native speakers. Of the 1.5 billion (20 percent) of the earth's population of 7.7 billion who speak English, fewer than 400 million (less than 25 percent) use it as their first language. As English progressively morphs by locality and function into diverse "World Englishes" (e.g., Singlish in Singapore) or Business English and myriad other hybrid and fluid varieties, it is argued that anglophone countries, and particularly the United States and the United Kingdom, no longer "own" English, as traditionally thought. And so they don't have the right to determine the standards for what is authentic or acceptable. English now belongs to the world.

While English, like other colonial languages, initially spread by "conquest, conversion, and commerce," a fourth process—"collusion"—has added greater momentum. The world is chasing after English for the opportunities it presumably offers.[19] Everywhere you turn, from the boulevards of major cities to the narrow streets of country towns, English language schools dot the landscape. The value of English on the global market is tied to its social appeal. Over the past half century, English has promoted what Joseph Nye coined America's "soft power" in shaping preferences and values to reinforce the country's economic and political stature as a world leader. Much of that attraction is related to American popular culture as idealized in film, TV, music, and fashion and a consumerist lifestyle, initially filtered through the lens of Hollywood and now readily accessible through social media and the internet. English has come to represent modernity, cosmopolitanism, and technological progress, especially in the imaginations of young people no matter where they live or what language they commonly speak.[20] Bucking attempts to turn back the clock on globalization, the first global generation shaped by the internet has come of age, and it passionately embraces English and the status and mobility it carries. Young people across the world are avid consumers of everything "American." Even when their English is halting at best, they pepper their conversations with English words to look "cool."

The popular appeal of English crosses generational, geographic, and class bounds. Walk through airports and down streets in any major city in the world, from Reykjavik to Rio de Janeiro, from Manila to Mexico City, and you will be bombarded with advertisements and signage in English. Take a taxi in Tokyo and it's likely to bear an "English Certified Driver" sticker. Visit a café-bar in any remote Italian hill town and you'll hear "American" pop music streaming into the piazza. Even some Paris theaters have acceded to showing English language films in the original with French subtitles. Bjork, an Icelander, sings in English. Korean mothers move their children to anglophone countries to learn in English. Dutch universities teach in it. ASEAN countries collaborate in it. Political activists tweet in it.

During the uprisings in North Africa in 2011, while protestors used French and Arabic to engage the local community, as one activist noted, they switched to English because "that's where we go when we want to influence the world."[21] In 2021, in the wake of the military coup in Myanmar, English dominated slogans, placards, and social media as young anti-coup protesters tried to gain the support of the international community. Messages like "Justice for Myanmar" and "We want democracy" were pervasive, even carved into rows of watermelons by chefs, despite exceedingly low levels of English among the overall population.[22] One can only wonder if the vaccine against COVID-19 could have been developed with such unprecedented speed without a common language for global collaboration. The first vaccine rolled out in Europe and North America was the product of partnering between the US pharmaceutical company Pfizer and the German biotech company BioNTech with two German scientists, the offspring of Turkish immigrants to Germany, playing a key role in development. This was globalization at its finest.

Around the globe, English makes headlines in the press, is the topic of talk show discussions, and is the preferred language of academic conferences and scholarly journals. Much of scientific knowledge is now disseminated in English in both print and digital form. More people of all ages now study English than any other language. In a growing number of countries it's compulsory, in some cases beginning in primary school. English accounts for over 60 percent of internet content.[23] Individuals who have access to both English and high-quality internet service enjoy entrée to a wide source of information and communicate with a sizeable public. Accessing news from anglophone and other countries via the internet and social media, they more clearly understand the competing interests and values that drive those countries. The more they utilize the language online, the more proficient they become. The more English savvy they become, the more they can move beyond their immediate surroundings and tap into cultural and economic capital worldwide. At the same time, as a new generation of world leaders become more skilled in English, they directly reach out to a larger political audience beyond their own constituents.

The global elite of all ages has almost a "mystical reverence" for the *Economist* and the *Financial Times*. French president Emmanuel Macron and his strategic use of English is a prime example of this "aspirational class" of cosmopolitan citizens.[24] Though Macron crusades to raise the international profile of French, he also recognizes the pragmatic importance of English to the French economy. While his official talks in other countries are often in French, he relies on the global value of English to communicate informally with world leaders and to establish his leadership on a world stage as he did at the World Economic Forum Meeting in Davos, Switzerland, in January 2018.

Though languages like French, Chinese, and Spanish carry weight in certain markets, and German is said to be gaining ground in Europe, English is becoming sufficiently unhinged from its national moorings, in perception if not totally in fact, to remain a vital force in driving global communication and the global economy. As the British Council noted back in 2013, English provides a "strong competitive advantage in culture, diplomacy, commerce, media, academia, and IT. It means a place at the heart of the global network."[25] That is still the case despite the Brexit debacle and four turbulent years of Trumpism having dimmed the "Anglo-American" glow. The long-term effects of those turns remain to be seen especially given a new administration in Washington. The United States is undeniably the biggest winner, but it is not the sole beneficiary. Other anglophone countries and their speakers have gained from the "English effect." The unspoken question is, "At what price?"

Can English Do It All?

Notwithstanding this worldwide flux, native English speakers tend to take the "rise of English" not just as a positive change but as an organic evolution. They can travel internationally for work or leisure with greater ease. Their political leaders can directly engage with foreign counterparts without interpreters. Business interests can make their way in the global economy without the burden of translation. Researchers can collaborate with foreign colleagues and present their findings in foreign venues. Students can enroll in European study-abroad and graduate programs offered totally in English and at a much lower cost than in the United States. From this vantage point, it is easy for Americans, along with the British, Canadians, Australians, and others, to conclude that other languages are not worth the effort. If the world is speaking English, then why bother learning other languages? There is a sense of English "exceptionalism" or privilege, an implicit belief that English is just part and parcel of globalization and progress. Any downside is simply "not their problem." Yet it is their problem. The dominance of English is fueling a debate on language with implications that impact anglophones and not just others.

Hidden beneath all the self-serving satisfaction lies the question of whether English can do it all. Or is there still a need, especially for anglophones but also for others, to speak other languages? Back in 2012, former Harvard University president and US secretary of the treasury Lawrence Summers attempted to tackle that question in an op-ed in the *New York Times*. Though not as definitively negative as some commentators understood, Summers questioned whether the "substantial investment" needed to learn to speak another language was "universally worthwhile" given rapidly developing machine translation and the "fragmentation of languages" worldwide. Over time, he said, mastering a language would become "less essential in doing business in Asia, treating patients in Africa or helping resolve conflicts in the Middle East."[26]

Subsequent years have proven Summers wrong. Perhaps he misunderstood the facts or misread the tea leaves, or both. Notwithstanding its wide cultural appeal and practical utility, English cannot do it all, nor is it steaming ahead unchallenged. While English has continued to be the favored lingua franca in many parts of the world, other languages like Chinese and Spanish are now giving English competition in different degrees. Six years prior to the Summers op-ed, David Graddol's much-cited analysis of global language trends was a wake-up call to anglophones that English, long considered the primary language for business, was perhaps not as universal or as sufficient as conventionally believed. Graddol warned that the gap in language skills was putting monoglot anglophones at a competitive disadvantage in the global job market when compared to their multilingual counterparts in other countries.[27]

That was a decade and a half ago. As the economy has become increasingly globalized, employers across sectors, from multinational corporations to small and medium-sized enterprises (SMEs) and government agencies, now look for workers with multiple language skills. With rising immigration and one in five people in the United States speaking a language other than English at home, the 2020 COVID-19 pandemic was a reality check on the critical need for multilingual workers, especially in the health fields, to communicate essential information on a human level with diverse language communities. The health crisis also revealed the limitations of machine translation and the false sense of comfort with English monolingualism that technology has created.

Most native English speakers are content to remain monolingual, unaware of what linguist Geoffrey Pullum calls "a social millstone" hung around their neck.[28] This indifference, or resistance, to learning other languages is a recurrent topic of finger-pointing in the anglophone press and handwringing among globally aware policymakers. From the pages of the *Guardian* to the *Atlantic*, commentators decry the "foreign language deficit" and the failure of countries to prepare young people for the global economy. Data from the United States is especially revealing. Though US students are enrolling in study-abroad programs in record numbers, most of them opt to take classes and even degree programs offered in English. Enrollment in language courses, with few exceptions, is steadily declining. Whether the reported uptick in online language learning during the 2020 "lockdown" remains after the pandemic is yet to be determined.

Meanwhile, the "Everyone speaks English" argument rings hollow on the facts. Only one-quarter of the world's population has some minimal degree of competence in English. Even those who claim to have conversational skills in English often don't operate at a very high level of proficiency. And so monolingual anglophones cannot effectively communicate with three-quarters of the world, nor can they tap into knowledge created in those languages. Relying solely on English as the language of global communication, not only do they limit their career and business opportunities, but they also risk the world talking over their heads as they become more politically and culturally isolated. Print and broadcast media as well as the global blogosphere still "speak in many voices and worldviews," and they are "powerful shapers of ideas and opinions."[29]

English ranks behind Mandarin Chinese and Spanish, and only marginally surpasses Hindi, in the number of speakers for whom the language is the first one learned, though with its overall total of 1.13 billion speakers worldwide, English ranks slightly above the 1.11 billion speakers of Mandarin Chinese.[30] Inasmuch as English now dominates the internet at 1.19 billion users, Chinese is not that far behind at 888 million, while a substantial amount of internet communication takes place in Spanish, with 363 million users, and Arabic, with 237 million.[31] Given the economic and political importance of those languages, the monolingual anglophone world is closed out of a vast amount of information critical to its interests. Though apps like Apple's Gentle Reader make newspapers and magazines from thirty major languages instantly available in English on computers and iPhones, much nuance gets lost in translation. The end product is only an imperfect facsimile of what speakers of the language are absorbing. As anglophones continue to rely on English as the language of global communication, they run the risk that others, and especially those looking to "upend democratic values," understand them far better than they understand the world.[32] English-speaking countries, the United States and the United Kingdom above all, unwittingly are becoming victims of their own "soft power."

The very way we characterize languages and their speakers, moreover, defies the complex diversity of today's linguistic landscape.[33] We typically talk in terms of the "native speaker" (versus the nonnative speaker), "first language" (versus second or third language), and "mother tongue" and "heritage language" (versus national language). The term mother tongue itself essentializes multilingualism and ignores vernacular languages as lived in many settings. With rising mobility for economic and other reasons, multilingual families are becoming commonplace. Some children speak to one parent in one language and to the other parent in another. In countries where many languages coexist, as in India and South Africa, children learn both a home language and a generally used indigenous or regional language. Which language is the "mother tongue"? These concepts mistakenly suggest that monolingualism is the norm and other practices are the exception.[34]

Despite the common belief among many anglophones, most of the world is multilingual or at least bilingual, with English often in the mix. The increasing use of multiple languages within EU countries, partly as the result of migration, and the vast store of intersecting languages in postcolonial countries in Asia and Africa lend credence to that assertion. In some parts of the world, rather than the monolingual model of using one language for all purposes, we find a multilingual model where speakers switch between and among languages depending on the context.[35] Many people in these countries and elsewhere are adding English to their diverse linguistic repertoire and to that of their children. To what degree that decision is a matter of choice, chance, or expediency varies widely within and between countries. The same can be said for anglophone countries, where the study of languages is selectively and unequally available depending on race, ethnicity, and social class. A form of "elite multilingualism" with English as a key component is spreading worldwide.

The overarching problem is twofold. Especially in the postcolonial world, what is considered a high-status form of English is often available only to those who are already more economically and socially advantaged, while the less privileged are denied a set of skills that carry significant personal and economic benefits. At the same time, the United States and the United Kingdom have fostered a similar socioeconomic divide in language study with inadequately recognized implications for upward mobility and economic security .

Why Education?

Nowhere have these concerns over English been more vigorously debated than in the arena of education, where national identity and educational access and quality have become increasingly salient and controversial. That fact is not surprising. Government-operated schools promote national stability by instilling in future citizens a shared sense of values. A common language is considered key to this common project.[36] It is generally believed that speaking and writing the same language help create social and political cohesion. Schools are the primary mechanism for making that goal a reality. This thinking goes back to the nineteenth century with the dawn of the nation-state, when the ideology of a national language, aided by print technology, took hold in western Europe. By mastering the dominant language, speakers demonstrated that they were willing to be part of an "imagined community" bound by a shared history and culture tied to a shared language. A common language was intended to make the inhabitants of a country feel like they were "members of the same nation."[37] In reality, many Europeans had to relinquish their own regional languages and identities in the process.

As already noted, western European powers carried that ideology to the lands they conquered. By will or by force, most countries embraced "one nation, one language" as a core principle. Whether the people actually benefited remains contested. The extent to which the colonizers succeeded in planting their language on colonized soil varied widely depending on how they selectively educated their subjects and on the multiplicity of languages they found. Yet unlike western European nations, these countries typically had no single ethnic-linguistic identity for building a national identity or a system of schooling. In Africa, in particular, that situation was partly the result of the way European powers had carved up the continent. Just as many countries were gaining their independence in the 1960s, English and its role in shaping a global economy appeared on the scene and further complicated language policies in the process of decolonization. The policies adopted mainly reflected the agendas of those in power, often motivated by an overriding interest in attracting foreign investment and loans to secure their political position rather than concerns for educational quality or workability.[38]

Six decades later, the idea that English can be a partner with and not a substitute for indigenous languages is only slowly gaining traction.[39] The foregone choice in many countries to use a colonial language as the medium of instruction has led to wavering education policies, gross inequities, and widespread language loss throughout the developing world. In various contexts and points in time, English has led to acrimonious debates over language and identity in newly independent colonies. English continues to push aside national and other languages in the name of economic progress. At the heart of the language problem lies the inequitable access to linguistic capital that English and other dominant languages carry and the parallel cost to smaller, less prestigious languages.[40]

At the same time, English has helped in reframing school knowledge to conform to the world of work, setting aside humanistic ideals like the pursuit of knowledge for its own sake. These changes align with the neoliberal drift of education and the emphasis on accountability and measurable outputs in standardized test scores geared toward a global economy. The importance that teachers, parents, policymakers, and the media place on results from the Programme for International Student Assessment (PISA), the standardized survey of performance among fifteen-year-olds, is clear evidence of that trend. Administered by the Organisation for Economic Co-operation and Development (OECD) every three years, the program aims to give countries comparative data on their education systems. With eighty-eight countries/regions participating in PISA 2022,

..ie OECD has promoted a worldwide "performance culture and an economic rationale" focusing on employability in the global labor market.[41]

This rescaling of education, tied to global capitalism and competition, reaches beyond primary and secondary schooling. It has equally captured higher education. As seen particularly in the European context, though gaining global ascendency, the market model has fostered an obsession with assessment, accountability, and university rankings that drive programmatic decisions, student recruitment, and faculty hiring and promotion. Much of the activity is focused on "internationalization," in which English plays a significant, and even a decisive, part. In the postcolonial world, the debate over the "commodity paradigm" has become further tied up in calls for "decolonizing" education and particularly freeing higher education from colonial, meaning European, ways of knowing and knowledge production. As Cameroon scholar and author Achille Mbembe critically tells us, "Who gets to be taught, what, where and how and for what purpose is an aspect of global trading in knowledge, in intellectual assets and cultural capital."[42]

That critique leads us back to the role of English throughout the cycle of education. State-run schools and universities are conventionally thought to be a force of liberation and social leveling. Yet they can merely reinforce class differences depending on how language, including English, is used from primary schooling upward. The elite, educated in well-resourced private English-medium schools, reap the consequent benefits of higher education, rewarding careers, and social status. Even beyond schooling, young people from economically secure and well-educated families are exposed to English through books, newspapers, films, computers, and travel abroad, all of which foster academic achievement and the ability to move freely in the global economy. Meanwhile the less advantaged are fed, at most, a diet of low-quality English instruction in state-run schools due in part to the uneven English proficiency of teachers.

English represents what the sociologist Pierre Bourdieu termed "cultural capital," using the concept of the "market" to symbolize the social context of language. For Bourdieu, language was not just a means of communication or knowledge sharing; it was an instrument of power. Along with the ability to use language, individuals acquire attitudes, knowledge, and ways of viewing the world through family and community socialization. These attributes, he maintained, bear cognitive and attitudinal consequences that benefit the most privileged. Looked at in reverse, as Bourdieu brought to light, the "combined effect of low cultural capital (including language) and the associated low propensity to increase it through educational investment condemns the least favoured classes to the negative sanctions of the scholastic market, i.e., exclusion or early self-exclusion induced by lack of success."[43]

But there is another side to this story. Taken to the extreme, the emphasis on English as representing "high cultural capital" can also prove counterproductive, most notably in countries where economic inequality is deeply entrenched. The global trend in introducing English at increasingly earlier ages inevitably leaves behind children in the poorest countries, including billions in Africa and South Asia.[44] Many parents push their children into English-medium schools or classes from the beginning to prepare them for university programs in English and for the global economy even where there is no English support in the home and community. They ignore or simply do not comprehend the conventional wisdom that first and second languages are mutually supportive and that children need to learn and initially develop literacy in a language that they understand. Once children have developed a certain proficiency threshold in their first language to succeed academically, they can then transfer those skills to the second language.[45]

Charting the Course

The costs and benefits of English as the dominant lingua franca have generated a deepening dialogue among linguists, economists, political scientists, and political philosophers. Some have taken a *human-rights-based* approach, whether group or individual, challenging the havoc of "linguistic hegemony" that English has inflicted around the globe, or in the least upholding the rights of minority language speakers. Others accept English as an inevitable and useful tool for international and intercultural communication, technological advancement, and empowerment. Still others have explored the effects on particular indices of social or economic progress, while others have looked through the lens of *linguistic justice*, striving to distribute the benefits and burdens of English in a fair, efficient, and democratic way. Yet to summarily conclude that English is universally bad, neutral, or good for the world is to sell short the nuanced effects of English and its global dominance on educational quality and access, identity, and democracy in diverse geopolitical settings—from former European colonies, whether English- or French-speaking, to Europe itself, and even to the United States. Searching for evidence of who's winning, who's losing, and who's pushing back on the rise of English demands looking at English and other languages in all their complexities—as conveyors of knowledge, as identity markers, as instruments of culture, as commodities, as tools of democracy, as human achievement.[46]

That global journey through time, place, and memory is at the heart of this book. Two interrelated precepts, guided by equality of opportunity and democratic participation, chart the course. The first is that politics, or the "interplay"

:tween conflicting interests and values in a given political setting, creates alliances and actions that shape and reshape language policies and languages over time.[47] The second is that government policies that create or sustain unequal relationships among languages carry serious economic, political, and social consequences for speakers of those languages and for the countries those speakers call home.[48] Proceeding in three parts, the book unpacks current debates over internationalization and English-medium instruction (EMI) in Europe, medium of instruction (MOI) in postcolonial countries, and the foreign or world language deficit in the United States as they confront both the rise of English and the forces pushing back on that rise.

The discussion starts in Europe, where the European Union has used multilingualism directly to promote integration and economic mobility and indirectly to temper the spread of English, and where France, Italy, and the Netherlands have faced heated conflicts over using English in university courses and programs. It then moves on to the postcolonial world beginning with an intense look at France and a brief look at China as they compete to override English and maintain or gain influence in Africa. From there it shifts to former French-speaking colonies, particularly Rwanda and Morocco, and their measured moves toward English set against distinct political and linguistic backdrops. It next turns to South Africa and India, two multilingual and relatively young constitutional democracies with low academic achievement linked to race and class, where disputes over English and education reveal longstanding grievances and the inequities of politically motivated language policies. It then crosses to the United States to deconstruct the monolingual mindset—the belief that monolingualism is the norm—and examine how the stars are aligning in unexpected ways to slowly turn that mindset around, with French influence once again in the forefront.[49] The discussion concludes with a look at popular market-driven arguments embraced by educators, parents, and policymakers supporting the advantages of both English and multilingualism.

Laying bare the "rise of English" across the arc of history and global politics, the book hopes to lay the foundation for a via media through which both anglophones and speakers of small and large languages can successfully navigate the intersecting paths of globalization, internationalization, and a knowledge-based economy in a world that is becoming paradoxically smaller and more linguistically diverse as it converges toward sameness.

PART I

MULTILINGUAL EUROPE

Myth or Reality?

In the popular film *L'Auberge espagnole*, the French director Cédric Klapisch presents the ups and downs of a young Parisian, Xavier, an economics student who goes to Barcelona through Erasmus, the EU-funded study-abroad program. His goal is to learn Spanish for the prospects of a job with the French Finance Ministry but also to escape his overbearing parents. He finds himself surrounded by Catalan while living in an apartment with a multinational group of six other Erasmus students. Like Xavier, they also speak English. Later writing on his computer from his bedroom back in Paris, Xavier describes the apartment as an *auberge espagnole*, a takeoff on nineteenth-century Spanish hostels where all nationalities brought their own food and ate together. As he explains the situation, "You get out of it what you put in." Told in flashbacks, the film uses the plot device of the Erasmus experience to explore the narrator's personal transformation and self-discovery as he accomplishes what the program promised; he broadens his horizons, and he does, in fact, learn Spanish. As the story progresses, we see Xavier and his housemates finding common ground as Europeans, acclimating to the rich diversity of Barcelona, and preserving and even defending their national identities. We also see them navigating their various languages and cultures while primarily using English as their lingua franca.

In the end, Xavier in voiceover tells us that he has decided to pursue his childhood dream of becoming a writer, hence this recount of his experiences in Barcelona. He describes himself as a composite of all the individuals he met over the year, as the image of each character flashes on the screen. "I'm French, Danish, English, Spanish. I'm not one but all. I'm like Europe. I'm all that. I'm a real mess," he says.[1] With that closing message, the film becomes more than just a "coming of age" or "study-abroad" story or a sentimental ode to the Erasmus program, which it clearly is. Set amidst the cultural and linguistic tensions of Barcelona, admittedly somewhat cliché-driven, it's also a metaphor for the diverse reality of the European project, for the people and countries that comprise it, and for the idea of holding on to singular identities while imagining and embracing a shared European identity.

In Britain, the film was titled *Pot Luck*, presenting a skeptical view of the European Union as an uncertain venture. Since 2002 when the film appeared, that venture has become more uncertain as the spread of English has interposed a mix of possibilities and challenges both within EU institutions and especially throughout the cycle of education. The United Kingdom's departure from the European Union has brought that mix to the fore as policymakers, scholars, and commentators weigh the benefits and costs of yielding to a single language outside the orbit of continental Europe. Meanwhile, national governments and academic institutions face competing demands both to prioritize English for its market value and to preserve and promote dominant European languages.

Throughout this time, the continent has been buffeted by intersecting forces and fallouts that have contributed, in one way or another, to both the Brexit debacle and the pressure from English on schools and universities. Globalization and its backlash, soaring youth unemployment, mass migration, resurgent nationalism, and fears of Islamic terrorism have all raised concerns for the future of European national languages and identity. As a generation of young Europeans from the continent's east and south have found job opportunities in countries to the north and west, they have added yet another language and culture to their stock and another dimension to the diversity landscape. Meanwhile, schools face an unprecedented influx of refugee and migrant students from beyond Europe. Some of those students speak rudimentary English, which they may have learned in the camps. All have an immediate need to learn the national language and a long-term need to learn English for accessing higher education and competing in the global economy. At the same time, many of them lead virtual translational lives, preserving aspects of their native language and culture through the internet and social media, which distinguishes them from migrants of the past.

Against this shifting landscape, the European Union has made repeated calls for multilingualism to promote European unification and job mobility, and less obviously as a bulwark against English marginalizing national languages. Some of those same European languages initially laid the groundwork for defining the nation-state on the principle of one nation, one language. That concept now weighs on the English question and on multilingualism both in Europe and in former European colonies, decades after colonialism formally ended. With those major linguistic roads leading back to Europe, it is only fitting to begin examining the "rise of English" on European ground.

Unity in Diversity

Speaking at a conference on the state of the European Union in Florence, Italy, in May 2017, Jean-Claude Juncker, then president of the European Commission, drew laughter and applause when he opened his remarks in English, only to note that he would continue in French. So why the switch? "Because slowly but surely," Juncker explained, "English is losing importance in Europe." He then added, "I would like [the French people] to understand what I'm saying about Europe and about nations."

Though the European Union has twenty-four official languages, in recent years it has increasingly conducted most of its business in English, much to French dismay. The multilingual Juncker usually addressed international gatherings in English. Yet he was looking ahead to the French presidential election the following Sunday, where the centrist and EU-friendly Emmanuel Macron was vying against his far-right anti-EU opponent Marine Le Pen. Juncker, who subsequently became an uncompromising Brexit negotiator, went on to discuss Britain's withdrawal from the European Union, which he called "a tragedy." The video of Juncker's remarks went viral across the European media. Back in Brussels, some thought the move "ill advised" as Juncker was in the midst of heated Brexit talks with British prime minister Theresa May. What the press called "Mr. Juncker's zinger" did not ease tensions with the British.[2] While some Brits sharply disagreed, it sent a decided signal that with the major anglophone country soon out of the picture, language changes might be afoot within the European Union.[3]

But Juncker may have been talking too soon. Barely a month later, less than two hours after the United States had announced that it would withdraw from the Paris climate accord, another video attracted even wider attention. With the French and EU flags in the background, newly elected French president Emmanuel Macron, speaking from the Élysée Palace in an unprecedented address partly in English, gave a rebuke that resounded worldwide. Looking directly into the camera, Macron "riffed" on the US president Donald Trump's signature slogan, "Make America Great Again," inviting "all scientists, engineers, entrepreneurs, responsible citizens who were disappointed by the decision of the United States" to join the French in working on "concrete solutions for our climate, our environment, to 'Make our planet great again.' "[4]

Within minutes, the phrase appeared on Twitter as a graphic accompanied by a renewed invitation to US scientists to "come to France and work with us together" (@Emmanuel Macron, June 1, 2017, 6:21 p.m.). This simple tweet generated over two hundred thousand retweets. In the following days, more than a million viewers had tapped into the video of the speech. Macron had hit a global nerve, in a way that was both clever and bold. It was a far cry from a decade earlier when French president Jacques Chirac, "profoundly shocked," walked out of an EU summit after the French head of the EU's business lobby addressed the meeting in English, "the language of business."[5]

Juncker and Macron were each using language to make a political point that implicated one or the other of the two leading anglophone world leaders. Yet the contrast between the two in style and subtext was striking. While the elder statesman's remarks were ostensibly a cri de coeur to the French people to save the European Union as they were about to go to the polls, his calculated use of French was also a wake-up call to Great Britain that multilingual Europe might no longer be tightly tied to English. And while the young diplomatic novice Macron seemingly took the reins of Western leadership on climate research, his use of English was not simply a reproach of the US president, using Trump's own words, for a decision that world leaders denounced as misguided. The combination of form and substance more deeply conveyed both an image of Macron as a global leader using the lingua franca of global power and an image of France as a country looking to the future and not only to the past. The French press, generally conflicted over English, praised Macron for expressing himself in "la langue de Shakespeare" (the language of Shakespeare), calling it "un coup de maître" (a master stroke).[6] Macron's strategic use of English would intermittently raise political hackles throughout his presidency. Even Juncker, a year later, stated that he believed English would continue to be the primary working language within the European Union.[7]

Both men obviously could use their skills in English and French to their political advantage. But what of the European politician whose English skills are less than proficient? A glimpse into the essential role that English plays in European diplomacy and business came to light in December 2018 when Switzerland's newly appointed economics minister, Guy Parmelin, found himself the object of much derision in the international press and on social media for his weak English skills. A cartoon in the Swiss German-language daily *Neue Zürcher Zeitung Sonntag* showed Parmelin, sitting under a Christmas tree, visibly upset that the instructions for his new post were in English. Given that his portfolio included research and education, some Swiss notables questioned whether he could negotiate a trade deal with China, engage in informal discussions within the European Union, or communicate in scientific meetings. As the *New York Times* reported, "Among world leaders, a command of English is often taken for granted, even when translators are present." The overall message was clear. In the diplomatic world, English is essential. Without it, you suffer a "handicap."[8] These scenarios speak to the changing shape of world politics and the power of social media. But the contrast and the subtext of each more pointedly speak to the ambiguous, and even oppositionist, yet critical place of English within a

Europe reeling from nationalist threats while priding itself on its commitment to linguistic diversity as a "normative component" of the European project.[9]

Pervasive fears over immigration's effects on national identity, political and economic pressure to establish an integrated European identity, and regional demands for linguistic and cultural recognition all bear heavily on both EU and national policies and practices. The lasting effects of colonialism, war-related shifts in national boundaries, the exodus from rural to urban areas, and the effects of mass migration further complicate matters.[10] With exceptions like Belgium, Finland, and Switzerland, European countries typically draw their national identity from one official language, an outgrowth of nation-state building in the early modern period. At that time, centralizing powers used a number of strategies, including a unitary system of laws, taxing, military, and language, to define and secure their borders. Individuals educated in private or state-run schools or drafted into the state's army learned the national language. Compulsory schooling laws eventually hastened the process.[11]

Multilingualism nevertheless has remained a fact of life for many Europeans. Regional languages like Breton in northwestern France, and postwar border languages like German in the South Tyrol of Italy and Italian in northern Croatia are examples. This complex linguistic terrain has posed challenges for the EU motto "Unity in diversity." The EU founders understood those challenges and addressed them from the beginning through a vision of protecting linguistic diversity among its member states while promoting individual multilingualism. Subsequent waves of immigration have added new hurdles to be overcome in maintaining the delicate balance implicit in that vision.

Linguistic rights vary widely across European countries. In recent decades, language advocates have looked toward supranational institutions, drawing on post–World War II concerns for human rights to fight for language and cultural recognition. In the aftermath of wartime atrocities, the idea of individual rights was more politically and philosophically acceptable than group claims to collective identity, which presumably would have threatened social and political cohesion.[12] Group rights hold an appeal, especially for linguistic minorities bound by a common cultural identity. On the other hand, they arguably run counter to liberal notions of individual choice and autonomy and fail to recognize that identities and languages change over time, including what individuals consider as their mother tongue.[13]

Setting aside these conceptual disagreements, even when language rights are recognized in international agreements, whether explicitly stated or implicitly tied to the right to freedom of expression or privacy or nondiscrimination, most often they apply to national minorities as opposed to migrants, though activists argue that non-nationals should enjoy the same fundamental human rights.[14] They typically are framed in a negative sense as *toleration*, that is, the right to preserve and use the language in the private sphere like associations and private schools. Meanwhile, they sidestep positive rights to state *promotion* or *accommodation* in the public domain with added deference for state discretion regarding what is "reasonable" or "appropriate" or "practical" in a given context. They also tend to be non-binding, without legal sanctions or a judicial remedy.[15] All these factors directly impact the rights of speakers of "small" or minority languages, with direct consequences for education.

Within the European Union, the wider discourse and institutional pronouncements on language have gradually taken a distinct turn, though, with similar space for wide discretion and digression and without any suggestion of legally enforceable rights. Except for intermittent bows to regional, national, and more recently immigrant languages, the European Commission, the European Parliament, the European Council, and the Organization for Security and Cooperation in Europe (OSCE) have largely framed the language narrative in terms of multilingualism in the collective interest of European identity and economic prosperity rather than the interests of individual speakers or the groups to which they belong.

EU officials, in resolutions, speeches, and formal communications, have likewise promoted multilingualism within EU institutions in the name of democracy, equality, and transparency. Yet here again, the reality falls short of the rhetoric.[16] The focus, in fact, has been on dominant national languages in descending order—English as lingua franca, national or official state languages of European countries, regional minority languages, and immigrant languages.[17] The result is a "segmented diversity," in which the EU's commitment to linguistic diversity benefits primarily the official languages of member states, with English at the top of the list.[18] EU language policies and practices reflect this linguistic hierarchy across the board.

In 1958, the six founding members of the European Economic Community— France, Germany, Italy, Luxembourg, the Netherlands, and Belgium—initially identified Dutch, French, German, and Italian as the official working languages.[19] With the language question directly tied to national identity, multilingualism including the languages of all members was the path of least resistance. Again, the EU now recognizes twenty-four official languages among its twenty-seven members. Any change in the EU institutions' language regime is subject to a unanimous vote of the Council of Ministers.[20] Spread throughout the member states are sixty regional or minority languages and more than 175 migrant languages. To effectively handle the twenty-four languages, EU institutions employ about forty-three hundred translators and eight hundred interpreters on the permanent staff in addition to a core of freelancers.[21]

All EU regulations and other generally applicable documents are translated into all the official languages, which are also used to communicate with the member states. Debates within the European Parliament and formal proceedings within the European Council can use any official language. Interpretation is provided in all of them. Budget cuts and cost efficiency have rationalized an increased reliance on English. Yet the EU Charter of Fundamental Rights, put into full legal force in 2009 with the Treaty of Lisbon, prohibits discrimination on the basis of language.[22] The question arises as to whether democracy, transparency, and especially equality should give way to practicality and cost-efficiency.

In theory, all the official languages are of equal value. In 2012, the commission expressly dismissed the idea of a single language for the European Union, calling it "undemocratic." The argument was that it would "prevent most people in the EU from understanding what is being done in their name and reduce accountability."[23] Yet in practice, the "working" languages are typically English and French, and to a far lesser extent German, though there are still calls to recognize German's equal status. The language in which documents are originally written has dramatically shifted from French to English over the years, especially within the commission. On that count, between 1999 and 2016, French dropped from 35 percent to 3.7 percent while, English rose from 48 percent to 82.5 percent.[24] By 2020, of the two million pages of commission documents translated each year, upward of 84 percent were initially produced in English.[25] A blog post in the French daily *Liberation* in 2012 said it all. Aimed at initial press releases in English, it opened with the iconic wartime poster of America's Uncle Sam pointing his index finger straight ahead with the play on the original call: "I WANT YOU To Speak English or Get Out!" For the author, the renowned French political journalist Jean Quatremer, it was a question of "democratic legitimacy."[26]

The commission is not alone in favoring English. The European Parliament has used English as the unofficial language, granting it the most airtime in parliamentary debates. Officials at the European Central Bank also communicate in English. Only in the European Court of Justice, located in Strasbourg, is the working language solely French, including deliberations, pleadings, and opinions, though proceedings are conducted in the official language chosen by the applicant. Outside of formal meetings, and especially in informal discussions, English and to a decreasing extent French prevail throughout EU institutions. The Parliament, commission, and council now all communicate on Twitter and Facebook in English. This progressive shift belies the Parliament's 2019 "briefing" titled *Multilingualism: The Language of the European Union*. The paper laid out the three goals of the EU's multilingualism policy: to encourage language learning and promote linguistic diversity; to give citizens access to EU legislation, procedures, and information in their own languages; and to promote a multilingual economy through a multilingual mobile workforce.[27]

As one parliamentary adviser summed it up, "English is Europe's common language in much the same way Latin once was."[28] With English as the foreign language most commonly studied throughout the member states, Europeans themselves reinforce the notion of English as the European lingua franca. While EU policy promotes linguistic diversity and rejects the idea of a lingua franca, political actors who cannot communicate in one of the working languages, and especially in English, operate at a serious disadvantage with lower visibility.

The fact that English has become so dominant within the EU has been a particularly sensitive issue for France. The French language was the common tongue of the Enlightenment and distinguished by its "universality," a belief immortalized in 1784 in a prize-winning essay by the Royalist writer Antoine Rivarol.[29] Like many of his contemporaries, Rivarol overlooked the fact that only the European bourgeoisie spoke French at that time, while the majority of French people spoke only their regional language. French continued as the language of international diplomacy until 1919, when the United States emerged as a world leader and, along with the United Kingdom, insisted that the Treaty of Versailles was drawn up in English as well as in French. In the end, the United States did not ratify the treaty. French dominated in the early days of what ultimately became the European Union. Yet any attempts on the part of France to make French the sole official and working language proved unsuccessful. France tried to stop English at the pass by twice vetoing Britain's entry into the European Economic Community (EEC).

In 1971, as Britain was negotiating membership in the EEC, the president of France, Georges Pompidou, told the Belgian newspaper *Le Soir*, "If with the arrival of the English, French no longer were the first working language in the Community . . . then Europe would never be totally European." English, he said, "is no longer the language solely of England. English is above all and in the eyes of the world the language of America; and Europe will not be Europe unless it distinguishes itself . . . from America."[30] The *Guardian* too quickly dismissed as "over-apprehensive" Pompidou's fears that English would become the Common Market's "common tongue" and that French would "wither away" to a "diplomatic whisper."[31] Even more can be read into the president's statement. Pompidou made a direct reference to American English and implicitly to American political influence, which he obviously saw as the greater threat to French and to France itself. Britain joined the EEC in 1973.

Institutional change came slowly. French continued to rule over communication among the member states and over the European Commission's daily press conferences for over twenty years. But as time wore on and English gained global force, the need for France to affirmatively bolster the French language became more pressing. In 1992, during the process of ratifying the Maastricht Treaty creating the European Union, members of the French Parliament expressed deep concerns that European integration would serve as the Trojan horse car-. rying English into the European Union and its institutions and threaten French national identity. French leaders needed to shore up their legal arsenal against "la langue de Shakespeare."[32] And so they carved French into the country's constitution as "la langue de la République."[33] In 1994, France adopted the Loi Toubon (Toubon Law), which made the use of French mandatory in certain public domains, including the media, commercial contracts, advertisements, the sale of goods and services, and official documents.[34] For French culture minister Jacques Toubon, sponsor of the legislation, "French prestige was at stake in a world hungering for an alternative to the stifling argot of Anglo-Americanisms."[35]

In the following years, France has continued to fight back against English as countries with "smaller" languages, like Sweden and the Netherlands, and newer members from eastern Europe, have more readily accepted English as the unofficial lingua franca for formal and informal EU business. In 2007, Nicole Fontaine, a former president of the European Parliament, led a failed campaign to make French the EU's standard legal language. The United Kingdom's Brexit vote in 2016 reinvigorated France's resolve for French to dominate within EU institutions.[36] In 2018, French president Emmanuelle Macron declared that English was "too dominant in Brussels," especially with Britain soon to exit the European Union. While promoting multilingualism, he pledged to step up efforts to "teach French to European officials" and promote a wider use of French abroad.[37] When the EU Commission's seven-year budget plan in 2018 revealed that "translation and interpretation services would remain unaffected," French politicians were outraged.[38] France's EU ambassador stormed out of a diplomatic meeting when the council proposed using only English in the meetings of a new working group on the EU's long-term budget.[39] In October 2019, a collective of associations with a shared interest in French urged Macron to vote against efforts to maintain the status of English within EU institutions, which would demand a unanimous vote in the European Council.[40]

Germany initially accepted French, and later English and French, as the working languages when the country became reunified in 1990. Eventually Germany and France signed an agreement to support each other whenever the working status of their respective languages appeared to be overlooked.[41] Germany, nonetheless, has been hesitant to assertively promote the German language against the rising role of English. With the departure of the United Kingdom and the loss of sixty million native English speakers, only two EU member states, the Republic of Ireland and Malta, still commonly use English as a co-official language. They respectively count Irish Gaelic and Maltese as their EU official languages. About 95 percent of the population of Malta speaks Maltese. Barely five percent of the population of Ireland is fluent in Irish Gaelic, which was inconsequential as long as Britain remained in the EU. That being said, the EU official website now expressly states that the EU has "24 official languages" and that "even after the withdrawal of the United Kingdom from the EU, English remains one of the official languages of Ireland and Malta."[42]

The triumph of English became strikingly apparent in September 2020 when the newly appointed European Commission president, Ursula von der Leyen, gave her State of the Union address. Reporting to the European Parliament, she overwhelmingly spoke in English with just a smattering of German and French. Yet fewer than twenty of the 705 members of Parliament spoke English as their mother tongue. All plenary sessions of Parliament, in fact, are interpreted into and out of the twenty-four languages, so no member needs to speak any language other than the mother tongue. As the press concluded, "The flight to English has been transformed by Brexit into a value-free, pragmatic choice."[43] Concerns over von der Leyen's attachment to English went to more than the State of the Union address. Within days of the speech, the Association of European Journalists sent a letter to von der Leyen and to council president Charles Michel charging that the executive was using too much English in press communications contrary, to the commission's three-working-language policy. The practice was giving the anglophone press a "competitive advantage," the letter stated, "and hampering the ability of European institutions to fight against 'disinformation.' "[44]

Though English will remain an official EU language, at least for now, Brexit is still a clear inflection point on the question of a common language within EU institutions. EU leaders have a number of options in moving forward on that count. They can do nothing and theoretically maintain the "multilingual" status quo as English unofficially glides into dominant use. They can choose English or another language (presumably French) as the official common language for conducting EU business. They can shift toward a modified multilingual model of perhaps English, French, and German. Or they can pragmatically adopt English as an official working language for "communication" both internally and internationally, while using and promoting the remaining twenty-three EU official languages as languages for "identification," thereby reinforcing the cultural identity of member states and the EU's strive toward diversity in multilingualism.[45]

In the long run, a common language might be more efficient in reducing the cost of interpreters while requiring nonnative speakers to learn only one or several additional languages. Yet choosing English, in particular, would still raise concerns over costs and benefits, parity of esteem, fairness, and equal opportunity.[46] In the short run, it would impose higher institutional and individual costs until the EU population at large gained the necessary English skills. The same goes for French, though a highly improbable choice. Native speakers undeniably enjoy an advantage that cannot be discounted.[47] An all-English regime arguably would prove undemocratic, as the European Commission has warned. It has been estimated that, depending on the indicator used, relying solely on English would exclude up to four out of five adult Europeans from understanding political and legal EU documents. Adding French and German would still "disenfranchise" as many as half of EU residents. The effects would be "regressive." The hardest impact would fall on individuals with the least education and the lowest income. Even chief executives, senior officials, and legislators would experience a loss in comprehension as compared with native speakers.[48] In an English-dominant regime, moreover, other languages and especially French and German could suffer a considerable loss. Not only might they become less attractive to study; they also could lose their cultural and political status and their influence as a form of global "soft power." Finally and fundamentally, to view English in purely instrumentalist terms, thereby separating the communication and identification functions of language, ignores the historical and political associations that languages carry and their impact on individual and collective identities.[49]

Given the weight of these competing interests and the political stakes involved, the EU's English language dilemma is likely to remain simply a matter of academic debate for some time. The failure to resolve or even address it systematically, however, will not be just a matter of inertia. As political sociology tells us, non-decision-making is also a form of decision-making. What the political scientist Peter Kraus suggested over a decade ago holds true today. Failing to settle the language question, or even debate it, suggests that the linguistic market will resolve it.[50] It remains to be seen whether France's plans to conduct all business in French when it takes over the rotating EU Council presidency in 2022 will seriously diminish the use of English beyond the council.

Ultimately the issue goes to the heart of the EU's political identity, which remains a "third rail" for discussion, especially since the failed attempt to adopt a European constitution in 2005. It can reasonably be said that Europe has met greater success as a market than it has as a polity.[51] Even putting politics aside, at least for the immediate future, EU institutional leaders have more pressing matters to address internally and externally, not the least of which are a post-pandemic weakened economy, mounting nationalism, random terrorist attacks, China's growing economic footprint, Russia's persistent power grabs, and threats of nuclear armament. All that leaves little institutional time and political bandwidth for tackling the highly contentious, though exceedingly important, question of language.

Panacea or Scourge?

The language used for doing business within EU institutions is part of a larger debate over the dominant role of English in all facets of European public and private life—from diplomacy to business, education, academic publishing, science, air travel, tourism, and the media. Europeans from all these sectors regularly speak English, typically with other nonnative speakers. That debate, initially driven by linguists and sociologists, has progressively engaged political scientists, economists, and political philosophers in a broader interdisciplinary discussion whose relevance reaches beyond Europe. At times the competing arguments move in extremes. Is English a "global communication panacea," or is it a "killer language?" Is it a barrier or a bridge to economic and social mobility? Is it neither, or both, or perhaps somewhere in between? Is it essential to creating and expanding a "transnational demos" for the powerful and the powerless to use to communicate and cooperate across borders? Some of the most positive claims seem overly optimistic and even myopic, while some of the most negative ones seem overstated and even outdated. Others are more measured. They vary in their philosophical grounding from liberal individualism, in its differing conceptions of language, to communitarianism. Yet all of them raise important questions for the future of European and national identity and for English as a common means of communication in Europe and beyond.

On the pro-English side, supporters maintain that equal access to English, the language that most Europeans "already perceive, study and use as a lingua franca," allows citizens to interact with each other across socioeconomic and national boundaries and to "push their old enmities further to the past."[52] For academics in poorer countries, they claim, publishing and teaching in English offer job mobility and career advancement.[53] Even within scientific research, there are those who believe that the benefits outweigh the burdens. A lingua franca, whether English or another common language, they argue, advances and spreads knowledge as scholars collaborate and share information across geographic borders.[54] In a more measured way, other commentators accept the dominance of English but also recognize the risk of "language death" when an entire worldview is lost, and so they promote preserving linguistic diversity for the good of society.[55] Some view English pragmatically as an inevitable trend that is irrational to resist as a "vehicular" language in creating a democratic space for pan European communication. Though multilingualism for all would be ideal, they say, in reality it is a privilege available only to the most highly educated, while English is a language of common citizenship for the majority of Europeans who can express themselves in the language.[56]

On the pro-multilingualism side, supporters look beyond assumptions of language as communication and underscore particular economic and political consequences. Some warn that as English spreads around the globe, it will become a new "baseline," removing any competitive advantage that native speakers now hold.[57] Multilingualism will be the norm. From an economic perspective, while multilingualism is not necessarily as cost-efficient as adopting English globally, it distributes the costs more equitably, it is said.[58] Some consider the role that languages play in the EU's political culture. They maintain that the polarization of English skills between the elites, including EU officials, and others limits democratic participation and skews it on a national level, feeding into rising Euro-skepticism and populist movements promoting the national language.[59] Still others, building on the Italian philosopher Antonio Gramsci's theory of "hegemony," consider the English question in light of its symbolic effects and inherent connection to power relationships and global politics.[60] The most vocal and prolific proponent of this view is Robert Phillipson, who has resolutely and stridently rejected global English as a form of Anglo-Saxon "linguistic imperialism," the product of nineteenth-century British colonialist expansion and twentieth-century US economic and military dominance.[61] This argument carries more than a kernel of truth. Yet starting from such an extreme vantage point, as a matter of policy, sheds more heat than light on how best to balance the equities given the dominant role that English now plays in global communication.

Political philosophers have moved the debate over English onto a normative plane. None has attracted more attention than the Belgian political philosopher and economist Philippe Van Parijs, a pragmatic yet controversial voice in the pro-English camp. His landmark work on linguistic justice has generated a wealth of critical but productive discussion. As a concept, linguistic justice looks toward a language policy that is democratic, efficient, and fair.[62] In the context of a broad theory that includes preserving individual languages and national identity, Van Parijs examines what has become "asymmetric bilingualism" worldwide through the lens of "cooperative justice." An ardent proponent of a unilingual English approach, Van Parijs maintains that a common global language promotes democracy and global justice by permitting everyone, regardless of their economic or social status, to communicate directly, in person or via the internet, without the burden or cost of interpretation and translation. The widespread use of English, he says, makes it the most reasonable candidate to fill that position. Yet he also recognizes that expanding English creates deep inequities between native speakers and "new speakers" and gives English-speaking countries a competitive advantage. Native competence is a valuable asset, he argues, which allows native speakers to get a "free ride" while English-speaking countries profit from offering English language courses and translation services.

To compensate for these inequities, Van Parijs considers a number of ancillary policies. For the free-rider problem, among other possibilities he proposes a linguistic tax on anglophone countries to help defray the costs of giving nonnative speakers the opportunity to learn English. As for inequality of opportunity, he suggests that governments "accelerate" the "dissemination of the lingua franca beyond the elite of each country." In addition to offering English in the school curriculum, he argues for a ban on dubbing movies based on evidence that countries where foreign films are subtitled and not dubbed have higher levels of English proficiency.[63] He does not suggest that English replace regional and national languages but that they function side by side, serving different purposes depending on context.

In the least, his proposals on schooling and dubbing are reasonable, assuming the legitimacy of a lingua franca in general and English in particular, which is a large assumption. His other proposals have run aground for lacking practical application. Without negating the "free rider" problem, for example, given the range of language proficiency among speakers, it would be difficult to measure the native academic advantage within any given country.[64] The advantage itself, moreover, can easily overlook the fact that native English speakers who have not mastered other languages, as is often the case, are also less able to negotiate meaning in multilingual settings than many nonnative speakers. The real difference may lie between those who possess the "flexibility" to engage language as "action" and those who are "imprisoned" in their own language."[65] Overall his theory, grounded in territoriality, has met criticism for favoring national minorities, failing to address linguistic identity and the symbolic aspects of language beyond the communicative, and ignoring the complexities of language use among multilingual individuals or the many varieties that English now encompasses.[66]

These varied theories and arguments and how they have intersected with other critiques in multiple scholarly venues go far deeper than this brief overview intends. Yet as scholars across the disciplines debate the costs and benefits of a lingua franca in general and English in particular, their insights seldom engage the public whose lives are intimately affected. Nor have they succeeded in moving decision-makers toward establishing coherent policies. Meanwhile, questions of opportunity or access, along with language preservation and national identity, continue to shape the type of political community the European Union is advancing toward or regressing from.

Whose English?

Moving from the normative to the descriptive, one contested matter is whether Brexit will change the nature of the English spoken among Europeans. People working in the EU institutions are said to speak what is called "Euro English," a fluid blend of jargon, British English, and the English spoken by nonnative speakers with grammatical and lexical borrowings from the other twenty-three official languages. English words like "information" become pluralized as in French "les informations." The word "what," as in "What do you call it?," becomes "how," as in "How do you call it?" similar to Italian, French, and German. Even EU staff members who are native English speakers slip into the pattern of using terms and phrases that would be considered incorrect in British English.[67] Some commentators predict that without frequent interactions with native English speakers, especially within EU institutions, these slight irregularities will morph into a distinct version of Euro English similar to the nativized post-colonial varieties of "World Englishes" in countries like India, Singapore, and Nigeria.[68] That assumes that those nativized varieties are "fixed" and not subject to regional differences, while officials within those countries refuse to recognize their legitimacy in the first place.[69] Besides, there are no "British clutches" from which European language practices need to be "liberated" to force a similar political countermovement.[70]

The idea of a distinct form of Euro English also assumes that Europeans on the continent are leaning toward more unity. Rising populist and related nationalist sentiments, together with the Brexit vote and the pushback against globalization, all seem to refute that assumption.[71] The 2020 COVID-19 pandemic with the resulting border closings, the EU Commission's slow response to the health crisis, and the initial reluctance of some EU member states to aid hard-hit countries like Italy or to vote unconditionally for a stimulus package as the pandemic continued to surge, made those cracks in the EU armor all the more visible. Without a clear cultural identity with shared characteristics, as seen in varied ways in former colonial countries after independence, widespread use of a distinct Euro English is unlikely to happen.[72]

Even if a spoken form does emerge to some degree, in all probability Europeans will continue to use standard British or American English in written communication, especially in formal settings like business, diplomacy, and scholarship. An alternative view foresees an "English within multilingualism" or English as a multilingual franca (EMF), in which Europeans will use their full multilingual repertoire (national, regional, immigrant languages) fluidly, depending on the context and the discussion partner without deferring to the norms of British native speakers and without necessarily using English at all.[73] In the post-Brexit world, it is argued, multilingualism will be the norm, reversing the "free riding" of anglophones, who will either bear the cost of learning other languages or be left behind.[74] Even so, any potential effect on the written word is highly speculative.

Whether looking at languages within EU institutions or among the wider population, many Europeans, their universities, and their school systems are investing time and effort in varying degrees to teaching and learning English. As we will take up later, English-language instruction particularly in university graduate programs is becoming increasingly dominant in some European countries. That is clearly the case in the Nordic countries and in the Netherlands. Across Europe, close to 100 percent of students study English at some point in their education, many of them as their primary foreign language. And so standard

English is not likely to be relinquished as a primary working language within EU institutions in favor of French or German or another variety of English.

Setting aside EU policy, Europeans and the European Union do business with the rest of the world, including regional associations in Asia and Africa that use English as their official common language. Even among EU countries, it seems implausible that a Romanian business manager will start conversing with or emailing a Greek counterpart in any language but English. At least for now, though individuals might informally speak to each other of necessity in non-standard English, the most valued common means of global communication is a form of English that is not simply mutually intelligible but one in which the written and spoken forms correspond with each other. That correspondence is especially critical in conducting official business. And while aspects of the national language might creep into the English used in individual member states or among individual speakers, for educational purposes British or American English will prevail, with perhaps slight variations, for the very reason that teaching materials are more readily available in those varieties.[75]

Regardless of whether or how the EU institutions resolve the language question post-Brexit, one can reasonably speculate that Europeans in general will fall more deeply under the influence of American English, which pervades film and TV, and especially American spelling, which dominates the internet and social media. Yet several demographic factors also weigh in favor of British English remaining on the continent. An increasing number of British nationals, looking for the career flexibility that EU residency offers, are resettling in countries like the Netherlands, where English is widely used. Between the 2016 Brexit referendum and early 2021, migration from the United Kingdom to the Netherlands increased by around 40 percent. In 2019 alone, over six thousand British citizens took that course.[76] There also are large numbers of British nationals, many of them retirees, who have second homes in France, Spain, and Italy, while others regularly vacation in those countries. Of course, that is not to deny that forces within the European Union, particularly France, will try mightily to push English to the margins.

The Council of Europe

Before continuing with the European Union, it would be remiss to overlook the Council of Europe (CoE) and the role it has played in marking the politics of language in Europe and establishing what it calls *plurilingualism* and *plurilingual competence* as shared goals. The CoE is not a supranational institution like the European Union where state members relinquish part of their sovereignty. It is, rather, an intergovernmental institution and the only such organization in

Europe that affirmatively promotes cooperation on the language of schooling among its members.[77] The CoE was founded in 1949, in the aftermath of World War II, to protect human rights and the rule of law and to promote democracy. Based in Strasbourg, it now encompasses forty-seven member states, including the twenty-seven members of the European Union, all of which have signed the European Convention on Human Rights.[78] The European Court of Human Rights hears claims brought by citizens of member states for violations of rights protected under the convention.

Since 1954, with the initial signing of the European Cultural Convention, member states have worked toward developing a framework for cooperation on language and education. Over seven decades, the CoE has contributed notably to language teaching, learning, and assessment. Its recommendations and practical instruments, while technically guidance documents and not legally binding, are considered authoritative. Implicit in the CoE's commitment to plurilingualism is an understanding that Europe's citizens need more than a lingua franca (English) to communicate with each other. While English has a place in the language curriculum, the CoE has warned, it is "far from sufficient to meet society's language needs."[79]

In contrast to the EU's apparent wavering, the CoE has more consistently addressed education policies as a matter of language rights. The CoE's overall focus on human rights naturally lends itself to that position. Unlike the EU's use of the term *multilingualism* directed at individual speakers, the CoE has drawn a distinction between *plurilingual individuals,* who are able to communicate in more than one language irrespective of their proficiency level, and *multilingual regions or societies,* where two or more languages are used, what the European Commission would consider *linguistic diversity.*[80] (This distinction seems to be unique to Europe. Elsewhere, the term *multilingualism* is used more widely in both the individual and societal sense.) In contrast to the European Union, the CoE places people rather than the languages they speak at the center of language policies. For the CoE, plurilingualism is fundamental in maintaining linguistic diversity and democratic citizenship in Europe as compared to the EU's "mother tongue plus two" project, which instrumentalizes languages in the name of job mobility and economic development.[81] Plurilingual competence not only "ensures communication" but "above all, results in respect for each language."[82] And unlike the EU's multilingualism project, which has focused primarily on the national languages of Europe's old nation-states, the CoE has affirmatively promoted the rights of regional and minority language speakers through the European Charter for Regional or Minority Languages adopted in 1992.

That is not to ignore that article 1 of the charter expressly excludes the "languages of migrants." Nor does the CoE have any clear enforcement powers against noncomplying member states.[83] Only twenty-five of the forty-seven member states have ratified the charter. Neither France nor Italy is among them. Among EU member states, creeping re-nationalization of decision making, especially since the eastern enlargement, has weakened the charter's ability to serve as a counterweight to the power and political proclivities of national governments and the entrenched hierarchies of "majorities" and "minorities" within their borders.[84]

The CoE's most notable achievement is the Common European Framework of Reference for Languages (CEFR), or Le Cadre européen commun de référence pour les langues (CECR).[85] The CEFR grew out of recognition in the 1980s that Europe was experiencing a new migration not only from southern Europe but also from other parts of the world, that language was key to mutual understanding and social cohesion, and that contact among European citizens could not occur solely through the use of a "certain lingua franca" (English). A series of thirty-one seminars between 1990 and 1996 led initially to Recommendation no. R (96) 6, which emphasizes intercultural communication and plurilingualism, and ultimately to the CEFR.[86]

Published in 2001 in English and French and officially adopted by the European Union the following year, the CEFR has become a guidepost for language teaching and learning within and beyond Europe. At its core are the Common Reference Levels, a six-point scale of detailed levels of competence (A1, A2, B1, B2, C1, C2) further subdivided and defined through "can-do" descriptors unrelated to any specific language. A companion volume, published in 2018, added new descriptors for mediation and plurilingual/pluricultural competence.[87] To its credit, the CEFR departs from the conventional measure based on high-level competence comparable to that of a native speaker and in one language (typically English). It rather innovatively provides a uniform standard for assessing real language skills and partial competencies as they progressively develop across each person's total linguistic repertoire.[88] In other words, it validates communication in different languages at different levels of ability for the purpose of communicating across cultures.

One criticism, nonetheless, is its "monolingual bias." In evaluating each language separately, the CEFR fails to imagine bi/plurilingual speakers and ignores their specific competencies. The European Language Portfolio, which is linked to the CEFR, comes closer on that point.[89] This is a personal document for recording an individual's language learning and cultural experiences, whether gained inside or outside of school. The idea is that every competence, however small (the basic A1 level), has social value and should be recognized. The problem is that the portfolio is rarely used in schools and not well understood by teachers.[90]

Much more can be said about the Council of Europe's initiatives and resolutions promoting linguistic and cultural rights and democratic citizenship. Yet keeping to the task at hand, it is within EU directives, resolutions, and reports that we find the most repeated references to English vis-à-vis Europe's other languages as they relate to the multilingualism agenda.

Mother Tongue Plus Two

The gap between the rhetoric and the reality of multilingualism in Europe spreads far wider than the EU institutions themselves. It permeates EU policy and national practices, especially in education. Part of the problem lies in institutional limits on the EU's policymaking powers. Under the principle of subsidiarity, the European Union has no jurisdiction over language or education. As noted, the EU multilingualism strategy does not grant or preserve legally enforceable language rights but merely encourages language learning. At most, it can prod member states in the direction of multilingualism through recommendations and the "soft power" of funding. The Erasmus+ program's study-abroad and "Strategic Partnership" initiatives are good examples. And while EU resolutions and directives have been sympathetic toward regional languages, they have been less so toward immigrant languages, which inevitably affects students belonging to those communities.

Beginning with the 1992 Maastricht Treaty creating the European Union, language learning and multilingualism have formed an official cornerstone of EU education policy. Article 126 (currently Article 165), however, left it to the member states to determine the "cultural and linguistic diversity" of their "education systems."[91] With this green light, individual countries have marched to the tune of English, some more decisively and extensively than others, despite repeated EU directives and warnings. Over the years, in document after document, EU institutions have endorsed learning two languages plus the mother tongue beginning in primary school. The focus has oscillated over time between preserving Europe's diverse languages in the name of cultural identity, intercultural dialogue, and social cohesion on the one hand and promoting language learning for its competitive advantage, economic benefits, and employment opportunities on the other. The Declaration on European Identity, signed by the nine members of the European Economic Community in 1973, focused on identity and cohesion.[92] Early EU pronouncements set the stage for developing language skills to promote European integration and build knowledge-based economies.

A seminal 1995 European Commission Paper, "Teaching and Learning," declared, "Multilingualism is part and parcel of both European identity/citizenship and the learning society." It called for all EU citizens to learn at least two "community" languages in addition to their mother tongue in order to benefit personally and professionally from the "border-free Single Market."[93] The European Union's Lisbon Strategy, implemented in spring 2000, more broadly confronted the challenges that globalization and the knowledge-driven economy, together with demography and the EU's enlarged membership, were then presenting. The goal was to make Europe "the most competitive and dynamic knowledge-based economy in the world, capable of sustainable economic growth with more and better jobs and greater social cohesion."[94] Since that time, EU pronouncements on language have gradually shifted toward economic concerns.[95] That shift is not surprising. As critics of EU language policy have argued, without regulation and protection, the economic inevitably triumphs over the cultural.[96]

The Council of the European Union, meeting in Barcelona in 2002, took a significant turn. Back in 1995, the council had passed a resolution, similar to the commission's paper that year, calling for students to learn two or more languages "of the Union" in addition to their mother tongue.[97] With a more inclusive view, the council in 2002 urged that the "supply of languages should be as diversified as possible, including those of neighboring countries and/or regions." Following up on the council's resolution, the European Commission adopted an action plan expressly "promoting language learning and linguistic diversity."[98] That set the call for "mother tongue plus two," which gradually shifted to "multilingualism" as the driving mantra of EU language policy. Either way, that mantra is intricately tied to the political and economic interests of an integrated Europe now set against rising nationalism, fears of Islamic fundamentalism, and massive migration from the global east and south. To what extent the economic fallout from the 2020 COVID-19 pandemic will further unravel that unified vision and fray what is already a fragile common European "project," only time will tell.

The English Undercurrent

The rising dominance of English has been a constant undercurrent in European discourse on multilingualism. Threaded throughout subsequent EU documents are direct references to English and its ascendancy as a lingua franca. In 2005, coincident with the EOP statement, the EU Commission issued its first report, "Communication on Multilingualism," and formed a High Level Group on Multilingualism made up of eleven language experts from across Europe.[99] The group's 2007 report underscored the career and cognitive benefits of multilingualism. For "a variety of reasons," it explained, many policy makers and other decision makers, including parents, believed that all their children needed was to acquire "a good command of English." In a strong counterargument, beginning with "sustainable" job mobility, the group laid out the case for every citizen to learn "practical skills" in at least two languages in addition to one's first language.[100]

From 2005 through 2007, the European Union more expressly tied multilingualism to intercultural understanding. During that period, multilingualism was added to the portfolio of the Commissioner on Education and Culture. In 2007, the EU Commission took several decisive steps as the discourse shifted more decidedly to economic arguments with implicit emphasis on the dominant languages of Europe.[101] It created a separate commission portfolio for multilingualism.[102] It also established a Business Forum on Multilingualism to explore ways to "open doors to new markets and new business opportunities" and reverse the trend toward business becoming "uniform" and "monolingual" (English-dominated).[103] Driving that decision were findings that a lack of language skills was causing thousands of European companies to lose business and miss out on contracts.[104] At the same time, it ended partial funding for the European Bureau for Lesser Used Languages, a nongovernmental organization established in 1982 with close ties to the European Parliament and the Council of Europe. The bureau's mission was to promote regional and minority languages.

With the global economy crashing in 2008 and staggering numbers of southern and eastern Europeans moving north and west, job mobility among citizens of the member states became a core feature of the multilingualism project. By then, nearly all EU member states had become multilingual and multicultural, which demanded national, regional, and local policies for promoting communication across languages and cultures. Yet despite those pressing demands and a multitude of programs supporting the EU's multilingualism agenda, English continued to become the most favored language among students and parents and businesses across Europe.

A 2008 commission report prepared by a group of ten intellectuals was a measured wake-up call to native English speakers and presumably to the United Kingdom. More fundamentally, it was a direct appeal for multilingualism and linguistic diversity. Headed by the Lebanese-born French author and 1993 Prix Goncourt winner Amin Maalouf, the group urged all Europeans to choose a personal adoptive language different from their language of identity and from the language of international communication (English). The idea was to overcome the "rivalry" that was weakening other languages and harming English and its speakers. Permitting a single language to dominate the "work of European institutions," the report warned, would prove "damaging" economically and strategically to Europe and to its citizens and run counter to the entire "ethos" of the European project.[105] At the same time, straightjacketing English into an "instrument of global communication" could potentially "impoverish" the language and put those who spoke only English at a competitive disadvantage in the job market.[106] The immediate response to the report was mixed. In a debate held on the eve of the report's launch, commentators including then–EU commissioner for multilingualism Leonard Orban sparred over whether multilingualism was a "bridge or a barrier" to intercultural dialogue within the EU.[107]

Following up on the "Maalouf Report," Orban officially positioned multilingualism in the "genetic code of the European project," as "not just the ethos, but [a] concept and philosophy as well." Though English had "its own important place," Orban explained, it was not "unique." While becoming ever more "present" within the EU, it also was progressively becoming less "sufficient."[108] Orban's words were rhetorically compelling, yet in practice they ultimately proved empty. Between 2007 and 2013, partially under Orban's watch, the lion's share of the commission's €50 million (US$59 million) yearly budget to promote language learning went toward learning English.[109]

Almost simultaneous to the "Maalouf Report," as the 2008 economic crisis was about to grip Europe and propel job mobility to the top of the multilingual agenda, the European Commission issued a "communication" that set the tone and direction for future pronouncements. In a section headed "Languages and Competitiveness," the commission noted that despite the leading role of English as the global language of business, "other languages" would provide EU companies with a "competitive edge" and permit them to "conquer new markets."[110] The force of that argument resonated in the following years as the European economy stagnated and youth unemployment, especially in the south, continued to mount.

The year 2010 was significant in showing signs that EU interest in multilingualism was faltering, or at least shifting. February saw the demise of the separate multilingualism portfolio. Responsibilities moved to an EU commissioner for education, culture, multilingualism, and youth. Orban's immediate successor, Androulla Vassiliou, expressly embraced Orban's DNA metaphor. She also challenged the widespread view that the "rise of English as the global lingua franca" was "inevitable" and "unstoppable."[111] This time, however, the rhetoric not only fell short of the reality; it became significantly less audible. Unlike Orban, who had addressed multilingualism 117 times in his three-year tenure, Vassiliou made only five speeches on the topic during her four years in office.[112] The commissioner's homepage offered no direct link to information on multilingualism despite a number of quick links to other areas under the portfolio.

Europe 2020, the EU's ten-year jobs and growth agenda adopted in 2010, made no mention of language even though "education" was one of its five target areas.[113] The commission established an expert group, Languages for Jobs, whose report the following year repeated the "competition" refrain but with a turn toward individual employability to meet employer demands for workers with language skills. The report accepted that English was "clearly an important language for international exchange and increasingly regarded as a basic skill." Yet, reminiscent of the 2008 communication, it also noted that "other languages" would provide a "competitive edge."[114] The multilingualism agenda had firmly moved onto a neoliberal course.

A 2011 report prepared by the Directorate-General for Translation of the European Commission looked at the implications of a lingua franca, specifically English, versus multilingualism and the relative benefits to European institutions in supporting participation and inclusion. With an in-depth discussion of competing views among prominent voices in the debate, the report recognized the utility of English but as an adjunct to strategies promoting multilingualism, including learning other languages as well as translation and interpretation. It also made clear that the more English spread and the world becomes multilingual, the "real losers" would be native English speakers who lacked the skills to effectively communicate in that world.[115]

Later that year, the Civil Society Platform on Multilingualism, representing twenty-nine nongovernmental organizations, made a more ominous observation in its report to the European Commission. For many Europeans, the report conceded, mastering English and another "big" European language was the "best way to success."[116] Yet it warned that the "overwhelming dominance of English" could dilute the importance of Europe's national languages especially in areas like science and scientific education. It could even lead, the report cautioned, to the complete extinction of other languages if English became the preferred language passed from one generation to the next.[117] That observation conceivably gave the commission members pause as to whether the move toward English, especially among the younger generation, was helping or harming efforts to promote broad scale labor mobility within the European Union.

The commission issued a "communication" in 2012 that once again struck the "competitiveness" chord.[118] Attached was a working document promoting proficiency in more than one additional language for "mobility and employability." It recognized that for "the vast majority of students" English was the first and at times the only foreign language studied. The clear "take away" was that, notwithstanding English's "special status," other languages should not be "disregarded." It proposed that by 2020 at least 50 percent of fifteen-year-olds should attain the level of "independent user" of a second language, while at least 75 percent of lower secondary school students should "study" at least a third language, but without indicating any level of proficiency.[119]

At that point, the commission more openly "re-branded" the multilingualism project from "unity in diversity" to the market value of language skills. The slogan on the commission's languages-related website switched from "Multilingualism: An Asset for Europe and a Shared Commitment" to "Supporting Language Learning and Linguistic Diversity," one of the six objectives in Erasmus for All which would combine seven existing international schemes for education, training, youth, and sport into one program. It seemed like the European Union was lowering its sights. The spread of English may have taken some steam out of the drive for "mother tongue plus two." Or perhaps there was growing recognition within the commission that for whatever reason, including mobility and changing demographics, the goal itself was unrealistic or politically fraught.[120] Meanwhile, the term "mother tongue" was gradually giving way to "national languages" to promote social cohesion.

With the 2014 inauguration of EU Commission President Jean-Claude Juncker, multilingualism was completely removed from the portfolio title. Language then fell under Education, Culture, Youth and Sports (changed to Innovation, Research, Culture, Education and Youth in 2019). At the same time, the continuing economic crisis and youth unemployment more noticeably shifted the "multilingualism" narrative, especially within the European Commission, from European integration and social cohesion as political ideals to the economics of language proficiency in the interests of job advancement, mobility, and competitiveness.

These commission directives and policy initiatives talk of multilingualism, but they refer only intermittently to linguistic diversity, and implicitly in the sense of preserving a diversity of national languages. They encourage individuals, in a utilitarian sense, to become proficient in multiple languages aimed at integrating Europe, preserving a strong economy, and enhancing employability. They sidestep the question of a multilingual society, which might suggest multiculturalism and threaten social unity within and between countries. The European Parliament has taken a broader view in supporting minority languages. In 2008, the Parliament noted that multilingualism and linguistic diversity were "sometimes conflicting policy agendas." Language learning policy, the Parliament stated, was influenced by "harder" priorities like "economic competitiveness and labor market mobility," and linguistic diversity by "softer" issues like "inclusion and human rights." The report concluded that multilingualism policy had enjoyed higher priority in terms of "concrete actions," while Parliament's repeated calls for initiatives promoting the use of minority languages, with over 460 million speakers in Europe, had run aground without any binding effect on member states.[121] A parliamentary resolution the following year specifically made reference to the role of languages in "shaping and strengthening identity" while warning against the European Union's limiting itself to a "single main language" (presumably English).[122]

The wavering tone and substance of these documents, especially comparing the commission and the Parliament, suggest that the European Union has yet to resolve the tension, within "unity in diversity," between promoting multilingualism as a marketable commodity and linguistic diversity as matter of human rights. Nor has it settled the question of what languages belong within each framework, whether solely national European languages (both large and small), or regional and immigrant languages as well.[123] A 2019 council recommendation appeared to make some progress on that count. Setting out specific goals and strategies, it promoted "multilingual competence," not simply for job mobility but also to provide a "better understanding of other cultures."[124] The following year, the commission put more detail into the council's recommendation, supporting literacy in the student's entire linguistic repertoire and valuing diversity as a matter of "social justice and inclusion."[125] It is noteworthy that both documents included within "multilingual competence" not just the languages of schooling and dominant foreign languages but also regional languages and the languages of children with a migrant or refugee background.

As noted in the discussion of English in EU institutions, part of the problem in resolving the EU language dilemma lies in the diverse stakes and stakeholders who, as commonly found in the politics of diversity, "rarely dance to the same tune."[126] Using the power of language to forge a common European identity out of a vast mosaic of national and local identities with many competing interests is indisputably formidable. Adding the unstoppable spread of English, along with the departure of the United Kingdom from the EU and the ongoing influx of migrants, has made the project all the more challenging and uncertain. As Robert Phillipson observed almost two decades ago, whether the European Union's practice of issuing occasional resolutions and directives, combined with various funding schemes for student mobility and collaborative research, can achieve any serious change in language policy is still an "open question."[127] More broadly, given the progressive move toward English within EU institutional practices, the narrative on multilingualism policy appears caught in a "self-contradictory gridlock."[128]

Multilingualism on the Ground

These numerous resolutions and directives suggest that for at least two decades the European Union has poured billions of euros into researching and promoting multilingualism and language learning, though the sum is admittedly minuscule as compared with expenditures in other areas. Data gathered over the years raise questions regarding the returns on that investment and the extent to which English has derailed the project.

As an early measure, a 2011 commission survey of approximately fifty-four thousand students in sixteen EU educational systems found results on the ground discouraging, while English clearly turned out to be the winner. Using the Common European Framework of Reference, by the end of secondary schooling, only 42 percent of students were able to have a simple conversation in their first foreign language and only a quarter in their second foreign language. Even more troubling, only 14 percent had achieved basic skills in their first, and only 20 percent in their second. France came in at only 14 percent in English, the most common language studied. The United Kingdom was at a stunning nine percent in French. At the opposite extreme, more than 80 percent of students completing secondary school in Norway and Sweden had reached the level of an independent user in English.

Even in systems where English was the second foreign language, the performance was higher than in whatever the first foreign language happened to be. Not only did students demonstrate better skills in English than in any other language, but they also judged English to be more "useful." For the vast majority of students, English had become the second and sole additional language. The findings varied by country. The Netherlands and Nordic countries, unsurprisingly, were at the high end.[129] One had to wonder how much of the fifty million euros a year spent on promoting language learning in the European Union were devoted to English and not to other European languages, contrary to what the multilingual agenda would have suggested.

Similarly, as of 2016 there was no indication of widespread multilingualism among European adults. Over one-third of working-age twenty-five to sixty-four year-olds in the then twenty-eight EU countries reported that they did not know any foreign language. A similar proportion knew one foreign language, though only a quarter of them could claim full proficiency. Just over one-fifth knew two foreign languages, and less than one-tenth knew three or more foreign languages. There was a noticeable gap between generations, with three-quarters of young adults between the ages of twenty-five and thirty-four reporting that they knew one foreign language, though only one-quarter with proficiency, as compared with slightly more than half in the fifty-five to sixty-four-year-old group. There also was a clear education gap. More than 80 percent of people who had completed tertiary education reported that they knew at least one foreign language, as compared to just over 40 percent among those with a low level of education. The results varied by country, occupation, and rural versus city residence.[130]

The poor showing on language skills in 2016 was unexpected given that in 2012 Europeans reportedly were embracing the "idea" of learning English. At that time, two-thirds believed that English was the most useful foreign language from a personal perspective, while 79 percent believed it was most useful for their children's future. English, spoken by 38 percent of Europeans, was the most widely spoken foreign language, followed by French (12 percent), German (11 percent), Spanish (7 percent), and Russian (5 percent). It also was the most commonly cited language for using the internet (26 percent) and the most widely mentioned language for following radio and television news and reading newspapers and magazine articles (25 percent).[131] In any case, it seemed that for many Europeans "mother tongue plus two" was turning into "language of schooling plus English." As linguist Suzanne Romaine rightly put it, as a result of "benign neglect" at the EU level, de jure multilingualism as a matter of policy was inadvertently veering toward de facto English monolingualism.[132]

The European Union is well aware that limited "multilingual competence" is often one of the main barriers to benefitting from European education, training, and youth programs. Learning a foreign language is compulsory in almost all European countries. Throughout most of Europe, all students must study a minimum of two languages for at least one year. Where that is not the case, the first language is required, while the second is offered as an option. In most countries, students begin learning their first mandated foreign language between the ages of six and eight and continue to the end of upper secondary school.

Among Europeans, the common view is for children to learn one or two additional "prestige" languages for economic reasons, not to create a multilingual society. The rapid spread of English ironically runs the risk of moving Europe in that direction. Again, English is by far the most preferred language and generally the first foreign language that students must learn. And so it is the language typically studied for the longest time. In 2018, nearly 100 percent of primary school students in Austria, Cyprus, Liechtenstein, Malta, Norway, North Macedonia, and Spain learned English as a foreign language. In Croatia, France, Greece, Italy, Latvia, Poland, and Sweden that figure was at least nine out of ten. Over 96 percent were studying English in upper secondary school.[133] The starting point varied by country.

As of 2016–17, students began learning English as a compulsory subject from the age of five in Malta; from the age of six in Greece, Italy, Liechtenstein, Norway, and Spain; from the age of seven in Denmark; from the age of eight in Portugal; between the ages of six and twelve in the Netherlands; and between the ages of seven and ten, though more typically at seven, in Sweden.[134] More recently, France has made a foreign language mandatory at age six. While eight languages are available on paper, over 90 percent of French children choose English. In a 2018 survey of over eight thousand young people between fifteen and thirty years of age from diverse social and demographic groups across the then twenty-eight EU member states, English was the most frequent language studied and the most frequently mentioned second language.[135] It also was the language that young people were most interested in improving, as high as 80 percent in Spain, 74 percent in France, and 69 percent in Italy.[136]

Notwithstanding the steady expansion of language programs across Europe, the 2018 survey once again showed that language competencies among young people were falling behind EU goals. While eight out of ten individuals could read and write in more than one language, only two-thirds could follow a course of study in more than one language. In the United Kingdom, 74 percent said they would only be "comfortable" studying in one language.[137] Once again, there was a clear socioeconomic divide. Both language scores and English study correlated with the level of education completed. Nearly six out of ten respondents with the lowest levels of education could only read and write in one language. Nearly half of those with the highest levels of education could read and write in two languages, and over a quarter in three languages.[138] Among high education level groups, four in ten had studied English, as compared to just over a quarter of those with the lowest education levels. Nearly half of those who had studied abroad had studied English, as compared with just over a third with no study-abroad experience.[139] Such economic disparities in English language skills bear consequences for democratic participation as EU institutions increasingly move toward English in the ordinary practice of EU politics.

Though no longer a member of the European Union, the United Kingdom has proved especially resistant to the EU multilingual agenda. A report, "A Language Crisis?" released in 2020 by the Higher Education Policy Institute, called for overturning the government's 2004 decision to drop compulsory study of languages at stage four when students in England, Wales, and Northern Ireland take GCSE (General Certificate of Secondary Education) exams. According to the report, only 32 percent of sixteen- to thirty-year-olds felt confident reading and writing in another language, as compared to 89 percent in the rest of the EU.[140] Between 2014 and 2018, the number of British students taking the GCSE in a modern foreign language fell by 19 percent. Most notably, French and German, the languages of two of the United Kingdom's closest trading partners, each dropped by 30 percent.[141] In a survey of young people between the ages of sixteen and thirty-four, only 31 percent reported that they could hold a basic conversation in a foreign language, and just 14 percent with a high level of proficiency. When traveling abroad, 65 percent still relied on locals who spoke English.[142] About 25 percent of secondary schools report that Brexit has had a negative impact on students' attitudes toward language learning.[143]

In response to these developments, an editorial in the *Guardian* warned that Britain had to remain fully engaged with the world and especially with Europe, and that meant "understanding what [its] neighbors and allies [were] saying." If not, the British mind would become "locked" inside an "Anglosphere prison."[144] The British Academy issued a similar "call for action" for national attention to focus on the language skills of UK citizens in filling the gap in qualified teachers.[145] In 2019, seven UK universities dropped their modern language degrees, which ordinarily would serve as a pipeline for preparing language teachers.[146] As of 2018, an estimated 35 percent of language teachers and 85 percent of language assistants in UK schools were non-UK EU nationals, a situation that Brexit has made more tenuous. Whether the United Kingdom will heed those warnings with a broad-based strategy including schools, businesses, and the civil service and whether it can convince resistant anglophones to embrace other languages remains to be seen.[147]

Some countries are slowly introducing content and language integrated learning (CLIL), in which certain subjects, like science or history, are taught in a language different from the language of schooling. Both the European Commission and the Council of Europe have promoted CLIL to advance the "mother tongue plus two" agenda. The approach holds promise for developing high-level language skills. Yet it ideally demands teachers both proficient in the second language and trained in teaching both language and the content area, and so schools utilize it sparingly and often ineffectively. The definition of CLIL, moreover, tends to be vague, while there seems to be no European consensus as to teacher training, time spent on each language, or student assessment.[148] Nor is there clarity as to whether and to what extent CLIL differs from language immersion programs in North America, which we will discuss later in chapter 12.[149] The overwhelming majority of CLIL programs offer English though some offer another European language like French in Germany or an ethnic minority language like Basque in Spain. School officials encourage certain students to enroll based on their grades in general, which makes these programs highly selective. As a result, CLIL programs, whether they focus on both content and language or primarily on content, can be socially divisive and create inequalities, closing out students from lower socioeconomic groups.[150]

More generally speaking, proficiency in a language is largely a function of contact and experience in actively using the language. Though students in Europe may study a foreign language for years, in many cases instruction is limited to only several hours a week. Even over the course of ten or twelve years, the cumulative time may not be enough to acquire an adequate level of proficiency to function at an academic level. Overall exposure to English, in particular, varies among student populations and across national settings. In some countries, the level of contact outside the classroom through TV and films is higher than in others, especially where subtitles and not dubbing are used. Students whose families expose them to other languages through travel, summer language camps, and private tutors have a decided advantage, which goes back to socioeconomic disparities. These out-of-school experiences overwhelmingly focused on English open doors to educational and career opportunities. While EU documents promote language learning for all students, it falls on member states to affirmatively compensate for differences in family background and social capital. The extent to which policymakers and educators even recognize those differences varies from country to country, locality to locality.

As the British Academy report noted, adding to the problem is a severe shortage of teachers proficient in foreign languages. That shortage is especially critical in English. It's a generational matter. Only in recent years have countries expanded English language programs. Older teachers are more likely to have studied French or German as their second language rather than English. And so there is a time lag between the potentially high student demand for teachers and the low supply in the adult teaching staff. As more of today's primary and secondary students reach adulthood, that gap might narrow provided those same students see language teaching as a desirable career choice. Generalist rather than specialized teachers, many with inadequate language skills, often teach languages in primary schools. Added to staffing deficits, school systems seldom require language teachers to have spent time learning the language in a country where the language is widely spoken.

The "mother tongue plus two" policy itself raises conceptual questions. Back in 2002 when that policy came to light, the concept of "mother tongue," in practice if not in theory, referred to the official languages of member states. It failed to recognize that for many European residents "mother tongue" and "official state language" were not one and the same.[151] Normative in its views on family, language, and identity, the concept in practice has not kept pace with Europe's changing demographics and the growing number of highly mobile populations and multilingual children. Aside from migration, the Erasmus program in particular has resulted in numerous transnational marriages and families that speak multiple languages. Nor has the notion of "mother tongue" kept pace with alternative perspectives on bilingualism, most prevalent in the literature on translanguaging. In its simplest form, rather than view the languages of bilinguals as two separate and autonomous monolingual systems, translanguaging considers the bilingual's entire linguistic repertoire without fixed bounds between languages, which bears directly on how they are used in the language classroom.[152] With the "mother tongue plus two" discourse overlooking these changing dynamics, schools in Europe are not moved to consider the range of language competencies that multilingual students bring to the learning table. In the end, they fall short on equipping all students, regardless of social class or migrant background, with the language skills they need to succeed at the university level and in the world of work.

Most students, regardless of their first or home language, put their major linguistic stock in learning English. Yet for all the suggested reasons, whether socioeconomic or systemic, some of them face a harsh reality when they enter the university and find themselves struggling to meet the level of English proficiency demanded in English-taught courses and programs. The language skills that students carry with them to the university and beyond rest in large part on those acquired in primary and secondary school and the degree of national support for that project. Much depends on clearly articulated national commitments to multilingualism and language learning and the intensity and quality of language instruction. What is lacking is a system-wide understanding of the "student journey" from start to finish. As a language consultant told the *PIE Review*, "There's no point in the university saying, 'We're going to do X Y and Z' if people leaving the secondary system at 18 are completely incapable of doing that."[153].

Erasmus Sets the Stage

That brings us back to the Erasmus program, now Erasmus+, which captures young people as they approach the end of that journey. The mobility program, named after Desiderius Erasmus of Rotterdam, the sixteenth century Dutch philosopher, Christian humanist, and one of the most famous "wandering scholars" of his day, is the most widely known of the EU's many measures to promote multilingualism. To what extent the humanist connection was merely symbolic given the program's instrumental objectives is debatable.[154] In any case, the program has slowly evolved along with the European project. The early architects of what became the European Union focused on joining together Europe's disparate economic communities.

As the 1980s approached and EU membership became larger and more diverse, the European Commission recognized that linguistic and cultural differences needed to be bridged for "unity in diversity" to have more than rhetorical force. One way to realize that mission was to offer young people the opportunity to physically immerse themselves in the language and culture of a European country different from their own. So began the Erasmus program in 1987. For 2014 through 2020, the European Union expanded the original model, merging language with other education and youth initiatives into the new Erasmus+. A key rationale was to tackle high levels of youth unemployment made worse in the recession of 2008. The program provides funding for students to study abroad for up to twelve months for each cycle. Among student participants, 91 percent state that their stay abroad has "improved their language skills."[155]

Initially begun with eleven countries and 3,244 students studying abroad, the program now benefits around three hundred thousand higher education students each year and covers thirty-three countries, including the twenty-seven EU member states as well as Iceland, Liechtenstein, Norway, the Republic of North Macedonia, Turkey, and Serbia. Over forty partner countries around the globe can participate in some aspects. Through the years, the program and its predecessors have served over five million students, apprentices, and volunteers. The Erasmus+ budget of €14.7 billion (US$17.3 billion), running from 2014 to 2020, was expected to support 3.7 percent of Europe's young population. That number was strikingly low as compared with widespread interest. A 2018 study across EU member states found that 45 percent of fifteen- to thirty-year-olds believed it was "very important" that young people have experiences abroad. Yet nearly three-quarters had not had a long-term experience studying, training, working, or volunteering in another country. Over a third of that group reported a lack of financial means.[156]

Since 2014 Erasmus+ has provided increased opportunities and granted funding to participants from lower socioeconomic backgrounds. In 2017, almost twenty-one thousand disadvantaged students and staff took part in higher education activities supported under Erasmus+, while more than one-third of youth projects focused on inclusion and diversity topics. For the next long-term EU budget cycle in 2021–27, the European Commission proposed doubling its Erasmus funding to €30 billion (US$35.6 billion), which would provide opportunities for twelve million individuals, a two-thirds increase from the existing program.[157] That increase affirms the commission's commitment to student mobility and empowerment with language as key factors in achieving those goals.

From the beginning, building language skills for job mobility has been a major goal of the program. The initial idea was that undergraduate students would spend time studying in the language of the host country and thereby promote the EU's multilingual agenda. That would have been the case in the early years. But as English started spreading across the globe, it became evident that a common language was an especially efficient vehicle for increasing the mobility that the Erasmus program envisioned. Subsequent reality is that Erasmus has helped set the stage for English-taught courses and programs across European universities along with the high stakes they inevitably carry.

A High-Stakes Movement

Facing a global knowledge economy, universities now navigate between being both international and national. For non-Anglophone countries, these conflicting pressures have given rise to a debate over the growing role of English in internationalizing universities and particularly the increasing number of English-taught courses and programs. The debate is especially alive in western Europe, at times reaching a feverish pitch as universities move toward English medium instruction (EMI) primarily in graduate-level programs and increasingly at the bachelor's level. The approach varies widely, from all-English programs in certain disciplines, to specific courses within programs, to select courses or classes determined at times by the availability of English-speaking faculty. In each case, subject matter rather than language development is the primary objective even though English is not the first language for most participants.

Beginning in the 1990s, northern European countries led the way on English language instruction. Some of them are now reassessing those decisions, as is the case with the Nordic countries and, as we will see more specifically, the Netherlands. With national languages rarely used elsewhere, English-taught programs were a means to attract international students who saw little or no value in learning the country's language to enhance job prospects beyond the country itself. The success of those programs further rested in part on primary and secondary schools, which equipped domestic students with the skills to study in English when they entered the university. English became mandatory in the public schools in Sweden as early as 1962, in Norway in 1969, in Denmark in 1970, and in the Netherlands in 1985, a stark contrast to the slow start in promoting English elsewhere in Europe. Countries like France and Italy have remained less linguistically prepared and less culturally attuned to widely adopt EMI.

The trend both supports and benefits from globalization as it ties universities into an economic network extending beyond education. Underlying the movement is a neoliberal emphasis on competition, metrics, and measurability with direct implications for scholarship and instructional quality. It also has implications for national identity, which has become a growing undercurrent of concern with the arrival in Europe of millions of migrants and the upsurge in nationalist parties whose members believe that their "way of life," including their language, is now under threat of erosion. Yet laws designed to preserve the national language often contain loopholes that universities freely use, underscoring once again the gap between the rhetoric of language policy and the reality of implementation.

EMI is intertwined with related policies and practices tied to internationalization, including student and faculty recruitment, scholarly research and publications, academic conferences, cross-national partnerships, and even academic administration. Together they are all bending university culture and governance toward English in ways that create benefits and burdens for faculty and students and challenges for institutions and policymakers. EMI is not simply one component in the internationalization project. It is emblematic of "internationalization," which has become synonymous with "Englishization."

Institutional Pressures

As English gains economic and intellectual capital, universities face the reality that English is no longer the wave of the future but an imperative of the present. For many graduates, English is not simply a "plus" on job applications. It's more akin to computer literacy in necessity. Meanwhile, European universities are racing to burnish their reputations and match their institutional peers, offering English-taught courses and entire programs in the name of internationalization. In many cases, the decision to teach in English is not grounded in an academic rationale or in a clearly articulated national vision. Nor is it necessarily the result of thoughtful planning among the stakeholders. It is often driven by internal budget demands under the weight of national directives and funding incentives. It is further propelled by external demands tied to globalization, including EU resolutions, university ranking systems, and Organisation for Economic Cooperation and Development (OECD) global assessments.[1] Those pressures are largely related to metrics-driven policies pushing toward a competitive advantage and global impact.

English instruction is moving across Europe despite pockets of resistance and a wide variance in English skills among students and faculty. In 2001, there were only 725 bachelor's and master's programs totally taught in English. Between 2007 and 2014, the number more than tripled from 2,389 to 8,089. Total institutions offering English-taught programs went from 18.1 percent to 26.9 percent. The largest increase by far was in the Nordic countries, which almost doubled from 31.5 percent to 60.6 percent. Southwestern Europe remained the lowest at

17.2 percent in 2014, up from 7.6 percent in 2007. Among the reasons that institutions cited for adopting EMI, revenue was the least often named. Attracting international students who would not enroll if the program were taught in the country's national language was the purpose most often stated. But it cannot be denied that additional students, especially from non-EU/EHEA (European Higher Education Area) countries who pay higher tuition, also bring additional revenue. Among institutions that did not adopt such programs, low levels of English among teaching staff and/or among domestic students proved most compelling in their decisions.[2] These figures are important for the institutional and national implications they carry, though they need to be kept in perspective. Despite the rapid increase in programs, the actual percentage of students enrolled in EMI courses across Europe remained small at only 1.3 percent, or about 290,000 participants.[3]

Between the end of 2011 and June 2013, master's programs, which dominate EMI, went from 3,701 to 5,258, a 42 percent increase in a timespan of only one and a half years. The Netherlands and Germany headed the list, while the sharpest growth was in Denmark and Sweden. In France, programs rose by 43 percent, despite limits in the French law on teaching in languages other than French. The *grandes écoles*, or elite institutions and business schools, led in the number of courses and programs. In Italy, during that same time span, English master's programs grew 60 percent. Yet they had started with 191 programs, a low base in a population of nearly 60 million people.[4] As in France, the Italian picture varied by sector. It also varied by region. English-taught courses were more commonly found in the relatively few and well-resourced private universities, which are more inclined to engage international partners. They also were more prevalent in the more prosperous north and center of the country, as compared to the south.[5] And so they appeared to perpetuate longstanding regional, social, and economic inequalities.

Even at the bachelor's level, by 2017 the number of English-taught programs within nineteen of the European Higher Education Area (EHEA) countries had risen to 2,900, a fifty-fold increase since 2009. Countries with the highest number of institutions offering these programs included Germany (69), the Netherlands (42), and France (41). The first two are understandable given the high levels of English proficiency within the population and the strong commitment to language learning. France may seem surprising, especially given purported legal constraints, yet the number of higher education institutions is relatively high as compared to other countries. Accounting for the total number of institutions by country, Switzerland and the Netherlands ranked highest in percentages. France and Italy were on the low end of the spectrum. That placed the Netherlands in the lead in both the number of programs and their spread across higher education institutions.[6] The overall demand for EMI could increase in the coming years as universities develop programs under the European Universities Initiative, a "bottom-up" network of universities across the European Union. Launched in 2018, the program envisions institutional partnerships where a student can complete a single-degree program while studying law in Paris, economics in Rome, and history in Athens, either in person or virtually, with their degree guaranteed recognition across countries.[7]

The numbers of English-taught programs could rise even higher as European universities anticipate an influx of students seeking an alternative to the United Kingdom where newly enrolled EU, other EEA (European Economic Area— Iceland, Liechtenstein, and Norway), and Swiss nationals would no longer be eligible for home fee status or financial support beginning in academic year 2021–22.[8] Following the announcement, among 2,505 EU nationals, 84 percent reported that they would "definitely not" pursue their plans to study for a bachelor's or master's degree in the United Kingdom if their tuition fees were doubled. About 49 percent said they would consider instead the Netherlands, followed by Germany (36 percent), France (19 percent), Ireland (16 percent), and Sweden (14 percent).[9] The Brexit referendum in 2016 had already set those changes in motion. By early 2018, more than 2,300 EU academics had resigned from UK universities in the preceding year over concerns with post-Brexit immigration status, job security, and research funding.[10]

A similar "Brexodus" of potential student applicants will drive up the demand for English-taught courses across the continent, especially in graduate programs. By mid-2020, IE Law School in Madrid and Amsterdam Law School in the Netherlands both reported a surge in international applications for their LLM programs.[11] In 2020–21, universities in the Netherlands saw a 13 percent increase in international student enrollments from EU/EEA countries but a drop of four percent in non-EU/EEA admissions.[12] The United Kingdom's decision on leaving the European Union to withdraw from Erasmus+ will drive that trend even further given the high fees in other Anglophone countries. The UK government's replacement, known as the Turing scheme, named after the mathematician and code breaker Alan Turing, is focused solely on sending UK students abroad.

These projections do not account for global shifts in international enrollments resulting from the 2020 COVID-19 pandemic. It has been estimated that student mobility, especially from outside the EU area, could take up to five years to recover from the crisis as universities wrestle with economic and programmatic challenges. With the loss of up to 10 percent of GDP worldwide, the global middle-class market for international education will shrink at least for the short term.[13] That said, in the interim, as institutions move to online and hybrid teaching with more sophisticated delivery, there arises the opportunity to recruit students from a wider range of countries and across the economic spectrum, which could reasonably heighten the demand for courses taught in English. That is not to suggest replacing physical mobility for the long term. The European Parliament's Committee on Culture and Education (CULT) issued a briefing paper roundly rejecting that very proposition. Though the paper was part of a study to examine ways to "green" Erasmus+ and other programs, it appeared in March 2020 just as the pandemic was spreading through Europe and online teaching became an immediate necessity.[14]

English-taught courses and programs are a direct outgrowth of two agreements: the Sorbonne Declaration of 1998, signed by the ministers of higher education of France, Germany, Italy, and the United Kingdom, and the Bologna Declaration of 1999, signed by twenty-nine European ministers of higher education.[15] Both agreements formed the basis for creating a European Higher Education Area (EHEA) with compatible programs, as well as a uniform European Credit Transfer System (ECTS). Over the years, membership in the EHEA has expanded to include forty-nine countries.[16] What is known as the "Bologna Process" required countries to reconfigure higher education into three cycles corresponding to bachelor's, master's, and doctoral degrees, though some countries have maintained isolated degrees outside the Bologna framework. The standardized system would allow students and graduates to transport their educational qualifications across national borders, promote mobility and employability, and put Europe on a more competitive footing in the global knowledge economy. These organizing agreements were noticeably silent on language policy, though the Bologna Declaration set a framework "taking full respect of the diversity of cultures [and] language."[17] English reportedly has been the sole language used in all conferences, workshops, and other forums relating to the Bologna Process as well as all documents emerging from those meetings.[18]

The bachelor's-master's model, adopted in 2003, effectively led to a "European paradox" of competing policies, one promoting multilingualism in theory for European integration and job mobility, and the other implicitly favoring English in practice to facilitate cross-national student exchanges.[19] The Erasmus+ program has given momentum to the overall effort. Since 2010, when the Bologna Process was completely standardized, the "stand-alone" master's degree has allowed students across the globe access to the relatively low tuition fees within Europe. At the same time, depending on funding levels in each country, it has permitted elite universities in particular to stabilize their budgets and improve job prospects for their own students while enhancing international rankings and institutional reputations.

In 2013, the European Commission called on member states to make internationalizing higher education a priority. The commission feared that Europe would lose its 45 percent share in global learners to rising competition from Asia, the Middle East, and Latin America. That total figure was expected to grow from four million to seven million by the end of the decade, and so the stakes were sizeable.[20] The commission recognized that English was a "de facto part of any internationalization strategy" to "attract talent which would not otherwise come to Europe." At the same time, it noted that multilingualism was an asset for Europe and that European language skills would enhance job opportunities.[21] To its credit, the commission understood that internationalization was more complex than simply enrolling more international students. It required programmatic changes, curricular innovation, excellent teaching, research opportunities, and strategic partnerships. Though well stated, the advice has not always been well taken. Experience has shown that university administrators often give these factors insufficient attention as they push to create both the optics and the metrics of an international program while they forego the necessary vision and substance. Administrators also equate internationalization with the dominance, and not simply the prevalence, of English in the interests of world rankings and global competition.

International rankings are a matter of serious concern to European universities, especially those on the continent, who consistently fall behind institutions in the United States and the United Kingdom. As Ellen Hazelkorn, a noted expert on the subject, put it, "Rankings—as a method of gauging competitiveness, providing transparency and accountability and aiding benchmarking of higher education performance—have spread like a virus."[22] A frequently cited assessment is the annual Times Higher Education (THE) World University Ranking. The results are based on responses from over sixteen thousand senior published academics as to the best university in their field. THE rankings depend on certain criteria clustered within five indicators. One specific indicator, "international outlook," weighs the percentage of international students and faculty (2.5 percent each), the amount of international collaboration on faculty research (2.5 percent), and the number of faculty publications cited by scholars globally (30 percent). The relatively heavy weightings on research and publications favor universities with large numbers of faculty members who publish in English language journals and who collaborate with researchers in other countries. The higher the rankings, the more international students the university attracts. The more international students, the greater the demand for English-taught courses. The more English-taught courses, the more international students enroll and the higher the demand for English-speaking faculty to teach, which all raise the rankings even further. It's an endless cycle.

A look at the Netherlands, France, and Italy, where controversies over EMI will be explored further, sheds some light on the link between English and world rankings. The Netherlands, with its high English proficiency and widespread English-taught courses, saw ten universities placed in the top 200 and six in the top 100 in the 2021 THE rankings. France, by comparison, saw five placed in the top 200 and three in the top 100. Italy had only three in the top 200 and none in the top 100.[23] The QS (Quacquarelli Symonds) World University Rankings 2021 showed a similar cut. The Netherlands had seven universities in the top 200, down from nine the previous year, and two in the top 100. France, on the other hand, had five in the top 200, up from four the previous year, and three in the top 100. Italy came up with only three in the top 200, up from one the previous year, and once again none in the top 100.[24]

English may have had some impact on this spread. France's rise over the past four years from one to three universities in the top 100 in the THE rankings may or may not be related to the increase in English-taught programs or to reforms in the French university system focusing on research, or both. When almost all French universities in the top 400 fell down on the list in 2014 in favor of universities in Singapore, Japan, and China, the editor of the THE rankings speculated that, aside from problems with branding, one likely cause was that France had "fallen behind" the growing number of universities in Europe and Asia in publishing research in English "to ensure the widest dissemination and impact."[25] Much has changed within French higher education in the intervening years to make French universities more competitive and boost rankings. Under the Law on Higher Education and Research adopted in 2013, universities have been joined into twenty-five clusters with an additional eight clusters supporting research and innovation, while the number of English-taught courses and French classes for non-French-speaking students have increased. Building on those changes, the Macron administration has emphasized enhancing the global reputation of French universities as research hubs.

One can question whether "internationalization" is a valid measure for ranking academic quality or assessing the overall role it plays in the outcomes. France, for example, showed a stronger placement in the 2020 Academic Ranking of World Universities (ARWU), known as the Shanghai Rankings, counting eight institutions in the top 200, as compared with five in both the THE and QS rankings for that year.[26] Whether the difference is a function of the ARWU not weighing internationalization measures is worth consideration. Again, it could have some connection to France having regrouped its universities in recent years, pouring funds into scientific research and international collaborations, along with institutions moving ahead on EMI.

Of course, there are weaknesses in any ranking system, as well as in the way findings are interpreted and used. Those weaknesses often go unnoticed, at least in the public eye. Correlation does not necessarily mean direct or sole causation. EMI may be just one piece in a larger puzzle of "neoliberal ideologies" embedded in the rankings.[27] One can also dispute the arbitrary weightings themselves. Changing the weightings can dramatically shift both the "absolute" and the "comparative" university performance. The apparent obsession with competition and hierarchy also ignores the fact that institutions have different missions.[28] Yet as long as the rankings continue to guide the decisions of institutions, policymakers, and the public, they remain a force to be watched with a critical eye.

The growth in English-taught programs is not simply directed toward rankings. It's also about economics, though the two are unquestionably related. Facing a declining college-age population, universities see high-fee-paying students as a source of additional revenue. Tuition rates for students from outside the EU/EHEA are typically higher while scholarship aid is limited, which makes recruiting students from countries like China and India particularly attractive. In a survey of European universities, 39 percent overall responded that one of the main drivers of enrollment increases was international recruitment. In the United Kingdom, it was as high as 92 percent; in the Netherlands, it was 86 percent.[29] With English being the most popular second language studied worldwide, English-taught courses lure students away from anglophone countries like the United States, the United Kingdom, Canada, and Australia, where tuition is considerably more costly. With upward of five million international students potentially seeking admission, up from two million in 1999, that market is extensive and profitable.[30] As the rector of a major European university told the French newspaper *Le Monde*, "Education has become an export product." And so universities consider languages an "obstacle to student mobility, like customs barriers." Creating a "free trade" in English offers them another vehicle for selling their "educational products."[31]

The swing toward teaching and scholarship in English, tied to English as a lingua franca, has raised cries that other national languages are losing their relevance in certain domains. These concerns are especially strong in the hard sciences, where English dominates the knowledge base and the terminology, especially in technology, and where universities are switching entire programs to English. Though the justification is to prepare students for careers where opportunities are quickly growing, the loss to German has been especially noted. Young German-speaking scientists and scholars now trained in English, as well as older generations who increasingly publish and lecture in English, have no reason to update scientific terms in German to meet the fast pace of technological advances. The fear that German, historically valued as a scientific language, will become stiff and outdated is not unreasonable.[32]

Countering that trend, the Working Group on German as a Scientific Language (ADAWIS), founded in 2007 by seven scientists, actively defends plurilingualism in research and teaching to support globalization. While its members agree that English is important in international academic communication, they make the case for using and developing German as an academic language within the German-language area.[33] In 2010, ADAWIS published an open letter to the federal ministries and other decision-makers dealing with higher education and/or science. The letter, signed by fifty-four scientists, laid out specific recommendations, including requiring that international students and lecturers learn the national language and that theses be submitted in German, with some exceptions.[34] Guidelines published in 2015 made similar points that covered students and faculty in addition to conferences, funding, and a European publication database. Using English exclusively throughout the academy, the group argued, ran counter to "integration, the pursuit of knowledge, and democratic principles."[35]

Scholars have expressed similar fears for other international languages. Scientific knowledge, they argue, is being compressed into an Anglo-Saxon discourse, rhetorical style, research models, and issue focus.[36] A manifesto drawn up in 2017 opposing English as a requirement for EU funding in the sciences raised many of these arguments. Drafted in Spanish with English, French, German, Italian, and Portuguese versions, the manifesto had gained over 120,000 signatures by 2021, with a goal of reaching 150,000.[37] It obviously struck a raw nerve in the academic community. Scholars from other disciplines, though not with the same collective outrage as in the hard sciences, have noted the loss in cultural and historical "perspective" in an academic regime dominated by English. By way of example, Peter Kraus argues that political science is not solely an "academic endeavor" but rather a "discursive field where a society reflects critically on itself." Language plays a critical role in both the conceptualization and the reproduction of "political knowledge," he says. He warns that separating political concepts from the language of local politics could have "alienating effects."[38]

Domains admittedly are not monolithic; they cover a range of activities that contextually lend themselves to different language choices.[39] Some researchers, for example, may choose to address certain audiences, orally or in writing, in their native language and other audiences in English. While that generally may be true, in the case of academic science in particular, and increasingly in other areas, the pressure on faculty to remain relevant and professionally secure is pushing them in a totally English direction—from teaching to publishing to conference presentations—denying them any real choice in the matter. The concerns are similar to those raised regarding the loss in "aggregate cultural capital" when parents stop speaking to their children in their native language. Even if the language is not totally abandoned, it may no longer be considered useful and worthy of further development for "high" or "modern" communication.[40]

Benefits, Burdens, and Challenges

Inasmuch as universities flaunt the gains to be made from English-taught courses and programs, those gains need to be weighed against the burdens on students and faculty and the challenges to national languages and identity.

Students

On the plus end, EMI is popularly promoted for preparing students to work in the global economy, including transnational jobs within their own countries. A 2014 study on the impact of the Erasmus program found that young people with international experience had an unemployment rate 23 percent lower five years after graduation than those who had not studied or trained in another country.[41] These findings admittedly raise the problem of causation versus mere correlation. The same social and economic factors that initially motivated or enabled students to study or train in another country may have positively influenced their employability. But that possibility does not negate the potential job and intercultural benefits of study abroad, which English-taught programs undeniably facilitate for students from across the globe. It just questions how robust the specific gains in employability might be. In some cases, English can "seal the deal" for graduates in hiring and promotion decisions. A growing number of multinational companies in non-anglophone countries now conduct business almost entirely in English. An article in the *Economist* fittingly called English the language "on which the sun never sets."[42]

The question is whether university students at the end of their program have acquired the necessary language skills. That depends in large part on the skills they brought to the university and whether they subsequently sharpened those skills over the course of their studies. The range in English proficiency among students underscores the burdens and challenges of EMI. The proficiency level needed to learn through a second language far exceeds the conversational ability typically acquired in secondary school world language classes. It requires an extensive academic vocabulary and the ability to critically evaluate facts, process information, and formulate opinions orally and in writing, at times under time-sensitive testing conditions. Students who are not up to the task fail to grasp the deeper meaning of what is taught. Beyond the classroom, writing a thesis or dissertation in a second language for wide dissemination, as English-taught graduate programs often urge or require, can prove especially challenging. The type of English language programs that US universities now offer second language users of English are only beginning to emerge in Europe. Even where available, they tend to be underfunded and not well developed.[43]

The language standards that universities use to screen applicants in the admissions process often fall short of the academic demands they will face. The Test of English as a Foreign Language (TOEFL) is one of the measures international programs commonly use to assess English language proficiency. The skills tested, however, are the minimum of what students actually need to succeed in English-taught classes and programs. TOEFL scores among European students vary widely depending on the home country. In 2019, the mean scores in France and Italy were 88 and 90, respectively, as compared with a high of 100 in Austria, 99 in the Netherlands, 99 in Switzerland, 98 in Germany, 97 in Denmark, and 93 in Sweden.[44] TOEFL scores correspond to measures of overall English competence within the population. In a study of English proficiency among 2.2 million adults who took English tests in 2019 in one hundred countries worldwide, France ranked twenty-eighth and Italy thirtieth as compared to the Netherlands and Denmark in the top two positions, Sweden fourth, Austria sixth, Germany eighth, and Switzerland eighteenth.[45]

Test scores of English "proficiency" raise the disputed native/nonnative binary and the question of "which English" should be used in EMI programs. Without digging too deeply into a highly controversial topic, two approaches rejecting the conventional English as a foreign language (EFL) "native-speaker" model demand further thought. The first is the notion of World Englishes based on Braj Kachru's landmark concept dividing the world of English users into three concentric circles. The inner circle is comprised of countries, including the United States, the United Kingdom, Ireland, Australia, Canada, and New Zealand, where English is the primary language. These countries are "norm-setting." The outer circle includes countries where English is the legacy of British (India, Singapore, Nigeria) or to a lesser degree US (the Philippines) colonization. These countries are "norm-developing" in that the localized variety has a "well-established linguistic and cultural identity," such as Singlish in Singapore. The expanding circle includes countries that are not former British or US colonies (e.g., western European countries other than Ireland and the United Kingdom) but that give English increasing attention in schools and universities. These countries are "norm-dependent" in that they rely on British and US standards without establishing any local norms of their own.

The World Englishes model undeniably has been important in highlighting both the diversity of English spoken around the globe and the exploitative ways in which English has dominated countries in the outer circle. It has been criticized, nonetheless, for being too "nation-based" while failing to recognize the sociolinguistic realities of individual speakers within and between the circles.[46] It also belies the fact that languages are not static but continue to evolve over time under the influence of migration and globalization. Sweden, where the pervasiveness of English throughout the media, film, music, education, and work have made it much less like a foreign language and yet not really a second language, is a clear case in point.[47]

The second alternative to the traditional EFL model is English as a lingua franca (ELF), which accepts more fluid socially embedded norms commonly used among nonnative speakers as they contextually rework the language to communicate with each other in the global market. Speakers of ELF, it is said, belong to a "virtual speech community" with no geographical boundaries.[48]

Unlike World Englishes, ELF is a "free language" disconnected from any particular country or ethnicity.[49] Whether that disconnection is real, given the
continued "soft power" of British and American English and culture, is understandably disputed. In any case, for ELF advocates, as long as intelligibility (the
listener understands the words spoken) and comprehensibility (the listener
understands the meaning in context) are not affected, then ELF is a suitable way
to communicate without any reference to native English.[50]

The relevance of ELF to higher education, its use by professors and students,
and the distinction between spoken and written English remain open to question. Academic institutions place utmost importance not only on international
intelligibility but also on lexical and grammatical accuracy especially in writing
(albeit according to a native US or British norm).[51] Two related issues arise here.
One is descriptive and addresses the way English and other languages are actually used in the EMI classroom. The other is normative and considers the standards of acceptability set by the professor and/or the institution for purposes of
student assessment and/or faculty hiring. On the descriptive side, the approach
varies from institution to institution and classroom to classroom. It depends in
part on the availability of faculty with native-like fluency, a group that is in short
supply in many countries. It also depends on the linguistic repertoires of the
students and the instructor within any given classroom. On the normative side,
universities aim to prepare students for the world of work. It is reasonable to
assume that unless and until such time as ELF gains wide professional acceptance, and it may in due time, university standards will maintain a conventionally
recognized form of English as spoken by native speakers. And as long as academic journals and textbooks are written in what is considered standard British
or American English, they will continue to influence the way students develop
their own writing skills.[52] All that is not to suggest that those norms need not be
reconsidered.

Aside from "which English" is or should be used in EMI, as noted, a critical
factor is whether universities make a serious effort to improve the English skills
of both domestic and international students in the course of their studies. While
English-taught programs presumably give students the opportunity to use academic English, depending on the English skills of the teacher, they focus on
content and do not teach students language skills per se. A related and equally
important factor is whether programs systematically enable visiting students
to learn the language of the host country. Unless required to take at least some
courses in that language, students enrolled in English-taught programs have minimal opportunities to learn and use the local language. That common situation
limits their ability to interact with local students and the local community, which
defeats the cultural benefits of an international experience.[53] It also limits their
opportunities for internships, as well as summer and post-study employment,

in the domestic labor market. At the same time, domestic students enrolled in English-taught courses also lose the opportunity to develop high-level academic proficiency in their own language, which they will need to succeed in the world of work and serve communities in their own country. For students from disadvantaged backgrounds, that loss carries serious career consequences.

English instruction in universities may effectively promote social and economic discrimination and reinforce existing inequalities, especially given the value of English for job opportunities. As English progressively gains prestige, the more privileged students, who have benefited from years of high-level English instruction and family exposure and encouragement, gravitate toward programs taught in English, whether in their own country or internationally. Meanwhile, students without the cultural awareness or language skills are left to an education of lower global value solely in their national language. Those deficits reflect, in part, inequities in primary and secondary education.

Faculty

As is the case with students, the EMI picture for faculty is also a mixed bag of benefits and burdens. For English speakers from outside the country, EMI opens the door to teaching either temporarily or long-term in a new linguistic and cultural setting. For those within the country, it allows them to sharpen their English language skills and remain relevant in their discipline. For both groups, it provides a setting for broadening their intellectual horizons and engaging with a culturally diverse group of colleagues and students. The flow of faculty moving from country to country presents opportunities for scholarly collaboration from diverse perspectives and intellectual traditions.

Nonetheless, the value placed on English also places a heavy burden on faculty members who lack proficiency in the language. Again, the demands are especially acute in the physical and life sciences, where US dominance grew following World War II while Europe struggled to restore itself. The war had raised the US scientific establishment to a height of productivity and status. The postwar years saw the US government pouring billions of dollars into scientific research, benefiting from the brain power of a highly educated generation with the help of talent recruited from abroad, including Jewish scientists who had fled Nazi Germany. English and technology worked in synergy to further that agenda.[54] By the 1980s, upward of 70 percent of international publications in science were in English; by 1990 it had risen to 90 percent in some fields.[55] Today, even where articles are published in English and another language, the English version attracts more readers. A clear example is the *Pan African Medical Journal*. While the journal publishes in English and French, English articles are accessed 70 percent more than the French.[56]

Publishing in English goes hand in hand with the reputational motives under-lying EMI. Particularly in the hard sciences, journal articles as compared to books or monographs are the norm. The questions examined tend to share a theoret-ical and methodological base that encourages collaboration and co-authorship across national and linguistic boundaries. Scientific research and publishing also lend themselves more to a common language.[57] That is not to deny that some terms and metaphors undeniably lose meaning in translation, while individual languages may use different patterns of argumentation. In English papers, for ex-ample, the argumentation is typically "linear," whereas in German, the grammar facilitates back-and-forth references.[58]

Large bibliographic databases of peer-reviewed literature, like the Science Citation Index (SCI) and Scopus, give priority to publications in English. The added global visibility is a powerful inducement for journals to shift to English.[59] Some journals that previously published in another language, such as German science journals, now publish mostly in English with a smattering of articles in the author's native language. Others have switched completely to English, with or without an abstract in the original language or in several languages, perhaps even with a change in their title. Still others have fallen off the publishing map al-together.[60] When the Institut Pasteur replaced its renowned journal, *Les Annales*, with an English journal, *Research in Microbiology*, it was a ground-shaking mo-ment in the world of science.

A growing number of prestigious journals now only accept manuscripts in English. "Prestigious" commonly means an indexed English language journal and preferably one with an international focus and high impact factor. For re-searchers, the more prestigious the journal, the better it promotes their career, which in turn enhances their institution's reputation, which attracts more in-ternational students, which requires more English-taught courses. University rankings highlight the role that citations play in maintaining a direction toward English. The 2019 ARWU (Shanghai Rankings) showed a clear connection be-tween institutional rank and inclusion in the Highly Cited Researchers (HCR) list, which ARWU uses to produce the rankings. Every institution ranked in the top 500 or 1,000 of ARWU had papers indexed in the *Science Citation Index* and the *Social Sciences Index*. An institution is unlikely to make it to the top 500 without a score in the HCR.[61] Again, the most highly cited papers from the most highly recognized journals are overwhelmingly in English. With faculty renown, recognition, and rank riding on citations, the rule no longer is "Publish or perish" but rather "Publish in English (or in a trimmed down 'Globish') or perish."

Across the disciplines, scholars whose English departs from native-like norms have fewer opportunities to make an impact. Even when they attempt to produce manuscripts in English, the process is more time-consuming and un-certain, often requiring lengthy negotiation with editors and reviewers. And so they inevitably publish fewer papers. Some turn to paid "literacy brokers" who refine manuscripts for content and/or language or completely translate them. Yet individuals with knowledge of the content area and the rhetorical style of academic journals are hard to find, and they charge hefty fees beyond the financial means of young or less economically secure scholars. Those added costs create unspoken inequities in a process that claims to be merit-based. Many scholars remain hidden in the shadows of their area of expertise, out of the view of global gatekeepers who select peer reviewers who, in turn, recommend articles for publication. Editors expect manuscripts to follow certain grammatical and stylistic conventions that are not necessarily related to intelligibility. Anglophone reviewers who raise editing questions about nonstandard use can sound the death knell for a manuscript submitted by a relatively unknown author.[62] Meanwhile, the large numbers of anglophone researchers, sitting high on their typically monolingual perches, cite only papers written in what is considered standard English.

To what degree open access journals will increase views and citations for scholars working outside the anglophone "center" remains to be seen. While open access can have a "democratizing" effect, it also carries potential problems. Some open access journals defy accepted norms of scholarly publication and lack transparency regarding board membership, disciplinary coverage, and selection criteria. They prey on the desperation of academics pressured to publish in English, many of them from Africa and Asia. Such "predatory" practices have delegitimized open access in general, which in turn has strengthened even further the dominance of journals recognized within the circle of anglophone gatekeepers.[63] Aside from publishing opportunities, as English has come to dominate scholarly research, it has become a sine qua non for accessing an almost infinite set of databases and sources from contemporary, to archival material, to news articles, blogs, scholarly articles, and treatises via the internet. Major academic websites are typically in English. Without English, access to information, and consequently to the breadth of knowledge that shapes ideas, is severely limited.

On the other hand, as noted in political science, much also is lost conceptually in viewing and producing knowledge and straitjacketing intellectual engagement into a monolingual English frame. Resting exclusively on English limits one's intellectual horizons and output, a fact that most anglophones foolishly overlook and other language speakers feel pressured to ignore. It's easy to dismiss information disseminated in other languages, especially in the hard sciences, as mere "folklore," silencing researchers of other cultural backgrounds until unique and important ideas simply "fade away."[64] In the end, the overall knowledge base suffers. Meanwhile, for anglophones to assume that they can access research in other languages through Google Translate is unrealistic. Running a scientific paper through translation software simply does not yield a totally meaningful result.

Given the dominance of public higher education in Europe, publishing solely in English or requiring student theses and dissertations to be written in English further denies the communities that finance the research, through their tax dollars, access to findings that may have a local or national impact.[65] This is especially problematic in areas like the environment, housing, health, law, and education that depend on local implementation. By way of example, a Google Scholar search of over seventy-five thousand documents related to biodiversity conservation, including journal articles, books, and theses in sixteen languages, found that 35.6 percent were not in English, while only about half of a random sampling of non-English documents included titles or abstracts in English. The other half was unsearchable using English keywords.[66] It's been said that useful solutions to the 2008 economic crisis were lost in the discussion dominated by English. The same may be said as we look back at the 2020 COVID-19 global pandemic.

English also has become the primary or sole language of most international conferences and of the published papers and proceedings they produce. Simultaneous interpreting, with its high costs and cumbersome logistics, is nearly obsolete. Even where it is still provided, debate and discussion commonly take place primarily in English. Communicating in one language facilitates the exchange of knowledge, but it also comes at a cost to nonnative speakers who have difficulty injecting humor into their presentations and fielding audience questions with ease. Their delivery tends to be scripted and wooden. And so they work at a disadvantage as compared with native anglophones whose ideas are taken more seriously simply by virtue of their comfort in navigating English. At the same time, conference organizers create the impression that the audience is sufficiently adept at English both as a sign of "modernity" and from a sense of shame to admit otherwise. As a result, native English speakers give rapid-fire presentations using idioms and Anglo-American references, which makes them less widely comprehensible than they believe.[67]

The essential role that conferences play in circulating research findings, establishing connections with possible collaborators, and advancing academic reputations makes the differences all the more consequential.[68] Scholars and researchers who lack English skills or speaking confidence in English avoid participating or even attending academic meetings, which effectively freezes them out of the networks essential to disseminate their findings and advance their careers. Despite the rise in EU research funding, from 1.87 percent GDP in 2008 to 2.18 percent GDP in 2017, higher education being the second highest sector, without a common language scholars cannot take advantage of opportunities like the Erasmus+ Strategic Partnership program to collaborate across linguistic borders.[69]

There seems to be a generational divide. Younger professors and researchers are more likely to have learned English through early school programs and sustained media exposure. They also are more likely to have studied internationally, especially through the Erasmus program, which began in 1987. They tend to be more at ease in presenting, writing, and teaching in English than their more senior colleagues, whose second language in school was more likely French or German. Yet universities understand that their rankings ride in part on the international reputations of their faculty, which ride on the ability to teach, publish, and interact in a scholarly universe dominated by English. That understanding shapes institutional decisions about faculty hiring, compensation, and course assignments. More senior faculty members, despite impressive scholarly reputations, may end up at the curricular margins as courses are increasingly switched to English.

Faculty proficiency in English and course assignments relate directly to the quality and integrity of the education program. Teaching at the university level in a less-familiar language is not a simple matter. Depending on the discipline, it can require the ability to think in that language at a high level of abstraction and to convey with clarity complex concepts. Many professors may publish in English, at times with editing provided by a paid network of outside sources. They may also be familiar with the relevant literature and terminology in English. Yet they lack the skills to teach effectively in English. Like the problem with conference presentations, when instructors lack competence and/or confidence in their English skills, their teaching can become scripted, lacking nuance and spontaneity, condensed into a drum roll of PowerPoint slides with endless bullet points. Discussion consequently fails to mine the diverse viewpoints that international students bring to the experience, a key objective of internationalization and of the EU multilingual project. To compensate for weaknesses in their own faculty, universities resort to hiring native English speakers, often as visitors. That strategy undoubtedly enriches the program with new perspectives. Yet if used in excess, it also creates a "revolving door" of instructors with no attachment to the institution or its mission and with little understanding of the local or national culture.

Institutions tend to overestimate the level of English skills among faculty members without providing careful monitoring and support, including intensive language workshops. They fail too often to set a standard for measuring faculty language skills, like a certain minimal score on the TOEFL or IELTS or level on the CEFR. Without a benchmark on proficiency, faculty and graduate advisers lose credibility when their language skills are noticeably lower than that of their students, or at least below student expectations.[70] Where both the professor and students lack adequate English fluency, classroom discussion is reduced to the "least common denominator" of oversimplified English. International students may consequently take from the experience far less than what the exchange program initially promised.[71] Managing the diverse levels of English among students can prove challenging even for instructors fluent in English who are trained in their discipline and not in language teaching.[72] Like their less fluent colleagues, they must adapt their teaching and content to accommodate students who struggle with comprehension and note taking. Unless properly trained, instructors may not know how to make those accommodations. Nor may they understand cultural differences that can chill or distort classroom interaction and impede student performance.[73] These problems may vary by subject. Some, like history and sociology, are more language dependent than others, like math and physics.[74]

Steps toward Moderation

The many challenges facing English-taught courses and programs are indeed cause for concern. Some countries and institutions have addressed the competing interests more thoughtfully and comprehensively than others. On that count, the Nordic countries, particularly Denmark, Norway, and Sweden, have made concerted efforts to preserve their "small" and globally unfamiliar national languages while preparing students for the global economy and reaping the financial and cultural benefits of an international student body. These countries have long promoted English in the schools and through the media. With a relatively high level of English proficiency among the population, they have used English for research and scholarly publications most widely since the 1950s but as early as the mid-nineteenth century. Over the past two decades, in response to the spread of English in classroom teaching and the threat it poses to using national languages across domains, the three countries have developed the concept of "parallel language use." The approach supports using more than one language in parallel in the same domains or contexts without one language dominating the others. It has gained heightened interest in recent years in the face of rising immigration and concerns over protecting linguistic and cultural identity.

The idea began in Sweden in 1998 as a draft action program from which a series of government reports emerged.[75] The Nordic Council of Ministers, an intergovernmental body covering Denmark, the Faroe Islands, Greenland, Iceland, Norway, Sweden, and the Åland Islands, formalized the concept in 2006. The Declaration on Nordic Language Policy promoted multilingualism though it focused on standard languages.[76] The Council's current policy as stated in the 2018 report "More Parallel, Please," is to use several languages, including English with one or more Nordic languages, concurrently without one "abolishing" or "replacing" the other.[77] Admittedly non-binding and subject to wide interpretation in practice, the report laid out eleven recommendations based on visits to leading Nordic and several other European universities. The recommendations took as their starting point that internationalization policies and language policies should be integrated closely for both to succeed, that EMI is not internationalization, that the entire curriculum has to be internationalized, and that the policy overall should relate to the role of the university in the local community.[78] The collective wisdom gained from the Nordic experience and its resource building has made these countries a model, in theory if not in fact, for constructive policymaking.

Like their European neighbors, these countries nonetheless still struggle with several issues, including language loss, particularly in the sciences.[79] In Sweden, those concerns led to the Swedish Language Act in 2009, declaring Swedish "the principal language." The law requires state institutions, including universities, to use and develop Swedish and to protect and promote the national minority languages.[80] And while the concept of parallel language use is "simple at first blush," it becomes more complex as it is applied to managing "language choices."[81] Given the flexible parameters, it has been difficult to gather adequate proof as to whether or not the approach yields positive results in language skills or overall learning.

The gap between national policy and institutional implementation, furthermore, is problematic. Evidence from Denmark, for example, has shown that while government policies have promoted the national language, university policies have favored English.[82] That trend came to a halt in 2018 when the Danish government announced cuts of between 1,000 and 1,200 university places for international students. The government claimed that a sizeable number of international master's graduates failed to remain in the country and contribute to the Danish economy. Yet Danish universities cannot discriminate against European applicants in admissions. And so the only way to reduce the numbers of international students was either to close degree programs completely or to switch the medium of instruction to Danish.[83]

In any case, despite its conceptual appeal, parallel instruction has not gained traction among other European countries, partially for the cost and logistical complexity in running parallel tracks. Nor have the guiding principles in the council's 2018 report noticeably influenced government or institutional policies in other countries. That takes us back more generally to EMI with its many loose ends. For all the reasons laid out, combined with wide variation in implementation, an exhaustive analysis of studies found the research evidence on EMI to be "remarkably flimsy" as to the benefits of learning English but also "insufficient" as to the possible harms to students in their learning academic content.[84] It thus remains unclear whether teaching through English is as effective as hoped or as harmful as feared. What is clear, however, is that without a national or institutional rationale with well-defined parameters and a comprehensive vision, many universities overlook their primary duty to preserve the integrity of the academic program as they rush toward a crabbed version of "internationalization." At the same time, they lose sight of the fact that poorly planned programs inevitably widen the socioeconomic divide. They give lip service to multilingualism without providing the motivation, deliberation, and support to make it a reality for all.

With all these challenges and limitations in mind, we now turn to three countries—France, Italy, and the Netherlands—where English courses and programs have raised academic and governance concerns provoking political conflicts and legal action. The surrounding events and the interplay among the key stakeholders provide distinct insights into education, national identity, and equal opportunity and the implications for European policies promoting multilingualism in the interests of European integration and job mobility.

Shakespeare in the Crossfire

In the spring of 2013, controversies over the use of English in university programs in France and Italy laid bare the political tensions and the legal consequences for universities moving in that direction. While the opposition in each country was distinct in tone and points of reference, both cases provoked public discussion that dug deep into cultural pride and the complexities of internationalization and globalization.

In May of that year, following months of rancorous debate invoking the nation's literary giants, the French National Assembly adopted legislation that would ease legal restrictions on teaching in languages other than French in the nation's universities. At issue was the Loi Toubon (Toubon Law) adopted in 1994, a wide sweeping mandate that made French the "language of teaching, work, and public exchanges and services."[1] Just one day following the French legislative decision, a regional administrative court in Italy went in the opposite direction. There the court struck down plans at the renowned Polytechnic Institute of Milan to move toward master's- and doctoral-level courses exclusively in English by the 2014 academic year.

These seemingly unrelated events unleashed impassioned arguments resounding across the Alps. Simmering beneath the surface was the fundamental question of how universities could compete on an international level while still preserving their national identity. In the following month, the European Commission added yet another wrinkle to this already contentious debate. In separate documents, the commission called on universities to more intensely internationalize their programs and to focus more directly on instructional quality.[2] As universities have found, and as these two cases demonstrate, the competing pressures of internationalization as a process, not an end in itself, and the goal of programmatic quality are difficult to resolve, especially when English is added to the mix.

France: A Legislative Compromise

In 2017, the former economy minister and presidential candidate Emmanuel Macron addressed in English a conference on the European Union at Humboldt University in Berlin. Macron explained that, given his "bad German accent," he chose English so that he and his audience could best understand each other. On the heels of a visit to the United States where he had enthralled the American press, Macron no doubt wanted to affirm his international stature.

The media quickly took note of the speech in the "language of Shakespeare," and even ran the full forty-eight-minute video. They seemed less interested in what Macron had said than how he had said it. The speech supplied grist for eye-catching headlines like "Macron Shocks by Speaking English" and "Macron Under Fire for Speaking English." The Twitter response of Marine le Pen, the far-right presidential candidate, "Pauvre France," spoke volumes on the use of English as a political flashpoint (@MLP_officiel, January 10, 2017, 7:24 p.m.). Florian Philippot, vice president of Le Pen's National Front Party, chimed in, "It's not just that [Macron] doesn't respect our language, he doesn't believe in France."[3] Yet save for some idle quibbling on social media, Macron's choice of language seemed to elicit little more than a yawn from the French people at large.

No doubt it was an unusual move for a French politician to speak in English even when traveling to English-speaking countries. As already mentioned, the story of former French President Jacques Chirac storming out of an EU summit meeting in 2006 to protest a French delegate addressing the audience in English is now legendary. But times were changing. According to a poll taken in 2016 by the language school ABC English, 64 percent of France's young people believed that their country's politicians had inadequate English language skills. A generation coming of age in a global economy, products of the Erasmus program and active on social media, recognized the value of communicating in a common language across borders and cultures. And that language was English. Neither of Macron's immediate predecessors, Nicolas Sarkozy and François Hollande, was comfortable with the language. Macron may be in the vanguard of a new wave of French public figures, though certainly the former French finance minister and president of the European Central Bank Christine Lagarde's impeccable English should not be overlooked.

What seemed to be but a brief tempest in a teapot over a political speech in English was a stark contrast to public controversies that had gripped the country in preceding years over English instruction in schools and universities. In 2011, Minister of Education Luc Chatel's proposal to teach English to preschool children beginning at age three unleashed a barrage of criticism on the educational merits and doability. Threaded through the opposition were shades of anti-Anglo sentiment. The government ultimately pivoted toward merely "raising aware-ness" of all languages in the environment and not actually "teaching" them.[4] Unlike half the countries in Europe, France made English mandatory only in 2016, and then only beginning in the sixth grade (age eleven), with four hours per week. That said, most French children begin to study English at the age of six, when twenty minutes a day must be devoted to a foreign language. The man-dates cover all public schools and a majority of private schools.[5] Marching be-hind the European "banner" of multilingualism, France offers students one of the widest ranges of language options, including numerous regional languages. At least on paper, France is trying to develop a generation with the language skills for global mobility, but with obvious ambivalence toward English.[6] The government education website barely mentions English, which belies its dom-inance as the second language of choice among French parents and students.

The controversy over the use of English in French higher education was even more pronounced and ultimately consequential. In April and May of 2013, the French minister of higher education and research, Geneviève Fioraso, presented to the Senate and the Assembly a comprehensive proposal to reform French uni-versities. Article 2 of the proposed Loi Fioraso (Fioraso Law), ignited a debate that plumbed the depths of French identity over the months that followed. The plan would allow university courses to be taught in another language (in reality English) if they were part of an agreement with a foreign or international educa-tional institution or if they were financially supported by the European Union. It would effectively loosen restrictions in Article 2 of the 1994 Toubon Law, which mandates that French be used in six areas of public discourse: consumer information, employment; education; demonstrations, colloquia, and meet-ings; media; and the civil service.[7] To best understand the controversy over the Fioraso Law, we have to first go back to the 1990s, and even much earlier, where the modern-day seeds of that controversy were planted.

The Toubon Law

Over the centuries, the French government intermittently has issued language decrees, beginning with the 1539 Ordinance of Villers-Cotterêts, which called for the use of French in all legal acts and documents and which is still used in part by the courts.[8] The objective was not to make French the national language but to replace Latin with French and reduce the power of the Catholic Church while strengthening the power of the king. As the first sign of growing central-ization, the ordinance also had implications for regional languages. In 1635, Cardinal Richelieu established the Académie française to maintain *bon usage*, or the purity of French. At that time, universities still taught in Latin. During the French Revolution, French became *la langue de la liberté*. More definitively, it became *la langue de la République* and the modern French nation, tying "linguistic unity" to "national unity and a sense of national identity."[9] In the 1880s, the Ferry Laws, named after the minister of public instruction Jules Ferry, created a free and compulsory national school system and mandated instruction in French, which effectively delegitimized regional languages.[10] Modern-day laws have aimed to preserve the French language by defining and regulating it while claiming to inform consumers and protect workers. Included among them was the Toubon Law's immediate successor, the 1975 Bas-Lauriol Law, which required that French be used in commerce, advertising, and other transactions. The law suffered from poor drafting and lax enforcement, and its application was largely limited to cases of fraud.

In recent decades, the French government has created numerous official entities designed to oversee language use. Currently operative is the Délégation générale à la langue française et aux langues de France (General delegation to the French language and languages of France; DGLFLF). Located within the Ministry of Culture and Communication, the DGLFLF forms a network with other terminology commissions, authorized associations, and the Académie française to monitor the use of foreign terminology and recommend French equivalents.[11] Yet as France entered into the 1990s, neither the Bas-Lauriol, nor the precursor to the DGLFLF, nor intermittent government decrees proved effective in fending off the spread of English.

In June 1992, when France signed the Maastricht Treaty creating the European Union, it amended Article 2 of the constitution to make French the official language of the country.[12] At that time, a confluence of forces were weighing upon France and creating a sense of insecurity over identity and global status. Immigration was stepping up in pace. Germany was assuming a more prominent leadership role following the country's unification. New member states from Eastern Europe were poised to embrace English over French as a common European language. English was beginning to take hold throughout academic life and definitively in the sciences. Fears were spreading that France had not only "lost any vestiges of its empire" but was being "Americanized, invaded by unwelcomed immigrants, and attacked by bureaucrats in Brussels."[13] Those fears, bundled up in language, were all the more immediate given the ineffectiveness of the Bas-Lauriol Law.

The month following the signing of the Maastricht Treaty, there appeared in the French newspaper *Le Monde* an appeal, "The Future of the French Language," signed by over 250 writers, diplomats, actors, academicians, and former ministers. Included among them were philosophers Régis Debray and Alain Finkielkraut; the controversial author Michel Houellebecq, the historian Marc Fumaroli, who later became director of the Académie française; and the playwright Eugène Ionesco. Urging President François Mitterrand to "do something," the call railed against "fanatics of *le tout anglais* [English for everything] who are more and more daring. They are making the French doubt their own language and . . . are weakening its worth in other countries."[14]

Shortly before the change in government in 1993, Catherine Tasca, who was in charge of the Francophonie and foreign cultural relations, answered the call with a proposal that received no further discussion as the legislative session was about to close. The minister of culture and Francophonie, Jacques Toubon, a longtime member of the conservative Gaullist party, took up the charge in marshaling what became known as the Toubon Law to insulate French from English terms and American cultural influence. Article 11 of the law required that "the language of instruction, examinations, and competitive examinations, as well as theses and dissertations in state and private educational institutions, shall be French, except in cases justified by the need to teach foreign and regional languages and cultures or where the teachers are associate teachers or guest teachers." Article L.121–3 of the Code of Education tracked that language.[15] In sum, it prohibited teaching in a foreign language in universities with few exceptions. Only activities carried out in French would receive government funding, while fines of three thousand to ten thousand francs would be imposed on private persons violating the law and fifteen thousand to thirty thousand francs on firms and societies.

Toubon's proposal sparked intense debate in Parliament and in the press. Toubon himself became an object of ridicule, especially among Socialists. Though the proposal emanated from the Socialist government of François Mitterrand, the center-right majority in Parliament was mainly responsible for the drafting. The left leaning daily *Liberation* dismissed the plan as a futile "patriotic beau geste."[16] Socialist members in the National Assembly abstained from voting on it. While they agreed that the government should work toward enhancing the status of French and France, they associated the measure with anti-immigration forces. Sixty deputies, mostly Socialists, took the proposed law to the Conseil Constitutionnel. In the French legal system, only the Conseil Constitutionnel can decide constitutional issues under limited circumstances. The president of the republic, the prime minister, the president of the National Assembly, the president of the Senate, or sixty deputies or senators can refer an act of parliament to the Conseil before the president signs it into law.

The deputies claimed that the law violated Article 11 of the 1789 Declaration of the Rights of Man and of the Citizen upholding the right to "the free communication of ideas and opinions."[17] They challenged two provisions in Article 7. One required that publications, reviews, and communications in a foreign language must be accompanied by a summary in French. The other mandated that research funded under grants from public entities must be published or

distributed in French, or translated into French. The court upheld the first provision but struck down the second. The Court, moreover, held that the government could require that French be used in public life and impose certain
language requirements on public entities or private individuals or entities that
carry out a public service. But it could not prohibit private citizens from using a
foreign term or expression under penalty of sanctions.[18] Freedom of expression
implied that "each person has the right to choose their own words in the manner
they consider best to express their thoughts."[19] As a commentary in Le Monde
noted, on that point the law became essentially "a set of principles without normative scope.... Only those who speak it can create the French of today."[20]

Underlying the Toubon Law and its clarification in the Education Code rests
a profound belief among many French citizens that their language is a symbol
of cultural preeminence and worldview. Though young people and French
elites of all ages now embrace English, which has infiltrated French everyday
life, 77 percent of respondents in a 2016 French poll reported that being able to
speak French was "very important" to being French.[21] France also places heavy
stock in education as the mechanism for creating French citizens. And so the
Fioraso proposal, legally permitting instruction in other languages (and notably
in English) at universities, was a stark retreat from a French-only policy with
deep historical, political, and cultural roots. English had become the "Achilles
heel of higher education."[22]

The Fioraso Law

Fast-forward from 1994 to 2013. Over the course of several months, the legislature addressed the government's arguments supporting the proposal. The importance of recruiting international students, especially from rapidly expanding
economies, was indisputable. The point of disagreement was whether English or
French instruction should be the means for recruitment. One side argued that
teaching in English would harm Francophonie and the status of French abroad.
The other side claimed that it would attract foreign students who would become
"ambassadors" of French language and culture. "Democratization" and equal opportunity arguments also came into play. Proponents declared that the changes
would allow the large numbers of French university students the same access to
learning English as enjoyed by students in the elite grandes écoles and business
schools.

Presenting the proposal before the Council of Ministers, Fioraso maintained
that it was "pragmatic." "If we do not authorize courses in English," she argued,
"we will not attract students from emerging countries like South Korea and
India." But when she suggested that refusing to move toward English could result

in "five of us discussing Proust around a table," she struck a collective nerve. Her faux pas dismissing one of France's literary deities proved blasphemous in intellectual circles where sitting around a table discussing Marcel Proust was quintessentially French.[23] Antoine Compagnon, a professor at the Collège de France, shot back in the pages of *La Liberation*: "In English, we talk about friendly fire to describe the kind of action the minister has just taken. Because Ms. Fioraso pulls us in the back as we climb to the front. . . . With friends like these, who needs enemies?"[24]

Fioraso's aim was to increase the number of international students from 12 to 15 percent by 2020, which presumably would boost the global reputations of French institutions. She insisted that foreign students would be required to take French language courses as part of their degree. At that time, France ranked fourth as a destination for international and foreign students, behind the United States and the United Kingdom (anglophone countries) as well as behind Germany, where universities offered a wide range of English programs. Not counting students who were permanent residents, including the high numbers of students from immigrant families, France did not even rank among the top twenty-five countries.[25]

The new legislation, Fioraso argued, would eliminate inequalities, granting all French university students and not just the most privileged the opportunity to reap the advantages of learning in English. She accused the opposing forces of "hypocrisy" for having ignored the grandes écoles and business schools that were openly flouting the Toubon Law with no questions asked. "Many people who criticize this law," she pointed out, "studied at the *grandes écoles*. They speak a high level of English and their children are in the same situation."[26] At that point, the Conférence des grandes écoles (CGE) estimated that member institutions offered between a quarter and a third of their courses in English. Some establishments, like INSEAD (master's of business administration) and the École d'économie de Paris (both master's and doctoral degrees), used only English.[27]

Fioraso urged policymakers to trust the institutions that were demanding these changes.[28] She argued that the French themselves had much to gain from expanding the role of English in French universities. English would prepare French students for jobs in the global economy and facilitate the work of French researchers, especially in the sciences. A large-scale study conducted between 2007 and 2009 had found that 77 percent of French researchers, across disciplines and ages, believed that English had become so essential that they had no choice but to concede. For those born in the 1980s, that belief rose to 90 percent, though 42 percent reported that they had limited use of the language. Younger researchers were less likely to equate English with Anglo-Saxon cultural dominance. Among laboratory directors in the hard sciences, 96 percent reported using English in their work.[29] That was over a decade ago. The level of English proficiency among young researchers undoubtedly would be higher today.

In the months leading to the legislative vote, strident voices emerged on both sides. Lawmakers, including members of Fioraso's own Socialist Party, denounced the proposal as a sign of the nation's "waning influence," a "humiliation to French speakers," and a "suicidal project."[30] Opponents repeatedly invoked the giants of French intellectual life and literature and the historical role of French as the language of international affairs. For many of them, yielding to English meant nothing less than conceding political defeat to the forces of Anglo-Saxon culture. How could the French replace the language of Molière with the language of Shakespeare? The Académie française immediately denounced "the dangers of a measure" that promoted the "marginalization of our language."[31] L'Observateur européen du plurilinguisme, a French-based organization that fosters linguistic diversity against the dominance of English, expressed fear that the changes would give rise to a uniformity of thought among scholars. Tied to a particular language and a particular culture's "history of words," the Fioraso proposal would "kill innovation."[32]

Prominent professors called the project a "self-destructive impulse," an assault on the French language.[33] Claude Hagège, a lecturer at the Collège de France and vocal critic of American English, warned that it was "no longer time" for the French to "close their eyelids." "We are at war!" he wrote on his blog in Le Monde.[34] Claude Truchot, professor emeritus at the University of Strasbourg and prolific critic of le tout anglais, urged that France learn from the negative consequences in Germany and the Netherlands, where English-taught courses had lowered the quality of teaching and learning in higher education institutions.[35] The philosopher Michel Serres assailed France for acting like a "colonized country whose language no longer could say everything," in essence abandoning its "linguistic sovereignty in the face of Anglo-American imperialism."[36] For author Frédéric Werst, a leader in the opposition campaign, the idea that the plan would attract the most qualified foreign students was "delusional." To the contrary, he said, the best English-speaking students would choose Anglo institutions, while French universities would only be a "fallback option." He accused Fioraso of being "blinded by a utilitarian ideology, which believes that knowledge is a commodity and a language is simply packaging." "Excellence," he argued, "is not just about speaking mediocre Globish but about mastering several languages."[37]

Jacques Attali, author, economist, and former adviser to President François Mitterrand, sounded an equally shrill note. "One cannot imagine," he said, "an idea more stupid, more counterproductive, more dangerous, and more contrary to France's interest."[38] Attali's position, nonetheless, was difficult to reconcile with a report he had published in 1998. There he had called on French higher education institutions to welcome more foreign students and researchers, to allow foreign students to take at least part of their coursework in English so that French would not prove an obstacle to their studying in France, and to permit professors to teach in English.[39] His more recent blog post in *Le Monde* undoubtedly proved both startling and distressing to Geneviève Fioraso. Not only did clause 2 of her proposal quote Attali's 1998 words almost verbatim, but she also relied extensively on the quote in her interviews with the press. One had to wonder whether the French landscape had so changed in fifteen years of globalization to justify Attali's making such an about-face without an explanation.[40]

Others raised more pragmatic and immediate concerns. Professors without job security, especially part-time faculty, feared losing their positions to native English speakers. Some teaching unions threatened to strike. Lawmakers repudiated using tax revenues to advance the interests of Great Britain and the United States. Political groups, from nationalists to socialists, jumped into the debate. The Union populaire républicaine, a hardline Eurosceptic political party founded in 2007, claimed to have gathered close to thirteen thousand signatures on a Facebook petition that spared no words in denouncing the proposal. "To kill one's own language," the petition read, "is a manifestation of an incomprehensible self-hate and a political will toward self-mutilation and self-colonization," reducing France to a "banal province of a vast English-speaking Euro-Atlantic group." It invoked Umberto Eco's oft-cited statement, "The language of Europe is translation," not English.[41]

The opposition crossed the political divide. On the far left, the Communist Party newsletter carried an image of a young woman with an American flag covering her eyes and a British flag covering her mouth, crying out, "Non au tout anglais" ("No to everything English"). For party leaders, the proposal was nothing but an "ultraliberal project . . . to destroy the French language." They raised the specter of English reinforcing social inequalities among students and displacing professors in favor of native English speakers from the United States, Britain, and India.[42] Looking at these developments from the outside, François Grin of the University of Geneva, an avid proponent of multilingualism, later remarked that the issue was not about "French against English" but about "plurilingualism against uniformity." He too feared that this kind of uniformity fosters a single way of thinking, which limits creativity and innovation. But in twenty or thirty years, he projected, it would help French students gain proficiency in English and give them access to the global economy.[43]

Amidst this deluge of opposition, Fioraso maintained some supporters within the academy and among the French intelligentsia. Chief among them was Jean-Loup Salzmann, president of the Conférence des presidents d'université (Conference of university presidents). Salzmann recognized the reality of English as the international language, regardless of what the "pessimists" thought.[44] Several Nobel laureates likewise warned of the dangers of "linguistic bunkerization." The international exchange of researchers and students, they contended, was indispensable to maintaining research and innovation at the highest level and reinforcing the image and role of France in the world.[45] For Pierre Tapie, president of the business school ESSEC and head of the Conférence des grandes écoles, the reform was "a step in the right direction."[46]

For the liberal press, it was a foregone conclusion. With the title "No English, No Survival," the French daily *Le Parisien* recounted the problems of laid-off adult workers who needed to learn English to re-enter the job market. To drive the point deeper, it cited France's relatively poor performance in English, at that time ranking sixty-ninth out of one hundred nine countries on the Test of English as a Foreign Language (TOEFL) and twenty-third out of fifty-four countries on the annual *English Proficiency Index*.[47] The title of the *Nouvel Observateur's* article, "Courses 100% en anglais à la fac: ça fait déjà, my dear!" ("Courses 100 % in English in the universities: it's already done, my dear"), spoke for itself.[48] The left-leaning newspaper *Libération* lent straightforward support in a front-page headline: "Teaching in English: **LET'S DO IT.**" The editorial board urged readers to "stop behaving like the last representatives of a besieged Gaulish village."[49] The reference was to the popular French comic strip hero Asterix and the inhabitants of his village, the "last corner of Gaul to hold out against Roman invasion."[50]

The Fioraso proposal became incorporated into French law in July 2013 as part of a broader set of higher education reforms. To appease the opposition, the bill adopted by the Senate and Assembly contained a number of modifications, incorporated in the Education Code: the use of English had to be justified by "pedagogical necessities," programs could only be offered partially in a foreign language, international students had to study French, and their French grades would count toward their final diploma score.[51] As Geneviève Fioraso later admitted, she agreed to the term "partially" in order to get the amendment passed, though she deliberately left the language vague to "leave room for maneuver."[52]

In the end, it was largely a win for Fioraso, who achieved with few concessions what she had set out to do. Yet she had not totally escaped the scorn of her detractors. Before the legislative battle had ended, the Académie de la carpette (commonly translated as the "English Doormat Academy") bestowed on her an "exceptional award" for having "legalized the teaching of English" in French universities, despite "numerous warnings."[53] The group, both admired and reviled for its tongue-in-cheek rhetoric, awards an annual prize to members of the French élite who relentlessly promote English over French in France and in European institutions. Previous awardees included the CEOs of Vivendi and Renault and the head of HEC, the prestigious French business school whose graduate programs are totally English-taught.

Side-Stepping Toubon

As instruction in English steadily grew in the years that followed, the question whether English was Anglo "soft power" and a "threat to French" hung heavily in the air. Critics decried the failure to apply the law as "scandalous." They took the administrative courts to task for not condemning institutions like the elite *grandes écoles* for offering programs exclusively in English.[54] With Brexit progressively becoming a reality and the anti-immigrant policies of Donald Trump deflating the US education market, France saw an opportunity to position itself even more favorably in recruiting international students. The government's aggressive efforts in India and anglophone Africa, as well as other non-francophone countries, put added pressure on French institutions to expand English courses and programs.

Managing outreach activities is Campus France, a government-funded nonprofit national agency established in 2011 to promote and manage international student mobility across public and private higher education institutions. With 225 offices in 124 countries worldwide, Campus France coordinates the diplomatic needs of French embassies abroad with those of French higher education establishments. Its English language website, marketing materials, Twitter postings, and recruitment fairs abroad all convey a clear message that speaking French is not essential to studying in France.[55]

Between April 2013 and January 2017, French higher education programs taught totally in English increased by more than 50 percent, from 631 to 951. Programs partially in English grew by more than 95 percent, from 161 to 315.[56] Those rising figures provoked the French advocacy group Avenir de la langue française (Future of the French language) and thirteen other associations to pursue legal action. In 2017, much to their chagrin, an appeals court affirmed the decision of the administrative court in Paris upholding the prestigious École normale supérieure's offering a master's degree in physics totally in English. The program, the court concluded, would operate within an international framework and "laboratory of excellence" designed to attract international students in compliance with the 2013 Fioraso Law.[57]

By January 2019, English-taught programs in France had risen to 1,328, of which 75 percent were entirely in English. Business, management, and engineering sciences represented two-thirds of the total. By January 2020, the total numbered 1,500, including 125 bachelor's and 1,200 master's programs offered mostly or entirely in English. The goal was to recruit students from China, India, and anglophone Africa who would not study in France if required to take French-taught courses. At that point, France was still the fifth most popular country for foreign students, and the second behind Germany among non-anglophone countries.[58] When the coronavirus pandemic sent shock waves through international

education in 2020, Campus French launched a hard-hitting recruitment campaign on social media (in English and French versions) addressing prospective students via video with a persuasive and timely message. It offered them a
"hybrid education" (in person and online) that would make them "distinct and
capable" of entry into "this new [post-COVID] economy" where "openness,
cultural, linguistic, and digital knowledge" would be "essential."[59]

The French government, in other ways, has sent signals that English is valued
and on the rise. In February 2018, France's prime minister, Edouard Philippe,
speaking at EDHEC, the prestigious French graduate school of business, announced plans to "accelerate" the teaching of English in France's secondary
schools and higher education. The plans were part of a wider set of measures,
what Philippe called "«game changers» comme on dit en bon français" ("as
they say in proper French") to enhance international trade and exports. "Because
a quarter of jobs are linked to export; because even those not working in export
still need English in their lives; because English is the 'first language' of globalization and to speak it well is to be in control of one's future," he explained. Philippe
was addressing a young and striving audience ready to "make an impact," as the
school's English language website invited them to do.[60] Reaffirming that view, he
unequivocally tweeted, "English is now the lingua franca" (@PhilippeEdouard,
February 23, 2018, 10.23 a.m.).

For the French government to deem English essential to making France more
competitive in global trade and to declare it "the lingua franca" was indeed historic. It was also ironic and baffling in view of subsequent events. The following
July, in a seemingly veiled barb at President Macron, Philippe reportedly criticized French people who interspersed their French with English words and
phrases. Perhaps it was simply *franglais* that he found irritating.[61] Just the previous month, the government had invited the French people to participate in
a two-month public consultation, "My Idea for French," followed by a two-day
conference of four hundred personalities and civil society actors from across the
globe. The aim was to generate innovative proposals that promote the French
language and plurilingualism. The project culminated in March at the Institut
de France with Macron rolling out a detailed plan, covering education, communication, and the arts, to "restore the French language to its place and its role in
the world."[62]

The administration obviously was struggling to ride the economic wave of
globalization through English while steering a pro-French course wrapped in
the mantle of multilingualism. Later that year, based on a commissioned report
cowritten by the French general inspector for modern languages and a British
journalist, the government launched an ambitious program to shore up foreign
languages in primary and secondary schools. The report specifically emphasized English. Making English mandatory for all students, it noted, would have a

symbolic effect in recognizing it as indispensable in the education of all students, regardless of social background and level of education. Adding more bilingual classes and teaching science, mathematics, and history in English and other languages, government officials underscored the importance of introducing children to English in the early grades.[63] Yet they failed to mention the Ministry of Education's data showing that over 90 percent of students in primary and secondary education were already learning English as a first foreign language.

The report drew a stark contrast, particularly in teaching English, between the success of northern European countries and the failure of France. At that time, France ranked fifteenth out of sixteen in a Europe-wide survey of how well foreign languages were taught.[64] By 2018, France ranked only thirty-first out of one hundred countries on the annual *English Proficiency Index*, down from twenty-third out of fifty-four countries in 2013. The Netherlands, Sweden, Norway, and Denmark ranked in the top four places.[65] Announcing the recommended changes, the French minister of education told the media, "We know perfectly well that if our Scandinavian neighbors are so good at English it is because they watch films in their original language." The state TV, he said, would be encouraged to follow that model for children's programming.[66]

With a target of attracting half a million international students by 2027 and doubling the number of students from emerging and mostly non-francophone countries, the government announced a series of measures to make France more appealing. It called for streamlining the visa process and loosening work eligibility for foreign students. It proposed doubling the number of students who would benefit from intensive training in French as a foreign language and from English-taught programs. It looked toward removing legal obstacles to permit programs taught in a foreign language as long as they enrolled international students. It made programs taught partly or entirely in English or in another foreign language eligible to receive support from the Bienvenue en France (Welcome to France) seed fund.

The plan emphasized fluency in English for both French and international students. At the end of high school and again at the end of the bachelor's degree, French students would have to pass an English test, financed by the state.[67] When the government adopted the requirement into law in 2020, prioritizing English over other languages and suggesting the use of Anglo-based tests like the Test of English for International Communication (TOEIC) and the Test of English as a Foreign Language (TOEFL), it met strong opposition, especially from foreign language teachers. The plan usurped their authority to assess the language skills of their students, they claimed, and needlessly expended public funds on the private sector. It also removed any incentive to learn other languages. Students would focus on passing the English test to earn their diploma.[68] Looked at objectively, aside from the debatable merits, the plan seemed to run counter to the

EU's multilingualism project and to the spirit of plurilingualism encouraged by the Council of Europe.

Language teachers are not alone in pushing back against the rise of English in the French educational system. While many professors have quietly acceded to publishing in English to maintain their academic standing, others continue to fight what may be a losing battle. In an op-ed published in February 2019 in *Le Monde*, one hundred management teachers and researchers (the maximum number allowed by *Le Monde*) called on French academic authorities to challenge the dominance of English language journals in evaluating their work. Touting the rich history of management science in France, they questioned the weight that French government research institutions like the Centre national de la recherche scientifique (National Center for Scientific Research) place on English language journals. The sole criterion used is the "impact factor," which measures the number of times that articles published in the journal have been cited in other articles over the previous three years. Obviously, there are far more English-speaking researchers in the world who read articles published in English and far more journals published in English. As the op-ed argued, the measure said nothing about the quality of work published in French journals.[69]

A petition airing those grievances, posted by the group known as the Collectif d'enseignants-chercheurs en gestion (Collective of management teachers-researchers), gathered upward of nearly four hundred signatures by early 2021.[70] The grievances may have struck a chord within the government. The following November, the minister of culture hosted a colloquium, "For Sciences in French and in Other Languages." Throughout the day, a stream of international scholars, government officials, and others denounced the "impoverishment" that comes with the dominance of one language (English) while they made the case for multilingualism in the sciences to preserve a "plurality of thought." One notable break in the thread came from a representative of the Ministry of Higher Education, Research, and Innovation who underscored the ministry's measures favoring a larger number of courses taught in English.[71]

The slow but steady move toward English in French universities is not the only area in which the Toubon Law is being bent. Browse through popular French magazines, ride the Paris metro, walk through Charles de Gaulle Airport, or wander past displays in French shop windows and you are met with a barrage of English phrases, slogans, and taglines. For retailers in particular, English "sells," it's "trendy," and it reaches a wide market. Even Air France draws international clientele with its company slogan "France Is in the Air." Take part in a business *meeting* and you encounter people talking about *les benchmarks, les startups*, and *le marketing*. Tune into French television or radio and you hear repeated references to *le news, le smartphone, les mails, le leader*, and *le challenge*, as if corresponding words did not exist in French. Though the Toubon Law requires radio stations to play at least 35 percent French songs (reduced from 40 percent in 2016), the remaining 65 percent is flooded with American music. Many young French artists themselves now sing in English to attract an international audience. And while France has a strong and well-subsidized film industry, about half of the major films playing in French theaters come from the United States.[72] An increasing number are shown in the original version (English) with French subtitles.

The Commission for the Enrichment of the French Language (CELF), a group of academics and cultural figures formed in 1996, takes these slights seriously. In 2017 it issued a ruling against using English words such as *gamer*, *dark web*, and *fake news*, in lieu of *joueur*, *internet clandestine*, and a completely new word, *infox* (*faux info* is more common). The ruling is quietly ignored among the limited group of young cosmopolitans in the French population that is most likely to use these terms in the first instance. Some of that dismissal is related to age, and some to class. And so the French are caught in the middle between their desire to be fashionable and their passion for preserving their cultural identity, of which the French language is a key part.

Symptomatic of that tension was the social media frenzy surrounding the slogan "Made for Sharing" on the Eiffel Tower as Paris competed for the 2024 Olympics. For purists, the organizers' claimed intent to give the French project a "universal character" in the competition did not justify once again casting aside "la langue de Molière."[73] On a more somber note, during the 2020 COVID-19 pandemic, when a new medical vocabulary, including anglicisms like *cluster*, *coping*, and *tracking*, spread across the globe as fast as the virus itself, the French minister of culture announced that these "notions imported from the Anglo-Saxon world" were often "obscure" to many French people. He understandably urged using the French equivalents.[74] Yet journalists still repeatedly used the term "cluster" rather than the French translation, "foyer d'infection."

Given all these developments, it was not surprising when the twenty-fifth anniversary of the Toubon Law triggered a government call for more vigilant application and enforcement. In February 2019, the French minister of culture, Franck Riester, warned against abandoning the French language in the interests of globalization. French is "essential to our republican pact and social cohesion," he said.[75] In June of that year, a French language collective (Le collectif langue française) published an open letter with one hundred signatures in the French newspaper *Le Parisien*. The letter could not have been more direct. It called on President Macron to protect French from the increasing "invasion" of English. "The French language is in a bad state," it read. "Stifled by British and American English, it sees its usage being ousted." The signatories asked the president to set an example by renouncing the use of "Anglo-American" abroad, by reinforcing a binding application of the law and reminding judicial authorities of their power to prosecute offenders, and by stopping the suicidal march toward the enthronement of the Anglo-American language as the second official language of the nation.[76]

The Macron government responded with what the press called a "crackdown on the English language."[77] On the anniversary of the law, Riester urged his followers on Twitter to "say things in French," the "language of the Republic" (@ franckriester, August 4, 2019, 5:41 a.m.). Critics pointedly reminded Riester that the president himself regularly used English idioms, while top French companies used English slogans like Renault's "Never Too Much" and again Air France's "France Is in the Air" posters.[78] The Académie française weighed in the following November, raising concerns with *franglais* and the "invasion of Anglo-Saxon terms." The statement, posted on its website, "solemnly" alerted "the authorities" and invited them, without naming names, to "respect the law themselves."[79]

To what extent these civil society demands and official pronouncements matter remains uncertain. Regardless of government and other pressures to enforce the language and spirit of the Toubon Law in general and the flexibility of the Fioraso Law in particular, as linguist Bernard Spolsky has explained, "Centralized language management plans do not achieve their goals." Among the primary components of language policy is "self-management." Speakers modify their own linguistic repertoire and proficiency, whether by socialization from their linguistic environment or by actively taking steps to improve their language skills.[80] With a young generation casually using English and less concerned than their parents with speaking *sans faute* (perfectly); a president flaunting his English as a badge of cosmopolitanism, even calling France a "start-up nation," while vigorously defending the glory of French; a now former prime minister promoting English as the dominant lingua franca; and a business sector chasing the bottom line where English carries economic capital, one has to wonder whether it's too late to rein in the steady march toward English within French universities and throughout French society.

For whatever it is worth, globalization and the internet have moved the French people a long way toward accepting, and even embracing, English as a dominant force because of, or in spite of, its ties to the United States. In 2020, France jumped from thirty-first to twenty-eighth the previous year in the world rankings on English proficiency.[81] English is now the language of electronic communication, while the internet has become the "new Académie française."[82] Online music streaming, as opposed to the radio, as well as streamed American films and TV series available on platforms like Netflix, are more widely exposing young people to English and motivating them to learn the language, which makes limits in the Toubon Law increasingly ineffective. These developments, added to the government's aggressive recruitment of students from non-francophone countries, are driving France toward English-taught university courses and programs.

In the end, one is left to wonder whether the wavering national angst over Englishization, especially among an older generation, will sustain itself and what effect a younger generation eager to embrace English will have not only on English in French universities but on French and its world status in the years to come. As France continues to struggle against the forces of English, it may be fighting in large part an enemy from within.

Italy: A Judicial Question of Rights and Governance

The controversy in France arose in response to a legislative proposal of nationwide scope set against a long history of laws and a constitutional provision giving primacy to the French language. It also took ground in a country where the national language is inextricably tied to national identity. The Italian controversy, in contrast, immediately concerned just one prestigious technical university in a country where language laws are negatively associated with Fascism, the constitution is silent on a national language, and late unification left a legacy of linguistic diversity uncommon in Europe. In a 2016 poll on language and national identity, only 59 percent of Italian respondents reported that being able to speak the national language was "very important" for "truly being Italian," the lowest among ten European countries and especially striking as compared to 84 percent in the Netherlands and 77 percent in France.[83]

Though the Polytechnic Institute's proposal to move all graduate courses to English evoked visceral responses, especially among intellectual elites, ideological hostility toward "Anglo-Saxon" dominance was not as evident as it was in the case of France. And unlike the repeated French invocations to the language of Molière, the need to preserve the language of Dante or to promote multilingualism only occasionally surfaced. Within the institute itself, the debate focused on the practical consequences for students, faculty, and the curriculum, especially in the sciences. As the dispute moved into the judicial arena, the legal conflict between individual rights and institutional autonomy took center stage, raising important questions that extended beyond the national borders.

To best comprehend the proposed plan and the competing interests at stake, one first has to consider the particular academic setting. Milan's Polytechnic Institute (POLIMI), often compared to the Massachusetts Institute of Technology (MIT) in the United States, is the premier technological institution in Italy. In 2020, its student body numbered upward of forty-six thousand, of which over six thousand were international students primarily enrolled in the master of science program. Founded in 1863 and state-funded, the institute has seven campuses that extend throughout the region of Lombardy in the north of Italy. The main campus is in Milan. Though not as old or as highly ranked as the University of Bologna, which dates from 1088, the Polytechnic University has a storied past and a highly regarded present. It hosted the first European center for electronic computing in the 1950s, laid claim to a Nobel Prize winner among its chemistry faculty in the 1960s, and was the birthplace of the European communications satellite Siro, launched in 1977.

A flagship institution for engineering, industrial design, and architecture, the institute counts almost one-third of Italy's architects among its alumni. It ranked first among Italian universities and among the top 150 universities worldwide in the QS World University Rankings 2020. For three consecutive years, from 2017 to 2019, it was named among the top five university incubators in the global rankings. The institute is located in a city steeped in Italian icons of both tradition and innovation, from the La Scala opera house and the soaring gothic architecture of the Milan Cathedral to its trend-setting fashion and modern design industries. And so the announcement that the school would offer all of its graduate courses in English by 2014 triggered what the BBC News called a "cultural earthquake" in a country that has been relatively slow to embrace English, including in its universities.[84] On the 2020 English Proficiency Index, Italy ranked thirtieth out of one hundred countries, up from thirty-sixth the previous year, but still the lowest in the EU next to Spain.[85] Even Italy's two largest cities, Milan and Rome, ranked lower than any other EU city included in the study.[86] Part of the blame rests on the lack of exposure to English, which dubbing of films and TV series rather than subtitling, a remnant of Fascism and of widespread illiteracy into mid-twentieth century, has made all the more intractable.

Institutions in the north were the first to embrace English instruction in the early 1990s. The Bologna Framework, adopted in 1999, ensuring mutual recognition of qualifications among twenty-nine (now forty-nine) participating countries, generated greater interest in internationalization and consequently English to accommodate foreign students.[87] Over the years, English instruction slowly increased, especially in graduate programs in science and engineering and among private universities, which are typically wealthier and more likely to forge international connections. In 2007, heads turned when the state-funded Polytechnic Institute of Turin, the country's oldest technical university, lowered university fees for first year students who followed a bachelor's program partially or totally in English.

In 2010, a questionnaire completed by 50 percent of Italian universities revealed that 86 percent of private and 71 percent of the public ones had introduced English-taught courses or programs. Among the principal reasons given, only 8 percent reported "to improve English proficiency" as compared with 32 percent "to improve the international profile," 21 percent "to attract foreign students," and 24 percent "to prepare Italian students for the global market."

Evidently the driving force was far more economic than academic, and so universities attached little importance to the language factor. The survey found that universities opting for English-taught courses almost totally lacked teacher-training programs, though 90 percent of the lecturers were Italian native speakers. Among 30 percent of the universities, the lecturers' insufficient competence in English posed the greatest challenge. For 31 percent, it was insufficient English skills among Italian students. In 71 percent of the cases lecturers were still delivering content through traditional monologues rather than the more typical "give and take" of an anglophone classroom.[88] A study of the Polytechnic Institute of Turin in 2012–13 similarly found that inadequate English language skills among lecturers was the problem most frequently cited (38 percent), followed by inadequate English language skills among Italian students (20 percent).[89]

Part of the drive (or justification) for English instruction comes from a law adopted in 2010. Known as the Gelmini Law after the minister of education Mariastella Gelmini, Law no. 240 reorganized the Italian university system along a 3–2-year axis: a three-year bachelor's degree followed by a two-year master's degree. Article 2 of the law calls for strengthening the internationalization process "*also* through" a number of strategies, including the offering of degree programs and selection procedures in a foreign language. The significance of the term *also* would later prove decisive in the courts.[90] Supporting the trend toward English instruction, the Italian ministry in 2012 introduced an Italian-English website, UniversItaly, listing all university courses, including those taught in English. Yet none of these developments foresaw what Milan's Polytechnic Institute proposed. Totally abandoning Italian in favor of English, even in graduate programs, was a first. And the plan's prime mover was a prestigious, cutting-edge institution, which others would closely watch as a model for success or a recipe for failure.

The Proposed Plan

The Polytechnic Institute started offering some courses in English in 2003, initially in its regional branches. Gradually the number grew to include master's courses in management science, mechanical engineering, civil engineering, and construction engineering. By the time the plan was first deliberated within the academic senate in November 2011, 30 percent of graduate coursework was in English. These courses were especially appealing to foreign students. They were limited in number, and the institute initially offered them in parallel with the same courses in Italian, which the Italian students favored. Foreign nationals, who represented 10 percent of the school's thirty-seven thousand students and a quarter of the graduate enrollment, never registered for any of the Italian-taught courses. A total of 55 percent of those students came from non-English-speaking countries, including Brazil, Russia, India, Vietnam, Turkey, and Iran.[91] The situation inevitably created two academically equal but socially separate streams where Italian and foreign students seldom, if ever, met. As the institute's rector, Giovanni Azzone, told the press, "I had a student from one of the Gulf states say to me that he could have had the same experience in Dubai."[92] Azzone resolutely believed that English would make the Italian students more employable, attract overseas students and researchers, and raise the institution's visibility in international rankings.

Between December 2011 and May 2012, the academic senate adopted three resolutions that set out the goals of the proposed plan and various strategies for developing and measuring competence in English among students, faculty, and staff.[93] The plan was designed to address the demands of internationalization and globalization. It would cap tuition at €3,500 (US$4,100) for non-EU students. Approximately a quarter of them would attend free of charge. It included a number of measures to ease the transition and ensure the program's success. Foreign students would be required to take Italian language and culture classes, accounting for ten of the 120 credits in master's programs. The institute would offer an extensive English language training program (contracted outside the university) for professors and administrative staff, though it set no specific learning outcomes. In 2012, almost three hundred professors and researchers, together with 238 support staff members, began weekly English classes, to continue through 2015.[94] Faculty could spend a semester abroad to develop English competency in their field of expertise. The school allocated €3.2 million (US$3.8 million) to cover the cost of English-speaking instructors, including fifteen professors, thirty to thirty-five postdocs, and twenty visiting professors.[95] It began actively recruiting native English speakers for the permanent faculty with a goal of reaching 20 percent non-Italian faculty. Initially, visiting professors would cover many courses.

The plan elicited passionate reactions from leading intellectuals, which became widely aired in the press. Though not as intense as responses to the Fioraso Law in France, where the immediate implications were more wide reaching, the competing views largely fell along a similar divide between the humanities in opposition and the sciences in support. In the months leading up to the Academic Senate's final vote, a debate erupted in the pages of *Corriere della Sera*, the country's oldest and most read daily newspaper. It began with an opinion piece by the philosopher Tullio Gregory. It was a direct response to the minister of instruction, universities, and research having endorsed the Polytechnic plan in the interests of internationalization. Gregory argued that imposing "English for all" does not make anyone "more modern or more 'productive'" but rather "damages humanistic culture and science."[96] The institute's rector Azzone's retort strategically focused on the advantages for Italy in making English mandatory. Not only would English offer foreign students greater access to Italian universities, he argued, but it would save Italy from losing a growing number of its own students who were open to the world and to training in a global context. For Azzone, time was of the essence, and there was no choice but to quickly make the changes.[97]

Over the next several weeks, other voices were heard. Some, like linguist Luca Serianni, claimed that the plan was excessive. If Italian students, who largely practice in English, relinquish their mother tongue, Serianni argued, they will "lose control of logical argumentative structure" and their "ability to reason." The linguist Tullio De Mauro similarly warned of the "negative effects on intelligence" and viewed it as "an unacceptable choice for a public university." The writer Sandro Veronesi called the plan "a completely Italian madness, a desperate choice." Through language, he explained, "thought is organized: it is good to know the dominant one, but one cannot cut out the mother tongue." Countering the opposition, Azzone's fellow scientists rallied to his support. The scientific director of the Italian Institute of Technology, Roberto Cingolani, saw no competition between English and Italian. English, he noted, was "indispensable" as a technical language, and the choice of the Polytechnic was "a great opportunity for technical education, for our children and for those who come from the outside." The president of the Order of Architects, Amedeo Schiattarella, agreed that the transition to English was "almost obligatory."[98]

To what extent this squabble over English at this elite technical institution mattered to the Italian public, or even to the academic community, is hard to determine. Yet no one, not even Giovanni Azzone, could foresee that it would ultimately be resolved in the country's highest court. The rector tried to reach consensus within the institute by giving the various constituent groups ample opportunity to air their views. Throughout the academic year, he held multiple meetings with the faculty senate and open forums with faculty and students. The faculty senate approved the plan by a 28:1 margin. The institute's doctoral students overwhelmingly agreed. For the president of the PhD student's association, it was purely a pragmatic decision. "What is the point," he asked, "of publishing in a language that no one else can read?"[99]

Some students still had serious reservations. An activist student association, La Terna Sinistrorsa, organized an open meeting with the rector. In a two-hour videotaped discussion, students respectfully but emphatically posed a list of questions presented in a written statement accompanying the meeting. The concerns raised were reasonable. Students focused on the two-year timeline, the level of English skills among the current faculty, and insecurities with their own fluency in English. They questioned the method of assessing English proficiency among incoming students and noted the potential impact on the quality of instruction as well as the danger of losing an Italian perspective on the subject matter. Azzone acknowledged that there would be problems during the transition period. But he also expressed confidence that the benefits in moving this highly regarded institution, its students, and its faculty into the global age would outweigh the temporary costs.[100]

As the weeks moved on, a number of faculty members expressed deep concerns with the all-English plan. Some feared that it was discriminatory and would have a negative effect on their careers if they were restricted to teaching undergraduate courses (in Italian) based on their limited knowledge of English. A particular conflict arose between the engineering and architecture programs regarding distinct ways of "disseminating knowledge." The head of the School of Architecture argued that few classics in the field had been translated into English. If international students did not read those texts in Italian, then what would be the added value of studying architecture in Italy?[101] The strongest and most consequential opposition came from a relatively small but vocal minority within the faculty that threatened legal action to keep the plan from being implemented. In a petition entitled "An Appeal in Defense of Freedom of Teaching," 185 of the total 1,400 professors challenged the plan's constitutionality. For the petition's leader, Professor Emilio Matricciani, who spoke fluent English, having lived in the United States as an exchange student, "the point [was] not English." It was that English was being "imposed on students as a kind of linguistic dictatorship." As he explained, "Speaking Italian to our countrymen is like watching a movie in colour, high definition, very clear pictures. Speaking English to them, even with our best effort, is like watching a movie in black and white."[102]

The Accademia della Crusca, dedicated to preserving the Italian language, denounced the plan. Dating from 1583, the society is located outside the city center in the imposing Villa Medicea di Castello , a favorite residence of Lorenzo il Magnifico. The surrounding lush gardens planted in 1540, among the most renowned in Italy, give the setting an air of tranquility and tradition. Yet the society and the roughly sixty Italian and foreign academicians who are its members frequently address language issues of the day, especially as they relate to Italy and Europe. As a case in point, in 2010 they hosted an invitational colloquium on multilingualism including Leonard Orban, then the EU commissioner for multilingualism, along with Amin Maalouf, author of the report on multilingualism prepared by a group of intellectuals, and other EU representatives and linguists.

The society is generally known as "La Crusca," which means "bran" in Italian; its emblem is a sifter, representing the founders' vision of straining corrupt words and structures from the Italian language, as wheat is separated from the chaff. The society's history is rich in twists and turns, from being rescued by Napoleon Bonaparte to being closed down by Mussolini's language police.[103] The society has made clear that it is not hostile to English, but it firmly supports preserving Italian and other national languages as conveyers of culture and national identity. In the spring of 2012, as the debate over the Polytechnic proposal heated up, La Crusca organized a roundtable discussion posing the question, "Is it useful and appropriate to adopt English monolingualism in Italian university courses?" Among the invited participants were Polytechnic's rector, Giovanni Azzone; the deputy minister for instruction, universities, and research, Elena Ugolini; the philosopher Tullio Gregory, who had triggered the *Corriere della Sera* debate; and an assortment of scholars, including scientists, mathematicians, and linguists, as well as members of the judiciary.

Looking to stimulate discussion among a wider audience, La Crusca subsequently gathered together the presentations, along with written submissions from academicians, authors, journalists, board members, and others. Many of them had publicly commented on the question in newspapers and on blogs. The writings, diverse in style, tone, and perspective, quickly went to print in a three-hundred-page compendium called *Fuori l'italiano dall'università* (Italian outside the university).[104] As the Accademia's president, Nicoletta Maraschio, explained in the preface, despite some differences, the contributors largely agreed that using English exclusively was neither useful nor effective. They especially raised concerns about the loss of Italian in certain areas of knowledge, particularly science, and the consequent loss to the public denied access to that knowledge. Most agreed that an Italian-English "parallel track" solution for individual courses or entire programs was preferable to a monolingual approach in a language other than Italian. But they also agreed that English was "essential" for gaining "access" to a "wealth of common knowledge (particularly in science and economics)" and for job mobility. Italian university students needed "a good, and even excellent," command of English.[105]

The institute and its rector were not willing to compromise on the total-English plan. For Azzone, the risk of not going forward on English was too high. The institute, he warned, would remain "stuck in the middle, between Anglo-Saxon countries which represent the traditional leaders in education, and the Asian countries which [Italy's] young people believe represent the future."[106] The opposing faculty members, ultimately one hundred in number, were equally resolute. Their only recourse was to take their grievances to the regional administrative court.

The Courts Have Their Say

In May 2013, the regional administrative court struck down the plan, taking the institute and its supporters by surprise. Even more remarkable was the court's rationale, which went well beyond the law per se. The opinion, in fact, showed an impressive understanding of university life, the competing interests at stake, and the scope and limits of judicial intervention in a constitutional system of law. It also set the course for the judicial decisions that followed as the case wound its way through the Italian courts over the next five years. Weaving together law and policy, the court drew on universal principles of fairness, freedom of expression, and equality in a sweeping but tightly reasoned narrative that effectively captured the nuances of "institutional self-governance, the rights of faculty members to teach, the rights of students to learn, the importance of language to teaching and learning, and the incontestable link between language on the one hand and thought and culture on the other."[107] For all those reasons, the details of the opinion are well worth examining.

The Italian constitution does not expressly state that Italian is the official language of the country. The court, however, relied on the Constitutional Court's repeated holdings that Article 6 and its protections for linguistic minorities implicitly recognize the constitutional status of Italian.[108] The court further relied on an Italian law dating from 1933 (during the Fascist era), which expressly states that Italian is the "official language of teaching and exams in all universities."[109] From there the court concluded that Italian could not play a subordinate role in higher education vis-à-vis other languages. A key part of the decision was the 2010 Law no. 240, the Gelmini Law, and the significance of the conjunction *anche* ("also"). Again, the objective of the law was to strengthen the internationalization process "also" through a number of approaches, including offering "degree programs and selection procedures in a foreign language."[110] The law suggests that internationalization can be achieved in a number of ways—greater mobility of lecturers and students, integrated study programs—and not just by using English. The law does not specifically mention English but refers generally to a "foreign language." The judges interpreted the law narrowly, requiring that any new courses in a foreign language had to supplement and not supplant existing courses in Italian, which the institute roundly contested. The judges recognized the value of internationalization in the abstract. They questioned, however, whether the institute's plan would actually achieve that end or merely promote instruction in a particular language and culture (English) at the expense of Italian.

The plan, the court noted, lacked "proportionality." It reached all graduate courses and all faculty members who teach them. But it failed to mitigate the burdens on some of the stakeholders, notably Italian-speaking professors and students who were not proficient in English or simply preferred to teach or learn in their native language. Here the court drew from Article 33 of the constitution and "the freedom of the arts and sciences, which may be freely taught," suggesting a "freedom to teach" in the language of ones' choice.[111] The plan, the court said, would inevitably consign the Italian language, and non-English-speaking faculty members, to teaching basic courses in the undergraduate program without considering which subjects might be more suitable to one language or the other. Some faculty members, unable or unwilling to teach in English, would not be assigned advanced courses that draw on their expertise and develop their research and scholarship. Others who agreed to teach in the program would have to revamp their teaching materials in line with English, a demanding task, especially for professors not totally comfortable with academic English. And though some graduate students would welcome taking courses in English, others would grudgingly give up using their native language in their chosen field. The court carried the discussion further to the nature of language learning, the importance of language in the university classroom, and the potential impact on the quality of the instructional program. Proficiency, the court said, does not necessarily translate into effective teaching in the language, nor into effective learning.[112]

For Maria Agostina Cabiddu, the Polytechnic professor of administrative law and lawyer for the one hundred claimants, the ruling was not only "their" victory; it also was a victory for "reason and culture."[113] The faculty members and students supporting the plan saw it otherwise. For them it was a poor reflection on Italy. The court decision, they argued, merely demonstrated the "provincialism" within Italian institutions. They contrasted Italy with northern Europe, where teaching in English was common practice, even in non-anglophone countries. Some critics questioned whether Italy lacked the "will" or the "courage" to open itself toward the outside and overcome the real crises facing universities.[114] Others found the ruling baffling. "Only in Italy would offering university courses in English be deemed detrimental to individual freedom," quipped one Twitter user. For another, "Even Dante would have understood." Adding ambiguity and political uncertainty to an already complex situation, the minister of education upheld the court ruling on the one hand and threw her support behind the institute's administration on the other. She "respected" the court's decision, she told the press. Yet she also understood the rector's position on English. Offering courses in English would allow students to "enter the world of work," she said, while the "debate on the importance of the Italian language" was better placed at "the primary school level."[115]

After much deliberation, the institute's academic senate and board of directors decided to appeal the decision to the Consiglio di Stato (Council of State), the country's high administrative court in Rome. In a public statement posted on Facebook, the institute affirmed its duty to guarantee to students the "right to the best possible education and training" and to preserve the institution's "autonomy" in defining the instructional program. At a hearing the following March, the appeals court ordered the institute to present documents outlining its plans for the 2014–15 academic year and indicating how it might offer parallel courses in English and Italian, a solution with a prohibitively high price tag.[116] The next academic year began with twenty-four out of twenty-eight graduate courses in English, of which only eight were also offered in Italian. Only eight of the second-level courses remained exclusively in Italian.

The Consiglio di Stato's ruling on the merits in January 2015 upended the lower court decision to a limited extent, but it did not lay the claims to rest. The court held that the institute had legitimately exercised its autonomy within the meaning of the 2010 law promoting internationalization. Nonetheless, it suspended the decision and transferred the case to the Constitutional Court to initially determine whether the 2010 law itself was "manifestly congruent" with the Italian constitution, namely Article 3, granting equality based on language; Article 6, safeguarding the rights of Italy's linguistic minorities; and Article 33, protecting the freedom to teach.[117] As both sides anxiously awaited the decision, the Italian journalist Beppe Severgnini shared his views in the *New York Times*. But rather than thoughtfully explain the problem to an international audience, in his characteristically breezy style Severgnini made a mockery of the important issues and ascribed much of the problem to superannuated professors for whom "all that matters is their cozy routine."[118]

The judicial wheels in Italy move slowly. The Constitutional Court did not publish its ruling until 2017, two years after the Consiglio di Stato had transferred the case and three years after the proposed Polytechnic plan was scheduled to take effect. In a well-reasoned opinion, the court upheld the constitutionality of the 2010 law on its face, which was a win for the institute. But much in tune with the regional administrative court, it also set constitutional limits on how universities might apply the law. Those limits fell short of an all-English university program. Within a framework of individual rights and institutional obligations, the court laid the ground rules for using languages other than Italian as the medium of university instruction. First, the court placed the Italian language front and center. Italian is important, the court noted, not just to transmit the country's heritage but as a modern-day cultural asset in itself. The court went on to Article 34's guarantee of "equal access to the highest levels of education."[119] All "capable" students, the court said, have the right to equal opportunities to learn English or the ability to enroll elsewhere, suggesting that universities have the obligation to provide "adequate [language] supports."

The court affirmed the freedom of professors to teach in Italian if they so chose. It disagreed with assigning them courses based on language skills rather than competence in their discipline. The court interpreted the word *anche* ("also") in the 2010 law to mean strengthening internationalization by using foreign languages as an "adjunct to" and not as a "substitute for" Italian. Universities could not offer entire programs in another language, the court warned, unless they offered parallel programs in Italian. But they could offer individual course units entirely in another language provided the choice of language would be "reasonable," "proportionate," and "appropriate" and did not reduce Italian to a subordinate position.[120] These terms, often used in the human rights context, lend themselves to broad interpretation depending on the surrounding facts.

The court's approach was measured and pragmatic. The justices undoubtedly understood that striking down the 2010 law on internationalization would have created institutional turmoil and political resistance across the country. They could not dismiss the growing reality of English language courses nationwide and the need for Italy and its universities to remain competitive in the global economy. They also had to protect the institutional autonomy that Italian law affords universities. Yet at the same time, they had to convey a clear message that universities could not ignore their obligations under the constitution. Nor could they deny the importance of the Italian language, its rich cultural heritage, and what it means to the nation and to its people.[121] With those guideposts and with those interests weighing in the balance, the Constitutional Court sent the case back to the Consiglio di Stato.

An Unending Debate

As conflicting headlines on the decision swirled through the press, the claimants spearheaded an open letter, "L'italiano siamo noi" ("We are the Italian language"), posted on the internet. On the face of the letter appeared the images of Dante, the father of modern Italian, and Galileo, the father of modern science: icons from Italy's storied past and symbols of what some feared was being forgotten in the race toward English. Directed to the president of the republic and other government officials, the letter called for a "new, diverse, and active Italian language policy." Within four days, the letter had gathered more than one thousand signatures. Within two weeks, the number had risen to twenty-four hundred. Among the first signatories were the president and president emeritus of the Accademia della Crusca, together with fifty-four professors from the Polytechnic Institute.[122] Meanwhile, the institute remained in a state of "suspended animation" under a new rector, Ferruccio Resta, who shared his predecessor's belief in an all-English graduate program.

In January 2018, after six years of the dispute winding through the Italian courts, the Consiglio di Stato gave what was thought to be the definitive ruling. The opinion was largely a summary and compilation of quotes from the

Constitutional Court with little additional rationale. It made clear that the goal of internationalization could not jeopardize three principles: the primacy of the Italian language, the freedom of students to learn, and the freedom of professors to teach. The Italian language, the court said, is a "fundamental element of cultural identity." Teaching courses solely in a foreign language, moreover, would remove Italian from "complete branches of knowledge." It would deny students, without adequate language support, the freedom to choose their own training and future and prevent them from reaching "the highest grades in their studies." It would affect how professors communicate with students. It would discriminate against professors in the assignment of courses based on criteria that have nothing to do with their competence in the subject matter they were hired to teach. In other words, for universities to change the "rules of the game" (the terms of employment) in midstream would be procedurally unjust.[123]

The Italian press either did not comprehend the court's ruling or simply decided to sensationalize it. Either way, it misled the public. Headlines announced that the court had "said 'No' " or "halted" or "blocked" courses in English, that English was "prohibited at Polytechnic." But the court had only declared that programs "entirely" in a language other than Italian would not pass constitutional muster. The rest was open to interpretation. Meanwhile, the president of the Accademia della Crusca, Claudio Marazzini, called the decision a "beautiful victory."[124] Maria Agostina Cabiddu, the professor and lawyer who had led the legal charge against the institute, set the ruling on a larger multilingual stage. It was not simply a victory for Italy. "The Constitutional Court's decision," she told the press, "marks a turning point in Europe." The ruling had already been translated into several languages and was attracting attention in other countries, including France and Germany. The "revolt," she said, was "widespread," and the point was "not to fight English but to protect national languages." By that point, "L'italiano siamo noi," the letter posted on the internet the previous year, had gathered over four thousand signatures, some from outside of Italy.[125]

Once the dust settled, the Polytechnic Institute had to find a solution that would keep it competitive in student recruitment and international rankings. It also had to remain within the somewhat "flexible" bounds set by the court. The rector asked for clarification from the Ministry of Instruction, Universities, and Research, which in the past had consistently approved the institute's courses in English. The response, from yet a new minister representing yet a new government, was that the institute would have to "rebalance" the plan, though the process of internationalization would be "maintained."[126] For that academic year, all doctoral courses at Polytechnic were in English. Out of forty-five master's courses, fifteen were offered in both languages and three solely in Italian. The remaining twenty-seven were only in English. The institute's English focus apparently was accomplishing what it had set out to do. Since 2014–15, enrollment in degree programs in English had risen from thirty-two hundred to eight-four hundred. Of the seventeen thousand master's students, six thousand were foreigners. These numbers, and presumably the English curriculum, had helped the institute climb the international rankings to first place in Italy in nine research areas and to tenth place among European universities in six areas.

It is said that sometimes the who of an argument can matter more than the what or the why and that a trustworthy intermediary or "surrogate" can influence the outcome more effectively. It also matters how the message is framed. As the Polytechnic administration mulled over its options and waited for formal guidance from the ministry, the institute's fifteen-member advisory board, individually and collectively, used the Milanese pages of the *Corriere della Sera,* Italy's most widely read daily newspaper, to gather public and official support for the institute and its English program. The argument centered on what was best for Italy's future and for its young people seeking employment at the highest levels. That was a most compelling argument for a country where youth unemployment had created a significant brain drain. In 2015, the rate of young people unemployed in Italy was over 40 percent. By January 2018, it was still a staggering 33 percent, the second highest in Europe after Greece. Italy also had the highest rate (19 percent) across the Eurozone of young people between the ages of fifteen and twenty-four in neither jobs nor education.[127]

On the heels of the court decision, board member Roger Abravanel, director emeritus of McKinsey Italia, published an opinion piece, "Prohibiting the Teaching of English Is Against the Interests of Students." He warned that English is the language of scientific progress and innovation and that forcing Italian to be used would "impoverish" the nation's "heritage of knowledge."[128] Two months later, the full board, including its most prominent graduates, purchased space in the *Corriere della Sera* to let their views be widely known. Among the signatories were famous architects, designers, and prominent leaders of business. Drawing on their collective experience at the top of large Italian and multinational firms, they masterfully turned the rights-based reasoning of the courts on its head. With knowledge of English being "essential" to young people entering the world of work, they argued, English did not deny the "right to study" but rather guaranteed the "right to work." It was a "responsibility" that the institute could "not avoid." To that point the rector Ferruccio Resta added the "national interest," that universities must offer an education of "international quality" or "risk losing talent."[129]

For members of the advisory board to publicly lend their professional weight to the institute was appropriate and strategically smart. What happened next was shocking: a member of the advisory board publicly mocked the professors who had taken the institute to court. The day following the board's paid statement, the *Corriere della Sera* ran a front page story that effectively distracted public attention from the board's measured position. The story recounted an insult-laden interview with board member and architect Piero Lissoni. In complete confrontational mode, Lissoni called the professors "provincial," "chauvinist," "chiefs without a future," lacking "foresight or curiosity."[130] Coming from a board member of such a prestigious institution, the tone and substance were inappropriate at best and harmful at worst. More fundamentally they were beyond the scope of the advisory board's function to "advise."

The interview provoked a pointed rebuke from Maria Gabriella Mulas, a Polytechnic professor who had not joined the legal action. A graduate of the University of California at Berkeley—the seat of the academic free speech movement in the United States—Mulas wrote a letter to the newspaper expressing her "indignation" at the accusations. She took Lissoni to task for overstepping his bounds as a board member and for his lack of understanding of the court's ruling, which did not ban all English instruction but only the "exclusive" use of English.[131] Mulas later noted that the newspaper had put her letter on "standby" for a week until she informed them that she would publish it elsewhere. The exchange moved the independent forum, Return on Academic Research (ROARS), to publish Lissoni's interview and Mulas's response on its website. Run by academicians concerned with the politics of higher education and research, ROARS jumped deep into the controversy, questioning how a rector could silently tolerate "such aggression" toward one hundred members of his faculty. The rector, they said, had no choice but to ask for the board member's resignation. They denounced the newspaper for publishing such an offensive diatribe.[132]

As the dust was barely settling on these events, the ministry declared that course offerings at Polytechnic would remain the same for the coming year due to time constraints in planning changes and notifying prospective students. While the declaration put the institute's officials somewhat at ease, it left universities throughout Italy guessing about how to comply with the court's ruling. As the next academic year was approaching, the Conference of University Rectors sent a letter to the ministry with a suggested interpretation of the law.[133] Once again, the ministry's letter in response was less clear than the problem demanded. The director of higher education and research (not the minister) approved the interpretation, giving universities the flexibility to offer Italian courses presumably taught partially in English, and to offer students the option to enroll in Italian-taught courses in other universities to fulfill the Italian requirement. At the same time, the director suggested that the interpretation would be subject to a more formal decree that would consider accreditation requirements and international courses. It also would take into consideration potential problems for students attending small universities or situated in regions where there were no comparable alternative courses.[134] At that point, the numbers for Polytechnic were still largely skewed toward English. Out of a total of forty master's degree programs, twenty-seven were in English, four in Italian, and nine in Italian and English.

Those figures propelled the opposing professors back into court, claiming that the institute was not in compliance with the court ruling. Yet despite the overwhelming percentage of English-taught programs, the Consiglio di Stato once again found in favor of the institute, which put a final end to the litigation.[135] One has to wonder whether the court simply believed it had gone as far as it could in setting academic policy or whether it felt the weight of professional opinion in favor of the institute, or both. In any case, the decision was the best that the university rectors could have expected. The question remained as to how specific the decision was to the facts of the Polytechnic Institute, a prestigious institution of technology and science whose graduates are more likely than most to pursue careers in the global economy where English dominates. Would it apply with equal force, for example, to a program in the humanities or the social sciences? It's impossible to predict how the Constitutional Court's reasonable, proportionate, and appropriate factors might weigh under other circumstances. In any case, seven years after this legal war had begun, it seemed that neither side had totally won or lost. That says as much about the complex nature of the issues as it does about the limits of the judiciary in weighing constitutional norms against institutional autonomy

The courts effectively gave Italian universities the green light to widely use English instruction so long as there was some pedagogical justification and some semblance of Italian remaining in the program. It was an open invitation to test those bounds, especially given the Italian ministry's weak oversight and the limits of court enforcement. English programs at Polytechnic, in fact, crept upward. In the 2019–20 academic year, the number of master's of science programs taught solely in English numbered thirty-one out of a total of forty-four, up from twenty-seven out of forty the previous year, with only nine programs still taught in both English and Italian and four solely in Italian. There was no discernible impact on foreign student enrollment, which remained steadily in the range of six thousand.[136] Only time will tell whether the institute can sustain the rising numbers of English-taught programs if the 2020 COVID-19 pandemic takes a sustained toll, especially on Chinese enrollment. If so, increased demand from domestic students or from countries like India may fill the void.

It is hard to determine whether the court decision has moderated in any way the spread of English-taught programs and courses throughout Italian universities. Though the pace has been relatively slow, especially in the southern regions, the Italians are turning the corner in recognizing the value of English, which has some bearing on higher education. In a 2018 poll of five hundred Italian students and workers between the ages of eighteen and fifty, 74 percent reported that learning English would become more important over the next five years.[137] That year, Italian universities offered 504 courses partially or totally in English, a 60 percent increase from 313 in 2016, though still considerably fewer than other western European countries including France.[138] In 2019, 262 of the master's level courses were offered in English, up from one 192 in 2016, while doctoral courses grew from 271 to 382.[139]

Yet the outcome of the litigation still was not a total loss for the professors who initiated the case or for the interests they represented. The courts refused to allow the institute to go forward with its all-English graduate program despite the risk of losing both native and foreign students who might seek English options in other countries. The slow pace of court action, with successive appeals, further tempered the move toward English instruction at the institute over the course of those years and ultimately preserved a place for Italian, albeit small and more definitively so in the sciences. The litigation also sparked a national discussion on Italian as a cultural asset and a unifying force in a relatively young country known for its regional fragmentation and historic local vernaculars. It motivated key stakeholders—students, professors, administrators, government officials, intellectuals, linguists, scientists, business leaders, and others—to air the competing interests. Whether that public introspection will result in any meaningful policies at the national level is another matter. In a country with re-peated turnovers in government, as occurred once again in early 2021, talk rarely transforms into decisive action.

The litigation, moreover, brought to light the national English language def-icit and the need to increase government support for primary and secondary schools to prepare students, across the economic and regional divide, for English instruction at the university level. In 2019, mean scores for Italian students on the TOEFL were ninety out of one hundred. Though reasonably high, the scores were still lower than those for Dutch and German students at ninety-nine, Danish at ninety-seven, and Norwegian and Swedish at ninety-three, though higher than those for French students at eighty-four.[140] The scores, moreover, represented a select group of students interested in studying in English and pre-sumably more proficient in the language than the larger student population. In recent years, Italy has attempted to address the problem as Italian parents are clamoring for their children to gain English proficiency.[141] English is now man-datory for all students beginning at age six in state-run schools. Content and language integrated learning (CLIL) has been incorporated into the national curriculum in upper secondary schools (of which the majority of programs are in English).[142] While those efforts are a noteworthy start, they are not enough. As in other European countries, the limited number of hours devoted to English have undercut the program in the primary grades, while language learning across the board suffers from a lack of teachers proficient in English, appropriate ma-terials, and adequate state funding.[143] If English-taught programs in universities are to succeed for Italian students, as well as for students in France, the government of each country must build a stronger linguistic infrastructure from the ground up.

In the end, the academically focused Italian litigation, combined with the public debate over the Fioraso Law in France, attracted widespread media attention, especially throughout Europe. It also helped energize a national reckoning already taking shape in northern Europe, especially in the Netherlands, where teaching through English is more widespread and has a longer history.

Headwinds from the North

Nowhere has the internationalization of higher education through English, and the resulting influx of foreign students, been more pronounced than in the Netherlands. And nowhere has the question embroiled the academic community, government officials, and the judiciary in such prolonged and polarized debate in search of a workable solution. The national uproar over the Fioraso law in France in 2013 and the institutional wrangling over the litigation against Milan's Polytechnic Institute both pale in comparison. Since the early1990s, when amendments to the Higher Education and Research Act were adopted, no fewer than six committees have discussed the place of "minor languages" in Dutch universities and their connection to university programs threatened with extinction. This endless cycle has raised questions regarding the accessibility and quality of university education along with preserving the Dutch language as a vehicle for intellectual engagement and knowledge production. As we have seen in France and Italy, these questions defy easy consensus among the many stakeholders. Each country presents a unique historical and political lens through which to assess the options.

Unlike France, where the French language is carved in constitutional stone, or Italy, where the courts have recognized the Italian language under statutory law, in the Netherlands higher education remains one of the few areas in which the Dutch language holds legal status. Any attempts to rule otherwise have failed to garner sufficient support in Parliament. Nor is there in the Netherlands an institution steeped in tradition that authoritatively preserves the purity of the Dutch language, comparable to the French Académie française or even the less dogmatic Italian Accademia della Crusca, both housed in architecturally imposing settings. The Nederlandse Taalunie (Dutch Language Union), by comparison, is an international regulatory institution on standard Dutch devoid of all the symbolic trappings and ties to the nation's literary giants of its French and Italian counterparts. Dating from1980, the Taalunie was re-established in 1995 by treaty between the Netherlands and Flanders. With offices in The Hague and

Brussels, it also promotes the Dutch language and teaching worldwide, similar in part to the British Council and the Alliance française.

This is not to suggest that the Dutch people are less emotionally tied to their language than the French or the Italians. In a 2016 poll on language as the "cornerstone of national identity," 84 percent of Dutch respondents reported that being able to speak the national language was "very important," while another 14 percent considered it "somewhat important," the highest among ten European countries studied, including France and Italy.[1] Generally speaking, they just don't draw the connection between their ties to the Dutch language on the one hand and higher education on the other, in large part from a sense of pragmatism on the utility of English in the global market. As we will see, that pragmatism runs through the academic and political debate over English and internationalization, which has now reached a fever pitch.

English Everywhere

Despite the EU policy of "mother tongue plus two," the Dutch people are progressively moving toward becoming bilingual rather than multilingual, dropping German and French as their historically second and third languages in favor of English. As linguist Alison Edwards put it, "If you can assume that you can walk down the street and that the hairdresser will be able to speak to you in English, and the bus driver, and the taxi driver, then functionally it's a second language not a foreign language."[2]

The exposure to English runs throughout the culture. English language films and TV programs are not dubbed as in other countries but subtitled in Dutch. Basic TV packages typically offer British and US channels like BBC and CNN. English music dominates popular radio channels. The "Longreads" section of the daily evening newspaper *NRC Handelsblad* posts articles only in English. English language advertisements dot the country's billboards, shopping areas, newspapers, and television. Product packaging, commercial signage, and business names and slogans increasingly use English. The government's official website is in Dutch and English. Official promotional campaigns are sprinkled with English. The police force designates some job titles like chief information officer and departments like Integrity and Security in English.[3] Dutch officials are well aware of the country's rich English language resources. Recognizing that "English is indisputably the language of international business," the Dutch judiciary in 2019 joined London, Dubai, and Singapore in establishing the Netherlands Commercial Court (NCC), an all-English court to resolve complex international business disputes.[4] It's easy to connect the dots between the court and the exodus of business interests moving to the continent in the wake of Brexit.

English now dominates education across sectors and levels. Wealthy parents, eager to prepare their children for universities abroad and for global careers, have the option of excellent international schools where instruction is totally or significantly in English. The Netherlands ranks sixth in the world for the number of students between the ages of three and eighteen enrolled in such schools, reaching 152,686 in the 2017–18 school year. Nineteen schools are government subsidized and teach in English; the remaining schools are private and teach primarily in English, though some teach in their native language. These schools largely serve families tied to the many international organizations and multinational corporations, the latter lured to the Netherlands by the favorable corporate tax system.[5] The number of students enrolled is astonishing given the country's relatively small total population of 17.1 million in 2018, as compared to China with a population of 1.42 billion and India with a population of 1.35 billion and where international school enrollments were upward of 459,000 and 296,000, respectively.[6]

Even in public schools, English is one of three required subjects, along with Dutch and mathematics. Students begin studying English in primary school at least by the age of nine, though some begin as early as four, and continue throughout secondary school. By 2017, 99.9 percent of upper secondary school students in the Netherlands were learning English.[7] A small but growing number attend publicly supported Dutch/English bilingual programs. A public bilingual secondary school program launched in the early 1990s included 132 schools by 2020. All offer instruction in Dutch and English, with the exception of one Dutch/German program.[8] They typically use the content and language integrated learning (CLIL) approach, with at least half the teaching time in English in the first three years.[9] Initially the program was offered only in schools within the pre-university and general education streams, where students are also required to study two other modern languages for two years. In 2009, it was extended to pre-vocational schools. A preliminary study of the pre-university programs from 2010 found that students scored significantly higher in English, and their language use was more "authentic" than comparable students in regular programs.[10]

In 2014, the government designated twelve national pilot schools at the primary level offering 30–50 percent of instruction in English, with additional schools joining the following year. Based on its success in teaching both languages, the government extended the pilot project to 2023. Other bilingual programs can be found throughout the country. These are largely grassroots efforts driven by the combined interest of parents and school officials, similar to what we will see in the dual language immersion programs taking off in the United States.

The presence of English is even more dominant in higher education, where the Netherlands stands with the Nordic countries at the forefront of English language instruction. Dutch universities offer the most English-taught programs in all of continental Europe. The Netherlands even outstrips Germany, where foreign students can attend universities relatively free of charge. Those rising student numbers further incentivize the drive toward English-taught courses and programs. In a similar vein, Dutch researchers were early in the movement to publish in English, surpassing their counterparts in countries like Germany, Italy, and France. Yet in contrast to Denmark, Norway. and Sweden, which have set parameters on language use in theory if not totally in practice, the Netherlands has given little practical attention to preserving the national language among domestic students. Nor has it assertively promoted Dutch among international students who can easily navigate Dutch life by simply relying on English.

Upward of 90 percent of the Dutch population claims to speak English reasonably well. The Netherlands ranked first among the one hundred countries analyzed in the 2020 *English Proficiency Index*, above Denmark, Finland, Sweden, and Norway.[11] It is not surprising that it is the only country on the continent that can compete with the United States, Australia, and the United Kingdom in recruiting non-European students interested in enrolling in English-taught programs yet not inclined to learn the Dutch language. It also is not surprising that Dutch is losing its place especially in graduate programs while some institutions are adopting English for academic administration. An extreme example is Erasmus University Rotterdam, where even the signage is totally in English. Walking through the campus, you are far more likely to see "Faculty Club" or "Food Plaza" than its Dutch equivalent.[12]

Beyond language, an equally compelling attraction for international students is the renowned reputation of Dutch education. In 2021, 13 of the Netherlands' research universities counted among the top 250 in the Times Higher Education World University Rankings, with 5 in the top 100 and 10 in the top 200.[13] That distinction is noteworthy in a system that depends on government funding without a US-style culture of fund raising. The Netherlands repeatedly outpaces all EU member states, relative to the size of their economies, in receiving prestigious European Research Council grants.[14]

The high quality of life in the Netherlands is an additional draw, as is the educational cost. Students from European Economic Area (EEA) countries—the European Union plus Norway, Iceland, and Liechtenstein—who enroll at a public university pay the same annual tuition fee as Dutch students, which for the 2019–20 year was €2,087 (US$2,460) and as low as €1,043 (US$1,230) for the first year for those enrolled in a bachelor's program.[15] Tuition fees for students from outside the EEA jumped to €6,000 (US$7,100). Yet they were still significantly lower than the 2020–21 average tuition of US$21,184 in state universities and US$35,087 in private universities in the United States and between £10,000 (US$13,600) and £26,000 (US$35,400) in Great Britain.[16] That difference diverts international recruitment from those countries toward the Netherlands.[17] The United Kingdom's exit from the European Union and from the Erasmus program further heightens the appeal of the Netherlands, especially among students from other EEA countries.

The government's direct block grant for higher education has progressively dropped by 25 percent on a per student basis since 2000. That drop is mainly the result of the growing influx of international students for whom the state does not fully compensate the extra costs. At the same time, the decrease has increased reliance on revenue derived from international students, especially those from non-EEA countries like China and India, an added incentive for universities to further expand English-taught programs. On the up side, about 25 percent of international graduates remain in the country after five years, which amounts to €1.5 billion (US$1.7 billion) in additional revenue for the Dutch economy.[18] On the down side, considerably more students from the EEA are enrolled full-time in Dutch public universities than Dutch students in other EEA universities, which amounts to a net loss for the Netherlands.

Mounting academic and economic pressures have moved the Netherlands' eighteen research universities and forty universities of applied sciences toward English. As of 2019, 76 percent of master's and 28 percent of bachelor's programs in research universities were totally taught in English, up from 74 percent and 23 percent the previous year. These programs intentionally drew recruits from across the globe. The change was especially notable in studies related to agriculture and environment. Upward of eighty-six thousand international students representing 170 nationalities were enrolled in degree-granting programs. The overwhelming majority (73.1 percent) of students were from countries within the EEA. Germany, with over twenty-two thousand students across the system, was by far the top country of origin. Italy, with a total of almost 4,814, had the largest increase, of over seven hundred students from 2018, outstripping China as the second highest source of students behind Germany. Driving the growth in the Italian market were a number of factors, including the large number of English-taught courses, low tuition fees, and Italy's high youth unemployment and stagnating economy, along with uncertainty over Brexit. The number of Syrian students nearly doubled for a total of 971, presumably a result of the influx of Syrian refugees since 2015.[19]

Obviously the Dutch place high priority on English. Yet even high interest, broad social exposure, and widespread English instruction from the early grades have not insulated the Netherlands from problems that frequently arise in internationalizing higher education through English. Basic English conversational skills among the general population and the availability of bilingual programs among a small number of students, though promising, say little about the level of "academic" English among the larger numbers of Dutch students or among their professors, and the relation to academic quality. English proficiency, moreover, is just one piece of the internationalization puzzle. Others relate to funding, cultural impact, and accessibility. The more English-taught programs have attracted international students, the more compelling the justification has become to further expand the programs. The further the programs have expanded, the higher the number of international students flocking to the Netherlands.

The Arc of the Story

A particularly important point in these developments came in 2018 in an interim lower court decision. The ruling said as much about the political potential and institutional limits of court action in shaping language policy as it did about the legal bounds of English-taught programs in Dutch universities. A chronological look at the events leading up to and following that decision, filtered through the press and social media and driven by multiple stakeholders, puts the implications for academic policy in bold relief

Seeds of Ambiguity

Back in 1994, an article appeared in *Times Higher Education,* a weekly London publication with a high academic readership. It was an interview with an Australian-born professor who had relocated to Amsterdam. After nineteen years of teaching at the University of Glasgow in Scotland, he had accepted the chair of English literature at Amsterdam's Free University. The article extolled the benefits of teaching in the Netherlands as compared with the United Kingdom. It also revealed an interesting historical backdrop to the ongoing debate over English instruction in the country's universities.

In 1989, as the Erasmus program sparked interest in English-taught courses and programs to promote student mobility, "wild rumors" that the Dutch education ministry was planning to "scrap Dutch" as the primary language of instruction in universities had moved the government to begin inspecting on a regular basis foreign language programs in the universities. Though a number of institutes for training students from developing countries had been using English as the common language for several decades, they were isolated from regular Dutch higher education and therefore considered less threatening.[20] The government's aim, the article noted, was to make sure that Dutch was not "under threat" and that students' ability in foreign languages would be adequately developed throughout their program. In those days, English instruction in the universities was limited to "components" of certain courses, especially in technical subjects, rather than entire programs as today. Foreign professors were contractually obligated to become competent in Dutch within two years. For the interviewee, that was "perfectly understandable." "My teaching," he said, "will be in English, but the administration is all in Dutch. If you have to fight your department's corner, you have to be able to communicate in the language of the country you're in."[21]

The rumors turned out to be not so wild. In December of that year, a news article entitled "English or Not, That's the Question" noted a proposal from the minister of education, culture and science, Jo Ritzen, to increase English instruction in Dutch universities.[22] Peter Kwikkers, now an independent consultant who at the time worked in the ministry, recalls that some of his colleagues thought the proposal "premature" and "politically extreme." Though the minister made clear that not all programs but only more courses should be offered in English, the media and politicians, interpreting the recommendation to encompass all programs and courses, launched a "campaign" discrediting it as "fundamentally undesirable."[23]

Parliament put the brakes on the proposal. The minister appointed an advisory Committee on Language Aspects on Education, which recommended that the decision of whether, and in which courses, instruction should be offered in a language other than Dutch be left to the universities.[24] While the minister agreed with the committee, he also thought it "conceivable" that the status of Dutch might be set in law. With only brief discussion, a large majority of the House of Representatives agreed to let universities decide whether and when to teach in languages other than Dutch, but with safeguards to preserve the Dutch language. The consensus ultimately led to amendments in the Higher Education and Research Act (WHW) in 1992.[25]

The revisions added a sentence to Article 1.3 of the Act that reads: "In the context of their activities in the field of education in relation to Dutch-speaking students, [universities] also focus on promoting expression in Dutch." A separate Article 7.2 was adopted, stating that education and examinations must be given in Dutch. Only three exceptions would hold: if (a) the teaching concerns a degree program respecting a foreign language; (b) the context is a lecture given by a foreign teacher; or (c) the "nature, organization or quality of teaching or the nationality of the students necessitates the use of another language." The exceptions must be built into a language "code of conduct" adopted by each university's executive board.[26] As Kwikkers now sees it, 1.3 plus 7.2 is "greater than the sum of its parts." Regardless of what the university's code of conduct says, the law is clear that an entire international recruitment of foreign students can never be used to justify invoking the "necessity" exception, and that the program must promote the Dutch language.[27] Others disagree. In any case, the open formulation in Article 7.2 offered loopholes that created a gap between the rhetoric of the policy in protecting Dutch and the reality of universities quietly promoting English.[28]

The changes in the 1992 Act put the debate over English-taught courses and programs to rest, at least for a time, except among a small group of language and culture "purists." There was general acceptance that English instruction was a "necessary evil" for universities to be a "player in the global educational market." A 1997 policy paper published by the Ministry of Education, Culture and Science seemed to suggest that even though the law stated otherwise, teaching in English was "accepted practice." While the paper specifically noted the legal restrictions on teaching in a language other than Dutch, it also offered the "more general view . . . that universities and colleges themselves have an interest in offering foreign language teaching as part of their courses."[29] A document issued by the ministry two years later made no mention of the growing number of courses taught in English. Yet it put notable emphasis on improving the profile of Dutch higher education abroad and investing in recruiting international students. Neither the media nor Parliament raised any questions on either count. Only within the academic community were concerns expressed regarding the quality of education on two main points—the learning performance of international students and the teaching performance of Dutch instructors in relation to their respective English language skills.[30]

The passage of time has shown how loosely universities have honored the provisions protecting Dutch in the Higher Education and Research Act and how laxly the government has enforced them. Universities often interpret the third exception as a free pass as long as their code of conduct states with few details why the "nature, organization, or quality of teaching or the nationality of the students necessitates" teaching in English."[31] A 2019 study of twelve Dutch higher education institutions found that at the master's level, the legal standard of "Dutch unless" apparently had morphed into "English unless." The exceptions typically covered study programs with specifically Dutch subject matter, like Dutch Law and Dutch Studies; or those directed toward the domestic job market, like teacher training; or public health services, like medicine, dentistry, and pharmacy.[32]

The Debate Takes Focus

The year 2014 marked a pivotal turn on the question of English instruction in Dutch universities. At that time, in keeping with a Dutch tradition of publicly posted declarations, four humanities lecturers from Vrije University and the University of Amsterdam posted on the latter's "notice board" a manifesto to preserve the Dutch language. The document raised concerns over students and professors who lacked proficiency in English and the danger that the Netherlands was "squandering" its own language and culture.[33] It received close to seven thousand hits on the internet.

The following year, the "Great Manifesto of the Dutch Language" further propelled the debate into action and laid the foundation for the court case to come. Published by the association Beter Onderwijs Nederland (Better Education Netherlands), popularly known as BON, the manifesto wove together a mix of reasonable points with what some might consider "nationalistic and inward looking sentiment." In any case, it was an "important wake up call," laying out ten points beginning with the need for universities and colleges to comply with Article 7.2 and to engage in open discussion among teachers, students, and staff on how to give meaning to the law.[34] It declared that decisions to use English should not be "economically or ideologically motivated" but rather substantively grounded. It underscored that Dutch was important to integrate immigrant youth and students from disadvantaged backgrounds, a point often lost in the discussion of English instruction in universities. It called for better preparing students as "critical citizens" and for careers in Dutch society. "Good English teaching," it concluded, "is something other than teaching in English."[35] With wide press coverage, the document gathered close to six thousand signatures from writers, professors, and researchers. Though noticeably short on precise recommendations, the document's forceful tone set in motion a more concerted government response and public discussion.

That summer, the Socialist Party education specialist Jasper van Dijk sent a series of written questions on monitoring compliance with Article 7.2 to the minister of education, culture, and science. The following December, the Socialist Party and the Christian Democrats held a hearing on the topic, followed by a debate in Parliament. A "Language Collective" of dozens of professors, scientists, and writers, as well as university staff, language experts, and representatives from the Landelijke Studentenvakbond (LSVb) (National student union), attended the hearing. Speakers expressed a spectrum of views, from the pointed concerns of BON president Ad Verbrugge to the passionate defense of Maastricht University president Martin Paul and everything in between. The gist of Paul's argument was that Maastricht is an "international university" whose goal is to prepare students for the international labor market by offering them an "international classroom" where students from different cultures can interact. Other speakers fell somewhere in between. As the education specialist van Dijk told the press, the idea was not to ban English from Dutch universities but to offer a "Dutch equivalent for every course given in English."[36]

Students, in the meantime, were gathering data that further questioned English-taught courses. On the eve of the parliamentary hearing, the LSVb student union released findings from a survey of 269 students. Almost 60 percent reported that they had encountered an incomprehensible lecturer in English. A large majority said that they had learned less from bad English lectures than from those given in Dutch. The group offered several reasonable recommendations. Students should have a choice between English and Dutch instruction. The decision to offer a course in Dutch should be based on the "added value" of education and not on "prestige or extra income." And teachers should receive advance training before instructing in English.[37]

A much larger survey, conducted in February 2015 by the Delft University student association ORAS, added fuel to the fire. At Delft, all staff teaching in English had to score at a minimum of C1 (proficient use) on the Common European Framework of Reference for Languages (CEFR), a set of guidelines established by the Council of Europe. The C1 level entails using English "flexibly and effectively for social, academic and professional purposes." Anyone who did not measure up when hired had three years to qualify. Yet many lecturers did not have the time to improve their English despite good intentions. Of the fifteen hundred Dutch bachelor's students polled, 32.5 percent said they had difficulty following lectures because of the teacher's poor English skills. At the same time, problems with their own English caused 21 percent of students to struggle with assignments or papers and 12 percent with lectures.

This was not the first time that Delft students had put English courses into question. Back in 2003, students took a symbolic approach where words seemed to be failing. Troubled with university plans to completely switch to English language master's degrees, they issued the "worst teacher award" to the lecturer with the most incomprehensible English. Using a clever play on words, the winner received a Gelderland cooked sausage, the word for sausage in Dutch being *worst*.[38] Despite the obvious message, it did not stop the university from moving forward. By 2018, the university's home page welcomed students to the "Opening Academic Year." In an overdone bow to popular culture, it invited them to "unchain your inner superhero" by joining Delft students and professors "delving into the superhero genre linked to science, engineering, technology and ethics." Not a hint of Dutch appeared on the page. It could have been pulled from the website of a British, American, or Canadian university.

An inventory of English-taught programs published in the centrist daily newspaper *de Volkskrant* in August 2016 once again brought English-taught courses under scrutiny. Having looked at 1,632 degree courses in the thirteen universities, the paper found that 60 percent overall were in English. As for master's degrees, only 30 percent were in Dutch, while three universities offered master's degrees solely in English.[39] The response from the Netherlands Association of Universities (VSNU), a key advocate of internationalizing higher education, was quick and decisive, with a spokesperson calling internationalization "an essential step for students on the international job market." The Council for the Dutch Language and Literature, the advisory body of the Dutch Language Union, saw the question somewhat differently. The following month, in the days leading up to the European Day of Languages, the group issued a forceful memorandum upholding Dutch as a language of science and higher education. Without discounting the role of English, the council maintained that Dutch remain a full-fledged language in science and that students in both bachelor's and master's programs learn Dutch at a high level within a policy based on multilingualism including English.[40]

From the view of outsiders, it seemed like the Netherlands' highly prized system of English-taught courses was imploding. In an apparent effort at damage control, Karl Dittrich, the president of VSNU, published a commentary in *Times Higher Education* roundly defending the Dutch system before the global academic court of opinion. The international environment, he maintained, enhanced the learning experience of Dutch students, exposing them to other cultures and to the latest in research findings from an international perspective. Teaching in English allowed that to happen, he said. He also defended the English skills of professors. They were not deterring native English speakers from enrolling, he argued, judging from the rising number of students from the United Kingdom.[41]

KNAW Stirs the Pot

As the debate continued to heat up, the minister of education, culture, and science commissioned the Royal Netherlands Academy of Arts and Sciences (KNAW) to conduct a study on language policy in Dutch higher education. KNAW convened an advisory committee of scientists and scholars to address the key question: On what basis should a Dutch research university or university of applied science choose Dutch or English as the language of instruction for a particular program or study? The committee was totally independent of any manifestos or interest groups. It rather relied on scientific sources, policy reports, interviews, and meetings with experts and constituent groups.[42]

Before KNAW was ready to publish its findings and recommendations, the Dutch press reported that BON, the "good education" association, was planning to take their grievances to court unless the newly formed government, which cut across political parties, included in its coalition agreement tougher rules on the use of English. BON president Ad Verbrugge took specific aim at the lack of English proficiency among many lecturers. "If we really want students to learn good English," he told the press, "we would be better off sending them to England or America."[43] In a separate opinion piece in *de Volkskrant*, BON board member Felix Huygen assailed the system for being guided by the "logic of cash flow" and "switch[ing] en masse to English [to] attract thousands of students who do not know Dutch well."[44]

Other voices within the system sharply disagreed. An opinion piece aptly entitled "Not Less But More English in Education" took exception to Huygen's warning on the "destruction" of Dutch university education and the threat that "we all use the language of Shakespeare more and more." To the contrary, it argued, internationalization makes the university atmosphere "more stimulating," while the whole society ultimately benefits from the "fresh perspective." It advocated improving the quality of English by making it an important part of the curriculum rather than banning it.[45]

KNAW's final report, *Nederlands en/of Engels?* (*Dutch and/or English*), issued in July 2017, took a measured approach that gave due deference to university decision makers. It recognized the "enormous importance" of internationalizing the university but advised that the "language of instruction must be a conscious choice, and not one that is simply made on autopilot." It recommended that the decision be made at the program or department level in consultation with the central board of the institution and that it be based on "good subject-specific evidence-based reasons" and "firmly anchored in a supportive language and internationalization policy." The report made clear that both students and lecturers needed to have a "good command of the language of instruction," whether English or Dutch. It raised equity concerns about the negative effect of English language instruction on students with a migration background and from disadvantaged communities, again a point too seldom heard in these debates. The report also warned that the loss of Dutch in academia could create problems with communicating scientific and scholarly research findings to the public.[46] Presumably mindful of the potential impact on university programs, the committee tiptoed around Article 7.2, that teaching in a language other than Dutch must be of "necessity."

The report's balanced perspective gained wide acceptance within the Dutch higher education community. As internationalization expert Hans de Wit later observed, it was an especially useful guide for the social sciences and humanities, where debates over English have been the most strident.[47] The following year, KNAW issued a more forceful report on language in the Netherlands. There KNAW questioned the government's failure to develop a national language policy that upheld the Dutch language, looked beyond English, and mobilized the multilingual skills of the Dutch people.[48]

Following on the heels of KNAW's university recommendations came a steady and seemingly endless stream of reports, speeches, petitions, meetings, and government activities. Taken together, they gave fodder to the Dutch press and laid the political groundwork for litigation. In September 2017, the

Rathenau Instituut, a science and technology think tank, issued a warning that Dutch universities were underfunded. Though bachelor's graduates had risen by a third and master's graduates by 29 percent since 2009, largely the result of active recruitment abroad, government spending had barely risen faster than inflation. Meanwhile, the technical universities, the hardest hit financially, were threatening to turn away students from some courses due to lack of staff and facilities.[49] Within days of the Rathenau study, a report from the European Association for International Education revealed that English-taught bachelor's programs at European universities had increased fifty-fold in the previous eight years, with the Netherlands' 317 programs at the top of the list.[50] VSNU president Peter Duisenberg confidently told the international press that "it's in the DNA of our universities to be international." He predicted that the number of international students would grow significantly until 2024–25 as the number of Dutch students declined demographically. For Ad Vebrugge, chair of Better Education Netherlands (BON), the danger remained that Dutch would become obsolete if university students no longer needed to use it to succeed. It would become a "language of ordinary people" and not the educated.[51]

As the actors in this Dutch drama continued sparring in the press, the language question became the subject of a masterful valedictory address at the University of Amsterdam. Annette de Groot, professor of experimental language psychology, embedded in her retirement lecture, "Dutch Is a Must," an eloquently updated version of the biblical Tower of Babel story where she made the case for Dutch in academic education and research. De Groot sharpened the narrative with cultural references to the Dutch struggle with the "omnipresent" water, portraying Frans Timmerman, a well-known Dutch polyglot and member of the European Commission, impersonating God and the VSNU (the organization of Dutch universities) as the biblical character of Nimrod. Weaving together strands of divine prescience, the dystopian world of George Orwell's *1984*'s "Newspeak," the connection between language and thought, the inherent tension in promoting linguistic diversity and EU integration, and the cognitive benefits of multilingualism, de Groot ended with a plea for a bilingual curriculum that gave Dutch and English equal status both in use and in the perception of the users.[52]

With the Dutch elite barely digesting this most unusual farewell to academia, yet another petition appeared on the internet. This time it was second-year psychology students in the Dutch track at Radboud University protesting the university's plan to merge their lectures with the English track. Aside from the midstream switch in language, the problem focused on the level of English among the teachers. As one student put it, "While the lecturers [speaking in Dutch] were able to draw freely from their knowledge" the previous year, they now said little more than what was on their PowerPoint slides. Lotte Jensen, a professor of Dutch literature and cultural history at Radboud, agreed. For her, the issue was not English instruction; it was the quality of the learning experience. "Many Dutch teachers who teach in English," she said, "teach with less humor, nuance, and irony. Students give less substance to their writing because of lesser language skills."[53] Though the petition got off to a swift start, garnering more than two hundred signatures on the first day, it ultimately had no effect on policy.[54] In the end, the university reserved its right to change the language of instruction.[55]

Just as the Radboud controversy reached a crescendo, the leaders of four parties in Parliament (VVD, CDA, D66, and the Christian Union) posted on the government website their new coalition agreement, "Confidence in the Future," in Dutch, English, French, and German versions. Despite disagreements on a number of policy issues, in the least the legislators agreed on what a "distinct Dutch identity" meant and how language fit into that identity. The Dutch language, along with the flag, the national anthem, commemorations, and the constitution, the agreement stated, "are not relics of the past, but emblems of the pride, freedoms, rights and duties that are a rightful part of the Netherlands, Dutch citizenship and... democracy." As for the role of English in higher education, the agreement made clear that the government would "step up monitoring" for compliance with the law. The aim was to assure that programs were taught exclusively in English only if the approach had "added value," if the quality of teaching was at a satisfactory level, and if there were a sufficient number of Dutch language courses. The agreement affirmed making "Dutch education more attractive for foreign students" while not "compromising accessibility" for Dutch students.[56]

The language of the agreement drew pointed criticism from Peter Kwikkers, the expert who had coauthored the 1992 Higher Education and Research Act. Kwikkers argued that the original intent of the law was to maintain Dutch as the language of instruction for the entire system of higher education. While there were "indeed exceptions," he explained, "that does not concern exceptions to the entire program" but rather "components of education, such as a guest lecturer or part of a language course in Chinese where practicing that language is the explicit intention." Kwikkers sharply disagreed with replacing the specific "exceptions" language in the Act with "added value," which he believed was a "misleading interpretation" of the law. "If there is already an English version of an entire program," he said, "then the legislative history indicates that there must always be a Dutch variant in principle at the same institution." Besides, he noted, monitoring compliance with the law was the responsibility of the Inspectorate of Education and the supervisory board of each institution and not Parliament.[57]

On the eve of the coalition agreement becoming public, KNAW hosted a debate in the Amsterdam public library to present its recently published report on language in higher education. The forum brought together a five-member panel of university administrators, student representatives, and members of the committee to thrash out the pros and cons of English and internationalization before an audience of concerned community members. The individual views of the panelists and the dialogue with the audience were enlightening. Writer and linguist René Appel made the stunning observation that "so far there has been no policy, or hardly any, but there are I do not know how many courses in English. Is it not insane that a university decides to allow all of this without policy being developed?" Paul Rupp, chairman of the Avans University of Applied Sciences and a member of the KNAW committee, noted that his university had made the deliberate decision to maintain Dutch as the standard. Yet with English playing such a dominant role in the labor market, every student must take an English course, which is tested.

Thom Palstra, the rector of Twente Technical University, gave a pitch for internationalization. His university, he explained, puts a high premium on the "international classroom," with the aim of producing "internationally global citizens." From Jan Roukens, chairman of the Dutch Foundation, which opposed the "narrowing" of Dutch, came the retort that the Twente policy was directly contrary to the Higher Education and Research Act, requiring that Dutch remain the language of education with few exceptions. Janneke Gerards, the chair of the KNAW committee, interjected that the law allowed room for the approach adopted by Twente and similar institutions. Several experts contradicted her interpretation. A student representative raised the question of educational quality and the fact that 15 percent of students do not pass the final English exam in secondary school and consequently enter university and enroll in all-English programs with inadequate English skills. Comments from the audience touched upon students' smaller vocabulary in English and the threat to Dutch as an academic language. Yet for some of those present, the discussion was merely a "hopeless rearguard action." Dutch as an "academic language" was a "world gone by," communication scientist Jo Bardoel declared. "Dutch has become an irrelevant language to publish in, while the labor market is in fact very much Dutch-speaking."[58] In the end, the meeting generated much heat while shedding some light on the need for a workable solution but without reaching any definitive conclusion.

That December, the Interparliamentary Committee of the Dutch Language Union (Taalunie), which again governs Dutch language issues primarily between the Netherlands and Belgian's Flemish community, held a public meeting in response to the KNAW report. Among the invited guests from the Netherlands were key academicians including Ad Verbrugge, Annette de Groot, Lotte Jensen, and Pieter Duisenberg of VSNU, as well as several members of parliament. An inevitable point of departure was the fact that Belgium, where the rights of

Dutch speakers have been hard won, had taken a far more cautious approach toward English-taught courses. Once again English and Dutch language proficiency in the context of quality, accessibility, and labor market needs, together with a broader view of multilingualism, came to the fore.

Several speakers underscored the question of equity and its relation to immigrant and other disadvantaged students. It was noted that internationalization based on English effectively segregates students in a way that favors those from more privileged families, who tend to be more fluent in English. At the same time, it creates "bubbles" where students with poor proficiency in either English or Dutch not only stay within their own groups but also are unable to engage in meaningful discussion or develop a sense of academic citizenship.[59] In the end, this was yet another meeting with interesting points raised but with no clear action plan. Even the chair, who called for developing a "careful language policy," noted that the "parameters of that policy" were not yet sufficiently clear.[60]

The Academy Takes Hold

As 2017 was reaching a close, an opinion piece in *de Volkskrant* by Lotte Jensen, the professor of Dutch literary history at Radboud University Nijmegen, ignited yet another round of discussion and debate in Dutch academic circles. This time the focus was on English in the humanities. Jensen described how one of her most talented students, "on demand of the examination committee," had to write her final paper on the prominent seventeenth-century poet and playwright Joost van den Vondel in English, including translating all the direct passages. "What is the added value of that?" Jensen asked. The "rhyme and the poetic meter" of the Dutch language was completely lost, she said. "Vondel's language was pressed into an English straitjacket to comply with the exam regulations." It was no longer possible, she lamented, to teach her specialization at the master's level. With most of the follow-up courses in English, she could not assign Dutch writers or secondary literature.[61]

The piece elicited a pragmatic response from Marrigje Paijmans, also a Vondel expert at Nijmegen. Paijmans regretted that she had not initially written her own dissertation in English, which she then had to translate for publication. "What is the purpose of a dissertation on Vondel?" she asked. "Do you write that only for Dutch people, or do you want to share Vondel with the whole world?" Dutch courses, she said, had to "reinvent themselves" to keep in tune with internationalization. The "specialists" will always return to the original texts. Though Jensen agreed, she saw a difference between education and research. "You also have to be realistic," she said. "If Dutch disappears from university education, you can no longer prescribe any Dutch texts to students."[62] Putting all this together, one had to wonder whether the debate was just about weighing costs and bene-fits or about something more intellectually and culturally important but not quantifiable.

Considering those broader interests, it seemed fit when Karen Maex, the Flemish rector of the University of Amsterdam, used the occasion of the institution's 386th anniversary to address internationalization and language policy. Delivering her speech, "The International Paradox," in English, Maex moved seamlessly from the height of education as "collective engagement and responsibility" and the current "cultural renaissance" to the nitty-gritty details of student housing and the pressure from international students displacing Dutch students. While Maex recognized the benefits of international classrooms that included students of diverse backgrounds and cultures, she called for English-taught programs with "specific learning objectives that also pay attention to Dutch language skills for Dutch-speaking students."

Maex cautioned against universities becoming "alienated" from their "native surroundings." Rather than cast Dutch aside, she said, offering both English and Dutch versions, especially in disciplines with large student numbers, would be "an enrichment." At the same time, allowing Dutch to evolve in new research areas would make findings "accessible to a wider audience." Venturing further into controversial territory, she proposed setting "limits for growth on interna-tionalization" so that the University of Amsterdam could continue providing "quality and added value." She called on the newly appointed minister of edu-cation, culture, and science to offer universities a "tool" for controlling the "in-flow" of international students, weighing diversity and international background in the composition of the international classroom.[63]

Little did Maex anticipate that her speech would unleash a transnational de-bate on the purposes and limits of internationalization, including ninety-five comments on the social media platform Reddit and commentary in the higher education press.[64] Hans de Witt, then director of the Center for International Higher Education at Boston College and a Dutch national, called for a "nuanced approach." Internationalization, he said, "should not be about the numbers of programs taught in English, international students, or branch campuses. The dis-cussion should be about why, what, how, and when, focusing on improving the quality of higher education." He warned that the current local-global balance has been "struck wrongly because politics and economics give wrong signals to do more or less [internationalization] based on political and economic sentiments and not on academic quality."[65]

Others were more supportive of the status quo. Markus Laitinen, presi-dent of the European Association for International Education, took issue with the claim that there were too many international students. For him, a quarter of the University of Amsterdam's first year class, though made up of foreign enrollments as Maex had noted in her speech, was not "even close to being excessive." Robert Coelen, professor of internationalization of higher education at Stenden University of Applied Sciences, argued that foreign students were not denying university places to local students but rather saving otherwise unsustainable programs for them.[66] Depending on how you looked at it, the glass was either half full or half empty.

The Dutch press chimed in, drawing views from within academia and the political arena on what NOS, the public broadcasting company, called the "English disease." Professor emerita Annette de Groot called for an immediate moratorium on English programs and for foreign students and lecturers to learn Dutch. The National Student Association LSVb suggested that a moratorium would give universities time to improve the proficiency of teachers already teaching in English.[67] Members of parliament took the minister of education to task for not acting quickly enough on the points laid out in the coalition agreement, proposing that members take up the issue immediately without waiting for the minister's vision plan.[68]

Adding a touch of drama, the award-winning Dutch novelist and philosopher of history Eelco Runia publicly announced his resignation from the University of Groningen in an opinion piece, "Why I Resign from the University." Runia ascribed his departure to the neoliberal "faith in the market" ideology driving higher education. To underscore the absurdity of "Anglicisation," Runia described how he had to give a lecture in English to a room full of students totally proficient in Dutch.[69] Runia's commentary was the most read article in the daily evening newspaper NRC, generating wide support on social media and in personal emails from politicians, scientists, and current and former students.

As the academicians publicly vented their angst and even rage, an article in de Telegraaf provocatively entitled "Stop the English Madness" brought the issue back to the students. Here the National Student Union (LSVb) raised concerns with denying Dutch students access to programs in psychology, which except for Utrecht University were all in English, despite a shortage of Dutch psychologists.[70] The reported figures on applications were startling. At the University of Amsterdam, a total of 594 Dutch students and 1,260 foreign students had applied for 600 places in psychology. The problem extended even more widely to other disciplines. At Erasmus University Rotterdam, 767 Dutch students and 2,605 foreign students had applied for 550 places in international business administration. As an LSVb spokesperson explained, English-taught programs ran the gamut from dentistry to pharmacology to Dutch law and even to Dutch literature.[71] Dutch universities bent on internationalization had seemingly become "hostage to their own success." An LSVb press release condemned English-only programs that often had "deteriorating quality" or suddenly put Dutch and international students in competition for a limited number of places. It called on universities to "be cautious and think their strategy through."[72]

There was some evidence that universities were already heeding the call. Delft University of Technology had announced that it would not enroll any students from outside the European Economic Area for the next bachelor's of computer science and engineering course. Others, nonetheless, were moving full steam ahead to broaden their English offerings in the interests of internationalization. In early 2018, the University of Twente (UT) initially announced that English would be the official working language beginning January 2020. All formal communications, official documents, meetings, and messages on the employee portal, as well as signage on the campus and information on LED walls, would be in English, with some exceptions. All legally binding documents, letters, and regulations would be in English and Dutch. Teachers would have to demonstrate a level of C1 competency in English on the Common European Framework of Reference for Languages (CEFR).[73]

This seemed like a bold move, given the heated tensions rattling Dutch academic and political circles. Yet at that point, all of UT's master's programs were already in English, and the last bachelor's programs were in transition. As the university's board chairman saw it, the political discussion on English language programs did not apply to technical universities like UT, which operated on an "international playing field." He predicted that internationalization would "no longer be an issue in three years' time."[74] Without the advantage of political foresight, the board chairman could not predict just how far the all-English strategy could go or how the government would be pressured to take the reins on English and international applications. Jump ahead to 2019 and we find the UT faculty council pushing back on guidelines issued by UT's director of computer science requiring that all formal and informal interactions on campus be conducted in English, even among groups of all Dutch speakers.[75] That same year the UT board, expecting changes in the law, adopted a stricter code of conduct on approving English-taught programs.[76]

Parliament and Ministerial Vision

Throughout the 2017–18 academic year, the coalition parliament and the newly appointed education minister engaged in a series of legislative questions and ministerial responses. In April 2018, the House of Representatives Permanent Committee for Education, Culture, and Science held a general hearing where the members held the minister's feet to the fire. In the course of pointed questioning, the discussion repeatedly circled back to quality, accessibility, and efficiency, with a side reference to equity and equal opportunity for immigrant and first-generation students. Along the way, it veered into the language of "necessity" in the 1992 law as compared to "added value" in the coalition agreement, a fundamental difference with serious implications. It also laid out the need for periodic inspection and stepped-up monitoring, as well as the importance of approaching the problem systemically. In the end, the minister rejected the idea of imposing a moratorium on new English-taught programs considering that her vision statement was due before the coming summer.[77] In the irony of this roller coaster debate, at the very moment that the minister was making that argument, Professor Annette de Groot, speaking at a symposium sponsored by BON, was again calling for a moratorium based on educational quality and preserving the Dutch language and Dutch identity.[78]

In anticipation of the minister's vision statement, the Association of Universities (VSNU) and the Association of Universities of Applied Sciences (VH) published a joint "internationalization agenda." Quality and accessibility once again were the central themes. The paper offered a list of options. Universities could coordinate the language of education at the system level to assure that at least one Dutch language program would remain available somewhere in the country. They might cap English-taught enrollment to guarantee accessibility and diversity. They might raise tuition fees and cap enrollment for non-EEA students in programs where the capacity was limited and the demand high. They could more effectively integrate foreign students into academic life. They might require a minimum C1 level of English for all lecturers in English classes and offer language modules to students in both English and Dutch.[79] In the end, the paper strongly requested more funding from the national government and tacitly underscored the need for more regulation.

The joint paper was a reasonable effort at reaching a middle ground on internationalization. Yet it glossed over critical points on implementation. System-wide coordination of English-taught courses could create barriers to accessibility. Some students might not be sufficiently mobile to move to another city where the only program in Dutch was offered in the subject that they hoped to pursue. That burden undoubtedly would weigh heaviest on less privileged students. Capping foreign enrollment seemed equally problematic. According to European agreements, EEA students, who form the majority of international students, have the same right to higher education at the same tuition rate as Dutch students.

The only way to indirectly lower student numbers would be to limit the number of English-taught courses or impose Dutch language requirements, which presumably would deter students unwilling to study Dutch. If that decision were left to individual campuses, however, universities could continue on their current course of increasing foreign enrollment as the Dutch college-age population continued to decline. That increase would put additional strain on a government budget that does not grow in proportion to the aggregate number of students enrolled but gets spread more thinly among increasingly more students. The system of funding provides no incentive for universities to limit the number of foreign students. It is quite the opposite: departments with larger numbers of students overall get a larger share of the education budget, which sets other universities in competition to increase their foreign enrollments. And so continues the recurring cycle of universities chasing funding through English-taught courses that attract foreign students in the name of "internationalization."

A Judicial Interlude

That brings us to the court decision in June 2018. As the Parliament and academic community awaited the minister's plan, with no meaningful political response in near sight, the Dutch Association for Better Education (BON) delivered on its threat to take the matter to court. The initial targets of the litigation were two examples of internationalization run amok—Maastricht University and the University of Twente—where all bachelor's programs in psychology were offered in English. The complaint also castigated the Education Inspectorate for failing to take action. BON asked the court to impose a one-year moratorium prohibiting the two universities from converting any additional programs to English while the government developed a new language policy. BON claimed that the programs impaired both the quality of teaching and the ability of Dutch students to access higher education. The group's ultimate intent was a broader challenge to English-taught programs and to the perceived failure of the government to enforce the law.

Leading the charge was BON's cofounder and chairman, Ad Verbrugge, a philosophy professor at VU University Amsterdam. As Verbrugge saw it, universities "do a lot of damage" by offering courses in English. For him, Dutch was an "essential part of academic education."[80] In a news article invoking "Shakespeare in trouble," Verbrugge called offering courses in English to "remain in the race" for international students nothing short of "linguicide." "Dutch students no longer master their native language," he argued. The article resonated beyond the Netherlands and even beyond Europe, finding its way into the foreign press as far away as Pakistan, Indonesia, China, Japan, and Qatar. Though Verbrugge was not certain if the lawsuit would succeed, he was heartened that at least it had "raised the issue for discussion."[81]

BON issued a press release, "BON Drags Universities to Court," laying out its arguments and asking supporters to sign a petition and donate to the litigation effort. Driving the point home, the release quoted from the Maastricht University Institutional Plan: "As a bilingual university, virtually all teaching takes place in English." For BON, this was a direct violation of Article 1.3 of the Higher Education and Scientific Research Act, which states that higher education must also focus on "promoting expression in Dutch."[82] The petition, posted on the BON website, called the rise in foreign students between 2000 and 2017, despite a drop in per student spending from about €20,000 (US$23,500) to €14,000 (US$16,500), an "improper use of public funds." By the time the case was brought in May 2018, the petition had gained seven thousand signatures and raised over €15,000 (US$17,600) to support the litigation, but that was hardly enough to mount a full-blown lawsuit.[83]

Before the court hearing took place, the minister of education sent to the House of Representatives her anticipated "vision" letter echoing themes of quality, accessibility, efficiency, and connection to the environment. She urged universities to take responsibility for balancing their Dutch and English courses and to coordinate their efforts so that every degree subject would be available in Dutch. She made a number of specific recommendations, including limiting both the number of student places in some English courses and the number of non-EEA students where legally possible, gearing language choice in any given course or program toward training students for the labor market, developing academic English skills among Dutch students while maintaining their command of Dutch, retaining Dutch as a language of science, and keeping closer checks on the English language skills of lecturers. Most importantly, the minister proposed that Article 7.2 be revised to shift the focus from "necessity" to "added value" and "accessibility" for Dutch students. She ordered the Inspectorate of Education, which she heads, to examine the codes of conduct that universities must develop under Article 7.2 and to determine the appropriate action for individual institutions. The inspectorate's findings would inform a wider investigation into internationalization in higher education through the coming year.[84]

The minister's letter met mixed responses from the constituent groups. Nuffic was "optimistic" and praised her focus on internationalization. It also appreciated her emphasis on the language skills of lecturers in English-taught courses.[85] The Association of Universities (VSNU) welcomed the vision statement but expressed slight discomfort with the implied regulation on the use of English.[86] The National Student Union (LSVb) was especially critical. Mere coordination among universities with oversight by the inspectorate was not enough. The group called for a national committee to oversee whether English-taught programs were jeopardizing accessibility for Dutch students.[87]

As competing views deconstructed the minister's letter, BON's claims against Twente University and the University of Maastricht went before the Rechtbank Midden-Netherland (Court of the Central Netherlands). The hearing extended over three hours. BON's attorney peppered his argument with dramatic metaphors ("The house is on fire and the fire brigade does nothing"), while the universities shot back with technical objections. They questioned whether Anglicization was essentially a political matter and demanded a change in the law. At BON's request, Peter Kwikkers—who had drafted the legislation adopted in 1992—argued that the law implicitly allowed parts of a course to be offered in English, but "never the entire program."

The decision, rendered several weeks later, dismissed the claim against the inspectorate, which, the court held, had no enforcement authority; it could only investigate, and there was an ongoing investigation ordered by the minister. As for Twente and Maastricht, BON had failed to counter the evidence presented by the universities that their decisions were not driven solely or mainly by revenue considerations, as BON claimed, but rather by factors demanded under Article 7.2. Those factors, the universities maintained, included both the international character of the field of psychology, where the academic literature was largely in English, and the universities' diverse student bodies, for whom English was a common language.

The court reserved judgment on the larger question of whether the codes of conduct and the method of implementing them complied with Article 7.2, since the article itself did not indicate the specific requirements the codes must meet. As the court noted, "It is not up to the judge to take a position in the debate on the importance of Dutch-speaking education for the quality of education." The court left that task to the inspectorate in carrying out the investigation it had already started and to the minister in acting on the findings.[88] The decision seemed reasonable given the way the complaint had been drafted. BON had merely asked for a moratorium, which the investigation rendered premature for court intervention. BON should have argued that the all-English psychology programs violated Article 1.3, which requires universities to "promote expression in Dutch" among Dutch speaking students. Apparently the court did not fully comprehend the connection between Articles 3.1 and 7.2.[89]

The court's exercising judicial restraint was not unusual but rather common practice. Courts are mindful of their limited capacity and legitimacy in deciding education matters. In this case, the nature of the lawsuit gave the court special reason to stand back. This was a provisional court proceeding heard by one judge; the interests at stake were enormous; the political discussion was continuing; and the minister and Parliament appeared to be acting in good faith. The court could only assume that their words would translate into action in reasonable time. Though the two universities made a victory lap in the press, it was uncertain how long-lived that victory might be. The court warned that once the inspectorate's investigation was completed and clearer standards for compliance with Article 7.2 were established, the picture could change. Dutch universities, including Twente and Maastricht, could still find themselves in court defending

English-taught programs unless they could prove "necessity" or "value added," however the law was finally resolved.

Like the Italian case against Milan's Polytechnic Institute, the claimants did not come away empty-handed. BON in the least could take credit for energizing the debate with its 2015 "manifesto" and for maintaining the momentum for a political response with its repeated threats of litigation. At the same time, the intermediate court ruling implicitly placed pressure on the minister and Parliament to make good on their word. The clock was ticking for them to find a workable solution to a policy problem with far-reaching implications for higher education, Dutch society, and the Dutch nation.

The Political Response

It was left to the legislature to clarify or revise the legal standards under Articles 7.2 and to remain true to the commitment to Dutch in Article 3.1. Meanwhile, it was left to the ministry to enforce the law in a way that addressed the quality and accessibility of education offered to Dutch students while preserving the integrity of the Dutch language along with a diverse and international student body. Reaching a political consensus among the interest groups was a tall order.[90]

The inspectorate's first report in November 2018 shed light on two related pieces of the internationalization puzzle: the codes of conduct and the use of a language (English) other than Dutch for education and exams.[91] The findings lent credence to concerns repeatedly raised over the years by voices inside and outside Dutch academic circles, including the BON petitioners. It was clear that numerous institutions were in violation of the law and that the inspectorate had failed to monitor a situation that was spinning out of control. Based on written responses from 125 government-funded universities and colleges, more than half (sixty-four) offered at least one complete program, and thirteen offered at least one training with a substantial part in a language other than Dutch. Among that total of seventy-seven institutions, only forty-three had developed a code of conduct as required by Article 7.2. Only about half of the forty-three codes began from the starting point in Article 7.2 ("Dutch unless . . .") or seemed mindful of Article 1.3's directive that higher education must promote the Dutch language.

There seemed to be a faulty assumption that as long as an institution had a code of conduct, it was in legal compliance. The report found that in many cases there was no compelling justification offered for teaching in a language other than Dutch, despite Article 7.2's requiring a showing of "necessity." In some cases, while the code adhered to the legal principle, policy documents were based on bilingualism. It was especially striking that while the law had been adopted in 1992, about half of the codes dated from 2017 and 2018, presumably in response to mounting concerns, legislative attention, and the threat of litigation. The report put pressure on the government to take action. The following January, the first version of proposed amendments to the Higher Education and Research Act were submitted for review and comment. Needless to say, they provoked a stream of responses.

As those responses publicly aired, an announcement from Vrije Universiteit in Amsterdam that it was dropping its bachelor's degree in Dutch language due to lack of applicants stoked the fires, provoking calls for "emergency measures."[92] The decision raised doubts as to whether the country was training young people to function in the Dutch labor market and to communicate with the people they serve. Would psychologists or medical doctors educated primarily or entirely in English have the terminology or Dutch language skills to address the needs of their clients or patients? Given these conflicting messages, a petition signed by 183 prominent academic and cultural figures raising well-worn concerns over the "Anglicization" of Dutch higher education should have come as no surprise to the political establishment.[93]

A second inspectorate report in June 2019 confirmed that the number of international students would continue to grow in the coming years, although the question of whether the increase might displace Dutch students was left for a subsequent study. The report found that institutions often could not explicitly state the effects of internationalization on their financial operations. Yet it found no evidence that universities or colleges were recruiting international students solely for financial reasons, which resolved one of the key questions left unanswered in the BON litigation.[94]

Though the minister expressed outrage at the number of violations found in the first report, she took no direct action against any institutions but rather set about drafting amendments to the Higher Education and Research Act. Her Language and Accessibility Bill, released in September 2019, followed the recommendations of an Interministerial Policy Review.[95] The review confirmed what had already become obvious: that internationalization "could threaten the funding, quality and accessibility of education" and that English-taught courses could undermine the proficiency of students in Dutch.[96] The less obvious question was how to preserve all the benefits of an international program while avoiding the inevitable fallout.

The minister's bill proposed a number of key changes in the law. Universities would be responsible for "facilitating foreign students' acquisition of Dutch," though students would not be compelled to study Dutch. Institutions offering courses in a language other than Dutch would need prior approval from the Netherlands-Flanders Accreditation Organization. They might set a student quota ("numerus fixus") on courses in which the language of instruction is not Dutch to guarantee accessibility to Dutch students. But they could only impose a quota where there was a capacity problem and where alternative solutions—like partnering with other universities—had proven unworkable, and then only with the approval of the minister. Tuition rates for students from outside the European Economic Area (EEA), many from China and India, would be raised. Funds previously channeled to the Netherlands Education Support Offices (NESO) for foreign student recruitment and run by the Netherlands Organization for International Cooperation in Higher Education (Nuffic) would be redirected toward providing study-abroad opportunities for Dutch students, including ethnic minorities and those with disabilities, who less commonly participated in these programs.[97]

The minister's recommendations were not as severe as university officials had feared. But they also were not as definitive as critics had hoped. Though the "Dutch unless" principle remained, universities would no longer have to demonstrate the "necessity" of using English instruction; they only had to show "value added." Instead of a code of conduct, they would have to develop more comprehensive language policies that described not only the rationale but also the official process by which the university decided to teach in a language other than Dutch. They would further need to describe whatever steps the institution would take to maintain the quality of teaching and the accessibility for Dutch students. Policies would be evaluated periodically to ensure compliance with the law.[98]

Given all the changes, the proposal elicited a seemingly endless string of questions that quickly circulated through the press and the corridors of government. Would the "value added" test lead to unnecessary bureaucracy? How would it be defined in any given case? Were there objective criteria for assessing the language policies of institutions? Was the numerus fixus at odds with accessibility and equal opportunity? Would it infringe on institutional autonomy? Would it lead to underutilized courses? How might universities accommodate the influx of students if the minister denied the numerus fixus? Would higher fees for students from non-EEA countries close out students from low-income countries? Would the Netherlands lose foreign talent needed to fill gaps in the Dutch workforce?

As government officials and stakeholders weighed in on the proposals, a newly published book, *Against English: A Plea for Dutch*, enlivened the public discussion.[99] The twenty-six essays included well-known academic voices, along with those of writers, journalists, editors, lawyers, translators, an entrepreneur, and a musician, some with roots not only in the Netherlands and Belgium but also in Denmark, France, Germany, Ghana, Italy, Morocco, and Turkey. In sum, the book inveighed against the "Anglicization" of Dutch society. Writing in different styles, the authors criticized the commercial motives of publishers who favored English over other languages and university leaders who claimed to promote "diversity" while creating an "academic monoculture" in displacing Dutch and scientific languages with "Globish." Some praised the power of language as a repository of cultural memory and a vehicle for becoming part of a society, especially for those arriving from another country. The book overall warned against the dangers of losing the nation's ties to the Dutch language and indicted the Dutch people for putting pragmatism and profit over national pride. At the same time, it paid homage to multilingualism and language as an integral part of identity, culture, and citizenship. The book became grist to the mill for a round of reviews along with yet more commentary from the book's authors and others.[100] The publication could not have been better timed, just as the House of Representatives was debating the minister's Language and Accessibility Bill.

Fanning the flames even further, the University of Twente (one of the universities in the BON litigation) took a radical turn on English and internationalization. It affirmed that, as of January 2020, it would finally put in place its plan, initially adopted in 2015, to make English the official university language. All lectures, research, application processes, interviews, press releases, promotional materials, and internal communications would be in English with few exceptions. The university even suggested that employees and students speak to each other in English on campus, though informal conversations in Dutch and any other language would still be allowed. If a non-Dutch speaker joined a group, the conversation had to switch to English. The response to the announcement from Parliament was swift and unequivocal. Both Christian Democrat and Socialist MPs described the plan as "bizarre." Some questioned its legality.[101] The University's university's website tried to allay concerns with an unconvincing assurance that "Dutch is and will definitely continue to be used on our campus."[102] As criticism mounted, the university's communications department posted a justification on Twitter that proved confounding at best: "The language in which we communicate must contribute to inclusiveness and diversity." Yet Dutch, which is the first language of most students and staff, was unquestionably excluded.[103]

Amidst this tsunami of overlapping developments, in December 2019 the House of Representatives adopted the minister's proposed amendments with some revisions. The following February, just as the COVID-19 pandemic was about to upend the Netherlands and the world, the Senate asked for further advice from the State Council. The question, bearing directly on EU and international regulations, addressed the "method for determining and assessing a capacity standard and the possible limitation of non-EEA students." Yet these concerns related more generally to national language policies and only tangentially to the specific "cause" of the problem, which was the Dutch/English language dilemma. If the Senate used the request as a delay tactic, the pandemic made it all the more effective. The State Council advised that the minister did not have the authority to place a fixed number in advance on international en-rollment absent evidence that Dutch students were being closed out of courses, which did not seem to be the case. Yet it also stated that it was not incompatible with European and international law to set a maximum number on courses for non-EEA students when the teaching capacity became inadequate.[104] As it hap-pened, the downturn in international enrollments from non-EEA countries re-sulting from the pandemic made the capacity problem a moot question, at least for the coming academic year.

A legislative election in March 2021, resulting in a new coalition government, put the proposal temporarily on hold. Even if the reconstituted government adopts all or most of the proposed changes, it is unlikely to put the issues to rest for longer than it takes for the ink to dry on the last signature. The law is more than likely to meet a court challenge, on its face or as applied to a particular uni-versity, as institutions stretch the bounds of legislative language and intent. If so, without arguably constitutional protections for the national language as in the case of Italy, it will be interesting to see how far the judiciary goes in preserving Article 1.3's mandate that universities "focus on promoting the Dutch lan-guage" against the weight of institutional autonomy and the demands of the global economy. Even English language proponents, who have pointed to the Netherlands as a success story on English proficiency and internationalization, are stepping back and waiting for the next chapter in this story.

In the meantime, international student applications and enrollments in the Netherlands remain uncertain. The United Kingdom's withdrawal from the Erasmus program and its elimination of the home-fee status for international students could make the Netherlands and its high number of English-taught courses even more attractive to students from other EU/EEA countries. Higher enrollments would put more pressure on capacity, which also affects quality in the absence of additional funding. On the other hand, a weakened global economy could decrease enrollments from countries like China and India, at least for the short term. Meanwhile, populist forces in Parliament, skeptical of "outsiders," could turn the Netherlands inward and dampen public support for educating students from other countries.

As these events continue to unfold, France, Italy, Germany, the Nordic coun-tries, and others, in search of a "roadmap" on English in internationalization, are keeping a watchful eye on what has evolved into a Dutch cautionary tale of both too much too soon, and too little too late.

PART II

SHADOWS OF COLONIALISM

The "New Scramble" for Africa

No country has resisted the spread of English and promoted its national language as resolutely as France. The driving force is not new, nor is it related solely to English. Over the centuries, France has fought three linguistic battles—displacing Latin, suppressing regional languages, and resisting Anglo-Americanisms—all the while fighting to maintain the global status of its national language.[1] Once considered the preferred language of diplomacy, literature, and intellectual endeavors, French has now fallen to a distant second place. The French government nonetheless strives mightily to regain its prominence not only for reasons of national pride but also for the economic perks that French once commanded in global commerce. France's most profitable and perhaps most challenging targets have been its former colonies in Africa. That is where the French-speaking population is predicted to grow exponentially in the coming decades and where the opportunities for trade and access to natural resources are abundant. The vigor with which France preserves these ties, especially through the Organisation internationale de la Francophonie (OIF), is striking as it resolutely pushes back against the force of English.

France's prime competitor is China, which also sees great potential in Africa's demographic dividend. Like France, China has set about using the soft power of language, along with intense resource investment, in what analysts describe as a "new scramble" to strengthen diplomatic, strategic, and commercial ties.[2] In the process, Chinese is slowly capturing the hearts and minds of African francophones, as well as anglophones. Each country and language, in its own way, threatens to impose another layer of colonialism on the continent and further marginalize indigenous languages and cultures as it intersects with English.

La Francophonie en Marche

Back in the 1880s, the French geographer Onésime Reclus, in his book *France, Algérie, et les colonies,* coined the term *Francophonie* to classify the French-speaking population worldwide irrespective of nationality. The concept of separating nationality from language was radical in an era when geographers charted the world by race, ethnicity, or religion.[3] Writing in the shadow of the Franco-Prussian War, Reclus was concerned with restoring France's standing vis-à-vis Germany. Colonial spread of the language would give longevity to the French nation.[4] Reclus predicted that one day the francophones in Africa and North America would outnumber all those in Europe.[5] Nearly a century later, in 1964, Léopold Senghor, the noted poet and president of Senegal, launched the term *Francophonie* as an organizing concept.[6] Senghor repeatedly said, "In the ruins of colonialism, we have found this marvelous tool, the French language."

The seeds of the OIF were initially planted in 1960 with a conference of fifteen education ministers from French-speaking countries. That meeting led the following year to an association of universities, the Agence universitaire de la Francophonie (AUF), which still exists with over one thousand member institutions across 119 countries. Three years later, 21 states and governments—led by Léopold Senghor, President Habib Bourguiba of Tunisia, President Hamani Diori of Niger, and Prince Norodom Sihanouk of Cambodia—signed the convention that created the Agence de coopération culturelle et technique, later reorganized into the Agence intergouvernmentale de la Francophonie in 1998, and ultimately into the Organisation internationale de la Francophonie (OIF) in 2005 with a more political agenda. For African leaders during the years of decolonization, officially joining together into a common organization would grant former colonies greater global influence.[7]

It is generally assumed that France was the driving force in launching the OIF. Yet unlike the British, who spearheaded the British Commonwealth of Nations, the French were initially hesitant to get involved for fear of being branded as neocolonialist. For the same reason, the term *Francophonie* was not used in French official documents until 1996. Charles de Gaulle, who served as president until 1969, never used the term in public. The French were not the only ones to associate the term with colonialism; so did North Africans.[8] Nonetheless, as the years wore on, France became anxious about losing influence in the postcolonial world in the face of English, whose global stature was on the rise. France understood that the Francophonie network could help protect the country's international interests.

Based in Paris, the OIF is now made up of eighty-eight member governments, of which seven are associate and twenty-seven are observer states, representing over nine hundred million people and over three hundred million French speakers across five continents. According to the OIF website, what binds the members together is not only the French language but also the "humanist values" that the language promotes. The general director of UNESCO explained it well in a 2017 letter celebrating March 20 as the Francophonie Day:

> The French language crystallizes centuries of culture and history. . . . It is in French that Pascal, Voltaire and Rousseau led the fight for tolerance, democracy and human rights. It was in French that Assia Djebar defended the rights of women and that Césaire, Senghor and so many others laid the foundations of modern humanist consciousness. On all five continents, hundreds of millions of men and women express their hopes for a better life in French. Apollinaire, Kundera and Beckett wrote some of their strongest works in French, and it was also in this beautiful language that Marie Curie wrote her thesis on uranium, which revolutionized modern science.[9]

While the organization's purpose is to protect and promote French, it also has taken a strong position on plurilingualism in promoting the use of multiple languages in international institutions and consequently by individuals within those organizations. Rather than target English directly or simply reject the "efficiency" arguments of English-speaking countries, plurilingualism ties language diversity to democracy as a "political" value.[10] In addition to promoting French language and culture, the OIF is a unifying force for political and economic cooperation and sustainable development among its members. French is an official language in thirty-two of the member states. The remainder includes countries like Mexico, Egypt, Moldova, Serbia, Poland, and Qatar that have little historical connection to France or the French language.

Many member states are in sub-Saharan Africa, though others span the globe from Vietnam to Canada. Beyond Africa, one Francophonie area that is often overlooked is the South Pacific, where there was a wave of French colonization in the mid-1800s. In French Polynesia, New Caledonia, and the territory of Wallis and Futuna, French is still both the national language and the language of schooling. In the Indian Ocean islands of Réunion, the Seychelles, and Mauritius, French also continues to have traction, though English is on the rise. In 2018, Ghana became the latest anglophone country to be admitted to full membership in the OIF, with an agreement to promote French throughout schooling. Bordered to the north, east, and west by French-speaking countries, Ghana recognized the trade and investment gains to be had in straddling the Franco/Anglo divide. In 2019, it adopted French as a second official language to English.

Leaders of OIF member states gather together biannually in a "summit" meeting over which the president of France and the president of the host country preside. While some members like to think that France, the former colonial master, is just one among equals within the organization, it remains a dominant force. The OIF receives a considerable portion of its budget from France. A good part of the funds go to French language and cultural programs across the globe, like the Alliance française and Radio France International. The OIF is an integral part of French foreign policy to preserve the French language and culture throughout the world. In Africa, in particular, it has helped France shift from military involvement and the negative connotations of "la françafrique," especially since the 1994 Rwandan genocide, to a softer form of influence that France strongly tries to maintain.[11]

The Haut Conseil de la Francophonie (HCF) (Commission for the French-speaking world) reports to the OIF secretary general. A key office within the HCF gathers data and publishes a report every four years on the state of the French language worldwide. The 2018 report, in close to four hundred pages, pays homage to the continued importance of French in the world. It covers a broad range of topics, including the increasing numbers of French speakers (three hundred million), French language learners (fifty million), students taught through French (eighty-one million), and international students studying in France (over three hundred thousand). It also covers the economic value of French in trade and the prevalence of French on the internet, where it is the fourth most used language and the third in terms of traffic. The French media chain TV5MONDE each week reaches an audience of sixty million viewers spread throughout more than two hundred countries and territories.[12]

France understands that francophone countries, especially in Africa and the Mediterranean, are key to protecting its global power and its language against the onslaught of English and US influence. The African continent is home to 59 percent of daily speakers of French. A relatively high birth rate and advances in schooling are projected to increase that number to close to 80 percent by 2070.[13] At the 2012 Francophonie summit in Kinshasa, former French president François Hollande declared that French "is now an African language." He also declared that speaking French meant speaking the language of "liberty" and "human rights," a bold assertion that must have rung hollow for Algerians and other Africans whose ancestors had suffered exploitation and even death under French colonial rule.[14] At the 2016 summit in Madagascar, Hollande drew on terrorist attacks against member nations, including France, Belgium, Tunisia, Chad, Burkina, and Ivory Coast, to rally the members around the French language. "We are targets," he told the crowd, "because French is the language of logic, liberty and emancipation. Because it is in French that the universality of the rights of man and of the citizen were declared and that is what fanatics do not accept."[15]

A follow-up article in the French daily *Le Figaro* put the problem in less varnished light. Preserving French, the article stated, is not just a problem of clashing worldviews between the forces of "good" and "evil." It's about access to valuable resources, as colonialism well understood. A good example is the Democratic Republic of the Congo (RDC), the most populous French-speaking country, where the constitution declares "la langue de Molière" the official language. Yet only 50 percent of the population speaks French fluently. The challenge for France is to gain greater access to the country's rich but untapped resources in oil, copper, and cobalt in the face of competition from the United States and Great Britain and most recently from China. That climb is especially steep in the eastern part of the country where English has overtaken French in some provinces.[16]

The French government drives home that the benefits work both ways. According to its website, membership in the French-speaking community accounts for 16 percent of the world's wealth.[17] The government understands that the only way to sustain the numbers is for countries with high population growth to keep the language alive through future generations. France has high stakes in making sure that children in these countries not only have access to schooling but that they also learn French. More fundamentally, it recognizes that it's competing with English, which holds a strong attraction as a gateway to global trade.

In 2011, with support from the French government, OIF launched the ELAN Program (Écoles et langues nationales en Afrique) in eight French-speaking West African countries, partnering with four institutions to promote joint literacy in African languages and French. Learning solely in French has caused students in French-speaking sub-Saharan Africa to fail, especially in rural areas where French is seldom spoken. And so the idea was to offer instruction in both French and the students' mother tongues. As of 2018, the project had grown to twelve countries, including upward of twenty-five hundred bilingual schools, more than thirty-five hundred bilingual classes, six thousand teachers, more than 225,000 students, and thirty-nine teaching languages in addition to French.[18]

In 2012, the French Ministry of Foreign Affairs and International Development (AFD) also launched the Francophone Initiative for Open-Distance Teacher Training (IFADEM), a project aimed at developing distance-learning programs. French embassies and African education ministries can use these programs for training teachers of French on the continent. In the Democratic Republic of the Congo alone, in addition to the €14.5 million (US$17.1 million) that flow each year from the OIF for education projects, the AFD invests another €70 million (US$82 million), all in the service of promoting the French language and consequently French business interests. Yet according to an anonymous source close to diplomatic circles in the capital, Kinshasa, French interests might best be served by developing a "selective francophonie" of elites in African capital cities. That may, in fact, be what's happening. Funded by the French Ministry of Education, schools like the Lycée René Descartes in Kinshasa charge tuition fees that make them accessible only to the children of government officials and business leaders, a throwback to colonial times.[19]

France also has a deep interest in remaining the destination of choice for African students studying abroad. In 2018–19, France hosted 358,000 foreign students from 196 countries, of which 46 percent of the total was from Africa and 22 percent from sub-Saharan Africa.[20] Ranking first and second in countries of origin were Algeria, with 80 percent of outbound students headed for France, and Morocco, with 58 percent.[21] Recognizing the rising appeal of English as the appeal of French declines, France is casting its international net beyond the Francophonie and reaching out to the anglophone sphere. It is especially eyeing sub-Saharan Africa, where the student population grew by 26 percent between 2012 and 2017 and is expected to reach 22 million by 2027.[22]

An increasing number of elite French *grandes écoles* and business schools are taking yet another approach. Rather than recruit African students for their campuses in France, they're opening branch campuses in Africa. The French engineering school ESIEE has campuses in Cape Town and Pretoria, South Africa. Sciences Po in 2018 announced the inauguration of its first recruiting office in Nairobi, Kenya, to attract promising students. Ironically, the websites and recruiting materials of many of these schools are in English, as are many of the courses offered. At the Rencontres Campus France 2016 meeting in Paris, the French minister of foreign affairs and international development, having visited Kenya and Tanzania, admitted that France needed to "address the linguistic question" by offering more courses in English.[23] That was a surprising statement given the controversy just three years previously over the Loi Fioraso, which loosened constraints on teaching in languages other than English in French universities.

Navigating the Colonial Narrative

The election of the young, charismatic Emmanuel Macron to the French presidency in 2017 took France's efforts to overtake English to another level. By any measure, Macron has proven to be a linguistic contradiction, especially in his love-hate relationship with English. His inclination to strategically slip into English charms his fans both at home and abroad but rankles his Francophonie detractors. At the 2018 World Economic Forum in Davos, he opened in English with "France is back, France is back at the core of Europe," before continuing in

French and then closing in English to a standing ovation.[24] In a subsequent visit to Washington, he easily used English in fielding questions from the press. His lengthy address to Congress invoked a string of US presidents.

At the same time, Macron is a passionate and pragmatic promoter of the French language to revitalize France's influence within Francophonie and beyond. He embraces globalization, which French leaders and intellectuals resisted in the past. They equated it with Americanization and the spread of English. He also realizes that English has made inroads, to a lesser or greater extent, in Francophonie countries like Rwanda, Gabon, and Morocco and even Lebanon. He has tried to reconcile the contradictions and to temper fears of neocolonialism under the inclusive umbrella of "linguistic pluralism," where French can reclaim its lost glory, charging forward against the overpowering force of English. He has turned that project into a crusade. Along the way, and despite such deep resolve, he has learned some hard lessons on language and politics and suffered some bruises in navigating a world dominated by English and locked in a colonial mentality of "otherness."

At first glance, it might seem that money is the cement of France's post-independence relationship with its former colonies. The real cement, however, is the soft power of language and culture.[25] Macron understands that well. Speaking to students in Burkina Faso's capital, Ouagadougou, in November 2017 during a whirlwind tour of West African countries, the recently elected Macron outlined an ambitious and conciliatory agenda for economic and educational support and for cooperation on human rights, terrorism, and migration. "The crimes of European colonialization are unquestionable," he told his young audience. "It's a past that needs to pass." He urged that French no longer be viewed as a "relic of colonial power. . . . It has a future and this future is playing out in Africa." He warned that "to restrict oneself to a particular language, to reject the French language because English is more fashionable in Africa is to ignore the future! French will be the number one language in Africa, maybe even in the world, if we play our cards right in the coming decades." To add action to his words, Macron announced that he was asking the award-winning Moroccan writer Leïla Slimani to represent him in the OIF. Her charge was to work on projects addressing education, culture, sex equality, and youth jobs and mobility. Together with other African intellectuals and the Académie française, she would compile a French dictionary reflecting the language as spoken not just in France but throughout the Francophone world.[26]

Driving Macron's grandiose forecast were recent and projected changes in the demographics of Africa. According to OIF data, the number of French speakers in Africa rose by 17 percent between 2014 and 2018.[27] The number learning French as a foreign language in sub-Saharan Africa and the Indian Ocean rose by a stunning 126 percent.[28] OIF has predicted that by 2050, when nine out of ten

French speakers will be African, French will have overtaken English on the continent. Even sooner, the number of French speakers worldwide could increase to 750 million by 2025, 80 percent of them living in Africa, where 70 percent of the population is under the age of thirty.[29] In 2017, an OIF official assured the French press that "the heart of the language of Molière will beat in former French colonies."

In riding what may be a demographic wave of opportunity, Macron has seized the possibilities for spreading France's political influence worldwide and tying its former colonies culturally and economically to France in the years to come. Yet his campaign to spread the language of Molière seems overly ambitious, resting on disputable claims and assumptions. Skeptics maintain that the OIF numbers and projections are misleading. Not all residents of countries claiming French as an official language speak it with any level of proficiency. In many cases, France's colonial policies, and more recent laissez-faire attitudes toward funding education in these countries, have merely preserved French for the elite.

Macron's Ouagadougou speech unwittingly unleashed a torrent of criticism, suggesting that he lacked sincerity and grounding in reality in his various displays promoting the French language. Michel Guerrin, the editor-in-chief of the center-left daily Le Monde, noted the "chasm" between Macron's words and his actions. He took Macron to task for his repeated interviews in English on foreign TV, using slogans like "Choose France" and "France is back." He criticized Macron for not appointing a minister of Francophonie, a tradition begun with Jacques Chirac in 1986, but rather naming a personal representative without a budget or an office. Guerrin pointed out that despite its 275 million speakers and potential for growth in Africa, French was losing its influence in key sectors—in universities, business, the sciences, tourism, sports, and culture. "English is crushing everything," he declared.[30]

Macron's major misstep in Ouagadougou was his failure to understand that while France remains the capital of the francophone world, a new generation of African leaders and intellectuals are not as tied to Paris as their predecessors. As the number of French speakers in Africa begins to dominate that world, and as French becomes unhinged from its Gallic roots, the narrative on the French language, its relationship to France's former colonies, and even the power of revered institutions like the Académie française need to be revamped. For a country so steeped in tradition and so enamored with its language and all its literary grandeur, that is indeed a challenge.

The Ouagadougou speech especially sparked a firestorm among African intellectuals, who found it not just out of touch with reality but neocolonial. References to the anglophone world, and implicitly the English language, intermittently surfaced in the debate. Touching it off was Alain Mabanckou, the acclaimed Congolese novelist, who published a biting letter to Macron in the literary site of the weekly French news magazine *Le Nouvel Observateur*. Strategically dated January 15 (Martin Luther King Day Jr. Day in the United States), the letter declined the president's invitation to help draft the plan promoting the French language. "You can't talk about the French-speaking world if you don't ask the question of democracy in Africa," Mabanckou said. He noted the "incongruity" of defending the French language and holding summits with dictatorships that are more numerous in the French-speaking than in the English-speaking world. He faulted the initiative and the French literary world for "clinging to a Paris-centric vision" while failing to recognize the work of French language writers outside of France as part of French mainstream literature.[31]

Mabanckou was not alone. Abdourahman Waberi, the Franco-Djiboutian writer and academic, directly rebuked Macron for praising the greatness of the French language at the Frankfort Book Fair the previous October without mentioning any writers from outside Europe.[32] The Cameroonian philosopher Achille Mbembe denounced la Francophonie for "muzzling" French, which needed to be re-envisioned. He called for a world where no language belongs to anyone in particular and where Africa would play as much a part as France in making French a "world language."[33] It should be noted that back in 2007 both Mabanckou and Waberi were part of a manifesto entitled "For a World Literature in French in Favor of a French Language That Would Be Liberated from Its Exclusive Pact with the Nation." Signed by forty-four writers, the manifesto called for a "literature-monde" (world literature) in French that would not distinguish between the works of authors in France and those from other parts of the French-speaking world. They rested the call on the end of la Francophonie, which they referred to as "une étoile morte" (a dead star).[34]

Leading figures within France also weighed in on the Ouagadougou speech. Pierre Astier, a French literary agent known for specializing in foreign authors, agreed that France dominated book production in the French language in an "imperialist" way, even down to the school textbook market. Of the 110,000 books published in French each year, he pointed out, ninety thousand come from francophone Europe (France, Switzerland, and Belgium), fifteen thousand from Canada, and only the remaining five thousand from other countries. In contrast, of the nearly six hundred thousand books published each year in the anglophone world, two hundred thousand are from the United Kingdom, three hundred thousand from the United States, and the remaining one hundred thousand from a broad swath of English-speaking countries including India, Australia, New Zealand, South Africa, Kenya, and Nigeria.[35]

As the weeks leading up to La Journée internationale de la Francophonie (The international day of la Francophonie) in March wore on, the demands for change escalated, and the pressure on Macron deepened. The left-leaning journal *Politis* ran a special issue, "La francophonie has been?" One article in particular entitled "Le français en liberté," written by Pouria Amirshahi, the Iranian-born former member of the French National Assembly, spoke directly to the question of France's lock on the French language and those who speak it. Amirshahi berated the French for not considering themselves as part of a "geocultural group" except when it came to "cultivating a sphere of influence." Linking the Francophonie debate to the sensitive question of migration, he called for the free movement not just of understandings and programs but especially of people across the Francophonie world. "Without mobility," he warned, "la Francophonie is without a future."[36]

Yann Gwet, the Cameroonian columnist for Le Monde, drew an insightful link between la Francophonie and France's "English problem." Gwet argued that those who looked for a more open and inclusive vision of French were not facing up to historical reality. The pursuit of la Francophonie, he argued, was purely "geopolitical" to accommodate the elite who created the language and not the "impoverished African masses." "He who speaks French, [also] thinks French, and acts French," he said. Gwet saw Macron's movement promoting la Francophonie as a continuation of age-old French-Anglo-Saxon battles, each side using its language to maintain a grip on Africa. First it was the British; now it's the United States. From the infamous white-knuckle handshake with Donald Trump that went viral to his "Make the Planet Great Again" in the wake of the US retreat from the Paris Climate Accord, Macron was using la Francophonie as just another lever for pushing his "tricolor pawns." The "real question" that la Francophonie poses, he said, is to figure out the role of French in an Africa that has to "deeply reinvent itself" in finding "its own way" in a "de facto Anglo-Saxon world."[37]

Leïla Slimani came to Macron's defense, countering "allegations" that he was "acting like an arrogant imperialist." She assured his critics that the aim of Macron's campaign was to open up the language with "real objectives in terms of human rights, gender equality and the defense of democracy."[38] A letter published in Le Monde took an especially measured view on the situation. Written by a doctoral student and directed at Mabanckou, it took the Congolese writer to task for "diverting the subject of la Francophonie into a personal battle" and underestimating the progress made in democratizing African regimes in recent years. Though admittedly slow, he said, it was the best that could be expected. He warned that Macron could risk even worse consequences if he tried to push for regime change as opposed to waiting for it to occur more securely through a popular movement.[39]

Macron soon realized that his boasts at Ouagadougou, particularly in making French the "first language of Africa," had landed with a thud. He admitted as much to a group of francophone intellectuals and artists invited to lunch at the Elysée Palace.[40] He also understood that the national narrative on the French language had to shift lest he continue offending the very group he was trying to engage. For la Journée internationale de la Francophonie, he knew that he had to soften the rhetoric and respond to his critics point by point.

Shifting Tone and Targeting English

Macron is big on symbolism. Standing under the imposing cupola of the Institut de France—home of the Académie française, the guardian of purity for the French language—Macron unveiled what the Académie's website called an "international strategy in favor of the French language and multilingualism."[41] More specifically, it was a sweeping plan to improve and spread the teaching of French throughout the world, particularly in Africa, where, he said, "the competition from English is intense." Sitting before him were four hundred distinguished invitees (three hundred of them young people), including Académie members known as the "Immortals." In the first row of dignitaries was Michaëlle Jean, the Haitian-born Canadian secretary-general of the OIF, whose presence Macron expressly acknowledged.

Others attending by invitation included the ambassadors of Nigeria, Africa's most populous and powerful country, and Ghana, which in 2017 Macron was the first French president to visit in sixty years. Both are primarily anglophone countries, with a combined population of over 216 million people. Both have an interest in learning French to do business with surrounding francophone neighbors and attract French investors. The target audience, however, was primarily French-speaking Africa. Underlying Macron's repeated call for multilingualism, there also was a more pointed message to convey to the world, that French was on the march in challenging the dominance of English and regaining its vaunted position in the global order.

In an hour-long lyrical address filled with references to writers from the wider Francophonie orbit and to French novelists who marked his youth, Macron laid out over thirty proposals covering three broad objectives: to learn, to communicate, and to create in French.[42] He talked about increasing the role of French in international institutions, supporting French-speaking artists and authors, encouraging more international students to study in France, and making French more widely utilized in the global media and the digital economy. He also spoke of opening the French publishing market to works in French "in all its plurality," giving students access to a broad range of French literature in schools and libraries and extending French lessons for refugees to assimilate them into French society. On the last count, he referred to the French language as not "simply a tool of integration; it is integration." He acknowledged that some of his proposals on education and economic matters were initiatives of the OIF.

A key component of the plan was to promote multilingualism by pouring money into teaching both French and "maternal languages," especially in French-speaking African countries. In defending the languages of former French colonies, like Swahili, Wolof, Haitian, and Martiniquais, Macron described la Francophonie as a place where "languages do not fade, where they move on," implicitly suggesting a contrast with English. He admitted that French was still associated with colonialism and autocratic regimes that Paris supported for years after independence. "It would be arrogant to say that French would be the only language of liberty," he said. "People have tortured in French and done wonderful things in French. There are always tyrants who practice tyranny in French."

In discussing linguistic pluralism, especially in commercial trade, Macron rejected the idea of imposing one language or setting up a "rivalry" between languages, taking yet another oblique shot at English. More directly, he emphasized teaching two languages in Europe in addition to the maternal language, because English, he declared, "is not destined to be the only foreign language spoken by Europeans." He expressed hope that French business schools would attract more international students and "contribute to a new surge of French as the language of business," undoubtedly to counter the dramatic increase in English-taught programs. Ironically, English instruction has made those schools especially competitive. In 2020, four French institutions ranked in the top ten in the *Financial Times* ranking of ninety European business schools.[43] All of them teach solely or primarily in English. On the question of Brexit, he saw the United Kingdom's departure from the European Union as an opportunity to recapture the rightful place of French and multilingualism in the European economy and in European institutions.

Macron assured his audience that la Francophonie and French, like no other language (presumably English), would give Europe entrée to a large part of Africa and to economic opportunities throughout the Mediterranean region. The dominance of English, he said, is not inevitable. "It's up to us," he declared, "to set some rules, to be present, and make French the language with which one has access to opportunities." Overall, he made clear that la Francophonie was not simply an extension of France but "a sphere of which France is a part, active but aware of not carrying alone the destiny of French."[44]

Macron, the master statesman, seemed to have landed on safe ground with the Francophonie community, at least for the moment. The Franco-Ivorian novelist Véronique Tadjo praised him for tying together multilingualism and la Francophonie. For her, the French language had for too long defended its "hegemony" in sub-Saharan Africa to the detriment of educating children in their mother tongue.[45] The young French-Rwandan writer and recording artist Gaël Faye welcomed the change in tone. Faye's widely acclaimed first novel, *Small Country*, written in French, is a moving account of the genocide seen through the eyes of a mixed-race child, not unlike the author.[46] "At Bujumbura [Burundi, where Faye spent his childhood], la Francophonie for a long time has been seen as a political hegemonic project coming from Paris," Faye noted. "Today, French is the language of connection, rich in its diversity."[47]

By promoting French under the veil of multilingualism, Macron dismissed the dominance of English and at the same time drew a picture of French opening doors internationally. That image resonated for French-speaking countries, which apart from France are all multilingual. At the same time, it appealed to China and India, which see French as a gateway to Africa and its rich resources. For Macron, French could redirect their entrée into continental Europe away from the United Kingdom. With 30,072 Chinese students studying in France in 2019 and 25,000 in the France Alumni global network, China has become a rich source of international students, only surpassed by Morocco and Algeria.[48]

India, with a population of six hundred million below the age of twenty-five—the largest in the world—is a particularly fertile field for student recruitment, especially in the STEM fields. Numerous French companies with subsidiaries in India now actively recruit Indian students who have studied in France or have basic skills in French. Visiting with Indian prime minister Narendra Modi just prior to La Journée internationale de la Francophonie in 2018, Macron sent out a series of tweets with exactly that end in mind. One tweet in particular, targeted toward Indian students, who traditionally have studied in the United Kingdom, caught the ire of Britain's foreign secretary, Boris Johnson, who later became prime minister. It said, "I want to double the number of Indian students coming to France. If you choose France you gain access to the Francophonie, you gain access to Europe." (@EmmanuelMacron, March 10, 2018). Without missing a beat, Johnson tweeted in reply, "We are proud too to have more than 14,000 Indian students coming to the UK in 2017—up a quarter over last year—choosing the home of the greatest universities, including four of the global top ten." He ended with the tag #educationisgreatinenglish (@BorisJohnson, March 11, 2018). The following July, the French consul general to Kolkata in India, attending the signing of an agreement to spread Alliance française branches throughout West Bengal, made a strong pitch for Indian students to learn French for its "added value" in a country where "everyone speaks [English]."[49]

Johnson failed to realize that studying in France is also "great in English," which the French consul general conveniently failed to reveal. In 2017, upward of fifty-three hundred Indian students were enrolled in French universities. By 2019, the number had reached seven thousand. Most of them chose among over thirteen hundred courses taught in English, a number that continues to grow. In 2018, the government agency Campus French had eased the way with pre-departure "Bienvenue en France" sessions held in English in thirteen cities throughout India.[50] In 2019, the agency rolled out the "Choose France Tour," a roadshow through five Indian cities to promote French higher education. France has set a goal of twenty thousand Indian students to be studying in French universities by 2025. With 570 French companies based in India employing over 350,000 workers, young people understand that a French degree carries weight in the job market back home.[51] And again, they can do it all, or primarily, in English while learning some rudimentary French.

Macron's speech on la Francophonie unfolded on well-trodden ground. The multilingualism theme and the idea of "mother tongue plus two languages" echoed European Union policies searching in part for a counterweight to English. The endearing tone of the speech and its valorizing la Francophonie as the embodiment of pluralism drew directly from a video entitled *Multilingualism: Why and How to Promote It?* The video was produced by the Organisation de la Francophonie to commemorate the tenth anniversary of the *Vadum-mecum* or reference work on the use of the French language in international organizations. Eloquently narrated in French by Michaëlle Jean, then OIF secretary-general, it was launched at a seminar on the challenges of multilingualism organized by the African Union in December 2016 in Ethiopia.

The text of the video is an uplifting and compelling homage to multilingualism and the nuances of different languages. The subtext is both an implicit and explicit rebuke of English as the dominant lingua franca. The presentation talks about language being the "foundation of cultural identity." It notes that "imposing one's language on another is imposing one's vision." It subtly critiques the numbers of international bureaucrats, diplomats, and representatives of state who put themselves at a disadvantage by expressing themselves in English rather than in their maternal language. It warns that "the model of a single hegemonic language [presumably English] is becoming obsolete" and that "monolingualism is on the brink of becoming the illiteracy of the twenty-first century."[52] Macron's speech wove together similar themes in laying out his inclusive and ambitious plan to promote the French language while acknowledging France's colonial and postcolonial sins.

Some of Macron's aspirations were still somewhat overstated. Even Jean-Claude Juncker, the European Commission president, who had tweeted that he was "an ardent supporter of multilingualism" (@JunckerEU, March 20, 2018), believed that English would continue to be the primary working language within European Union institutions (despite his claim the previous year that English was "losing importance in Europe").[53] Though Juncker took the European Union to task for having become "so anglicized," he conceded that EU institutions would continue to use English as a daily working language post-Brexit because eastern Europeans had become accustomed to speaking in English.[54] The Belgian linguist Michel Francard, in an interview with *France Culture*, agreed that English had become "dominant" and that trying to "supplant" it should not be the objective.[55] As the international press covered Macron's speech, other skeptics and even critics joined the debate. Some agreed that it would be an uphill battle for French to counter the lure of English even on its own ground. As Cyril Gaillard, the head of Bénéfik, a Paris-based branding consultancy that described itself as an "agence de naming," observed, "Business people think it's more funky, more fun, and more modern to use English. They think French is an uncool language."[56]

Others noted inherent contradictions in Macron's vision of the French language. Anticipating his "grand discours" to "revive la Francophonie," an incisive article in the newspaper *L'Express* declared that for Macron to be "credible," he had to "modify his vocabulary and his decisions." Suggesting a baffling show of cosmopolitan sophistication, the author admonished Macron for strategically using "anglicisms" even when speaking to the French people. An accompanying video presented a series of quick flashes with Macron using terms like "la start up nation," "le business model," "silver economy," and "job mentoring." His assertive promotion of multilingualism, the article noted, defied his own actions at home toward France's regional languages, most recently opposing demands by Corsican nationalists to grant their language co-official status.[57] Another commentator chided Macron for limiting la Francophonie simply to the French language itself without considering other aspects, like how it plays out in local and regional communities, in economics, in the environment, or in the French public's appreciation for sports stars from other French-speaking countries.[58]

Problems Left Unspoken

Looked at objectively, there were any number of pressing economic and political problems related to la Francophonie that Macron could not remedy in the course of a speech, no matter how inspiring or well crafted. Perhaps it was best not to address them as a starter. Yet these issues inevitably would surface as his five-year term unfolded. Despite constant references to the French language as the glue that binds Francophonie countries in a common purpose, that purpose, as Macron's critics have noted, has less to do with the glories of France or its values than with trade, geopolitics, and demographics. It also has much to do with the soft power of French and seizing the moment to wrest global dominance from the clutches of the anglophone sphere, particularly the United States. And though the OIF boasts a community of 1.5 billion people, representing 16 percent of the world's population among its eighty-eight state members and governments, French is the official or one of the official languages in only thirty-two of them.

Clearly there is hard work to be done in solidifying the language both within and without the Francophonie community. There's also much effort to be made in convincing the younger and numerically dominant generation that France has an essential role in helping to liberate young Africans and build a new relationship with the continent. In any case, the fact remains that sub-Saharan Africa, which is twice as vast as the European Union and counts close to 300 million inhabitants, is now one of the world's principal emerging markets for foreign investment. Were it not for the language and monetary ties, France, which is a major trading partner, could well redirect its sights toward eastern European countries, whose closer proximity and comparable production costs make them competitively attractive. The problem is that most of those countries, once freed from the yoke of the Soviet Union, have eagerly embraced English.

Even accepting la Francophonie as a business or trade relationship, one point should not be taken lightly. As symbolically important or politically useful as some might think the OIF biannual world summits are, they also place a media spotlight on the parade of dictators and autocrats that head up many of the its member states, especially in Africa. That spotlight shone bright at the 2018 OIF meeting in Yerevan, the capital of Armenia, where France wholeheartedly endorsed Louise Mushikiwabo of Rwanda, a country rife with human rights problems, to head up the organization. Once again Macron, calling for a francophone "reconquest," promoted French as a language not only of trade and diplomacy but also of "creativity." He praised it as a language "respectful of the world, far from any hegemony," a language that does not "crush" but rather "nourishes" others, a not so veiled aim at English.[59]

Peeling away the captivating cultural theater surrounding these meetings inevitably raises questions as to France's complicity or passivity, depending on how you look at the facts, in helping these leaders to rise to and remain in power in the years since independence. A contrast can be drawn with the British Commonwealth of Nations, which has rightly expelled countries like apartheid South Africa for failing to comply with the organization's basic values and principles. One has to wonder to what extent the blatant violations of human rights and the perpetuation of poverty associated with these leaders tarnishes the image of the French language and of France.

That being said, and fully recognizing the ulterior motives, Macron at least has faced up to historical wrongs and tried to begin establishing a more equal and inclusive relationship between France and its former colonies. And while some of his assertions on the future of French seem overstated, he cannot be faulted for aggressively moving France into the global economy and trying to push English aside, especially given the void that Brexit and Trumpism created. To what extent he succeeds on any count depends in part on how much time French voters allow him to lead the country and to what extent francophone countries cooperate. Certainly the seemingly endless, and at times violent, *gilets jaunes* (yellow vest) demonstrations from 2018 to 2019, the extended strikes over the government's efforts to reform the retirement system, and legislative disputes over Islam tested his political mettle. The COVID-19 pandemic with the slow rollout of the vaccine in 2021, followed by protests over the government's "health pass" policy limiting access to indoor venues, further challenged his leadership skills.

Meanwhile, whatever the negative optics of the OIF summit meetings and the undeniable wrongdoing among some of its members, they're outweighed by the more enduring economic and political benefits that la Francophonie offers. By numbers alone, the vast Francophonie network challenges trade policies that make globalization work to the benefit of the well-off and to the detriment of developing countries. It also helps temper the dominance of English, making French a more significant force in driving the global conversation.[60]

As French linguist Louis-Jean Calvet described the paradox, the United States has spread its language and culture not by design but incidentally, by imposing its political and economic hegemony; France, conversely, has consciously used it language to impose its economic and political hegemony. Here, language is the decided driver, while politics and the economy are the result and not the tool. Facing the "immense American machine," says Calvet, the defenders of the French language now engage in "trench warfare" defending French as the language of a "cultural community."[61]

The Awakening Giant

The conventional wisdom that the future of French rests in Africa depends on whether those former colonies can resist the pull of English. It also depends on whether English remains dominant in the global economy or gradually loses ground, along with French, to Chinese. Two centuries ago Napoleon Bonaparte warned of China's rise: "Içi repose un géant endormi. Laissez le dormir, car quand il s'éveillera, it étonnera le monde" ("Here lies a sleeping giant. Let him sleep, for when he awakes, he will shock the world").[62] Napoleon's prediction has become reality as China assertively shapes the economy of African and other countries in myriad ways. Not only has China resumed its economic journey along ancient roads and routes; it is using its language to gain political advantage over Western competitors, particularly the United States, whose language and culture now dominate the globe.

According to a 2017 McKinsey report, China is now the major trading partner and investor on the African continent. Since 2000, Africa-China trade had increased by about 20 percent each year and was expected to reach US$400 billion by 2020. Meanwhile, foreign direct investment had seen an annual growth of 40 percent. Over ten thousand Chinese firms are now doing business in Africa.[63] Unlike Western countries, China places no human rights or other political conditions on its aid (other than the "One China" principle tying Taiwan to China), which is especially attractive to autocratic African governments. And unlike French and English, Chinese has no colonial past in Africa. Understanding the potential implications of these developments for both languages demands a brief digression into China's strategic use of its language as a political and economic wedge.

A decade ago, after much debate among Chinese academics, the Communist Party decided to "revive the Chinese nation" through the use of "soft power," or *ruan shili*, a concept originally coined by the American academic Joseph Nye. Nye argued that countries could not rely solely on the ability to coerce through the hard power of military and economic might. They also needed the soft power of attraction and persuasion. Force, the threat of force, or economic sanctions and inducements were not enough to exert influence and achieve foreign policy goals. According to Nye, a country can gain "soft power" in three ways: through its political ideals, through its culture, or through its foreign policies.[64] Culture is not just about attraction and appeal. It's also about opportunity. Each side must believe it is gaining something from the interaction. The economic and the cultural reinforce each other. A country's economic success generates interest in its culture. At the same time, cultural understanding engenders interest and confidence in that country's economic undertakings.[65] Certainly China is not alone in the effective use of soft power for economic and political gain. In its own way, China has followed the path paved by the United States and colonial powers like France and Great Britain.

Looking to satisfy its need for raw materials and to control the flow of global trade, China decided to use what might be called "smart power," or a combination of moderated hard power through economic investment—building roads, railways, and factories—and soft power in promoting its culture to create a benign image that glosses over its authoritarian domestic politics.[66] Along with Asia and Latin America, Africa became a prime destination. Built on the Forum on China-Africa Cooperation (FOCAC), launched in 2000, the strategic effort has resulted in a series of "action plans" detailing a long list of aid programs from education to trade, agriculture, infrastructure development, and tourism. At the 2015 inauguration of the ultramodern €38 million (US$45 million) national government building in Kinshasa, the capital of the Democratic Republic of the Congo, the general director of BTP China opened his speech in French, a symbolic gesture with a powerful message.

Intent on reaching markets in French-speaking Africa, China has forged especially strong ties to Morocco. The connection gives China "preferential access" to fifty-five markets where Morocco has free trade agreements, including EU member states, the United States, and Arab countries. A number of actions in recent years furthered those ends. The Central Bank of China negotiated a monetary exchange agreement with Morocco. The Chinese company HAITE Group, Morocco-China International, and BMCE Bank of Africa launched an investment fund to build a US$1 billion industrial park in Tangiers. The information technology company Huawei built new headquarters for Francophone Africa in Casablanca. In 2017, China's Ningxia University and Morocco's University of Hassan I signed an agreement to establish a joint institute focusing on "belt and road" studies and promoting trade and higher education cooperation between the two countries. With all this at stake, China keeps careful track of France's steadfast hold on Morocco's economy.[67]

In 2013, China's President Xi Jinping, in a move toward realizing his China dream, launched the multi-trillion-dollar Belt and Road Initiative (BRI; formerly known as the "One Belt, One Road Strategy"), a geopolitical/geo-economic enterprise of intertwined trade deals, investment, and infrastructure projects. The idea was to revive the ancient trade routes along the Silk Road economic belt from China to Europe and the maritime Silk Road crossing between Asia and East Africa. With support for globalization waning in the United States and Europe, upward of seventy countries encompassing over four billion people across all three continents were cashing in on the offer. By 2019, thirty-nine African countries and the African Union Commission had entered into BRI cooperative agreements.

Again, unlike the attention and selective limitations western donors impose on human rights violations and corruption, China's no-strings-attached funding and look-the-other-way approach makes these projects widely appealing. In 2018, during the sixty-ninth Chinese National Day in Lusaka, the Chinese ambassador to Zambia, Li Jie, made it clear that China would continue its aid without interfering in the "internal affairs" of any state.[68] Many analysts see the initiative as more about politics than trade or development, a diplomatic effort to "win friends and influence people" on the way to eclipsing the United States as a dominant superpower. To what extent China can sustain this effort over the long term is another question. Burdensome financing terms and turbulent markets in emerging economies, combined with a perceived "odor of neo-imperialism," have moved some countries to cancel projects.[69] As the Chinese economy slowed in 2018, spending on the initiative dropped to some degree. The 2020 COVID-19 pandemic brought some projects to a halt amid calls from African leaders for emergency debt forgiveness, which China selectively granted. Helping move this wave of globalization are China's international media, including the China Global Television Network with journalists in seventy countries and a burgeoning film industry, which has built a platform for creating China-Africa "narratives." Xi Ping has pushed the media to "tell China's story well, spread China's voice well, let the world know a three-dimensional colourful China."[70]

"Smart Power" in Action

So how do language and education play into this scenario? And what are the implications for English? The short answer is that Chinese is slowly gaining ground in Africa, arguably at the expense of French and English. The long answer is far more complex. To solidify economic ties and counter negative images of China as a threat to the world order, the Chinese government has effectively used this "smart power" strategy by combining investment in education and language learning, at home and abroad, with cultural appreciation. China understands that education now plays a strategic role in African development. The game plan is for the continent's growing population of young people to look toward China for intellectual vision and social and economic grounding while pivoting away from the United States and Europe. Since 2000, China's Forum on China-Africa Cooperation (FOCAC) summits have committed the country to financially and politically support African education on the African continent and in China.[71] At the 2018 Beijing meeting, Xi Jinping referred to the Africa Forum as a concrete step for "building a shared future." He promised to "fully honor" the promises made to its "African brothers."[72] Among the African leaders attending the summit were South African President Cyril Ramaphosa and the Rwandan president and chair of the African Union, Paul Kagame, both representing anglophone countries.

Included in the Beijing Action Plan 2019–21, an ambitious program to improve "institution building" on the continent, the government pledged to provide fifty thousand scholarships to African students and fifty thousand training opportunities through seminars and workshops. It also made a commitment to carry out a "tailor-made" program to train one thousand "high-calibre Africans" who presumably will become Africa's political leaders of tomorrow.[73] That program goes well beyond education or the status of French and English; it has far-reaching implications for the future of African political values and governance.

China's commitment to higher education has pushed two of its institutions into the top thirty rankings. As the *Times Higher Education*'s editorial director noted in 2017, "China's leading universities are truly now part of the global elite and overtaking universities in the US, UK and Europe."[74] At the same time, with a combined population of over 1.3 billion, a median age of 19.4 years, and a lack of funds going into higher education, Africa is a ripe source for recruiting international students. African students who once would have chosen the United

Kingdom or the United States or France are now setting their sights on China as a study destination. Facing difficulties obtaining visas to study particularly in the United States and the United Kingdom while becoming familiar with Chinese trade and employment prospects through local projects, they find China increasingly attractive. Affordability combined with not having to take the International English Language Testing System (IELTS) proficiency exam required for most English-taught programs in Europe are yet additional advantages. In an odd twist, China falls second behind France as a destination even for African students studying English, outstripping the United States and the United Kingdom, where fees are considerably higher. Learning Mandarin is becoming more, or at least equally, important as learning English or French.

Between 2003 and 2018, the number of African young people studying in China rose from 1,800 to over 81,500, increasing by 4,549 percent in a fifteen-year period and surpassing the typical 40,000 African students that the United States and the United Kingdom host each year. They accounted for about 17 percent of China's foreign students.[75] They commonly study Chinese and/or engineering, often offered in English for international students. Chinese and African universities have signed numerous memoranda of understanding, while plans are under way for the Chinese government to open several research centers on the African continent.[76] To what extent these university ties will shape global politics to come or solidify Africa as a base for trade and raw materials remains just a matter of speculation. Meanwhile, Chinese citizens are settling in Africa in growing numbers to make their fortune in industries as broad as chicken farming, telecommunications, and construction. From doctors, teachers, and entrepreneurs to less fortunate migrants, they are building a "new empire in Africa" through formal and informal networks in what has been called "China's second continent."[77]

Most commentators would agree that the most widespread vehicle for China to burnish its world image and create a cultural footprint has been its language and culture program. The program is a multibillion-dollar enterprise run by the Office of Chinese Language Council International, commonly known as Hanban, a public institution affiliated with the Chinese Ministry of Education and tied to the Communist Party. Begun in 2004, the program aims to project a benign image and open up wider communication between China and the world.[78] For developing countries in particular, accepting the program sends a clear signal of interest and affinity that increases the likelihood of Chinese investment. For the Chinese government and investors, developing language skills eventually reduces transaction costs in doing business in the country. The two motivations work hand in hand.[79]

By the end of 2018, Hanban claimed to sponsor 548 Confucius Institutes and 1,193 K–12 Confucius Classrooms in 154 countries worldwide. The Institutes numbered 125 in Asia, 59 in Africa, 182 in Europe, 161 in the Americas, and 21 in Oceania, while the classrooms covered 114 in Asia, 41 in Africa, 341 in Europe, 595 in the Americas, and 102 in Oceania. The number of full-time and part-time native Chinese and indigenous teachers had reached 47,000, with 1.86 million students instructed face-to-face and 810,000 registered online.[80] The program provides a Chinese director, Chinese teachers, materials, and equipment—something like a "class-in-a-box kit"—to spread the Chinese language, culture, and worldview among young people across the globe. The institutes typically are joint ventures between Chinese and foreign universities.

Mounting Opposition

While Asia and Africa have welcomed the opportunities, Confucius Institutes have become a flashpoint for rising concerns, especially in the United States and to some extent in Europe and Canada. No doubt they fill a void in African universities, which have been slow to engage academically with China, unlike their US and European counterparts. Yet for that very reason, they create a dependency on resources that can give them power over academic content and potentially infringe on academic freedom. The institutes have been linked to the Chinese Communist Party and its efforts to promote party policies abroad. They reportedly place clamps on their carefully selected teachers discussing sensitive subjects like Chinese political history, rampant human rights abuses, the role of the Dalai Lama, or the government's suppression of the pro-democracy movement in Tiananmen Square in 1989. Critics describe them as "academic malware" and "soft power propaganda tools" for the authoritarian Chinese state.[81]

Organizations in the United States, across the political spectrum, have raised similar concerns. In 2014, the institutes drew criticism from the American Association of University Professors, warning of commonly found nondisclosure clauses and accessions to academic freedom. The report contrasted the program with the British Council, the Goethe Institute, and the Alliance française, which admittedly have similar soft-power objectives but are not embedded in college campuses where the contract terms remain secret. It urged universities to break ties with the institutes unless they could renegotiate their contracts to maintain control over all "academic matters" and protect the academic freedom of institute teachers.[82]

A study published in 2017 by the National Association of Scholars underscored the lack of transparency in agreements signed with over one hundred Confucius Institutes operating on US college campuses in return for US$150,000 in start-up funds and $100,000 a year thereafter.[83] A similar report prepared for the Hoover Institution by a working group of leading China scholars called for "protecting American values, norms, and laws" from Chinese interference, though it also warned against unfairly "demonizing" any group of "Americans" or visitors to the United States.[84] Based on extensive interviews, Human Rights Watch issued a statement in March 2019, including a twelve-point code of conduct advising academic institutions worldwide to "refrain from having Confucius Institutes on campuses, as they are fundamentally incompatible with a robust commitment to academic freedom."[85]

In February 2018, the director of the US Federal Bureau of Investigation, testifying before Congress on worldwide threats, disclosed that the agency was "watching warily" the activities of the institutes. He raised concerns about the "naïveté" of the "academic sector," suggesting that Chinese operatives may have "infiltrated" university and college programs nationwide.[86] Federal lawmakers likewise charged the programs with serving as hubs for espionage and propaganda and urged that they register as foreign agents. Several congressional members sent letters to colleges and universities in their respective states urging them to close their Confucius Institutes or refrain from starting any new initiatives.

In August 2018, Congress signed into law the National Defense Authorization Act, which prohibits the federal Department of Defense from funding Chinese Language Flagship programs at institutions that host Confucius Institutes unless the institution obtains a waiver from the department. Since 2002, the Pentagon has funded the Language Flagship Program for graduate study in Arabic, Chinese, Persian, Portuguese, Russian, and Turkish to meet the needs of national security agencies. The response from China has been dismissive. The Beijing-based *Global Times* called the criticisms a "witch hunt by members of the US elite" and "a form of hysterical American nationalism."[87] A 2019 bipartisan report by a US Senate subcommittee, following an eight-month-long investigation, warned that Confucius Institutes are funded "with strings attached that can compromise academic freedom" and that many contracts contain non-disclosure provisions. The report, nonetheless, found no evidence connecting the institutes with Chinese espionage.[88] A report released at the same time by the US Government Accountability Office (GAO) raised similar transparency concerns over constraints on "campus activities and classroom content."[89] At that point, there were over ninety Confucius Institutes in the United States, more than in any other country, and 519 Confucius Classrooms in elementary, middle, and high schools.

Over the past several years a stream of institutions, including the University of Chicago, Pennsylvania State University, the University of Illinois at Urbana-Champaign, Texas A&M University, the University of Iowa, Indiana University, Michigan University at Ann Arbor, the University of Minnesota at Twin Cities, the University of North Carolina, the University of Rhode Island, Ontario's McMaster University, Stockholm University, France's University of Lyon, the

University of Leiden in the Netherlands, and Vrije Universiteit Brussel have closed their Confucius Institutes. Some claim that budget cuts, curricular realignment, and shrinking enrollments drove those decisions, while others have expressed academic freedom and, in the case of Vrije Universiteit, espionage concerns. Several others, like Cornell University and the University of Manitoba in Canada, rejected offers to establish an Institute in the first place.

As one Australian educator described the problem, "Education [is] the perfect microcosm for understanding the choices we're facing on a grand scale about the China relationship and how these choices effect our future."[90] Among US institutions, fear of jeopardizing Chinese Language Flagship programs funded by the Defense Department has become a significant factor.[91] In 2019, the Pentagon denied a waiver to all thirteen institutions that had applied, stating that it was "not in the national interest to grant waivers to this provision."[92] The denial led to another spurt of institute closings, bringing them to a total of at least fifteen in the previous fifteen months. Some university administrators nonetheless defend the institutes for the study-abroad and other opportunities they offer students. They deny any threats to academic freedom or institutional autonomy.[93] Some credit Hanban with being flexible and willing to adjust contracts to conform to university rules.[94] Others claim that the concerns raised are bound up in racially "politicized othering" and "historical fears of a yellow peril."[95] It remains to be seen whether the Biden administration's withdrawal of proposed rules requiring universities and K–12 schools to report ties to Confucius Institutes suggests a more tolerant approach.

There are no signs that any of these developments or apprehensions are stemming the spread of Confucius Institutes throughout Africa. Though much ink has been spilled on the impact of China's economic ties in Africa, little has been said about its cultural diplomacy, of which the Confucius Institutes are the driving engine. The simple truth is that Chinese language skills translate into jobs. The Confucius Institute at the University of Rwanda is a case in point. Rwanda, a former French-speaking Belgian colony, has replaced French with English as the language of schooling, though many educated Rwandans still speak French. In partnership with Chongqing Normal University, the institute opened in 2009 with sixty students to serve local business people who needed basic Chinese for trade with China. By 2018 it had trained more than four thousand students at its ten teaching posts throughout the country. Many of its graduates speak Chinese without ever having set foot in China. They consequently have found jobs with Chinese companies, Chinese-run projects, or the Chinese embassy in Rwanda. Some have worked part-time in Chinese restaurants, garment factories, and construction companies while completing their studies.[96]

In 2019, the China-Rwanda partnership rose to another level when the School of African Studies of Beijing Foreign Studies University (BFSU) introduced a course in Kinyarwanda. The language is spoken by twelve million people, including almost the entire native population of Rwanda, as well as others in eastern Democratic Republic of the Congo and neighboring parts of southern Uganda. It's also mutually intelligible with Kirundi, the official language of neighboring Burundi. For the University of Rwanda, it was a way to socially integrate students from the two universities.[97] For China, it undoubtedly was a way to strengthen its economic and political footprint in Africa.

Another notable example is the Confucius Institute at the Cheikh Anta Diop University in Dakar, the capital of Senegal, a former French colony and one of the most economically stable democracies in West Africa. Beijing now covers the institute's operational costs, including the salaries of twelve staff members. The institute's new building opened in 2016 with an initial Chinese investment of US$2.5 million and includes seven lecture halls, a multimedia hall, an amphitheater, and a library serving five hundred students. Besides language and culture, students can take courses in subjects like history, vocational training, and IT. In an interview with the *South China Morning Post*, the institute's director, Mamadou Fall, noted that not only is "Chinese gaining momentum," but "the languages of former colonial powers—such as English, French, and Portuguese—may also now be under threat." As far as he could see, "Very soon Chinese will be in a good position vis á vis a language like French." "In 50 years," he said, "the lingua franca in Africa may well be Chinese."[98] The Senegalese director's bullishness on the future of Chinese in Africa sounded like it had been torn from the Macron playbook on French. By 2018, China had opened thirteen Confucius Institutes and four Confucius Classrooms in ten Arab states, including the most recent in Tunisia, a former French protectorate where French is still considered an important social marker and actively utilized by intellectuals, the business sector, and the scientific community.[99]

Faced with mounting criticism in North America and Europe, the Chinese government rebranded the institutes in 2020. The Hanban was renamed the Ministry of Education Center for Language Exchange and Cooperation. It would continue to train teachers and develop textbooks for operating the Confucius Institutes. A separate nongovernmental nonprofit organization, the Chinese International Education Foundation, would fund and oversee them. Whether these arguably cosmetic changes will allay commonly expressed concerns is still speculative.

French or English?

That circles us back to the implications of China's involvement in Africa for French and English. Back in 2006 David Graddol, in a report for the British Council, predicted that China (and India) probably held the "key" to the "long-term future of English as a global language." Graddol in no way could have imagined the course of geopolitics in the years that followed, from Brexit, to Trumpism, to rising nationalism, to France's assertive re-engagement in Africa, and finally to a pandemic that put the world on hold and shook the global economy to its core. But he could see the rise of China as a world power.

In terms of numbers, France and the United States each has more than twice as many cultural institutes in Africa than China does. Despite the strong US presence, China's growing engagement in Africa is more likely to pivot attention away from English than it is to upend French, particularly in francophone countries. That prediction reflects US policy, focusing in recent years on trade and countering terrorism, while China and France aggressively have deployed the soft power of language and culture as they jockey for position as global powers. China's interest in tapping into African markets has triggered an increased demand for French language courses in China as well as an increasing number of Chinese students enrolled in African universities. According to the OIF, about 120,000 Chinese students are studying French with an eye toward doing business in Africa. To the extent that this trend takes off, it might not bode well for English in China or in French-speaking Africa. That being said, the long-term impact of the COVID-19 crisis on international student mobility is yet to be seen. Much depends on whether China can maintain its Belt and Road commitments amid the resulting economic turmoil. In the meantime, under the global vision of Emmanuel Macron, the French language has eased the way for France to partner with China in its development efforts in Africa. On his visit to China in January 2018, among numerous economic proposals, Macron expressed hope that French would gain additional ground in the Chinese education system. Beyond organizing university exchange programs and professional training, Macron suggested that the Confucius Institutes play a greater role in promoting the two languages, together with French schools and the Alliance française.[100] In 2018, more than on 110,000 people were learning Chinese in France. Chinese is the third most common foreign language taught in French primary and secondary schools. For French parents and their children, it is slowly moving into the territory of English as a key asset in the job market, though probably without the same social and cultural appeal.[101] China's place in world politics, with pressure mounting over human rights abuses against ethnic Uyghurs in Xinjing and the erosion of freedoms in Hong Kong, could possibly reverse that trend.

In recent years, the United States has appeared to close its eyes as China and France have tried to upend English in francophone Africa. A changed administration in Washington may reverse that course. The United Kingdom, meanwhile, seems ready to face the challenge, reviving the engine of English language support to secure its diplomatic presence and increase trade. In April 2019, the

British government announced funding for a new £4 million (US$5.5 million) English language program in French- and Portuguese-speaking countries across Africa. The English Connects program, based at the Université Virtuelle du Sénégal in Dakar, aimed to reach 7.5 million young people in each of two years primarily through online learning. While Brexit was looming on the horizon in 2019, Foreign Secretary Jeremy Hunt, in a show of grandstanding, explained, "In a future where Britain is no longer a member of the EU, I want to . . . set out the stall for the UK to be the new partner of choice across Africa. . . . There is an enormous appetite from among young people across Africa to learn our language because English is the language of opportunity."[102]

Some francophone countries in Africa in fact are weighing in favor of English while also keeping their economic options open to the French-speaking world. With the United States, like the United Kingdom, now primed to more actively engage in global partnerships and development, France as well as China may be facing yet again two old competitors in the "new scramble" for Africa. To what extent each uses the soft power of language to gain competitive advantage will be interesting to see.

Adieu to French

Africa offers fertile ground for exploring the tension between English and French and the present-day consequences for schooling. Going back in time, both classical antiquity and Arab conquest shaped Africa's early development in the north. For the rest of the continent, the Berlin Conference in 1884–85 laid the foundation for much of what Africa is today. No Africans were present. Fourteen Western powers participated in the negotiations, which were conducted in French. France, Germany, Great Britain, and Portugal were the major stakeholders, as they controlled most of Africa at that time. In the end, in what was the original "scramble for Africa," they carved 90 percent of the continent of diverse peoples into fifty irregular colonies defined by the languages of Europe, irrespective of existing linguistic and cultural boundaries. West Africa went to France, most of East and South Africa to Great Britain, and other parts to Belgium, the Netherlands, Portugal, and Spain. What happened subsequently is the subject of a conntinuing body of scholarship. One essential yet often overlooked piece of the story rests on language and its effects on identity, democracy, and educational opportunity, with English playing an increasingly key role.

The colonizers initially taught their respective languages to a small group of natives, who served as interpreters and low-level civil servants. They divided, however, on the overall approach to language in the schools. The British were torn on the question, though like the Belgians and Germans they generally followed the path set by early Christian missionaries. They respected local traditions and promoted instruction in the local languages in the first three years of primary school. They progressively introduced and selectively switched to English to train a class of "elites" who would help the British communicate with the rest of the country's population.[1] For everyone else, the cultural gap was presumably "unbridgeable," which made assimilation unthinkable.[2]

The French imposed their language across government administration and education. The policy supported the French understanding of citizenship and a unified Republic based on the notion of "one nation, one language" inspired by the French Revolution. It also reflected the French belief in the superiority of their language and culture and furthered France's "civilizing mission."[3] If the colonized subjects were going to share a common destiny with the French, they had to adopt France's language and cultural values and abandon their own. In that way, the new territories were considered part of France.[4] French became the major language of government, law, and education. As the linguist Einar Haugen described the English-French dichotomy: "The English were tolerant of native tongues but unwilling to accept their speakers as equals. The French were willing to receive natives of all colors into the French community provided they gave up their identity and learned French."[5] No doubt that was an overstatement on community membership.

Over the past sixty years, former French-speaking colonies in North Africa and parts of West/Central Africa have struggled to resolve conflicted feelings toward France and even wrest themselves from its perceived grip, some more decisively than others. The reasons lie in history, in politics, and more recently in the economic appeal of English. In the North African Maghreb, specifically Algeria, Morocco, and Tunisia, historical roots in Arabic and the force of postcolonial Arabization intermix with competing claims from speakers of Tamazight and other Berber languages and the tenacity of French-speaking elites to maintain the status of French in the schools. Some sub-Saharan countries have added English as a co-official language with French in order to benefit from economic ties to both the francophone and anglophone worlds. For Rwanda, a former Belgian colony in East Africa, the official transition from French to English was directly related to the disputed role that France played in the Rwandan genocide of the 1990s. In most cases, wavering language policies have had profound consequences for education, especially within poor and marginalized communities. English, with help and prodding from international organizations, has played a significant role in shaping those outcomes.

Flirting with English

Several former French-speaking colonies, answering the siren call of English, have shifted in varying degrees away from French, though not necessarily from the economic network of the Organisation internationale de la Francophonie (OIF). Disregarding the raw fact of British imperialism among their neighbors, they see English as a "neutral" language, refusing to equate it with Anglo military, economic, and cultural power. At the same time, memories of the Franco-Algerian war and the Rwandan genocide, along with France's continued involvement in African affairs, still cast colonial shadows on French despite the French government's efforts, through the Francophonie network, to symbolically link the language to its national origin.[6]

On a national scale, government officials look toward English to modernize the workforce, expand employment opportunities for skilled workers in Europe and in English-speaking Africa, and open access to world markets including Asia and the Middle East. English-speaking countries like South Africa, Kenya, and Nigeria increasingly drive the African economy, and so English has become the default link language among African countries. On a personal level, English permits the lower classes, whose French skills are weak at best, to bypass French entirely and directly access the global economy.[7] That is not to suggest that adopting English is a win-win. As elsewhere, the switch to English reinforces social and economic inequalities, at least for the short term and often for the long term. It also carries political undertones, undermining democratic participation and threatening national identity.

Countries like Tunisia have considered replacing French with English in government and in schooling but have backed off in the face of public opposition and a realization that their fortunes were best tied to the francophone world.[8] Yet even there, enrollment in English language schools is on the upswing, as are English language blogs and news websites. Aside from economics, the subtle bottom-up shift away from the colonial language is part of an Arabic affirmation following the 2011 Arab Spring uprising that placed Tunisia in the foreground of the Arab world.[9] Where English fits in that gradual changeover is hard to predict.

The Democratic Republic of the Congo (DRC), the French-speaking country with the largest population after France, made English an official language along with French in 1998. With similar intent, Madagascar in 2007 raised English to the status of a "national" language alongside French and Malagasy after exiting from the Franc Zone and closing the French military base. Gabon adopted English as the second official language in 2012. While embracing English gave Gabon significant economic advantages, there was a compelling political backdrop to the story. After years of quietly acquiescing to blatant corruption in the country, the French government was looking into the assets of African leaders, including Gabon's ruling family, at the request of two anticorruption NGOs.[10] It behooved Gabon to free itself from the scrutiny of France. Burundi added English as an official language along with Kirundi (a Bantu language) and French in 2019, though English has not relieved the poverty, civil strife, and violence that has racked the country for decades. In some sense, these linguistic revolts against the French language reflect a feeling of hostility toward the way that France has used the Francophonie concept to maintain its influence over former colonies.[11]

Perhaps nowhere is that hostility more palpable than in Algeria. Though the country, with sixteen million French speakers, counts one of the largest French-speaking populations outside of France, Algerians still have a conflicted relationship with the language. Algeria stands alone in the francophone world in not having joined the OIF. Yet it supports other semiofficial French channels. In 1961, it was a founding member of l'Agence universitaire de la Francophonie (AUF), a global network of 944 French-speaking higher education and research institutions. Next to France, with 174 establishments in the AUF, Algeria counts second with 62, even above Canada at 33. In July 2019, the Algerian minister of higher education and scientific research, Tayeb Bouzid, stunned Paris when he declared, "Le français n'a aucune valeur" ("French has no value"). He sent a letter to university rectors asking that official correspondence be written in Arabic and English and announced that the country's seventy-seven universities would move instruction from French to English. As he said,

> If we put online modules taught in Arabic, there are 200 or 300 million people who will read them. If you put them in French, nobody speaks French. If we want foreign students to come, we have to use the English language. . . . We [also] want to give Algerian students every chance to have a place in this world[12]

In a two-week online national referendum, launched by the ministry, 94 percent of the more than ninety-four thousand participants expressed their approval.[13]

Following a national symposium of Algerian universities, Bouzid posted on Facebook in Arabic that he was establishing a think tank of specialists and administration officials to draw up proposals for promoting English in higher education and scientific research.[14] The posting elicited mixed responses from faculty and students. Some raised concerns over the lack of English skills among faculty and the ability of students educated in French to keep up with instruction in English. The minister of vocational education and training soon announced a similar measure to gradually introduce foreign languages, notably English, into programs under his charge. The intent was to put Algeria in tune with technological advances internationally and give the work of researchers greater visibility.[15]

Two countries—Rwanda and Morocco—stand out in the move toward English in different degrees despite distinct ancient and modern histories. The lessons learned from those experiences reveal much about the politics surrounding the changes, the challenges encountered, and the impact on education and equity in each setting.

Rwanda Takes the Lead

In 2019, Netflix released an eight-episode fictionalized series set against the historic facts of the Rwandan genocide of 1994.[16] With all the intrigue of an international thriller, the story lays bare the unanswered questions and unsettled scores that still remained twenty-five years later. One seemingly minor, though significant, point can easily go unnoticed to anyone not familiar with the course of events. The lead characters that identify as Tutsi bear Anglo given names and primarily speak English. In contrast, the few Hutu characters bear French given names and primarily speak French. How this former Belgian colony arrived at this linguistic and political divide, and the psychological scars it has left, lies deep in Rwanda's not so distant past. Watching the story unfold in eight spellbinding hours only scratches the surface of this riveting drama where English continues to play a key role in a complex and even violent history.

Rwanda is a relatively small country where global pressures, a horrific civil war, and international factors have swayed education policies on language. It was the first francophone country to abandon French for English. Once a colony of Germany, Rwanda fell under Belgian control following Germany's defeat in World War I. Under the Treaty of Versailles, the League of Nations gave Belgium administrative power over Rwanda and Burundi (Ruanda-Urundi). Following World War II, Ruanda-Urundi became a United Nations Trust Territory with Belgium again granted administrative authority. Belgium's influence on Rwanda's language, culture, and education dominated throughout the twentieth century.

When Rwanda (and Burundi) gained independence in 1962, the new Rwandan government decided to maintain French as the official language along with Kinyarwanda, which it also designated as the national language. Rwanda was one of a few newly independent African nations to grant an African language any official or national status. French and Kinyarwanda remained the country's two official languages until 2003, when the constitution formally adopted English as a third. In 2017, it added Swahili as a fourth to solidify economic ties with the East African Community, whose three founding countries—Kenya, Tanzania, and Uganda—use Swahili as their official languages, along with English. Laws are published in all four languages.

Unlike its neighbors, Rwanda is practically monolingual. Though divided among three ethnic groups: Hutu (85 percent), Tutsi (14 percent), and Twa (1 percent), upward of 99 percent of the population speaks Kinyarwanda, which is widely used in Uganda and eastern DRC and spoken as a mutually intelligible language with Kirundi in neighboring Burundi. With no need to rely on English as a common language, the amount of English in everyday life—in taxis, churches, markets, and shopping centers—is limited, especially outside the capital of Kigali.[17]

By 1962, the year of independence, a Belgian-led Hutu uprising had forced the Tutsi king into exile and resulted in the deaths of many Tutsis. Tens of thousands of Tutsis sought refuge in neighboring Uganda, Burundi, and Tanzania. Under Hutu rule, Rwanda adopted a constitution, making primary education free and compulsory. Constitutional stability, however, was short-lived. Discontent among northern Hutus who dominated the army led to a "bloodless coup" in 1973, followed by a brief period of military rule, which eventually brought to the presidency Juvénal Habyarimana, a Hutu who had been the army chief of staff. From that time to the beginning of the civil war in 1990, primary school enrollment rose from 46 to 65 percent. As education had worked to the benefit of the Tutsi elites under Belgian rule, it now favored the Hutus. That inverse in fortunes helped set the stage for the political turmoil that followed.[18] A look into the events surrounding "the genocide" is essential to understand Rwanda's embracing English while maintaining a tenuous relationship with France and the French language.

The Genocide

In Gaël Faye's haunting novel *Small Country*, the narrator describes the genocide as seen through his eyes as a child living in Burundi with his French father and his Rwandan mother. He recalls questioning his father about the war between the Tutsis and the Hutus as clouds begin to gather over their tranquil lives.[19]

> "Is it because they don't have the same land?" he asks.
> "No, they have the same country."
> "So . . . they don't have the same language."
> "No, they speak the same language."
> "So, they don't have the same God?"
> "No, they have the same God."
> "So . . . why are they at war?"
> "Because they don't have the same nose."

It is true that Tutsis are thought to be visibly distinguishable from Hutus by their longer nose and their tall and slender countenance, though intermarriage between the two groups has softened those distinctions. They also share the same land and the same God. As for their language, that's a more complicated story. In the 1990s, some Tutsis no longer spoke their native Kinyarwanda. It depended on where they had settled in the aftermath of the political turmoil of the 1960s. Having lived under Belgian colonial rule for over four decades, educated

Rwandans like the narrator's mother, whose family had fled to Burundi, spoke French as well as Kinyarwanda. For the large number of Tutsis exiled in Uganda, their children grew up speaking English.

Rwandans subsequently came to favor English over French not just for the trade and educational advantages but also for deeper political reasons that date back to the departure of the Tutsi exiles in 1959 and the subsequent return of their children in the 1990s. Many of the returnees came from English-speaking Uganda. At that time, a rebel group of exiled Uganda-based Tutsis, the Rwandan Patriotic Front (RPF), invaded Rwanda in an attempt to regain power. Paul Kagame, the Tutsi who masterminded the RPF movement and commanded the forces that moved across the border in 1991, has ruled Rwanda since 2000. France saw the RPF invasion as part of an "Anglo-Saxon" plot to destabilize "one of their own" and undermine France's influence in central Africa. As the historian Gérard Prunier describes it, that is how Paris "found itself backing an ailing dictatorship in a tiny distant country producing only bananas and a declining coffee crop without even asking for political reform as a price for its support."[20]

The Arusha Peace Agreement, negotiated in 1993, aimed to establish a transitional government that would lead to a democratic election. Immediately sparking the mass slaughter was the shooting down of a plane carrying the Hutu president, Juvénal Habyarimana, an ally of France, on the night of April 6, 1994. Accompanying him was his Hutu counterpart from Burundi, Cyprien Ntaryamira. Habyarimana allegedly was about to sign a peace treaty with the RPF. Hutu extremists quickly set up a provisional government and charged the RPF with the assassination. France and Rwanda continue to trade accusations of culpability for the attack, but to this day the question remains unanswered.

France armed and trained the Rwandan Armed Forces subsequently responsible for the mass murders of up to a million Tutsis, three-fourths of the Tutsi population, and the displacement of another two million refugees within the span of one hundred days. The US government was equally involved on the other side in giving generous foreign aid and selling weapons to Uganda, which passed them over the border to support the RPF.[21] The carnage spared nothing. Schools were ravaged, Tutsi teachers and students were killed, and the Ministry of Education was destroyed. The unimaginable horrors were such that both Western and African authors have repeatedly described them as "hell."[22]

Though the vast majority of those killed were Tutsi, it has since been reported that the RPF also staged brutal killings of innocent Hutus and Tutsis, adults and children, in the years leading up to, during, and after the genocide.[23] Western leaders and most journalists failed to acknowledge anything but Kagame's counter-narrative concealing his alleged crimes, portraying a battle between good and evil, despite reports to the contrary by groups like Human Rights Watch.[24] Ignoring direct warnings, the international community, including the

United States, refused to intervene in what even reporters in the field mistakenly viewed as "ancient tribal hatreds" rather than genocide. US officials avoided using the g-word for fear of being obligated to take action under the United Nation's 1948 genocide convention.[25] The details of what transpired through those years, and what the world may have understood at the time, are far too complex, contested, and remote from the central question of language to outline here. Suffice it to say that for the new Tutsi-led government, while French was necessary in that the government institutions had functioned in the language for over half a century, English was the language of "resistance and victory" and would ultimately prevail.

In the twenty-five-plus years since the genocide, tension between the French and Rwandan governments has run high. This is where English more definitively enters the picture. A French parliamentary commission report from 1998 concluded that France had played no role in supporting the massacre but had actually taken the lead in the international response. In 2006, a French antiterrorism judge charged that Kagame had been involved in the plane attack that provoked the genocide. Kagame has long claimed that Hutu military forces shot down the plane. Unable to indict Kagame because of his position as president, the French judge issued arrest warrants for nine high-ranking RPF officials and requested that the International Criminal Tribunal for Rwanda address the case. Kagame's response was to close down the French embassy and the French cultural center and remove Radio France International from the air.[26] A 2008 report, spanning almost three hundred pages and prepared by a panel of international specialists lent credence to Kagame's claim that France had helped arm the Hutu forces and could have stopped the massacre but failed to do so.[27]

For over two decades, France denied any claims that it was complicit and refused to open archives on the genocide, though it admitted to having made some political errors. Rwanda likewise refused to recognize crimes committed by the rebel army led by Kagame and the Rwandan Patriotic Front. In 2016, France reopened the investigation into the assassination of Habyarimana, based on incriminating evidence from a former RPF member. Rwanda, in turn, opened a formal investigation into twenty French officials suspected of having been involved in the 1994 genocide. The formal report, issued in 2017 and prepared by a United States law firm, affirmed the involvement of France and French officials in supporting the government responsible for the genocide.[28] The backstory to this steady stream of accusations and counter-accusations left a mark on French-Rwandan relations and helped finalize Rwanda's shift in language policy toward English.

In addition to Kagame and his key advisors harboring ill feelings toward the French for political reasons, they were all primarily English speakers. After the RPF under Kagame's leadership took control of the capital in 1994 and declared a ceasefire, over three hundred thousand former Rwandan refugees returned from neighboring Tanzania and Uganda. Many of them had played important roles while in exile. Like Kagame, they had acquired English and a British perspective, and so they made little effort to learn French on their return. The country consequently drew closer to the United States and Britain, while the sizeable back migration boosted the status of English and solidified the political influence of English speakers. It also brought education policies and practices rooted in British models—what has been called "second generation colonialism."[29] The United Kingdom's Department for International Development, which remains a significant donor, was partly responsible for those changes.

The English Advantage

Given the course of events, it was not surprising when the Ministry of Education announced in 1996 that, as of the following year, instruction in grades one through three would continue in Kinyarwanda, with English added to French as a subject. Instruction would then switch to English in grades four through six. Secondary schools could choose either French or English. A new constitution adopted in 2003 declared Kinyarwanda the national language and Kinyarwanda, French, and English the official languages of the country.[30] Schools would teach in Kinyarwanda in the first primary cycle, though the minister of education could authorize French or English. The second cycle would switch to French or English.

In a 2004 interview with the pan-African weekly news magazine *Jeune Afrique / L'intelligent* regarding Rwanda's waning relationship with la Francophonie, Kagame said: "Nous avons ici trois langues officielles: le kinyarwanda, l'anglais et le français. Chacun évolue, progresse ou régresse dans le cadre d'un marché linguistique ouvert e libre. L'état n'intervient pas." ("We have here three official languages: Kinyarwanda, English, and French. Each one evolves, progresses, or regresses within the framework of an open and free language market. The state does not intervene.")[31] That laissez-faire approach ended in 2008 when, having terminated diplomatic relations with France two years earlier, the government sidestepped the constitution and removed French as an official language. English would take its place in government, commerce, legislation, and education. Yet the vast majority of people spoke only Kinyarwanda, and only about 5 percent, largely members of an elite class of Tutsis, spoke English.

The officially stated motivation was a mix of globalization, economic development, and unification. English would improve the economic status of Rwandans, help transform the country from an agricultural to a high-tech knowledge-based economy, attract tourism and business, and lead to reconciliation by eliminating ethnic affiliations to create a single national identity. But there also was a political undercurrent. That year, the government demanded that thirty-three accused French military and political officials stand trial for their involvement in the 1994 genocide.

Despite the switch to English, in 2009 French president Nicholas Sarkozy successfully restored relations between the two countries. Sarkozy's interest in a rapprochement was strategically timed. While Rwanda remained part of the Francophonie community, that year it also joined the Commonwealth of Nations (formerly the British Commonwealth), a fifty-three-member association primarily of past British colonies spanning Africa, Asia, the Americas, Europe, and the Pacific. Following Mozambique, Rwanda was only the second country with no colonial ties to Britain to take that step. Two years earlier Rwanda had become a member of the English-speaking East African Community (EAC). This economic and political bloc of what is now six partner states, including neighboring Uganda and Tanzania, has a combined market size of 146 million people. With EAC membership came fewer trade barriers and free labor mobility.

It made sense for Rwanda to align itself culturally and economically with anglophone countries. For a small, mountainous, land-locked nation with no rail system and few significant natural resources, trade with its neighbors was important. The route to the coast through Tanzania and Kenya, its English-speaking neighbors to the east, was far more travelable than the one through its western French-speaking neighbor, the Democratic Republic of the Congo, with whom relations were also less than peaceful.[32] Education through English, moreover, would help develop the country's human resources. Kagame, whose critics continue to attack him for his autocratic style, set his sights even wider, using the country's growing use of English to draw business from the United States, Europe, and China. As Rwandan trade and industry minister Vincent Karega explained at the time, "French is spoken only in France, some parts of west Africa, parts of Canada and Switzerland. English has emerged as a backbone for growth and development not only in the region but around the globe."[33]

The immediate effect was striking. English-speaking investors raced into the country. Trading ties with Uganda, Kenya, and South Africa brought in luxury hotels and shopping malls. Especially in the capital, Kigali, local English language schools brimmed with students. Taxi drivers carried French-English dictionaries on their route. Bookstores were stocked with English books. Government officials peppered their speeches with English words.[34] Churches were offering English services or using English interpreters when preaching in Kinyarwanda. Banks, migration offices, and hospitals were asking clients to complete forms in English and advising them to learn English if they wanted better service.[35] By 2015, Rwanda's leading daily newspaper, the New Times, declared the switch to English in the schools as "yet another of those brilliant initiatives by this government specifically to earn Rwanda a place as a global player in business, diplomacy, media, and entertainment." Learning English, the paper predicted with confidence, would "make Rwandan workers highly prized in a global business world."[36]

In hindsight, Rwandan officials claim that whatever challenges the country had to overcome in switching to English have paid off economically. The numbers seem to support that view. In 2009, Rwanda was the first sub-Saharan African economy to lead the world in *Doing Business* reforms.[37] Between 2009 and 2010, it leapt from 143rd to 67th.[38] Between 2009 and 2015, the country witnessed a groundswell of global investment totaling about US$3 billion, or 40 percent of its GDP. In 2014 alone, 111 projects worth US$390 million were registered. According to government figures, the economic boom had lifted two million people out of poverty.[39] The government maintained that the poverty rate had dropped from 57 percent in 2006 to 40 percent in 2014, an amazing accomplishment in stark contrast to neighboring countries like the DRC and Burundi where Tutsi-Hutu violence still reigns. In 2018, the MasterCard Foundation launched a five-year US$100 million project focusing on developing the country's tourism and hospitality industry and improving the quality of secondary education.[40]

World leaders, including former US president Bill Clinton and philanthropist and Microsoft cofounder Bill Gates, have praised Kagame, respectively calling him a "visionary" and one of the "greatest leaders of our time.[41] Others roundly disagree. Amnesty International maintains that the country is still plagued by widespread poverty and suppression of human rights.[42] Scholars especially denounce Kagame for using both legal and extralegal means to control expression in the media, civil society, and academic inquiry. Ironically, he was one of the first African leaders to set up a website and develop a presence on Twitter, Facebook, Instagram, and Flickr.[43] While Kigali's high-tech industry is thriving, the new prosperity has yet to reach the many rural Rwandans whose livelihood depends on subsistence farming. Economists question Rwanda's statistics, including its claims to impressive economic growth, decreased poverty, and increased consumption. This is not simply quibbling over numbers. Both Kagame's reputation and his development model are at stake.[44] In the end, while the switch to English apparently attracted foreign investment, the resulting benefits may not have benefited many who needed it most.

The Education Fallout

The education picture has been less upbeat than even presumably the economic one. It is reasonable that a country looking for foreign investment and international trade would turn to English. It's also understandable, as the Ministry of Education itself noted, that maintaining education in three languages was expensive in terms of instructional materials and teacher training.[45] Especially in the sciences, though textbooks in English had a high cost, they also had a quality advantage. Yet the speed of the change to English and the way it came about were problematic. The language question was also sensitive. It related not only to access, learning, and completion rates but also to race and identity in a society that was still reeling from an extreme political conflict over those issues.[46] With a top-down approach, the elite of a small ethnic minority imposed its language without allowing the overwhelming majority any say in the matter or giving the education sector much forewarning or guidance.

When the Rwandan Cabinet adopted the English resolution in October 2008, it did so without a clearly articulated plan or empirical findings informed by practice. The 2008–12 Education Sector Plan, in fact, made no mention of the shift in language. Despite contrary recommendations from the African Union, UNESCO, and other donors and international nongovernmental organizations, government officials removed French and Kinyarwanda from instruction in primary and secondary schools and directed teachers to begin teaching through English in under four months. Teachers would have preferred using textbooks written partly in Kinyarwanda to ease the transition, but the government believed it would slow down the process.[47] With the advantage of a common language (Kinyarwanda) distinguishing Rwanda from countries struggling with multilingualism, it seemed counterintuitive to totally eliminate it as a language of instruction even in the early grades. The country would soon encounter that truth in practice. Though the resolution applied only to public and subsidized institutions, private schools followed along to remain competitive. Meanwhile, university programs had to begin transitioning to English by January 2009, regardless of whether students had been taught in French or English in secondary school.

The plan was to roll out the change in primary and secondary schools gradually. It would begin with math and science and then move on to the social sciences and language arts in subsequent years. The changeover to English, nonetheless, was daunting. At that time, advanced primary and secondary school students theoretically were instructed in French or English while they studied the other language and Kinyarwanda as subjects. In reality, over 95 percent of the schools taught in French to students beginning at age nine. Lacking both English materials and English-speaking teachers—many teachers had been trained in francophone teacher training institutes—the program was questionable from the start.[48] Of the country's thirty-one thousand primary school teachers, only about forty-one hundred (15 percent) had been educated in English. Of the twelve thousand secondary school teachers, that number was a mere six hundred (5 percent).[49] Beyond the language itself, teachers had to shed the traditional teacher-focused approach left over from Belgian occupation and adapt to a student-centered Anglo style of teaching.

To help fill the immediate need, the government recruited English-speaking mentors and teachers from neighboring Kenya and Tanzania. The move heightened the anxieties of French-speaking teachers who feared that their jobs were in jeopardy. The supply also fell far short of the demand. Rwandan teachers in French-dominant schools took evening and weekend English classes at their own expense as they strained to teach their students in English during the day.[50] Anyone who openly opposed the new policy would face government reprisals. Some school officials banned using other languages (including Kinyarwanda) in class and even elsewhere on school property, denying students the benefits of using all their linguistic resources to fully comprehend what they were learning. Multilingualism became a problem rather than an asset.[51]

Aligning the changes with the anglophone world eased some of the financial and strategic problems. The British Council in Kigali took an active part in the transition. It provided free consultant services, English tutoring for all French-speaking teachers, and iPods with all English language courses.[52] The Peace Corps supplied English-speaking teachers to rural secondary schools. The British Department for International Development increased funding for education in the country by over 50 percent between 2010 and 2015, allotting upward of 27 percent of its budget to Rwandan education projects.[53] The British Council later touted its support in training eighty-five thousand English teachers in 860 centers over a five-week winter holiday break.[54] Yet the program was too short to convey both English language skills and how to teach through the language. It focused on basic English and lumped primary and secondary teachers into the same classes with no regard for level or subject area. As of 2012, 93.5 percent of Rwandan teachers still had a low level of English proficiency.[55] Only six hundred of the projected one thousand had been hired.[56]

Despite all the initial problems with implementing the plan, a 2012–13 study of Kigali public secondary schools found students and school officials optimistic. As far as they could see, Rwanda's new English policy would open employment and study opportunities, promote diplomacy and international relations, and integrate the country regionally and globally.[57] The following years would prove their optimism overblown. Meanwhile, education officials remained resolute in what turned out to be an abrupt policy change fraught with problems. As the director of the Rwanda Education Board told the British press, "We were not prepared to wait the conventional ten or twenty years to adopt a more strategic longer plan, because the interests of this country are more paramount than the difficulties that people can face in the shorter term." But he also understood that Rwandans' mother tongue, Kinyarwanda, remained "central" to their "identity and . . . values." "We adopt English, he explained, "for us to be able to compete globally, but we are Banyarwanda [people of Rwanda] and this is number one and not negotiable."[58]

In other words, English was purely instrumental, tied to Rwanda's economic development goals and divorced from identity. The Ministry of Education's 2010 strategic plan said it all. The plan's mission, it explained, was to "transform the Rwandan citizen into skilled *human capital* for socioeconomic development of the country by ensuring equitable access to quality education focusing on combatting illiteracy, promotion of science and technology, critical thinking and positive values."[59] The neoliberal agenda had captured the country.

Eventually the schools overcame some of the logistical problems and textbook shortages. What remained, unfortunately, was a sizeable number of students who had moved through the system with poor skills in any language and limited subject-matter knowledge. At the same time, the general population lacked fluency in English and had few incentives to learn French. Kinyarwanda still dominated daily life. As teachers grappled with English, so did their students, whose contact with the language was largely through the schools. As of 2011, 90 percent of grade 6 students could not respond correctly to more than half of the questions on an English reading test designed for grades 1 and 2 classes. Sixty-two percent could not respond to even one question.[60]

The national high-stakes exam-based curriculum put additional pressure on teachers and students to cover materials under time and language constraints. Class discussion often shifted back and forth between English and Kinyarwanda. One teacher noted that "many students fail the General Paper [upper secondary composition course] on the national examination . . . due to language skills, to some expressions, informal languages, and so on and so on."[61] International donors and nongovernmental organizations tried to convince the government, to no avail, that there might be a connection between the new language policy and increased dropout rates.[62] As one commentator put it, "If Rwanda was committed to delivering education to the poor it was also, unfortunately, delivering poor education."[63] At some point, the Rwandan government had to come to terms with reality. In March 2011, under pressure from international organizations like UNICEF, which was supporting primary teacher training, the government partially reverted to teaching in Kinyarwanda in grades one through three. Afterward, the schools would introduce English instruction gradually subject by subject, again beginning with mathematics and science and then moving on to social studies and language arts.

As part of a strategy to improve the quality of teaching, in 2014 the Rwanda Education Board announced that it would administer English proficiency tests to assess language skills among the teaching staff. The following year, teachers would undergo more rigorous exams that would affect their career advancement and mobility.[64] A diagnostic test administered in February with follow-up testing in October showed that teachers participating in a nationwide mentoring program still had not gained the skills they needed to effectively teach in

English. Measured on the Common European Framework of References for Language (CEFR), only 9 percent could function at the B1 independent level, while 73 percent only had the "ability to deal with simple, straightforward information" (level A2). The remaining 18 percent were still at the beginner stage (level A1).[65] A 2014 British Council study of over six hundred primary and secondary school teachers found that English competency for the majority of them was at the "elementary" (41.8 percent) or "intermediate" (43.4 percent) levels.[66] A test administered in 2018 found that among 800 mentors in the schools, 500 were still on lower level (A1) and needed intensive English training to reach standard A1 and B2 levels. The 500 subsequently participated in a six-month training program through face-to-face and online self-lecture designed to close the gap.[67]

The teacher problem, tied to other factors related to English, has created deep economic and social divisions in the quality of education. National exams administered in English at the end of primary 6 and primary 3 serve as filters to secondary and upper secondary school and ultimately determine who goes on to higher education. Some teachers fail to cover the entire curriculum in English, which has moved more privileged families to engage the services of after-school coaches who prep their children for the exams. And while Rwanda's technically fee-free system of education has led to nearly universal enrollment at the primary school level, large numbers of students never go beyond that point due in part to hidden costs in attending school. According to the World Bank, only 68 percent of Rwandan first graders eventually complete six years of primary schooling, and only 38 percent of them complete the full nine years of basic education.[68] Parent-teacher associations impose voluntary fees that vary by school and are typically used to supplement teacher salaries. Families in poor communities are less able to contribute, as compared to those with greater family wealth. In some cases, students are expelled or not permitted to take exams until they pay the PTA fee. If they fail to pay, they risk repeating a year.[69]

As would be expected, the children of the ruling anglophone elite have no worries. They speak English at home, attend private or well-resourced public anglophone schools, are taught by well-paid and qualified teachers competent in English, and have the advantage of private tutoring when needed. The consequences of this two-tiered system on learning outcomes have been alarming. As the 2018 World Bank report further noted, only 45 percent of second and fifth graders tested in 2014 met grade-level expectations in Kinyarwanda and in English. The report suggested that children could benefit from delaying to fifth grade or even sixth grade the transition of all courses to English while learning English as a subject up to that point. Combining those changes with targeted teacher training in English and well-sequenced textbooks and materials would help children make better progress in all areas of the curriculum.[70]

The situation has proven equally problematic at the university level. Four years after converting to English, students at the Kigali Institute of Science and Technology were still struggling to follow what lecturers were saying. As the vice-rector for academics explained in 2012, the source of the problem was the shortage of primary and secondary school teachers fluent in English.[71] University graduates were finding it difficult to compete with their anglophone neighbors on the job market. In March 2018, the minister of education denounced the low English competency of graduates from the nation's universities. Some institutions formed committees to examine the matter and developed strategies to improve English skills.[72] The ministry subsequently finalized a plan whereby teachers in colleges and universities would undergo assessment two or three times each year to determine their competency in English. Those scoring below required levels would be considered unfit to teach. Students entering universities would also take an English exam to determine their proficiency and, if necessary, would receive help parallel to their coursework.[73]

Notwithstanding the action plan, in March 2020 the minister of education once again raised concerns over the low levels of English competence in Rwanda's universities and the impact on teaching and learning. In 2019, the average score among Rwandan test takers on the Test of English as a Foreign Language (TOEFL) was 75 out of 120, as compared to 98 in South Africa.[74] Adding to the problem was that learners and lecturers, uncomfortable with English, were reluctant to use it outside the classroom, so there was little reinforcement. As one university lecturer told the press, "Except for a few students who grew up in good families and went to good schools in primary and secondary [level]; . . . there is limited knowledge for the majority."[75]

The grand plan to convert the educational system to English, especially in rural areas but also throughout the country, is taking years to sort itself out. It's been estimated that it will take an entire generation to develop a corps of teachers who were themselves taught in English, though often poorly. It will take yet another generation before the English taught in Rwanda's schools is worth learning and able to prepare students to succeed at the university level.[76] Looking at the current language situation throughout the country, that estimate, however disheartening, seems accurate. In a 2019 study of English proficiency among 2.2 million adults in one hundred countries worldwide, Rwanda ranked ninety-fifth, the lowest in Africa and well below countries like South Africa (twelfth), Kenya (twenty-second), and Nigeria (thirty-fourth) where English also is an official language.[77]

A Practical Détente

As for Rwanda's relationship with France, the ice seems to be thawing, though France has not had an official ambassador in Kigali since 2015. In a cordial meeting with Rwandan president Paul Kagame, in the course of the "Tech for Good" summit in Paris in May 2018, French president Emmanuel Macron agreed to convene a commission of historians to research the role that France played in the 1994 genocide. The following year, Macron announced the appointment of the commission's fifteen members who would examine, over a two-year period, classified documents from 1990 to 1994. Macron also promised to speed up the prosecution of genocide suspects living in France.[78] In a stunning twist of irony, Kagame used the 2018 Paris visit to announce, in English no less, the candidacy of Rwanda's minister of foreign affairs, Louise Mushikiwabo, to head up the Organisation internationale de la Francophonie in the upcoming election in October. Just as ironically, Macron gave the proposal his full endorsement. Kagame was serving as president of the African Union that year. Mushikiwabo, as head of the OIF, was key to Kagame's gaining support among some member countries that were less than enthusiastic about his reform agenda.

Mushikiwabo tried to set the record straight, explaining to the press that Rwanda's move toward English and the East African Community was not a rejection of French. Not only was it "necessary" for Rwanda to join the "club of English-speaking countries," she argued, but it also was "pragmatic" for such a small country to embrace bilingualism. As the Rwandan historian Antoine Mugesera put it, "We are at the crossroads of both worlds. One language is poverty, two languages is wealth." There is some truth to those assertions. French news, satellite TV channels, newspapers, and books are still popular, especially among the Kigali elite. Primary schools once again offer French as a foreign language, while the French school in Kigali, reopened in 2010 following a four-year closure, now has a long waiting list for admission.[79] The nongovernmental organization Reporters without Borders nonetheless questioned how an official of a state that "stamps out the right to information and represses journalists" could lead an organization committed to pluralism in the media and freedom of the press.[80] Kagame denied any claims that Rwanda's freeing two thousand political prisoners that September was an "act of good will" for France's endorsement of Mushikiwabo.[81] Yet for some African commentators it was shades of *francafrique*, the infamous policy of intermeddling that France claims to have abandoned long ago.[82]

The commission's report, issued in March 2021, stopped short of finding that France was "complicit" in the actual massacres. Yet it forcefully concluded that the country bore "heavy and overwhelming responsibilities" for having remained "blind to the preparation" of the "genocide" and for having reacted too slowly to the killings that followed. France's prime interest in Rwanda at that point, the report noted, was defending la Francophonie from the "threat of an Anglo-Saxon world" represented by the Rwandan Patriotic Front, Uganda, and their international allies.[83] On the heels of the report, France announced that it was opening to the public its government archives from the genocide, including about eight thousand documents examined by the commission. For Macron, the report was a "major step forward" toward understanding France's actions.[84] The response from Rwandan officials was cautiously positive as they awaited the conclusions of their own soon to be released report.

France undeniably hopes that this evolving détente with Rwanda will also strengthen its position in Africa. For Kagame, it might simply be a useful reset in a wider geopolitical power grab. It is hard to predict to what extent it will promote French language and culture in a country where only 6 percent of the people speak French and many still harbor ill feelings toward France. In any case, the opportunistic softening of relations is unlikely to derail English as it slowly makes its mark in educating the next generation of Rwandans who search for the upward mobility and job opportunities that English now offers.

Morocco in Small Steps

To shift the focus to North Africa, an apt way to start is with the American novelist Edith Wharton, who spent one month in 1918 traveling through Morocco in the closing days of the First World War. In her evocative chronicle of that journey through mosques, markets, sultans' palaces, and ruins of past invaders, Wharton observed that "'everywhere . . . lurks the shadowy spirit of instability. . . . Change is the rule in this apparently unchanged civilization."[85] Though much indeed has changed over the last century, Wharton's words fairly sum up Morocco's enduring tension between clinging to the old and embracing the new with each succeeding government. They also evoke unresolved conflicts arising from the country's geographical, linguistic, and ideological position between east and west and its ambivalent feelings toward France, its former colonial ruler. Those tensions and conflicts have especially played out on the question of language in schooling, with English more recently taking center stage.

Morocco's strategic position at the crossroads of Africa, Europe, and the Middle East brought it under the influence of multiple cultures and languages long before English became an incontestable force in the mid-twentieth century. A former protectorate acquired partially by Spain in 1884 and largely by France in the 1912 Treaty of Fez, Morocco has joined the pro-English march, though at a more measured pace than Rwanda. Like Algeria and Tunisia, its French colonial neighbors, Morocco's national and official language has been Modern Standard Arabic since it gained independence from France in 1956 and became an Arabic monarchy the following year. At that time, Spain also ceded to the new state most of its land in the north except for two enclaves on the Mediterranean coast. That former relationship with Spain and the close geographical distance has afforded Spanish a continued presence in education and the media. In the following decades, French has maintained a guarded role in perpetuating a form of neocolonialism through long-term economic and political strategies and partnerships, including the OIF. French, along with Modern Standard Arabic, is the language most often used in government, business, and diplomacy.

Most educated Moroccans speak at least one foreign language, commonly French, in addition to Moroccan Arabic (Darija) and/or Tamazight and Modern Standard Arabic. Darija, a vernacular Arabic heavily influenced by the Berber languages and to a lesser extent by French and Spanish, is the language spoken by nearly 90 percent of the population. Moroccans often use Darija even in more formal settings including schools and Parliament. Tamazight (a Moroccan version of Berber) is a generic term that encompasses three indigenous Amazigh dialects—Tarift (in the north), Tamazight (in the center), and Tashelhit (in the south)—together spoken by upward of 50 percent of the population. It is the oldest language in Morocco and in the Maghreb region, which covers Algeria, Libya, Mauritania, Morocco, and Tunisia. In the northern regions close to Spain, many Moroccans also speak Spanish. And so while the official ideology claims that Arabic is the "language of the country," the average citizen is bound in a mix of languages and dialects. Some Moroccan writers now publish in English, a language with which they have no national, local, or cultural ties.[86]

To appease the Amazigh population in the face of protests during the 2011 Arab Spring and the February 20 Movement, Morocco amended its constitution to add Tamazight as a second official language and declared that it would promote Tamazight in the public arena, including public education. The change proved especially troubling to traditionalists who placed Arabic at the very core of what it meant to be Moroccan. In announcing the proposal, King Mohammed VI's reference to the "diverse fabric of Moroccan society" reignited disagreements over the nature of Moroccan identity and the primacy of Arabic.[87] The king subsequently created the Institut Royal de la Culture Amazighe (IRCAM), which has since developed a usable written form of the language. While the uprisings did not produce significant political reforms, they marked a pivotal point for language advocates, shifting from the discourse of unity in promoting Arabic to equity and justice as the primary legitimating principle across languages.[88] Shaping this landscape are the indelible stamp of French colonization, the enduring challenge to the Arabization project, the rise of English in the global economy, and gross inequalities in accessing language skills.

Arabization

The arrival of the Arabs in the seventh century brought both Islam and Arabic into the country. The Amazigh embraced Islam, yet they maintained their own language in daily communication, particularly in the mountainous areas. When the French arrived in 1912, they imposed yet another cultural and linguistic layer. Under the protectorate, the Moroccan public school system developed with French at its core, though it largely benefited the children of French settlers.[89] In 1930, the French issued the infamous Dahir Berbère, a proclamation requiring the Amazigh to attend bilingual Amazigh-French schools where they would not learn Arabic. In this way, the French strategically used the language of schooling to divide and conquer racial and ethnic groups that had a common religious bond. Eradicating Arabic through French was a way of cutting the Berbers off from Islam and suppressing overall the unifying religious element in Moroccans' national identity.

That stratified colonial history laid the foundation for what happened following independence, when Morocco adopted the "one language, one nation" principle. Between 1957 and 1964, the country incrementally Arabized primary and secondary education while suppressing the use of Tamazight/Berber. The process finally reached completion in the 1980s at the same time that the country witnessed the rise of conservative Islamism. In 1983, the government officially changed the language of instruction in science, math, and technical classes in middle and high school from French to Arabic, allowing teachers just two weeks of training from the Ministry of Education. Those same classes remained in French in the universities, which created problems for students instructed in Arabic and left an advantage to the French-speaking elite. The idea was to culturally detach the country from France the colonizer and return it to an "imagined" past of Arab-Islamic identity that would unite the country.

Despite repeated official messages that French was "purely instrumental," the general public still associated French with modernity, social progress, and economic development and Arabic with Arab-Islamic tradition.[90] Arabization especially failed to undo the hold of French on many private schools. Members of the Moroccan elite, including the chief of the nationalist movement, made sure that their children continued to be educated bilingually in French along with Arabic. As for the long term, the colonial practices used under the protectorate assured a lasting attachment, albeit ambivalent, to la Francophonie.

In 1999, the government adopted the National Charter of Education and Training, which implicitly recognized the shortcomings of the Arabization project. Intended to be a roadmap for a "decade of education" and built on a pillar of national unity, it set three major goals on language. It strengthened the teaching of Modern Standard Arabic, which had started replacing French in education, employment, and everyday conversation, though about half the population spoke French to some degree. It endorsed more French in the second year of primary education and a second foreign language (English, Spanish, or German) in the third year of the *collège* (lower secondary school). Most importantly for language rights, it allowed mother tongue instruction for speakers of Tamazight in the first four years of primary education.[91] Opening the school doors to Tamazight was a significant step toward a politics of recognition—that many Moroccans are not Arab—as a condition to the unity project. The Amazigh activists' slogan, "Unity in diversity," is emblematic of that joint commitment.[92] The charter also instituted tax incentives to encourage the private school sector. The resulting growth in private schools offering instruction in French effectively put public school students at a linguistic disadvantage. When the charter did not deliver on its promise to improve educational performance overall, an emergency plan in 2009 introduced new reforms with additional funding without any apparent change in language policies.

The French Divide

Over the years, critics have increasingly described the Arabization policy in education as a "social disaster" in need of an "immediate remedy." Using a variety of Arabic that students do not speak outside the classroom, it has failed to eradicate illiteracy and has led to high dropout rates and high unemployment even among college graduates. Serious gaps in education with only 5.5 mean years of schooling ranked Morocco 121st out of 189 countries on the 2019 Human Development Index report.[93] More broadly, the policy has created a backward mindset rejecting linguistic and cultural diversity and has fostered traditional and nationalist views among the younger generation.[94] Even the king addresses his people not in Darija, the country's primary mother tongue, nor in Tamazight, the other official language, but in Modern Standard Arabic.

The limitations of Arabization have strengthened the position of French, which has remained an essential though controversial tool for social mobility and political power. While Moroccans rarely speak French as their first language, the urban middle and upper classes tend to use it as their operational language in business, finance, science, technology, the media, and higher education.[95] Morocco has a vibrant publishing market in French literature. Some of the country's most popular authors write in French. Morocco also is the preferred destination for high-profile French business and engineering schools looking to open campuses in Africa. ESSEC Business School in Rabat and the EIGSI Engineering School in Casablanca are prime examples. The kingdom has embraced these connections to build bridges between Europe and Africa.[96]

Private schools begin introducing French in preschool and at a high level of quality, which inevitably lures parents from a public school system plagued with problems. France maintains forty-four elite mission schools in Morocco with forty-four thousand students and where the all-French curriculum prepares students for the French baccalaureate. Modern Standard Arabic is taught as a second language. Other private schools use English or Spanish for instruction in a similar way. Government and education ministry leaders, largely graduates of French education, send their children to French language schools where they typically learn English as a subject despite the official push toward Arabization. Between 2009 and 2015, enrollment in private schools increased from 9 to 15 percent. The figure dipped to 11 percent in 2020 when bankruptcy from the COVID-19 crisis caused sixty-eight private schools to close and 140,000 students to transfer to public schools.[97] On the other side of the linguistic divide, less privileged students schooled in Arabic ultimately face the reality of French, which is the dominant language of most university faculties. They then encounter a primarily francophone and growing anglophone job market that considers many of them as "multilingual illiterates" and "unemployable."[98]

A 2015 report of the United Nations Committee on Economic, Social, and Cultural Rights warned that "uncontrolled" growth in private education in the country was "generat[ing] discrimination" and was a "source of human rights violations."[99] A parallel report submitted to a UN committee in 2014 by a collective of Moroccan and international organizations raised similar concerns with private schooling and the differential impact on student performance.[100] The uneven availability of French has been a key factor contributing to those inequities. Meanwhile, the growing demand for English, especially among more privileged Moroccans, has generated a lucrative after-school and weekend instructional market. As elsewhere, English language schools run by private interests, like the American Language Centers, the British Council, and AMIDEAST, have seen a dramatic spike in enrollments, especially among middle- and upper-class students. Public school English teachers have jumped on the bandwagon, offering more reasonably priced options.[101]

Veering toward English

Franz Fanon, the renowned postcolonial theorist, noted that "tout peuple colonisé . . . se situe vis-à-vis du langage de la nation civilatrice" ("all colonized people . . . position themselves in relation to the language of the civilizing nation").[102] Throughout the former colonial world, that positioning and repositioning has lasted long after independence, especially in countries like Morocco where French increasingly confronts English. The conflicted feelings that Moroccans hold toward French have indirectly influenced their positive attitudes toward English, a language devoid of colonial baggage (at least for them). Morocco's relationship with Great Britain goes back several centuries, and with the United States to 1777, when Morocco recognized the new country's independence. That said, Morocco is a relative newcomer to English. The first significant connection dates from World War II with the opening of US military bases while Morocco was still a French protectorate. Anyone who came into contact with the "Americans," from taxi drivers to store owners, had to learn at least rudimentary English. The long-term impact, nonetheless, was minimal.

A conference in Rabat in 2013 with the pointed title "Strengthening the Position of English in Morocco for Development" signaled a change in the air. According to the conference program, the aim was to bring together language experts, business people, education officials, industry actors, and others to "debate and make their cases about the foreign language they would want to adopt and use as they trade and communicate with the rest of the world."[103] When the government announced in 2014 that students applying to scientific, technical, and economic universities would have to demonstrate mastery of English, it came as no surprise. The country's most prestigious institution, Al Akhawayn University, opened in 1995 on an American model, had already paved the way for totally teaching in English just at the time when the internet was enhancing the role of English in global communication. Private engineering, business, and computer science schools had likewise made English a mandatory subject to help students pursue graduate studies in anglophone countries. As one university president explained, English offers "a fresh start. We don't have bitter memories. There's no bad blood, bad history."[104]

In 2013, King Mohammed VI stated publicly that "the state of education [was] worse . . . than it was twenty years ago." Calling for an overhaul of the system, he convened a Supreme Council for Education, Training, and Scientific Research. After wide consultation and heated debate, the council recommended adopting English instruction in all Moroccan schools.[105] The head of government, Abdelilah Benkirane, appeared on YouTube supporting English as the "language of today's science, technology, and commerce." Though he recognized that Morocco and France had "very strong bonds" that could not be "broken" and that the country had to teach students "to be excellent at both English and French," it was not Morocco's "destiny" to continue using French.[106]

Echoing those concerns, a report submitted to the council in 2015 by the Rabat Center for Political and Strategic Studies warned that without mastering English, Moroccan students could not compete on the job market.[107] English, the report stated, was fast becoming the preferred language in European universities. Upward of 90 percent of publications and research in Europe, including France, were published in English.[108] The argument resonated with an overwhelming majority of Moroccans. A survey by the Arabic news website *Hespress* found that out of 41,526 people responding, 86 percent were in favor of replacing French with English in the Moroccan education system.[109] Others within the government roundly disagreed. The Justice and Development Department pushed to maintain instruction in Arabic, while forces within the Supreme Council lobbied to keep French as a second language.

The opposition from French supporters apparently gave decision-makers pause. A year later, in a backpedal reminiscent of Rwanda, the minister of national education announced that primary schools would introduce English instruction gradually beginning in fourth grade, depending on teacher availability, while technical schools could use French to teach some scientific subjects.[110] More dramatically, the government reversed its thirty-year Arabization policy, which appeared to be holding back public school students in a private labor market dominated by French. Beginning with the 2017–18 school year, French would be taught in the first year of primary education.

The Debate Intensifies

With Arabic increasingly shunted aside, despite resistance from traditionalists, and Tamazight making only small inroads on mother tongue instruction, the larger debate over language and schooling in Morocco today is shifting toward French and English, neither of which has official status under the Moroccan constitution. Tamazight and Darija only intermittently come into play. That debate picked up steam in January 2019 when the Moroccan education minister, Said Amzazi, announced that French would remain the "second language [after Arabic] in Moroccan public schools, at least throughout the next ten years." It would take that long, he said, to develop a corps of teachers competent to teach in English. Moroccans immediately took to social media, arguing that English, the "language of globalization," should be the primary foreign language.[111] For many Moroccans, French is considered an undesirable remnant of French colonization. At the same time, Amzazi proposed legislation calling for science, math, and technical subjects in secondary schools to be taught in one or more foreign languages, rather than in Arabic. The aim was to combat the high dropout rates in public universities where the teaching language was French and which the proposal implicitly endorsed.[112]

The plan called for "linguistic alternation," the equivalent of content language integrated learning (CLIL)—an approach promoted in the European Union—whereby certain subjects are taught through one or more foreign languages. The draft law also stressed that students should master the two official languages, Arabic and Tamazight, as well as two foreign languages (presumably French and English) by the time they complete high school. Though the move toward French surprisingly occurred under an Islamist government, it was not a total shock. French seemed a more workable choice, at least for the short term, than English.

In any case, the following week, at the World Education Forum in London, the minister quickly embarked on moving Morocco toward English within his ten-year window. Speaking to *Maghreb Arab Press*, he laid out three projects between Morocco and the United Kingdom. The first focused on English language training for twenty thousand teachers of non-language subjects. The second would increase the teaching of English especially after the opening of the first British school in Marrakech the following September. The third called for presidents of Moroccan universities to visit the United Kingdom and update existing agreements with British universities. The minister explained that this was not a shift from French but a new opportunity for Moroccan university graduates to "continue their studies in British schools."[113]

Whatever the long-term strategy, the minister's plan presumably promoting French fired up an intense public discussion where Arabic, French, Tamazight, and English coalesced in dizzying combinations of support. It divided members of parliament even within the ruling party. Critics charged the government with falsely assuming that all teachers could teach in French and that all students could learn in French, which was far from reality. The minister's reference to French as the country's second language brought an especially sharp rebuke from Tamazight activists. Leaders of the pro-Arabic opposition party also took exception to the minister's supporting the teaching of science in French. For conservatives in Parliament, the proposal was a "betrayal" of the constitution and the status of the Arabic language. Some saw it as "a crime against students and against Morocco."[114]

The former head of government, Abdelilah Benkirane, still influential in the Islamist movement, called on his successor to resign if the law succeeded. Appearing in a twenty-six-minute video on Facebook, Benkirane strongly criticized the proposal, chalking it up to the "French colonial lobby." Teaching science in French before college, he warned, could increase student failure rates. Between French and English, he would choose English. "If [higher] education in a foreign language is necessary one day," he said, "there is a better language for it than French."[115] The head of the International Union of Muslim Scholars, Ahmed Raissouni, agreed. "If science should be taught in a foreign language," he believed, "English should come first, Spanish second, and then French."[116]

Organized groups of medical and engineering students posted a petition inveighing against the "neo-colonialist" proposal.[117] A similar petition, "For Linguistic Justice," launched by more than 150 politicians, activists, linguists, academics, and public figures drew over eighteen thousand signatures. Supporting Arabic and Tamazight for scientific and technical subjects below the university level, the group called for an "open national dialogue involving all parties, from civil society activists and students to linguists." The aim, according to the coalition's president, Fouad Bou Ali, was to denounce the "Frenchification" of public schools."[118]

At the other end of the argument, eleven Amazigh (Berber) associations issued a joint statement backing the government's proposal. They condemned supporters of Arabic as driven by ideology. Not only would teaching science in Arabic have "adverse effects on the quality of education," they argued, but it contradicted the "essence of science."[119] In a searing swipe at official hypocrisy, some backers of the government's plan denounced leaders who supported Arabic in the public schools while sending their own children to private French language schools.

Others were torn over whether French or English would allow Morocco greater access to scientific developments outside the Arab world. The Conference of University Presidents (CPU) expressed a well-worn concern that public school students were experiencing a "linguistic divide between high school and university." Having studied science in Arabic from primary through secondary school, students had difficulty adjusting to French instruction at the university level. This was especially the case for students of modest means who did not have the benefit of private schools where science was taught in French. In the end, the group recommended teaching science subjects at all levels in French while laying the groundwork for teaching these subjects also in English.[120] Other voices hostile to French but supportive of English roundly rejected the French "monopoly" over "intellectuals, thinkers, and students." Meanwhile, the Moroccan press was torn between defending Arabic and supporting foreign languages in view of the high rate of unemployment, which hit one out of four young people in urban areas.[121]

Despite all the fundamental disagreements, the various camps seemed to agree on one point. If education shifted from French to English, it would take time and it would not be easy. Yet they also seemed to suggest that, with proper planning, English would provide a neutral and even necessary compromise. As the debate raged on, the education minister did not waver in his defense of the proposal. It was not simply a "policy preference," he explained; it was a way for Morocco both to address "persisting social inequality" and to become more competitive in the "global knowledge market." Citing data showing one in four students dropped out of the university before completing the first term, he argued that Arabization had resulted in "two Moroccos" divided by socioeconomic status often tied to fluency in French."[122]

Ultimately both houses of the legislature passed the law based on the "two pillars of *equity* and *equality of opportunity* on the one hand, and *quality for all*, on the other," according to its preamble.[123] Though scheduled to go into effect in the 2019–20 academic year, it was delayed by one year. Between the two votes, a Moroccan newspaper posted a compelling video on YouTube. A voiceover in American English is heard saying, "The tide of African revolt washes over Morocco, completely overwhelming the efforts of firefighters" as a newsreel from the 1950s shows Moroccans marching and rioting in the streets. The video ends with the question "Is Morocco taking a step backward?"[124] Following the second vote putting the plan in place, a group of political, civil, human rights, and Islamic activists, including the former prime minister Benkirane, warned that the conflict would continue to intensify.[125] Undeterred by the opposition, and despite the challenges of the COVID-19 pandemic, the Moroccan government was able to move forward on the plan with the help of a US$500 million loan from the World Bank. In December 2020, the World Bank together with the British Embassy in Morocco signed an additional £217,000 (US$299,000) agreement providing technical assistance to help maintain a reform momentum in a post-pandemic context.

Politics and Pragmatism

Given this turbulent backdrop, sparring over whether English in Morocco is useful, whether replacing French with English is realistic, and whether Arabic is either essential to national solidarity or an economic liability is not likely to end for some time, if ever. The shift away from Arabic, nonetheless, is a sign that Morocco is bending toward the west as the Middle East and North Africa are lurching toward Islamism. Though the wounds of French colonization have yet to heal among many Moroccans, language cannot be separated from politics. France is one of Morocco's most significant allies and, as already noted, its largest foreign direct investor. Large French companies, like carmakers Renault and Peugeot, employ tens of thousands of Moroccans. The educated class widely speaks French. France maintains cultural ties through a broad network of cultural centers in major cities. Morocco, moreover, is the largest source for international students in France. Ironically, a large part of the attraction is the growing number of English-taught courses both in France and in French satellite campuses on Moroccan soil. France understands that alliance and what the French government gains from it. Both in spite of and because of the inroads that English is slowly making in Moroccan education, especially in private schools and universities, France continues to reclaim its lost prestige in Morocco as in other former African colonies.

Early in his term, French president Emmanuel Macron made clear that the future of the French language lies in Africa. He vowed to increase the number of francophone students from Africa in French higher education institutions. In 2018, the French and Moroccan governments signed an agreement to build French language programs in all Moroccan youth cultural centers. The announcement was made just at the time when controversy was swirling around new French legislation on university fees for foreign students. The changes required, as of the 2019–20 academic year, that non-EU students studying in France pay 30 percent of the cost of their university degrees, which was considerably more than the amount students from France and other EU countries paid. Critics argued that rather than attracting more students to France, the new law would redirect students to anglophone countries like Canada, the United States, and England despite their even higher tuition fees. Moreover, it would undermine France's efforts to preserve the French language unless students from former French-speaking colonies were allowed an exemption.[126]

That being said, all the overtures toward reinforcing French, especially in universities, have not stopped the Moroccan government from incrementally embracing English. As of 2015, students must master English as a condition for admission to STEM university programs, while faculty hiring in those programs likewise hinges on English language proficiency. As of 2017, doctoral students must meet certain English requirements in preparing and defending their doctoral thesis. In January 2020, the Moroccan minister of national education, vocational training, higher education and scientific research announced that Morocco was switching from the *licence, master, doctorat* (LMD) system used in francophone countries to the bachelor's degree system used in the anglophone world. A preparatory year would help students develop needed skills, including mastering English. The change would open Morocco and its students to international education systems, especially in English-speaking countries, and provide an extra year for students to develop both soft and hard skills that meet the needs of a changing workforce. A UK-Morocco Higher Education Commission would work to forge new partnerships between Moroccan and British universities and research institutions.

The government publicly launched the idea at a conference organized with the United States embassy in Morocco and the Moroccan-American Commission for Educational and Cultural Exchange. Despite assurances that French would remain the language used in all technical and scientific university courses, the change indicated that Morocco was broadening its horizons beyond France.[127] The Moroccan government understands the need to strengthen the country's position in Africa and in the world economy and to attract more foreign investment. The way to do that is to train a workforce proficient in English. At the same time, a post-Brexit United Kingdom is looking toward developing trade connections beyond Europe, and Morocco is among its strongest allies in Africa. Meanwhile, a new administration in the United States is re-engaging on the international front.

The move toward the bachelor's system was not surprising considering the events of the previous months. Just as the controversial language changes had taken effect, a government reorganization plan had brought in Driss Ouaouicha as the newly appointed minister of higher education and research. Ouaouicha held a PhD in linguistics from the University of Texas in the United States and had served as president of Al Akhawayan University in Ifrane, a basically anglophone institution. He also held the position of secretary general of the Morocco-British Society—a cultural, academic, and economic exchange institution. This was yet another sign of Morocco's moving beyond the francophone orbit while slating English to gain more prominence in higher education. If that is the case, it seems inevitable that the shift will gradually filter down into primary and secondary schools by way of necessity.

Changing to an English-based higher educational system undoubtedly has its advantages. It would ease the way for Morocco to integrate into the Economic Community of West African States (ECOWAS) and the African Union, positioning the country to navigate between anglophone and francophone countries in the bloc, as does Rwanda, and to create the human capital for attracting multinational corporations. More immediately, it would set the stage for establishing exchange programs of teachers, education specialists, and professors from West Africa while sending French-speaking teachers to anglophone countries like Ghana and Nigeria.[128] The challenge is how to reap those benefits without weakening economic ties with France or losing the country's historical identity and multicultural landscape. The added wrinkle here, as compared to Rwanda, is Morocco's roots in Arabic tied to a particular religious faith, Islam.

Young Moroccans in particular prefer English to French, as the growing number seeking university degrees in English attests. That being said, though they may speak English with reasonable fluency and are "digitally literate" in English, their academic English is severely deficient. In 2019, Morocco ranked seventy-fourth out of one hundred countries and regions worldwide on the *English Proficiency Index*. Though up from eighty-sixth the previous year, it was still at the very bottom of the "low proficiency" band.[129] Much of the blame for the limited English skills of many Moroccan students can be laid at the door of primary and secondary schools, wavering language policies, and a shortage of English-speaking teachers.

In the end, over sixty years since independence, Morocco still struggles to resolve its relationship with France and the French language as it weighs the global advantages of English for the short- and long-term. Whether and how quickly Morocco will follow the lead of Rwanda, with English dominating education and government, may be just a matter of time. It depends on the drift of Moroccan politics; the continued vitality of the Arabization project, especially among the younger generation; the government's commitment to strengthening its English teaching capabilities; and the ability of France to convince Moroccan leaders and the Moroccan people otherwise.

Redress and Transformation

In February 2018, South Africa's president, Cyril Ramaphosa, in his first State of the Nation address, proclaimed "a new dawn" that would "confront the injustices of the past and the inequalities of the present." Invoking the memory of former president Nelson Mandela, Ramaphosa assured South Africans, "We are continuing the long walk he began . . . in which all may be equal before the law. . . . We are building a country where a person's prospects are determined by their own initiative and hard work, and not by the color of their skin, place of birth, gender, language or income of their parents."[1]

Ramaphosa struck a timeless chord in recalling that race and language have divided South Africans for centuries. The historical connection between the two is a complicated one fraught with layers of colonial oppression and hazy racial boundaries. Here the dominance of English assumes a particular importance set against constitutional, legislative, and administrative commitments guaranteeing language equity and advancing indigenous languages. Yet beneath the rhetoric of equity and multilingualism lies the reality of a neoliberal economic agenda with post-apartheid shades that, despite professed legal protections, fosters English monolingualism to the exclusion of Afrikaans and local languages.

Politically divided under the Population Registration Act of 1950, the population of South Africa today falls within four major racially identified groups: Black Africans (80.7 percent), "Coloureds" (multiracial of varying Khoisan, Malaysian, Indonesian, European, and Bantu-speaking African descent) (8.8 percent), Indian/Asians (2.6 percent), and Whites (7.9 percent).[2] As the numbers reveal, though the South African Parliament repealed the Act in 1991, these racial categories remain embedded in the social and political fabric and are still officially used. The term "Coloured," which dates back to the British Cape Colony but acquired sharper meaning under apartheid, is highly contested. Grounded in a socially constructed hierarchy based on "racial purity," it suggests with political certainty a fixed identity of "otherness" as "unclassifiable," neither Black nor White.[3] Individuals whom the Act would have designated as Coloured based on "physical appearance and social acceptability (inc. linguistic skills)" self-identify by it, some more easily than others. They generally speak Afrikaans, the language associated with white Afrikaners. Within these groups lie various ethnic clusters, including African isiZulu and isiXhosa, White English and Afrikaners, and Hindu and Muslim Indians who may speak Hindi, Tamil, or another Indian language, though they primarily speak English. Each cluster struggles in different degrees to maintain its language, culture, and identity against the irresistible pull of English.

The first European settlers to South Africa in the 1600s were from the Netherlands, first landing in the territory that is now Cape Town in 1652. In 1658 they began importing a Black and Malay population for slave labor, which created early on a multiracial society dominated by Europeans. An Indian population of about one hundred fifty thousand began arriving primarily as indentured laborers in the 1860s to work the sugar plantations. Subsequent arrivals of French Huguenots and Germans added to the European mix. The Dutch had no interest in learning the local languages, and so the indigenous population of Khoikhoi and San gradually learned a simplified variant of Dutch. What evolved into Afrikaans was a creole language with Dutch roots mixed initially with Khoikhoi and San and later with Malayo-Portuguese spoken by laborers working for White landowners in the Cape Colony.[4]

Tension between the English and the Dutch/Afrikaners (referred to as "boere" or "farmers), including their respective languages, goes back centuries. When the English arrived, unlike the Dutch, they communicated directly with the people and taught them in their own languages. In 1814, British control of the Cape Colony replaced Dutch with English throughout public life. English became the language of schools, churches, and government, which in turn helped shape an opposing Afrikaner identity. In 1875, a group of teachers and clerics in the Cape banded together in the Society of True Afrikaners under the banner "Our language, our nation, our land." The group's newspaper, published in Afrikaans, declared its "God-given destiny."[5]

Afrikaner resistance led ultimately to the second Anglo-Boer War of 1899–1902, which the British won. They subsequently declared English the sole official language. Resentment toward the policy, fueled with the spirit of eighteenth- and nineteenth-century nationalism, reinforced a nationalistic mindset among the Afrikaners. Hostility toward the British and speakers of English lasted through the twentieth century, when fascist discourses in Germany and religious fervor helped cement the apartheid regime.[6] In 1910, the Union of South Africa was formed as a self-governing autonomous British dominion along the lines of Australia and Canada. A new constitution granted Dutch and English equal status as official languages in theory if not in practice, especially in schooling. English was a condition for state aid to education.

In 1925, the Official Languages of the Union Act included Afrikaans as a variant of Dutch and effectively made it an official language. At that point, Afrikaans was taught in all primary schools to accommodate the Afrikaner poor who could speak neither Dutch nor English. The language was still in a state of development and without a noteworthy body of literature to claim, while Afrikaners on the high end of the class spectrum were moving toward English.[7] By 1929, the Afrikaner Cultural Broederbond, established in 1918, had morphed into the Federation of Afrikaner Cultural Associations with a mission to unite Afrikaners around a collective identity centered on language, culture, and race. As historian Hermann Giliomee describes, "A new type of Afrikaner was born: the 'organization Afrikaner,' prepared to wage the language 'struggle' on an organized and sometimes secret basis."[8]

This unsettling past, carved into the White Afrikaner psyche, produced negative feelings toward the English language and an enduring attachment to Afrikaans. Initial opposition to British domination, later interwoven with a sense of Afrikaner privilege, led to lasting anxieties over cultural survival in which language still plays a major role. Nowhere are those sentiments better summed up than in the inscription *Dit is ons erns* ("This is our passion") on the path leading up to the Afrikaans Taalmonument (Afrikaans language monument) opened in Paarl, South Africa, in 1975.[9] The same "passion" gave rise to a version of White nationalism that evolved into the politics of apartheid, or "separateness," based on racial lines. That mix of history and emotions explains why many White Afrikaners in particular, though with growing exceptions, have resolutely educated their children in Afrikaans from preschool through the university.[10] It also explains, in part, why Black South Africans have favored educating their children in English, a post-apartheid antidote to Afrikaans though some send their children to Afrikaans-only schools for the better quality education.

Here we see linguistic diversity bumping up against race in a country where racial lines are blurred, marginalization crosses the language divide, and language has come to be used as a proxy for race. We also see two visions of democracy confronting each other, one grounded in a liberal notion of individual human rights supporting an all-English society and private sphere, and the other based in a communitarian notion of group rights looking toward a multilingual society and public sphere. Yet even within the Black argument for English, there is a sense of group redress for past wrongs. The ambivalence is rooted in the compromise negotiated back in 1996 in the post-apartheid constitution.[11] As we will see, that ambivalence is graphically displayed in conflicts over language and schooling and in the challenges that repeatedly confront the Constitutional Court in mapping out rights to equity and redress from primary school to the universities.

Apartheid from Beginning to End

The country and the official position toward English took a definitive turn in 1948 when the Afrikaner-led National Party gained power from the British and became a dominant political force for the next half century. Ironically, this was the same year in which United Nations representatives from across the globe signed the Universal Declaration of Human Rights.[12] South Africa decided to move in another direction, making the country a moral outcast for over four decades. The White voting majority's support for the National Party's racially segregated system of apartheid led the Commonwealth of Nations to break ties with the country in 1961.

Though racial segregation and educational inequalities had existed under British control, apartheid was more firmly tied to an ideological worldview of White supremacy, whose undercurrents remain palpable today. The new regime ushered in racial separation and marginalization in all aspects of South African life, including language and education. During this time, languages were significant markers of ethnic identity and served as effective tools for organizing social relations. The ideology of apartheid demanded that each group be taught in separate institutions, by members of that group, and given the skills that the government in power thought suitable. Even Whites were separated into distinct English and Afrikaner school systems.[13] Separate schools brought separate language policies.

Under the Bantu Education Act, passed in 1953 and implemented as of 1955, the government took control of all state-funded schools, then largely run by churches and missionary societies and typically in English. With the Bantu system in place, Black children learned through their mother tongue in the eight years of primary school. Afrikaans and English were introduced as separate subjects. Instruction switched to English and Afrikaans in equal proportions in secondary school. The idea was to divide and conquer the Black population by tribal language and loyalties and to prevent African language–speaking students from setting their sights beyond their own communities.[14] The government established language boards to develop dictionaries and grammars. It even set up separate radio and television stations for different African languages. Schools educating Black students received about a fifth of the funds allocated to White schools while barely teaching math or science.[15] Schools educating Indian and Coloured children received something in between. Hendrik Verwoerd, the leader of the National Party, reportedly hoped that by minimizing the likelihood of Black children's gaining competence in English, the Bantu policy would limit their future job opportunities and life chances.

Bantu education coincided with a landmark 1953 UNESCO report promoting teaching in the child's home language.[16] Whether the apartheid regime
consciously claimed any connection between its language policy and the report
remains uncertain and irrelevant. The Bantu policy's insidious motives defied
the report's very intent to affirm the value and uniqueness of the child's cultural heritage. The policy was racist and segregationist. It placed Black children
outside the mainstream, essentially locking them into culturally and linguistically distinct identities much in line with nation-state thinking of the day. As
Albert Luthuli, the 1960 Nobel Peace Prize winner and president of the African
National Congress (ANC), described it, "Using only the many vernaculars as
media of instruction ... cut children off deliberately and violently from access to
influences and ideas—and the heritage of much of the civilized world."[17] Setting
aside the negative implications, for Black South Africans, a key part of that "economically developed world" was English. With the intent of training Black
people for manual labor, Bantu education created a future generation of parents
unable to guide their own children toward higher education levels. That cycle of
poverty and underachievement continues to the present.

Ironically, despite the resistance to mother tongue instruction and despite
the poor quality of primary schooling, at least for the small percentage of African
language–speaking students who completed secondary school, the pass rate dramatically rose under the Bantu regime from 43.5 percent in 1955 to 83.4 percent
in 1976. Students had the primary school years to learn English and Afrikaans
before they had to actually study through them.[18] Solid research has shown that
while students might learn basic interpersonal communication skills (BICS)
for everyday conversation in one or two years, it can take four to seven years
for them to develop the cognitive academic language proficiency (CALP) they
need to transfer knowledge and successfully learn through a second language.[19]
Neither parents nor government officials understood the connection at that
time. Many still don't.

When South Africa became a republic in 1961, Afrikaans and English remained the two official languages. The government continued to promote the
use of Afrikaans throughout public life, including education. Meanwhile various
liberation movements led by a small group of elites, some in exile and operating
from abroad, promoted English. This was not out of any affinity for the language but as an ideological tool to express Black opposition to Afrikaans, which
the government used to enforce oppression.[20] In June 1976, a bloody uprising
erupted in Soweto, a Black township outside Johannesburg, when twenty thousand students, inspired by the Black Consciousness Movement, protested the
government's stepped-up enforcement of the Bantu Act's 50–50 rule of instruction through Afrikaans and English in Black schools.

The official directive in Soweto and other schools in the southern Transvaal was that mathematics had to be taught solely in Afrikaans even though most teachers and students had no command of the language. Demonstrations spread throughout the country. The firestorm of police violence, leading to 167 deaths in the first six months, displayed the injustices of apartheid before the world and changed South Africa's sociopolitical landscape.[21] In 1979, the government conceded and reduced learning in the mother tongue to four years of primary school with the choice of English or Afrikaans thereafter. The majority of schools chose English. By the early 1990s, instruction in the home language was "whittled away" even further to a maximum of three years, while many schools moved to English even earlier. By 1992, the pass rate had plummeted to 44 percent, which has been attributed largely to the rapid and early switch from mother tongue instruction, combined with the poor English skills of teachers.[22]

In 1990, the apartheid government under F. W. de Klerk admitted defeat and negotiated with Nelson Mandela the transition to majority rule. Mandela would become the country's first Black president under the first democratic election in 1994. That momentous act set the country, still reeling from years of Black oppression, on a tortuous and unending course wherein the "obsession with race for segregation" became an "obsession with race for redress," with English driving the momentum.[23] It also paved the way for a constitution that affirmed linguistic diversity in law if not entirely in fact.

Constitutional Beginnings

The 1996 constitution, adopted in the wake of apartheid and negotiated through English, has been called "the most admirable constitution in the history of the world," a "vindication of decades of human rights activism."[24] Widely hailed as "transformative," it was designed to tear down the walls of racial segregation and economic exploitation and to help build a society where all could live with dignity. Though not expressly stated, the concept of "transformation" is implicit in various provisions beginning with the preamble, which recognizes the importance of "honour[ing] those who suffered for justice and freedom" and the role of the constitution to "heal the divisions of the past based on democratic values, social justice, and fundamental human rights."[25]

Modeled on the German Basic Law and the Canadian Charter of Rights and Freedom, the constitution's comprehensive Bill of Rights is rooted in individual choice and nondiscrimination.[26] It's also grounded in international agreements, including the Universal Declaration of Human Rights and its promise of dignity and equality.[27] It prohibits both direct and indirect discrimination, recognizing that discrimination can be expressed both intentionally and unintentionally.[28] In deciding whether a right may be limited, the Constitutional Court uses a flexible proportionality approach based on "transformative pragmatism," weighing a given right against the resulting benefit to society. In interpreting the Bill of Rights specifically, it uses a "generous and purposive" approach.[29] In that way, the court espouses "substantive equality" that looks to the end result in benefitting groups that have historically suffered discrimination.

The constitution's provisions on language and its apparent commitment to multilingualism draw on the most enlightened understandings of "language rights and language use."[30] They state that all have "the right to receive education in the official language or languages of their choice in public educational institutions," but only "where . . . reasonably practicable." In fleshing out the scope of that right in any particular case, the state must "consider all reasonable educational alternatives, including single-medium institutions," while taking account of "equity, practicability, and the need to redress the results of past racially discriminatory laws and practices."[31]

The constitution also retains an aspect of the republican-nationalist tradition in recognizing some notion of group rights. It states that "persons belonging to a cultural, religious or linguistic community" have the right "with other members of that community to enjoy their culture, practice their religion and use their language" and "to form, join and maintain cultural, religious and linguistic associations."[32] As for any positive obligation on the part of the state, the constitution merely provides that the state "must take practical and positive measures to elevate the status and advance the use" of all of the country's eleven official languages, and that all those languages "must enjoy parity of esteem and be treated equitably." The official languages include English and Afrikaans, along with nine African languages—isiNdebele, Sepedi, isiXhosa, Tshivenda, Setswana, Sesotho, isiZulu, SiSwati, and Xitsonga.[33]

Despite these and other protections, there remain significant gaps between the constitutional guarantee to language equality and actual government practice. In Parliament, for example, all members theoretically have the right to use any of the eleven "certified" languages, while citizens also are entitled to address the central government in any one of them. Yet there are no funds dedicated to translating between English and Afrikaans or between either of them and the other nine languages. Ordinary citizens are likely to get no response when they try to communicate with government authorities in any language other than English or Afrikaans. And so at least in the workings of government, these rights seem little more than symbolic, or perhaps best viewed as intended for a "distant future."[34] Enforcing equal use and treatment among eleven official languages, including nine formerly unrecognized African languages that are not considered equal in social practice, has proven challenging.[35]

By the time the post-apartheid constitution was drafted, Afrikaans was one of only a handful of languages in the world that in the course of the twentieth century had become standardized and used in higher education, science, technology, the courts, and the media. Its meteoric rise in less than half a century was made possible through a well-oiled state-funded machine of schools and universities, newspapers, magazines, and publishing houses. That fact set it apart from other African languages, which White missionaries and linguists attempted to address and Black linguists and activists continued to debate even during the banning of liberation movements from the 1960s to 1990. Despite diverse positions on African languages within liberation politics, English increasingly gained wide currency as the "language of aspiration" in looking toward democracy and international participation.[36] Perhaps the only exception on standardization was Kiswahili, which is one of the official languages of the African Union and rivals French and English as the dominant lingua franca in East Africa.[37]

The constitutional drafters could have taken a more practical route and chosen English as the only official language. Some commentators claim that in yielding to demands from White Afrikaners to protect Afrikaans, the drafters focused instead on setting aside longstanding divisions, reaffirming the constitution's preamble that South Africans were "united in their diversity."[38] Others, like historian Hermann Giliomee, maintain that the politicians who drew up the constitution gave "surprisingly little attention" to the language question despite its fundamental significance to the country's minority groups, including Afrikaans speakers. As Giliomee reports, they ignored proposals from Afrikaner leaders to establish a post-apartheid policy incorporating language into a bill of rights and giving more than lip service to multilingualism. Giliomee suggests that throughout the constitutional negotiations, the ANC party had every intention of making English the primary public language once it officially gained power.[39] Whatever the intent, the failure to effectively resolve the Afrikaans-English conflict, especially in education, increased racial tensions in communities and universities over the next two decades. Meanwhile the clawback language of "reasonably practicable" in Article 29 (2) of the constitution's provision on education, commonly found in constitutions and human rights treaties to avoid controversial issues, undermined in practice the nation's purported commitment to multilingualism.

The constitution provided for the creation of a Pan South African Language Board (PanSALB) to "promote, and create conditions for, the development and use of all official languages."[40] In 1999, PanSALB's independence became compromised when it was made accountable by law to the Ministry of Arts, Culture, Science, and Technology (the Ministry of Arts and Culture since 2004), which also oversees the National Language Service (NLS). These two agencies handle all official language planning and draft language policies. PanSALB plays a watchdog role, investigating and hearing complaints on language rights violations, while NLS is more concerned with language policy development and translation. In 2016, the minister of arts and culture dissolved the entire board of PanSALB after a damning report by the auditor-general. In addition to findings of financial mismanagement and corruption, the board had done little to oversee and monitor the implementation of the Official Languages Act of 2012. Less than 20 percent of national departments had a language policy.[41] The board challenged the decision, which the South African High Court upheld.[42] PanSALB continued to function as the government wiped the slate clean. A new thirteen-member board was appointed in 2019.[43]

The Language in Education policy, adopted in 1997, like the constitution, was hailed as one of the most forward thinking worldwide. Unlike the inherited European model, the policy saw no contradiction in maintaining both a core of common values, practices, and beliefs on the one hand and distinct communal cultures on the other. It promoted multilingualism beginning with the child's home language and extending out to other languages, without prescribing any one method.[44] Yet again, these commitments to "language equity" and the development of "marginalized languages" carved into law and policy belied the reality of English and its close connection to promoting a more encompassing market-driven agenda.[45] What followed proved not much different than the typical postcolonial situation. From the very beginning, there existed a wide gap between the policy's guiding theory of additive bilingualism and the perception among many parents and school administrators that learning English was paramount to upward mobility and that "time on task" was the essential route to that end.

In subsequent years, South Africa's much heralded turn toward equality and linguistic pluralism has defied a reality that goes beyond schooling. Despite dogged optimism, the new South Africa is deeply divided by both culture and language. Though Whites are a numerical and political minority, overall they fare far better in education and socioeconomic status. That is not to overlook a small wealthy class of elite Black political appointees and entrepreneurs or a sizeable class of poor Afrikaners. The country also is far more officially monolingual, though socially stratified, than claimed. English has become a pragmatic language used across ethnic lines, though it undeniably gives the upper and middle classes, both Black and White, an advantage.[46] It dominates every sector—government, the courts, business, finance, science, the internet, education, broadcasting, the press, advertising, street signs, and the music industry. Parliamentary debates are in English. As of 2017, English is the only language of record in the courts. Government positions are largely advertised in English, which has become a ticket to a civil service appointment. Even the instructions on prescription drugs are only in English or Afrikaans.

Notwithstanding the dominance of English among the elite and in government, and the country's distinction in English literature with two Nobel laureates (Nadine Gordimer and J. M. Coetzee) to its credit, the 2011 census confirmed PanSALB's findings from 2001. Only 9.6 percent of the population spoke English as a first language. A majority of the people did not speak English in all of the nine provinces. Meanwhile, upward of 75 percent spoke an African language, the most common being isiZulu (22.7 percent) and isiXhosa (16 percent). Afrikaans accounted for 13.5 percent. Many people, especially in the townships, spoke various African languages. The distribution of English, as a first language among the major racial groups, varied from only 2.9 percent for Blacks to 20.9 percent for Coloureds, 35.9 percent for Whites, and 86.1 percent for Indians and Asians. Though 48.6 percent of Blacks spoke isiXhosa or isiZulu, a staggering 75.6 percent of Coloureds and 60.8 percent of Whites counted Afrikaans as their first language.[47]

These figures do not reflect the rising socioeconomic status of English or the extent to which individuals speak English as a second or third language or in education or work. Some White Afrikaners nonetheless resent having to use English as a lingua franca to communicate with Blacks who, in the past, had to communicate with Afrikaners in Afrikaans. They also see Afrikaans as an indigenous African language entitled to protection against the rising dominance of English. What it means to "speak English" itself is confusing. Black South Africans often integrate features of local African languages and Afrikaans into new forms of Black South African English (BSAfE) that convey "resistance and power."[48] A form of South African Indian English also has emerged. Migrants from other parts of Africa, some speaking French, Portuguese, or a local African language, continue to expand the linguistic terrain.

Language and Schooling

English poses its own inequities even within the Black and Coloured populations. Though there are some excellent public schools in South Africa, many Black and Coloured children attend under-resourced state-operated schools where they learn English poorly from teachers who themselves have difficulties with the language. While many South Africans, including teachers, claim English as their first language, the form of English some of them speak is far from the academic English needed to succeed at higher levels of education. Children of the Black and Coloured elite as well as the rapidly growing middle class, on the other hand, often attend English language private schools where the level of English instruction is considerably higher.[49]

Private schools are mushrooming. Between 2000 and 2016, enrollments jumped by 130, percent while the number of independent schools grew by

91 percent. In the Eastern Cape, the increase was a stunning 431 percent. Though White flight from government schools was partially to blame, the lion's share of growth came in the low-fee private school sector, where the majority of students are Black. An online survey of 28,380 parents in twenty-nine countries in 2017 found that 82 percent of South African parents whose children attended no-fee schools said they would be "fairly likely" or "very likely" to send their children to a fee-paying school if they could afford to do so. This was the highest rate of any country excluding India at 85 percent.[50] Some low-fee schools are owned and operated by private companies like Curro. Others schools, like Sparks Schools, are operated by entrepreneurs.[51] Not-for-profit low- and middle-level-fee schools are eligible for state subsidies. They also hold protection under the South African Constitution provided they don't discriminate by race, are regis-tered with the state, and maintain standards comparable to those of the public schools.[52]

The other option for parents looking to escape failing public schools and deficient English programs are former "Model C" schools. The now informal Model C designation, a holdover from the waning days of apartheid, signifies formerly White government schools that must now admit students regardless of race. Negotiations ending apartheid intentionally maintained their privileged status. They charge modest fees and are governed by a parent board that often re-mains all or primarily White despite an increasingly diverse student population. A White "ethos" continues to prevail.[53] These schools are deeply assimilationist, as protests in 2016 by Black female students against rules prohibiting certain hairstyles and African languages revealed.[54] Through language, and specifically particular forms of English, White teachers impose norms of whiteness on Black students, who are enrolling in growing numbers.[55]

Model C schools are relatively well resourced and rank among the highest achieving schools nationally. A dwindling number have continued teaching in Afrikaans and offer English as a second or additional language. Provincial ed-ucation departments, at the request of Black parents, have pressured Afrikaans schools to offer parallel English classes, which some school governing boards have resisted even to the point of litigation. Many former Model C schools have totally shifted to English instruction. For many Black children these schools are the first step into the middle class.[56] Even many middle-class White Afrikaners, who historically viewed English as the language of the enemy, now send their children to English-medium schools whether public or private. In some cases, exposure to English begins in the home and community even before children start school. Bilingualism with English as a second language is common among very young children from more affluent households. Increasing numbers attend English nursery and preschools, which prepare them for learning in English when they enter formal schooling.

For many South Africans, English remains nevertheless "unassailable but un-attainable," as the activist Neville Alexander's pointed out in his oft-cited 1999 lecture. It wasn't the dominance of English that troubled Alexander, who had spent ten years in prison during the struggle against apartheid and later led a task force to develop a national language plan. It was the hegemony, "the feeling among non-English-speakers that without English there is no power, the feeling that African languages are worthless, that we cannot empower ourselves by means of African languages." For Alexander, multilingualism carried economic and political capital that would potentially bring democracy and mobility to the masses.[57] This seemed to be a slight shift in position for Alexander. Back in 1989, discussing language policy for a free South Africa, he had proposed that English be the official national language and that all other languages have official status on a regional level, which diminished the value of indigenous languages and their importance to the identity of their speakers.[58]

In any case, it is hard to refute Alexander's later proposition on multilin-gualism. Yet among many Black South Africans, multilingualism that entails school instruction in an African language evokes memories of education under apartheid. That system denied Black children, who did not continue on to sec-ondary school, meaningful access to the two national languages, English and Afrikaans. English has played a key role in the struggle to overcome that history and its lasting effects. That does not deny that, aside from schooling, in rural areas African languages remain valued symbols of ethnic identity and cultural continuity. In urban areas Black tribal or ethnic identity is giving way to a more general "race consciousness" among a politicized younger generation.[59]

The government has tried to promote multilingualism and even mother tongue instruction while remaining mindful of the past. Its most recent policy on African languages is a clear example of the stresses and strains those efforts entail. The current National Curriculum Statement requires schools to offer two languages, one as a language of learning and teaching and the other as an additional language. Most public schools choose English as the first. In 2013, the government announced a policy making it compulsory for schools to offer an African language as a subject beginning in grade one. The stated aim was to promote social cohesion, economic empowerment, and nation building.[60] It's been suggested that the decision was motivated by "sheer panic" over the low performance of South African schools and that English was thought to be the problem.[61] Though the policy stopped short of mandating instruction in the child's mother tongue, the Department of Education hoped that the pro-gram would encourage parents to "choose their own languages as languages for learning and teaching."[62] The following year, a Global Monitoring Report con-firmed the vital connection between the language of instruction and effective learning.[63]

After piloting the 2013 policy across the provinces and allowing for wide public consultation, the government extended the program to all public schools beginning in grade one by 2018 and gradually moving up to grades ten to twelve by 2027–29. As of 2017, only 3,558 out of 25,000 public schools did not offer an African language as a subject. As a department official explained, "Schools are incubators of future citizens. Many people believe African languages don't have currency; they won't take you overseas. That's the misconception, but languages can sell. You can exchange experiences."[64]

Nonetheless, implementing the plan was less than straightforward. The Ministry of Education's claim that there was a sufficient stock of African language teachers was overstated. Merely speaking the language did not necessarily mean being able to teach in it. Nor did the government foresee the conflicts that racial, linguistic, and class differences, along with high inter-country mobility, had created. In rural areas there was a wide distribution of regional languages, some with multiple local varieties. Internal and external economic migration had further added to the number of English speakers. Many classrooms, especially in urban areas, were linguistically heterogeneous beyond imagination. As the principal of an English language primary school described the situation, "In our school . . . the children are now being taught in a second or third or fourth language which is not their home language. We have got children from Nigeria . . . Burundi . . . Mozambique, Zimbabwe, all over Africa. . . . The problem lies with the ability of children to speak the language [English] when they enter the school."[65] Adding a marginalized African language to that mix was a formidable challenge for students and teachers. It also presented steep hurdles for school officials charged with finding instructors able to teach in a wide assortment of indigenous languages.

That is not to deny the merits of the policy or its goals. Requiring all students to learn an African language is a positive step toward healing the wounds of apartheid. For students who speak an African language when they enter school, however, a critical part of their education is not merely to learn the language as a subject but to initially learn through the language. While an early version of the policy proposed just that, the final document skirted the issue. Apparently the government feared resistance from parents fixated on English as the entryway into the global economy. And so many students begin learning through English rather than a language they understand, even though studies from South Africa and elsewhere suggest that introducing English too early in the school cycle is counterproductive; children end up learning neither English nor their mother tongue well.

The situation only widens the student achievement gap between disadvantaged schools and private and formerly White privileged schools where many students are exposed to English before they begin the primary grades.[66] It does not prove much better for African language–speaking children who are instructed in their home languages through the third grade, with only several hours each week of English as their "additional" language. They abruptly switch to English instruction in grade four, when they are expected to use the same English learning materials and to function at the same level as students taught in English from grade one. The transition to learning in English needs to be more gradual.

Inasmuch as English is a vehicle for upward mobility, it also is an obstacle, especially for the many Black and Coloured South Africans with inadequate formal schooling and no opportunity to learn the language well, if at all. At the same time, the declining fortunes of lower-middle-class Whites, whether Afrikaans- or English-speaking, are also reflected in the declining academic achievement of their children.[67] Results from the last Progress in International Reading and Literacy Study (PIRLS) on reading among grade four students revealed the distressingly poor state of South African education across race and language groups. The study included 12,810 students in 293 schools. A total of 23 percent took the test in English, 9.2 percent in Afrikaans, 21.8 percent in isiZulu, and 15.9 percent in isiXhosa, with the remaining students scattered among the seven other official languages. Among the fifty participating countries, South Africa landed at the very bottom of the list.

After four years of schooling, 78 percent of South African students could not read for meaning, as compared with the international average of 4 percent. South Africa even fared poorly among other middle-income countries like Iran at 35 percent and Chile at 13 percent. Students from rural areas were more than two years of schooling behind students from suburban and urban areas. The language in which students took the test proved significant. Less than half of the learners who wrote the tests in English or Afrikaans could read for meaning; 80 percent of those learning in one of the other nine official languages effectively could not read at all. Only 21 percent of the students tested in English reported speaking the language at home, as compared with 75 percent on average for students tested in the other ten official languages. For Afrikaans, it was 89 percent.[68]

These findings speak volumes on the high levels of illiteracy throughout the country, the scarcity of programs teaching in the child's primary or home language, and the overwhelming difficulties for the 2,946 (23 percent) of students who learned in English, a language many of them only encountered at school and rarely, if ever, in their communities. The low reading levels among children learning in African languages, presumably their home language, is especially striking, perhaps reflecting rural schools that lack materials in those languages along with poorly educated and untrained teachers. As the advocacy group Equal Education put it, "Children who have not learned to read, cannot read to learn. . . . They cannot acquire new knowledge." Without those skills and knowledge, they cannot effectively "participate in democracy."[69]

Language Rights and School Governance

The fact that for Black South Africans English is both the language of historical resistance and the "aspirational" language of upward mobility has found its way into the South African courts, pitting Black parents and provincial education departments against historically White Afrikaans schools. In some cases, school officials have refused to admit Black English-speaking students, ostensibly based on language or lack of space. In other cases, they have refused requests to offer dual or parallel instruction in both Afrikaans and English. Either way, Black parents are using English as a sword to gain entry into high-performing White schools, while the schools allegedly are using it as a shield to keep Black students out.

One particular controversy, ending in a landmark Constitutional Court decision, opens a window onto the role of English as it intersects with racial disparities and parental ambitions.[70] It began in 2006 when the Hoërskool Ermelo, an Afrikaans middle school with a prestigious academic record, refused to provide a separate English language program for twenty-seven Black eighth grade students who could not be accommodated in any of the province's overcrowded English language schools. By the following year, the number of Black students still left without schooling had grown to 113. The school claimed that it was full to capacity, even though its enrollment was dwindling. Class sizes were below the national average of 35 students and far below those of the neighboring Black schools, which ranged from 33 to a high of 62. The school had been built originally to accommodate 2,000 students. By 2007, its enrollment had dropped to 587. School officials maintained that the curriculum—offering a wider choice of subjects than the national average—demanded more teachers and more classrooms and consequently resulted in smaller class sizes. Freeing up classrooms to accommodate English learners would force the school to cut down on its curriculum offerings.

The Constitutional Court decided the case *Head of Dep't, Mpumalanga Dep't of Educ. & Another v. Hoërskool Ermelo* as a matter of administrative governance. While it upheld the authority of the provincial Department of Education to intervene in the school's language policy, it found that the procedures the department had followed—suspending the school's principal, withdrawing the functions of the School Governing Board, and determining the school's language policy contrary to the board's decision—were invalid. At the same time, the department had failed to address the "unacceptably high level of overcrowding" in the district's high schools.[71] The Court nevertheless understood that there was an immediate problem that needed to be resolved. Rather than impose a specific remedy, it ordered the School Governing Board, in line with constitutional and statutory law, to devise a language policy that considered not just the interests of its current students but also the needs of other learners in the community.[72] School and department officials had to report back to the Court by a given date on how they were each addressing the matter. The school complied with the Court's order. It conferred with the parents and the community, modified the language policy to accommodate the English-speaking children, and made available some of its teaching positions to hire teachers for the English program.[73]

The Court recognized that this was not an isolated occurrence of Black students denied access to White Afrikaans schools. Nor was it simply a dispute over language policy. The constitutional mandate could not be separated from the historical backdrop. And so the justices seized the moment to establish a substantive constitutional framework that not only guided the parties in the case but has given the *Ermelo* decision importance well beyond its facts. "The case arose," the Court noted, "in the context of continuing deep inequality in [South Africa's] educational system, a painful legacy in apartheid history."[74] The only way to constitutionally address this "social unevenness" was by "a radical transformation of society as a whole and of public education in particular."

The Court referenced the South African Schools Act, which called for a "new national system of schools" to "redress" past educational "injustices."[75] It invoked a "cluster" of constitutional rights including "human dignity," "equality and freedom," nondiscrimination on the basis of "race and language or social origin," and the "right to enjoy and use one's language and culture."[76] Most directly and significantly, it relied on the constitution's guarantee that students have "the right to receive education in the official language or languages of their choice" where it is "reasonably practicable." The constitution required that in implementing these rights, the state had to "consider all reasonable educational alternatives" and take into account "equity," "practicability," and "the need to redress the results of past racially discriminatory laws and practices."[77]

At first glance, the language of "reasonably practicable" might seem to permit school officials to hide behind administrative convenience or financial constraints. Yet as the Court suggested, combined with "redress" and "equity," it forces them to justify their actions and demonstrate that they have fairly weighed the competing interests. As the end result in *Ermelo* indicates, these three factors taken together can tip the balance in favor of Black parents and students depending on the facts and claims. They provide a means to develop a record for courts, if they are so inclined, to sniff out local language policies that seem neutral on their face but that effectively use language to justify preserving White privilege. The *Ermelo* decision, with its contextual framework, has since become the guidepost for language rights in education. In this instance, English was the lever for asserting rights to equal educational access for Black students. Yet as the following discussion reveals, the constitutional right to education in the language of "one's choice" can also cut different ways as English, Afrikaans, and other African languages intersect with the law in post-apartheid South Africa.

Universities as Battlegrounds

Almost two decades ago, Neville Alexander predicted that "language divisions" would become "eminently exploitable for purposes of mobilization." He warned that the "danger of language-based conflict within the next generation . . . makes the policy of promoting multilingualism and individual plurilingualism such an urgent and critically important imperative."[78] Alexander's cautionary words have become reality. While language rights in South Africa are typically invoked to protect languages spoken by the Black majority, the White minority has steadfastly claimed rights of its own. Activists within the White Afrikaans-speaking population have come to understand that it is in their interest to conceptually promote "multilingualism" among all South Africans with the same zeal that they defended Afrikaans under a white supremacist regime. Alexander has called this "tacit but tension-filled alliance" between Afrikaans and indigenous African languages "one of the defining and most creative features of language planning in South Africa today."[79] The paradox has reopened old apartheid wounds within higher education, a ladder into the middle class.

The legal arguments hinge on several grounds. First are the constitutional rights fleshed out in the Court's opinion in *Ermelo*. Second is the 2012 Use of Official Languages Act, requiring government departments, including universities, to choose and use three official languages.[80] Third is the Language Policy for Higher Education, adopted in 2002 by the Ministry of Education. That policy echoes the words of Nelson Mandela, that Afrikaans should "continue growing as a language of scholarship and science," that "non-speakers of Afrikaans should not be unjustly deprived of access within the system," and that "no single language should, either intentionally or unintentionally, be made the basis for the furtherance of racial, ethnic, or narrowly cultural separation."[81]

When democracy came into being in 1994, participation rates at universities were racially disproportionate. Though 89 percent of the population was Black, Coloured, or Indian, only 52 percent of students came from those groups.[82] A majority (18 out of 21) of the universities were officially monolingual. Two-thirds (13) were English-medium, and one-quarter (5) were Afrikaans-medium. Three were officially bilingual, though what counted as "bilingual" varied from one university to another.[83] Neither English nor Afrikaans was a home language for the country's majority Black population. As the country inched toward democracy and universities opened their doors to more Black students, language policies became a source of controversy.

Tension over language came to a head in 2015 and 2016, a period of intense disruption on campuses across the country. It began in March 2015 with the Twitter initiative #RhodesMustFall, demanding that the statute of Cecil John Rhodes, a prime minister of the former Cape Colony, be removed from the University of Cape Town campus. The dispute progressively evolved into a nationwide call #FeesMustFall, which then grew into #AfrikaansMustFall and #OpenStellenbosch at Stellenbosch University. Threaded throughout were demands for "decolonializing" higher education and for all-English instruction at former White Afrikaans universities. The Open Stellenbosch Memorandum of Demands, published on May 13, 2015, called for discontinuing translators and translation devices; using English in all official communications, administrative meetings, and signage; and developing isiXhosa.[84]

Leading the protests were mostly poor and working-class Black students, which added an element of class struggle to race. Their support for an English instructional policy that not only was silent on their own languages but also privileged a language that many of them did not speak well has been characterized as a case of "complicity in self-harm." They seemed to assume that the use of English would serve as a "leveler," putting the White Afrikaans-speaking students at an equal disadvantage. Yet the White Afrikaans-speaking students, as compared to the Black and Coloured students, more than likely had attended better-resourced schools where higher-quality English teaching had prepared them for English instruction at the university level.[85]

Faced with escalating violence, the police intervened to stop the destruction of property. As the controversy continued to heat up, a YouTube video of interviews with thirty-two Black students at Stellenbosch University went viral. Filmed by four White University of Cape Town students over six hours, the video, called *Luister* (the Afrikaans word for "listen"), portrayed the racist abuse, discrimination, and marginalization that Black students in the undergraduate program suffered, along with the learning challenges they faced in predominantly Afrikaans classes. Through harrowing personal stories, it presented a clear message on language. Afrikaans was a tool of exclusion; English, as a common language, would right the wrongs of the present and the past.[86] The university published a swift response defending its efforts at making the institution more inclusive.[87]

As Jonathan Jansen, the former vice-chancellor of the University of the Free State (UFS) later recalled, "In many ways the campus protests were a proxy for deeper concerns about the South African transition. The promise of democracy in 1994 did not deliver. This generation of post-apartheid students was angry and anxious about what this meant for their futures."[88] The universities embodied African society's failure at "transformation" and its legacy of "institutional racism" and "Eurocentrism."[89] Language became a pivotal point for airing those grievances. The language of White Afrikaners, who had oppressively ruled over the country for over four decades, was high on the list.

The demands to transition to English centered on three universities that were formerly bilingual (English and Afrikaans) under a 1919 Department of Education directive but gradually evolved into monolingual Afrikaans institutions: Free State, Pretoria, and Stellenbosch.[90] All three used only Afrikaans from 1932 until 1993, when the twenty-one public universities were organized by race and ethnicity. With the end of apartheid, Free State, Pretoria, and Stellenbosch introduced English on a limited scale to accommodate non-White students, many of whom arguably spoke English to a degree. Free State and Pretoria, and to a lesser extent Stellenbosch, later formalized parallel (separate English and Afrikaans) or some form of dual-language instruction as a compromise between maintaining Afrikaans to please their traditional "clientele," alumni base, and donors and opening access to satisfy national policy demands on transformation and multilingualism.[91] By 2016, facing intense pressure from Black students, each institution had announced that it would redirect its program toward English.

The University of Pretoria proposed to offer all lectures in English but to continue using Afrikaans and Sepedi, one of the official languages, to support "multilingualism and student success." The University of Free State similarly agreed to phase out Afrikaans and move all courses to English over a five-year period. To ease the transition, it would offer an expanded tutorial program for first-year students in Afrikaans and several African languages. It would maintain parallel classes in English, Afrikaans, Sesotho, and isiZulu in teacher education and theology where there was greater market demand. Stellenbosch took a more measured approach in re-examining its parallel language policy, adopted in 2014. The revised plan would provide dual language with simultaneous translation in first-year classes. In subsequent years, it would offer simultaneous translation in dual-medium or English classes depending on student needs and available resources. Each college within Stellenbosch would be able to customize its language implementation plan. At the same time, the university would promote isiXhosa in the interests of social cohesion. In all three cases, university officials maintained that the move toward English was more than a response to student demands; it aimed to advance racial integration and remedy historical wrongs.

The Pretoria, Free State, and Stellenbosch plans ignited heated clashes between Black students and the White student members of AfriForum Youth, the young peoples' wing of AfriForum. Founded in 2006, AfriForum describes itself as a civil rights organization committed to equality and justice. Many Black

South Africans challenge that description. They claim that AfriForum is "deep-rooted in Afrikaner nationalism" and is solely focused on preserving Afrikaner language and culture.[92] Some White Afrikaners claim that the group has "hijacked" the mainstream, damaging the "popular perception" and "parading" as the "true face" of Afrikaners.[93] About 90 percent of its members are Afrikaans speaking and White. Some of its leaders are from the old conservative Afrikaner guard. In recent years, AfriForum has "rebranded" Afrikaners from the "oppressors" to the "oppressed," allegedly to shield them from losing a place in South African society.[94] The group now trumpets the rights of the Afrikaans-speaking Coloured population."

Backed by a solid membership, which grew from nine thousand in 2010 to over 230,000 in 2020, AfriForum had the resources to take its grievances to court, which it did in the cases of Free State and Pretoria.[95] In an interesting twist, leading the legal charge against Stellenbosch was a group of White Afrikaners with a more liberal political bent. The initiative called itself Gelyke Kanse ("equal opportunities" or "even chances"). Among the individuals launching the organization were celebrities from a variety of sectors including the prominent South African poet and anti-apartheid activist Breyten Breytenbach, who had spent seven years in jail under the apartheid government. The group claimed to support mother tongue education for all. In the case against Stellenbosch, it argued that Afrikaans and English should have "equal status" and that the university should make a "significant commitment" to developing isiXhosa as an "academic and teaching language." Gelyke Kanse's initial goal was to raise a million South African rand (US$68,000 or €57,800) to legally challenge the Stellenbosch plan. Of the four universities in the Western Cape, home to a large historically disadvantaged Afrikaans-speaking coloured population, Stellenbosch was the only one that was not solely teaching in English.[96]

As the universities became battlegrounds for equity and inclusion, each racial/ethnic group brought a unique history that shaped its response and participation. The economic and education issues at stake were real and not just symbolic. The generation of "born frees," that is, all South Africans born after 1990, with no personal memory of apartheid, had not fully realized Mandela's dream of reconciliation. Language was a flashpoint in a society where a relatively small minority of White individuals, many of them English speaking, still held most of the wealth. Black students were impatient with the still unfinished business of rooting out the effects of years of apartheid oppression. Meanwhile, White Afrikaans speakers were fearful of losing their language, identity, and status in a country where young Blacks were becoming more radically bent on transformation. As former Free State rector Jansen later explained, it was largely about power and the enduring memory of the Anglo-Boer War, where the enemy for Afrikaners was not simply "the English" but "English" itself. "Emotions run very deep," Jansen told the press, "and you do not travel far in provinces like the Free State without encountering memorials to ensure you do not forget the fact."[97]

The fiery exchanges between these two groups made interesting fodder for the nightly news. It was difficult to determine whether these were grievances shared by many or by just a small group of radicals on each side. Noticeably absent from public view were the many Coloured students, predominantly Afrikaans speakers, who kept a low profile throughout the protests. Though at least some of them lacked English skills, with the evils of apartheid still fresh in their collective memories, they arguably saw English as the language of aspiration. For the visible and vocal Black students, the language question had more to do with "decolonization." English offered them not only social and economic mobility; it also provided a neutral alternative to Afrikaans and the role it had played in the country's racist past.

Transformative Justice

Over the next year and a half, the cases against Free State and Pretoria Universities wound through the South African courts in tandem. At the same time, Gelyke Kanse, along with six White and Coloured Afrikaans-speaking students and the president of the convocation of the University at Stellenbosch, engaged the small Cape Town law firm of West and Rossouw to take legal action against the University. Though the three cases differed to some extent, they all raised questions of language rights, mother tongue education, and the role that English plays in redressing past wrongs and promoting educational equity and access. With the exception of one decision subsequently overturned, the lower courts consistently upheld the constitutionality of each university's program, repeatedly recounting the country's shameful legacy of apartheid.

University of the Free State

The first case to reach the Constitutional Court was the University of the Free State where the Court extended its reasoning in *Ermelo* into the realm of higher education. Here the Court struggled to maintain a constitutional vision that embraced both language as a "basic human right" and multilingualism as a "national resource."[98] The conflicting views once again placed in bold relief the role of English in South Africa's racially charged politics. But before getting into the details, some background is needed to better understand the competing interests and the differing perspectives they elicited among the justices.

The University of the Free State has three campuses with seven faculties and more than forty-one thousand students from forty countries. It is located the heart of the Free State, an area settled by the Dutch in the mid-nineteenth century. It is the founding home of the Afrikaner National Party, associated with apartheid. Opened in the early 1900s, the university initially offered instruction in English. It was the first South African institution to conduct classes in Afrikaans. UFS was essentially all White until the early 1990s when all public institutions had to integrate as the apartheid regime came to an end. Integration seemed to go smoothly until the mid-1990s, when Black enrollment reached about 30 percent. Black students began to resist White Afrikaner campus traditions, some of which, like freshman hazing, they found offensive and reminiscent of apartheid power dynamics. At the same time, White students became equally resentful and insistent on maintaining a sense of "campus life" as several generations of Afrikaners had known it. The dorms consequently became increasingly resegregated, and racial tensions flared. As journalist Eve Fairbanks explained, the students were merely playing out "a greater national drama" where the mood and first priority had shifted from the "emotional reconciliation" of Nelson Mandela to "economic and social transformation."[99]

In 2003, the university formally moved to a parallel language program offering English and Afrikaans instruction in separate classes. The change responded to a policy adopted the previous year by the Ministry of Education denouncing "the use of language policy as an instrument of control, oppression and exploitation."[100] The parallel program proved problematic from the start. Two years into its operation, Fred Fourie, the sitting rector and vice-chancellor, admitted that the policy had what he called the "unintended consequence" of segregating students in lecture halls along racial lines. In the following years, it became a source of racial tension and complaints among students and staff. By 2016, the UFS vice-rector, Lis Lange, described the "persistent challenge of racial segregation" as "untenable on a post-apartheid campus." "It was absolutely impossible," she said, "to provide language of choice without indirectly discriminating on the basis of race."[101] A 2008 audit report from the Council of Higher Education had raised similar concerns regarding racial separation as well as administrative problems.[102] It was difficult to recruit teaching staff equally competent to lecture in both languages and willing to take on the workload of teaching each class twice. Offering a number of classes in two languages, moreover, was costly to maintain.

By that point, Jonathan Jansen had taken over as rector when Fourie resigned in 2008. The South African media portrayed Jansen, UFS's first Black rector, as a "healer" for his efforts to create racial cohesion at UFS.[103] A speech Jansen made in September 2013 before the English Academy of South Africa nonetheless provoked a storm of reaction. Jansen was convinced that English and not Afrikaans was the "only language of reconciliation" for South Africa. He even suggested that it could be the "one major solution for the crisis in education." Every child, he proposed, should be instructed in English from the beginning of schooling.

Jansen condemned the hypocrisy of Black elites who "trumpet the value of indigenous languages in schools while their own children attend middle-class
private and public schools in English." He commended Black parents for prefer-
ring that their children learn in English. It's a "correct calculation that the entire
economy is organized on English terms and therefore the chances of success are
much greater in the colonial language." He went so far as to say that exclusive or
dominant Afrikaans White schools and universities held a "serious threat to race
relations in South Africa."[104]

Jansen's positioning English above mother tongue instruction, and above
Afrikaans in particular, received stinging rebukes across the country, from the
halls of academia to the Afrikaans press. Professor Russell Kaschula of Rhodes
University called Jansen's proposal "simplistic" in its view of the educational
challenges facing South Africa. He questioned whether "a sustained democracy" could operate "in a language in which most people are functionally il-
literate."[105] The Christian Democratic party dismissed Jansen's suggestion as
"not scientifically sound and in conflict with the Constitution."[106] "There is no
way," Jansen responded on Twitter, "in which young people across divisions
can heal past rifts without a common language; that is English."[107] Educated
in the United States at Cornell and Stanford Universities, Jansen was a strong
proponent of internationalization, which he believed English would facilitate.
Postgraduate students and world-class faculty recruited from across the continent, he argued, would serve as role models, heighten standards, and challenge stereotypical views of Black people among White students.[108] It would
take another two years before student protests gave Jansen the ammunition to
put those views into action and to officially undo the parallel program with institutional support.[109]

This brings us back to the closing days of 2017, when a divided Constitutional
Court upheld the language policy. In an opinion written by Chief Justice
Mogoeng and joined by six justices including two acting, the Court denied
AfriForum an oral hearing on the grounds that the remaining questions were
purely legal with no facts to be clarified. Threaded through the opinion were repeated references to the country's apartheid past, including the events that gave
rise to the Soweto uprising in the 1970s and the need to redress the inequalities suffered by the Black population. The majority movingly recalled the history of apartheid and its lasting legacy of social and economic inequality. With
quotes from the Court's decision in *Ermelo*, the majority recounted the "many
scars" left by apartheid, the worst being the "hierarchy of privilege and disadvantage," which left the "most abiding and debilitating legacy" of "unequal distribution and competencies acquired through education." "These truths," the
majority stated, demanded a "radical transformation" of the country's formerly
all-Afrikaans universities.[110]

The claimants had argued the case on two legal grounds: Section 29 (2) of the constitution granting the right to "receive education in the official language" of "one's choice" where "reasonably practicable," and a 2002 ministerial policy that allowed universities to establish their own language policies, but in conformity with government directives including those laid out in the constitution. While it might be "practicable," the majority conceded, to "retain Afrikaans as a major medium of instruction," it was not "reasonably practicable" where it led to "race relations" that were "poisoned."[111] The constitution expressly requires, the opinion noted, that "practicability" be guided by "equity" and the "need to redress the results of past racially discriminatory laws and practices." The majority accepted the university's argument that the parallel program had perpetuated segregation and racism, running counter to building a "common sense of nationhood." To let it stand would "leave the results of white supremacy not being redressed but being kept alive and well." While the 2002 Language Policy for Higher Education Act recognized Afrikaans as a "language of scholarship and science" and a "national resource," the majority conceded, it also required that the language of instruction conform to "constitutional imperatives like access, equity and inclusivity."[112]

The majority's unblinking focus on past racial oppression, without considering the other rights at stake, elicited an equally sensitive and more nuanced dissent. While the majority aimed to undo any signs—real or symbolic—of racial subordination, the dissenting opinion, written by Justice Froneman and joined by Justice Cameron and Acting Justice Pretorius, focused on the present harms that non-English-speaking students would suffer under an English-only system and the need to move beyond history. It warned against "disproportionately and uncritically" burdening future generations with the "undeniable injustices perpetrated by white Afrikaans speakers in the past."[113] Turning the university's "privilege" argument on its head, the dissent described the struggle that Afrikaners had waged against British imperialism and the dominance of English, which even the 2002 language policy recognized.[114] And while it agreed that the country must still reckon with "claims of justice" on language matters, it invoked Tolkien's advice to distinguish between languages and their speakers and to remember that languages "are not hostile one to another." It is only when "men are hostile [that] the language of their enemies may share their hatred.'"[115] "True unity in diversity" meant "creat[ing] space for other languages."

One of the most compelling points the dissent made was on procedure. It questioned the majority's refusal to allow a full review of the facts in an oral hearing, despite the claim that "reasonableness" depended on "all the relevant circumstances of each particular case," citing the Court's 2010 landmark decision in *Ermelo*.[116] There were questions that begged for answers before reaching a conclusion on whether the parallel language program was "impracticable" within the bounds of "equity" and "redress." What "reasonable alternatives" to the all-English program had the university considered in trying to "redress" past wrongs? What factors should determine "equity" and "practicability" beyond resource limitations? What role should other constitutional rights to language, equality, and culture play in defining the appropriate objective criteria?[117] The Court had never before addressed the question of sanctioning an approach that deprived speakers of one of the country's official languages the constitutional right to receive education in the language of their choice. Yet, the dissent maintained, that question had "enormous implications" beyond the university.[118]

The fact that all three dissenting justices were White while the nine justices in the majority were Black suggests racial divisions on the Constitutional Court itself. Nonetheless, contrary to what might be believed, the dissenters were not old-line conservative Afrikaners upholding the White privilege of Afrikaans. In fact, they were among the most politically liberal White South African judges one could find. And they arguably were upholding the right of all students to learn in the language of their choice.

Public reaction to the decision was immediate and direct, underscoring once again deep divisions about race and reconciliation within South African society. University officials assured the press that the ruling was "not a victory against Afrikaans" and that UFS would "continue to develop Afrikaans as an academic language."[119] Other responses were more overtly political. The South African National Civic Association (SANCO) hailed the decision as "the defeat of forces opposed to radical socio-economic transformation and cultural tolerance" and charged AfriForum with "preserv[ing] pigmentocracy and domination of the Afrikaans language."[120] The Higher Education Transformation Network (HETN) saw the ruling as the "official flattening of AfriForum's racist campaign to retain Afrikaans as the sole medium of instruction in formerly Afrikaans-only universities."[121]

Responses on the other side were equally caustic. The Christian Democratic Party called the decision "punishment for Afrikaans speaking students."[122] AfriForum found the Court's focus on race especially troubling. Within hours of the ruling, Alana Bailey, AfriForum's deputy CEO for cultural and language issues, posted a retort on the group's website. English monolingualism, she warned, would privilege only a small group of English-speaking students while leaving "very little hope" for indigenous languages.[123] Meanwhile, "the 58 percent non-White Afrikaans speakers," she said, "will again be disregarded and White Afrikaans speakers will be reminded that their years of privilege have now come to an end." She feared the ruling could foment "increased tensions and even violence.[124]

The opposing views had a tense history behind them. But looked at objectively, the majority's reasoning raised some problems. The exact cause of the racial tensions remained uncertain. It was unclear whether the arguable inequities related to language per se or race, or both. Or perhaps they had something to do with the administration's failure to provide additional English classes to better manage enrollment. To what extent were Afrikaans-speaking "Coloured" and White students pragmatically choosing the English classes, leaving the Afrikaans classes to the most committed White Afrikaaners and with the advantage of lower enrollment? The majority text was all about the harms of racial separation and the implicit force of English as a unifying neutral language. Connecting the dots, the subtext was about the symbolic association of Afrikaans with the racially motivated wrongs of apartheid and the settling of old scores with its speakers. It's undoubtedly difficult to imagine White Afrikaners as the newly "oppressed." Nor can it be denied that under apartheid Afrikaans was a tool of nationalist ideology, white supremacy, and violence.

Nonetheless, one still had to consider who exactly were the speakers of Afrikaans at UFS and whether they had any ties to those now repudiated beliefs. Some Afrikaans-speaking students, in fact, were not privileged White Afrikaners but rather Coloured students from disadvantaged and rural backgrounds, who have the lowest higher education participation rate in the country. Yet without delving into the facts, the Court majority may have let fall by the wayside the right to equal educational opportunity for the Coloured Afrikaans-speaking students in particular in the quest to arguably achieve substantive equality on an institutional level. The justices appeared eager to convey a political message that all but obliterated Afrikaans in the name of "redress" and "social cohesion."

In using language as a proxy for race, at the core of the controversy was the unresolved problem of what Afrikaans represents in South Africa today, and from whose perspective. Does it denote a White Afrikaner racial identity grounded in apartheid nationalism and White supremacy? Or does it signify a non-ethnic linguistic identity initially forged in opposition to British colonialism and now also used by the "descendants" of those pressed into slavery, "indigenous people," and others who were "simply poor"?[125] Should it at least be "reset" to no longer reflect the language of racists and oppressors but rather its varied histories, embracing all its speakers regardless of race? If primarily the latter, then those speakers had rights that demanded constitutional protection.

The majority disregarded the country's multilingual landscape and the constitutional obligation under Chapter 1, Article 6 (2) to "elevate the status and advance the use of indigenous languages" and not simply promote English.[126] The ultimate outcome was that universities could no longer hold White Afrikaans-speaking students as the norm. Yet by simply falling back on English without that broader discussion, the Court failed to understand that true transformation for social justice should take diversity as its "point of departure."[127] As some critics saw it, the Court's reflexive reaction against Afrikaans ended up being a "win for the English-brigade and neocolonialism."[128]

Removing Afrikaans completely from higher education, in fact, might cause more social and academic harm than good and ironically undermine the reconciliation project itself. It depends on the group under consideration. English classes without "scaffolding" in Afrikaans might reinforce inequities and might pose additional obstacles for the numerous less privileged Coloured Afrikaans-speaking students. Many of them come from underfunded rural schools in the Northern and Western Cape where shortages of competent English teachers produce graduates with poor English skills. Many are said to initially process information through their mother tongue and then translate into English before participating in classroom discussion.[129]

The same inequities and difficulties hold for many Black students from African language communities. These students decidedly call for English instruction, though they have been found to overestimate their proficiency in English, for a number of reasons. Being multilingual, they likely measure their English skills against their other languages, which they rarely read, and compare themselves favorably to members of their community. They may not consider or understand the difference between informal conversation and academic language skills. Yet between Afrikaans and English, English with all its global benefits is still a rational choice for them.[130]

Getting back to the *Free State* decision, the Court accepted the university's view of the facts at face value. In failing to give voice to White Afrikaners' concerns in an oral hearing, the ruling caused deep resentments that conceivably heightened racial tensions. The majority seemed insufficiently concerned with process and the appearance of fairness, apparently unaware that individuals are more inclined to accept official decisions when they believe the decision makers have thoroughly and impartially addressed their concerns and interests. The question remained as to whether the ruling would have an impact across education. The *Stellenbosch* case was yet to be resolved, while legal claims pitting English against Afrikaans in primary and secondary schools continued to surface.

University of Pretoria

The South African government, in any case, was not ready to throw all its weight behind English. Nor was it about to completely abandon Afrikaans, while it appeared interested in shoring up indigenous languages in some way. In February 2018, on the heels of the Constitutional Court's *Free State* decision, the South African Department of Higher Education and Training issued for public comment a revised Language Policy for Higher Education that put more teeth into multilingual teaching. It appeared to run counter to the direction in which the universities and the courts were moving. The document recognized that South African higher education had become more diverse since the "inception of democracy" and acknowledged the challenges facing university students whose first language was not English. It called for a comprehensive language plan for regulating and funding public universities. University language policies would identify all official languages "in addition to English" as "languages of scholarship, teaching, and learning," and each campus would cultivate a "culture of multilingualism." It required universities to "diversify the languages of instruction to include indigenous official languages."[131] The plan gave no guidance on the specific role that English should play in university instruction, effectively leaving it to the courts to decide on a case-by-case basis.

It's difficult to predict whether the government's ringing endorsement of multilingualism will save Afrikaans in universities in any measure or significantly increase the presence of African languages. Or will the demands of the global market prevail on the side of English? The University of Pretoria's January 2019 announcement that all first-year students would only be taught in English was a sign as to where these questions may be moving, and presumably with the imprimatur of the Constitutional Court, whose decision in the *Free State* case governed language policy at Pretoria. The announcement further stoked the debate over language and identity. Once again, social media was set ablaze when the finance minister, Tito Mboweni, known for his outspoken tweets, disagreed with the decision to phase out Afrikaans teaching. Mboweni warned university officials, "You are shooting yourselves down. You will regret it in 30 years' time" (@tito_mboweni, January 24, 2019, 2:46 p.m.). It was indeed ironic that Mboweni, a member of the ruling ANC party, appeared to be siding with AfriForum, whose unsuccessful suit against the university had delayed full implementation of the plan for three years.

Within a week of the Twitter posting, close to seven thousand people had joined the discussion. When one Twitter user called on "every Black student from the University of Pretoria to share their experiences regarding Afrikaans lectures" (@sindivanzyl, January 24, 2019, 7:52 p.m.), the invitation let loose a torrent of responses. Current and former Black students described being marginalized and discriminated against in Afrikaans classes. "Lecturers would walk in an English lecture room and tell us, 'My English is bad, so I'll mostly revert to Afrikaans and if you can't understand that's not my problem'" (@Its_Neo, January 25, 2019, 3:04 a.m.). "Afrikaans was used to give the Afrikaans speaking university students a distinct advantage over the rest of us. The lectures were NOT the same. The tutorials were NOT the same" (@sindivanzylJanuary 24, 2019, 8:56 p.m.). Others saw the policy as a "self-fulfilling prophecy." Why would these students apply to a university that would deny them the right to study in

Afrikaans? Meanwhile, Pretoria University officials defended the change, in part, on the declining number of students reporting Afrikaans as their home language, down from 85 percent in 1992 to 18 percent in 2019.[132]

Stellenbosch University

In the wake of these developments, in October 2019 the Constitutional Court rendered its long awaited decision in the case of *Gelyke Kanse v. U. of Stellenbosch and Others*.[133] To best understand the Court's ruling and its importance demands some background on the role of the university in the apartheid regime. Stellenbosch gained university status in 1918 with a grant from a local resident on the condition that at least half the courses be taught in Afrikaans or Dutch. The institution was initially intended to accommodate Afrikaans-speaking students whose language was essentially excluded from the University of Cape Town. Though Afrikaners made up half the Cape Town student body, instruction at that time was totally in English.[134]

Stellenbosch eventually became an elite stronghold of Afrikaans tradition and the academic engine driving Afrikaner apartheid ideology. That cloud still hangs over the institution. In the 1990s, the university had to open its doors to all South African students. English was introduced as a second instructional language. Afrikaans and Afrikaner culture remained dominant despite a gradual increase in Black enrollment. As of 2018, the student population was only 58.1 percent White, and not all of them were Afrikaners.[135] Nor were all Afrikaans-speaking students White Afrikaners. Many of them were Coloured students who had remained noticeably in the shadows throughout the protests that had led to the changes in language policy.

The plan adopted by the university senate in June 2016, by a vote of 113–10, set the course for the litigation. The plan came into effect in January 2017. A documentary filmed the following month by a Stellenbosch student and titled *The Other Side* expressed the concerns of Coloured students. In a series of interviews with leading language experts, the filmmaker posed the question "What do we stand to lose should Afrikaans be abolished in South African universities?" The responses were incisive. For Rhoda Kadalie, former human rights commissioner, making all students speak English amounted to "recolonizing the mind of Brown and Black students." For Danie Marais, manager of PEN Afrikaans, it would be a "shame" to lose the many Afrikaans schools in the Western Cape where "learners earn good grades in math and science." He likened it to "taking good infrastructure and throwing it overboard." Abraham Phillips, the novelist best known for his work on the impact of Anglicization on South Africa, warned, "If Afrikaans is terminated at the Stellenbosch University, poor Coloured communities will be lost because there will be no future for them." Dr. Willa Boezak, the commissioner of rights of cultural and linguistic communities, expressed dismay that the "drivers of Anglicisation" at Stellenbosch were the "Afrikaans-speaking academics—professors and doctors."[136]

The arguments, though compelling, failed to influence the legal outcome. The Constitutional Court's unanimous decision upholding the policy favoring English proved important in both substance and tone for its evolved narrative on language, race, and historical wrongs. As in the case against the University of the Free State, the Court addressed the constitutional right, under Section 29 (2), to "receive education in the official language" of "one's choice" in public educational institutions where "reasonably practicable," taking into account "equity," "practicability," and the need to "redress the results of past racially discriminatory laws and practices." It also considered the state's obligation, under Section 6 (2), to "take practical and positive measures to elevate the status and advance the use" of the country's eleven official languages, including English and Afrikaans, and under Section 6 (4) to treat all official languages "equitably."

Though the Court reached the same conclusion as in *Free State*, the facts were slightly different, while the analysis was strikingly so on several counts. In *Free State*, the policy changes were reportedly designed to relieve racial tensions; here the targeted problem was the marginalization of Black students. There the new policy effectively eliminated Afrikaans; here it "diminished" its presence and use in the classroom. The 2016 policy at Stellenbosch increased the number of English-taught classes so that students who could not speak Afrikaans could receive all their instruction in English. While Afrikaans-speaking students inevitably had to take most courses in English, all first-year lectures were also offered in Afrikaans. Beyond the first year, Afrikaans-taught classes would be subject to demand and available resources. In *Free State* the Court's ruling elicited three dissenting opinions; here the decision was unanimous with two concurring opinions. There the central theme was redress and "radical" transformation, including repeated references to "healing, reconciliation and reparation" to move beyond the history of "racial supremacy." Here the justices acknowledged the past, but only fleetingly. And though bound by the prior ruling, both the majority and two concurring opinions conveyed a tone and message that were more conciliatory and pragmatic and less politically charged.

In a unanimously endorsed opinion written by Justice Cameron, following the context-sensitive analysis laid down in the *Ermelo* decision, the Court ruled that judging what is "reasonable" under the constitution could take financial considerations into account, an issue not addressed in *Free State*. The justices agreed with the university that offering parallel streams in English and Afrikaans on an equal basis, as Gelyke Kanse proposed, would be "enormously, even if not prohibitively, expensive," raising the cost to students by 20 percent.[137] In balancing the equities, the justices recognized that a significant minority of first-year students lacked the skills to learn in Afrikaans, while the former Afrikaans-dominant policy made those students—predominantly Black—feel "marginalized, excluded and stigmatized."[138] At the same time, most of their Afrikaans-speaking classmates could be taught in English. Despite the net effect in favoring English, the justices attempted to place the language question and "equitable treatment" on politically neutral terrain. Noting the "global march of English" and its impact on the country's linguistic heritage, they recognized the cost to the country and to the world in diminishing Afrikaans at the university. Yet, they concluded, that was not "the University's burden."[139]

The two concurring opinions, one by Chief Justice Mogoeng, who had written the majority opinion in *Free State*, and the other by Justice Froneman, who had dissented in that case, underscored the importance of indigenous languages. Justice Froneman, pointedly writing in both English and Afrikaans, was especially insightful in viewing the "big picture" on language and schooling. While he concurred with the reasoning and outcome of the Court's opinion grounded in practicality and cost constraints, he also saw a "cautionary tale" on the implications for multilingualism and language rights throughout schooling, in South Africa and beyond.[140]

Focusing on the present and the future, he highlighted the connection among race, language, and poverty, along with the importance of language in shaping self-identity. He specifically supported mother tongue instruction in Afrikaans and other languages, not simply as a legal matter but as a matter of sound pedagogy and research. He recognized that English, as the dominant global language, favored privileged White first-language English speakers, as well as privileged White, Coloured, and Black second-language speakers, who often attended English language private or well-resourced public schools.[141] Yet he also made the case for marginalized Coloured students whose home language was Afrikaans. These students, he noted, were the lowest in numbers in higher education and "suffer[ed] most" from an English-only education. While acknowledging that Afrikaans was a means of power and oppression in the past, he called for moving to a place where Afrikaans speakers could be proud of their language and where speakers of other indigenous African languages could claim their right to "use their language anywhere and everywhere."[142]

The ruling overall was historic for the university. It also was significant for the Constitutional Court and for South Africa. The majority and concurring opinions suggested a forward-looking direction in resolving the tensions among English, Afrikaans, and other indigenous languages. Without dismissing the wrongs of the past, the Court set its sight on present inequities within a more inclusive multilingual narrative. It is hard to tell what moved the Court to take this mollified approach with a symbolic nod toward multilingualism. Was it looking to place the decision within the wider global discourse on multilingualism prevalent in the European Union and, as we will see, gaining ground in the United States? Or were the justices trying to turn the corner on "transformation," moving in step with policymakers on the language question? Perhaps it was related to the revised language policy that the government had referred to the Council on Higher Education subsequent to the *Free State* decision. The minister of higher education and training, science and technology, Dr. Blade Nzimande, praised the ruling. He noted that it would inform the outcome of the policy, whose "particular focus" was on the "development of African languages as languages of scholarship, teaching, learning and communication at universities." Afrikaans, he said, had "to be located in a democratic South Africa and be rescued from a right wing agenda."[143]

Decolonizing the Globalized Mind

Despite the rulings in favor of both Free State and Stellenbosch Universities, the concerns that Coloured South Africans raised over English in the Stellenbosch video should not be dismissed. Others have expressed similar qualms about the roots of colonialism in the onrush of English. As Rozena Maart, director of the Centre for Critical Research on Race and Identity at the University of KwaZulu-Natal explained, "English traps us. We can't think outside that particular language, we are schooled in the coloniality of that language."[144] Yet government officials, educators, and ordinary South Africans remain locked in an English-Afrikaans debate. At the same time, while Black parents are seduced by the global pull of English, their own indigenous languages receive lip service at best. As it was a hundred years ago under British rule, Afrikaans is the sole counterweight to the domination of English, while English, once again, has gained the upper hand as the language of nationalism.

Back in 1990, addressing how universities might serve the interests of South Africans "dispossessed and dehumanized during apartheid," Nelson Mandela asked, "What does [a university] need to address about itself in order to become an instrument of [its] empowerment?"[145] Mandela would have agreed with African intellectuals like Ngũgĩ wa Thiong'o who have made the case for linguistic diversity, and especially for developing African languages and literature as crucial pillars of decolonization. Reflecting on his own schooling in Kenya in his landmark book *Decolonising the Mind*, Ngũgĩ compared the corrosive effect of English language instruction to a form of "spiritual subjugation."[146] More recently, speaking to the Kenya Editors Guild, he made headlines across the continent when he advocated a three-language policy throughout Africa: mother tongue, Kiswahili, and English for every child. "If you know all the languages of the world but you do not know your mother tongue," he told the group, "that is mental enslavement. But if you know the language of your culture and add all these other languages, that is empowerment."[147] The impact of his proposal on linguistic diversity would be endless—from arts and culture to education, politics, technology, scientific discovery, health care, industry, commerce, the environment, and the media.

Some South African activists now propose political campaigns, like #EnglishOnlyMustFall, #FrenchOnlyMustFall, that directly confront former colonial languages within a broader movement to decolonize the curriculum and rescue it from the European and Western canon.[148] Still others look toward a shift from a national focus on language policy to the nine provinces, where majority languages differ and should be promoted equally alongside English and Afrikaans.[149] Both proposals call for moving African languages from the periphery to the center of knowledge production, rather than totally replacing globally important Western languages.[150] Despite claims that African languages are unfit for university learning, proponents point to cases proving otherwise. Rhodes University uses isiXhosa as a medium of instruction in certain courses. At the University of Limpopo, master's and PhD students write their theses in any official language of their choice.[151]

In recent years there has been growing interest in promoting Kiswahili, which is one of the working languages of the African Union and recognized as a lingua franca alongside English within the East African Community. In 2015, Tanzania went to the extreme in dropping English as its official language and switching to instruction in Kiswahili throughout the school years. Some commentators welcomed the change in giving Tanzanians a sense of "collective identity" while facilitating trade within the region. Others questioned how the move would work in a globalized economy, especially with foreign investors who place a high premium on English in the labor market.[152] In 2018, South Africa took a more measured approach. Kiswahili would be introduced as an optional subject in public, private, and independent schools beginning in 2020 to promote unity and social cohesion with other Africans. The general public barely noticed the announcement, though several media outlets hailed it as an effort to decolonize the continent. People would no longer have to resort to a European language, particularly English, to communicate across national borders. The "language of freedom" would replace "European languages of the oppressors."[153]

Meanwhile, young Coloured activists are challenging the English-Afrikaans binary and validating alternate forms of expression, like AfriKaaps, a form of Afrikaans spoken in the West Cape and now promoted by hip-hop artists. It's a way of politically reclaiming the creole history of Afrikaans and asserting the humanity of multilingual speakers of the language in a post-apartheid South Africa that has "disempowered" them. As Quentin Williams, a senior lecturer at the University of the Western Cape who has studied AfriKaaps and its speakers sees it, "The future of language in South Africa lies in the hands of 'Coloureds' who speak Afrikaans."[154] Yet they too understand the importance of English for upward mobility. It's not an either/or matter. The challenge is for the education system to recognize and tap into these dual sensibilities.[155]

The call to multilingualism is culturally affirming and politically appealing. Nonetheless, it can easily get drowned out in the euphoria of South Africa's economy, which has become increasingly globalized and internationally influential. The signs already are there. Afrikaans is fading from university classrooms by court order, market forces, or changing demographics. Afrikaans-speaking academics, as elsewhere, are publishing their scholarship in English under the pressure of internationalization within higher education. Meanwhile, other African languages receive mere lip service at most within academic circles. University officials, like their counterparts in Europe and across the globe, have fallen under the spell of international rankings despite warnings that South African universities lack the resources to compete in that race to the top. In the end, as Hermann Giliomee warns, it causes them to neglect the very "communities they were supposed to serve in the first place."[156]

English also is a draw for foreign students.[157] South Africa ranks third, close behind France and the United Kingdom, as the most common study destination for students from other African nations. Even the Potchefstroom campus of the North-West University, the only institution nationwide offering Afrikaans instruction in all undergraduate courses, has established a target figure of 52 percent non-Afrikaans speaking students for 2022, which undoubtedly will increase pressure for more English instruction.[158] A new generation of Black South Africans, regardless of their home language, is feeling less ideologically grounded solely in memories of the past and broadening its present-day sights toward English with its promise of upward mobility in the global economy. Yet much still needs to be done to improve public schooling and English instruction to make those dreams a reality in the job market. Employers persistently raise concerns over the shortage of qualified English-speaking workers.

English has proven essential to South Africa's membership, since 2010, in the BRICS (Brazil, Russia, India, China, South Africa) association of newly industrialized and fast-growing economies, representing over 40 percent of the world's population. In 2018, South Africa took the lead in hosting the group's tenth annual BRICS gathering. Movement toward a "BRICS-Plus," inviting non-BRICS countries to BRICS summits, could bring a total of thirty-five countries into an expanded geopolitical orbit, with English as the common means of communication.[159] With the largest economy in sub-Saharan Africa, accounting for about a third of the region's GDP, South Africans might pragmatically bury not just Afrikaans but also other African languages along with the colonial past, casting their lot with English with its high global currency. It's already happening in the schools where tomorrow's leaders and followers are being shaped. As the chief justice noted in the *Ermelo* case, the "collateral irony" is that parents who speak one of the country's indigenous languages at home demand that their children learn in English despite all the research pointing in favor of mother tongue instruction .

As African languages struggle for institutional recognition and Afrikaans declines as a language of teaching and learning, the constitutional commitment to language equality in South Africa is aspirational at best. It remains to be seen if the Constitutional Court's emerging multilingual turn can reshape public discourse and language polices across education. The even bigger question is whether it can move South Africa toward the constitution's promise of transformation and redress.[160] In the meantime, English reigns supreme for its economic power, while its role in navigating colonialism and modernity remains a source of political and legal conflict.

Confronting the Raj

India presents a kaleidoscopic view on how English has created conflicting possibilities of inclusion and exclusion in what was considered the "jewel in the crown" of the British Empire.[1] Over the seven decades since independence, English in India has evolved from a much-resented instrument of colonial domination, to a grudgingly adopted lingua franca, to a symbol of social status, and most recently to an essential second language (and even a first language for a thin layer of elites). Several brief examples by way of stark contrast, from bourgeois angst to impoverished resolve, offer an entrée into the complex role that English now plays and how these incongruities have affected identity and educational equity over time.

First from the world of popular culture are two films. Typical of the Bollywood genre identified with the post-1990s Hindi film industry, both underscore the uneven distribution of English and the social capital it carries among upper-class metropolitan Indians. In the first film, *English Vinglish*, the main character is a Hindi-speaking mother and wife of a busy executive living in the city of Pune. Though Pune is Marathi-speaking, the film used Hindi to accommodate the late well-known South Indian actress Shridevi, who played the leading role. The woman's husband and teenage daughter treat her halting English with both amusement and contempt, while she anxiously tries to avoid speaking English in social settings. The fact that her husband is fluent in English underscores the gendered nature of education and particularly English in India. When she visits New York City on her own to help organize her niece's wedding, she encounters repeated humiliations. Determined to redeem herself, she decides to enroll in a four-week crash course in English, where she becomes increasingly self-assured as she conquers the language. Along the way, she encounters similarly situated individuals whose English, or lack thereof, and the treatment each merits from others illustrate sharp class distinctions.[2]

The second film, *Hindi Medium*, tells the story of a young middle-class couple living in Delhi. We see the couple going to extreme lengths, including fraudulently feigning poverty, to game the system so their child can gain admission to a selective private English language school under a mandated quota for the disadvantaged. In the end, the couple is forced to reckon with their misdoings. Both films, box office hits in India, offer a seemingly light but decidedly critical spin on the shallow foibles of an elite segment of Indian society. The second especially highlights the appalling state of government schools and the enormous gap in economic equality. Together they convey a pointed message about the value that English holds in the minds of present-day Indians and its currency for becoming an insider within a privileged world of English speakers. As the female character in *Hindi Medium* tells her Hindi-speaking husband, "English isn't just a language in this country. It's a class."[3]

That resolute statement takes on a deeper meaning at the other end of the social spectrum. Here, we have the gripping story of the two hundred million Dalits in the northern state of Uttar Pradesh and the failed attempt to build in the small village of Banka a black granite temple to house the "Goddess of the English Language." The district administration allegedly halted construction for lack of the required permission. Last reported, the goddess remains in the home of the local primary school principal who had donated land for the temple. To understand what the temple and the goddess represent, you have to understand the caste system. Rooted in ancient India, the system is divided along four *varnas* defining occupation and social status: Brahmans (priests—learned people/people of books), Kshatriyas (warriors, rulers/administrators, and nobility), Vaishyas (farmers, merchants, artisans), and Shudras (tenant farmers and servants). Dalits ("untouchables") were considered so low in social status that they fell totally outside the caste system. The term "Dalit" in Hindi means "crushed, oppressed," from the Sanskrit *dalita*. Included in this class are the Balutedars, who carried out professions such as pottery making, carpentry, blacksmithing, and weaving/textiles. Though Article 17 of the 1949 constitution abolished "untouchability" and made its practice in any form a crime, oppression and academic exclusion have persisted. While circumstances for many Dalits have improved, the literacy rate is only 80 percent for males and 64 percent for females, as compared to 84.7 percent for males and 70.3 percent for females nationwide. Higher education enrollment among Dalits is a shocking 18 percent.[4]

In an odd twist of history, Dalits designed the still unrealized temple in honor of the infamous Lord Macaulay, whom the nationalists now revile for his plan to create an English-speaking middle class. The bronze "goddess," modeled after the Statue of Liberty in New York harbor, stands two and half feet tall. She wears a sari and an English straw hat, the hat being a symbol of rejecting the traditional Indian dress code. In her right hand, she holds aloft a giant pink pen to show that she is literate. In her left hand, she holds a book representing India's constitution, which gave Dalits equal rights. She stands atop a computer to signify that Dalits will use English "to rise up the ladder and become free forever." For Chandra Bhan Prasad, the Dalit writer who conceived of the "goddess" idea, "If your child learns English it's as if he or she has inherited 100 acres of land."[5]

Like many reformers, Prasad argues that Indian languages all carry the "legacy of caste," while adopting an egalitarian language like English can offer a tool of empowerment. In a 2007 interview, Prasad explained that "if you replace Hindi or Tamil by English you will greet by saying 'good morning.' The other person will respond saying 'good morning.' Both will look into the eyes and equality is established." That suggests that the traditional Hindi greeting "Namaste," meaning "I greet you / I respect you," is of lower social value. Unlike most Indians who condemn Macaulay for making India "bilingual," Prasad praises him as the "father of Indian modernity."[6] Not surprisingly, Dalit activists are among the most vocal supporters of English-medium schools.

A main vehicle for deconstructing these contradictions is a postcolonial literature rooted in the early nationalist movement. That movement effectively used English as a tool to confront the British imperial rulers with the injustices of colonial domination. Educated in Western democracy, nationalist leaders were able to vent their outrage on the rulers' own liberal democratic grounds and in the rulers' own language.[7] Contemporary writers from across the former British Empire have similarly used their former subjugation and lingering marginality as a "counter discourse" and source of creative inspiration with English amplifying their voices.

The Indian-born author Salman Rushdie's groundbreaking article "The Empire Writes Back with a Vengeance" makes that point clear. As Rushdie tells us, this body of work lays bare the residue of past wrongs, "placing politics at the centre," while "decolonizing" English with "new rhythms, new histories, and new angles on the world."[8] Evoking a transnational identity, it upends the notion of languages situated at either the center or the periphery, evoking a transnational space inhabited by people traveling across linguistic and cultural boundaries.[9] Of course, there are Indians and others who rail at what they believe is an "orientalist bias" in anglophile writers like Rushdie. They question the ability of such writing to capture the same historical and cultural significance as a vast body of less recognized yet "complex" and "stimulating" works in the Indian languages seem to do.[10]

These examples suggest a mix of history, politics, and economics roiling beneath English as it works its way through modern-day India. English indisputably enjoys favor despite wavering national policy, an enduring caste structure, and an evolving class system tied to language access and ability, now under the watch of a pro-Hindi government. As elsewhere, it grants access to global markets, attracts foreign investors, selectively opens doors to prestigious national and foreign universities, and promotes job mobility to anglophone countries among the more privileged. English also serves as a "link" language throughout the country's multilingual landscape. In recent years, English has become caught in a high-stakes tug of war between nationalist fervor promoting Hindi and the consequent pushback from speakers of other Indian languages. That clash bears serious consequences for the quality of education that the economically and linguistically diverse population of Indian children receives.

English Then and Now

English in India competes on a vast linguistic terrain of regional politics where multilingualism is built into a federal system of twenty-eight states and eight union territories defined largely by language. India is almost unique in the large numbers of people who speak more than one language. Its legally enshrined multilingualism distinguishes it from other postcolonial countries, like Namibia and Nigeria, where official English monolingualism has been considered critical to nation building and developing a national identity. That is not to deny, as we will see, persistent efforts of Hindi speakers to impose their language on the entire country.

Data from the 2011 census, completed over seven years, showed that India had 19,569 different overlapping languages or dialects reported as "mother tongues" within a population of 1.21 billion. The census winnowed the 19,569 down to 156, including twenty-two scheduled languages, ninety-nine non-scheduled languages with ten thousand or more speakers, and thirty-five "others" with fewer than ten thousand speakers classified under a particular language. More than 43 percent of the population spoke Hindi, up from 41 percent in 2001. Hindi was the fastest-growing language, adding one hundred million speakers over those years.[11] These figures and the method of identifying languages nonetheless have been hotly contested. One commonly invoked alternative source, the People's Linguistic Survey of India, conducted over four years with three thousand volunteers beginning in 2010, found that India counts over 780 languages.[12]

Many Indians speak both a local and a state language, which may or may not be the same. Some also speak Hindi or English to a greater or lesser degree. On one end of the economic spectrum, the educated classes speak and read either or both languages. On the other end, illiteracy runs rampant. This diverse linguistic backdrop magnifies other disparities, posing significant challenges to equalizing educational access across socioeconomic lines. Yet the constitution, theoretically modeled on the European nation-state of a culturally and linguistically homogeneous people, merely pays lip service to the country's linguistic pluralism.

English ranks only forty-fourth in native speakers among India's languages. It ranks second after Hindi in those who speak it to some degree as their first, second, or third language. Though English is the preferred second language among about a third of Indians, it has been estimated that as few as 4 percent are proficient in it. On the 2020 *English Proficiency Index*, India ranked only fiftieth out of one hundred countries, placing it within the low-proficiency band far behind other former British colonies like Kenya, ranked at twenty-second, and Nigeria, at thirty-fourth.[13] Fluent English speakers are a privileged minority, just as they were in colonial times when the British strategically used English to maintain their power by creating a class of loyal government workers. British colonialists set their sights on modernizing Indian society. A key part of their agenda was to spread Western knowledge and Enlightenment ideology to the masses and to replace the Hindu religion with Christianity. The purpose was both economic and moral. Yet they disagreed widely over whether that project could best be carried out through English or the vernaculars—a view favored by traders, merchants, and business owners—and what role, if any, the classical languages should play.[14] English won out for a time.

The most memorable legacy of that dispute was Thomas Babington Macaulay's ill-reputed "Minute of 1835," presented to the British Parliament in discussions leading up to the English Education Act. Macaulay, a law member of the Supreme Council and chairman of the Committee on Public Instruction, firmly believed in the overall superiority of English—that it was "better worth knowing" than Arabic or Sanskrit, and that it stood "preeminent" even among the Western languages. His startling dismissal of centuries of scholarship in Sanskrit and other languages of India brings clarity to more recent efforts supporting decolonization. "Whoever knows that language," Macaulay said, "has ready access to all the vast intellectual wealth which all the wisest nations of the earth have created and horded in the course of ninety generations." Macaulay most infamously asserted that English would create a class of Indians sufficiently "Anglicised" to bridge the gap between the British and their Indian subjects—"Indians in blood and colour, but English in taste, in opinion, in morals and in intellect."[15] That view held sway for what became the Indian upper classes. Macaulay's pro-English position had important short-term effects on education policy in India. It also had lasting effects on a discourse that made English the critical medium for conveying knowledge. Yet despite the prominence it has gained especially in modern times, Macaulay's "Minute" had virtually no impact in the South; nor did it end the controversy over English versus vernacular schooling.

As the British spread education, they eventually reached a compromise between the orientalist view that the most efficient way to spread European knowledge was through vernacular languages and the anglicist position insisting on English.[16] Policy gradually shifted away from universal English and toward local languages for the middle castes. The elite were educated in English from primary school through to university. Both types of schools, separated by class, were common in the major cities. English was necessary to gain entry into secondary schools and, for the select few, into British universities. The lower oppressed castes, whose members rarely made it beyond primary school, were educated if at all in their indigenous languages. The cultural and economic capital attached to English made it a desirable skill, which the masses wished they could acquire.

Between 1858, when the British East India Company transferred power to British Crown rule (the "British Raj"), and 1947, when India gained independence, English gradually developed into the language of government and education. It allowed the Raj to maintain control by creating an elite gentry schooled in British mores, primed to participate in public life, and loyal to the Crown. It also helped cultivate a scientific and technical base that served the needs of Europe's Industrial Revolution. This "English-vernacular divide" has had lasting effects on India's language policy, identity, and class structure.[17] It has given English-medium instruction both symbolic and real capital, which translates into upward mobility. Meanwhile, the country has no national language to serve as a unifying force in shaping a national identity.[18]

An Uneasy Compromise

The constitution adopted in 1949 reached a fragile and arguably majoritarian compromise on the language question. In the debates over language policy, nationalist leaders disagreed on which Indian languages should be included and what role English should assume. The two leading figures were Mohandas Karamchand (Mahatma) Gandhi and Jawaharlal Nehru. Gandhi, who had led India to independence and admired the Boers' language pride when he lived in South Africa, supported Hindustani—the vernacular spoken by Hindus and Muslims in the North—as the national language. He feared that English would hurt efforts to organize the masses in freeing themselves from colonialism. He also believed that all children should be taught in their local language. "Parents who train their children to think and talk in English from their infancy," he warned, "betray their children and their country."[19] Gandhi described his own painful introduction to English in the schools.

> For the first three years the mother tongue was still the medium. . . . The pillory began with the fourth year. Every thing had to be learnt through English—Geometry, Algebra, Chemistry, Astronomy, History, Geography. . . . I know now that what I took four years to learn of Arithmetic, Geometry, Algebra, Chemistry and Astronomy, I should have learnt easily in one year, if I had not to learn through English but Gujarati. My grasp of the subjects would have been easier and clearer.

My Gujarati vocabulary would have been richer. I would have made use of such knowledge in my own home. This English medium created an impassable barrier between me and the members of my family, who had not gone through English schools. . . . I was fast becoming a stranger in my own home.[20]

The anglophone writer Keki Daruwalla has described the intensity of that alienation even more graphically. "Colonial history," he says, "shows that language can be as domineering as any occupational army. It supplants myths, whole iconographies, worldview, ideology. It ushers in its own symbols and its own values. An armada of new texts sails in. Old dogmas and bigotries are swept away and exchanged for new ones."[21] Gandhi did not live to see his dream of a constitutional democracy realized. In January 1948, he died from three bullets fired at point-blank range. The perpetrator believed that Gandhi had forsaken Hindus by opposing the "two nations" approach creating a separate Muslim-dominated East Pakistan (now Bangladesh) and West Pakistan (the current Pakistan).

Jawaharlal Nehru, the prime minister following independence, and whose first language was English, was equally clear-eyed on the language question. While English, he recognized, had "opened the doors and windows of foreign thought [and] and science," it had "created a gulf between [those] who knew English and those who did not . . . and that was fatal for the progress of the nation." He agreed that India needed its "own language" and accepted Hindi as long as it was not forced on non-Hindi speakers but left to evolve over time. Yet he also saw that English was an emerging international language that large numbers of people had to learn, perhaps even under compulsion. He especially believed that English was key to advancing science and technology.[22] On that last point, time and the growth in India's technology sector have proven Nehru right.

The *Report of the University Education Committee* of 1949, the country's first statement on higher education, echoed those concerns. "The use of English," the report noted, "divides the people into two nations, the few who govern and the many who are governed, the one unable to talk the language of the other, and mutually uncomprehending." Yet the committee also recognized that English had exposed India to "the ideas of modern civilization, to modern science and philosophy." Seeing English as the "world language" on the near horizon, the report maintained that English was essential to keep the country connected to the rest of the world.[23] From that report, independent India set the course of language policy for future decades, building an educational barrier that those without adequate English skills still cannot overcome.

In the end, the 1949 constitution reflected a compromise between the Anglo-educated leaders in the independence movement and traditionalists from the Hindi heartland. By a narrow vote, the framers adopted a Sanskritized Hindi as the "official" though not the "national" language. They also set out to develop Hindi in place of English within fifteen years, though pro-English forces had argued for a more widely used colloquial form of Hindi that they might understand.[24] Neither Hindi nor English held any connection to the masses that felt especially alienated from the elites educated in English. Those class distinctions have remained through the years.[25] So has a national reverence for Hindi. Even today, National Hindi Divas (Hindi Day) is observed across India every September 14 to mark the adoption of Hindi as the official language by the Constituent Assembly in 1949 and to promote the language as the country's *matru bhasha* (mother tongue). The day is marked by Hindi-centered events, including literary festivals, essay writing competitions, and poetry sessions. Awards are given to the heads of select government departments and ministries for outstanding efforts in promoting Hindi.

The constitution included a list of fourteen languages, which were spoken at that time by over 90 percent of the population. The list has since grown to twenty-two in what is called the "Eighth Schedule." Upward of thirty-eight additional languages now look to be recognized. Some of them fall under the umbrella of Hindi. Though it's difficult to determine objective selection criteria, languages included in the schedule are more widely used in government, education, and the media and consequently receive government funds to help make them even more accessible.[26] The constitutional framers failed to appreciate that the "essence" of India was multilingualism, both individual and societal, and that each area was linguistically and culturally heterogeneous. Nor did they understand the role of language in constructing and transmitting knowledge for all students, including many underprivileged groups. It has been suggested that if they had recognized that importance, especially to education, then India would be in a better situation today.[27]

English is not among the languages in the schedule. Article 348 of the constitution nonetheless states that "all proceedings in the Supreme Court and in every High Court . . . shall be in the English language."[28] Though the constitution has been amended several times in the intervening years, this remnant of colonialism remains in force and largely unchallenged. Given the small percentage of English speakers in the country, it prevents many individuals who cannot afford high-priced English-speaking lawyers from seeking or successfully gaining redress in the country's highest court. The limited number of judges and lawyers who can speak the Queen's English, moreover, has created a huge backlog of cases. The situation, however, seems to be slowly changing in practice. Since 2019, the Supreme Court of India has made judgments available on its website in six languages: Assamese, Hindi, Kannada, Marathi, Odia, and Telugu. And though Article 348 also requires that English be used for all bills and acts of the central and state legislatures, these are now published in English, Hindi, and other languages. Below the national level, the legal system is more accommo-dating. Many state high courts also have moved to the regional language with the approval of the president.[29]

Article 30 gave minorities, "whether based on religion or language," the right to "establish and administer educational institutions of their choice.[30] As for public schools, the amendment gave a nod to India's linguistic pluralism with priority to teaching children in their home language, yet the wording was not mandatory. It provided that "it shall be the endeavor of every State and of every local authority within the State to provide adequate facilities for instruction in the mother-tongue at the primary stage of education to children belonging to linguistic minority groups." It authorized the president to issue directions to any state that he considered "necessary or proper."[31] The term "endeavor" effectively weakened the law, while the categorization of "linguistic minorities" was mean-ingless, since all languages in India can be numerically considered "minority" languages.[32] Practically speaking, with the large number of mother tongues. in-cluding numerous dialects, even considering the reportedly undercounted 156 identified in the 2011 census, it was simply not feasible to comply. And so mother tongue education became schooling in the regional language or in the majority language in areas where the population did not speak the state's official language. This limited strategy put speakers of tribal languages at a serious disadvantage.[33]

Over the years, it became clear that the constitution's plan to "Hindi-ize" the country could not be accomplished in fifteen years. The Official Languages Act passed in 1963 continued English as a "subsidiary official language" in ad-dition to Hindi for official purposes including deliberations in Parliament. The Act met regional opposition. Hindi activists in the North, fearing that English would threaten national unity, passionately opposed it.[34] Non-Hindi speakers, including Tamils in the South, believed it betrayed Nehru, who in 1959 had as-sured them that the government would not impose Hindi without their con-sent.[35] For the speakers of Tamil, a Dravidian language with a classical literature on a par with Sanskrit, English was and remains a shield against Hindi. As the fifteen-year sunset for English approached in 1965, those lingering concerns ig-nited riots in the state of Madras among non-Hindi-speaking groups who feared losing government jobs and promotions in favor of Hindi speakers. Led by Tamil-speaking students, the uprisings continued for several weeks. Schools and colleges were closed. Hindi books were burned. Hindi signs were torn down. Five people set themselves on fire in protest as a mass movement in neighboring states reached epic proportions and provoked police violence. The death toll mounted to over sixty.

In the following months, the government tried to reach a compromise, but to no avail, maintaining the status quo by default. The crisis revealed once again the language question to be a chronic point of contention in Indian politics. It also was a harbinger of things to come. In 1967, the government, under Indira Gandhi, amended the Official Languages Act to guarantee that Hindi and English would be used indefinitely as official languages. Individual states could adopt laws to officially use their regional language. The language compromise underestimated, but also facilitated, the dominant role that English would come to play in the global marketplace. Educated Indians would realize in the years to come that their well-recognized skills in mathematics and science had a global economic value that could be marketed both at home and abroad, especially through the internet. The one condition was proficiency in English.[36] Development policy built on science and technology has since made English the preferred language in higher education, government, and business.

In 1968, following the recommendation of the National Education Commission (1964–66), popularly known as the Kothari Commission, the Parliament adopted the "Three Language Formula" into the National Policy on Education.[37] The "formula" is not a formal policy but merely a "strategy" for using English and Hindi as "link languages" taught as subjects in all schools throughout the country indefinitely. The idea was for students to learn the mother tongue or regional language as their first language. The second and third languages would be English and another modern Indian language in Hindi-speaking states (primarily the northern and central regions) and English and Hindi in non-Hindi-speaking states. Though accepted in principle, the formula has not been widely implemented. Some states have honored it more in the breach than in the observance depending on resources, linguistic politics, and the availability of teachers who speak regional languages. The official medium of instruction is typically the regional language and not the students' mother tongue.

Southern states like Tamil Nadu have resisted teaching Hindi and only include English and the regional language in the curriculum. A number of Hindi-speaking states have likewise not included any South Indian language but rather teach Sanskrit as the third language. Meanwhile, the constitution effectively leaves the choice of language to parents. Some states have used this fallback to encourage English-medium schools, even permitting private entrepreneurs to enter the market. Private schools do not follow the formula. Many of them use English as the first language.

From a political perspective, the attempt of the Three Language Formula to reach a balance between diversity and uniformity was understandable. But from a practical point of view it was inequitable and unworkable. It meant two languages for Hindi-speaking states (Hindi as the regional language plus English) and three languages for all the others, which gave Hindi speakers in the North an unfair advantage. It also ignored the local languages spoken by millions of Indian children. Switching from the mother tongue to a "school language" was complicated enough. In a country like India, where millions of people don't speak any of the twenty-three acceptable school languages or even a standard local language, complying with the policy proved formidable.

The Push toward Hindi

The language question is a recurring subtext in Indian politics. When the nationalist Bharatiya Janata Party (BJP) took control of the government in 2014, the newly elected prime minister Narendra Modi's pro-Hindi actions sparked vigorous debate across broadcast and social media. The BJP stood in stark contrast to the Indian National Congress, the legacy of Mahatma Gandhi and Jawaharlal Nehru's struggle for independence. Rather than embrace the European concept of one nation, one language, Gandhi and Nehru had envisioned a secular India built on diversity. The rise of the BJP to power came as a shock to English-speaking drawing-room bureaucrats who had dominated Indian politics for nearly six decades.

Modi was the first prime minister born after India's independence from Britain. He ran on a platform of breaking India loose from its "imperialist, anglophile past," rejecting English as the country's lingua franca. There also was a hint of egalitarianism or leveling in his rhetoric. Having risen from poverty helping his father sell tea at a railway station, Modi promised to uplift India's "dejected millions" and to realize the potential of India's demographic advantage in young people eager for well-paying jobs beyond the informal sector. He believed that promoting Hindi, the "language of the masses," would boost that agenda. In 2019, Modi won reelection by a landslide, once again appealing to nationalism and tapping deeper into widespread angst over illegal immigration and fears of terrorism.

To what extent Modi has made good on his original promises is highly questionable. While India's place in the world has risen and its economy has modernized to some degree, the consensus among Indian activists and liberal political analysts is that the gap between upper and lower castes has become wider. Modi has barely moved the needle on educational opportunity, while his language policies promoting Hindi have swelled the rolls of private English language schools that it has taken a world pandemic and economic crisis to pull back. Many Indians argue that he has polarized the country and created a "poisonous atmosphere that has dehumanized minorities."[38] Following his reelection in 2019, *Time* magazine's cover story featured Modi as "India's Divider in Chief."[39] It has been said that with his "populist" rhetoric, Modi claims "the moral monopoly of representing the majority, while declaring the opposition as illegitimate, morally bankrupt and fiscally corrupt."[40] Modi and his party have proven that the push toward Hindi is not simply about language. It is a key component in turning India into a Hindu nation, excluding Muslims in particular. His Hindu-nationalist agenda came to full light in September 2019 when he upended seven decades of history, repealing Articles 370 and 35a of the Indian constitution and thereby stripping Indian-controlled Kashmir, India's only Muslim-majority state, of its statehood and its autonomy.

Modi's initial moves toward Hindi upon taking office were not unexpected given the anti-English position of nationalist party leaders, who often refer to India's English-speaking elites as "Macaulay's children."[41] Modi, his ministers, and party members of parliament all initially took the oath of office in Hindi, and some even in Sanskrit. The day following the inauguration, the Ministry of Home Affairs issued a memo advising that all government employees and corporate and bank officials "should . . . give priority to Hindi" on all official social media accounts, including Twitter, Facebook, Google, YouTube, and blogs. The government later explained that the directive only applied to the Hindi-speaking northern states. The Official Languages Act of 1963 provides no penalties for not using Hindi in official communications. The national government can only promote Hindi through persuasion and encouragement. The not-so-subtle pressure sparked a rash of criticism, especially from the southern states. Yet even in the North, as one midlevel bureaucrat in New Delhi told the press, "many of us have not written in Hindi for years. We're really struggling with this new directive although it is by no means mandatory. Frankly, if a letter takes 10 minutes to write, I am now spending 30 minutes on it. It's quite frustrating."[42]

Modi soon announced that he would conduct all government business in Hindi, though he spoke English reasonably well. He delivered on his word. And though he informally used English as a common language with world leaders, he used Hindi in his 2014 address to the United Nations and in official meetings when US president Barack Obama visited India the following year. He did the same when French president Emmanuel Macron visited in 2018. The government even created a separate division within the Ministry of External Affairs to promote Hindi abroad.

In 2017, Modi's information and broadcasting minister at the time, Venkaiah Naidu, whose mother tongue was Telugu and who, like Modi, was fluent in English, declared it a "misfortune" that Indians were giving "too much importance" to English, developing what he called "an English mindset." Naidu hailed Hindi as a "national" language and "an important link all over [India]."[43] Political pundits were quick to point out that the Indian constitution made no mention of a "national" language but rather designated Hindi as the "official language of the Union" and English to be used for "official purposes."[44] Later that year, following anti-Hindi protests, Indian president Ram Nath Kovind urged doctors and lawyers to use Hindi and other regional languages to better connect with the people they served. In response to claims that without English India could not prosper economically, Kovind queried, "How come China has become an economic power by speaking Mandarin?"[45]

The Hindi question flared up once again in early 2018 when the government announced that it was willing to spend US$63 billion to make Hindi an official language of the United Nations. Opponents pushed back at yet another sign of "hyper-nationalism gripp[ing] the ruling Bharatiya Janata Party." For Hindi film director, producer, and screenwriter Priyadarshan, not only was Hindi not the national language; it was "not the language aspiring India wants to learn."[46] Again, according to the 2011 census, only 43 percent of Indians spoke Hindi or one of its fifteen major dialects. In fact, Hindi was spoken by more than 50 percent of the population in only eleven of the country's twenty-eight states, all of which were concentrated in what is known as the "Hindi heartland" of north-central India. In 2017–18 the government allocated Rs 50 million (US$750,000) to spread Hindi worldwide through international conferences, endowed university chairs, and scholarships and fellowships for foreign students to study the language.[47]

Venkaiah Naidu, who had since become vice president, once again got his comeuppance when he called English an "illness" left behind by the British. Making the case for primary schooling in the mother tongue, he cited studies suggesting that the preference for English was causing children to develop feelings of inferiority.[48] His intent was not simply anti-English or even pro–mother tongue instruction. It was clearly pro-Hindi. Naidu praised Hindi as "the symbol of social, political, religious and linguistic unity of the country." It was not possible, he said, to progress in India without it.[49] The remarks went viral through the Indian press and social media. The response from the Indian diaspora was especially sharp. English was "a boon, not a burden," argued a *Wall Street Journal* opinion piece directed to an international audience. It gave India "an economic advantage" while holding a "dizzyingly multilingual country together." Though some Hindi activists might condemn the "India love affair" with English as a mark of "mental slavery," it said, "were it not for English India's 'multibillion-dollar-IT-services industry'" would not exist, nor could the country "ward off the threat of Hindi imperialism."[50]

In a similar vein, Naidu's speech set off a Twitter storm of criticism requesting him to "stop using English language, mobile phones, electricity, internet, planes" (@Tufailelif, September 15, 2018); "hop[ing] all ministers take cue from this message and call back their children who are in foreign universities" (@vivek1307, September 15, 2018); and claiming "the disease is not English . . . [but] this kind of constant and pseudo-nationalistic attempt to make us forget our history while giving us no alternative" (@theshashidhar, September 14, 2018). One tweet best summed it up: "Language wars are embers that are always burning and such statements only stoke them" (@PradRham9, September 14, 2018).

A similar Twitter frenzy erupted in early 2019 when the press reported that the central government's New Education Policy would make Hindi compulsory for students up to grade eight. Most of the more than two thousand tweets defended English and regional languages against the onslaught of Hindi. Yet a small minority recognized that Hindi carried capital in the job market in the South as well as in the North, a reality that younger non-Hindi speakers are just beginning to comprehend (#StopHindiImposition, January 9, 2019). The government immediately disavowed the press report as "mischievous and misleading."[51]

Notwithstanding all the official pro-Hindi posturing, Modi the avowed nationalist ascribes to capitalist economics. He understands that English is vital to continuing the country's rapid economic growth. In 2015, on a visit to France, Modi brokered an agreement with the French government to attract more Indian students to French institutions, where courses are now increasingly offered in English. While the original 2020 goal was ten thousand students, in only two years the number reached seven thousand.[52] By 2019, it was at ten thousand, a year ahead of the target date.[53] Modi has relied on his English skills to visit other industrialized democracies including Germany, Canada, and Sweden with the intent of forging political alliances and attracting more businesses. All three countries have strong English language skills within their populations. In 2019, there were more than 160 English-speaking Swedish companies in India, including furniture giant Ikea and fashion retailer H&M, which had over thirty-five hundred people working in the country in addition to an online store. Meeting with global business leaders at the Bloomberg Business Forum in New York City that year, Modi used India's strength in English to promote foreign investment in the country. "India's democracy and judiciary, and reliance on English, give investors confidence," he said.[54]

As these developments reveal, the controversy over Hindi has laid bare age-old tensions over English. Nationalists consider English a threat to India's linguistic and cultural diversity. Despite their leader's strategic use of English in the global economy, they argue that economic and political success is not necessarily contingent on learning English and that Hindi symbolically represents India as a unified nation internationally. For some, the dominance of English throughout government and the courts limits public discourse to a small elite class, denying most Indians basic rights and an equal opportunity to participate in public life.[55] Back in 2014, civil service exams in English had sent Hindi speakers to the streets, protesting that the exams were biased against them. Supporters shot back, insisting that English is a "must-have skill" for an effective "bureaucrat."[56] As one commentator described the situation, "India finds itself sandwiched between a relentlessness that assumes semi-religious overtones to banish English and a vehemence with latent subnationalism to reject Hindi."[57]

That being said, the debate over language in India is not confined to Hindi and English. Modi's rise to power has coincided with rising interest in India's regional languages and identities. An organized movement toward "language equality" is on the march. Speakers of scheduled languages push for official status on a par with Hindi and English. Speakers of non-scheduled languages look to be included in the "Schedule." A language rights conference held in Chennai in Tamil Nadu in 2015 resulted in the Chennai Declaration of Language Rights, modeled on the Universal Declaration of Linguistic Rights adopted in Barcelona back in 1996. Among its demands, it called for all "citizens of the Indian Union" to enjoy the "rights to get all education in their mother tongues."[58] A group called the Campaign for Language Equality and Rights (CLEAR), including representatives of forty languages in India, has become a vocal proponent for recognizing the "mother tongue" as a "basic cultural right" linking speakers to their "economy" and "socio-cultural system."[59] Meanwhile, momentum is slowly building to unite non-Hindi states against the central government's push toward Hindi in public life.[60] Supporters chafe at the cultural hegemony of Hindi and the loss in political and economic power that comes with it.

The organized action supporting India's vernacular languages reflects wider trends in Indian society. India's leap into global capitalism, accelerated with a loan in 1991 from the International Monetary Fund, brought with it liberal economic policies. Those policies have given rise in smaller towns to a new Indian middle class whose growth in consumption has brought a proliferation of newspapers and consumer advertising and a growing demand for transacting business in regional languages. In 2012, the *Times of India* launched a newspaper in Bengali. Another prominent English daily, the *Hindustani Times*, has put more staff and resources into its Hindi "sibling" *Hindustan*.[61] Even the domestic call center industry has expanded its scope beyond anglophone countries and is targeting the domestic Indian language market.[62]

Private Schooling

Before looking at recent language in education policies promoting Hindi, an overview of public and private schooling and the relationship to English puts the Hindi question in clearer perspective. Many Indian parents, from the wealthiest to the poorest, still press for their children to be taught in English notwithstanding the political sparring over Hindi, the nationalist resistance to English, and the resurgence of interest in regional languages. These attitudes and values are tied to the aspirations that parents have for their children, whose success is a measure of family background, identity, and status. In a country infamous for its caste system, building a social hierarchy around English is not surprising. The fact that Indians equate English with social status and quality schooling is not a new phenomenon. As in other former British colonies, English has long held symbolic and real value as the language of power, prestige, and spatial mobility with higher employment opportunities.

This trend has become increasingly pervasive. It also has moved deeper down into the social strata due in part to the reforms in 1991 carrying free market economic policies and an ideology of competition. The ensuing software boom and expanding service sector have made learning English all the more compelling. Even among parents who speak no English or speak it poorly and where English is not spoken in the community, the demand for English is inconceivably high. For some it is the way to break the cycle of poverty and servitude. Even public schools that use Hindi or another local language are introducing English as a subject in the early primary grades in response to parental pressure and private school competition.

Indian schools fall into three main categories: government, government aided, and private unaided (with subcategories "recognized" or "unrecognized"). Government schools are plagued with systemic problems including insufficient funding, high teacher absenteeism, crumbling infrastructure, high dropout rates, and uneven compliance with laws and regulations. Like South Africa, the English program in India suffers from inadequately trained teachers with poor English language skills who teach by rote memorization rather than developing the ability to communicate. With wide economic migration across India, from rural to urban areas and across regions, schools enroll children from a wide mix of ethnic and language backgrounds. As a result, students may not share a language in common with each other or with the teacher. The idea of teaching in the mother tongue may have no practical meaning, while adding English into the mix makes a difficult situation impossible. To make matters worse, teachers are often assigned to rural areas where they do not speak the local languages. With fifty students in a class, teaching becomes even more problematic. India's performance in the 2009 Programme for International Student Assessment (PISA) was so shockingly low, coming in second to last among seventy-two countries, that the government bowed out of the 2012, 2015, and 2018 rounds. The scores were related, in part, to "reading literacy."

The results of a 2018 household survey across rural school districts were especially eye opening. Only 72.8 percent of students in rural schools left grade eight with basic reading skills in any language. And while the gap between government and private school students had narrowed slightly, it was still significant. Among students in grade three, only 20.9 percent in government schools could read a grade-two text, while the number for private school students was almost double at 40.6 percent. Among students completing grade eight, only 69.0 percent of government school students could read a grade-two-level text as compared to 82.9 percent in private schools.[63] These figures were scant cause for celebration on any count. Even the bar for private schools was set quite low regardless of the economic and social disparities between public and private school students. Given the multilingual nature of many Indian states, this widespread failure in learning outcomes was at least partly the result of many students in both sectors, whether taught in English, in Hindi, or in the state language, learning in a language that they did not fully understand.

India's schooling problem is to some extent a legacy of the first decades of independence. Article 45 of the 1949 constitution's "Directive Principles of State Policy" stated that within ten years the state "shall endeavor to provide . . . free and compulsory education" for all children up to the age of fourteen.[64] Deciding who was going to pay for it was another matter. The central government largely left it to the provinces, which later became states, and to private initiative, as was the pattern under the Raj. The system suited the middle and upper middle classes, who were content with the elite private schools and looked toward government-aided higher education for upward mobility. Denying primary and secondary education to the less privileged classes would keep them socially in their place and politically powerless. From the very beginning, the government allocated a disproportionate share of funds to technical and higher education, which left large swaths of the poor without basic schooling.[65] That explains why India counts millions of primary school children out of school and at the same time boasts one of the highest number of students receiving bachelor's degrees in science, technology, engineering, and math (STEM) subjects.

Part of the push for private schooling, especially among the middle and lower classes, lies in government policies that ignore the benefits of learning English as a subject at an early age. The Three Language Formula suggests that government schools defer teaching either Hindi or English as a second language until grade five. Some public schools have started introducing English sooner, and even offering English-medium instruction in grade one despite the benefits of learning initially in the mother tongue. The numbers, however, remain small.[66] And so parents who equate education quality with early and intensive English have few options outside of private schooling.

As the *Financial Times* reported in 2015, parents were "voting with their feet" and choosing to place their children in English-medium and primarily private schools, whatever the cost.[67] The prime value placed on English instruction is adding a new dimension to the caste system based on English proficiency. Driving the growth in India's private school market are the same forces operating in other emerging economies. Rising incomes offer families greater spending power. For upper- and middle-class professional families, elite private schools, some requiring English for admission, set their children on a track to study abroad at English language universities. In 2019–20, over 193,000 students from India attended colleges in the United States alone, second only to China.[68]

Growing competition to gain a place at a prestigious anglophone university has generated a booming sector of private international schools, primarily in English. In 2017, 268,500 students between the ages of three and eighteen attended these relatively high-priced schools, an increase of 70 percent over the previous five years.[69] By 2019 the number of students had jumped to 373,000.[70] By 2020, international schools affiliated with the Cambridge International Examination (CIE) numbered over four hundred, while those affiliated with International Baccalaureate (IB) boards numbered 185, with more expected to come given the high demand among Indian parents.[71] At the secondary level, both boards require students to study a foreign language, most commonly Spanish for its broad utility on the job market. Mandarin, Korean, and Japanese are slowly attracting interest with the rise in multinational companies establishing offices in India.[72]

Private schools brand and rebrand themselves to appeal to consumerist cravings for elite global schooling. English is a critical part of the draw. Walk through major cities during the admissions cycle and you will find billboards reaching forty feet into the sky offering opportunities for success and upward mobility— an advertisement depicting a middle-school student playing golf with the words "Nurturing, excellence, the future begins here"; another showing a young child gazing up at a miniature airplane that he holds high above his head, with the words "Learners wanted for exploration" for "classes Pre-Nursery to IX."[73] While the associations seem out of sync with conventional educational values and purposes, the message and the target audience could not be more direct. Some families give their children a head start in private preschools to prepare them for admissions interviews at age four. Educated mothers proficient in English are now considered essential for children to succeed in school, causing high anxiety for those not up to the task.[74] Parents engage the services of English language coaching schools and tutoring centers to keep their children competitive.

For families further down the socioeconomic ladder, the private school picture is strikingly different. These families make enormous financial sacrifices, up to 30 percent of their incomes, to pay modest tuition fees. Some reportedly sell family property held for generations.[75] When families cannot afford private schooling for all their children, they choose in favor of their sons. Education in largely unregulated or semi-regulated private English-medium schools is presumably their child's ticket out of poverty and into the middle class, or so they are led to believe. Some opt to send their daughters to so-called convent schools originally founded by English-speaking Christian missions. Here, too, the teachers are often poorly trained and lack English proficiency. Not unlike the state-run schools, students are still caught in a never-ending cycle of memorization and translation from Hindi or whatever the state language is. The results prove less than satisfactory, especially for students hoping to advance to higher education where instruction is primarily in English.

The trend toward private English-medium schooling extends down to the most disadvantaged communities in the Hindi heartland. That brings us back to the opening story of Dalits and the Goddess of the English Language. For some Dalit intellectuals, the idea of English freeing Dalits from their "stigmatized identity" is simply an implausible assumption. For others, the campaign to promote English brings to light the great divide between those who speak English and those who do not, which has much to do with caste, class, and gender. The temple met especially strong opposition from nationalists. For them the term "Macaulayite" is a negative reference to the Anglicized Indian elite.[76] Even those in the region who support teaching English argue that it should not come at the cost of not learning the home language and culture. Prominent intellectuals maintain that learning in the mother tongue, at least until secondary school, keeps children connected to their social and spiritual roots. For Dalit activists, however, that argument is simply an "upper-class ploy" to deny Dalits opportunities as the Brahmans denied them Sanskrit in the past.[77] English can be the passport to a white-collar job, even for Dalits. As Dalit scholar D. Shyam Babu put it, "English is no longer just a language—it's a skill. Without it you remain an unskilled labourer." That notion is especially salient given the link between English and a new middle class rising up through India's booming technology industry.[78]

Neerav Patel, the acclaimed Dalit poet and critic, has raised the related question of whether mother tongues in India evoke the same meaning, or the same status, for everybody. He argues that the concept of mother tongue is not homogenous. It puts those like Dalits, who may speak a nonstandard variety of a regional language, at a disadvantage. Considering the social significance and the role that languages play in identity politics, he says, English offers Dalits the possibility to redefine themselves. Like Chandra Bhan Prasad, the Dalit political commentator, Patel sees English as separating "destiny from system," enabling Dalits from diverse regions to imagine a "pan-Indian Dalit unity" in a language that does not "normalize" caste discrimination.[79] It frees socially marginalized groups like the Dalits from the "rigid linguistic hierarchies" common to Indian languages.[80]

English for the Poor

At the lower end of the economic ladder, the rush toward English has created an explosion of low-fee private (LFP) schools. Dating from 1991, when free-market economic policies ushered in a spirit of privatization and market competition, these schools now cover 95 percent of the private school sector. As of 2018, about 70 percent of fee-paying schools charged less than US$13 a month. Roughly 45 percent charged less than US$7 a month. Between 2010–11 and 2016–17, their rolls swelled from forty-four million to sixty-one million. At the same time, enrollment in government schools fell from 126 million to 108 million in the twenty-one of the country's states for which data is available.[81] That said, in 2020, the loss in family income and school shutdowns during the COVID-19 pandemic generated a clear swing back from private to public schools, with private school enrollment down from 37.2 percent to 33.6 percent for boys and from 30 percent to 27 percent for girls. The decline was most evident in rural India.[82] It remains to be seen whether those losses will revert after the pandemic. In the meantime, poor and marginalized communities remain disproportionately represented in government schools.

A small number of commentators extol the benefits of LFP schools on various measures of "quality," however defined, and see them as "democratizing" access to English.[83] A much larger chorus of critics argues that the level of instruction in no sense measures up to that of the 5 percent of schools that serve the elite and are affiliated with major education boards. LFP schools, they claim, are English in name only and merely reproduce existing social and economic inequalities.[84] They fail to provide an education of any higher quality than the government schools in the same locality.[85] Teachers are typically paid a fraction of what their government-school counterparts earn. Some teachers have no more than a secondary education, and many have poor English skills. As the owner and operator of a chain of schools in Hyderabad admitted, in some of these schools the teachers "[could] not speak English let alone teach in English."[86] Unlike the elite fee-paying schools where all classroom interactions are in English and students are encouraged to speak English both in and out of class, even the best LFP schools, like English programs in government schools, often teach through rote learning and make active use of the students' home language despite English being a key deciding factor for parents. Classroom assessments typically use a multiple-choice format in lieu of questions that require critical analysis and longer written answers.[87] It is not unusual for students to achieve passing grades during their ten years of education only to fail the English common high school exams.[88]

Critics dismiss the positive findings on these schools for their questionable assumptions, faulty methodology, and case-specific conclusions. The vast range of models used and the diverse populations served make the evidence on outputs admittedly inconclusive. Comparing LFP schools to government schools, to other private schools, or even to each other demands more rigorously controlled studies than may be possible. Studies cannot adequately account for the input factors that affect learning outputs, not the least of which is the language of instruction and assessment—whether English, a vernacular language, or both. Schools differ across categories in many other ways, including grades covered, management style, their definition of the "poor," and parental education background and level of support. Many of the studies, moreover, cover small samples of schools.

A 2014 report by Human Rights Watch on more objective input measures painted a damning picture.[89] Many of these schools were housed in makeshift and even open-sided buildings. Some lacked adequate plumbing and restroom facilities. Some were in the homes of providers, who lacked any educational background. Some offered instruction for only part of the day while students attended public schools for the rest of the day to take advantage of free lunch, remain eligible to take state and national exams, and maintain the option to transfer to another government school should the private school close down.

Often found in urban slums and rural areas, LFP schools are largely "unrecognized" (unregulated under state law). They have faced special challenges in the wake of India's landmark Right of Children to Free and Compulsory Education Act (RTE), which took effect in 2010. Adopted over six decades after independence, the Act tracks the 2002 amendment to the Indian constitution, Article 21A, making free and compulsory education a fundamental right for every child between the ages of six and fourteen. It also directs how the article must be implemented.[90] All primary schools, both aided and unaided, must now be "recognized" by the government for meeting standards covering teacher qualifications, facilities, and curriculum. The RTE has caused thousands of unrecognized schools to close, though many remain open due to lax enforcement. Private unaided schools, as well as government and aided schools, must reserve 25 percent of seats in each class for economically weaker students (EWS), that is, children from marginalized groups in the community. The state assumes the cost. With more applicants than seats, students are chosen by a state lottery. That is exactly the "system" that the middle-class parents in the film *Hindi Medium* were trying to exploit to their child's advantage.

The Act was not well received among the more privileged classes and especially within the elite private school network. Both administrators and parents feared that the presence of poor and unprepared students would diminish the quality of education and harm their students' "right to learn."[91] Those concerns led the Society for Un-aided Private Schools to mount a legal challenge to the constitutionality of the 25 percent mandate. In 2012, a three-judge panel of the Supreme Court, in a 2–1 decision, gave a lengthy and nuanced response. The Court held that while Article 19 (1) (g) of the Indian constitution granted the right to establish private schools, the state under Article 19 (6) could impose reasonable restrictions in the public interest, since education is recognized as a "charitable" activity. Yet the Court also held that unaided schools established by religious or linguistic minorities were exempt from the mandatory quota under Article 30 protecting the right of "all minorities, whether based on religion or language" to "establish and administer educational institutions of their choice," and Article 29 (1) protecting the right of citizens to conserve their "distinct language, script or culture."[92]

In 2014, the Supreme Court extended the ruling to include minority schools receiving government aid.[93] The exception remains controversial. A question not before the Court but equally significant was the practical limits of Article 30 as applied. Whatever language the school chooses for instruction has to be a language in which final exams are offered. Yet outside of the major scheduled languages, exams are not held anywhere in many smaller minority languages, which puts those communities at a serious disadvantage in running their own schools.[94]

Some advocates have hailed the RTE Act as a long overdue effort to equalize educational opportunities for the poor. Others have denounced it for ignoring how to manage linguistic diversity within the classroom and protect the rights of children who attend English language schools and are expected to learn in a language that is either unfamiliar to them or is not their home language. Still others have condemned the government for partially handing over to non-state actors its constitutional obligation to provide free and compulsory education. In practice, the 25 percent mandate has fallen short of its transformative potential. It has opened the door to higher quality English instruction only for the minute number of disadvantaged students fortunate enough to land a place in a well-resourced school. Though the EWS population accounts for more than 80 percent nationwide, less than 10 percent of eligible children attend private schools under the RTE provision.[95] In 2016–17, only 16 percent of the covered schools nationally were even participating in the program. Only 20 percent of the available seats were filled, much of the fault lying with the schools.[96]

A number of factors dissuade or prevent the poorest families from seeking admission to the most elite schools under the RTE allowance. High out-of-pocket expenses despite tuition waivers, distance from home, lack of adequate information on school quality, burdensome administrative procedures, negative experiences during the admission process, fear of discrimination after admission, and resistance on the part of private school leaders have all swayed family decisions on school choice. And though the Act purportedly aims to promote educational equity, it requires no additional academic support to level the playing field for the 25 percent who must compete with students who begin school with significantly more linguistic and social capital.

A closer look at the LFP school sector raises yet more concerns related to English and how it bears on access, quality, and equality. Here we enter the world of "budget private schools" or "micro schools." These are fee-paying for-profit schools organized or funded by business philanthropists, private entrepreneurs, and investors who have seized the opportunity to fill a gap in the market. They typically operate through networks of transnational advocacy groups wedded to a market agenda.[97] Some of these schools belong to a "school chain" and peddle a "brand" of low-cost education. A main selling point to poor parents is that they provide English-medium instruction at minimal cost.[98] In some cases, the sponsoring companies also offer a higher quality parallel program to more privileged students at equally inflated tuition fees. In other cases, they have totally abandoned initial projects serving the poor and moved on to more profitable "affordable" schools for the middle class. While the Indian government does not permit for-profit schools, a common operating structure is for the school to be owned by a trust. The trust contracts out management to a private company that earns profits from the fees paid for its services.[99] Investment and venture capitalists are known to provide the funds for low-cost private schools where conventional banks are unwilling to lend to not-for-profit organizations, especially ones with such high-risk profiles.[100]

Bridge International Academies, with investors like Mark Zuckerberg of Facebook, Bill Gates of Microsoft, the World Bank, and a list of well-placed venture capitalists, is a leading example of initiatives focused on poor populations. It also is the most controversial of the low-cost for-profit chains of schools and an anathema to unions and NGOs.[101] Beginning with its first school in a slum area in Nairobi, Kenya, in 2009, Bridge runs or supports nearly two thousand schools and has educated a million children in the past decade. In 2016, Bridge opened four schools in India. The chain's website promises "quality education at a price point [on average US$8 per month] accessible to families living on US$2 a day per person or less," though in reality the total costs are much higher. It boasts an average teacher attendance rate of 100 percent, addressing a problem that continues to plague India's public schools. It also boasts a high student achievement rate. In 2019, Bridge students in Kenya outperformed the national average for the fifth consecutive year in their primary leaving exam.[102]

Bridge's website makes no mention of local or regional languages. The assumption is that all instruction is in English. Despite all the website accolades, using an "academy in a box" model, which aims to deliver high quality education through standardization, has opened the teaching methods to question. To save costs on teacher training and monitoring, teachers reportedly read scripted English lessons from centrally linked computers. Ministerial officials and school inspectors familiar with the approach have described it as "robotic," "too controlling," "lacking creativity," and even "neocolonial."[103] Whether such "teacher-proof" robo-instruction is better than what the government schools provide is uncertain. It depends in part on how you define "better" beyond basic literacy and numeracy. Whether it provides poor children with the critical analytic skills and broad-based knowledge they need to prepare them for college or for middle-class jobs as their parents imagine, the response is more likely to be negative. Whether foreigners should be making a profit from educating poor people more fundamentally raises serious political and humanitarian questions.

Given the troubling state of primary and secondary education across sectors, it is not surprising that parents are also seeking other private avenues as an adjunct to compensate for the deficits of mainstream schools. In most of India, private supplementary tutoring (PST) has become a critical adjunct to schooling. The chief motivating factors are high performance on exams and on university admissions tests. The trend is more common in urban areas among parents who are better educated, have the requisite funds to spare, and feel a sense of group pressure and competition.[104] Yet it filters down into rural areas as well. Private tutors and tutoring companies hawk their services in ads posted in schools, trains, buses, and metros and on lampposts and trees. Websites for companies like TutorVista and My Private Tutor promise to identify the ideal academic support in person or online. A mushrooming number of coaching centers now offers spoken English lessons through smartphone apps.

This "shadow school system" is variously considered as "social opium," a "status symbol," and an "assertion of low-caste ambition."[105] And though the support offered cuts across the curriculum, the demand for English is significant and plays a key role in perpetuating a quality/inequality dilemma. In a perverse way, it also has increased dropout rates, pushing out of formal schooling some of the poorest students whose parents believe that all hope for their children's future is lost if they cannot afford private tutoring.[106] As the Indian author Arundhati Roy put, it, "We are witnessing the re-Brahminization of education, this time fitted out in corporate clothes."[107] And English is doing its bidding.

English clearly is driving education policy across the board. To stem the mass exodus to the private sector, some states have moved toward English instruction. Jammu, Kashmir, and Nagaland have made English the main medium of instruction in all public and private schools. Andhra Pradesh announced in 2018 that its elementary schools would convert to English. Other states are experimenting on a more modest scale. Tamil Nadu, Maharashtra, and Delhi offer English-medium instruction as an option in state schools.[108] In April 2018, five thousand schools in Uttar Pradesh converted to English. As a head teacher told the *Economist*, the changeover to English increased the school's enrollment by over 50 percent from 117 to 185. Yet again, with many parents lacking literacy in any language, children face even more hurdles when forced to initially learn in a language that no one speaks at home or in their community.[109]

A Drawn-Out Legal Battle

In 1994, the authority of private schools to teach through English exploded into a legal battle that engaged the Indian courts for the next two decades. At that time, the state of Karnataka, by government order, mandated that the language of instruction in grades one through four in all "government recognized schools" had to be either the mother tongue or Kannada. Schools found in noncompliance would be closed down. When the state rejected applications from 1,400 schools that sought permission to teach through English, the schools formed the Associated Management of (Government Recognized—Unaided—English Medium) Primary and Secondary Schools in Karnataka and challenged the order on constitutional grounds. The state argued in response that it had the constitutional right to impose "reasonable" regulations on education institutions. As the litigation moved in fits and starts through the lower courts, the state introduced English as a subject beginning in grade one in all government and aided Kannada-medium schools. The policy was believed to empower the disempowered, and particularly Dalits, who could not afford to send their children to private English-medium schools.[110]

It took twenty years for the case to reach the Constitution Bench of the Supreme Court of India. In an opinion spanning sixty-six pages, the Court wove together constitutional strands of free speech, individual autonomy, and the limits of state interference with quotes from the philosopher John Stuart Mill, political theorist Harold J. Laski, and US Founding Father and fourth president James Madison. In the end, the Court held that the state could not prevent private unaided schools from teaching in English notwithstanding the state's expert testimony on the benefits of mother tongue instruction. Nor could the state require linguistic minorities to learn only through their mother tongue in primary schools.

The Court found that the government order violated the constitutional right of linguistic minorities, even in state-funded schools, to "conserve" their language and culture (Art. 29.1) and to "establish and administer" schools "of their choice" (Art. 30.1). The Court extended the argument to non-minority unaided schools. Here it affirmed the right of private school parents and children to "freedom of speech and expression" (Art. 19.1), including the right to both impart and receive knowledge, and from there the right to "establish and run" schools and choose the language of instruction. It even recognized the right of teachers (Art. 19 (g) (1)) to "carry on any occupation." "Freedom," the Court said, meant "absence of control by the State."

The infringement on constitutional rights, the Court concluded, had no direct bearing on education standards and went beyond the state's interest in protecting children from harm or protecting national interests. As for schools run or aided by the state, with the exception of linguistic minorities, the Court allowed them to mandate learning in the mother tongue in the primary grades as long as parents could decide what their child's mother tongue might be.[111] This proved to be an empty right for many migrants, especially in the capital Bangalore, the hub of India's business processing industry. It was impossible to find teachers with the range of language skills needed, while most families could not afford private schooling in English. And so in the end, it effectively was a partial win for Kannada.

The decision was reminiscent of two landmark US Supreme Court rulings from the 1920s—*Meyer v. Nebraska* and *Pierce v. Society of Sisters*—upholding the rights of parents to control their child's education as a matter of substantive liberty in the economic realm.[112] US law has since abandoned the economic underpinnings of those rulings, though the courts still cite the decisions in cases addressing parental rights. Here the Indian Court decided the case within a liberalized (or modern-day neoliberal) economy where the medium of instruction could ultimately determine one's future opportunities in the job market.

But this was not simply a case about education and parental rights. The implications reached deep into the limits on government authority to mandate the use of languages by private actors. The Court weighed on the side of "liberty of choice" and individual autonomy. Given the high consumer demand for English, the ruling constrained without eviscerating the government's ability to promote Indian languages.[113] At the time, there were only 422 officially recognized English-medium lower primary schools across the state of Karnataka. The real numbers were in the thousands. By one estimate, the number of English medium schools had grown from 6,033 in 2006–7 to 10,647 in 2012–13, while the number of Kannada schools had progressively declined.[114] In the wake of the Court ruling, the government had to update its records while it faced a flood of applications to start new unaided primary schools free to teach in English. The number of private schools teaching in English soared.

In another way, the decision was a blow to equality. Though it directly protected the interests of the private school community, it indirectly denied children in government schools equal access to English instruction. It took another five years of political pressure and new leadership for the Karnataka government to turn the policy around. Once again, English and its role in maintaining a class divide became the focus of controversy. In 2018, the state announced that it would open English-medium sections in 947 government schools beginning in grade one in the 2019–20 school year, extending to grade two the following year. A motivating factor was the sharp decline in public school enrollments as parents opted for English-medium programs in the rapidly growing private school sector. Campaigns like #SaveGovtSchools were pressing the new government to address the problem. The education department deployed teachers to visit local households and promote the program.[115]

Kannada activists, including noted literati, strongly opposed the initiative for its cultural implications. The award-winning Kannada poet, playwright, and film director Chandrashekhar Kambar likened the decision to that of Thomas Babington Macaulay. As discussed earlier, Macaulay is often credited (or blamed) for solidifying English as the administrative language in British colonial India.[116] Yet many poor parents, and especially the Dalit community, welcomed the opportunities for higher education and employment that English would offer children from lower socioeconomic backgrounds. Dalit leaders pointed to the hypocrisy of certain writers who advocated learning in Kannada yet sent their own children to private English language schools. They questioned why disadvantaged students in government schools alone should be responsible for "safeguarding Kannada."[117]

Finding the Link

The competing arguments for and against English instruction in Karnataka reflect similar strains on the national government as it pushes its pro-Hindi agenda. In 2019, an emphatically pro-Hindi draft national education policy, prepared by a committee established by the Ministry of Human Resource Development, pushed back heavily against using and relying on English and the power it wielded in the hands of the upper classes. Extolling the clarity of Indian languages and the vast store of ancient, medieval, and modern literature, the report railed against the "unfortunate trend in schools and society toward English as a medium of instruction and as a medium of conversation" despite the small numbers of speakers. It spoke directly to members of the "economic elite," who had "adopted English as their language" and often used it "as a test . . . for the jobs that they control," thereby "marginaliz[ing] . . . large sections of society based on language." This "power structure of language must be stopped," the report said, for society to reach "true equity and inclusion." While English had become *an* international common language in areas like science and technology, the report claimed, it had not become *the* international language as expected back in the 1960s. It called upon everyone to value native languages and to increase their use in the workplace, education, and daily conversation.

High on ideology but low on new vision, the report once again reaffirmed the Three Language Formula. It promoted education in the home language until grade five but preferably until grade eight and continued as a subject wherever possible. All students would be "immersed" in three languages from preschool and grade one so they could read "basic text" by grade three. The report's original text required the teaching of Hindi in non-Hindi states. In a flash of déjà vu, the proposed plan sparked protests in southern states, and especially in Tamil Nadu, which has resolutely used a two-language formula of English and Tamil and made clear that it would not change that policy. #HindiIsNotTheNationalLanguage began trending on Twitter. Attempting to do damage control, the minister also took to Twitter, clarifying in a video that the report was only a draft, that the government supported all Indian languages equally, and that it would not impose any language on educational institutions (@DrRPNishank, June 1, 2019). In a head-spinning turnaround, the committee dropped the provision mandating the teaching of Hindi in non-Hindi states, claiming it was an "inadvertent error" in the original text.[118] An editorial in the *Indian Express*, aptly titled "Tongue Twisted," excoriated the committee for promoting native languages at the expense of English.[119]

The final policy, adopted in August 2020, definitively stated that no language would be imposed and that the three languages would be the choice of states, regions, and the students so long as two of the three languages were native to India. The medium of instruction until at least grade five but preferably until grade eight, in both public and nonpublic schools, would be the home language, the mother tongue, or a local or regional language "wherever possible." The implications of that requirement for the numerous English medium schools remained uncertain, though the conditional "wherever possible," along with lax enforcement, might result in little change. The plan only fleetingly mentioned English, particularly in reference to bilingual textbooks and instructional materials in science and mathematics and "high quality" offerings in languages, including English, in secondary schools.[120] It was silent on the role of English in the overall curriculum.

In view of India's vast linguistic diversity, its high level of internal migration, and the political sensitivity of Hindi, the remaining question is what role English and schooling together might play in linking Indians to each other and to the world. The answer lies in weighing the benefits and burdens of English in the context of India's colonial past and the economic and social strains of the present. To start demands a look at English itself. With some exceptions, Indians view English as a neutral language between Hindi (which is actually many dialects) in the North and the commonly used local languages in the South. At the same time, it remains a "foreign" language, evoking for some Indians memories of colonial subordination with any hope of economic progress tied to the language of the colonizer. The form of English spoken runs along a spectrum of Englishes, from pidgins influenced by the country's indigenous languages, to a form of "nativized" English used by "vernacular elites," to Standard British English used by urban professional elites.[121]

The profile of first-generation English speakers has been described as "schizophrenic." They continue to think and feel in their mother tongue, yet they need English in their professional lives. But it's not just enough to communicate. Living in the shadow of the Raj, you need to talk with "style," with a "modern touch," and in an "impressive manner" to display that you are socially skilled and well educated. The eagerness of many Indian youth to shed their "Indian accent" has given rise to an industry of private English coaching centers that benefit those who can afford to pay. As the cofounder of Kings Learning, an English language teaching company that targets Indian nationals, put it, "There is a glass ceiling in English and if you don't speak English, there is only so far you can go in the corporate world."[122]

English proficiency is both a form of social capital required for those who claim membership in the middle class as well as a means of ranking oneself and others by level of proficiency. Reminiscent of the Bollywood films noted earlier, a woman interviewed for a study of middle-class Indians in Bangalore, the capital of Karnataka, put it well. "If you know English," she said, "people look at you differently" (i.e., with approval/respect), even if they themselves "don't understand what you're saying." Other interviewees talked of the transformative power of English.[123] The director of the Centre for Media Studies in New Delhi noted that "people still think that if you know English, your life is set." But he also believed that the " 'myth' [had] been broken that only English, and English alone, can earn you an assured future."[124]

There was a time when young people who studied English became teachers or entered the civil service. The new economy has opened up a range of career options including call centers, business processing offices, and multinational corporations as well as British and American publishing houses looking for editors with English language skills. English dominates university education, opening doors to high-paying professional, managerial, and scientific careers. In the southern region in particular, 75 percent of university students study in English.[125] Tamil Nadu, where Hindi instruction is rare, accounts for twenty-six of the top-ranked institutes of higher education in the country as measured by the National Institute Ranking Framework. All the Hindi-belt states combined account for only twenty-one.[126]

Numerous students in the STEM fields have traditionally been drawn to the first-rate research laboratories and facilities in the United States, the United Kingdom, and Canada. They are now broadening their sights to English-taught programs in the Netherlands, France, and China. English translates into higher income even controlling for age, social group, schooling, geography, and ability. As the coauthor of a report on the "English edge" told the *India Times*, "Politicians who don't like English are captains of a sinking ship. Higher education in English helps us get better integrated into the globalized organized sector and labour market. Those without access to higher education in English are being left out.[127]

Far more Indians, in fact, are fluent in a hybrid third "language" of sorts, "Hinglish," than in English. That is not surprising, since most Indians are not exposed to English on a regular basis. They combine their limited English with Hindi, which remains the language of Bollywood films, of four of the five news-papers of wide circulation, and of the most popular TV news and entertainment channels. Even among young well-educated urban dwellers, Hinglish holds a certain cachet as a "modern but locally grounded" way to be "bindaas" (cool). Over the years, Hinglish has moved from the streets to television, films, ad-vertising, fiction novels, and even business and politics, raising the hackles of purists on both sides of the debate. Films with titles like *Jab We Met* ("When we met") are becoming commonplace.[128] Young bestselling authors like Anuja Chauhan pepper their prose with jokes and references in Hinglish that readers presumably understand.[129] "The new first generation elite," says novelist Namita Devidayal, "don't have that old snobbery about the Queen's English." Yet many of them, educated in English language schools, still have "the Queen's English" to fall back on as they ride the crest of the global economy and compete against other new English speakers from countries like China and Argentina.[130] For the Indian author Pavan Varma, "The truth is that for most Indians English has largely become an instrument of social exclusion; the upper crust of India has presided over this linguistic apartheid, while the rest of India has consisted of victims or aspirants."[131]

That said, unless thoughtfully managed, English could be a hidden trap for disadvantaged students, especially if they are the first English learners in their family.[132] This is especially the case for lower-caste students and those from so-called other backward classes. English might be their fourth language alongside their home language, the local link language, or the school or state language. These students theoretically understand the value of English for job oppor-tunities and advanced study, yet they lack social supports like internet access, English newspapers, TV programs, and films, as well as the cultural and prac-tical motivation to learn the language well. They also lack reinforcement at home from parents whose English skills are poor at best and who may lack literacy in any language. Meanwhile, particularly in rural areas, English is less relevant to their everyday lives and the way they construct the world. Even for the most eager and ambitious students, schooling solely in English can alienate them from their families and communities despite its promise of material privileges. Compared with most other countries where younger people have considerably better English skills than those who are older, in India the gap between young graduates and adults over forty is narrow. That suggests that schools have failed to make progress on English over the past decades.[133]

In the final analysis, English is neither the problem plaguing India and its education system, as Hindi nationalists claim, nor the total solution as others like the Dalits suggest. Aside from inadequate funding and poorly trained teachers, the real problem is that, especially given the multilingual nature of many states and the high rate of internal migration, far too many children—whether educated initially in English or Hindi or in a state or regional language in government or private schools—are initially learning through a language in which they lack full proficiency. And so the challenge is twofold. First, it is to convince parents across the economic spectrum that children succeed best when they first learn in a language that they understand. Second, it is to assure that schools, both public and private, provide early and sustained instruction in English, properly timed and with needed supports—in addition to and not in lieu of initial mother tongue instruction—to guarantee upward mobility and to preserve India's place in the global economy.

Beyond schooling, the even larger challenge is to convince extreme nationalists that using Hindi as a lever to create a monopoly in language and thought defies, and can destroy, the very essence of India as a multilingual and multicultural democracy.[134]

PART III

DEFYING THE MONOLINGUAL MINDSET

Defining the Deficit

The United States traditionally has been ambivalent toward languages despite the country's diverse origins and makeup. In August 2016, two headlines in the *New York Times* captured that ambivalence. The first, "Bilingual Invitation to Arizona Mayor Draws an Angry Reply, in English," was disturbing.[1] The second, "Know English? For New York Cabdrivers, That's No Longer Required," was baffling.[2] Each presented a different picture of the country's changing linguistic landscape and the competing attitudes those changes have evoked.

In the case of Arizona, the issue was a message from the US-Mexico Border Mayors Association inviting members to a meeting to discuss common concerns the two countries faced in the global economy. The invitation drew the ire of Mayor Ken Taylor of Huachuca City, who refused to accept an invitation sent in, what he called, "Spanish/Mexican." In a strident email Taylor shot back, "One nation means one language and I am insulted by the division caused by language." He would not tolerate the association's "putting America subservient to Mexico." With the local press weighing in on the exchange, an *El Paso Times* editorial got to the core of it. What seemed like a "passing kerfuffle," the editors concluded, was "symbolic of the shortsightedness in the national conversation about language." An invitation intended as an "inclusive" gesture was interpreted as "divisive."[3]

Taylor's diatribe was not just about language. With Hispanics projected to soon outnumber Arizona's white non-Hispanic population, it reflected deeper concerns over changing demographics. The forty-one million people nationwide who speak Spanish as their first or home language are a particular target of hostility. Taylor was the only mayor to decline the invitation, and so there is no way to know if others shared his views. If they did, Taylor's public display and the media response evidently gave them pause. As the *New York Times* explained, the "fuss" echoed an enduring disagreement over the use of Spanish that has reared its head in other contexts, from singing the national anthem in

Spanish over the radio to students reciting the Pledge of Allegiance in Spanish or speaking Spanish on school buses.

The alleged Spanish "threat" entered the 2016 presidential primaries when Donald Trump blasted a rival, former Florida governor Jeb Bush, who is married to a Mexican American, for speaking Spanish on the campaign trail. "He should really set the example by speaking English while in the United States," Trump quipped, signaling what became an administration openly hostile to "foreigners" and the languages they speak. On the other hand, in a presidential debate that same election year, Marco Rubio, the Republican senator from Florida, questioned whether Ted Cruz, his Republican senatorial rival from Texas, actually spoke Spanish.[4] The early Democratic Party presidential debates in 2019 once again brought language to the fore with candidates trying to outdo each other in speaking a few words of Spanish, some more convincingly than others. Spanish seems to be a litmus test for how "American" or "Hispanic" you are, or how culturally sensitive you are, depending on which voter base you're trying to engage.

The week following the Arizona story, the New York taxi driver article presented a different narrative in a part of the country with different views on multilingualism. Here the issue was not whether Spanish was permissible but whether English proficiency was essential for New York's cabdrivers. With 96 percent of yellow taxi drivers coming from 196 countries other than the United States, New Yorkers more often than not encounter drivers who primarily speak languages like Bengali, Spanish, Haitian Creole, and Wolof. The issue was to what extent they must also speak English. Responding to concerns that English was presenting a barrier for immigrants looking for work, the city council eliminated the English proficiency exam as a requirement for obtaining a taxi license.

The announcement met mixed reactions from New Yorkers. Some thought the English question was immaterial as long as riders reached their destination. Others worried about safety or the ability of drivers to discuss directions and fares. Taxi drivers of various nationalities voiced similar reservations.[5] Yet none of the responses even touched on identity or whether it was acceptable to publicly communicate in a language other than English. Nor did they target the immigrant population, even indirectly. This was New York City, perhaps the most ethnically diverse city in the country, where multiculturalism is celebrated in scores of parades, feasts, and street fairs that dot the calendar year—from the St. Patrick's Day Parade in March to Bastille Day street fairs in July to the West Indian Parade in September.

That is not to suggest that all New Yorkers welcome newcomers and their languages. In the first two years of the Trump administration, even the Big Apple witnessed a 20 percent increase in reports of discrimination based on national origin and immigration status. A video from May 2018 that went viral will stay etched in the city's memory for some time. In it we see an angry customer at the Fresh Kitchen, a casual eatery in Manhattan, ranting against employees who were addressing each other and customers in Spanish. We hear the man, a lawyer, threatening to call immigration authorities and shouting, "Speak English; this is America."

Immediate responses from city officials and the general public were palpably condemning. The mayor made clear on Twitter that New York is a "welcoming city" where 8.6 million residents speak over two hundred languages. The city's commissioner of immigrant affairs told the press that such incidents, "while horrifying, are not commonplace—they also don't belong in our city." Social media lit up with a similar level of collective outrage.[6] Protestors held a "Latin party," complete with mariachi bands and a taco truck, outside the lawyer's home. The lawyer apologized on Twitter and insisted that he was not a racist. In an effort to clear the political air, the following fall the city's Commission on Human Rights, in partnership with *El Diario* and *Univision 41*, hosted a community forum under the slogan "Habla Español, esta es América!" ("Speak Spanish, this is America!") to inform immigrants of their rights.

Arizona and New York arguably sit at different points on the spectrum of cultural and linguistic diversity and public attitudes toward those differences. The scenarios might vary in countless communities in between, as other videos and news stories have since suggested. Nonetheless, the juxtaposition of these three accounts is still eye opening. In the first, we see a closed "America" that lashes out at linguistic differences when feeling threatened by outsiders, especially the dominant number of Spanish speakers. In the second, we see a more open "America" that refuses to let those same differences prevent immigrants from pursuing the "American dream." In the third, we see much of the second but a shade of the first.

That apparent dichotomy, however, can also be misleading. Underneath the two visions lies a linguistic passivity along with an unspoken belief that English monolingualism is the norm. Even though multilingualism is admired among the educated elite, when the young mayor of South Bend Indiana, Pete Buttigieg, threw his hat into the 2020 presidential campaign, left-leaning media outlets sarcastically referenced his signature "polyglottery" in speaking eight languages.[7] Overall, some segments of the population grudgingly tolerate linguistic diversity in society given the country's immigrant undertones, while most others merely give it lip service at the level of public policy. These competing sentiments, officially welcoming outsiders into the fold but fearing ethnic strife and divided loyalties, have been shaping attitudes and policies on the primacy of English since the beginning of the republic. They also have marginalized the place of other languages in the school curriculum and led to a deficit in language skills that sets the United States behind in a world that is moving further toward multilingualism.

Past to Present

Given its a history as a settler nation, the country's conflicted view toward language is not surprising. Language and culture have long been disputed terrain. Building and maintaining a cohesive political community from successive waves of newcomers has been an ongoing challenge. Though English is the common language, it is not carved into law as French in France or Italian in Italy. It simply functions that way through a maze of customs, institutions, and policies that legitimize English throughout public life. And while the nation's Founders shared a late eighteenth-century worldview where equating language and national identity was just gaining ground in the Western European notion of the nation-state, they also understood that they were embarking on a unique nation-building project. During and following the Revolutionary War, English held no special status as a symbol of national unity. In fact, the national government issued many officials texts in French and German to accommodate new immigrants. The only early hint of a national language came from Noah Webster, whose reference works promoted a brand of "American" English distinct from British English.[8]

Through the following decades and centuries, as immigrants have poured into the country in numbers beyond the Founders' imagination, each successive wave has brought another surge of angst over potential threats to English or to national identity and security. In the late 1800s, when Germans in the Midwest pressed to maintain their language in public and private schools and industrialization brought new groups of immigrants from southern and eastern Europe into the country, tolerance turned to hostility. What had begun as an unspoken "English first" policy in the nation's early days slowly morphed into "only English." In 1889 and 1890 alone, eight states faced legislative proposals to limit the use of languages other than English in schools.[9] In 1891, the National Education Association affirmed the "right of the child to an education in the English language."[10] In 1905, a commission on naturalization convened by President Theodore Roosevelt recommended that English language ability become a precondition for US citizenship. The next year, the mandate was put into effect. It was later expanded during the 1950s Cold War era to reading and writing English.[11] That requirement remains intact, with some exceptions for age and ability.

Following World War I, suspicion of foreigners and their languages reached unprecedented heights. Just three days before he died in January 1919, in a letter written to the president of the American Defense Society, Roosevelt wrote, "We have room for but one language here, and that is the English language, for we intend to see that the crucible turns our people out as Americans, of American nationality, and not as dwellers in a polyglot boarding-house."[12] Roosevelt was not alone in unabashedly expressing those sentiments. Commissioner of Education P. P. Claxton, addressing a conference on "Americanization" that same year, declared, "English is the language of the United States. . . . It is the common means of expression; it is the air that we breathe, and without a knowledge of English one can never begin to know the American People and American ideals."[13] By 1923, thirty-four states had adopted laws mandating instruction only in English, either in public schools or in both public and private schools. Some states, like Texas and Nebraska, deemed it a crime for teachers to use a language other than English in the classroom. Ultimately the US Supreme Court, in the case of *Meyer v. Nebraska* in 1923,[14] struck down similar legal prohibitions. Yet psychologists still warned that bilingualism was not only "un-American;" it harmed children's cognitive ability.[15]

Languages other than English and their speakers still evoke in some quarters a sense of "otherness" and even danger to the nation's political and economic interests, as the Arizona "invitation" story points out. In recent decades, an "Official English" movement has gained force, most notably in response to the growing number and visibility of Spanish speakers. Over thirty states now declare English as the official language by law. In a 2019 survey, 77 percent of respondents nationwide believed that English should be the official language of the United States.[16] The movement nonetheless has failed at the national level despite repeated congressional proposals.

In any case, one would assume that a nation so rich in diversity would also be rich in language skills. Yet assimilationist attitudes of a century ago have been slow to change. Despite policies promoting education access and inclusion growing out of the 1960s civil rights movement and purported interest in other languages and cultures, the advantages of bilingualism too often remain beyond the reach of the foreign-born and their children. Differing views of how best to educate what we now call "English learners" or "dual language learners" have led to ambivalent and inconsistent statutes, regulations, and guidelines that draw on anti-discrimination principles grounded in race and national origin.[17] They speak in the language of "deficiencies" and "barriers" that children who speak another language at home bring to school.

For immigrant students, maintaining the home language is still widely viewed with skepticism; it is thought that it may impede academic achievement and social integration. Becoming what is considered a "true American" entails abandoning the home language, except perhaps for the small number of educated multilingual elites. The "good citizen" is one who honors the country's core symbols and principles (reasonable requirements), visibly embraces the ways of living and dress of an idealized mainstream, and does not speak an immigrant language in public. It's presumed that anyone who fails on any of those counts harbors feelings of social difference at best or lacks civic commitment and national allegiance at worst.

Adding to the language deficit is widespread resignation among the native born that they are not "good" at languages. They simply lack a "language gene." That belief is counterintuitive. A sizeable portion of the population of the United States is made up of immigrants or descendants of immigrants who hold genetic ties to countries where multilingualism is becoming more the norm than the exception. With so many individuals now searching for family members far and wide through popularized DNA testing, you would think they would question their faulty assumptions on language learning. But the problem goes even deeper than perceived inability. They see little incentive in learning another language when the rest of the world is acquiring English for its economic and social capital.

Yet all is not lost. Other forces, driven by technology, are challenging those misguided attitudes and broadening the country's linguistic horizons. The dominance that English has held for decades in modern-day media and the global soft power the language has gained from that privileged position now face competition. Capitalizing on the global multilingual turn, media giants like Netflix and HBO are using streaming services to spread local productions worldwide with the help of social media. Changes in the way people consume entertainment on any number of digital devices and the fact that more actors from across the world now welcome the opportunity to work in multiple languages have helped fuel these developments. Netflix, represented in 190 countries, offers subtitles in over thirty languages to market the content worldwide.

In the United States, the number of Netflix subscribers who view shows with English subtitles, like the Spanish thriller *La Casa de Papel* (*Money Heist*), is growing by the month and setting soft power in reverse. As the *Indie Wire* put it, with upward of one hundred non–English language series in production in 2018, Netflix was taking "binge-watching global."[18] As the 2020 COVID-19 pandemic sent the world into lockdown and online viewing became the prime source of cultural entertainment, Netflix engaged viewers across the globe with non–English language dramas like Spain's social allegory *The Platform* and the French mystery series *Lupin*, which attracted seventy million households in the first twenty-eight days of its release.

That is not to suggest that subtitles capture the deep meaning of the original language. Nor does it suggest that Netflix has thrown dubbing into the dustbin of history. In an effort to extend beyond what may or may not be a niche US market in non-English programming, Netflix is building an alternate production chain and recruiting actors to elevate the quality of its English versions. Netflix claims that in our "multitasking age," many subscribers in the United States find subtitles cognitively taxing or simply annoying. Among American viewers,

85 percent chose "dubs" over "subs" for *Money Heist*.[19] Netflix also dubs in over thirty other languages to reach a global market. Yet for foreign film aficionados, dubbing is a cultural travesty.

In 2018, HBO boldly laid new ground with its first non-English series, a thirty-two-episode, four-season adaptation of *The Neapolitan Novels*. The epic tale of female friendship evolves over six decades through four novels by the mysteriously pseudonymous Italian author Elena Ferrante. With more than thirteen million book copies sold worldwide in multiple languages and 2.6 million sold in the United States, the initial eight episodes, filmed largely in the Neapolitan vernacular, with English subtitles, were met with intense media fanfare. HBO sold the broadcast rights in fifty-six countries. Few American (and even few Italian) viewers could understand the dialogue. Yet much of the passion of the characters and the intensity of their interactions, amplified in the local accent and slang, would have been lost if the series had been dubbed either in English or in any other language. The gradations of local language and the code switching with Italian did not just signify social class and psychological tensions within and among the characters; they effectively drove the plot.

Such exposure to other language entertainment fosters cross-cultural awareness, especially when presented in the original voice. That incontrovertible fact came to light in 2020 when the Korean language film *Parasite* swept the Oscars and showed promise that even American viewers can overcome the "one-inch barrier" of subtitles. The class-struggle thriller, a US$35 million box office hit, was the first non–English language film to take home the Best Picture prize, along with three other Oscars, in the Academy of Motion Picture Arts and Sciences' ninety-two-year history.[20] The media coverage and the artistic quality and compelling story of the film itself opened a soul-searching discourse on intercultural diversity in the film industry, and also on American attitudes toward viewing films in a language other than English.

It remains to be seen whether that conscious awareness, on both counts, will push monolingual English speakers out of their comfort zone and inspire them to learn other languages. In the meantime, the United States is left with a "foreign language" deficit, with eye-opening numbers and failures in policy that merit close scrutiny.

Waning Numbers

In 1979, a Commission on Foreign Language and International Studies convened under President Jimmy Carter declared that "Americans' incompetence in foreign languages" was "nothing short of scandalous." The report warned that the country's "moat mentality" was obsolete and was harming the country's economy and diplomatic efforts. It highlighted an "untapped resource of talent" in the nation's racial and ethnic minorities, who could reach out beyond the country's borders. The hope was that Congress and the newly created Department of Education would effectively implement the commission's recommendations.[21] The following year, in what the *Los Angeles Times* called "a blistering indictment of our smug monolingualism," commission member Senator Paul Simon in his book *The Tongue-Tied American* added detail and immediacy to the commission's "call to action." Revered as Congress's most passionate promoter of language study, Simon warned that "cultural isolation is a luxury the United States can no longer afford, but we are culturally isolated."[22]

Looking back over those four decades, the commission's hope was never fulfilled. Simon's warning rings equally true today. The country's weak language capacity is as "scandalous" now as it was then despite even more pressing economic, social, and security needs. Language advocates continue to decry how the country is lost in a monolingual daze. The numbers tell it all. Three-quarters of the American population who speak a language other than English proficiently are "heritage speakers" who initially learned the language at home and not in school.[23]

The low numbers of individuals studying foreign languages and the limited languages they study paint a troubling picture of a country failing to develop a workforce in sync with pressing demands. As of 2014–15, the most recent year for which data is available, only 10.6 million, or 20 percent, of K–12 students in the United States were studying a foreign language or American Sign Language, down from 14.7 million in 2008.[24] Contrasting that number with close to 100 percent in countries like France and Romania and 96 percent in Spain reveals a deep "transatlantic divide."[25] Spanish, with 7.36 million students, was the most popular language in the United States across the grades, followed by French (1.29 million), Chinese (227,086), German (331,000), and Latin (210,030). Chinese enrollment had doubled since 2009. Noticeably absent from enrollment data were Arabic, Hindi, Bengali, and Urdu despite the increase in their reported numbers as languages spoken in the home.[26]

The disparities in language enrollments among the states were especially striking. In nine states, the figure was below 13 percent. In Montana, it was 8.5 percent. In Arizona and Arkansas, it was 9.1 percent. New Jersey was by far the highest at 51.1 percent.[27] Among K–8 programs, Spanish was overwhelmingly the most common language taught, followed by French, Chinese, and Latin.[28] At the high school level, Romance languages were the most common, with Spanish counting for 46 percent and French 21 percent. Chinese, German, and Latin were the only other languages that counted for more than 5 percent of language courses in secondary schools.[29] One of the most noteworthy developments was the mounting popularity of Chinese language classes, which were offered in primary and secondary schools nationwide with the exception of South Dakota.[30] These numbers presumably have shifted in the intervening years.

The United States has no nationwide foreign language mandate at any level of education. That's not surprising given the country's legal and political culture of deferring to the states on education matters while using the carrot of federal funds to incentivize state action in meeting federal interests. As a result, the states vary widely on foreign language policies. In 2014–15, a total of eleven states required a foreign language for high school graduation, sixteen states had no requirement, and twenty-four had graduation requirements that could be met by a number of subjects including a foreign language. Some twenty states did not even gather data on foreign language study.[31]

In some states, students now have a choice between a foreign language and another specific subject. In California, it's the visual and performing arts or technical career education. Oklahoma and Texas permit students to take computer-coding classes to fulfill their foreign language requirement. In Oklahoma, the results of this "swap-out" have been devastating. In 2015–16, only 12.6 percent of Oklahoma students were enrolled in a foreign language class. Between 2007 and 2017, one-quarter of the state's high schools eliminated these classes entirely. Rural schools suffered the most, in part the result of teacher shortages. Schools in forty of Oklahoma's seventy-seven counties, up from twenty-seven in 2007, offered no advanced-level foreign language class. The classes that did exist were mainly in urban areas, putting rural students at a particular disadvantage.[32]

The trend toward trading languages for computer coding has proven controversial. Language advocates argue that while computer skills prepare students for the world of technology, those skills are not comparable to the global and interpersonal understandings of language learning. Professor Simon Gikandi of Princeton University put the difference in perspective. "When I ask Google to translate 'Call an ambulance' into Swahili," he said, "it suggests 'beat up the vehicle that carries sick people.'" To that, Paula Krebs, MLA executive director, responded, "Code gives you Google Translate, but only context will get you the ambulance."[33] The inevitable question is whether it must be one or the other. With limited funds and an emphasis on preparing graduates for the job market, many educators and policymakers see no choice and mistakenly dismiss the personal value of language skills and their marketability. When budget cuts are made, enrichment programs like foreign languages and the arts are the first to go. Part of the problem is the general public, which underestimates the importance of language skills needed in a changing workplace. In a 2016 report, "The State of American Jobs," only 36 percent of respondents believed that foreign language proficiency was "extremely important" or "very important" for success in today's economy. Another 43 percent believed it was only "somewhat important."[34]

The downward slide in primary and secondary school language enrollments and policies is mirrored in higher education. Despite widespread growth in international programs, foreign languages have not weighed heavily in the equation. Almost three-quarters of 1,164 US colleges and universities reported in 2016, up from 64 percent in 2011, that they had expanded international offerings in recent years, primarily to prepare students for a "global era." Yet the number of foreign language programs, and the students enrolled, is moving in the opposite direction.[35] A hundred years ago, 89 percent of four-year institutions in the United States required previous study of a language other than English for admission. By 2020, the number had dropped to 25 percent.[36] Once students are enrolled, many institutions don't require any foreign language coursework as a condition for graduation.

Even many highly selective institutions, including Harvard, Columbia, and the University of Pennsylvania, permit students to "test out" of coursework if they can demonstrate proficiency, for example, through a high score on the SAT II or Advanced Placement exams. Columbia is the only member of the Ivy League where there is a foreign language admission requirement. The prestigious Middlebury Institute of International Studies in Monterey, California, known for preparing students to work in cross-cultural/multilingual environments, announced in 2019 that it would no longer require foreign language proficiency for admission. Nor would language study be part of the required curriculum. The motivating rationale was to increase the applicant pool and decrease costs in the face of declining enrollment. Along with the changes came a significant reduction in language faculty.[37]

As degree requirements have dropped, foreign language enrollments have fallen even further in a seemingly endless cycle. In the most recent reporting from the Modern Language Association (MLA), undergraduate enrollments declined by 9.2 percent between fall 2013 and fall 2016, the second largest decrease since the MLA began tracking this data in 1958. The largest decline, 12.6 percent, was in 1972.[38] While the drop between 2009 and 2013 could have been a blip following the 2008 economic downturn, recent data point to a continuing trend. Even accounting for demographics, the ratio of modern language course enrollments compared with the total number of students enrolled in colleges and universities fell from 8.1 percent of students in 2013 to 7.5 in 2016, a dramatic slide from a peak of 16.6 in 1965.[39] Especially notable is the 20.9 percent decline, between 2006 and 2016, in language course enrollments at community colleges, which typically serve less advantaged students. The drop at four-year institutions was only 6.7 percent.[40]

While the 2008 economic recession hit foreign languages harder than many other programs in the humanities, the underlying cause remains open to debate. One likely factor is the priority that colleges, along with educators and policymakers, now give to STEM programs, which in turn has influenced student interests. Another is the long-term effect of colleges' eliminating language requirements for admission or graduation. The MLA report questions whether the falloff might be the result of a 36.9 percent drop in federal funding for major international education programs between 2010 and 2016.[41] Those cuts, combined with other funding pressures on higher education, have whittled away at some of the institutional supports for language study.

Both private colleges lacking substantial endowments and public universities facing cutbacks in state support have eliminated smaller language programs or consolidated larger ones. In some instances, even majors in more heavily subscribed languages like Spanish, French, and German, have come under the axe as part of an overall retrenchment in liberal arts and the humanities in favor of job-oriented programs.[42] More recent data suggest that the full impact of the 2008 recession took several years to reach foreign languages. Between 2009 and 2013, higher education lost just one program. From 2013 to 2016, it lost 651. Spanish declined by 118 programs, French 129, German 86, and Italian 56.[43] Revenue shortfalls from the 2020 COVID-19 pandemic may drive the number of language programs down even further.

Program losses track the decline in student numbers. Even Spanish, despite capturing 50.2 percent of language enrollments, has been steadily declining since 2009, with a drop of 9.8 percent between 2013 and 2016. But it's not simply a matter of declining numbers. It's also a question of patterns of change that have wavered depending on political developments and social trends. Some of the enrollment loss may reflect tapering immigration from Mexico in the face of stepped-up border patrols and federal enforcement policies. Similarly, Arabic, a former standout with 46.7 percent growth between 2006 and 2009, has since been on a continuous downswing reflecting hostility toward predominantly Muslim countries, especially during the Trump administration. The only commonly taught languages on the upswing since 2013 are Japanese, increasing by 3.1 percent, and Korean, increasing by 13.7 percent.

The rise in Korean is especially noteworthy from both a cultural and a political perspective. Despite Korean being one of the most difficult languages for English speakers to learn, between 2009 and 2013 enrollment jumped by a phenomenal 45.1 percent.[44] More recent data show that upward of fourteen thousand college students in the United States are now learning Korean as compared to only 163 students two decades earlier. When Duolingo, the internet-based language program, launched a Korean course in 2017, in no time it attracted over two hundred thousand users. Taking a page from China's soft power playbook, the South Korean government has opened 130 language institutes in fifty countries, including support for an Institute for Korean Studies founded in 2016 at George Washington University.[45] Rising numbers of students from Korean immigrant families, as well as increased political focus on the Korean peninsula, are contributing factors.

Perhaps the greatest drive is the growing appeal of South Korean popular culture, or Hallyu, which the *Financial Times* described as a "gradually expanding stream to the west." Roughly translated as "Korean wave," it includes "K-pop" and "K-drama," where the South Korean entertainment industry has heavily invested in music and TV programs.[46] K-pop's trendy music and its heartthrob singers have inspired a cultural invasion disseminated through YouTube, Instagram, Twitter, and other social media. In October 2018, the number-one album in the United States featured lyrics sung primarily in Korean, a first for the industry. That year, K-pop helped entice 120,000 international students to choose South Korea for study abroad, a 40 percent increase from 2007.[47] The Korean Cultural Center in New York, a branch of South Korea's Ministry of Culture, Sports and Tourism, even offers summer courses tailored toward learning Korean through K-pop.

Though largely apolitical in South Korea, K-pop took a political turn in 2020, at least in the United States. In the midst of a pandemic, a polarizing presidential election, and racial protests, K-pop's "digital warrior" fans flexed their collective muscles and caught the attention of the media in a show of political empowerment.[48] That added visibility could well make the Korean language even more popular among young people searching for an outlet to make positive social change. In a less extensive way, Japanese pop culture, including anime, manga, pop music, and fashion, is moving students in the United States to study Japanese. The College Board's Advanced Placement Japanese Language and Culture Program and interest among young people of Japanese descent to reconnect with their ethnic roots are helping to cultivate the Japanese revival. The United States is not alone in its attraction to Asian languages. And it is not just the "superstars," Korean and Japanese, for which travel and culture are important motivators. The five fastest growing languages worldwide, among language learners of all ages, also include Chinese, Hindi, and Turkish, though for purposes more related to global politics.[49]

These unpredictable spurts of interest in one language or another make long-term programmatic planning problematic, especially for teacher hiring at the local level. The hiring problem is directly related to the declining number of young people taking advanced language courses. In 2016, only 16.5 percent of students studied beyond the introductory level.[50] That leads to progressively fewer college students specializing in foreign languages, and consequently fewer teachers and professors to help reverse the enrollment downslide and ultimately the national deficit. Even states and localities with the will to expand programs and with a stable level of language interest among students inevitably hit a roadblock when it comes to staff recruitment. In the 2016–17 school year, forty-four states and the District of Columbia reported a shortage of language teachers.[51]

"Sorting" through Languages

Examining the language deficit in numbers of students, programs, and languages is but an entry point into the larger question of winners and losers as English continues to mask the global multilingual landscape. Buried within those numbers lie concerns, often going unnoticed, that bear on access, opportunity, and social capital. Especially salient is systemic exclusion based on race and social class. Related to that factor are discriminatory assumptions underlying policies and practices that reflect educational inequalities and the role of transnational human capital in defining opportunities and benefits.

Throughout much of the twentieth century in the United States, bilingualism was considered a skill that only a select group of students could master. This aura of elitism excluded certain groups, including the economically disadvantaged and racial minorities. In 1961, former Harvard University president and noted educator James B. Conant wrote in his landmark book *Slums and Suburbs* that teaching "foreign languages" to urban school students was "educationally futile."[52] Like Conant, school administrators, counselors, and language teachers believed that these students would gain no benefit from studying another language. They were not headed for college, they would not travel to other countries, and they would probably fail the course in any case. So it would just be a "waste of their time."[53] Though an emphasis on English literacy was understandable, in the end this view denied certain students any exposure to other languages, cultures, and worldviews beyond their narrow enclaves.

More recent discourse on "languages for all" runs counter to these outdated attitudes. Researchers and language advocates now tell us that with employment opportunities and job mobility increasingly tied to language proficiency, the opportunity to learn a second language is essential to equalizing educational access across the racial and economic spectra. The implication is that schools can no longer justify treating language learning as merely an "enrichment" activity available to the most academically "gifted" students who typically are better recognized and served in more privileged communities.

Yet the rhetoric still falls short of the reality. The figures suggest "sorting" practices and inequities that get lost in the current whirl of testing, accountability, and "job readiness." The key to engaging in the global knowledge economy remains unavailable to most economically disadvantaged and racial minority students, who often attend under-resourced schools with bare-bones academic programs. That group includes a large segment of the 22 percent of school-age children who speak a language other than English at home and arrive at school with linguistic potential that schools seldom fully realize. A 2009 study showed that public schools in rural areas and schools whose students were on the lower end of the socioeconomic scale were less likely to offer foreign languages classes. At the elementary school level, three times the number of private schools offered language instruction compared with public schools.[54] The figures are not likely to have improved in the following years. That head start on languages gives more privileged students additional years to develop their skills through high school and on to college.

Many disadvantaged students are academically challenged as a result of poverty or inadequate English skills, or both. Elementary and middle schools feed them a steady diet of basic skills in math and reading to improve results on standardized tests. Little or no time is left for "enrichment" of any sort.[55] Black and Hispanic students are more likely to attend schools that offer few advanced courses, if any, or simply deny them an equitable share of seats in the courses offered.[56] Secondary schools too often steer these students away from college preparatory courses, tracking them into vocational programs where foreign languages are not part of the curriculum. Even where students are placed on an academic track, school officials may not encourage them to learn another language with any intensity, believing they're not up to the task or that it would prove worthless. The traditional Eurocentric bias of the language curriculum itself and its failure to explore diverse cultural perspectives that relate to the experiences of real life further deter some students from taking up language study, continuing on to higher levels, or considering a study-abroad experience. Should learning French only focus on the "hexagon" and France's literary giants? Should learning Spanish merely consider Spain? Or should the curriculum also represent former European colonies in Africa and Latin America?

Racial and ethnic data and success rates of students who persevere to advanced study shed added light on disparities in language learning. In 2020, the percentage of Advanced Placement test takers and their average scores on the French Language and Culture exam were as follows: Whites (53.9 percent; 3.55); Asians (14.03 percent; 3.54); Blacks (7.06 percent; 3.40), and Hispanics/Latin (15.33 percent; 3.22). For the Spanish Language and Culture exam, the numbers ran as follows: Whites (22.51 percent; 3.53), Asians (6.26 percent; 3.69), Blacks (1.69 percent, 3.10), and Hispanics/Latinx (63.87 percent; 4.02).[57]

Admittedly these figures do not reflect the total number of students from each group studying a foreign language. Yet they do represent those who studied at the highest levels and who were most likely to benefit in their future careers. The percentage of participating Black students was particularly low, as were their scores in both French and Spanish when compared to other groups. While Hispanics performed relatively well in Spanish, one would expect the schools to have brought their performance up to an even higher level given the home language advantage.

Formal schooling is not the only source of language inequities. A "shadow system" of informal language experiences also promotes language skills in unequal ways. Just as more privileged parents across the globe use private language tutors, after-school and weekend classes, and specialized summer camps to give their children a leg up in English, parents in the United States do the same for other languages. Families with the economic resources further offer their children trips abroad that create an interest in and familiarity with other peoples and places. Those experiences carry "transnational human capital," opening doors to study-abroad experiences and ultimately to careers on the domestic and international fronts.[58] On that score, both Black and Hispanic students are underrepresented in study-abroad programs. In 2018–19, Hispanics, who made up 19.5 percent of the college population, were only 10.9 percent of those who studied abroad, up from 9.7 percent in 2015–16. Blacks, who made up 13.4 percent of that population, were only 6.4 percent of those who studied abroad, up from 5.9 percent in 2015–16.[59]

Disparities in study abroad are not simply a matter of race. They are also about class and how the two factors intersect in distributing social capital and economic opportunity. Findings from over 2,700 freshmen in the United States showed that lack of finances not only presented a barrier in the end but also shaped students' intent to study abroad. That intent tracked parental education, a measure of economic and social capital.[60] The NAFSA: Association of International Educators warns that, "like the digital divide of a generation ago, today we face a growing 'global divide' between those who have access to an international education and will be primed for success in our globalized world, and those who will not."[61]

Children belonging to certain ethnic groups enjoy the advantage of private heritage language programs. These after-school and weekend classes typically operate out of local community centers or houses of worship. Some programs rely on volunteer teachers; others hire paid staff. Some focus on preserving the ethnic culture; others combine culture with language lessons.[62] In the past, these programs were common in "old wave" immigrant neighborhoods of Germans, Italians, Poles, Yiddish-speaking Jews, and other Europeans. Today, they're most often found in solidly middle-class Korean, Japanese, Chinese, Greek, Armenian, and Arab communities and funded in large part by tuition fees. Less frequently, they receive support from foundations like the United Way or from the government of the parents' home country. A thriving example is the Huaxia Chinese School, a nonprofit organization, which offers Mandarin Chinese language and culture classes beginning at age four. It includes twenty-two branch schools serving over seven thousand students across New York, New Jersey, Connecticut, and Pennsylvania. It provides scholarships to young people who cannot afford the relatively modest fees. Launched in 1995, it initially served students with a Chinese family background. It now runs classes in Chinese as a second language to meet the increasing demand of non-Chinese English-speaking parents eager to prepare their children for the global economy.[63]

Community language programs of this sort are rarely available to economically disadvantaged students, including large numbers of Spanish speakers. These students are equally capable of becoming fully bilingual, biliterate, and bicultural, yet public efforts to make that happen have been insufficiently focused or funded. Since the turn of the millennium, when the National Foreign Language Center and the Center for Applied Linguistics launched the Heritage Language Initiative, many public secondary schools have offered heritage language classes designed for students who speak a language other than English at home. These programs, however, are not universal and often depend on public-private partnerships that are difficult to establish and sustain. Nor do school officials necessarily encourage students to enroll. And while special courses and internship opportunities at the postsecondary level more commonly address the needs of this growing demographic, the success and endurance of these initiatives frequently hinge on volunteers and faculty commitment rather than on institutional support.[64]

Missing the Mark

Over the past six decades, the federal government, in fits and starts, has attempted to address this growing deficit in the nation's language skills. Those efforts typically have responded to an international or domestic crisis threatening national security and have largely involved the oversight of the Department of Defense. During the Cold War of the 1950s, Sputnik was a wake-up call to the threat of Soviet power. While the Soviet satellite set a focus on Slavic languages and especially Russian, it also triggered a flash of federal interest in languages overall, including funding for foreign languages in elementary schools (FLES) programs. The September 2001 al-Qaeda-led terrorist attacks in New York and Washington, and what evolved into the global "War on Terror," set the spotlight on so-called critical languages essential to the country's strategic and economic interests, including Arabic, Chinese, Hindi, Indonesian, Korea, Russian, and Turkish. Subsequent reports emanating from Washington have continued to make the case for more decisive and broad sweeping action, but to little avail.

In 2008, a congressional committee roundly criticized American education for ignoring concerns with national security and economic competitiveness. It laid out a strategy for developing a "robust expertise" in foreign languages and area studies to help avoid communication gaps and misunderstandings between military personnel and international partners. The report opened with a sobering quote from a military leader in the 2003–5 Iraqi campaign saying, "Even a fundamental understanding of the language would have had a significant impact on our ability to operate."[65] A 2012 congressional hearing, as well as an earlier 2006 report issued by the nation's business and education leaders, sounded similar alarms. To "confront the twenty-first century challenges of our economy and national security," the report noted, it was vital for the education system to increase Middle Eastern language skills and cultural awareness in particular.[66]

In 2010, the Central Intelligence Agency (CIA) and the University of Maryland cosponsored a Foreign Language Summit. Gathering together policymakers, congressional members, intelligence community officials, and leading language educators, the meeting ended in yet another "call to action." CIA Director Leon Panetta and Secretary of Education Arne Duncan each affirmed the nation's "foreign language deficit" and forcefully argued for a national commitment to address it. Panetta, who had made language capabilities a top CIA priority with a five-year Language Initiative, called language skills "fundamental to U.S. competitiveness and security."[67] Quoting President Barack Obama, Duncan hailed this time as "our generation's Sputnik moment."[68] By that point the language gap was at least as pressing as the STEM gap in science, technology engineering, and math, which continues to attract far wider support nationally.

What Duncan failed to acknowledge in his remarks was that Sputnik predated significant demographic changes. Immigration reform in the mid-1960s opened the nation's borders to global migration, while postcolonial strife and civil wars brought new waves of refugees and asylum seekers to the nation's shores. The linguistic diversity these newcomers brought with them was a resource just waiting for schools to develop. The fact that this obvious solution to the language deficit eluded the education secretary revealed much about attitudes toward newcomers and their languages, even at the highest levels of national decision-making.[69]

In the following years, changed demographics combined with an increasingly globalized economy and tensions in foreign relations have heightened the relevance of language skills even beyond the warnings of the past. Yet the deficit remains, as does the lack of meaningful federal support for language programs in the schools. Meanwhile, the gap between the national demand and the local supply of students studying strategically important languages continues to grow wider. Even Chinese seems to be wavering in appeal despite China's growing political and economic influence across the globe. Though educated parents are flocking to Chinese programs for their school-age children, enrollments in colleges and universities declined in 2016 by 13.1 percent for the first time in a decade. Between 2011–12 and 2018–19, the number of American students studying in China fell by 20 percent.[70] That drop is partly the result of China's constraints on free speech and the political risks of being detained while studying or doing research in the country.

Arabic has suffered a similar decline. While enrollments peaked in 2009 at 35,228, incentivized by the infusion of federal funds and intense government interest in hiring speakers fluent in Arabic, only 31,554 or 0.22 percent of college and university students studying a foreign language took an Arabic course in 2016. That same year, only 1,426 college and university students were taking a course in Hindi, down from 2,173 in 2009.[71] The picture for elementary and secondary school programs looks no more promising. As of 2016, ten states had no K–12 offerings in Arabic. Meanwhile, eight times as many K–12 students were studying Latin, a so-called dead language.[72] That is not to deny the value in studying classical languages. The overall numbers nonetheless underscore the narrow set of languages offered to students, which is grounded less in national needs or world diversity and more in historical and cultural factors related in part to the continued dominance of the Western European canon.[73]

The deficit in critical language skills especially impacts areas of geopolitical interest to the United States. In 2016, Foreign Service officers who lacked the appropriate language skills filled 23 percent of overseas language-designated positions. The largest gaps were in the Near East (37 percent), Africa (34 percent), and South and Central Asia (31 percent).[74] Within the ranks of foreign ambassadors, among the 30 percent of political appointees between 1980 and 2014, excluding ambassadorships to English-speaking countries, only 28 percent possessed prior skills in the principal language of the receiving state. Even among the larger group of career diplomats, only 56 percent held those same skills. The gap in language ability was greatest in Europe, the Middle East, and East and Southeast Asia, all areas with pressing diplomatic challenges. Yet the need for language skills to communicate with a wider group of key actors in countries like China and Iran and understand what makes them tick cannot be overlooked. Nor can the importance of speaking the language as a sign of respect for the people and their culture.[75]

Related to these concerns are differences among languages that reflect differences in one's view of the world. Certain terms used in diplomatic discussions and documents can cause serious misunderstandings in translation. Chinese is a case on point. A National Security Strategy document released in December 2017 repeatedly used the term "rival" to refer to China. While the document consciously avoided presenting China as an enemy, the Chinese translation of "rival" (duì shǒu) is more akin to an "opponent in conflict" than the English notion of "adversary" or "challenger." In recent years, it has become common to refer to China as a "strategic competitor," which in Chinese is translated as zhànlüè jìngzhēng. In English the term does not necessarily connote "war" or "conflict." In Chinese, on the other hand, the first character for the word for "strategy" (*zhàn*) can be translated into "war," and the second character (*lüè*) into "plan" making it a "war plan" or "war strategy" of sorts.[76] Unless diplomats who negotiate agreements and staff members who draft documents are aware of such subtleties in meaning, the consequences for international relations can be dire.

Perhaps nowhere was a mistranslation more globally noted and ridiculed than the British government's 2018 bungled rendition of its Brexit white paper "executive summary" in twenty-two European languages. What was intended as a combination of "charm offensive" and "olive branch gesture" became a reputational disaster. A "principled Brexit," for example, became *un Brexit vertueux* in French, presumably adding a moral element to the process. The Croatian version used a now obsolete term for the United Kingdom. The Dutch, Maltese, Polish, and especially German versions displayed other gaffes. The numerous errors and awkward irregularities in several of the translations left Twitter abuzz with cries of "clumsy," "absurd," "unreadable," "embarrassing," "reckless," and even "a national humiliation." From the Netherlands came a pointed tweet: "Dear UK government. We appreciate the effort and you probably have no clue, but please stick to English if you want us to understand you. This is horrible. Kind regards. The Netherlands."[77] As the *Financial Times* concluded, the mistakes affirmed the perception, among some Europeans, that the British had become "lazy and inward looking."[78] In the least, the errors made them appear oblivious to the level of proficiency and the deep understanding of nuance that language in diplomacy demands.

National security and diplomacy are important drivers of language education policies at the federal level. In recent years, globalization and the needs of business, based in a market-oriented agenda, have become an even more direct force in changing the attitudes of students, parents, and educators toward language learning. But here too there is a perplexing disconnect between the languages offered in the schools and the fastest-rising international markets. It is hard to reconcile the 3,738 French and 1,548 German language programs in high schools as of 2016 with only 37 programs in Portuguese, despite Brazil's growing economy.[79] Nor do the 175,667 college and university students studying French and 80,594 students studying German make economic sense when compared with only 9,827 studying Portuguese.[80] This picture was understandable in the days when French was considered the language of high culture and literature and German the language of science. But it defies present day political and economic realities. In a similar disconnect, while the dominance of high school Spanish programs, numbering 8,177, understandably served the Latin American global market, India's economy is projected to rival that of all of Latin America in the years ahead. Yet only nineteen high school programs reportedly taught Hindi, which did not even make the list of the fifteen most commonly taught languages in higher education. The same went for Mandarin Chinese, with only 1,144 high school programs, though China will soon become the world's largest economy.[81]

These divisions across languages have created a notable gap between the demands of the market and the supply of college graduates with both language skills and an academic background relevant to a particular profession or industry. Closing that gap requires close collaboration between educators and the business community.[82] It also demands close articulation between college and university language programs and disciplinary departments. Gone are the days when studying a language solely meant exploring the great works of literature. It is increasingly common for students to take courses in sociology, history, and political science in a language other than English. And while the numbers of students majoring in a foreign language has dramatically declined over the years, language departments now encourage students majoring in other disciplines to pursue a language minor.

Whether used to promote national security and diplomacy or to access the global economy, language is key to intercultural understanding. You cannot deeply comprehend a nation's core values and politics unless you can access its art, literature, news media, government documents, and policy reports. As the diplomacy examples show, cultural subtleties including idioms and tone get lost in translation. Yet advances in technology and social media now permit other nations to absorb "American" or "Anglo" language, culture, and politics. Meanwhile, they themselves promote not simply bilingualism but multilingualism, especially in the younger generation as the adult population rushes to catch up. Europeans in particular have long been avid consumers of American television and films, and consequently the country's culture and values. Individuals of any given age inevitably recall the popular television shows that helped sharpen their English skills. Today young people across the globe use Netflix as a "virtual immersion course."[83]

The irony of all this is that the figures on the language deficit belie the fact that a steady and diverse stream of immigration is making the United States more multilingual. According to Census Bureau data for 2019, a record 67.8 million United States residents over the age of five speak a language other than English at home. Among that population, 8 percent (25.6 million) reported that they speak English "less than very well," which means that about forty million individuals are fully bilingual. And the languages they speak have become more diverse. Spanish still tops the list at 41.7 million, or two-thirds of individuals who speak a language other than English in the home. The remaining one-third speaks around 350 languages, including 169 Native American and indigenous Alaskan languages. Since 2010, Telugu, Bengali, Tamil, Arabic, Hindi, Punjabi, Urdu, and Chinese have experienced the largest percentage increases in speakers.[84]

One in five or upward of twelve million school-age children (age five to seventeen) speaks a home language other than English. About 80 percent of those children also speak English "very well," with 85 percent of those born in the United States. The overall number has doubled since 1990 and nearly tripled since 1980. Spanish is by far the most common home language among students identified as English language learners, accounting for 74.8 percent of the five million students in that population. Arabic at 2.7 percent and Chinese at 2.1 percent are the next home languages in line.[85] Beyond the local level, this young bilingual cohort, with proper academic support, can easily engage in the global economy, mediating across linguistic and cultural boundaries.

These figures reveal a case of unmet demand and potential supply. On the demand side is a growing non-English-speaking population whose everyday lives depend on bilingual service providers—government agents, teachers, health care professionals, sales and banking personnel, court interpreters, and hotel and hospitality workers, as well as journalists and marketing experts—who can communicate in their languages and understand their cultural differences. On the potential supply side are large numbers of students from immigrant families who could conceivably serve their communities. They also could serve on the international front, especially in regions like Latin America, East Asia, Africa, and the Middle East where the United States holds important economic and geopolitical interests.

As noted, snuffing out the home languages of children from immigrant families is a significant factor contributing to the language deficit problem. The education system has squandered the linguistic and cultural resources of these heritage language speakers, failing to stem the tide of progressive language loss from generation to generation. A look at Hispanic immigrant communities, the largest of all groups, is telling evidence of what has become the country's "language graveyard."[86] A 2015 Pew Research Center survey of 1,500 Hispanics found that while 97 percent of immigrant parents spoke Spanish to their children, that share dropped to 71 percent among the US-born second generation and even further to 49 percent among the third generation and beyond. And though 82 percent of first-generation Hispanics said that they often encouraged their children to speak Spanish, only 53 percent of the second generation and 33 percent of the third generation did the same.

Fluency in Spanish among young people between the ages of sixteen and twenty-five followed a similar decline, from 89 percent in the first generation to 79 percent in the second, with a dramatic drop to 38 percent in the third.[87] By any objective measure, these are lost assets for strengthening economic and diplomatic ties with Latin America. Just as importantly, they rob succeeding generations of a linguistic and cultural dimension grounded in ancestral roots. Other immigrant groups, including Chinese, Koreans, Vietnamese, and Filipinos, are

similarly at risk of losing their language and their cultural identity with each succeeding generation except for the efforts of community-run programs.

As the linguist François Grosjean tells us, "The more monolingual a group or
country is, the more difficult it is for the society to understand that bilinguals are
a real asset to a nation in terms of what they can bring to cross-cultural communication and understanding."[88] Moving the needle toward that understanding
would take a serious turnaround in American views on immigrant languages and
on language learning for all. It would take an equally serious commitment on the
part of policymakers to provide the needed resources.

Reframing the Narrative

Globalization, transnational lifestyles, and a diverse population of newcomers are slowly raising public awareness and shifting attitudes on languages and language learning in the United States. Educators, business leaders, and government officials are joining together to promote policies and programs aimed at developing a workforce to meet the needs of the global economy. In challenging the monolingual mindset, they are reframing the narrative and changing the way Americans think and talk about English vis-à-vis other languages with direct consequences for social integration and especially for schooling. With spurts of support from the federal government, advocates are striving to build a sustained national momentum, while individual states and local school districts are taking the lead toward making multilingualism a reality. Armed with research findings, student performance data, and the political and economic realities of the day, they now forcefully make the case for "world languages" as they loudly proclaim, "Monolingualism is the illiteracy of the twenty-first century."

As noted in the previous chapter, concerns with national security following the 9/11 terrorist attacks sparked renewed interest in language education in Washington. In the following decade, federal agencies examined the high demand and the short supply in language skills and global understanding. Not since the Cold War period and Russia's Sputnik launch in 1957 had the federal government more decisively recognized the importance of language skills. At the same time, the explosion of borderless communication via the internet, the lingering impact of the 2008 economic crisis, and the rise of China as a global power put languages on the radar of business leaders. Research into the cognitive advantages of bilingualism further offered an arguable justification that has resonated among educated parents, state policymakers, and local school officials. Those research findings, and the history that preceded them, place in sharp focus the momentum driving the current movement. And so that is where we begin to explore the evolving narrative on language learning.

The Bilingual Advantage

Looking to the world of popular culture, the film *Arrival* offers a mind-bending entrée into that discussion.[1] Here we encounter linguist Dr. Louise Brooks, played by the actress Amy Adams. Brooks has been enlisted to assist a team that is investigating aliens who have landed on earth in spacecrafts. In trying to communicate with the heptapods, Banks learns that the way they perceive and talk about time is circular rather than linear, which permits them to see into the future. Her efforts to understand them reshape her view of the world, irreversibly rewiring her brain so that she begins to live out precognitive experiences of her own future. While this sci-fi film, based on Ted Chiang's short story "Story of Your Life," goes well beyond linguistic science, it nonetheless exposes an aspect of language long debated by linguists.[2] Do the languages we speak influence or even determine the way we view and interact with the world?

The most extreme arguments on both sides of this debate have outstripped the evidence. With origins lying in late eighteenth- and nineteenth-century Germany, the notion that language defines our sense of reality or the way we think (*linguistic determinism*) became popularized in the mid-twentieth century in what became known as the Sapir-Whorf hypothesis, named after the linguist Edward Sapir and his student Benjamin Whorf, a chemical engineer who studied linguistics with Sapir at Yale University.[3] While the two men collaborated closely for years, they never published a "hypothesis" on language and cognition together. It seems that Whorf ran with the deterministic view after Sapir's death. The term *linguistic relativity* has subsequently gone through several phases of acceptance and rejection since Sapir conceived of the idea of "relativity" as an anthropological observation, which later morphed into a psychological research hypothesis. Much of the negativity came at a time when linguistic diversity was viewed with suspicion in the United States and educational policies promoted monolingualism.[4]

Modern-day linguists now debunk the extreme version, popularized in the media, that language "determines" thought, as they have the *Arrival* character's brain rewiring.[5] At the same time, more recent studies in neurocognitive psychology have made promising inroads into the connection between language and thought and spurred a neo-Whorfian movement.[6] While much more needs to be done to arrive at a definitive conclusion, a moderate and widely accepted view suggests that language influences, to some degree, how we "categorize, evaluate, and remember the world" and "make sense of the human experience."[7] If so, then it is reasonable to conclude that speaking more than one language gives us a wider vision on life encounters, which supports the argument for linguistic diversity. This conclusion leads to the broader question of whether being bilingual, or even multilingual, carries a net advantage that sweeps across social and psychological domains.

That certainly is not the way anglophone countries traditionally saw it. For many years there was a fear, particularly among anglophone researchers and educators, but also among others, that bilingualism had a negative impact on child development. Back in 1890, Simon Somerville Laurie, the noted Scottish educator and Professor at Edinburgh University, warned that children who were raised with two languages would be so confused that it would halve their spiritual and intellectual growth.[8] In 1922, the Danish linguist Otto Jespersen argued that a child who learns two languages does not learn either of them as "perfectly" as the child would have if limited to only one. Though appearing to speak like a "native," the child would not "really command the fine points of the language." Jespersen asked the rhetorical question, "Has any bilingual child ever developed into a great artist in speech, a poet or orator?"[9] He obviously did not recall the many eminent bilingual individuals, not the least of which were the Renaissance writers who wrote in Latin and not in their vernacular, the Polish-born writer Joseph Conrad, who wrote in English; the Russian-born writer Vladimir Nabokov, who wrote in French and English; or the Syrian mystic Khalil Gibran, who wrote in English.[10] Nor could he imagine the American Pulitzer-winning novelists Jhumpa Lahiri, whose first language was Bengali but has since written in English and more recently in Italian, an adopted language, or the Dominican-born Juno Díaz, who spoke only Spanish until the age of six.

Laurie and Jespersen were not alone in their unsupported and biased conclusions. Similar studies on child bilingualism in the United States date back to the early twentieth century with the development of standardized IQ tests. At that point, researchers took to examining the negative effects of family bilingualism on the children of newly arrived southern and eastern European immigrants, comparing their test performance with that of northern Europeans and "Americans." They typically offered two explanations for the lower performance of immigrant children. Either these children were genetically inferior or, again, speaking two languages was causing mental confusion. The American psychologist Florence Goodenough, writing in 1926, claimed that it was not bilingualism that was causing "mental retardation" but rather the inferior average intellectual ability of these immigrant children that prevented them from learning English.[11] Either way, the assertions and underlying assumptions did not bode well for immigrants or for bilingualism.

These early studies have since been thoroughly discredited.[12] Judged by modern experimental standards, their methodological flaws were striking. They commonly used small samples. They failed to consider that poor test performance might have been the result of living in a non-English-speaking home with little if any exposure to English. Nor did they account for the education and socioeconomic level of parents, the attitudes of parents toward education, or the relative status afforded each group and its language within the wider community. The tests were administered in English, a language that many of the immigrant children did not fully understand. Though some researchers urged caution in drawing conclusions on the innate capacity of children from immigrant families, the findings collectively took on a life of their own. They created a professional and popular mindset that bilingualism was developmentally harmful, that monolingualism was the norm, and that learning a second or third language was a "cognitively unnatural" endeavor. Those beliefs and assumptions, feeding off suspicion of foreigners and belief in the superiority of English following World War I, remained broadly accepted for close to a half century.

The tide began to turn in the 1960s, initially with studies examining the effects of bilingualism not in families but in school settings. Elizabeth Peal and Wallace Lambert's groundbreaking research on French immersion programs in Canada showed that bilingual students outperformed monolinguals on almost all tests of cognition, both verbal and nonverbal.[13] Looking back, there admittedly were limitations to their findings. The study looked at a specific population of middle-class ten-year-old children in Montreal who were "balanced" bilinguals. There also was the problem of cause and effect. Did their bilingualism enhance their cognitive ability or vice versa?[14] Peal and Lambert's work nonetheless was significant in that it shifted the understanding of bilingualism from detrimental to additive. The possibility that bilingualism might positively influence the "structure and flexibility of thought" soon received confirmation in other settings, from Singapore to South Africa to Switzerland and Israel.[15] These encouraging findings inspired bilingual schooling for a new wave of immigrant children in the United States.

In the intervening years, attitudes toward bilingualism have changed, at least in the popular culture. In the past decade alone, there have been a rash of articles in the anglophone press telling us "Why Bilinguals Are Smarter," and waxing poetic over "The Joys and Benefits of Bilingualism."[16] These compelling stories draw on the work of psychologists who now claim that bilingualism may offer benefits beyond language ability itself. Neuroscience, with the use of brain imaging, has helped reveal that the human brain has far more plasticity than previously thought. Contrary to beliefs of the past, exposure to two languages beginning in childhood does not cause confusion but rather regulates the pace and direction of language development. Studies continue to show that bilingualism may carry cognitive advantages throughout the life cycle, from infancy to old age. Researchers describe bilinguals as "mental jugglers" adept at maintaining both languages in play, with most obvious consequences for the old and the very young.[17]

Intelligence is now considered to be a multidimensional construct. What is termed "emotional" intelligence, for example, shows in traits that relate to multilingualism, like adaptability and social competence.[18] The more proficient that bilinguals are in their second language, the more closely they emotionally align with native speakers in dealing with moral issues.[19] Speaking skills in more than one language may allow greater communicative sensitivity. Frequently using those languages has been linked to higher levels of cognitive empathy. It enables individuals to recognize what other people are thinking or feeling and to predict their behavior, which could be interpreted as a sign of multi-competence.[20] Interacting on a social level demands being aware of cues that trigger when to use each language. The implication is that bilinguals may be more adroit at reading the mental states of others and seeing the world from the other person's point of view, undoubtedly useful skills in cross-cultural communication.[21] This social "advantage" may extend to monolingual children raised in a multilingual setting, perhaps with grandparents who speak other languages. The mere exposure to other languages appears to make these children as able as bilinguals to consider the perspective of others, which carries over into their personal interactions.[22]

Bilingualism has been associated with several cognitive outcomes, including increased attention control, working memory, metalinguistic awareness, and abstract and symbolic representation skills.[23] Bilinguals seem more adept at solving certain spatial tasks that require mental manipulation, which may have some connection to mathematical ability.[24] Bilingualism may also influence unconscious processing, like divergent thinking, which helps lay the foundation for creativity. It could be that multilingual/multicultural individuals see the world through "two different conceptual prisms" and view events against a wider range of experiences.[25] At the same time, using a second language appears to promote deliberation and reduce emotional resonance, which lead to less biased decisions.[26]

Individuals who grow up bilingual appear to learn new languages more easily than others, which supports the merits of early bilingual education programs.[27] The advantage may stem from being able to focus on new information while suppressing interference from the language the speaker already knows.[28] Bilingualism may even affect the aging process, preserving the structure of white matter in the brain and warding off dementia as people age. That applies not just to individuals who have been bilingual from childhood but even to those who learn a second language later in life and actively use both languages.[29] In a similar way, bilingualism may act as a "protective factor" for certain difficulties that children with autism spectrum disorders experience, like switching from one task to another, though the findings are very preliminary.[30]

Skeptics, Critics, and Defenders

Much of the research on the "bilingual advantage" builds on the work of the Canadian psychologist Ellen Bialystok and her research primarily on children but also on adults. Bialystok, a distinguished research professor at York University in Toronto, has found that children raised bilingually have higher levels of selective attention, even in nonverbal spatial perception, than their monolingual peers. In having to select which languages to speak, she explains, they learn to screen out irrelevant information, which helps with problem solving and is fundamental to overall academic achievement.[31] Even six-month-old babies who are raised in a bilingual environment, she has found, show better attention control than infants exposed to only one language. It's not the language itself that makes a difference later in life, she notes, but the early networks for developing attention, which is the basis for all cognition.[32] She suggests that bilingualism may lead to more "fluid intelligence" that translates into more creative thinking.[33] To counter arguments that the effects on cognitive development might be related to socio-economic status, Bialystok along with others studied children from low-income Portuguese families in Luxembourg. As compared with monolingual children in Portugal, the Luxembourg group confirmed earlier findings of cognitive advantages in executive control.[34]

More recently Bialystok studied a sample of eight- and nine-year-old Spanish-English bilingual children of low socioeconomic status (SES) in California, who similarly faced a variety of risk factors for cognitive development and academic achievement. The children were enrolled in either a dual immersion (English and Spanish instruction with an equal number of native speakers of each language) or a transitional/English-only classroom. The two groups were comparable in their daily use of Spanish and in their country of origin. Avoiding the problem of between-group comparisons, she posed a more nuanced question, namely, whether among low-SES bilingual children being more bilingual leads to better performance outcomes, all else being equal. She found that the more balanced the children were in their language skills, the better their performance on nonverbal tasks of cognitive function. Bialystok maintains that these results have implications for social and education policy. Children's level of executive control, she says, predicts "educational achievement, long-term health, and earning potential." Children from minority language families, she notes, are "known to be at risk for all these outcomes."[35]

Though intuitively appealing and widely touted by language advocates, findings on the "bilingual advantage" have encountered challenges on several fronts. Critics and skeptics argue that the sample sizes tend to be small, that the subjects studied tend to be immigrants as opposed to other bilinguals, and that attempts to replicate the studies have produced inconsistent results. They claim, based on a review of abstracts of papers presented at professional conferences, that there may be a bias in favor of publishing studies with positive rather than null findings.[36] Bialystok justifiably replies, "There is no way of knowing how many abstracts that reported positive results and how many that reported negative results were submitted for publication."[37]

Bialystok's most vocal critic has been Kenneth Paap, a professor of psychology at San Francisco State University. According to Paap, bilingual advantages in executive function in particular "either do not exist or are restricted to very specific and undetermined circumstances."[38] Yet Bialystok takes exception to researchers who equate findings of null results (no differences) with negative results. "Absence of evidence," she says, "is not evidence of absence." She also warns that research results are only as good as the quality of the study, and "not all studies are equally sound." Some studies have measured tasks where there was no reason to expect any differences between bilinguals and monolinguals.[39]

Other researchers have qualifiedly come to Bialystok's defense. Thomas Bak, a lecturer at the University of Edinburgh's School of Philosophy, Psychology and Language Sciences, has most directly questioned some of Paap's conclusions. He and his colleagues have confirmed Bialystok's findings on the bilingual delay in dementia irrespective of gender, socioeconomic status, education, or immigration even in "passive" bilinguals who no longer use the second language actively. As Bak explains, multilinguals are constantly dealing with two or more languages, and so they need to select, monitor, and suppress linguistic information as needed. He suggests that learning a second language may leave "lasting cognitive traces" unrelated to later use.[40] Studies conducted between 1991 and 2012 in the United States, Canada, the United Kingdom, India, and Sweden, including Bak's research, have shown that dementia symptoms appear up to five years later in elderly bilinguals than in elderly monolinguals.[41] Bak recognizes methodological weaknesses in past studies as a given. "When you have something as complicated as bilingualism interacting with so many variables," he explains, "you'd expect varying results, depending on the circumstances and populations."[42]

Bialystok herself concedes that more rigorous studies may not yield the "exciting" results of earlier ones. She also admits that the research evidence on bilingual children is "disproportionately thin."[43] "Much remains unknown," she says, "but that does not overrule what *is* known."[44] She holds fast to the conclusion that increased levels of executive control in bilingual children are the result of bilingualism itself and are independent of other factors like the similarity of the two languages, cultural background, or language of schooling.[45] She also continues to defend the "bilingual advantage" in mental functioning across the lifespan, including the proposition that bilingualism "reorganizes the brain," despite flaws in the tests used.[46]

The results of a five-year study that she and others conducted on 158 patients of comparable education background who had been referred to a memory
clinic confirmed that belief. Bilingual individuals with mild cognitive impairment showed delayed symptoms of dementia as compared with monolinguals,
though full-blown Alzheimer's disease progressed more quickly for the bilinguals once the symptoms finally appeared. Bialystok credits the delay to "pre-
existing processes" that "help the brain cope with pathology." What is known as
"cognitive reserve," she suggests, holds back the onset of symptoms. In the least,
it enables bilinguals to live independently and maintain connection with family
and friends for a longer period of time.[47] "Experience shapes our mind," she says,
"just as our mind selects from the array of experiences in which we potentially
engage. . . . Experience is powerful, and bilingualism may be one of the most
powerful experiences of all."[48]

In an effort to explain the variability of findings across studies, Bialystok
and colleagues have broadened their sights from simply comparing bilinguals
and monolinguals, as if each group were monolingual, to exploring bilingualism as a spectrum of experiences. Treating bilingualism as a "monolingual variable," they have concluded, does not adequately account for "all the
potential adaptations." They suggest that experience-based factors, like the
duration and extent of language use and the time at which the second language is introduced, influence neurocognitive adaptations in different ways
depending on how those factors align in forming different groups, and even
in individuals within those groups.[49] This more nuanced take on the "bilingual brain" promises to unravel some of the mystery behind the inconclusive
findings in the existing literature.

As Bialystok and others continue to mine the depths of the "bilingual advantage," either affirming or refuting it in whole or in part, more fine-grained
studies are slowly yielding more insightful conclusions.[50] A two-part study creating a "vetted research trail" of published empirical research, from multiple
databases, conducted in multiple countries from 2005 to 2019 lent encouraging
support on a number of themes, including gains in cognitive abilities, academic
achievement, creativity, intercultural competence, and positive aging.[51] One
point, nonetheless, is incontrovertible. There is no firm evidence that knowing
two or more languages imposes any long-term cognitive or social harm as once
thought, while it increasingly appears to offer cognitive and interpersonal benefits across the life span.

Whether, when, and to what extent, the "advantage" concept will definitively enter the realm of perceived wisdom is still on the horizon. Perhaps what
is needed, as psycholinguist Aneta Pavlenko suggests, is more interdisciplinary
collaboration among linguists, psychologists, and ethnographers to critically explore the connection between cognition and linguistic diversity.[52] That said, the

bilingual advantage has become a key element in reshaping the narrative on bilingualism and language learning.

Signals from Washington

As noted, the federal commitment to language learning has wavered over time, typically in response to immediate concerns over national security. Most programs have been long on vision but short on funding and impact, making the federal government a very limited partner in the language enterprise. Over the past two decades several programs, though noteworthy in their intent and design, stand out on both counts. The most comprehensive effort joining national, state, and local interests is the Language Flagship Program, an initiative of the Department of Defense National Security Education Program initially created by Congress in 1991 with a small US$2 million a year budget. In the wake of the 9/11 terrorist attacks and during the administration of President George W. Bush, the program got a significant boost when Congress once again turned its sights on the country's language deficit and its impact on national security. It awards grant to colleges and universities in the United States and to Flagship Centers abroad.

The network is currently made up of thirty-one Flagship programs at twenty-three institutions of higher education and seven Overseas Flagship Centers. It focuses on developing new models of language learning to produce graduates fluent in one or more languages, including Arabic, Chinese, Korean, Persian, Portuguese, and Russian, critical to the country's competitiveness and security. In 2021–23, a separate competition focuses on African languages, including Akan/Twi, Swahili, Wolof, and Zulu. Emphasizing culture and media, the approach departs from the traditional focus on literature. The point is to give students the tools to function as professionals using their language skills. While the program has succeeded in producing college graduates with high levels of proficiency in another language, it has never realized its initial goal to "socialize" the Flagship model across higher education.[53]

The Flagship Program also funds projects that promote language learning and cultural understanding in elementary and secondary schools. A practical outcome of the K–12 initiative is the Roadmap to National Language Excellence. The concept emerged from the Language Flagship Centers initially funded at the University of Oregon, the University of Texas, and Ohio State University in 2006. The centers each supported research into current and future demands for language and cultural skills in business and government. Language summits held the following year brought together educators, representatives from state and local governments, and more than seventy business leaders to discuss each state's strengths and weaknesses in responding to the need in foreign languages. Working groups within each summit developed a strategic plan, or "Language Roadmap," outlining initiatives to promote foreign language and cultural education over the short and long term.

Hawaii, Indiana, Rhode Island, Utah, and Wisconsin have since undertaken the same process and developed similar plans. In each case, the stress has been on developing a world-class workforce to better access global and domestic markets. That being said, with only eight states having developed language roadmaps in over a decade and a half, the program has had little national impact. Meanwhile, most of the roadmaps have not produced significant changes in policies or practices. The one notable exception is the state of Utah, whose roadmap led to the most robust statewide and sustainably funded commitment to language education in the country. The fruits of those labors will come to light when we look at Utah's dual language immersion programs.

Federal interest in foreign language learning continued into the administration of President Barack Obama. Speaking at a national symposium on multiliteracy and learning in 2016, Secretary of Education John B. King, Jr., told the crowd of educators: "We are preparing all young people for a global economy in which they are likely to work alongside someone different from them, they are likely to have a supervisor who may speak a different language than they do, they may be serving clients and customers in other countries with vastly different language and cultural backgrounds."[54] In June of that year, the Department of Education and the Department of Health and Human Services issued a thirty-two-page joint policy statement supporting bilingualism in early childhood education. The focus was on dual language learners, that is, children who speak a language other than English at home.[55] At that point, upward of 22 percent of children aged five to seventeen fell into that category. The numbers in federally funded early childhood programs was 29 percent. These students spoke over one hundred forty languages, though the overwhelming majority (71 percent) spoke Spanish. While almost 96 percent of them were born in the United States, three-quarters came from families where both parents were foreign born.

The document was a policy statement, and so it technically imposed no legal obligations on state or local school officials. Yet it was a ringing endorsement of dual immersion models and a clear recognition that the child's home language is an asset and not a barrier to learning English. To prove the case, the statement included a comprehensive review of the literature and empirical findings supporting the social-emotional, cognitive, and academic advantages of bilingualism. Especially striking was yet another important shift in terminology from the suggestively subtractive "English language learners"

(ELLs) to the more inclusive and additive "dual language learners" (DLLs) who would make up a "sizeable proportion of the workforce" in the years to come. "Preparing them for school," it counseled, is an "economic imperative that will directly influence the competitiveness of the United States in the evolving global economy."[56]

The nod to market forces did not satisfy detractors who read more legal weight into the statement than intended or even legally possible. A searing "issue brief" from the conservative Heritage Foundation challenged the president's authority to require that schools maintain "cultural assets." It warned of the dangers of divisions along ethnic lines. The brief called on Congress to conduct hearings to investigate the president's actions and to make clear that states would not lose federal funding if they failed to implement the recommendations.[57] Congress, in the midst of a turbulent presidential election year, took no action. Meanwhile, the policy statement was merely hortatory without funds allocated to the states for implementation.

In the closing days of the Obama administration, the Department of Education gave a final nod toward bilingualism. The *Framework for Developing Global and Cultural Competencies to Advance, Equity, Excellence and Economic Competitiveness* said much in its title alone. Covering early childhood through postsecondary education, the tightly worked chart went from "developing language skills in English and other languages" in preschool to "advanced proficiency" or the "ability to work or study in at least one other language" in college. These measures were only recommendations. Anything more mandatory would have impermissibly intruded on state and local control over education. Taken together with other national, state, and local developments supporting bilingualism and language learning, they reflected growing national interest in moving the country into a world where multilingualism is the norm. What was lacking, however, was a funding stream to the states to make those recommendations a reality on the ground.

In any case, the symbolic force of the recommendations and the supportive view they represented soon evaporated in the "America First" air of the Trump administration, where language skills were ignored at best and rejected at worst as a sign of national disloyalty. Riding a wave of popular nationalism, the administration divested in public education and fomented a misguided view that speaking other languages was anti-American. With the Biden administration taking the helm in 2021, there is a strong expectation that bilingualism and multilingualism will be considered assets and not threats. Yet given pressing concerns with restoring education in the wake of the pandemic, perhaps the only foreseeable hope for actual funding is where language learning can be tied to the federal interest in equity and justice.

Building Momentum

Concrete policies continue to emerge from a high-profile nationwide study, the first in over three decades, conducted by the Commission on Language Learning. The seeds of that commission were sown over several years, beginning in 2012 through the joint efforts of the Center for Advanced Study, the federal Department of Defense, the American Academy of Arts and Sciences, and the British Academy. That collaboration led to a series of conferences involving key stakeholders in language learning and teaching. The point was to address the question of "equal access to education for all children."[58] Building on that conversation, in 2015 the Academy of Arts and Sciences convened the Commission on Language Learning at the request of a bipartisan group of members of Congress and with support from private foundations. The academy, founded in 1780 during the American Revolution by John Adams, John Hancock, and sixty other "scholar patriots," is one of the country's oldest and most respected independent policy research centers. The commission's membership, drawn from the ranks of national leaders in education, research, business, and government, gave the projected findings further weight. Its mission was to examine the current state of language education in the United States, to assess future education needs, and to make recommendations to meet those needs.[59]

The legislators who initiated the 2015 study understood the immediacy of the problem. They also understood the changing landscape of the country and the world. As they wrote in their letter to the Academy:

> English is no longer sufficient as a *lingua franca*—neither at home nor abroad. The percentage of the world's population that speaks English as a first language is declining rapidly; if current demographic trends continue, only 5% will be native English speakers by 2050. At the same time, the ability to communicate in languages other than English has never been more important as: American jobs and exports are more dependent than ever on foreign markets; [t]he American population is increasingly multilingual; [and] Americans are more engaged diplomatically and militarily around the globe than ever before.[60]

Following a series of white papers targeting specific issues, the final report, *America's Languages: Investing in Language Education for the 21st Century*, appeared in 2017, a banner year for reports addressing language study and the potential for developing language resources. To the commission's credit, the end product was a well-documented storehouse of information grounded in social science research on the country's deficit in "world" languages, the cognitive and economic benefits of bilingualism, the shortage of language teachers, and the potential use of technology in developing language skills. The report's shift in terminology from the traditional "foreign" to the more neutral "world" languages was significant, placing all languages on an equal plane without suggesting that languages spoken by newcomers are of lesser importance.

The report noted that the United States, with only 20 percent of the population able to speak a language other than English, fell behind most nations in the percentage of individuals with some ability in a second language. It pointed out that languages other than English fade from immigrant families by the third generation, and that the number of K–12 schools teaching languages and the number of students taking language courses in college had declined over the years. The report underscored the emerging consensus among business, educational, and political leaders that English was critical "but not sufficient to meet the nation's future needs." It described how language barriers impeded international business interactions, science and technology innovation, national security, and international relations.

The findings were eerily similar to those of the President's Commission on Foreign Languages and International Studies, convened back in 1979 during the administration of President Jimmy Carter. As Leon Panetta, a member of Congress in 1979, observed almost forty years later as a member of the new commission, "In times of great national security challenges, such as those we face today, as well as in times of great opportunity, such as the opening of new international markets, we find ourselves scrambling for people who can speak, write, and think in languages other than English." For Panetta, who had gone on to become Director of the Central Intelligence Agency and Secretary of Defense in the Obama administration, neglecting "training and education in languages other than English" was "evidence of a dangerous myopia."[61]

The 2017 report had a clear agenda promoting both action and advocacy. It focused on five "capacity building goals": (1) increase the number of language teachers at all levels of education so that every child in every state has the opportunity to learn a language in addition to English; (2) supplement language instruction across the education system through public-private partnerships; (3) support heritage languages already spoken in the United States; (4) provide targeted support and programming for Native American languages; and (5) promote opportunities for students to learn languages in other countries.[62]

The National Academies of Science, Engineering, and Medicine, that same year, published a report with a similar tone and substance. Focusing on English/dual-language learners, the report affirmed the diverse cultures, languages, and experiences of these students as "assets for their development, as well as for the nation."[63] *The National K–12 Foreign Language Survey Report*, sponsored by the Department of Defense Language Flagship, added weight to those conclusions.

Prepared in collaboration with leading language advocacy organizations, as already discussed, this first-of-its-kind national survey presented compelling data on the shortfall in school language programs across states and languages.[64] Both documents recognized that the national language deficit could only be addressed through a conscious shift in values giving world languages the same priority as math and science. The year 2017 continued to roll on with the New American Economy's report *Not Lost in Translation*, making the case for "foreign" language skills in the US job market.[65] That year also saw the Council on Foreign Relations convene a meeting of experts to discuss the link between languages and the country's national security. A clear message emerging from the discussion was that while the Department of Defense and state governments were actively growing the country's linguistic capacities, there was still much work to be done.[66]

Building on all these efforts, the American Council on the Teaching of Foreign Languages launched Lead with Languages, a multi-year national public awareness campaign aimed at encouraging government leaders and university, corporate, and nonprofit partners to join together in making language learning a national priority. The campaign came on the heels of a national opinion poll that found that parents and students were generally uninformed on the connection between "foreign" language proficiency and career opportunities.[67] To fill that gap, the project launched a website with a wealth of information on language programs, scholarships, study-abroad and career opportunities, and tips on language advocacy.[68]

An added outgrowth of the commission's report was the America's Languages Working Group, an informal group of experts and organizers that maintains a running map of best practices in language education. In 2018, the group issued a call to action signed by thirty-five individuals and 150 organizations, including businesses, academic and professional associations, universities, and school systems, promoting a "more forward-thinking strategy" to meet the country's language needs. Along with trade, diplomacy, and scientific innovation, the document underscored the "social obligation" to offer critical services in languages other than English.[69] When the salience of that point vividly came to light in the 2020 coronavirus pandemic, the group launched a petition, "Language Education in the Time of COVID-19," calling for immediate and long-term funding to support language education and services for disadvantaged children and adults. The petition soon gathered over five thousand signatures.[70]

As the pandemic surged and resurged throughout 2020, the American Academy of Arts and Sciences once again took the lead in an unprecedented joint "International Call to Action" on language education signed by five academies from nations where English is the primary language—the British Academy, the Academy of Social Sciences in Australia, the Australian Academy, and the Royal

Society of Canada. The document underscored the demands of business and diplomacy and especially the need "to share accurate information" in situations like the global health crisis. It called on the countries represented to support access to education in a range of languages, including minority and indigenous languages, while working toward improving literacy in English.[71]

These related developments reveal a shifting landscape toward multilingualism, not just in the United States but also in the wider anglophone world. Those promising changes are due in large measure to the initial impetus of the Commission on Language and Learning's 2017 report. Several years earlier, the Academy of Arts and Sciences had conducted a similar study on the humanities and social sciences, again in response to a bipartisan congressional request. The 2013 report recommended greater national support for language and study-abroad programs, and even a federal "National Competitiveness Act" to fund international affairs and transnational studies.[72] The intent of those recommendations was never fully realized. In the years following the 2017 report, there has been more sustained action and determination among a broad coalition of actors to build both grassroots and government support for language education. In continuing to press for federal legislation, their efforts have met some losses, but they also have seen some promising gains.

On the "loss" side, a federal bill called the Biliteracy Education and Seal Teaching (BEST) Act, which would provide funds for the administrative costs of establishing and administering Seal of Biliteracy programs, has repeatedly faltered in Congress. In the meantime, as we will see, the state Seal of Biliteracy remains a "patchwork of policies and standards" across the country.[73] On the gain side, in late 2019 Congress adopted the World Language Advancement and Readiness Act despite Skopos Labs having given the bill only a 2 percent likelihood of being passed.[74] This was the first major piece of federal legislation on languages in a generation. Focused on national security, the legislation provided three-year competitive grants to local school districts that hosted a unit of the Reserve Officers' Training Corps (ROTC) and to schools operated by the Department of Defense Education Activity. The Act was a visible sign that congressional support for language programs was slowly growing.

In November 2019, members of the House of Representatives formed the America's Languages Caucus, a bipartisan language policy forum. It was a direct outgrowth of the 2017 Commission on Language and Learning report. The goal was to develop a national strategy in raising the nation's awareness and to direct resources toward world language learning, especially as it bears on economic and national security. The caucus is a major milestone for language education. Unlike past language initiatives reacting to specific national threats like Sputnik and 9/11, this was an affirmative move toward a more systemic commitment.[75]

Instrumental in establishing the congressional caucus was the Joint National Committee for Languages—National Council for Languages and International Studies (JNCL-NCLIS), a mission-driven membership organization that has worked tirelessly to promote language programs and raise awareness of the benefits of multilingualism particularly in Congress. Representing a network of over three hundred thousand language professionals and specialists from the education, nonprofit, and industry worlds, the group annually organizes a Language Advocacy Day and Delegate Assembly in Washington, DC. In 2020, the two-day program brought together upwards of 185 administrators, educators, researchers, analysts, translators, interpreters, language industry leaders, and representatives of leading language associations from forty-five states and the District of Columbia. As in the past, the agenda was to discuss advocacy techniques and to lobby Congress and the executive branch for stepped-up support for language programs. In the end, it tallied 220 meetings with Senate staff while reaching a million people on social media.

Each year, the organization has added sponsors to the Senator Paul Simon Study Abroad Act[76] and the World Language Advancement and Readiness Act.[77] The Simon Act, first introduced in 2006, would increase the number of minority students, first-generation college students, students with disabilities, and students studying in developing countries through study-abroad programs. The World Language Advancement and Readiness Act, initially introduced in 2017, finally passed in 2019.

Finally, one brief but encouraging note should be made on the international front. At the April 2016 G7 education ministers meeting in Japan, representatives from Canada, France, Germany, Italy, the United Kingdom, the United States, UNESCO, and the Organisation for Economic Co-operation and Development (OECD) agreed to develop a measurement of global competency for the OECD to include in its 2018 Program for International Student Assessment (PISA). Following up on that agreement, a student questionnaire asked students across countries how many languages they learned at school and how many they and their parents spoke sufficiently well to converse with others. As the OECD summed it up, "When individuals establish meaningful and deep connections across languages and cultures, they build their capacity for understanding and their dispositions for valuing other cultures."[78] This new addition to the PISA assessment suggests a change in perspective among key international actors that language learning should no longer be a mere footnote in the education of future world citizens; rather, it should be part of the essential curriculum alongside science, math, and the humanities. That change, together with findings on the cognitive advantages across the life spectrum, broadens the rationale for developing language skills beyond career opportunities and national security.

The State Seal of Biliteracy

One of the most ambitious and successful efforts to promote language learning in the states has been the Seal of Biliteracy. By 2021, forty-three states plus the District of Columbia had either a state seal, commendation, or endorsement posted on diplomas and transcripts. The seal serves as evidence that students have attained proficiency in standard academic English and at least one other language by the time they complete secondary school. Participation has been highest among states with larger percentages of English language learners. Within some states and localities, the selling point is less about honoring students and more about industry and boosting the economy.

Programs vary in their goals and target populations. Most look toward bilingualism for all students. Others focus on maintaining heritage languages among English learners and, more generally, students from linguistically diverse communities. Some have gone the route of state legislation. Others have originated in policies adopted or approved by the state education department or the local board of education.[79] The choices cover modern world languages, Latin and classical Greek, Native American languages, and American Sign Language. The criteria for awarding the seal are challenging, including a variety of assessments, course requirements, and student work. Most states use a rating scale developed by the American Council on the Teaching of Foreign Languages similar to the Common European Framework of Reference (CEFR). Some states simply base the award on "seat time," that is, completing a certain number of courses and maintaining a minimum overall grade point average. Some have developed incremental tiers of awards based on proficiency. The language level reached can potentially earn advanced placement, college credit, or scholarships and save students thousands of dollars and even college semesters.

The Seal of Biliteracy concept originated in 1992 in the Glendale, California, school district despite state restrictions at that time on bilingual programs for English learners. Deciding to formally recognize the linguistic potential of its growing diverse student population, the district developed the Bilingual Competency Award for graduating seniors who demonstrated proficiency in a second language. Beginning with Spanish and English, the program soon expanded to accommodate the district's large Armenian population, as well as Arabic-, Korean-, and Tagalog-speaking newcomers.

In 2011, California adopted the Seal of Biliteracy statewide, largely through the efforts of Californians Together, a research and advocacy group committed to advancing the rights of English learners. It was the first state legislative measure to effectively counter policies adopted in California, Arizona, and Massachusetts in the late 1990s and the early 2000s that prohibited or strictly limited support for the home language of English learners.[80] The move was especially significant for California, where 40 percent of K–12 students enter school with knowledge of at least two languages. The following year, New York adopted the Seal of Biliteracy by gubernatorial executive order. Thus began a national movement for recognizing biliteracy skills and making language learning central to the curriculum. The rest is history, as they say. In 2015, the American Council on the Teaching of Foreign Languages, the National Council of State Supervisors for Languages, the National Association for Bilingual Education, and the TESOL International Association jointly issued a set of implementation guidelines for states to follow.[81] In 2020, despite school closures over the pandemic, over sixty-five thousand students in California received the Seal of Biliteracy in forty-one different languages. Forty-seven percent of them were once English learners.[82]

Data from California further show that the Seal of Biliteracy has value in the job market. In a statewide survey of 289 employers, the likelihood of respondents hiring a bilingual candidate over a monolingual English candidate jumped by 10 percent, over an initial 57 percent, when they were asked if the seal would be an advantage.[83] Recognizing that "multilingualism is an essential skill," in 2015 the state's superintendent of public instruction launched Global California 2030, an initiative intended to "vastly expand" the number of students who know at least two languages.

The Seal of Biliteracy is similar in form and intent to the European CertiLingua Label of Excellence, which originated in the North Rhine-Westphalia region of Germany and in the Netherlands. First awarded in 2008, the Label of Excellence has since spread to other European partner countries. By 2021, there were nine countries and more than three hundred schools participating in the program. Students must demonstrate that they have acquired written and oral proficiency in at least two languages on level B2 of the Common European Framework for Languages (CEFR) and that they can use at least one of those languages in one or more content-related courses. They also must show that they have participated in an international cooperation project in the second language. Validating the label's value are CertiLingua "partners" or sponsors including universities, local chambers of commerce, corporations, and foundations throughout Europe. The goal is to develop communication skills and to enhance student mobility for personal and professional purposes.[84]

In contrast to CertiLingua, the Seal of Biliteracy in the United States varies from state to state in the level of proficiency required, the number of proficiency levels recognized, if any, the English language requirements, and the measures used to test proficiency in English and in the other language. The District of Columbia is the most demanding on assessment. California accepts four years of study plus evidence of oral proficiency. New York is perhaps the most flexible in offering a number of ways to meet the requirements, including a portfolio and coursework. While seat time is not the most accurate measure of language proficiency, it arguably is more equitable given the prohibitively high cost of language assessments like Advanced Placement and International Baccalaureate exams. Schools generally participate in the program at their discretion, except in Hawaii, which is a single school district. Indiana, Kansas, and Nevada allow private schools to offer the state's seal.[85]

With over twelve million students in the United States speaking a language other than English at home, advocates for English learners have raised a number of concerns regarding equity and access within these programs. Approximately two-thirds of the states do not explicitly mention English learners in their Seal of Biliteracy policy purpose. Some states give priority to dominant world languages while ignoring many of the more than three hundred languages that students speak at home. Students who speak Haitian Creole and Vietnamese, which are among the top five languages for English learners, are often denied the opportunity to prove what they know in their native language. As of 2018, for example, no student had earned a Seal of Biliteracy in four of Minnesota's twelve most common languages (Vietnamese, Lao, Amharic, Khmer).[86] Some states require English learners to demonstrate proficiency in English in the tenth grade, as in Florida and Massachusetts, or in the eleventh grade, as in California and Rhode Island, as compared to the twelfth grade for other languages. Some demand a comparably higher level of proficiency in English than they do in the other language.[87]

Only a few states monitor the demographics of students earning the Seal of Biliteracy. For example, 27 percent of the 4,031 students who had earned the award in New York State in 2018–19 were current or former English learners.[88] The majority of other states maintain no data on whether or not English learners are reaping possible advantages, including college credits or job opportunities. Nor do the assessments used to measure proficiency recognize that heritage language speakers and learners have not necessarily learned the topics, tasks, and language varieties they would have learned in language classes. Seal of Biliteracy programs, moreover, are not mandatory, and so parents, educators, and other advocates are left to push for adoption at the local level.

Critical studies focusing on California and Minnesota confirmed such deficiencies in the way policies were enacted and implemented in the schools of each state. They also echoed findings from a Utah study on dual language immersion, where programs tended to be wrapped more in a discourse of "global human capital" and student marketability and less in the language of "equity and heritage."[89] Drawing on lessons learned, a group of seven organizations—including Californians Together, the American Council for the Teaching of Foreign Languages, and the National Association for Bilingual Education—published a detailed set of implementation guidelines aimed at strengthening existing strategies and encouraging expansion at state and local levels.[90]

Most states offer the Seal of Biliteracy only to public school students. To fill the gap in the private sector, Avant Assessment, a private company offering online tests of language ability, launched the Global Seal of Biliteracy program in 2019. Available in over one hundred languages and open to private, independent, international, and home schools as well as colleges, universities, and individuals currently in the workforce, the Global Seal certifies language skills in two or more languages at three levels to schools and employers across state lines and national borders. In 2020, colleges and universities accounted for nearly 20 percent of Global Seals. Some public school districts use the STAMP and WORDSPEAK tests developed by AVANT.

The flaws in implementing the state Seal of Biliteracy undeniably demand attention to make it more effective and widely available. That fact, nonetheless, does not negate the program's conceptual importance. When appropriately presented, it motivates students to study other languages and cultures for both the intrinsic and extrinsic gains. When equitably designed and offered, it sends a clear message to students who speak English but come from immigrant backgrounds that educators and policymakers value the students' home language and implicitly their home culture. And as a matter of policy, it moves the country another step forward in developing a linguistic infrastructure to meet the demands of the global economy and national security.

Building on these collective efforts, state and local officials, parents and advocates are forging ahead, continuing to reframe the narrative in the direction of dual language learning from pre-kindergarten through secondary school.

A Revolution in the Making

The prevailing justifications for language learning—from the personal to the economic and the diplomatic—are giving visible momentum to a growing movement across the United States driven by a combination of findings and forces, both domestic and international. Beyond the Seal of Biliteracy, powering that movement is the concept of "dual language immersion" which forward-thinking communities from California to New York are enthusiastically embracing. Abandoning the deficit narrative, these programs respond to several demands, all related in different degrees to globalization and migration.

State policymakers and local school officials see dual immersion as a way both to develop the potential of dual language learners who live transnational lives, either physically or virtually, and to prepare all students for the global economy. Immigrant communities, in fact, are not necessarily the prime movers or intended beneficiaries of these programs as they once were. In some cases, the grassroots drive comes from educated native-born American families looking for the economic and cognitive benefits of early bilingualism. Joining them are assorted expats eager to maintain their children's home language and culture.

National interests like the soft power of language in politics and in diplomacy weigh more or less heavily in the balance at the state and local levels depending on the involvement of foreign governments. A clear example is the growth in Mandarin Chinese immersion programs, up from ten in 2009 to over 250 in 2018.[1] Another striking case, with a similar mix of political, economic, and culture undertones, is the rapid spread of French immersion programs with support from the French government, the French president himself, and the well-organized French business community in the United States. By 2021, there were upward of 170 French dual language immersion programs across the country.

This current wave stands in sharp contrast to the bilingual education programs of the 1960s and 1970s. Those programs grew out of the civil rights movement and the quest for ethnic consciousness. They were designed principally for Spanish-speaking Cubans in Florida, Mexican Americans in the Southwest, and Puerto Ricans in the Northeast, with a sprinkling of others. They became increasingly criticized for segregating students by ethnicity and language. Most of the programs aimed to transition students into mainstream English classes without necessarily preserving the home language and culture. In some cases students languished in bilingual classes for years without showing marked progress in English or in overall achievement.

As data mounted on the failure of transitional programs to adequately develop English language skills, so did public opposition. That opposition eventually translated into highly restrictive language policies in states like California, Arizona, and Massachusetts, propelled in large part by anti-immigrant sentiment. As a countermovement, language advocates found in dual language immersion a more pedagogically promising and politically palatable alternative, replacing the deficit model of bilingual education with an "assets" or "resource" approach that extended beyond language minority populations. The concept appealed to English-speaking families encouraged by widely publicized findings on the cognitive advantages of bilingualism and the marketability of languages in the global economy.

Dual immersion integrates native English speakers and English second-language speakers using each of the languages for varying portions of the school day. Programs teach subject matter in both English and the partner language and develop reading skills in both. They use only one instructional language in the classroom at a time and try to maintain a student balance between the two groups, though in some cases they are weighted more heavily toward one group or the other depending on demographics. They begin in kindergarten or first grade and continue through elementary school, ideally through eighth grade. The number of hours spent on each language varies from program to program, as do the populations served.

According to *Guiding Principles for Dual Language Education*, which practitioners consider their Bible and now in its third edition, these programs rest on three pillars: bilingualism and biliteracy, academic achievement in both languages, and sociocultural competence. Essential to their vision of multilingualism and multiculturalism is the concept of "additive bilingualism," that is, students acquiring a second language while maintaining their home language.[2] By 2019, these programs numbered about three thousand, up from an estimated two thousand in 2017, in at least forty states and the District of Columbia. Two groups, the National Dual Language Forum, sponsored by the Center for Applied Linguistics, and the Association of Two-Way and Dual Language Education, serve as resources for schools interested in developing high quality programs.

The growing popularity of dual immersion shows how politics and place shape educational policy and practice. Louisiana, for example, was a forerunner in serving a long-existing community eager to revitalize its heritage language. Home to an estimated 250,000 French speakers, the state counted by 2020 twenty-six programs in eight parishes supported by the Council for the Development of French in Louisiana (CODOFIL), a program launched in 1968 under the state's Department of Culture and Tourism.[3] In 2018, the state became an observer member of the Organization internationale de la francophonie (OIF), which provided grants for French textbooks and other materials and offered opportunities to collaborate with the francophone world.

Delaware has followed a different model in which a key element has been the state's favorable incorporation and corporate tax laws that historically have drawn businesses to create a foothold there. With the global economy growing, state government and industry leaders have joined together in providing funds and other resources to develop a multilingual workforce serving the needs of multinational corporations that place high value on language abilities. By 2020, Delaware's World Language Expansion Initiative enrolled four thousand students in thirty programs, either one-way immersion with native English speakers or two-way immersion with native English and native Mandarin Chinese or Spanish speakers.[4]

Across the country, Spanish programs are by far the most numerous. Yet growing diversity among immigrant groups is giving rise to programs that target other languages.[5] Language immersion programs typically appear without much fanfare. One, however, created a storm of controversy that had everything to do with global politics and nothing to do with education. In 2015, the Houston School District launched the Arabic Immersion Magnet School in response to demands from the city's Arabic-speaking population, which had grown by more than a third since 2009. Protestors waving American and Israeli flags claimed the school was "anti-American."[6] One protestor carried a sign reading "Qatar out of our school." The reference was to the Qatar Foundation International, which had awarded the school district US$85,000 to help train teachers and develop curriculum. While some community members claimed that immigrants should be "assimilated," the school proved popular with parents. In the end, it attracted nearly five hundred applications from a mix of Black, Latinx, and White families hailing from forty zip codes and vying for 132 kindergarten and pre-kindergarten seats.[7] The program, now covering grades pre-K through five, has grown and thrived.

As desirable as dual language immersion programs are from a policy point of view, like the Seal of Biliteracy they too have raised equity and access questions. It has been argued that these programs can leave behind the very students whom dual immersion originally was designed to serve. Federal law requires school districts to identify students with limited English skills and to provide them with an equitable program based in sound research. As Michael Bacon, the director of dual language education in Portland, Oregon, told *Education Week*,

"Dual language immersion is a game-changer, especially for our emergent bilingual children whose first language is not English. From an equity lens, it's about valuing those kids' linguistic and cultural assets, and leveraging them for their academic [benefits], but also in terms of their own self-identity."[8] These pressures, combined with a shortage of immersion teachers and an increasingly diverse immigrant population, have opened debate in some communities over which schools and which student groups should get priority in accessing this coveted opportunity. At least some of the problem with student selection is often resolved through a lottery system. But there still remain issues of school selection and intra-school dynamics.

As a study on the gentrification of Utah's dual language immersion programs suggested, the emphasis on language as a marketable skill drives policymakers and more privileged parents to consider dual language as essential enrichment. These programs are often found in upwardly transitioning (and even affluent) neighborhoods while failing to offer equal opportunities to many students of color attending schools in racially segregated low-income communities. Given the historical link between enrichment programs and tracking (Advanced Placement courses, honors classes, STEM programs), that approach can easily shut low-income and other underserved students out of language education.[9]

Even for students who are included, dual language programs can generate a power imbalance between English-speaking families who at times are the driving force and non-English-speaking families who may lack the time, the awareness, or the cultural norms to actively participate in school governance. It has been argued that school districts risk operating what essentially is an elite world language program, treating low-income children from non-English-speaking homes as a "commodity" to "boost the resumes" of privileged white middle-class students.[10] Dual language programs, at times products of "broader racialized histories," can serve to reinforce the power relations that they claim to challenge.[11] Treating language merely as a resource, which is common within the discourse on dual language programs, fails to recognize "intrinsic nonquantifiable" aspects, including the "psychological, cultural, affiliational, aesthetic, and historical."[12] Experience has shown that the longer these programs run and prove their worth academically, the more the community and the school become whiter, wealthier, and more demographically English dominant. A clear case on point is the forty-year-old Oyster-Adams Bilingual School in Washington, DC. Created in 1971 to serve the Latinx community, the school by 2020–21 had a population that was 34 percent White, 55 percent Hispanic/Latino, and only 28 percent English learners.[13]

While these problems are serious, they are not insurmountable. They simply demand that policymakers and school officials consciously devise ways to avoid them from the start and vigilantly address them if they arise over time. As they say, the devil is in the details, and those details must be ironed out program by program. Some states and localities have been more successful at avoidance and vigilance than others. Of all those that have implemented immersion programs, California, Utah, and New York City are especially worth a close look. All three offer eye-opening views on the changing face of bilingualism and language learning as they wind through a maze of competing interests from the local to the international. The organizing ecology, ranging from top-down to bottom-up, and the continuing spread of these programs across language communities give clear signs of a "bilingual revolution" in the making.

The California Turnaround

Perhaps nowhere are the changing attitudes toward multilingualism more evident than in California's dramatic turnaround on bilingual schooling. That reversal ironically occurred on the same Election Day in November 2016 when a newly elected administration in Washington set about moving the nation in the opposite direction. The history behind the California course of events says as much, if not more, about immigration and political will as it does about language per se.

In the closing decades of the twentieth century, language became a surrogate for concerns over the flow of Latin American immigrants crossing into states at the country's southern border, including California. By the 1980s, those concerns had become widespread and emotionally fraught, as the 1986 law making English California's official language demonstrated. Over the next decade, the debate found a new focal point in the nationwide backlash against bilingual schooling. That backlash came to a head in 1998. Following a US$6 million ad campaign spearheaded by Silicon Valley multimillionaire Ron Unz, 61 percent of California voters approved Proposition 277, which effectively dismantled the state's bilingual programs. Unz and his supporters inveighed against an approach that relegated the state's largely Spanish-speaking students to separate Spanish-only classrooms, some for years. The vote, riding on the slogan "English for the children," followed a wave of California anti-immigration laws tinged with racism.

Proposition 227 mandated that students spend one year in an English-immersion class before moving into the mainstream. If parents signed a waiver, schools could offer a program in the home language. The waiver requirement had a chilling effect. Parents who themselves could not speak English were at the mercy of school administrators who might or might not fully inform them of their options. Even if informed, the negative press in the debate over Proposition 227 had convinced many parents that bilingual education would harm their children academically. Bilingual education thus became by far the exception and English immersion the norm. Meanwhile, in an unexpected turn, the small number of programs that opened under waivers gained from a supply of trained bilingual teachers then exceeding the demand. They also benefited from school administrators and parents committed to making the programs work, as well as from the experience of new models, particularly dual immersion, from other parts of the country. These were not the old bilingual programs targeted by Proposition 227 organizers.

As time passed, testing became a deciding factor. Results for English-only immersion programs proved progressively disappointing. Though scores in English language and reading rose in the first few years, subsequent testing found no further significant effects. Meanwhile, results from the few remaining bilingual programs were far more encouraging. A 2014 study of eighteen thousand English learners who had entered kindergarten between 2002 and 2010 in the San Francisco public schools found that by fifth grade not only were students equally proficient in English—whether they had received bilingual or English-only instruction—but the bilingual program students had gained the added advantage of developing their Spanish skills.[14]

The San Francisco findings came as no surprise to researchers in the field. They confirmed a number of previous studies consistently supporting the benefits of language immersion programs in particular. On that count, the steadfast work of Virginia Collier and Wayne Thomas stands out. Over a period of thirty-two years, Collier and Thomas analyzed 7.5 million student records covering grades K–12 in thirty-six school districts and sixteen states. Their long-term longitudinal studies from 1985 to 2017, which have been replicated in other countries, demonstrated that the most effective way to close the achievement gap for English language learners in their second language (English) was through dual language programs. Particularly impressive data from North Carolina attested to the sweeping benefits of two-way immersion for White, Latinx, and African American students as well as for English speakers and native Spanish speakers, including students of low-income background and students with special education needs.[15] The researchers maintained that it takes an average of six years of quality dual language schooling, beginning at kindergarten, for students to reach grade level achievement across the curriculum and to remain at grade level throughout their school years.[16]

Other findings refute claims that these programs succeed because they serve selective populations. A four-year study from Portland, Oregon, a leader in dual language immersion, offers convincing evidence. In that case, 1,625 kindergarten applicants were randomly assigned, through a lottery process, to Spanish, Japanese, Mandarin Chinese, and Russian one- or two-way immersion programs. As compared to a control group, the immersion students had everything to gain and nothing to lose. Not only did they all outperform their English-taught peers in English reading by about seven months in grade five and by about nine months in grade eight, but the native English-speaking students assigned to the two-way programs also reached on average intermediate proficiency in the partner language by grade eight. As for math and science performance, there were no benefits or losses.

That finding was especially significant. Students had received between 25 percent and 100 percent of mathematics and science instruction in the non-English partner language as they progressed to grade five. Meanwhile, the probability that native speakers of the partner language would still be classified as "English learners" declined by six percentage points at grade five and by fourteen points by grade six. As the researchers concluded, well-planned immersion programs beginning in early childhood might be the "next frontier" in promoting educational equality and opportunity.[17] The success of the Portland program, combined with the Collier and Thomas findings, helped lay the foundation for what ultimately came to be in California.

Looking back, there was indeed a silver lining in the cloud of Proposition 227. The law mobilized advocates to counter attempts by English-only forces at discrediting the few existing bilingual programs and to develop an organized strategy to turn the law around. In the end, it made California a leader in creating innovative programs to promote both the education of English learners and the benefits of multilingualism for all students. The relationships forged in fighting the Proposition 227 campaign led to the creation in 1999 of Californians Together, a statewide coalition of twenty-five parent, teacher, education, advocacy, and civil rights groups. As Shelly Spiegel-Coleman, the group's first executive director and one of the original organizers, later recalled, "We wanted an official body to protect the rights of English learners. But we knew we had to change hearts and minds to make it work."[18] They started with a legislative proposal for a statewide Seal of Biliteracy, building on the success of the original Glendale program. Though the state legislature approved the measure twice, both times it was vetoed by then-governor Arnold Schwarzenegger. Not to be defeated, Californians Together campaigned for school districts to adopt the seal; fifty-five agreed. With the election of Jerry Brown as governor in 2011, the legislation finally passed and set in motion a national trend.

The group then moved on to dismantling Proposition 227, which demanded legislative action to put a new proposal on the ballot. A key part of the coalition's agenda was to build a strong relationship with minority leaders, and especially with the "Latino Caucus" in the state legislature. By that time, California's demographics and politics had changed in significant ways. The number of Latinx and Asian voters had increased. The number of elected officials from those groups had also grown. Some of those officials had been English learners themselves and had seen the negative effects of Proposition 227 play out in their own schooling. Leading the charge in the state legislature was Ricardo Lara, a Democratic state senator who regretted his own experience as a student in English-only immersion classes.[19] Meanwhile, Californians Together had built a constituency among parents, teachers, and business leaders. As positive findings on bilingual programs nationwide mounted, along with the demand for multilingual workers, so did support among Californians to repeal Proposition 227. Among the committed allies were chambers of commerce and associations of physicians, lawyers, and firefighters.

In 2016, having raised $4.95 million to gain public support, Californians Together saw victory when 73 percent of the voters adopted Proposition 58, the California Education for Global Economy Initiative. That was a stunning reversal from the 61 percent of voters who had approved Proposition 227 in 1998. As of July 2017, school officials would have to offer the program "to the extent possible" where twenty parents within a grade level or thirty parents within a school requested a "language acquisition program," including dual language immersion. At the time, under 5 percent of California's public schools offered multilingual programs despite the state's 1.4 million English learners, 80 percent of them Spanish-speaking.

The turnaround in California was not just about demographics and politics. The world of bilingual instruction had experienced a sea change since 1998. The solid research findings supported new bilingual education models that departed substantially from those targeted in the Proposition 227 movement. Again, dual language immersion mixed native English speakers with English language learners, avoiding the years-long ethnic and linguistic segregation of earlier programs. Californians Together underscored these findings and distinctions. Just as importantly, the people of California were facing globalization and a strained economy, which changed their attitudes toward language learning and multilingualism, a twenty-first-century skill. They also heard the voices of their children, which program organizers effectively used to their advantage. In radio ads leading up to the vote, young supporters urged their parents to prepare them for "the jobs of tomorrow." The question the ads posed—"Are your kids ready?"—spoke volumes.[20]

As the president of the California Teachers Association stated, "We are really a diverse state now, and we are participating in a worldwide economy. For our students to only know one language puts them at a disadvantage, and the research bears that out."[21] The California Chamber of Commerce reminded the public, "Top education systems in the world all require students to learn multiple languages. Yet California, with its natural reserve of diverse linguistic resources, has failed to develop a multilingual workforce."[22] The new order of dual immersion programs appeared to be a win-win for native English-speaking students and English learners alike. What remained to be said was what a generation of California's English learners had personally lost in the intervening two decades. For state senator Ricardo Lara, the bill's sponsor, this was "an attempt to right a tremendous wrong."[23] A journalist looking back on his own experience under Proposition 227 even more pointedly recalled, "The 'no-Spanish dictate' amounted to a form of cultural erasure. It was a cruel, shortsighted act, born of ignorance and intolerance." For "Latino immigrant children," he declared, "Spanish is the key that unlocks the untranslatable wisdom of their elders.... It's a source of self-knowledge, a form of cultural capital."[24]

The Proposition 58 organizers realized that they essentially were fighting an ideological battle. Bent on building a wide consensus, they carefully crafted the language of the measure and the message, shifting the discourse away from civil rights and compensatory education toward economics and competition. The selling points to the public were carefully designed. The measure made clear that public schools had a "moral obligation" to teach all the state's children "literacy in the English language." It also highlighted the cognitive, economic, and academic benefits of "multilingualism and multiliteracy." Multilingual skills would promote the state economy.

In contrast to Proposition 227's "language as problem" (and English as the solution), Proposition 58 spoke in terms of "language [economic] resources". It dropped the term "bilingual" with its negative connotation and the stigma of failed and segregated programs. In its place appeared "multilingual" with its positive association with "innovation and cosmopolitanism." It abandoned Propositions 227's state and national references focusing on the past. In its place it offered a future-looking perspective on internationalism and the global economy. It spoke of parental "choice and voice" and broadened the program's beneficiaries from immigrant children to all children, along with California businesses, the state itself, and the nation. In marketing the proposal in a neoliberal discourse, the proponents were able to attract the necessary political and financial support from a wide constituency.[25]

"Going global" and extending the base to include majority parents and business interests, including multinational corporations, were crucial to saving dual language education. Yet some might ask, "At what cost and for whom?" The original intent of dual language programs in California and elsewhere was to provide equal educational opportunity to disadvantaged English learners who would gain English language and literacy skills by interacting with native English speaking students throughout the school day. As already noted, time has shown that their needs can get lost at the local level amidst those of students whose parents exercise more voice in school matters. There also is the danger that with so much weight and community support on the economic value of language, the ideology of the market might pervade the entire educational program.

The Californians Together organizers have remained consciously aware of these dangers. Though Proposition 58 does not convey a civil rights or access message, the group drafted the proposal to highlight that the prime objective was to realize the potential of English learners.[26] Subsequent developments prove this point. While not abandoning support for multilingualism for all, in the years following the measure's adoption, the group has refocused its energies on its core mission to "protect and promote the rights of English learners," who make up 23 percent of the state's K–12 population. Its website is replete with initiatives promoting those rights, including a report entitled *Unveiling California's Growing Bilingual Teacher Shortage* as well as publications geared toward "long term English learners" and "immigrant and refugee students." The group's English Learner Leadership and Legacy Initiative brings together mentors and fellows in an effort to train the next generation of advocates and educators. The group was instrumental in spearheading the English Learner Roadmap, a state Department of Education document providing guidance materials and resources to school districts in meeting the needs of English learners.[27]

When the State Board of Education unanimously adopted the roadmap in 2017, it marked a historic moment for those who had resolutely worked to undo Proposition 227.[28] Global California 2030, an initiative launched the following year, was further proof that the state's commitment to "quality education" included students achieving high levels of proficiency in English and at least one more language.[29] Among the initiative's ambitious goals, the state projects that by 2030 half of all K–12 students will participate in programs that lead to proficiency in two or more languages, that world language classes will reach one hundred thousand, and that the number of dual-immersion programs will quadruple from about four hundred to sixteen hundred.[30] In 2018, the school superintendent in Los Angeles predicted that by 2025 dual language programs in the district would grow from fourteen thousand to a stunning fifty thousand students who would be biliterate when they graduate (@AustinLASchools, May 30, 2018).

The California turnaround undeniably has been a tour de force, though it is difficult to predict how intense the demand for the Seal of Biliteracy or for language immersion programs might be in the years to come. It depends on the sustained commitment of state and local school authorities and on the level of information provided to parents on both their options and the benefits of multilingualism. It also depends on a number of external factors, including a steady stream of positive research findings, the continued pull of the global economy, and the winds of politics, from the international to the local, in the face of demographic changes. Whatever the outcome, the events in California have had a pronounced effect on language policy across the nation. They have inspired other states to adopt the Seal of Biliteracy and to embrace language immersion programs. They also laid the political groundwork for a similar reversal in Massachusetts, where the legislature in 2017 lifted a fifteen-year-old law that had placed severe constraints on bilingual and dual language programs.[31]

Utah and the Politics of Pragmatism

As interesting a case study on language and politics as California may be, the state of Utah is equally so, and for somewhat different reasons. Utah, in fact, has produced the most ambitious state-led immersion program, despite being the state with the lowest per-pupil spending on education combined with an "English only" law adopted in 2000, though with no direct implications for education. And it has done so through unswerving political backing from an alliance of business interests and language advocates, with an influential overlay of religious pragmatism.

The state's large Church of Jesus Christ of Latter-Day Saints (LDS) population, which counts for over 60 percent of Utah's residents, understands the benefits of bilingualism. Though church headquarters are in Salt Lake City, about half of the fifteen million church members live outside the United States. The most devout among them, in their late teens or early twenties, go abroad on a two-year proselytizing mission, which both demands and improves language skills. Before embarking, many of them undergo intensive religious and language training at one of the church's Missionary Training Centers, the most notable being the campus in Provo, Utah. In nine weeks at most, they acquire a working competency in one of fifty-five languages. They return home from abroad with sharper language skills, a broader worldview, and an understanding of different cultures.

It is not accidental that Brigham Young University, which the church owns and operates, houses one of the most well regarded Centers for Language Studies. The center supports twelve departmental major and minor language programs and provides instruction in over forty additional languages. It awards a Language Certificate for advanced coursework and places an official language proficiency notation in nineteen widely used world languages on undergraduate student transcripts.[32] Upward of 70 percent of students attending Brigham Young are bilingual. Language immersion programs align with the religious needs, cultural mindset, and openness of the modern-day LDS Church, especially toward the state's growing Spanish-speaking immigrant community. In most states, any overt religious ties to public education would invite charges of violating church-state separation under the First Amendment to the US Constitution; but that is not the case in Utah. Among the responses to the question "Why Portuguese?" the Office of Education's information brochure openly notes that "LDS returned missionaries . . . have served in over thirty-five Portuguese-speaking missions around the world."[33]

Utah's rise as a leader in dual immersion has evolved over the course of forty years. It began in 1979 when a family in the state's Alpine School District pressed for a dual Spanish-English immersion program. From there, the concept spread to other school districts. The idea was to support dual language learners, improve achievement, and challenge gifted and talented students. As totally local initiatives with limited resources, some of these programs did not survive. But the seeds had been sown and left to germinate for almost three decades.

Two improbable allies are credited with getting the Utah program off the ground. The first was Howard Stephenson, a conservative state senator, LDS Church member, and self-proclaimed "government watchdog" from a Salt Lake City suburb. Stephenson chaired the Senate Public Education Appropriations Subcommittee and cohosted a conservative Saturday morning radio show called *Red Meat Radio—Inside Utah Politics*. As Stephenson tells it, while visiting China in 2008 he had an "epiphany." Meeting a number of Chinese students who spoke fluent English, he wondered what he could do to help the United States connect with a rising nation like China.[34] The second ally was Gregg Roberts, who would become the world language specialist in the state's Office of Education. Roberts was a former French teacher, self-described "liberal," and non–LDS Church member. As the world language specialist at Granite School District in Utah in 2007, Roberts had implemented pilot immersion programs in two elementary schools modeled after similar programs in another district.

Governor Jon Huntsman, an LDS Church member who spoke Mandarin and later served as American Ambassador to China, recruited Roberts and Stephenson to lay the groundwork for offering Arabic and Chinese in Utah's secondary schools. "Legislation seemed to be the best way to create a multitude of bilingual programs," Roberts later recalled.[35] Stephenson was responsible for convincing his colleagues in the Senate that language skills were essential to engage with emerging economies like China. A bilingual workforce would attract business and revenue to the state. As Utah has a 76 percent white population, framing the program as a way to enhance global competitiveness while steering clear of cultural arguments was a sound strategic decision. In 2007, the state legislature approved US$100,000 of ongoing funding for a full-time world language specialist position, which Roberts filled, and US$230,000 over six years to create the Critical Language Pilot Program in Chinese and Arabic in twenty secondary schools.[36]

Stephenson and Roberts realized that beginning language study in high school was too late. And so they made the case for starting in the elementary grades. Their initial focus was on Spanish, French, and Chinese—languages with a world market. To win over the skeptics, and there were many, they drew on psychologist Ellen Bialystok's research on the cognitive benefits of bilingualism along with Virginia Collier and Wayne Thomas's findings on the academic benefits of two-way immersion.[37] The state's LDS heritage and its tradition of sending missionaries all over the world were an added selling point. It was natural for Utahans to embrace language learning.

Their efforts paid off. In 2008, the Senate adopted the International Education Initiative (Senate Bill 41), allocating US$270,000—$6,000 to $18,000 awarded to twenty-five elementary schools—for dual language immersion programs in Chinese, French, and Spanish. Portuguese, German, and Russian have since been added. Cloaking the program in the mantle of state law increased the chances for continued state funding.[38] When Huntsman resigned in 2009 and Gary Herbert took over as governor, three summits were held under the auspices of his office, bringing together business, education, and government leaders in various groupings to discuss and create a new model for language education. The meetings sparked the development of the Utah Language Roadmap for the 21st Century. The goal was to address the state's need for language skills in education, government, and business.

Most of Utah's dual immersion programs begin in the first grade, with a few starting in kindergarten. They include mostly one-way immersion (majority of native English speakers with limited or no proficiency in the second language) but also two-way immersion (both native English speakers and speakers of the second language) using a fifty-fifty model. Elementary grade students spend half of the school day in the target language and the other half day in English. In the upper grades, they shift languages in math, science, and social students to some extent. One course is offered in grades seven through nine. Students take the Advanced Placement class in the particular language in grade nine or ten.[39]

To avoid problems with teacher certification requirements plaguing other states, Utah created a special International Visiting Guest Teacher license. The license can be used for any country with which Utah has signed a memorandum of understanding as long as the teacher is certified in the home country and holds a J-1 visiting teacher visa. It remains valid for the duration of the visa.[40] This arrangement has allowed the state to hire native teachers from Brazil, China, France, Germany, Mexico, Peru, and Spain who remain for three to five years. For guidance on teacher hiring, the state's Dual Language Immersion Advisory Council developed criteria for measuring "five discriminating characteristics of effective DLI teachers." The list included language proficiency, a coachable disposition, a collaborative disposition, strong pedagogy, and classroom management.[41]

Over time, the Chinese program has grown exponentially. It was initially launched in response to the business community's need to communicate with counterparts in the Chinese market. That growth is due largely to support from the Chinese government agency Hanban and the Confucius Institute, launched in 2007. By 2018, it was the largest Chinese dual language immersion program in the country, with over twelve thousand students from preschool through senior high participating.[42] That year, despite serious concerns raised elsewhere over Confucius Institute programs, Utah officials including Howard Stephenson and former US senator Orin Hatch publicly praised the institute's program and its teachers for being "very critical and crucial" to the program's success.[43] The Chinese press reported that Utah officials hoped to introduce the Utah model to other states.[44] Arizona, Colorado, Delaware, Georgia, Indiana, Rhode Island, and Wyoming have subsequently adopted it.

In 2018, Stephenson hosted a public event at the State Capitol with guests from the military, universities, business, law enforcement, and civic groups to witness the proficiency of dual immersion ninth graders presenting their language skills. Entitled "Utah's New Natural Resource: Dual Language Immersion," it was a tribute to the senator's ingenuity in tapping into the diverse interests of key stakeholders. By that point, the program had grown from fifteen hundred students in twenty-five schools to thirty-five thousand in 195 schools. By 2020–21, it was serving sixty-five thousand students in 285 schools. As Gregg Roberts says, "Not bad for a small state in the middle of nowhere."[45]

A consortium of five institutions of higher education in the state have partnered with the Utah Office of Education in the Bridge Program, which offers upper division language courses that take students beyond the Advanced Placement Language and Culture exam. Students can receive up to nine college upper division credits, allowing them to begin college just two or three courses short of claiming a minor in the language. Between 2016–17 and 2020–21, the program served approximately forty-nine hundred students and awarded 14,700 upper division university credits, saving Utah families an estimated US$17.6 million in tuition.[46]

As successive waves of students move through Utah's dual immersion programs, they progressively add to the state's sizeable bilingual workforce. Along with a flat 5 percent corporate tax rate, bilingual workers have attracted multinational corporations including eBay, Goldman Sachs, Oracle, and Procter and Gamble.[47] In 2019, Utah was named among the top three in Forbes Best States for Business for the ninth time since 2010. It's simply a matter of supply and demand. As the schools (and colleges) produce workers with language skills, more corporations move into the state. More corporations translate into more jobs and a higher tax base. Everyone gains in the end.

This almost unique combination of state factors—smallness in size, focus on economic development, changing demographics, and a dominant population with practical language demands, cultural sensitivities, and global experience—has made Utah, one of the most politically conservative states, overwhelmingly receptive to bilingual schooling, an approach typically identified with political liberals.

New York in French

Just as Utah brought about statewide change in a top-down model, a similarly compelling local story of bottom-up change comes from New York City, where a convergence of forces has made the city the epicenter of a "bilingual revolution." Unlike French programs in Louisiana, where state legislation has undone years of stigma attached to Creole speakers, the New York experience has evolved through public-private partnerships. Inspired by parents and supported by a diverse coalition of actors, the city's mix of low-income immigrants and professional urban dwellers, including many French nationals in particular, has helped make this happen.

The meteoric rise in French programs in New York is part of a broader citywide effort that cuts across an ever-growing list of languages and communities. By 2018–19, the total number of dual language programs was 572, of which 79 percent were Spanish and 13 percent Chinese, with the remaining programs now spread among Arabic, Bengali, French, Haitian Creole, Italian, Japanese, Korean, Polish, Russian, Urdu, and Hebrew. From the Department of Education's perspective, the primary goal has been to increase access and to develop the bilingual potential of the city's diverse and disadvantaged population of English learners. It's also a way to make schools more racially and economically integrated by attracting middle-class educated families to neighborhoods that those families ordinarily would not have considered. Meanwhile, as the city rebounded from the 2008 financial downturn and the economy diversified, it drew an educated population of foreign-born families looking for their children to develop literacy in both their home language and English.[48] To what extent the economic fallout of the 2020 COVID-19 pandemic will affect these demographics remains uncertain.

Aside from the DOE's efforts, the grassroots momentum for dual language programs has mainly come from the French community and its tenacity in preserving its language and culture. That would all seem unremarkable in the iconic melting pot of New York, were it not for the role the French community has played in building public-private partnerships across the Atlantic. This is an odd turn of events on several counts. Of all the language groups in New York, the French historically have not been a driving force in shaping public school policy. Nor, until recent years, has French been a commonly heard language on the streets of the city. That is not to suggest that the French are new to New York. French speakers have lived in the Big Apple since colonial times. In the late

1800s, part of what is now SoHo in lower Manhattan was reportedly a thriving "Quartier Français." According to *Scribner's Monthly* from 1869, "The people are nearly all French. French too is the language of the signs over the doors and in the windows."[49] Yet over the years their numbers have been relatively small and their presence rarely noted, as compared to the widely known French-speaking communities in Louisiana and Maine.

As of 2019 there were over eighty thousand New Yorkers above age four who primarily spoke French, accounting for 1.6 percent of the city's total population. French ranked eighth among the top ten languages of immigrant New Yorkers with limited English proficiency.[50] The expatriate population has tended to prefer private French schools. The demographic profile, however, is shifting in response to economic developments, natural disasters, and political unrest in parts of the francophone world. About sixty thousand French expatriates live in New York. Between 2015 and 2016, those who were registered with the French consulate increased by 6.5 percent, though the number has leveled off and even declined by one percent in 2018.[51] The population is presumably much larger. The reported numbers reflect neither the numerous expats who don't bother to register nor the many French speakers from former French colonies spread throughout the five boroughs. In Brooklyn alone, there are an estimated two hundred thousand Haitians and Haitian Americans in addition to a sizeable population of French speakers from France. West Harlem in Upper Manhattan and the Bronx are home to scores of West Africans, while North Africans have clustered in western Queens.

The city's French-speaking community is a combination of three social groups that share little in common, save for an abiding concern that their children preserve the French language and culture. The first is the international business and diplomatic elite from France or from former French colonies, some assigned to the United Nations, whose jobs have taken them to New York for a defined period. The group also includes a smaller number of restaurant owners, both recent and longstanding, and a smattering of others. They typically send their children to a handful of private French schools, with tuition (and the family's housing) in some cases paid by their employer. Some of these schools form part of a unique network of 494 establishments, educating 330,000 students in 135 countries. They receive funds from the French government under several types of agreements. About 60 percent of the students are not French nationals.[52] The French consulate grants scholarships ("bourses scolaires") to the children of low-income families to cover a portion of the tuition fees. In New York City, the awards amount to about US$3 million each year. For France, the idea is not simply to meet the needs of French families living abroad. Most importantly, it is to promote France's mission of cultural diplomacy and the socialization of French citizens while spreading the French language around the globe.[53]

The second group, moving toward the other end of the economic spectrum, is made up of new immigrants from former French colonies in West Africa, the Caribbean, and the Middle East whose children typically attend public or Catholic schools. Many of them struggle in low-wage jobs and see English as the ticket to social mobility for their children. In the past they put minimal weight on French. A notable exception is the Malian community in the Bronx and Harlem, where Saturday French classes for young children give testament to the community's deep attachments to the language. Within this diverse group, a growing number have come around and followed along with a more sizeable and organized third group of French-speaking families too wealthy to receive the "bourses scolaires" to attend private schools in the French government's network but not wealthy enough to pay private school tuition on their own.

This third group is a young educated population. Some of them are in the arts. Many of them are connected to the city's vibrant startup network and plan to remain in the United States indefinitely. Greasing the gears of this network is French Tech NYC, one of a number of worldwide online hubs accredited by the French government and designed to promote the development of French startups both in France and abroad. To support these efforts, the Consulate General of France has created the French Tech Club in New York. The club hosts conferences and breakfast meetings that draw linkages among entrepreneurs and investors and give recent arrivals to the city immediate access to an active network.

The election of Emmanuel Macron to the French presidency in 2017 and his repeated calls to make France a "startup nation" have given added impetus to developing French-American connections. Between the early 2000s and 2018, French companies invested US$7.2 billion and created over twenty-one thousand new jobs in New York.[54] In April 2018, the Consulate General of France and the city of New York joined with French Tech NYC in forming a partnership to promote further investment between the two countries' ecosystems. By that point, the city was home to 180 French startups with thirty more companies expected to expand by the end of the year. Another addition to the New York tech scene is FrenchFounders, a worldwide association launched in 2014. By 2021, it counted over four thousand members, including French-speaking investors, entrepreneurs, and CEOs in over thirty countries on five continents.

With the support of both the growing French business community in the United States and the French government, these initiatives reflect a wave of French nationals, both accomplished and still reaching, riding the crest of globalization. They find New York particularly attractive for a number of reasons: its ready access to private investment; its community of designers, artists, and publicists; its rich multicultural life; and its shorter traveling time and distance from France than California's Silicon Valley. Many of these newcomers have studied in other countries through Europe's Erasmus program and are open to other languages and cultures. They are especially familiar with all things "American" through film, TV, and social media. These are change makers who actively pursue what the city has to offer, including the possibility of quality public schooling on their terms.

In a more general way, dual language programs are bringing socioeconomic and racial diversity to New York City's public schools, while revitalizing aging or economically challenged neighborhoods, for better and for worse, in a tsunami of gentrification. The community in Brooklyn, just over the Brooklyn Bridge from lower Manhattan, is a prime example. Carroll Gardens, a former working-class Italian American neighborhood of one- and two-family stone and brick houses, surrounded by low-income apartment complexes of African Americans and Latinx, is now home to a thriving population of young French-speaking families and others attracted to the French "vibe" that the neighborhood has acquired. French cafes intermix with a fading number of Italian food shops and Hispanic bodegas. Walk down Smith or Court Streets on any given day and you are as likely to hear French as English spoken. In July, local businesses and community groups host a series of events celebrating Bastille Day. The main street is closed off to traffic, French flags fly from the buildings, crêpes are eaten in abundance, and pétanque competitions draw enthusiastic crowds.

A significant part of the neighborhood's appeal is the French dual immersion program in the local public school. The seeds of the program were planted in 2004 when a group of parents, troubled by the lack of affordable education options for French-speaking families, formed the association Éducation Française à New York (EFNY). Aiming to explore the possibility of French bilingual schooling within the public schools, they had two key factors working in their favor—a critical mass of eager French-speaking families and the interest of the French government in promoting the language abroad. They also understood that under New York State law, if there were twenty or more students at the same grade level in a school district who spoke the same home language, the district had to provide a bilingual education program in some form. In New York City, the requirement is only fifteen students. The number of students whose home language was French was sufficiently sizeable to comply with the Department of Education's mandate that each immersion classroom must be two-way, that is, it must have at least half English language learners. That hurdle has proven challenging for less widely used languages like Italian, Japanese, and Polish.

Over the next several years, the group was able to engage the logistical and financial support of the French government. The point person was Fabrice Jaumont, the education attaché for the embassy of France in New York and a program officer of the French American Cultural Exchange (FACE) Foundation, a nonprofit partner of the embassy. Jaumont first encountered immersion programs back in 1997 as an education liaison for the French consulate in Boston. Moving to New York in 2001, he has since carried the gospel of language immersion to other parts of the city and beyond. Along the way, he started *New York in French*, a "free, apolitical, community-oriented" blog where Francophiles can exchange information and share interests. By 2021, the blog had upward of twelve thousand members.[55]

EFNY strategically decided to begin at the local level. As Jaumont now explains, the French bilingual revolution started in 2007 with three schools in three boroughs serving a diversity of families. Through EFNY's efforts, a program primarily for West African students opened at PS 125 in Harlem. Jaumont also worked with Shimon Waronker, the principal of MS 22 in the Bronx, listed in 2004 as one of the most dangerous schools in the city. Waronker, a member of the Chabad-Lubavitch sect of Hasidic Judaism, wanted to open a French dual language program for his African students, who were being bullied by other students in the school.

The third school, in Brooklyn, set the revolution in motion. Why the momentum emerged from Brooklyn at that time is a story in itself. Jaumont links it to the 9/11 terrorist attacks, when many young people left lower Manhattan for Brooklyn and mingled with teachers, artists, and local restaurant owners. They started to have families, and the Lycée Français de New York in Manhattan was too far and too expensive.[56] In any case, in 2006 three determined mothers approached Gisele Gault McGee, the principal of PS 58, the Carroll School, where a small French community was forming. By that point, the Language and Laughter Studio, a private French bilingual preschool opened in 2005, was serving the demand for early childhood education.

McGee was the daughter of a French mother born in Toulouse whose family came from the north of France. At the age of five she announced to her mother that she no longer wanted to speak French, as none of her friends spoke the language. The year was 1960, before the advent of bilingual education. Immigrants in New York were still looking to assimilate into the mainstream. Later mindful of her own linguistic loss, McGee had a personal attachment to the language and an intuitive understanding of the benefits of bilingualism.[57] On a more pragmatic note, opening new French immersion classes would help resolve the school's dwindling enrollment and attract additional funding from the Department of Education. Without replacing the monolingual English program, the dual immersion classes would offer both French- and English-speaking families an appealing option and infuse new life into the school.

When the first kindergarten class opened in 2007, applications were double the number of available places. For the first year, the program accepted students from outside the school zone. In following years, it limited enrollment to students living in the area. By 2014, the school's overall student numbers had jumped from three hundred fifty to nine hundred, of which three hundred were in the French program. The program now runs from kindergarten through fifth grade, two classes per grade. Families move into Carroll Gardens specifically for their children to attend PS 58, creating what has come to be called "Little Paris" in the heart of South Brooklyn. The enthusiasm of parents gives testimony to the role the program plays in building a sense of community. For French-speaking parents, it maintains their children's ties to France while allowing them to intermix with American students. For English-speaking parents, as their children learn French, they too are drawn into the language and culture.[58] They also see the career opportunities for their children down the road. French-owned companies employ close to seven hundred thousand workers in the United States. France is the third largest foreign employer in the country.[59] As one parent recalled, "Entering P.S. 58 [was] like winning the lottery. All my friends called to congratulate me."[60]

In neighboring Boerum Hill, the School for International Studies now offers a French dual language program for grades six through twelve in an extended school day as part of its International Baccalaureate program, the first of its kind in a United States public school. Opening in 2015, the school partnered with the French Embassy and the Smith Street Workshop, a Carroll Gardens learning center, in designing the school's innovative interdisciplinary French IB curriculum. The workshop, the brainchild of Olivia Ramsey, a former kindergarten teacher at PS 58, has grown to include a French immersion preschool and an assortment of French programs for toddlers to adults. In the past, many of the preschoolers have moved on to the French dual language program at PS 58 or to the International School of Brooklyn, a private nonprofit school in Carroll Gardens that offers both French and Spanish bilingual tracks from pre-K through grade 8.[61]

As word of the PS 58 developments traveled through the city's French community, French-speaking parents pressed for similar programs in their neighborhood public schools. In 2010, the city's first French-American Charter School, now covering pre-K through eighth grade, opened in Harlem's "Little Senegal" through the efforts of parents and partner organizations. Other language groups, including Russian, Italian, Polish, and Arabic, encouraged by the success of the French programs and armed with the "roadmap" developed by Fabrice Jaumont, promoted their plans to local school officials. By 2021, French dual language programs in New York were serving fifteen hundred students with sixty-five teachers in seven elementary schools and three middle schools, with a high school soon to be opened.

Fabrice Jaumont had set out to start a revolution, and he did. As he explains, it's a "social" revolution aimed at upending a system where education in a world language has been available only to children whose families can afford private schooling. His book, *The Bilingual Revolution: The Future of Education is in Two Languages,* inspirationally recounts the triumphs and challenges in realizing that dream.[62] Initially published in 2017 in both English and French, it is now available in eleven languages. "We underestimate the impact of motivated parents," Jaumont says. Programs would "multiply," he maintains, if parents realized that they have the ability to get them off the ground and if they knew how to do it. "This book," he says, "tells parents, 'you are capable.' "[63] With the success of the book in hand, Jaumont went on to initiate a podcast, *Révolution Bilingue,* a series of talks with practitioners and experts on bilingualism. He then brought together his blog *New York in French,* the podcast series, book publishing, and advocacy under the umbrella of the Center for the Advancement of Languages, Education, and Communities (CALEC), a nonprofit organization that he founded as a wider platform for promoting bilingualism and dual language programs.

As school administrators understand well, language immersion programs do not come cost free either in administrative effort or in resources. They are a strain on severely strapped public school budgets. They demand additional staff fluent in each language, special instructional materials often purchased from abroad or translated from English, and targeted staff development. Even with adequate funding, finding materials aligned with state content standards in languages other than Spanish can prove challenging. Understanding the severity of the funding issue, Fabrice Jaumont used a bit of French ingenuity. He took to crowdfunding, with a goal of US$50,000 targeted toward realistic objectives like purchasing iPads. He launched an "Adopt a School" campaign where donors could support a particular project, like certifying a teacher or purchasing books. He encouraged parents to create a tax-exempt nonprofit organization where donors could receive a tax deduction.[64]

In 2013, the French Embassy and the French American Cultural Exchange (FACE) Foundation launched a campaign to raise US$2.8 million and reach seven thousand children within the next five years. One of the objectives was to make these programs available in less privileged francophone immigrant communities across New York's boroughs. Funds raised went toward purchasing French children's books for school libraries, providing scholarships for teachers to pursue a master's degree in bilingual education, and organizing workshops for teachers. Staffing is a particular problem for language immersion programs, though less so in a large city like New York. In more remote places such as Utah and Louisiana, school districts have resorted to working with private agencies to find qualified teachers abroad and help them secure visas with the United States Department of State. Yet with visas valid for only five years, visiting teachers have to return home just as they hit their stride, sending the school district back to square one on recruitment.

The French government has given special recognition to New York's dual language programs. In 2012, the government, by legislative decree, launched the LabelFrancÉducation seal, which the Ministry of Foreign Affairs and Education awards to schools that promote French language and culture as part of their curriculum.[65] The stated goal was educational, creating a "club of excellence" alongside the French lycées abroad. The larger goal was political, overtaking English as the global language. As the ministry noted at that time, there were signs that the era of "English domination" was over. French-speaking countries were seeing "strong demographic growth," while a new middle class in emerging countries like India was looking for "cultural and linguistic diversity."[66] To be eligible, a school must offer French language in addition to at least two other subjects in French, which together make up at least a third of weekly instruction. By 2020, 395 schools in fifty-nine countries on five continents had earned the seal, including thirty-five schools in the United States. Nine of them were in New York City.[67]

As these facts suggest, it takes a village to get dual language programs off the ground and maintain them. A key member of New York's "village" is *French Morning*, an online magazine published since 2009 in French. Its English edition, *Frenchly*, is geared toward anglophone Francophiles worldwide. *French Morning* is the brainchild of expat Emmanuel Saint-Martin, a French journalist and correspondent for *France 24* in New York. Saint-Martin saw the need for an online news source to serve the city's growing French community. In May 2017, the parent company, French Morning Media Group, launched *Maudits Français* in Montreal, followed by *French Morning London* in partnership with French Radio London in January 2018.

By mid-2017, FrenchMorning.com had close to sixty thousand subscribers. In April and May of that year alone, it reached upward of 270,000 individual visitors. The company's revenue had increased by 61 percent from the previous year. Its growth potential seemed so promising that it offered its readers the possibility of investing in stock in the company for as little as US$100, which allowed the company to enter the Montreal and London markets. By 2019, French Morning Media Group had six local editions in the United States, including New York, San Francisco, Los Angeles, Miami, Texas, and Washington, DC. The total enterprise was attracting about five hundred thousand separate visitors each month, while its subsidiary website, Frenchly.us, was reaching 110,000 monthly users. At that point it launched yet another fundraising campaign to expand to Asia. This was French cultural entrepreneurship at its most creative.

To say that *French Morning* is a cornucopia of information on each city's cultural and community life is an understatement. Stories run the gamut from practical advice on immigration, education, health, beauty, and learning English to film reviews and political commentary. Advertisements lead you to

French-speaking lawyers, real estate agents, psychotherapists, and young French speakers looking for au pair positions. A yearly competition on the best baguette in New York gathers a crowd of mostly young people to celebrate the final announcement with a celebratory brunch. The magazine keeps the French connected with each other and helps them navigate city life. *French Morning* also brings France into the lives of ardent Francophiles, who are a sizeable part of its readership. During the coronavirus pandemic of 2020, it was an informational lifeline for the French-speaking community in the city, addressing support networks, services, and coping mechanisms.

French Morning has been a key factor in the bilingual education "revolution," especially in New York City. The group's *Guide de l'Éducation Bilingue* is an invaluable source of information on raising a bilingual child. It reminds readers that 50 percent of the world's population is bilingual, fifty million such people living in the United States. The guide includes a list of French bilingual schools, after-school activities, and summer camps for New Yorkers.[68] From the online magazine grew the idea for an annual Bilingual Fair held each fall at a local college in New York. Since 2014, *French Morning* has organized and co-sponsored the fair in partnership with the French Embassy, the Québec Générale New York, the French-American Foundation, and other language communities including CityKinder, a lifestyle and community platform for German-speaking parents. Each year brings additional language groups into the mix. *French Morning* has co-sponsored similar Bilingual Fairs in San Francisco, Los Angeles, and London. In 2020 in the midst of the pandemic lockdown, the Bilingual Fair moved online over multiple days in two cycles, one in the United States and the other in London.

The New York City fair consistently attracts over five hundred attendees, gathering in a single space all the players in the metropolitan area's bilingual education community. This is a festive family event where children keep busy with fun activities as their parents gain insights they need to make informed decisions. Each year, the exhibition hall is lined with learning materials and staff from private and public school programs eager to share the benefits of raising and educating children in more than one language. Panel discussions with titles like "Understanding the Bilingual Mind and Brain" and "Becoming a Teacher in a Bilingual Program" generate lively discussion. The Q&A sessions have an "alternate universe" quality even for cosmopolitan New York. Audience members give glowing testimony to their experiences either growing up themselves or raising their children in two, three, and even four languages. It's a bit like a religious revival meeting. If you entered with any doubts, by the end you are a confirmed believer not just in bilingualism but in multilingualism.

You also come away with a sense of sea change and generational shift. These are educated and involved parents who understand that parental commitment, including help with fundraising and even tutoring, is an essential component of these programs. They also have an expansive view of language and culture. They understand the benefits of bilingualism and especially the market value of English. They want their children to easily navigate the American mainstream with native-like English but without losing their French language and identity. As Emmanuel Saint-Martin put it, "There's something specific about the French identity that believes in the language, about the way they see themselves in the world. It's at the core of the movement."[69] But the racial makeup of the group cannot go unnoticed. Participants in the annual Bilingual Fair are overwhelmingly White, with lesser representation from the city's wider francophone community.

Among the Bilingual Fair exhibitors, two have played an especially notable role in the promotion of French language and culture in New York. The first is Albertine, a bookstore devoted solely to books in English and French from over thirty francophone countries. A project of the Cultural Services of the French embassy, Albertine's home is the landmark Payne Whitney Mansion, which also houses the French Cultural Services, on Fifth Avenue in New York's toney Upper East Side. Beyond its extensive selection of books, Albertine has woven itself into the intellectual and cultural fabric of New York. Throughout the year, it hosts debates and discussions on contemporary and classical culture. Its annual festival gathers together a wide range of American and French artists, writers, and thinkers around a particular theme.

The second exhibitor is the French American Cultural Exchange (FACE) Foundation. Among its many educational and cultural projects, FACE operates a French Heritage Language Program (FHLP) in partnership with the French embassy and the Internationals Network for Public Schools (INPS). By 2020, INPS included twenty-eight public schools and academies for new immigrants across the country, sixteen of them in New York City.[70] The FHLP program began in 2005 when its president and founder, Jane Ross, a recent retiree from the Lycée Français de New York, began meeting with representatives of the French embassy along with school administrators, private foundation staff, and students from INPS to explore ways to offer French classes to the growing number of West African and Haitian immigrants in the city. From there emerged the first free French afterschool program, offering a two-hour weekly class at the Manhattan International High School. Many of these students were refugees from the Democratic Republic of the Congo, Guinea, Ivory Coast, Mali, and Sierra Leone.

The program, now run by FACE in partnership with the French embassy in the United States, connects students to internships and job opportunities where they can use their bilingual and multicultural skills. In 2020, it served seven hundred students from elementary to high school in New York, Florida, Maine, and

Massachusetts, 485 of them in New York City including several community centers.[71] Schools have recognized the quality of the classes in allowing students to take the Advanced Placement French exam. A survey of students enrolled in FHLP programs in New York underscored the positive impact these initiatives have had on the attitudes and aspirations of participants. Among the 115 respondents, 97 percent affirmed that it was important for them to continue learning French in the United States; 90 percent stated that they were planning to continue taking French classes in college; 73 percent noted that they were doing so for a future job or career; and 69 percent believed that their schools valued their speaking French.[72]

Much of the lead for these coordinated efforts has come from the French embassy and directly through the efforts of Fabrice Jaumont. By 2021, the French dual language network covered thirty-three states, ninety-four cities, 170 schools, and over thirty thousand students.[73] The embassy's 2017 report's reasons for "Why French?" are convincing. France, being the fifth global economic power, shares close trading ties and cross-investment with the United States. A total of twenty-eight hundred French companies in the United States earn a combined US$1.7 billion annually in technology, medicine, banking, defense, publishing, and tourism among other sectors, while French businesses in the United States count over thirty-six hundred affiliates with over 560,000 employees. The embassy has forged partnerships between French and American universities to train teachers and administrators and recruit interns. It also has signed memoranda of understanding with school districts to hire teachers certified by the French Ministry of Education. As the embassy's report states, "We're bringing France closer to the U.S."[74]

The force of those words was thrust into public view in September 2017 when the president of France, Emmanuel Macron, visited New York for opening meetings of the United Nation's General Assembly. Over the course of several days, Macron established himself as a measured counterweight to "oppositionist" thinking from the Trump administration, winning the hearts of many New Yorkers. As French presidents before him had done, he met with the French community in New York, a consular district that had endorsed him the previous spring with 52 percent of votes in the first presidential round and 95 percent in the second. Addressing nine hundred handpicked guests, mostly entrepreneurs, Macron spoke of "France's special role" in "reinventing" international relations. He invited the expats to return to France. "Come back, spread your knowledge, exchange ideas. Come to conquer!" he urged the crowd. "And for those who want to stay in the U.S. . . . We'll be by your side, so that you're proud of your country, and your children are well educated here."[75]

Macron continued his upbeat message the following day at an event cohosted by the Graduate Center of the City of New York and the French embassy. Macron had already demonstrated his support for bilingual education in France. The New York gathering was to officially launch the French Dual Language Fund, an extension of the fundraising campaign begun in 2013 to support French-English bilingual programs. Spearheaded by the embassy, with corporate funders including Chanel, Axa, Bic, and Best Buy, the program over the next five years would fund projects in two hundred schools, award scholarships to 120 future bilingual teachers, and provide stipends for seventy-four French teaching interns. At that point, the fund had reached US$1.4 million of its US$2 million target.

The auditorium was packed with VIPs and other select guests, including artist Patti Smith and the French minister of education, Jean-Michel Blanquer. Amidst flashing cameras, the charismatic Macron gave a powerful and touching vision of bilingualism and the possibilities of speaking both *la langue de Shakespeare* and *la langue de Molière*. "If cosmopolitanism makes sense," he said, "it is through multilingualism, and not through the domination of one language over the other, which will result, in a way, in blending many imaginations into one imagination." The oblique reference to the dominance of English was subtle but pointed. His words nonetheless were in tune with the program as young children from the Carroll School sang the American and French national anthems with gusto and teens from the Boerum Hill School for International Studies performed a moving playlet on the plight of child refugees. This was a celebratory event for the city's French-speaking community and for the parents, teachers, and advocates whose vision and tenacity had made these programs happen. It certainly was a victory lap for Fabrice Jaumont, whose "bilingual revolution" was changing hearts and minds on both sides of the Atlantic.

The event also was ironically historic for both its message and the setting. New York is a city that, despite opening its arms to successive waves of newcomers, had told immigrant children in earlier times that the price for "belonging" was to abandon their home language for English. Now a hundred years later, many of their offspring heard the president of France, a country with a similar assimilationist past and present, turn that message on its head. And they heard it in the grand hall of a public university that calls itself "the American Dream Machine" and vaunts its role in educating first- and second-generation Americans. The occasion was indeed revolutionary. The following March, in what *French Morning* called "Noël pour les programmes bilingues aux Etats-Unis" (Christmas for bilingual programs in the United States), fifty-eight French-English public schools and programs received US$150,000 for projects serving twenty-four thousand students. Louisiana with eleven projects was the biggest of the state winners. New York came in second with six projects, all in New York City.[76]

In the end, Macron's visit and the surrounding events brought to light how no other country has made such a determined effort as France, or its people, to promote its language and culture against the onslaught of English and to enhance its role as a key player in the global economy. Using the soft power of language, dual immersion programs are becoming a well-trodden path for helping move that project forward across the landscape of France's prime competitor for linguistic dominance.

Marketing Language

The belief that language is a tool for economic mobility is driving language policies and personal choices around the globe. Whether it's English-taught university programs in Europe, English instruction in primary and secondary schools
in former colonial countries, or world languages in the United States, the principal argument shaping this mindset rests on the value of language in the global
economy. While there are many other laudable reasons to promote language
learning, including the cognitive and cultural benefits, the economic argument
demands critical attention for its universal salience and appeal.

On that note, we begin with Mark Zuckerberg, the poster boy for unbridled
global ambition and success. In October 2014, long before Zuckerberg fell from
grace over data breaches, charges of antitrust violations, and creating a platform for hate-mongering on Facebook, the media were abuzz when the young
Facebook founder, to cheers and applause from students and faculty, carried out
a thirty-minute Q&A entirely in less-than-perfect Mandarin. The setting was
Tsinghua University in Beijing, where the university's School of Economics and
Management had named Zuckerberg a board member. When Zuckerberg returned to the university a year later with his skills somewhat sharpened, he self-
confidently gave a twenty-minute speech once again in Mandarin, describing
Facebook's origin, story, and mission.[1] The video, with English subtitles, quickly
became a popular item in China.[2]

The young entrepreneur, estimated to be the fifth richest person in the world,
claims to have taken up Chinese in 2010, initially to win over the family of
Priscilla Chan, whom he later married and who grew up speaking Chinese at
home. Yet underneath this personal story lies a compelling and quintessentially
"Zuckeresque" business motive. The Chinese government had blocked access to
Facebook since July 2009, when independence activists used the site to communicate during riots in the northwest city of Urumqi.[3]

As the *New York Times* reported in 2014, Zuckerberg's affiliation with
Tsinghua University demonstrates how Facebook is "playing the long game" in

China. The video, in particular, was a deliberate move to engage Chinese users. The unstoppable wunderkind has publicly praised China as "a great country" despite its blatant censorship problems. He credits his studying the language with his better understanding the culture. Apparently, speaking Chinese has helped him reach not only into the hearts of his Chinese-speaking in-laws but also into the minds of the Chinese people, from young students to Chinese technology innovators and President Xi Jinping himself. He first met the Chinese president at an industry forum in Seattle where the two spoke in Chinese.[4]

Whether Zuckerberg has used his language skills and cultural understanding in a socially responsible way would take a full-length book and then some. Nonetheless, he is not alone in understanding their market value in the global knowledge economy. As neoliberalism has re-envisioned the role of the state and placed greater emphasis on individual choice and fulfillment, it also has recast language learning not merely as a talent or a marker of ethnic or national identity but as a measurable skill and a saleable commodity on the market. Technology, mass migration, and affordable travel options are now making multilingual societies and cross-border transactions the norm rather than the exception.

Just about the time Zuckerberg was wooing the Chinese and trying to impress the world with his linguistic prowess, a book focusing on the benefits of multilingual skills for business struck a resonant chord across the globe. The book's title, *Fluent in 3 Months: How Anyone at Any Age Can Learn to Speak Any Language from Anywhere in the World*, boosted its popularity.[5] It quickly reached the top 100 sellers' list on Amazon in the United Kingdom, Canada, and France. In the United States it rose to number one in several Amazon categories. In Norway it was sold out on arrival. Calling the United States a "shockingly monolingual nation," *Forbes* ran a feature article warning US entrepreneurs to "take note" of the book's message that learning another language is worth the investment for potential business gain.[6]

Certainly this is not a new idea. As already recounted, when former European colonies gained independence in the mid-1900s, the elites justified retaining the colonial language for practical reasons, including its economic benefits and national cohesion, stripped of political and ideological baggage. Meanwhile, local and regional languages remained as symbols of cultural identity. That dichotomy began to shift in the latter decades of the twentieth century as mass migration and technological advances coalesced in making linguistic diversity a factor that could not be ignored. Political economists, in response to global movements and developments, began talking more generally about languages, both world and indigenous, as economic resources and valuable commodities. As people, goods, and ideas began circulating across national borders, they moved languages through multi-local markets. No longer were certain forms such as "standard" English merely a sign of breeding or education or taste. They transformed into a skill that could be exchanged for goods and even money.[7] Language became a type of human capital that individuals invest in, whether for their children or for themselves, based on the benefits and costs.[8]

Most commentators credit Jacob Marschak's seminal 1965 article, "The Economics of Language," with beginning this inquiry into the connection between material wealth and language. Marschak maintained that worth was not measured in money but in the probability of "attaining a goal." His point of departure was the theory of evolution. In other words, a language has value if it endures based on certain properties in the environment.[9] Those properties might include the number of speakers, the language community's economic and political power, and its cultural status in the international arena. Several strands of research subsequently emerged from this early work.

In recent years, studies have mainly focused on the effect of different language skills on earnings and trade. A useful model, suggested by François Vaillancourt, distinguishes between the mother tongue as both an "ethnic attribute" and a "form of human capital" and an individual's other languages as solely "elements of human capital." The mother tongue can either increase or decrease earnings. Knowing other languages, on the other hand, cannot reduce earnings. And while it can potentially increase them, it need not necessarily do so.[10] On that count, the work of Swiss economist François Grin is especially noteworthy.[11] As Grin explains, viewing language in terms of human capital is grounded in deep-rooted theory whereby professional experience, formal schooling, and the like are "assets" that increase personal earning power.[12]

A related line of inquiry, building on the writings of French sociologist Pierre Bourdieu, uses the concept of the "linguistic market." For Bourdieu, language is a form of "social capital" to which users and the market attach a value. "On a given linguistic market," he says, "some products are valued more highly than others."[13] The differential valuation itself provokes debates over "variability." Which languages or forms of a language and what types of speakers carry sufficient social capital to merit "legitimacy or authority or value as commodities?" In postcolonial settings, for example, while former colonial (i.e., western European) languages maintain value in managing global business transactions, other varieties may have added value in managing local transactions. As linguist Monica Heller sums it up, "The commodification of language confronts monolingualism with multilingualism, standardization with variability, and prestige with authenticity in a market where linguistic resources have gained salience and value."[14]

There are a number of ways to look at language from a market perspective. Some studies consider the demand among business sectors for multilingual workers as measured by responses to questionnaires, often on a point scale from "most important" to "least important" or from "strongly disagree" to "strongly agree." Others look at the percent of advertisements that mention foreign language skills as a requirement or as a plus in hiring. Some draw conclusions from self-reports by managers or workers on the importance that foreign language skills hold in their own work. Others look for a correlation between low levels of foreign language proficiency and corporate revenues and business gained or lost in the overall national economy. Still others try to measure the impact of language proficiency on an individual's earning power.

It would be remiss not to mention at the outset the limitations of each of these approaches. Drawing the link between linguistic and various economic variables, determining how these variables impact one another, and sorting out cause and effect pose serious difficulties, as François Grin himself has cautioned.[15] Questionnaires rely on the subjective assessments of individuals in a variety of work settings. Correlations between language skills and market factors, like lost or gained corporate revenues or individual earnings, do not necessarily mean a direct causal effect. Any number of outside factors—the country context, the corporate culture, the particular industry, or the sample size—might influence the outcome in some way. Job advertisements that call for specific language skills, moreover, tell us nothing about actual job offers or hires. Meanwhile, advertisements may not mention language skills simply to attract the largest number of applicants or to keep hiring costs down.[16]

The same goes for the survey responses of managers declaring the extent of a company's language needs or the weight placed on language in recruitment and hiring, which may be over- or underestimated. The economic impact of language deficiencies also can be overstated. Merely tallying up business lost due to inadequate language skills, for example, does not reveal situations where the company ultimately was able to close the deal with a more linguistically compatible business partner resulting in no net economic loss but merely a "trade diversion."[17] Finally, as Grin further suggests, the economic model is not intended to "dictate policy decisions" but should be considered alongside other perspectives in making "principled and transparent choices."[18]

These concerns are indeed noteworthy and should not be lightly dismissed. Yet they do not negate the value of overwhelmingly positive results. They merely call for assessing those results in the context of the larger picture, looking beyond the precise data to the general direction in which the evidence seems to point.

Marketing English

From the business perspective, when we think of marketing English, multinational corporations and high-end employment in developed countries immediately come to mind. Individuals who speak English well are rewarded with job mobility and higher earnings. Businesses that communicate in English are able to reach new markets and increase their profits. At the same time, however, English creates tensions in the global economy, especially for businesses and workers lacking the requisite language skills. There also is a hidden dark side to English as it intersects with the world of work particularly in emerging economies where globalization, fueled by English, is reshaping cultural norms and in the process redefining individual and national identities. Nowhere are those experiences more striking than in labor outsourcing, where aspects of authenticity and standardization are played out in real time. It is in that arena that we begin to examine the marketing of English, and the use of English in marketing, before moving on to the well-traveled multinational corporate discussion.

Outsourcing

English opens paths to labor outsourcing that run both ways. The essential idea is to increase profits by containing costs. Low-cost countries, particularly in Asia and Latin America, are a fertile source of immigrant workers for high-cost anglophone countries like the United Kingdom and, in particular, the United States. The remittances these workers send back to their families are a mainstay of the home economy. In the reverse, English enables high-cost countries to outsource a wide range of "knowledge-based work," including insurance claim processing, tax return preparation, computer programming, legal research and brief preparation, medical data entry, financial data analysis, CAT scan readings, airline reservations, and accounting. The Philippines and India, along with Brazil, Chile, China, Indonesia, and Malaysia, count among the top ten offshoring destinations.[19]

The Philippines opened its first call center in 1992. With its large young population (90 percent of its one hundred million people are under the age of fifty-five) and its standard of English close to that spoken by Americans, the country now leads in customer service jobs worldwide. Filipinos overall have relatively strong English skills compared to other Asian populations. On the 2020 English Proficiency Index, the Philippines ranked twenty-seventh among one hundred countries, well above India, ranking at fiftieth, based on test data from over 2.2 million adults.[20] The English advantage is due to several factors, not the least of which is the lasting effect of the American occupation on the school system and on familiarity with American culture and jargon. Filipinos, moreover, benefit from extensive media exposure to English language TV channels and movies and from widespread use of English across public signs.

An economy poor in natural resources has forced Filipinos to work abroad and businesses to attract international clients. As a result, English has proven invaluable in keeping the country financially afloat. The Philippines is considered the number one country globally for business process management (BPM) jobs, initially known as business process outsourcing (BPO). These jobs tend to demand no direct verbal contact with the public, which makes speaking skills of lesser importance than reading and writing.[21] Typically revolving around English, though increasingly around other languages, these opportunities permit countries to participate in a globalized service economy.

Both the Philippines and India, countries with conflicted colonial roots in English, are also commonly known for their call center industries. There the market value of English, along with questions of ownership and authenticity, are especially visible (or audible) while decoupling language from place and identity. Call centers capture the undesirable aspects of offshoring and the dangers of "feminizing," "racializing," and exploiting labor, as the focus shifts from producing tangible goods to providing information in a way that is mediated by language.[22] Both countries provide Anglo-American corporate clients with a large pool of highly qualified low-cost English-proficient labor. The globalized commodity is not simply language but accent, which as Bourdieu would say, is a measure of the speaker's linguistic capital exchanged for material prosperity and social mobility. Call centers provide both inbound and outbound services. On the inbound side, they employ "help desk" personnel who give technical, customer, or transactional support to clients in Western countries, particularly the United States and the United Kingdom. At all times of the day and night, workers process insurance claims, answer computer and software questions in the telecom industry, and respond to billing and payment inquiries in the banking and utilities sectors. On the outbound side, they provide services like telemarketing and sales. India dominates information technology outsourcing.

The call center industry has become symbolic of the tensions within the global economy. It has given birth to a type of local cosmopolitanism explored in films, TV programs, and novels with suggestive titles like *Stilettos in the Boardroom*[23] and *Bangalore Calling*.[24] The 2005 bestseller *One Night @ the Call Center* took middle-class India by storm. It reportedly sold more than one hundred thousand copies in its first few months of publication in a country where only 61 percent of the population can read.[25] Like most novels of this genre, it conveys an idealized sense of empowerment, material autonomy, and liberation from gendered norms and traditional family structures, especially for the female characters. But the price to be paid can be steep. At the core of these narratives lie the harmful effects of forced hybridity and emotional labor. Workers must assume a Western identity while oscillating between sympathy and detachment as they calmly deal with "disgruntled" callers across the world demanding a speedy resolution to a problem.[26]

In fiction and in real life, for the typically young employees, English is both a blessing and a curse. It provides quick money—in Manila more than some general physicians earn. But it also leads to an irregular and unhealthy lifestyle.

Restaurants, bars, and cafes in Metro Manila's Makati District remain open around the clock, offering after-work happy hour at 8 a.m. The pressures of working under constant surveillance through the night to accommodate time differences with customers, handling upward of a hundred calls each shift, create an abusive environment where workers risk losing their identity as they strain to pass for Western anglophones. As a longtime accent trainer in Mumbai explained, the obligatory night work and the intense nature of the job tend to attract young people who "don't speak very well and are not from the best schools." Many of them are college dropouts.[27] The hierarchy within these work settings, with owners and managers often educated in English-medium private schools, has come under criticism for recreating language-based relationships of power and privilege reminiscent of colonialism.[28]

Workers undergo rigorous voice and accent retraining programs to neutralize any mother tongue influence and to remedy pronunciation and grammatical mistakes. In the 1990s, it was all about acquiring either an "American" or a "British" accent. That dichotomy locked workers into a particular country and denied managers the flexibility to move call agents as needed. More recently, the focus has shifted to a "neutral" accent, one that suggests no particular regional or national ties (though it decidedly slants toward the American side).[29] To build rapport with anglophone clients, workers must assume a new identity, adopting conventional American/British names. For American marketing, centers teach workers to get into the "American psyche," considering how Americans think, what they value, how they can be moved to decide in a certain way.[30] Workers use a prepared script so they keep to a prescribed discourse style.

Unlike other back-end BPM jobs, the synchronicity of call center work where the call agent and the customer are interacting on the telephone in real time makes the cultural distance both relevant and difficult to overcome. The negative impact on the agent's sense of self cannot be underestimated. As a young Indian who started call center work at age seventeen, became addicted to heroin from the stress, and later switched to a lesser-paid trainer position put it, "Your mentality changes. The conservative nature, the ethnicity, it gets lost. You try to think like an American, but you're not really an American, you're an Indian."[31] For Filipinos who learn American English in first grade, eat hamburgers, follow American sports teams, and watch American TV shows long before they encounter a call center, the adjustment is somewhat easier, though not seamless.

Not surprisingly, client dissatisfaction with the quality of service, poor accent skills of foreign workers, and criticism over robbing Americans of work have led companies like Capitol One and Delta Airlines to quietly move at least some operations back to the United States. Easing the way are technological advances in software and the option of using home workers instead of brick-and-mortar facilities. Between 2010 and 2015 alone, call center contacts with a significant onshore delivery presence in the United States jumped from 35 percent to 53 percent.[32] More recent data shows a slowdown in hiring, though service providers have continued to earn higher revenues, which indicates more automated work. As voice-based interaction is giving way to chat, email, and other nonvoice contact and technological and analytic skills are becoming more in demand, spoken English is becoming of lesser importance. India, with its high supply of science and technology graduates, may ride this wave more successfully than the Philippines or other less developed countries. As of 2018, India still held 37 percent of the global offshoring market.[33]

Beyond call centers, computer programming, and back-office jobs like accounting and billing, a second wave of offshoring is on the rise in the form of academic tutoring services. Here, the "accent" is irrelevant, because the contact between tutor and client is totally in writing. With increased emphasis on standardized tests and "outputs," particularly in the United States, companies like TutorVista offer online tutoring from kindergarten through undergraduate school for a flat rate per month. Started in 2005 by Krishnan Ganesh, a forty-five-year-old Indian entrepreneur, within two years the company had raised more than US$15 million from investors, signed up ten thousand subscribers in the United States and one thousand in the United Kingdom, and employed six hundred tutors in India.[34]

Tapping into the leisure habits of a tech-absorbed generation, the company's website states, "We use the computer, which your child associates with entertainment and fun, to make learning more interesting."[35] For the company and the child's family, it's a win-win situation. Low wages in the Indian economy maintain the fees at a reasonably low level, providing individual tutoring to the anglophone masses well below the hourly cost of tutors based in the United States or the United Kingdom. Meanwhile, Indian-based tutors have the freedom to work from home with somewhat flexible hours, no constant surveillance, and no worries about whether the client at the other end can understand their spoken English. Yet the question of wages still carries more than a hint of exploitation.

Accenting the Accent

The politics of "neutral" English is not limited to offshore call centers. It also ties into a global industry of short-term programs focused on voice training, intercultural communication, and British or more commonly American pronunciation. All these skills meet the demands of the wider job market.[36] The internet abounds with companies, in the United States and in major cities abroad, peddling American-accent-learning packages. These websites play on the common view of English and the "imagery of American cultural symbols" as frontrunners in global mobility.[37] Like the call centers, they suggest that the American accent is an "unmarked" neutral tool, a "normal" and "efficient" language. Once you acquire it, you will communicate with "confidence, clarity and accuracy" and realize your dreams of success.[38]

A marked example is Accents International, formerly known as the Accent Reduction Institute, located in Ann Arbor, Michigan, which is a leading provider of American accent training. It offers courses in real time through a virtual classroom as well as individual face to face, telephone, and webinar communications coaching. Its staff includes certified linguists and speech pathologists. The company promises to help "non-native English speakers become culturally competent while maintaining their unique cultural identities."[39] Boasting a greater than 70 percent improvement in English pronunciation after twelve sessions, it presents persuasive testimonials like "This course has been a breakthrough in my career development."[40]

In a similar way, though less overtly focused on accent and with a more conventional business model, Wall Street English (formerly Wall Street Institute) runs over 420 centers in twenty-nine territories with a total enrollment of more than 180,000 students through a stream of franchises. With a main base of operations in Barcelona (despite the New York–suggested name), its website invites potential clients, whether individuals for travel, socializing, or business or corporations looking to compete on a global scale, to tap into a flexible program that "follows the natural way of learning English." The message is that through English you can "change your future" and "realize your dreams." In other words, English will put you in charge of your destiny. It invites those looking for a career teaching English or for a business investment to join an exciting and dynamic enterprise with opportunities around the globe.[41] This is yet another aspect of language marketing at its most persuasive.

The English language learning market is one of the most rapidly growing sectors within education. In 2017, the adult market was over US$34 billion and forecast to increase by more than 80 percent within the next five years. The continuously regenerating pool of potential English learners has been estimated at around 1.4 billion worldwide.[42] One in seven of the world's population, an estimated 1.75 billion people, were learning English in 2016. In China alone, there were an estimated four hundred million English language learners. Many of them, looking to expand their career options, were preparing for language tests like the Test of English as a Foreign language (TOEFL), the International English Language Testing System (IELTS), and the Graduate Record Examination (GRE), which are required for admission to graduate schools in the United States, Australia, the United Kingdom, and Canada.

The popularity of these programs is understandable. The ability to function professionally in English is now compared to computer literacy and even to literacy itself. Across the globe, English proficiency correlates with gross domestic product, average gross income, ease of doing business, and service exports. The one hundred most influential scientific journals all publish in English, and there's a strong positive correlation between the number of technical and scientific articles per million people and a country's level of English skills.[43] These developments have had a significant impact on career advancement worldwide, from Europe to the Middle East and to Latin America.

Opportunities and Earnings

The high demand for learning English reflects growing evidence that English carries positive labor market returns across the globe. Outsourcing is just the tip of the iceberg. The effects have been especially striking in central and eastern Europe. Freed from the Soviet yoke, post-socialist countries have become more open to trade and foreign investment and have enthusiastically embraced English as the economic lingua franca. A study of seventy-four thousand job advertisements published on leading online job boards across Czechia, Hungary, Poland, and Slovakia found that 52 percent of the vacancies required English. In Poland, with its high pre-Brexit migration flow to the United Kingdom, the figure jumped to 64 percent. The demand for English skills appeared to increase as the occupations became more complex. In Czechia and Slovakia, the higher the share of vacancies mentioning English in given occupations, the higher the hourly wages. Yet only 25–33 percent of the population in those countries can hold a conversation in English.[44] The economic importance of English has also hit workers in western Europe. In a study of French adults enrolled in English courses, 55 percent of those between the ages of twenty and forty-five reported that their lack of English skills hindered their ability to advance professionally. Among all age groups, 66 percent believed that English was becoming increasingly important for French workers.[45]

Findings from less developed economies likewise suggest that English can be key to employment and higher salaries. A Euromonitor International study from 2012 found that salaries in the Middle East and North African (MENA) countries were generally higher for English speakers. Employees who were more proficient in English earned salaries from 5 percent (Tunisia) to a stunning 200 percent (Iraq) more than their non-English speaking counterparts. A direct link between unemployment and lack of English fluency was also evident. Yemen and Iraq had the lowest English levels (18.3 percent) and the highest unemployment (19 percent).[46] Though English proficiency in most of the Middle East has improved slightly in recent years, particularly in Iran, the United Arab Emirates, and Kuwait, it is still the weakest region on that count. Inadequate public schooling and weak labor markets have slowed any progress on adult proficiency in English.[47] Arabic speakers, who make up a large portion of the region, generally place at or near the bottom in world rankings on the TOEFL[48] and IELTS[49] tests of English language skills.[50]

Studies from Latin American countries show a similar correlation between income and English learning. Except for Argentina, English proficiency in the region is generally low. According to a British Council study from 2015, respondents in the higher income levels were more likely to have studied English, though both income and English skills admittedly could be related to a combination of other factors such as social class, education, and family wealth. In any case, an overwhelming percentage of employers in the region (69 percent in Mexico, 90 percent in Argentina) believed that English was an indispensable skill for managers and directors. Among 110 Mexican and 130 Argentine business managers and directors from different industries, over 80 percent agreed that English was essential to the growth and progress of their organization, while 94 percent in Mexico and 85 percent in Argentina believed it was important to them in their job.[51]

On a similar survey of 137 employers from different industries in Peru, more than three-quarters (78 percent) strongly agreed that English was an essential skill for managerial staff, but only 38 percent indicated the same for non-managerial jobs, indicating that English is a gatekeeper for higher level employment.[52] For non-White men in South Africa, the ability to read and write English "very well" has been found to increase earnings by approximately 50 percent. When combined with a post-secondary education, that premium jumps to 90 percent.[53] In an online global learning survey of more than eleven thousand people between the ages of sixteen and seventy years in nineteen countries across the globe, over 60 percent of respondents in the United Kingdom, South Africa, Brazil, Hispano-America, and the Middle East responded that English would help them to compete better in the global economy.[54]

Foreign Investment and Corporate Benefits

Language plays a significant role in foreign direct investment (FDI). Considering English language skills as a form of human capital, a critical mass of English speakers in a given region can attract FDI, which in turn creates jobs. FDI takes a number of forms, from buying shares in foreign companies, to reinvesting the profits of a foreign-owned company back into the country where it is located, to a parent company's loaning funds to its foreign branches. A study of forty-nine emerging economies found that English language proficiency was directly related to FDI and consequently to income per capita. Many of these countries relied on FDI as a funding source to develop skills, acquire technology, and gain access to international markets in the wake of the 2008 economic downturn.[55] Across the globe, there appears to be a correlation between English proficiency and key economic and social indicators like service exports, internet access, and investment in research and development. It has been suggested that "as English facilitates the exchange of ideas and services, more people gain access to international opportunities, which in turn improves English proficiency," and so the cycle continues.[56]

English language skills affect business in even more direct ways. Sixty percent of directors and managers of international businesses with more than one thousand employees across the globe reported that lack of English had cost them a business opportunity. A total of 80 percent would have considered dropping a supplier that lacked adequate English skills, while 85 percent would have paid an average of 16 percent more to work with an organization that had a higher level of English proficiency. The report estimated that an employee with a professional command of English could add US$128,000 in sales, efficiency, and productivity in just one year.[57]

A survey of five hundred human resource and business leaders across seventeen countries found that companies that provided language training for their employees (46 percent of the total group) reported higher growth in revenue and a more innovative spirit than their competitors. Among these so-called global fluency leaders, 51 percent required English as an essential skill for all workers as compared to 45 percent across the sample. At the same time, 88 percent of them reported that their cross-border teams worked together "well" or "very well," as compared with 65 percent across the sample, while 74 percent noted that their employees had "the will and desire" to generate new ideas as compared with only 48 percent of the overall sample. The report concluded that global fluency leaders understand that "in a large multinational, multicultural organization, with workers dotted all over the globe, so much can be lost in the corporate fog" without "smooth communication between colleagues."[58] In contrast, according to a senior vice president at Pearson English, multinational clients who had used the language development company's resources claimed on average a gain of forty-five hours each year in improved productivity for each staff member who had gone through the English program.[59]

Corporate English

An increasing number of multinational companies outside the anglophone orbit have adopted English as their official language. The trend began in countries with "small populations and global ambitions" like the Nordic countries and Switzerland, as well as Singapore, where English is a holdover from British colonialism.[60] In the 1980s and 1990s, as countries within the EU opened their economies, mega-corporations like Germany's Deutsche Telekom and France's Alcatel moved beyond borders in a spate of mergers and acquisitions that made a common language essential. When France's Rhone-Poulenc and Germany's Hoechst Marion Roussel combined in 1999 to form the multinational pharmaceutical company Aventis amid a matrix of prior and subsequent mergers, they established their headquarters near the border city of Strasbourg and adopted English as the neutral company language "to defuse cultural tensions." As the CEO of an Italian lighting company put it back in 2001, "Europeans who don't know English are 'running a marathon in house shoes.'"[61] But it's not only European companies that have come to that realization. Lenovo in China and Samsung in South Korea, as well as Honda and Bridgestone Tires in Japan, have joined the ranks of Audi and Lufthansa in Germany, Nokia in Finland, Heineken in the Netherlands, Electrolux in Sweden, and Renault in France in the march toward corporate English.

Especially for countries with declining populations like Germany, the Netherlands, and Italy, English makes tapping into global talent and global markets possible. When the quintessentially German company Volkswagen, maker of the "people's car," announced in 2016 that it was shifting its official language to English, it raised more than a few eyebrows. Yet as VW's personnel chief told the press, "We need the best people in the world."[62] Even where English is not the official corporate language, depending on the type of international business, it can become a must for all levels from upper- and mid-level management to the secretarial staff and even to line workers in manufacturing plants looking to advance to team leader. At KPNQwest, the former Netherlands-based pan-European phone company, which fell into bankruptcy in 2002, all email messages were written in English, even between German engineers. The idea was to avoid excluding anyone in a string of communiqués as they traveled across language borders through the corporate system.[63]

A study of 111 job offers posted on the website of Sapienza University in Rome found that 75 percent of multinational companies and 50 percent of national companies explicitly sought competency in English. While in prior years, language skills were considered secondary in the Italian job market and a privilege of an elite group, by 2013 they had become "fundamental to communication and trade negotiations."[64] Among 66 engineers working in twenty multinational corporations, including General Electric, Deloitte, Nestlé, and Unilever, headquartered in nine different countries and operating in French West Africa, 85 percent identified English as the corporate lingua franca. Though French dominated among French speakers, in some workplaces all respondents reported using English with global teams. They also emphasized that English was an essential requirement for employment and promotion. As one Deloitte engineer noted, "You must speak English, if not no Deloitte."[65]

Rakuten, Japan's largest online retailer, is perhaps the most radical and the most well-documented global changeover to English. Here, the company did not choose English to remain neutral between two equal parties, as was the case with the Hoechst Marion Roussel and Rhône-Poulenc merger, but rather adopted it to expand the enterprise across countries with diverse national languages. In 2010, the company's celebrity CEO, Hiroshi Mikitani, announced that from that day forward, workers at all levels would gradually move toward English. All meetings, presentations, training sessions, documents, and emails would be in English. The following day, all cafeteria menus and elevator signs switched from Japanese to English. Rakuten sent some of its employees to the United States or the United Kingdom for English immersion classes. Others attended multi-week language programs in the Philippines. Most of the seventy-one hundred Japanese workers attended on-site language training during the workday. Within two years they would have to score above 650 on the 990-point Test of English for International Communication (TOEIC) or risk being demoted or dismissed. In the meantime, the company would monitor their progress through test scores and monthly reports from managers.

The company had set a goal to become the premier internet services provider, not just in Japan but also in the world. And it needed to break the language bottleneck that was preventing it from getting there. Mikitani believed that a lingua franca, and specifically English, would allow the company to extend the reach of its operations to twenty-seven countries and increase overseas revenue to 70 percent in ten years. The *Japan Times* praised Rakuten for recognizing that English was an "absolute necessity" to compete against rivals like Amazon and Alibaba.[66] "Englishization" proved to be a total win for Rakuten. By 2015, the company had made billions of dollars in acquisitions, joint ventures, and new regional development centers in North and South America, Europe, and South Asia.

Yet as Harvard professor Tsedal Neeley, who studied the transformation over the next five years, recounts, the process was painful. Many of the Japanese employees, she explains, had to "detach from their native language and cultures in order to move into this third space." Many felt like "expats" in their own country. The majority of employees were not able to achieve native-like ease in English. Some fell by the wayside as Rakuten hired significantly more non-Japanese engineers even in their Japan offices.[67] By 2018, 80 percent of the new engineers in the Tokyo offices were non-Japanese, while the company had grown from 200 million users to 1.1 billion by expanding beyond the home market.[68]

Mikitani's grand plan for a total two-year transition to English was undeniably extreme in speed and scope. His assessment on the rise of English, however, is one that many corporate leaders share. In an Economist Intelligence Unit survey of 572 executives in Europe, Asia Pacific, North America, and Latin America, more than two-thirds responded that English was essential, distantly followed by Mandarin (8 percent) and Spanish (6 percent).[69] Given the scarcity of jobs and the high mobility of young people across the globe, these findings are significant. In a 2016 study of fifty-three hundred employers in thirty-eight countries or territories and twenty different industries, over 95 percent in nonnative-English-speaking countries reported that English skills were important. That figure varied from 100 percent in Germany to 96 percent in Italy, 90 percent in India, 85 percent in France, 78 percent in Mexico, and 63 percent in China.[70] Upward of 80 percent of job tasks outside the anglophone world required advanced or intermediate English.[71] About half of all employers where English was not an official language offered a more attractive starting package to applicants with good English language skills.[72]

Aside from hiring preferences, much has been written on English as an instrument of power within the multinational corporate hierarchy and the potential challenges and distortions it can create. Most of the research has been in-depth case studies of one or several companies. Managers tend to rate native speakers more favorably, resulting in nonnative speakers losing power and status. Differences in language proficiency, especially within global teams, can create feelings of job insecurity. Team members with lesser language skills may avoid approaching their bosses or interacting with coworkers, marginalizing them from decision-making and denying companies the benefit of other cultural perspectives. It takes time, effort, and motivation to learn not simply grammar and vocabulary but appropriate levels of politeness and formality and how to recognize cues in business settings, from emails and videoconferences to small talk at cocktail parties. These abilities well exceed the formal English skills that are traditionally learned in school.

A large-scale study of more than eight hundred multinational corporate subsidiaries representing various industries in thirteen countries with headquarters in twenty-five countries put the question in broader scope. The study concluded that where English is the corporate language, which is common in anglophone and Nordic countries and increasingly so in continental Europe, foreign subsidiary employees with lesser English skills than headquarters managers risk being perceived as "less capable" and may not receive promotions commensurate with their managerial skills. The proficiency gap also works the other way. Local subsidiary managers with better English skills than headquarters' bosses might get the upper hand in corporate debates and negotiations.[73] And so English is not just about accessing the job. It's also about being taken seriously when you get there and moving up the corporate ladder. As the chair of UBS Financial Services London put it, "We are being told that there's a 'glass ceiling' for monoglots" within global businesses." Staff will not get into "the more rarified atmosphere" of the senior ranks unless they have "overseas experience, cultural awareness and probably [another] language."[74]

There is still another side to this story that should not go unnoticed. While some employees resent being forced to speak English and being judged on a native standard by managers and colleagues, in other settings they pragmatically use what has come to be called business English as a lingua franca (BELF). Here the focus is on communication and not on "correctness." English is a means to an end and not an end in itself. As a manager in a German multinational technology company, where English was indispensable but managerial expertise came first, explained, "There is simply no better solution. I don't speak Chinese, I don't speak Indian, I don't speak Japanese. . . . This morning I talked to a Japanese partner on the phone. It was awful English, but we sort of understood each other."[75] It depends on the corporate culture. As more nonnative speakers use English to communicate with each other than with native speakers (which Brexit may accelerate in Europe), BELF with its contextual fluidity and lack of national grounding may well gain a sense of normalcy as the business "English" of the future.

Marketing Multilingualism

Just as not speaking English is a drawback in many countries, so is speaking only English for much of the anglophone world. As English spreads and becomes more commonplace worldwide, it will offer less of an advantage in business and the workplace. It's simply a matter of supply and demand. There is now mounting evidence that while a common language facilitates communication in multinational work settings, relying solely on one language that may not be the native language of some clients or, as in non-anglophone countries, of most employees has significant drawbacks. Even multinational corporations both in the United States and abroad that adopt English as the common language for "in-house" business must localize their services if they want to remain competitive, and that demands multilingual staff. As the term "glocal" expresses, the global and the local are inextricably intertwined. Doing business with global clients often means negotiating in local languages, understanding local cultures, and comprehending local contracts, rules, and legislation, which customarily are written in the local language.

The "American" Landscape

The pressure to meet today's language demands is especially acute in the United States, a country with a notoriously low commitment to developing its linguistic capital and an intensely high level of global business transactions. The Council on Foreign Relations has predicted that growth in the US economy will increasingly rely on the sale of goods and services in markets abroad where English is not necessarily spoken.[76] Much of that business will transpire via technology, which has spread the global market beyond time and location barriers. "User generated content" (websites, blog posts, and social media including Twitter) is the new frontier for interacting with customers and markets. While English is the identified content for over 60 percent of websites, only 25.9 percent of internet users are English speaking, as compared with 19.4 percent Chinese and 7.9 percent Spanish.

Since 2000, the number of native speakers using the internet has grown exponentially by 2,650 percent (Chinese) and 1,511 percent (Spanish).[77] At the same time, more than half of internet users worldwide (53.1 percent) come from Asia, as compared with only 6.5 percent from North America.[78] And so as an effective marketing strategy, businesses must communicate in a number of languages on a sophisticated level. One example of where the need for languages is acute is the growing IT service industry. US- and UK-based multinational corporations, eager to reach markets abroad, face difficulties in finding local professionals with a combination of technical and language skills. Some, like Cognizant, a multinational corporation providing IT services, conduct in-house training in these languages for candidates from other regions while also making sure that local employees are proficient in business English.[79]

Upward of twenty-three million jobs in the United States are tied to international trade in goods and services. In California those numbers reach over 2.5 million and in New York and Texas over 1.6 million.[80] As business increasingly crosses national borders, languages spoken in emerging economies, particularly in China and Latin America, have become a significant part of the corporate skill set. As the lead manager of a real estate development company with interests in Spanish-speaking markets noted, "We have been raising more capital from abroad and need employees who can communicate with our foreign investors."[81] Companies find that it is far easier to hire bilingual individuals already in the country than bear the administrative burden and cost of obtaining visas for foreign workers.

Findings show that externally 16 percent of international business agreements are made through a "cocktail of languages." Where functional multilingualism falls short, "cognitive divergence" between and among the parties leads to misunderstandings and lost opportunities.[82] Considering the multilingual glass as half-empty/half-full, researchers now look at language diversity within work settings not as a barrier, as conventionally believed, but as a resource that needs to be managed. This "multilingual turn," or concept of a *multilingual franca*, recognizes how internal individual and group language diversity can enhance communication and productivity within global management teams.[83] That does not necessarily negate adopting a "company language." The two strategies are not mutually exclusive but can complement each other. A company language facilitates communication especially within but also outside the organization, while a linguistically diverse staff can directly solicit and transact business in countries where the "company language" is not widely spoken.

The internet now enables even the smallest company, unconstrained by time, space, or travel, to become multinational. Many businesses have expanded beyond their national borders, while many investors are putting their money into other countries. Economists now talk of the "born-global firm," the early and rapid internationalization of young, entrepreneurial companies. A novel concept two decades ago, these firms are now growing in number.[84] A Forbes Insights survey of more than one hundred executives in large US businesses showed that overseas assignments were becoming more common, while bilingual skills in promoting corporate efficiency, collaboration, and productivity were becoming increasingly important. Over 70 percent of respondents agreed that overseas assignments were an important factor in moving up the corporate leadership ladder.[85] Apple and its success in launching the iPad simultaneously in nine countries in 2012 are an example of a company where language was the engine for growth and international competitiveness. In the first three days alone, iPad sales topped three million units, bringing in over US$1 billion in revenues. The following week, Apple released the iPad in twenty-five more countries. What allowed this to happen was Apple's product platform (iOS), which was available from day one in thirty-four languages. Coordinating the engineering, sales, marketing, and distribution was a major coup for the company.[86]

On the other end of the language spectrum, the cost of language specialists, commonly employed by global companies, is often beyond the reach of most SMEs. When they do venture internationally, they tend to be thin on bilingual staff, which makes it difficult to build and maintain long-term relationships with overseas clients and partners. Meanwhile, negotiating business deals through document translations and ad hoc interpreters runs the risk of missing cultural nuances and the benefit of personal interactions. The cultural question is especially critical for companies trying to enter new markets.

In countries with high levels of English proficiency like the United States and the United Kingdom, companies need multilingual workers to do business with countries low on English speakers. A series of discussions with business leaders offers a bird's-eye view of the price that companies in the United States pay for not having readily available staff with language and cultural skills. As the operations director for the US-Algeria Business Council pointed out, "The lack of language skills is an enormous barrier to increasing greater US participation in overseas markets."[87] And as the vice president of global workforce management for a major corporation summed it up, "Without the ability to communicate clearly, concisely, and effectively [between workers in different geographies], significant risks begin to enter the equation, including lower quality, lost pro-ductivity, and increased training costs."[88]

From local airports unable to accommodate international clients, to FedEx drivers unable to communicate with customers, to businesses missing formal proposals and informal leads on opportunities abroad, the report graphically laid out the problems that businesses in the United States face in remaining afloat in global competition. Non-US companies vying for international cli-ents, it noted, often have language skills that "surpass American businesses."[89] An event endorsing the report brought together business and education leaders, policy makers, and the press. It ended in a national Call to Action. In a partic-ularly sobering statement, a former CEO of Tyco China, equating the crucial business needs to the Cold War era, warned that despite a global "shift in para-digms," the United States was "not well prepared for a 21st-century world in which economic competitiveness, not military power, is central to our security and well-being."[90]

Other findings reflect similar concerns. A survey of more than one hun-dred executives at large US companies with annual revenues of more than US$500 million found that "language barriers" had a "broad and pervasive im-pact" on business. Two out of three respondents said that language barriers ex-isted between company managers/executives and other workers, while two out of three reported that miscommunications were leading to inefficiency. About one-third of respondents were sending more US nationals on assignments abroad than two years previously. Two out of three firms expected employees who took positions where English was a secondary language to have basic or intermediate proficiency in the host language. Overall, 93 percent agreed that bilingualism makes for more successful managers.[91] In a survey commissioned by Rosetta Stone, of 493 senior and upper management-level business profes-sionals at leading US corporations, half agreed that at least 10 percent of their employees would benefit from training in languages other than English.[92]

In a 2018 survey of twelve hundred US employers, nine out of ten reported that they relied on US-based employees with language skills other than English. One-third reported a high dependency. More than half said that their needs would increase in the next five years, while 46 percent reported a demand for language skills exclusively for the domestic market. The most likely projected increases (64 percent) were in health care and social assistance. One in four employers reported losing business due to a lack of language skills. The most sought-after languages were Spanish (85 percent of employers), followed by Chinese (34 percent), French (22 percent), and Japanese (17 percent).[93]

Job advertisements, hiring, and employer preferences show a rising demand for bilingual skills in the United States. An analysis of fourteen million job post-ings found bilingual/multilingual skills were among the top eight required for high-wage occupations, accounting for 11.5 percent of new hires and 28 percent of job growth by 2020.[94] A survey of twenty-one hundred US human resources departments struck a similar note. Among over two thousand respondents, 66 percent considered foreign language skills when recruiting employees, while 41 percent gave a hiring advantage to multilingual candidates, 34 percent to candidates with multicultural experience, and 22 percent to those with international experience.[95] In a survey of more than twenty-one hundred companies that actively recruited on college campuses, 60 percent identified foreign language skills in the hiring process, 41 percent gave an advantage to multilingual candidates, and 34 percent specified levels of linguistic competence. Employers recruiting for service industries, which comprise 80 percent of the US economy in number of employees, were the most likely to place priority on language in their recruitment and hiring practices.[96]

Findings from a study by New American Economy, a coalition of mayors and business leaders supporting immigration reform, are eye-opening. Language or cultural misunderstandings, the report noted, cost Americans close to US$2 billion each year. Between 2010 and 2015, job postings for bilingual employees more than doubled, from roughly 240,000 to about 630,000. Over that time, ads for Chinese speakers tripled. The number of jobs listing Spanish and Arabic as a desired skill grew by approximately 150 percent. The highest demand for bilingual workers was in jobs that involve high human interaction like customer service and sales representatives, retail salespersons, and health service managers.

At Bank of America, more than a third of the positions advertised required language skills. At H&R Block, the tax preparation company, it was just under a quarter. At the health insurer Humana, close to one in four postings required the same, including almost 40 percent of listings for registered nurses. Mobile service providers like AT&T and T-Mobile saw a spike in bilingual sales positions to accommodate a growing bilingual customer base. Though the largest increase was in high-prestige jobs like financial managers, editors, and industrial engineers, 60 percent of the occupations with the highest demand for bilingual workers did not require a college degree. The fact that one in five persons in the United States (63.1 million) speaks a language other than English at home makes the demand for bilingual workers all the more pressing and the pool of potential workers all the more apparent.[97] As the *Boston Globe* summed it up, even as the Trump administration was looking to cut down on immigration, employers were trying to "woo immigrants as consumers—and employees."[98] A survey conducted by the American Management Association in 2012 found that more than 13 percent of high-performing companies only hired multilingual candidates for management positions.[99] Among eight hundred US business executives across sectors, between 59 percent and 69 percent agreed that foreign language proficiency and an appreciation for cross-cultural differences were the most important skills at the entry level.[100]

Europe and Beyond

Findings from abroad are equally noteworthy. In a study of 801 French businesses, 70 percent of the respondents reported that workers with linguistic competencies were essential to their enterprise. And though 76 percent most frequently mentioned mastering English, they also cited no fewer than twenty-one foreign languages, including German at 39 percent and Spanish at 35 percent. Foreign languages helped employees to acquire senior positions and enhanced job mobility.[101] An analysis of French job advertisements between 2016 and 2018 found that while English accounted for over 890,000 postings, over seventy-two thousand looked for German and over fifty-six thousand for Spanish language skills.[102]

Findings from Spain yield similar results. In a survey taken by Adecco, a worldwide temporary staffing firm specializing in middle managers and directors, among 1,947 Spaniards between the ages of eighteen and sixty-five, 47.3 percent reported that their last job interview required knowledge of Spanish plus one other language, 24.9 percent two other languages, and 3.8 percent three other languages. English was by far the most commonly sought at 61.3 percent, with French a far distant second at 11.3 percent, German at 10.7 percent, and Portuguese at 1.7 percent. Another 14 percent of respondents put weight on other languages including Chinese, Romanian, Polish, and Arabic, with smaller demands for Spanish regional languages.[103]

A British Council survey of nine countries, including the United States and United Kingdom, confirmed that employers were looking for workers who understood people from different cultural backgrounds and who spoke other languages.[104] An Economist Intelligence Unit study of 572 companies around the globe likewise found that for one-half of the respondents, at least one in five workers needed to speak another language on the job. One-quarter said that a majority of their workforce required some foreign language skills.[105] An overview of thirty case studies on businesses in France, Germany, Austria, and Italy concluded that while employees overall did not necessarily receive additional remuneration for their language skills, many reported that they would not have been hired without those skills.[106] In the same way, a European Commission report found that in seventeen member states, adults who knew at least one foreign language were more likely to be employed than those who did not know any foreign language.[107]

Aside from enhancing employment opportunities, there appears to be a link between language and income earned. A study of more than 124,000 native residents from thirty-one European countries suggests that foreign language skills can boost earning power. Based on data from Eurobarometer surveys between 1990 and 2012, individuals who spoke at least one foreign language were at least 5.8 percentage points more likely to have a high income (at the top 25 percent of the income distribution) and about 3.2 percent less likely to be unemployed. English and German had a stronger effect on both factors than French, Spanish, or Italian. Foreign languages overall proved more effective in increasing income than in decreasing unemployment.[108] An earlier study from Switzerland, which is divided into four distinct language regions, found that even controlling for education and prior experience, the individual advantage of language skills was greater than the average value of one additional year of schooling.[109]

In a widely cited study, MIT economist Albert Saiz shed particular light on earnings by examining the 1997 income levels of individuals in the United States who graduated college in 1992–93. He found that the premiums varied by language, with Spanish at 1.5 percent, French at 2.3 percent, and German at 3.8 percent. While those figures seem unimpressive at first glance, they can translate over a lifetime into earnings of US$51,000 (Spanish), US$77,000 (French), and US$128,000 (German). The interesting question is: Why the differences among the three languages? The answer lies, Saiz explains, in supply and demand. On the supply side, the returns for Spanish study were lower in states with higher Hispanic populations. On the demand side, Germany's position as a "trade powerhouse" gave the language more economic value for the smaller number of outsiders who spoke it.[110] The same conclusions can be drawn for the relative earning power of languages in other countries. A large-scale study of native individuals in Germany, Italy, and Spain found a similar "scarcity" component in correlating knowledge of English with employment. Among male workers in particular, English language skills were less rewarded as they became more widespread among the population and where the employment rate was higher.[111]

In many parts of Europe and beyond, English is now considered more a basic skill than a foreign language. Given the many connecting "open" borders and the short distances between and among European countries, there is a need to develop languages beyond just English. The European Commission and others have repeatedly declared that a multilingual workforce is especially critical for Europe to create job mobility, maintain strong economies, and develop a shared European identity among member states. A growing body of research bears witness to that assertion. The ELAN study, the first and most frequently cited macro-level study, commissioned by the European Commission in 2005, found that among two thousand SMEs a lack of language skills had cost 11 percent of the respondents a contract. For as many as thirty-seven of them, the loss was valued at between €8 million (US$9.4 million) and €13.5 million (U $15.4 million). Another fifty-four businesses had lost potential contracts with a cumulative worth of between €16.5 million (US$19.5 million) and €25.3 million (US$29.9 million). Over three years, the average loss per business was €325,000 (US$385,000).[112] As Grin and others have pointed out, however, the sample here was relatively small; the extrapolation may not have been representative of actual losses; and factors other than language could have been in play.[113]

Other studies have used different measures to assess the value of languages in the global economy. The PIMLICO (Promoting, Implementing, Mapping Language and Intercultural Communication Strategies) study, a follow-up to ELAN, found that while employees were expected to maintain high-level skills in English, recruiting multilingual staff was a prominent feature among forty European SMEs selected for their growth in trade and progressive language strategies. Findings from case studies revealed that 43 percent reportedly had increased their turnover by more than 25 percent by introducing new languages. There was "a common recognition . . . that a competitive edge comes from their multilingual and multicultural capability."[114]

A consultation conducted by the EU's CELAN (Companies' Linguistic and Language Related Needs in Europe) project across twenty-nine member states found that among 543 respondents, 90 percent of businesses and 95 percent of business representative organizations believed language skills were important for their particular enterprise.[115] In a survey of over seven thousand EU companies recruiting higher education graduates, 30 percent ranked foreign language skills as the most important skills for the next five to ten years. That figure jumped to 40 percent when limited to the private industry sector. Within twenty-four countries, at least three-fourths of the companies surveyed ranked foreign languages as "very" or "rather" important.[116]

A study of SMEs in France, Germany, and Sweden found that businesses exporting abroad increasingly used the language of the country to maintain a competitive edge in emerging markets like Brazil, Russia, India, and China. The higher the multilingual skills of exporting SME companies, the larger the number of export countries and the higher export performance to each country.[117] A series of interviews with employers and reviews of online vacancy databases in all EU member states revealed that for a fifth to a quarter of employers, a language other than English was the most useful foreign language. About one-quarter believed that language skills gave their competitors a decided advantage.[118]

These studies all look at countries with advanced economies where global demands increasingly drive business and hiring decisions. Yet as the call center industry in India and the Philippines has shown, the need for multilingual skills equally extends to emerging economies that may lack natural resources. A case on point is Morocco. An analysis, between February and August 2017, of job postings related to Morocco's offshore sector found that while French was by far the most needed language, there also were smaller requests for English, Arabic, Spanish, and German. Just as anglophone companies outsource their business processing to call centers in India and the Philippines, so too do France and other francophone countries to a lesser extent, utilize the services of Morocco's vibrant call center industry concentrated in Casablanca.[119]

The United Kingdom Post-Brexit

To what extent the United Kingdom's leaving the European Union will shift the emphasis away from English throughout the continent is a matter of speculation. It seems more predictable that the stakes in multilingualism are bound to rise for the United Kingdom, which like the United States and other anglophone countries has ignored the linguistic demands of the global market. According to a 2016 Cambridge University report, "The Value of Languages," companies in the United Kingdom blame lost business opportunities on the country's foreign language deficit. Employers list global competency, including foreign language proficiency and intercultural viewpoints, among the key skills they look for in prospective employees. The report calls for a national strategy to promote language learning.[120]

A 2016 survey found that the most wanted language skills among UK businesses were French (50 percent), German (47 percent), and Spanish (30 percent).[121] Language barriers have prevented businesses in the United Kingdom from tapping into emerging economies like BRICS (particularly Brazil, Russia, and China), which represent over 50 percent of the world GDP, as well as more developed economies like France, Germany, and Japan, where the trade potential is significant. Language is the single greatest source of perceived cultural gaps even accounting for information, relationships, and legal difficulties.[122]

Despite this compelling data, according to the 2018 CBI/Pearson Education and Skills Survey, only 27 percent of UK businesses surveyed reported that they were dissatisfied with the foreign language skills of young people applying for jobs within the previous twelve months, down from 49 percent the previous year. The drop can be interpreted several ways. Either foreign language skills had improved or employers had changed their expectations and mistakenly believed that foreign languages would be of less importance post-Brexit. The report, however, warned that without a "wider emphasis" on foreign languages in the schools, "UK business will suffer and be unable to seize global opportunities effectively." Major European markets were the "largest export markets for British goods" and were "likely to remain so after Brexit." As in previous years, French, German, and Spanish were the languages most in demand. The growing demand for Spanish, the report pointed out, reflected its widespread use both in Europe and in Latin America.[123]

The need for second language skills will become even more pronounced as the United Kingdom emerges from the 2020 pandemic and the global economic effects of Brexit per se become more apparent. If that demand is not met, the notable exodus of businesses from the United Kingdom might extend even further. An Adzuna survey one year out from the Brexit vote found that the highest paid jobs in the United Kingdom had shifted demand from German to Chinese, followed by Japanese, though German still offered the most job opportunities.[124] Yet between 2000 and 2016, the number of students in the United Kingdom taking German A-levels fell by nearly half.[125] The British Academy, the United Kingdom's national academy for the humanities and sciences, has repeatedly raised concerns about the state of foreign languages in the country. According to Bernadette Holmes, principal researcher for the British Academy's Born Global Initiative, languages are not only critical for business; they also impact legal liability. "Businesses can fall foul of all sorts of regulatory issues and cultural misunderstandings," she warns.[126]

The impact of language on the UK economy and its world standing became a point for action in the British Parliament in 2014 when the all-party parliamentary group (APPG) on modern languages presented to the main party leaders a *Manifesto for Languages*. Baroness Coussins, the chair of the APPG, sounded the alarm that poor language skills in the work force were costing the UK economy upward of £50 billion (US$69 billion) a year in "lost contracts." And it was not just high-level posts. The language deficit was causing administrative and clerical jobs to remain unfilled. The manifesto warned, "In the 21st century speaking **only** English is as much of a disadvantage as speaking **no** English." Backed by over one hundred businesses, organizations, and leaders, it called for a bundle of programs, including tax incentives for companies who invest in language training.[127] Reforms to the British curriculum effective that year required that all children begin learning a foreign language from the age of seven.

The manifesto's call to action is likely to become louder and more pressing as the United Kingdom searches for markets and trading partners outside the European Union to secure its economic position. As Baroness Coussins told the House of Lords in 2017, the United Kingdom was "overdependent on Anglophone markets," with 83 percent of SMEs doing business solely in English while over half of them claim that language skills would increase their export capacity.[128] Similar to other surveys, a British Council report identified Spanish followed by Mandarin, French, Arabic, and German as the most important languages for the British to master. The ability to communicate, the report noted, is especially critical where the level of English language proficiency is low, as in many Latin American countries.[129]

Domestic Needs

The high demand for language skills in the job market is not limited to international business and trade. It also is clearly evident on the domestic front, as data from the United States, by way of example, demonstrate. Government agencies and private domestic service industries—including hospitals, nursing homes, hotels, tourism, banks, delivery companies like UPS and FedEx, and translation/interpreting companies—are all looking for foreign language speakers. Federal agencies, including the State Department, the Agency for International Development, and the Central Intelligence Agency, as well as many others, are the most active employers of individuals proficient in foreign languages. Many of these positions are related to national security and international development.

Just two months into 2018, federal government spending on language services exceeded US$100 million, according to data from USASpending.gov. That same year the US Drug Enforcement Administration awarded five contracts worth US$260 million to just three language providers, while the Department of State renewed a US$15–20 million contract looking for one thousand linguists for diplomatic and foreign affairs activities.[130] Despite rapid advances in computer translation, the US Bureau of Labor Statistics projects that employment opportunities for interpreters and translators will grow much faster than the average of all other occupations, increasing by 20 percent from 2019 to 2029.[131]

Besides globalization, the mounting number of non-English speakers is an especially potent force driving the demand for language skills. According to the US National Census Bureau, upward of 67 million residents in the United States speak a language other than English (LOTE) at home, approximately equal to the entire population of France.[132] Though the US Census Bureau has not conducted a city-by-city breakdown since 2015, at the time the LOTE population accounted for more than half the population in ninety US cities. In Los Angeles, it was 59 percent; in New York, it was 49 percent; in Houston, it was 50 percent; in Phoenix, it was 38 percent; and in Chicago, it was 36 percent. Spanish speakers were by far the most numerous nationwide.[133] Further fueling the demand is a wide array of federal, state, and local laws and regulatory policies mandating translation and standardized services. New York City law, for example, requires government agencies to appoint language access coordinators, to translate documents into ten languages, and to provide telephonic interpretation in at least one hundred languages. Most recently Arabic, French, Urdu, and Polish were added to the list. In the first eleven months of 2017 alone, the US government spent US$517.2 million on translation.[134]

Jobs in health and medicine in particular, where the stakes in communicating effectively are exceedingly high, demand language and cross-cultural skills. A nationwide study of more than sixty thousand US physicians found a significant language gap between the respondents and their patients. Languages from sub-Saharan Africa, Southeast Asia, and parts of the Middle East were the least represented among the physician population. Patients in large metro areas were the most likely to have difficulty finding a physician who spoke their language.[135] As of 2018, in the state of California, there were only six hundred certified medical interpreters for the more than four million Spanish speakers with limited English—about one interpreter for every sixty-five hundred people. At that time, Parkland Health and Hospital Systems in Dallas, one of the country's largest public hospital systems, reportedly planned to spend over US$1 million in doubling its in-house team of Spanish interpreters.[136] Between 2016 and 2017, Boston Medical Center's outpatient clinics hired 315 bi- or multilingual staff, which counted for more than 40 percent of new employees. As the head of a Boston nonprofit that trains medical interpreters noted, "[It's] changed over the last five years, from just having open positions to kind of a desperate tone. We're getting pleading calls and e-mails at this point."[137]

The need goes beyond "world languages." In recent years migrants and asylum seekers crossing the US border from Mexico and Central America have created a critical demand for border patrol staff as well as immigration and asylum attorneys and interpreters who speak indigenous languages. It has been estimated that as many as a third of migrants crossing the Mexican border into Arizona do not speak Spanish. As one researcher explained, "We have an entire infrastructure set up where the default language is Spanish, but there are thousands of people coming to the southern border who can't communicate that way—and they basically become invisible."[138] In December 2018, the death of two children from indigenous Mayan communities in Guatemala while in US Border Patrol custody shed a spotlight on the potential dangers when a parent cannot adequately report a child's medical condition to border officials.[139]

Social service agencies, especially in urban areas with large pockets of immigrants, need bilingual professional and administrative staff to work on housing, education, domestic violence, child abuse, unemployment, and immigration cases. The same goes for the criminal justice system, where federal and state laws and federal constitutional protections mandate interpreters in criminal and certain civil cases.[140] In Santa Clara County in California, court interpreters have raised concerns that a lack of professional linguists is creating a "two-tier justice system" where persons with limited English get their hearings delayed or cannot file claims in the first instance. In New York City, where some nineteen thousand police officers speak upward of seventy languages other than English, that still might not be adequate to serve the limited-English-speaking population of 1.8 million.[141]

In the state of Massachusetts, there were nearly fifteen thousand online job postings for bilingual workers in 2015, a 159.5 percent increase since 2010. The bilingual share of postings cut across business sectors. It was especially large among many of the state's top employers, including Radio Shack (71.2 percent), CGS Incorporated (70.9 percent), Community Healthlink (37.6 percent), and Bank of America (35.0 percent).[142] One of the fastest-growing business sectors is the tourism industry. Notwithstanding terrorist attacks, political instability, and natural disasters worldwide, international travel and tourism have exploded in recent years, creating jobs and driving exports. In 2019 alone, tourism contributed US$8.8 trillion (10.4 percent of the global GDP and the equivalent of one in ten jobs) to the global economy, up from US$2.3 trillion in 2006. Hotels, restaurants, and retailers also pay a premium primarily for workers who speak English but also for other language skills, especially in anglophone countries.[143] While the COVID-19 pandemic effectively put a halt to these industries, they are gradually rebounding as life progressively returns to normal.

At no time has the global need for multilingual workers in the public sector been more visible and essential than during the pandemic. With so many migrants living in countries across the globe, it became essential for national, state, and local governments to disseminate accurate life-saving information to these communities on how to protect themselves from infection, what to do if they became infected, and how to comply with official directives. And they needed to convey that information in a language that these communities could understand. The meaning of "official advice" easily got lost if literally translated. The anglophone term "social distancing," which was critical in managing the crisis, proved ambiguous among non-English-speaking communal cultures accustomed to socializing collectively. As the virus rapidly spread, it also was essential for health care workers to personally communicate with the mounting numbers in dire need of medical assistance and with their families.

Where governments dragged their feet, civil society stepped in. Translators without Borders, a non-profit organization, translated reliable information from agencies, including the World Health Organization, in over twelve languages while monitoring and translating misinformation online. The group posted a call on its website for volunteer translators especially in Eastern languages like Tagalog, Vietnamese, Malay, and Hindi.[144] In Italy, when the numbers stricken by the virus spiraled out of control, leaving over thirty thousand dead, a social cooperative in Bologna launched a social media campaign in eleven languages to explain the emergency to more than five million migrants from more than fifty countries in Africa, Asia, and the Middle East who did not speak Italian.

In the United States, when the federal government failed to provide comprehensive information, the task fell to state and local governments to fill the gaps. New York City, where 23 percent of the population has limited English skills, posted guidance materials in twenty-two languages other than English. As well intentioned as these efforts were, they soon revealed the limitations of machine translation. California's Coronavirus Response website, having posted information in over one hundred languages, included a disclaimer that the state "cannot guarantee the accuracy of any translation provided by Google Translate," and is therefore "not liable for any inaccurate information" resulting from the use of the translation application tool.[145] Considering the gravity of the consequences, there could not be a more compelling case for the human element in translation.

Language Services, Training, and Technology

That brings us to a rapidly growing worldwide language services industry and the potential and limits of technology. Fueling that growth are business trends in "on demand" offerings including support chats, texts, and tweets in regional and national languages. Language providers offer translation, global website design, and marketing services. In 2017, Lionbridge Technologies, Inc., the language industry's top-ranking provider of services that year, managed the business of more than eight hundred global brands across platforms and languages. Companies like LanguageLine connect clients to a team of eleven thousand on-demand interpreters via audio or video in seconds. It also provides training to help in-house interpreters and bilingual staff reach limited-English customers. As the founder of the market research firm Common Sense Advisory put it, "People are much more likely to purchase products in their own language," while "localization reduces customer care costs and increases brand loyalty."[146]

A rise in corporate language training is an evident trend as companies look toward extending their international reach. Just a few of the major players show the enormous magnitude of this market. Communicaid, a multinational organization, provides cross-cultural training and business language courses in more than sixty-five foreign languages and dialects to major corporate and public organizations worldwide. Rosetta Stone, the leader in technology-based learning, has worked with over twelve thousand corporate clients in more than thirty languages. The International Association of Language Centres boasts a membership of 141 year-round and summer centers in ten languages in over one hundred destinations in twenty countries.[147]

Universities have jumped on the bandwagon, offering combined business and language degrees that enable graduates to "hit the ground running" in the global economy. As employers set their sights on new markets, recruiters are urging business schools to direct students toward language classes as part of their program. Longstanding cultural organizations like the Alliance française, the Goethe-Institut, and the Instituto Cervantes offer courses in business French, German, and Spanish customized to the needs of individuals, employers, and industries. Opportunities to self-learn are seemingly endless. Companies like

Duolingo, Busuu, Jump Start Games, Yabla, and Rosetta Stone are part of a growing market in global language programs and games, projected to be worth US$2.5 billion by 2026. Typically presenting material in short segments without high time demands, they cater broadly to academic, corporate, and distance learning markets, though the "kids" segment is the fastest growing.[148]

Meanwhile, technology is moving in to make up for human shortcomings, though with some limitations. Both individuals and businesses increasingly use translation software, which has dramatically improved in recent years. The options are growing rapidly. So too is the level of accuracy, as anyone who has used Google Translate over the years can attest. This free app now uses artificial intelligence to power its translation engine. Through neural machine translation, it supports over one hundred languages.

Microsoft Translator claims to have achieved "human parity" in the quality of translations. Google's wireless in-ear headphones, called Pixel Buds, can now translate forty languages in real time. The Pilot Translating Earpiece developed by Waverly Labs, a New York based start-up, can purportedly translate fifteen languages and forty-two dialects. Yet both devices are still less than perfect, especially for less spoken languages. Pixel Buds at times produces awkward results that miss the linguistic mark. The Pilot Earpiece is bulky in size and suffers from a short time lag. In early 2019, Google rolled out Interpreter Mode, which by the end of the year could translate forty-four languages in real time. The translated text appears on a smart display so that all parties to a conversation, not just the one wearing earphones as with Pixel Buds, can understand what is being said. Yet here again the experience falls short of ordinary conversation. Exchanges are capped at about fifteen seconds. The result is somewhat unwieldy. The speaker has to wait for a tone, say a few words, wait again, and listen to Google Assistant to respond. In 2020, Google Translate went a step further with a Transcribe feature allowing Android users to listen to speech in one language and transcribe the text in another. Yet the result is less accurate and the flow less natural than human translation.

To what extent, and how soon, these programs and devices will significantly reduce the need for bilingual workers is an open question. A 2016 article in the *Wall Street Journal* stated with conviction, "The Language Barrier Is About to Fall." Just as English propelled globalization, the article projected that the "next wave" of exponential technological progress would eliminate the need for any shared language, making each of us a "master of the Tower of Babel."[149] While that prediction seems plausible on the surface, it depends on how high you perceive that barrier to be and what level of accuracy and understanding you're trying to achieve. It also depends on the communication stakes. That precise issue arose in the early days of the 2020 US presidential campaign when Democratic Party candidates were trying to court the growing number of Latinx voters. Spanish postings on a number of websites appeared strikingly similar to the less-than-accurate Google-generated translation. Mistakes ranged from "minor typos" to "truly incomprehensible passages." One candidate wrote that she had "wasted" (intending "spent") her life defending American democracy. As the press noted, "While Google Translate can serve as a workable starting point, more often than not it needs a human hand to produce Spanish that would pass muster with a native speaker."[150]

Artificial intelligence and deep neural networks may one day resolve many such inaccuracies as the quantity and quality of the data fed into computers increases. Yet they may never replace the human interaction, personal give and take, and sensitivity to nuance, cultural references, puns, and humor that are essential to business, government, and social interaction. Translation is not simply a question of matching words. It's about finding a corresponding meaning. Understanding a word or phrase can depend on deciphering contextual clues along with volume and pitch in spoken language.[151] As George Lakoff and Mark Johnson's influential book *Metaphors We Live By* explains, much of language is figurative, which unconsciously shapes our perceptions.[152] Phrases in one language may not have a word-to-word match in another or may need several words or an entire sentence to convey the same meaning. For example, a number of words regularly used in English, like "feedback" and "judgmental," have no direct single word counterpart in many languages.

Researchers in the Netherlands report that while neural machine translation has substantially improved translation quality, it still has problems with infrequent words and phrases, and especially with idioms. The French phrase *l'appel du vide*, which literally translates as "the call of the void," is intended to mean "the urge to do something crazy." Translating that something is "a shoo-in" or telling someone to "catch my drift" in Mandarin is still a challenge for computers. Nor can translation software keep pace with slang or detect sarcasm or irony, which often is conveyed by emphasizing a word in a sentence.[153] Machine translation cannot capture metaphorical or figurative language. And so it's not surprising that Unbabel, which peddles to the business community its "AI-powered, human-refined" translation service, touts as a selling point that it uses thousands of "native" translators across the globe to "improve" computer-driven translations, providing "authenticity that can only come from a native speaker."[154] The system, called Machine Translation Post Editing (MTPE), produces quicker translations with a minimum of errors.

Translators and interpreters are often used in situations that demand critical on-the-spot decisions, like health care or national security, and where relying on a machine could prove risky or strategically unfeasible. Translating content for pharmaceutical products and medical devices or interpreting in emergency rooms or in war zones are just a few pointed examples. A 2014 study found that

Google Translate translated twenty common medical phrases in twenty-six languages with only 57.7 percent overall accuracy."[155] African and Asian languages scored the lowest, yet these are the languages more frequently used to compensate for the shortage of human interpreters. Some of the errors were serious. The English phrase "Your husband had a cardiac arrest" rendered in Marathi as "Your husband had an imprisonment of heart." Similarly, "Your wife needs to be ventilated" translated in Bengali to "Your wife wind movement needed." In 2017, Facebook apologized when a man was arrested by Israeli police for having uploaded a picture from his job at a construction site with the text "Good morning" in Arabic, which Facebook's auto-translating service, used by the officers, translated as "Hurt them" in English and "Attack them" in Hebrew.[156]

On the global front, the price to be paid for a misinterpreted phrase can be extraordinarily high, causing financial losses, embarrassment, and reputational harm for individuals, companies, and even countries. A clear case occurred in January 2019 when a mistranslated word created a scandalous cause célèbre for China. The occasion was the 2019 China-Africa Friendly Night in Beijing. As top African and Chinese diplomats and business leaders gathered together for a social evening with representatives involved in China's ambitious Belt and Road Initiative, a giant video behind the stage described the relationship between the two sides with four English words: Innovation, Efficiency, Transcendence, and "Exploitation," accompanied with corresponding Chinese characters. The gaffe apparently was a thoughtless translation of the Chinese phrase 开拓 (kaituo), which can be translated as "development," "exploration," "openness," and even "pioneering." A screenshot posted on Twitter by a reporter ignited a storm of reactions from China-Africa observers worldwide. Some saw the mistake as not merely a careless error but rather a revealing "Freudian slip." The timing could not have been worse for China, coming in the midst of worldwide criticism for its use of "soft power" as a form of neocolonialism entrapping African countries in debt.[157] In any case, it was a pointed lesson on the critical role that languages play in the global political economy and how one misstep can potentially threaten fragile relationships.

As one expert put it, "[Translation] requires a cultural literacy across languages, across generations, that is sort of impossible to keep up with."[158] The way humans engage in spontaneous communication or maneuver through conversations still eludes current technology. The problem is especially acute with interpretation in real time, which is not necessarily linear. Interpreters are part of the "communication flow," asking questions or clarification from the speaker before moving on. Can technology adequately handle those pauses? And while it is true, as already noted, that programs like Google Translate are constantly improving their language translation algorithm, even Google advises that machine translation is not "intended to replace human translators."[159]

In the end, the economic and social value of multilingualism—including both English and other languages—should not be underestimated despite the personal effort demanded. At the same time, the essential human element in translation and interpretation should not be dismissed despite advances in technology and the compelling convenience those advances offer. The data incontrovertibly make the case on both points.

CONCLUSION

Looking Back, Moving Forward

As English weaves its power through the global politics of language, with points of competition and resistance, it is creating winners and losers in expected and unexpected ways. Deciding who falls on either side of that divide demands weighing the gains and losses within and across countries—social class being a constant factor. Even countries that are pushing back on English are at the same time embracing it for its value in the global economy. France leads the way on that count. Amidst these stresses and strains, English is shaping language policies—from the supranational to national and local—that influence individual decisions. Those policies and decisions affect rights to education, democratic participation, and knowledge dissemination in significant ways. They also raise serious concerns over national languages and identity.

Beginning with the European Union, whatever the status of multilingualism among EU member states and their people, the EU multilingual agenda as originally conceived seems to be running aground in the face of English. All signs point to English winning out despite repeated EU pronouncements promoting "mother tongue plus two," steady efforts on the part of France to stem the use of English within EU institutions, and charges among academics of linguistic imperialism. In response to market demands and parental pressure, English is now the dominant non-national language in primary and secondary schools across the European Union and, for some students, the only one offered. It is not surprising that students participating in the Erasmus+ program use English as a shared vehicle of communication regardless of the language of the country where they are studying. Even the departure of the United Kingdom is unlikely to diminish the importance of English as a working lingua franca within EU institutions without any decisive action on its official status. EU officials will continue to defy their own rhetoric, favoring English in their informal contacts and, when legally permissible, in their formal transactions. Given the scope and number of EU directives across a wide range of policy areas, Europeans who lack proficiency in English will also continue to lose access to important information bearing on their interests.

English especially dominates international programs in European higher education. Here the victory of English over other languages has proven the most contested and the gains and losses the most publicly disputed. The controversies in France, Italy, and the Netherlands over English-taught programs, aimed at internationalization and reputation, reveal much about the limits of the law in shaping official policy, institutional practices, and public attitudes. They also reveal how ideology, historical memory, and national fervor can inflame the discourse while only marginally affecting what happens in real life. Notwithstanding the Italian Constitutional Court's affirmative statements on the rights of Italian students to learn and of professors to teach in the national language, the vast majority of courses and programs at Milan's Polytechnic Institute are still taught in English. Similarly, despite all the high-minded French pronouncements on linguistic superiority and republican values surrounding the debate over France's Fioraso Law, English-taught programs continue to spread throughout French universities, and especially in the elite *grandes écoles* and business schools, where they dominate the curriculum. Meanwhile, revisions in Dutch law, dating from 1992 and designed to preserve the Dutch language, have not stemmed the tide of English washing over higher education in the Netherlands. Despite years of intense debate over that trend, additional changes in the law still await definitive legislative action.

The Italian and Dutch scenarios, in particular, underscore the widespread nature of the concerns raised and how national conflicts can stimulate transnational discussion and inform the course of events elsewhere. In the case of Italy, as each successive court decision caught the attention of the international press, the constitutional and other legal issues aired and the policy options explored proved noteworthy beyond the country's borders. Following on the heels of Italy, the most recent iteration of the longstanding Dutch debate dug even deeper into the academic and economic consequences of English and internationalization, including the loss in instructional quality and diminished access to courses for Dutch students. Those arguments, and others, engaged Dutch officials and the university community in a heated dialogue intensively dissected in the popular press. They also touched on questions of equality and access less visible in the Italian and French debates, save for references to English programs inequitably concentrated in the French elite institutions. Most notably, the debate in the Netherlands intermittently mentioned less privileged students, including immigrants, who are less prepared to learn in English at the university level. Yet in none of the three countries did the controversy over English-taught programs generate a sustained discussion directly addressing differences in social capital underlying the English opportunity gap in education from preschool through the university.

The Dutch debate continues to evolve against a shifting backdrop of rising nationalism, increased migration, a declining native-born population, and a waning global pandemic with broad implications for student mobility and institutional finances. For some of those same reasons, the public debate over English in both France and Italy ironically appears to have lost steam or temporarily receded in the face of more pressing economic and political developments, including a revolving door of changed governments in Italy and massive demonstrations in France over government policies and reforms unrelated to language, again all followed by a health crisis and economic uncertainty. Yet with widespread attacks on academic freedom and higher education showing signs that internationalization is under global threat, any cutback in Dutch programs may set a wider trend.[1] That said, there might be one bright spot in the dark cloud of the COVID-19 pandemic. The downturn in international student enrollments has inadvertently forced universities to step back and rethink internationalization, which is a far more complex undertaking than merely offering courses and programs taught in English.

Moving from Europe to former European colonies presents yet another perspective on language as it relates to equality, identity, and opportunity with distinct historical and political underpinnings. Languages, and colonial languages in particular, play many roles long past independence. They can be a vehicle of domination or of liberation, an engine for social mobility, or a "gatekeeper" of the elite, a means of inclusion or exclusion.[2] Adding China to the age-old Anglo-French rivalry for the soul of Africa puts yet another angle on neocolonial imperialism.

In recent years, France and China have invested significant resources in promoting the "soft power" of language, combined with financial aid and development, as a political and economic wedge into the continent. France has assertively used the Francophonie network to blur its colonial past, though with greater success among political leaders than among African intellectuals and activists. China has, with equal resolve, used its language as an adjunct to wide sweeping infrastructure spending, lending, and trade deals. While both countries have made some headway in cross-national language programs, English still holds a privileged place in Africa as long as market forces maintain the language's appeal and global value. English-speaking African countries, moreover, carry the weight of economic, diplomatic, and military power on the continent. Whether francophone Africa continues to realign its collective regional interests to capitalize on that power will be linguistically significant. There already are signs pointing that way.

The extent to which English or French now dominates public life, including education, in French-speaking Africa hinges on a number of factors that have shaped how the "people" in each country define themselves. That shared self-definition is developing country by country as English gains global economic dominance. In former French colonies, it is tied to ambivalent and even hostile feelings toward France as the former colonizer. In the north or Maghreb, specifically Algeria and Morocco, it also is rooted in an Arab past and present. In Rwanda, though formerly a Belgian colony, it is mired in the lingering memory of France's failure to adequately intervene in preventing the 1990s genocide. Weaving through this intricate matrix is the role of English with its promise of social and economic mobility and the attraction it holds both for parents eager to educate their children for the global economy and for government leaders equally eager to ride the crest of that wave.

Both Algeria and Morocco in recent years have made difficult and politically controversial choices in weighing English and French in the educational balance. Looked at objectively, the Algerian government's plan to shift to English instruction in the universities was reasonable, given broad support particularly from young people who view English as the language of opportunity. The Moroccan government's plan to teach science, math, and technical subjects in French in secondary school was equally reasonable, given the fact that these subjects are taught in French in the universities and that the current system of switching from Arabic to French has led to high university dropout rates. An alternative compromise might have been to switch to English instruction from preschool through the university in view of strong anti-French and pro-English sentiments among segments of the Moroccan people. But that change requires years to develop a corps of teachers fluent in English. Either language, though especially English, would allow Morocco greater access than Arabic to scientific developments outside the Arab world.

Whatever future direction language policies in these countries take, it should be seamless and with due regard to the languages children bring to the school setting. Changes must be thoughtfully planned, as Rwanda learned through trial and error. They also must build on political consensus, as Morocco has struggled to understand. At the same time, countries like Morocco and Algeria should not lose sight of Tamazight, which, except for the elites, many more students speak at home than French and certainly than English.

In South Africa, the role of English is even more politically fraught. In a country where the wounds of apartheid and White Afrikaner supremacy still run deep, the Black population sees English as the language of liberation and Afrikaans, though also spoken by the Coloured population, as the language of oppression. Nonetheless, it remains uncertain whether English can produce the radical social transformation and reconciliation that the Constitutional

Court pursues and the unity that the constitution promised. If so, then what price will be paid, and at whose expense? Or, as Neville Alexander asked, is a multilingual society the only way to avoid "ethnic fragmentation" and "civil conflict" based on "linguistic affiliation?"[3] Can there be unity in multilingualism?

From that vantage point, the discussion of language in South African education moves beyond the traditional nation-state/group-rights dichotomy. It rather looks toward preserving equal access to knowledge through English, Afrikaans, and other African languages. All are vital, in differing degrees, for South Africans to fully participate in the economy and in the democratic political process. The problem is how to measure those degrees and effectively layer those languages into an education system that can gain the confidence of parents and students across the racial and economic divide, while also promoting social justice, equal opportunity, and political cohesion.

These issues have progressively rattled South African universities as well as local communities in recent years. The Black community continues to seek equal justice through English and rejects the multicultural arguments of White Afrikaners and the Coloured population to preserve Afrikaans. In keeping true to the transformative ideals of the South African constitution, the Constitutional Court has struggled to resolve these conflicts, trying to move beyond the past without abandoning the reconciliation project or the country's rich multilingualism. In the end, English is gaining the lead across education, though not necessarily to the advantage of all students. Stark economic and social disparities remain in the quality of English instruction between predominantly Black and White schools. Many Black students, in fact, might be served better by initially learning in the African language spoken in their home and community. Yet Black parents, as parents elsewhere, go to extreme lengths to educate their children totally in English for its economic advantages.

Similar inequalities and misguided decisions arise in India, where language policies and practices have not changed significantly since the end of the Raj, or rule by the British Crown, nearly three-quarters of a century ago. Caste and religion still intermix on a rich multilingual landscape, while English and Hindi compete for political prominence. A significant segment of the country's upper class has in some respects picked up where the Raj left off and remains deeply attached to English. Some even proudly profess their incompetence in Hindi. The nationalist government, nonetheless, is now set on a politically motivated course to unite a linguistically diverse, socially stratified, and religiously divided country through Hindi. And while its education policy, adopted in 2020, supports multilingualism through mother tongue instruction in the primary grades, it guardedly diminishes the place of English in the Three Language Formula with little more emphasis than other "foreign" languages.

Though English technically shares co-official status with Hindi, that status remains only as long as the non-Hindi states hold their ground and use English as a barricade against Hindi. Some Indians still see English not simply as a bridge language but also as the social and economic glue that holds India together. At the same time, the government is trying to move forward in a knowledge-based global economy reliant on English with all its benefits and trappings. These problems underscore the conflicted role that English continues to play in shaping Indian politics and education policies long after Gandhi and Nehru debated what the future might hold for guarding India's unity through diversity.

Despite the hopes of the most fervent Hindi activists, English in India cannot simply be wished away. As most of the population would agree, it should be embraced, however enthusiastically or grudgingly, for the competitive advantage it has provided India in the global market, especially as compared to other emerging economies. Not only has English provided the knowledge that has given India a jump-start in science and technology and created jobs in the outsourcing market; it also has enabled a mutual sharing of ideas and cultural understandings between east and west. The question is how to equitably spread that advantage socially and economically and in a way that is pedagogically sound for children, protective of regional languages and cultures, and mindful of the wide range of linguistic capital that children carry with them to school.

The Indian government needs to more aggressively enforce the Right to Education Act, which now extends from ages three to eighteen, in providing equal educational opportunity, including access to high-quality English instruction, across social classes. It especially needs to enforce the Act against the numerous unrecognized low-fee private schools where poor students presumably receive education in English that is far below their parents' expectations. Given the government's wavering and ineffective efforts to resolve the Hindi-English dilemma, organized regional forces have taken the matter of schooling, language, and cultural identity into their own hands with varying success. Meanwhile, parents across the socioeconomic spectrum wrap their children's identity and future in the mantle of English proficiency, some for better and some for worse, depending on family resources and the quality of English they can afford to purchase in the exploding market of private fee-paying schools.

For people worldwide, native English speakers are presumably the big time winners in the language lottery. They admire, envy, or resent native anglophones for their ability to communicate professionally and personally in English with great comfort, wherever they go. Yet they fail to understand, as do many anglophones themselves, that English cannot do it all and that there is a downside to the Anglo "myth of monolingualism." The global economy, mass migration, and diplomatic tensions have created a need for speakers with multiple language skills that most anglophones sorely lack. Data on the American "language deficit," including racial and economic inequities in access to language learning and study abroad, have brought to light a "monolingual mindset" that has given inconsistent and uncoordinated attention to world languages.

The United States is slowing reckoning with that reality. Language advocates now optimistically talk of making "multilingualism for all" the "new normal" throughout schooling and society. A key part of that argument draws from a growing body of research suggesting that bilingualism may carry cognitive and even emotional advantages from birth to old age. In making the case, however, a common mistake is conflating world language study with bilingualism—that is, equal proficiency in two languages. Research and experience have shown that the first does not necessarily lead to the second. Producing students who can communicate with ease in a second language demands far more than the several hours per week of instruction typically begun in middle school and dropped after several years. On the other hand, if language instruction is begun intensively in the elementary grades, spread contextually throughout the curriculum, and continued through secondary school and even college, sustained exposure and active use could develop an intermediate to advanced level of proficiency in many students. That caveat applies equally to language programs in Europe and beyond, where English and other languages suffer from similarly short student contact hours and years.

A number of American states and local school districts are now making impressive inroads in turning the situation around. Yet even in some dual language programs—the most promising and favored approach—students reportedly reaping the greatest benefits are at times those from more privileged homes. The challenge going forward is for programs to assure participation across racial and socioeconomic groups and to valorize cultural and ethnic identity, especially for linguistic minority students. As the experiences in California, Utah, and New York City demonstrate, achieving equity and sustainability depends on a number of factors. Chief among these are enthusiastic support from local school officials, a continuous source of funding, and parental commitment over six to eight years. Also needed is a steady stream of newcomers to maintain a 50–50 balance between native English and second language speakers, a close relationship with non-English-speaking communities, and a working partnership with the private sector. A prime example is New York City, where the French-speaking community, with support from the French government and local education officials, has successfully hit all these points in fueling a "bilingual revolution" that has spread to other language groups.

The key challenge facing world language programs in the United States is one also common to countries reaching for the "gold ring" of English. It is to convince policymakers, educators, parents, and students of both the intrinsic and extrinsic value in learning not just English but also other languages, which the neoliberal narrative and its instrumental motives favoring English have overshadowed. That challenge applies with equal force to European countries working within the EU's multilingual agenda; to South Africa and India, where multilingualism is part of the social fabric; to Algeria and Morocco, caught in the struggle among French, English, Tamazight, and Arabic; and to Rwanda, trying to resolve its tenuous relationship with France. Treating languages solely as commodities that increase economic productivity risks creating an elite class of English-speaking multilingual cosmopolitans who speak dominant world languages and easily navigate the global economy while marginalizing those who lack the social capital to develop those skills. In the postcolonial world, it casts shadows of cultural and linguistic domination.[4]

Lost in the discourse of marketability are the many reasons for learning other languages beyond landing the job of one's dreams, or any job for that matter, though undeniably important. Languages are not interchangeable. They open windows to other people, their culture, their literature, their way of viewing the world, the context in which they live, and how they interact. There also is something to be gained in preserving languages beyond those typically taught in language programs in schools. Languages bear communal, cultural, and political significance for ethnolinguistic communities, including immigrants and speakers of regional and indigenous languages.

There is no reason, in fact, why language as both an expression of self-realization and a source of material "profit" cannot exist side by side.[5] The social, psychological, and economic benefits are not mutually exclusive but rather mutually supportive. All are important in creating a global citizenry with the sensitivities and skills needed to maintain a thriving world economy and political stability. Observing life through a wide linguistic and cultural lens leads to greater creativity and innovation that not only is personally gratifying, but also has a potentially broader economic impact. Even where business is conducted in English, simply understanding a country's language and culture promotes empathy and trust. The task ahead is twofold: to persuade young people to maintain a balance between these mistakenly competing views on language learning, and to avoid losing sight of a generation that is moving into a global economy where language skills and cultural understandings are becoming useful and even essential in some sectors. Anglophones who speak only English, as well as non-anglophones who do not, will find themselves personally bound in cultural myopia and professionally unprepared to compete for some of the most available and desirable jobs.

And so ending where we began with Condorcet, it does indeed matter "who speaks which language."[6] In the global politics of language, it is left to policy-makers at all levels to realize the opportunities and mitigate the damages of a common language, English for now, in all its complexities. It is not unreasonable to foresee another lingua franca pushing English aside someday, though which one is highly speculative. French is unlikely to make much headway on that score beyond the Francophonie countries at most. And while Mandarin is a commonly mentioned candidate, China's repressive policies on human rights are dimming the glow of its appeal in many parts of the free world. Spanish, officially or unofficially spoken on all five continents, might prove to be the most viable successor. In the meantime, rather than reveling in English as a global "godsend," tolerating it as a necessary evil, or using other national languages as a bulwark against it, key decision-makers should accept English as a core component of multilingualism in its most inclusive sense and decisively move toward educating informed world citizens who can transcend linguistic and cultural borders.

In the words of the 2020 joint International Call to Action from anglophone academies, "To solve the problems we face, we must increase our capacity to speak with each other as part of a global community."[7] The COVID-19 crisis has made that call all the more forceful and meaningful. As the global economy reshapes in a post-pandemic world and countries reconfigure their transnational alliances, language skills will prove ever more critical to achieving a shared vision for the future.

NOTES

Preface

1. *The Inferno of Dante*, trans. Robert Pinsky (New York: Farrar, Straus & Giroux, 1994), Canto 34, 303.

Introduction

1. Marie Jean Antoine Nicholas de Caritat, Marquis of Condorcet, *Outlines of an Historical View of the Progress of the Human Mind*, translator not credited (Chicago: G. Langer, 2009).
2. Ibid., 237–39.
3. Dante Alighieri, *The Divine Comedy = La Divina Commedia*, trans. Henry Wadsworth Longfellow (Oxford: Benediction Classics, 2012).
4. Ibid., 374–75; 405; Will Kymlicka, *Politics in the Vernacular* (New York: Oxford University Press, 2001), 216–17.
5. "The Great English Divide: In Europe, Speaking the Lingua Franca Separates the Haves and the Have-Nots," *Bloomberg Businessweek*, August 12, 2001, https://www.bloomberg.com/news/articles/2001-08-12/the-great-english-divide.
6. *Europeans and Their Languages*, Special Eurobarometer 386 (June 2012), http://ec.europa.eu/commfrontoffice/publicopinion/archives/ebs/ebs_386_en.pdf.
7. Fernand de Varennes, "Language Rights and Social Cohesion: A Balance for Inclusion and Stability," in *Languages and Social Cohesion in the Developing World*, ed. Hywel Coleman (London: British Council, 2015), 23.
8. *Dante: De Vulgari Eloquentia*, ed. and trans. Steven Botterill (New York: Cambridge University Press, 1996), 25.
9. Nicholas Ostler, *The Last Lingua Franca: English until the Return of Babel* (New York: Walker, 2010).
10. Ibid., 277–78.
11. Bill Ashcroft, Gareth Griffiths, and Helen Tiffin, *The Empire Writes Back: Theory and Practice in Post-Colonial Literatures* (London: Routledge, 2002), 7.
12. UNESCO, *The Use of the Vernacular Languages in Education*, Monographs on Foundations of Education 8 (Paris: UNESCO, 1953), http://www.tolerancia.org/upimages/Manifiestos/unesco_1953_english.pdf.
13. World Bank, "In Their Own Language . . . Education for All," *Education Notes*, June 2005, 2, https://documents.worldbank.org/en/publication/documents-reports/documentdetail/374241468763515925/in-their-own-language-education-for-all; John Simpson, *English Language and Medium of Instruction in Basic Education in Low-and Middle-Income Countries: A British Council Perspective* (London: British Council, 2017), https://www.britishcouncil.org.np/sites/

default/files/pub_h106_elt_poseng_nep_ition_paper_on_english_in_basic_education_in_ low-_and_middle-income_countries_final_web_v3.pdf.

14. Intrac for Civil Society, *Respecting Communities in International Development: Languages and Cultural Understanding*, June 2018, https://www.intrac.org/wpcms/wp-content/uploads/ 2018/06/Listening_zones_report_-EN.pdf; Angela Crack, Hilary Footitt, and Angela Crack, Hilary, and Wine Tesseur, "Many NGO Workers on the Ground Don't Speak the Local Language—New Research," *The Conversation*, August 8, 2018, https://theconversation.com/ many-ngo-workers-on-the-ground-dont-speak-the-local-language-new-research-100845.

15. Joan Pujolar, "Bilingualism and the Nation-State in the Post-National Era," in *Bilingualism: A Social Approach*, ed. Monica Heller (New York: Palgrave Macmillan, 2007), 81.

16. Thomas Ricento, "Language Policy and Globalization," in *The Handbook of Language and Globalization*, ed. Nikolas Coupland (Oxford: Wiley-Blackwell, 2013), 122–41.

17. Joseph Sung-Yul Park and Lionel Wee, *Markets of English: Linguistic Capital and Language Policy in a Globalizing World* (New York: Routledge, 2012), 161.

18. Ibid., 124.

19. Abram de Swaan, *Words of the World: The Global Language System* (Cambridge: Polity, 2013), 142.

20. Joseph S. Nye, Jr., *Soft Power: The Means to Success in World Politics* (New York: Public Affairs, 2004), 5.

21. British Council, *The English Effect: The Impact of English, What It's Worth and Why It Matters* (British Council, 2012), 7.

22. Reuters, "English First as Myanmar Protesters Appeal to the World," *U.S. News and World Report*, February 23, 2021, https://www.usnews.com/news/world/articles/2021-02-23/ english-first-as-myanmar-protesters-appeal-to-the-world.

23. "Usage Statistics of Content Languages for Websites," Web Technology Surveys, https:// w3techs.com/technologies/overview/content_language.

24. Simon Kuper, "Globish Just Doesn't Cut it Anymore," *Financial Times*, January 11, 2018, https://www.ft.com/content/981379a8-f58f-11e7-88f7-5465a6ce1a00.

25. British Council, *The English Effect*, 3.

26. Lawrence H. Summers, "What You (Really) Need to Know," *New York Times*, January 20, 2012, https://www.nytimes.com/2012/01/22/education/edlife/the-21st-century-education.html.

27. David Graddol, *English Next: Why Global English May Mean the End of "English as a Foreign Language"* (London: British Council, 2006), https://web.archive.org/web/20201113004353/ http://englishagenda.britishcouncil.org/sites/default/files/attachments/books-english-next.pdf.

28. Geoffrey K. Pullum, "The Anglophone Millstone," *Lingua Franca* (blog), *Chronicle of Higher Education*, October 4, 2016, https://www.chronicle.com/blogs/linguafranca/ the-anglophone-millstone.

29. Rosemary Salomone, "Why English Is Not Enough," *University World News*, January 30, 2015, http://www.universityworldnews.com/article.php?story=20150128065508699.

30. "What Is the Most Spoken Language?," *Ethnologue: Languages of the World*, https:// www.ethnologue.com/guides/most-spoken-languages.

31. World Stats, "Top Ten Languages in the Internet in Millions of Users—March 31, 2020," https://www.internetworldstats.com/stats7.htm.

32. Rosemary C. Salomone, "The Foreign Language Deficit: A Problem in Search of an Obvious Solution," *Teachers College Record*, January 28, 2011, http://www.tcrecord.org/ PrintContent.asp?ContentID=16317.

33. Stephen Vertovec, "Super Diversity and Its Implications," *Racial and Ethnic Studies* 30, no. 6 (2007): 1024–54; Jan Blommaert and Ben Rampton, "Language and Superdiversity," *Diversities* 13, no. 2 (2011): 1–21.

34. Ingrid Gogolin and Joanna Duarte, "Superdiversity, Multilingualism, and Awareness," in *Language Awareness and Multilingualism: Encyclopedia of Language and Education*, 3rd ed., ed. Jasone Cenoz, Durk Gorter, and Stephen May (New York: Springer, 2017), 379.

35. Rani Rubdy and Peter K. W. Tan, eds., *Language as Commodity: Global Structures, Local Marketplaces* (Malden, MA: Wiley-Blackwell, 2008), 2.

36. Rosemary C. Salomone, *Visions of Schooling: Conscience, Community, and Common Education* (New Haven, CT: Yale University Press, 2000), 10.

37. Benedict Anderson, *Imagined Communities: Reflections on the Origin and Spread of Nationalism*, 2nd ed. (London: Verso, 2006), 46; Will Kymlicka, *Politics in the Vernacular: Nationalism, Multiculturalism and Citizenship* (Oxford: Oxford University Press, 2001), 312.

38. Thomas Ricento, "The Promise and Pitfalls of Global English," in *The Politics of Multilingualism*, ed. Peter A. Kraus and François Grin (Amsterdam: John Benjamins, 2018), 209.

39. Nkonko M. Kamwangamalu, *Language Policy and Economics: The Language Question in Africa* (London: Palgrave Macmillan, 2016), 117.

40. Nancy Hornberger and Viniti Vaish, "Multilingual Language Policy and Linguistic Practice: Globalization and English Language Teaching in India, Singapore and South Africa," *Compare* 39, no. 3 (May 2009): 316.

41. Tonia Bieber, *Soft Governance, International Organizations and Education Policy Convergence* (New York: Palgrave Macmillan, 2016), 137.

42. Achille Joseph Mbembe, "Decolonising the University: New Directions," *Arts and Humanities in Higher Education* 15, no. 1 (2016): 29–45, 41.

43. Pierre Bourdieu, *Language and Symbolic Power*, ed. John Thompson, trans. Gino Raymond and Matthew Adamson (Cambridge, MA: Harvard University Press, 1991), 62.

44. Suzanne Romaine, "Linguistic Diversity and Global English: The Pushmi-Pullyu of Language Policy and Political Economy," in *Language Policy and Political Economy: English in a Global Context*, ed. Thomas Ricento (New York: Oxford University Press, 2015), 259–60.

45. James Cummins, "Linguistic Interdependence and the Educational Development of Bilingual Children," *Review of Educational Research* 49, no. 2 (1979): 222–51.

46. Joseph Lo Bianco, "Real World Language Politics and Policy," in *Language Policy: Lessons from Global Models*, ed. Stephen J. Baker (Monterey, CA: Monterey Institute of International Studies, 2020), 25.

47. François Grin and Peter A. Kraus, "The Politics of Multilingualism," in Kraus and Grin, *The Politics of Multilingualism*, 7.

48. Michele Gazzola, Bengt-Arne Wickström, and Mark Fettes, *Towards an Index of Linguistic Justice*, Working Paper No. 20–1, Research Group "Economics and Language," Ulster University, October 9, 2020, 2.

49. Michael Clyne, "The Monolingual Mindset as an Impediment to the Development of Plurilingual Potential in Australia," *Sociolinguistic Studies* 2, no. 3 (2008): 347–66.

Chapter 2

1. Cédric Klapisch, dir., *L'Auberge espagnole*, directed by (Paris: France 2 Cinéma, 2002), DVD; Mana Derakhshani and Jennifer A. Zachman, " 'Une histoire de décollage': The Art of Intercultural Identity and Sensitivity in *L'Auberge espagnole*," *Transitions: Journal of Franco-Iberian Studies* 1, no. 1 (2005): 126–39; Jean M. Fallon, "Ni Pour, Ni Contre: Conflict and Community in Films of Cédric Klapisch," *Foreign Language Annals* 40, no. 2 (Summer 2007): 214.

2. "Diplomats Applaud Juncker's Switch to Speak in French Rather than English—Video," *Guardian* video, May 5, 2017, https://www.theguardian.com/politics/video/2017/may/05/jean-claude-juncker-speech-english-french-language-brexit-video; James Kanter and Michael Wolgelenter, "E.U. Leader Says (in English) That English Is Waning," *New York Times*, May 5, 2017, https://www.nytimes.com/2017/05/05/world/europe/jean-claude-juncker-eu-english.html.

3. "Britain Is Leaving the EU, But Its Language Will Stay," *Economist*, May 13, 2017, https://www.economist.com/news/europe/21721861-despite-jean-claude-junckers-joke-anglophones-should-rest-easy-britain-leaving-eu-its.

4. *Business Insider*, "French President Excoriates Trump in English over US Withdrawal from Climate Deal," June 2, 2017, YouTube video, https://www.youtube.com/watch?v=BLzlwqtmuoI.

5. Nicholas Watt and David Gow, "Chirac Vows to Fight Growing Use of English," *Guardian*, March 25, 2006, https://www.theguardian.com/world/2006/mar/25/france.eu.

6. Marie-Sandrine Sgherri, "#MakeOurPlanetGreatAgain: Le coup de maître d'Emmanuel Macron," *Le Point*, June 2, 2017, http://www.lepoint.fr/politique/comment-emmanuel-macron-est-devenu-leader-du-monde-libre-02-06-2017-2132311_20.php.

7. Marine Pennetier and Ingrid Melander, "Macron Says Too Much English Spoken in Pre-Brexit Brussels," *Reuters.com*, March 20, 2018, https://www.reuters.com/article/us-france-politics-macron-french/macron-says-too-much-english-spoken-in-pre-brexit-brussels-idUSKBN1GW2JP.

8. Palko Karasz, "'I Can English Understand,' New Official Says. The Swiss Have Their Doubts," *New York Times*, December 19, 2018, https://www.nytimes.com/2018/12/19/world/europe/guy-parmelin-switzerland-english.html; Lise Bailat, "L'anglais de Guy Parmelin divise les élus," *24 Heures*, December 13, 2018, https://www.24heures.ch/suisse/anglais-guy-parmelin-divise-elus/story/22022224.

9. Peter A. Kraus and Giuseppe Sciortino, "The Diversities of Europe: From European Modernity to the Making of the European Union," *Ethnicities* 14, no. 4 (2014): 492.

10. Tariq Modood, *Multiculturalism: A Civic Idea* (Cambridge: Polity, 2007), 10–14.

11. Sue Wright, "The Elephant in the Room," *European Journal of Language Policy* 1, no. 2 (2009): 98.

12. Lisanne Wilken, "The Development of Minority Rights in Europe," in *The Tensions between Group Rights and Human Rights*, ed. Koen de Feyter and George Pavlakos (Portland, OR: Hart, 2008), 89–104.

13. Will Kymlicka, *Multicultural Citizenship: A Liberal Theory of Minority Rights* (Oxford: Clarendon, 1995), 45–46; Lionel Wee, *Languages without Rights* (New York: Oxford University Press, 2011), 58–63.

14. Fernand de Varennes, "Language Rights as an Integral Part of Human Rights," *MOST: Journal of Multicultural Societies* 3, no. 1 (2001): 17–18; John Edwards, "Language Economics and Language Rights," in *Bridging Linguistics and Economics*, ed. Cécile B. Vigouroux and Salikoko S. Mufwene (Cambridge: Cambridge University Press, 2020), 237.

15. Tove Skutnabb-Kangas and Robert Phillipson, eds., *Linguistic Human Rights Overcoming: Linguistic Discrimination* (Berlin: Mouton de Gruyter, 1995), 79–100; Stephen May, "Justifying Educational Language Rights," *Review of Research in Education* 38 (March 2014): 224.

16. Cornelius J. W. Baaij, "The EU Policy on Constitutional Multilingualism: Between Principles and Practicality," *International Journal of Language and Law* 1 (2012): 15–18.

17. Guus Extra, "The Constellation of Languages in Europe," in *The Routledge Handbook on Heritage Language Education*, ed. Olga Kagan, Maria Cariera, and Claire Chik (New York: Routledge 2016), 11.

18. Peter A. Kraus and Rūta Kazlauskaitė-Gürbüz, "Addressing Linguistic Diversity in the European Union: Strategies and Dilemmas," *Ethnicities* 14, no. 4 (2014): 533–35.

19. Council of the European Economic Community, "EEC Council: Regulation no. 1 Determining the Languages to Be Used by the European Economic Community," *EEC Council Official Journal* 1, no. 1 (April 15, 1958): 385–86, https://eur-lex.europa.eu/LexUriServ/LexUriServ.do?uri=CELEX:31958R0001:EN:HTML.

20. Consolidated Version of the Treaty on the Functioning of the European Union, Article 342, https://eur-lex.europa.eu/resource.html?uri=cellar:2bf140bf-a3f8-4ab2-b506-fd71826e6da6.0023.02/DOC_2&format=PDF.

21. European Union, "EU Administration—Staff, Languages and Location," https://europa.eu/european-union/about-eu/figures/administration_en.

22. *Charter of Fundamental Rights of the European Union* (2009), article 21, https://www.europarl.europa.eu/charter/pdf/text_en.pdf; Treaty of Lisbon Amending the Treaty on European Union and the Treaty Establishing the European Community, December 13, 2007, 2007 O.J. (C 306), http://publications.europa.eu/resource/cellar/688a7a98-3110-4ffe-a6b3-8972d8445325.0007.01/DOC_19.

23. "FAQs on Multilingualism and Language Learning" (memorandum, European Commission, September 25, 2012), https://ec.europa.eu/commission/presscorner/detail/en/MEMO_12_703.

24. "Chiffres et données clés sur la language française 2017," Langue Française et Langues de France, Ministère de la Culture, February 22, 2018, https://www.culture.gouv.fr/Sites-thematiques/Langue-francaise-et-langues-de-France/Actualites/Chiffres-et-donnees-cles-sur-la-langue-francaise-2017.

25. European Commission, Directorate-General for Translation, "Translation in Figures 2020," May 13, 2020, https://op.europa.eu/en/publication-detail/-/publication/c29be934-9588-11ea-aac4-01aa75ed71a1.

26. Jean Quatremer, "I Want You to Speak English or Get Out!" *Liberation*, May 31, 2012 (updated February 16, 2015), http://bruxelles.blogs.liberation.fr/2012/05/31/peut-on-gouverner-une-zone-euro-qui-compte-330-millions-de-citoyens-dans-une-langue-qui-nest-parlee-que-par-moins-de-5-mi.

27. "Multilingualism: The Language of the European Union" (briefing, European Parliament, September 2019), http://www.europarl.europa.eu/RegData/etudes/BRIE/2019/642207/EPRS_BRI(2019)642207_EN.pdf.

28. Anna Codrea-Rado, "European Parliament Has 24 Official Languages, but MEPs Prefer English," *Guardian*, May 21, 2014, http://www.theguardian.com/education/datablog/2014/may/21/european-parliament-english-language-official-debates-data/.

29. Antoine de Rivarol, *De l'universalité de la langue française* [On the universality of the French language] (Paris: H. Didier, 1930).

30. Charles Rebuffat, "Comment la France conçoit l'idée européene" [How France conceives of the idea of Europe], *Le Soir* (Brussels), May 19, 1971.

31. "French Worry about Fate of Molière's Language," *Guardian*, May 17, 1971, https://www.theguardian.com/theguardian/2012/may/21/archive-1971-language-french-english-common-market.

32. Michel Feltin-Palas, "La langue de la République est le français" [The language of the Republic in French], *L'Express*, May 12, 2020, https://www.lexpress.fr/culture/la-langue-de-la-republique-est-le-francais_2125721.html.

33. Anne Judge, "France: 'One State, One Nation, One Language?'" in *Language and Nationalism in Europe*, ed. Stephen Barbour and Cathie Carmichael (New York: Oxford University Press, 2000), 46.

34. Loi 94–665 du 4 août 1994 rélative à l'emploi de la langue française [Law 94–665 of August 4, 1994, relating to the use of French language], *Journal Officiel de la République Française*, August 5, 1994, 11392, https://www.legifrance.gouv.fr/affichTexte.do?cidTexte=LEGITEXT000005616341.

35. Charles Bremner, "Gaulists Outlaw Draft Bill to Outlaw English Patois," *The Times* (London), April 14, 1995, 12.

36. Guy Chazan and Jim Brunsden, "Push to Bid Adieu to English as EU's Lingua Franca," *Financial Times*, June 28, 2016, https://www.ft.com/content/e70b5042-3c65-11e6-8716-a4a71e8140b0.

37. Pennetier and Melander, "Macron Says Too Much English Spoken in Pre-Brexit Brussels."

38. European Commission, "EU Budget: Commission Proposes a Modern Budget That Protects, Empowers and Defends," press release) May 2, 2018, https://ec.europa.eu/commission/sites/beta-political/files/communication-modern-budget-may_2018_en.pdf; Nick Gutteridge, "Sacre Bleu! French Politicians Furious after European Commission Signals English Will Be Main Language after Brexit," *Sun* (London), May 9, 2018, https://www.thesun.co.uk/news/6230982/french-politicians-furious-european-commission-brexit.

39. Maïa de la Baume and David M. Herszenhorn, "English Only? Try Au Revoir, French Ambassador Tells Council," *Politico*, April 27, 2018, https://www.politico.eu/article/english-only-try-au-revoir-french-ambassador-tells-council-philippe-leglise-costa.

40. Collectif Résistance Francophone, "A Monsieur Emmanuel Macron, Président de la République" (letter, Défense de la langue française, October 22, 2019) [letter, In defense of the French language], http://www.langue-francaise.org/2019_index_lettre_emmanuel_macron.pdf.

41. Ulrich Ammon, "Language Conflicts in the European Union," *International Journal of Applied Linguistics* 16, no. 3 (2006): 319–38.

42. European Union, "EU Languages," https://europa.eu/european-union/about-eu/eu-languages_en..

43. Tim King, "Ursula von der Leyen's Speech Shows English Still Dominates," *Politico*, September 17, 2020, https://www.politico.eu/article/ursula-von-der-leyens-speech-shows-english-still-dominates-state-of-the-union.

44. Letter from l'Association des Journalistes Européens to Ursula von der Leyen and Charles Michel, September 23, 2020, https://www.euractiv.com/wp-content/uploads/sites/2/2020/09/Association-of-European-Journalists-to-VDL.pdf.

45. Elżbieta Kużelewska, "*Quo Vadis* English? The Post-Brexit Position of English as a Working Language of the EU," *International Journal for the Semiotics of Law*, 2020, https://doi.org/10.1007/s11196-020-09782-x.

46. Diarmait Mac Giolla Chríost and Matteo Bonotti, *Brexit, Language Policy and Linguistic Diversity* (Cham, Switzerland: Palgrave Macmillan, 2018), 56–76.

47. Michele Gazzola and François Grin, "Is ELF More Effective and Fair Than Translation? An Evaluation of the EU's Multilingual Regime," *International Journal of Applied Linguistics* 23, no. 1 (2013): 103–4.

48. Michele Gazzola, "Multilingual Communication for Whom? Language Policy and Fairness in the European Union," *European Union Politics* 17, no. 4 (2016): 546–69.

49. Stephen May, "The Problem with English(es) and Linguistic (In)justice: Addressing the Limits of Liberal Egalitarian Accounts of Language," *Critical Review of International and Political Philosophy* 18, no. 2 (2015): 136.

50. Peter A. Kraus, *A Union of Diversity: Language, Identity and Polity-Building in Europe* (Cambridge: Cambridge University Press, 2008), 179.

51. Peter A. Kraus, email to author, January 8, 2021.

52. Alessandro Carlucci, "Language, Education and European Unification: Perceptions and Reality of Global English in Italy," in *Antonio Gramsci: A Pedagogy to Change the World*, ed. Nicola Pizzolato and John D. Holst (Cham, Switzerland: Springer, 2017), 145.

53. James A. Coleman, "English-Medium Teaching in European Higher Education," *Language Teaching* 39, no. 1 (2006): 1–14.

54. Scott L. Montgomery, *Does Science Need a Global Language?* (Chicago: University of Chicago Press, 2013), 61.

55. David Crystal, *Language Death* (Cambridge: Cambridge University Press, 2000), 33.

56. Abram de Swaan, *Words of the World* (Cambridge: Polity, 2001), 192; Pierre Bourdieu, Abram de Swaan, Claude Hagège, Marc Fumaroli, and Immanuel Wallerstein, "Quelles langues pour une Europe démocratique? [What languages for a democratic Europe?]," *Presses de Sciences Po* 2 (May 2001): 54.

57. David Graddol, *English Next* (London: British Council, 2006), 66.

58. François Grin, Claudio Sfreddo and François Vaillancourt, *The Economics of the Multilingual Workplace* (New York: Routledge, 2010).

59. Jean-Claude Barbier, "English Speaking, a Hidden Political Factor of European Politics and Europe Integration," *Social Policies*, May–August 2015: 190.

60. Peter Ives, " 'Global English and the Limits of Liberalism: Confronting Global Capitalism and Challenges to the Nation-State," in *Language Policy and Political Economy: English in a Global Context*, ed. Thomas Ricento (New York: Oxford University Press, 2015), 62–65.

61. Robert Phillipson, *Linguistic Imperialism Continued* (London: Routledge, 2009), 125.

62. Astrid von Busekist, "Justice linguistique," in *Dictionnaire des inégalités et de la justice sociale* [Dictionary of inequalities and social justice], ed. Patrick Savidan (Paris: Presses Universitaires de France, 2018), 1693.

63. Philippe Van Parijs, *Linguistic Justice for Europe and the World*, (Oxford: Oxford University Press, 2011), 77–116.

64. Gibson Ferguson, Carmen Pérez-Llantada, and Ramón Plo, "English as an International Language of Scientific Publication: A Study of Attitudes," *World Englishes* 30, no.1 (2010): 55.

65. Sue Wright, "What is Language? A Response to Philippe Van Parijs," in *Linguistic Justice: Van Parijs and His Critics*, ed. Helder De Schutter and David Robichaud (London: Routledge, 2016), 35.

66. Helder de Schutter and David Robichaud, "Van Parijsian Linguistic Justice—Context, Analysis and Critiques," *Critical Review of International and Political Philosophy* 18, no. 2 (2015): 87–112; Thomas Ricento, "Political Economy and English as a "Global" Language," in Ricento, *Language Policy and Political Economy*, 31–33.

67. Lindsey Johnstone, "World English Language Day: So You Speak 'Euro English'?" *EuroNews*, April 23, 2020, https://www.euronews.com/2020/04/23/world-language-day-do-you-speak-euro-english.

68. Marko Modiano, "English in a Post-Brexit Union," *World Englishes* 36, no. 3 (2017): 313–15.

69. Mario Saraceni, *World Englishes: A Critical Analysis* (London: Bloomsbury, 2015), 172–73.

70. Mario Saraceni, "Post-Brexit English: A Post-National Perspective," *World Englishes* 36, no. 3 (2017): 351.

71. Edgar W. Schneider, "The Linguistic Consequences of Brexit? No Reason to Get Excited!" *World Englishes* 3, no. 3 (2017): 353–55.

72. David Crystal, "The Future of New Euro-Englishes," *World Englishes* 36, no. 3 (2017): 330–35.

73. Jennifer Jenkins, "An ELF Perspective on English in the Post-Brexit EU," *World Englishes* 36, no. 3 (2017): 343–46; Barbara Seidlhofer and Henry Widdowson, "Thoughts on Independent English," *World Englishes* 36, no. 3 (2017): 360–62.

74. Jennifer Jenkins, "Trouble with English?" in *Languages after Brexit*, ed. Michael Kelly (Cham, Switzerland: Palgrave Macmillan, 2018), 32.

75. Marinel Gerritsen, "English in the EU: Unity through Diversity," *World Englishes* 36, no. 3 (2017): 339–42.

76. Deborah Nicholls-Lee, "Meet the Brexiles Who Have Swapped the UK for the Netherlands to Escape Brexit," *Dutch News*, January 11, 2021, https://www.dutchnews.nl/features/2021/01/meet-the-brexiles-who-have-swapped-the-uk-for-the-netherlands-to-escape-brexit.

77. Jean-Claude Beacco, "Le Conseil de l'Europe et les langues de scolarisation" [The Council of Europe and languages of schooling], *La revue international de l'éducation de Sèvres* 870 (2015): 155.

78. Council of Europe, *European Convention on Human Rights*, https://www.echr.coe.int/Documents/Convention_ENG.pdf.

79. Marisa Cavalli et al., *Plurilingual and Intercultural Education as a Project* (Strasbourg, France: Council of Europe, 2009), 13.

80. Rosemary C. Salomone, "Multilingualism and Multiculturalism: Transatlantic Discourses on Language, Identity, and Immigrant Schooling," *Notre Dame Law Review* 87, no. 5 (2012): 2046.

81. Marisa Cavalli, "Bilingualism, plurilingualisme et politiques linguistique éducatives en Europe," in *L'éducation bilingue en France: politiques, linguistiques, modèles et pratiques*, ed. Christine Hélot and Jürgen Erfurt (Limoges, France: Lambert-Lucas, 2016), 553.

82. Jean-Claude Beacco and Michael Byrum, "From Linguistic Diversity to Plurilingual Education: Guide for the Development of Language Education Policies in Europe" (Strasbourg, France: Council of Europe, 2007), 10, https://rm.coe.int/16802fc1c4.

83. Council of Europe, "European Charter for Regional or Minority Languages," https://www.coe.int/en/web/conventions/full-list/-/conventions/rms/0900001680695175.

84. Peter A. Kraus, "Between Minority Protection and Linguistic Sovereignty," *Journal of Language and Law* 69 (June 2018), 15.

85. Council of Europe, "The CEFR Levels," https://www.coe.int/en/web/common-european-framework-reference-languages/level-descriptions..

86. Council of Europe, "Recommendation No. R (96) 6 of the Committee of Ministers to Member States Concerning Modern Languages" (recommendation, Strasbourg, France, March 17, 1998), https://rm.coe.int/16804fc569; Guido Reverdito and Sarah K. St. John, "Breaking the Language Barriers: Free Movement and Language Learning in the European Community," in *Education and Public Policy in the European Union*, ed. Sarah K. St. John and Mark Murphy (New York: Palgrave Macmillan, 2019), 129–31.

87. Enrica Piccardo, Brian North, and Tom Goodier, "Broadening the Scope of Language Education: Mediation, Plurilingualism, and Collaborative Learning: The CEFR Companion Volume," *Journal of e-Learning and Knowledge Society* 15, no. 1 (2019): 17–36.

88. Guus Extra, "Trends in Policies and Practices for Multilingualism in Europe," in *Plurilinguismo Sintassi*, ed. Carla Bruno, Simone Casini, and Francesca Gallina (Rome: Bulzoni, 2015), 30.

89. Council of Europe, "European Language Portfolio (ELP)," https://www.coe.int/en/web/portfolio.

90. Christine Hélot, email to author, May 19, 2020.

91. The Maastricht Treaty: Provisions Amending the Treaty Establishing the European Economic Community with a View to Establishing the European Community, art. 126 (February 7, 1992), https://europa.eu/european-union/sites/europaeu/files/docs/body/treaty_on_european_union_en.pdf.

92. European Union, "Declaration on European Identity" (declaration, Copenhagen, Denmark, December 13, 1973), https://www.cvce.eu/en/obj/declaration_on_european_identity_copenhagen_14_december_1973-en-02798dc9-9c69-4b7d-b2c9-f03a8db7da32.html.

93. Commission on the European Communities, "Teaching and Learning: Towards the Learning Society" (White Paper on Education and Training, Luxembourg City, November 29, 1995), 44, https://publications.europa.eu/en/publication-detail/-/publication/d0a8aa7a-5311-4eee-904c-98fa541108d8.

94. "The Lisbon Strategy in Short," ECON Commission of the Regions, 2000, https://portal.cor.europa.eu/europe2020/Profiles/Pages/TheLisbonStrategyinshort.aspx.

95. European Council, "Speech by the President Nicole Fontaine: Presidency Conclusions" (bulletin, Luxembourg City, March 27, 2000), http://www.europarl.europa.eu/bulletins/pdf/1s2000en.pdf; Michał Krzyżanowski and Ruth Wodak, "Political Strategies and Language Policies: The European Union Lisbon Strategy and Its Implications for the EU's Language and Multilingualism Policy," *Language Policy* 10, no. 2 (2011): 115–36; Peter A. Kraus and Rūta Kazlauskaitė-Gürbüz, "Addressing Linguistic Diversity in the European Union: Strategies and Dilemmas," *Ethnicities* 14, no. 4 (2014): 517–38.

96. Humphrey Tonkin, "Language Inclusion and Individual Exclusion: Patterns of Communication in Bilingual and Multilingual Polities" (paper presented at the MIDP Symposium on Multilingualism and Exclusion, University of the Free State, Bloemfontein, South Africa, 2006), 11–12, https://citeseerx.ist.psu.edu/viewdoc/download?doi=10.1.1.499.4232&rep=rep1&type=pdf.

97. Council of the European Union, "Council Resolution of 14 February 2002 on the Promotion of Linguistic Diversity and Language Learning in the Framework of the Objectives of the European Year of Languages 2001," *Official Journal of the European Communities* 50, no. 1 (February 23, 2002), https://eur-lex.europa.eu/legal-content/EN/TXT/PDF/?uri=CELEX:32002G0223(01)&from=EN.

98. Commission of the European Communities, "Communication from the Commission to the European Parliament, the Council, the Economic and Social Committee and the Committee of the Regions, Promoting Language Learning and Linguistic Diversity: An Action Plan 2004-2006, at 5–6" (communication, Luxembourg City, July 24, 2003), http://eur-lex.europa.eu/legal-content/EN/TXT/PDF/?uri=CELEX:52003DC0449&from=EN.

99. European Commission, "Communication from the Commission to the Council, the European Parliament, the European Economic and Social Committee and the Committee of the Regions, A New Framework Strategy for Multilingualism," November 22, 2005, https://www.europarl.europa.eu/RegData/docs_autres_institutions/commission_europeenne/com/2005/0596/COM_COM(2005)0596_EN.pdf.

100. European Commission, "Final Report: High Level Group on Multilingualism" (report, Luxembourg City, 2007), 8–9, http://biblioteca.esec.pt/cdi/ebooks/docs/High_level_report.pdf.

101. Michał Krzyżanowski and Ruth Wodak, "Hegemonic Multilingualism in/of the EU Institutions: An Inside-Outside Perspective on European Language Policies and Practices," in *Sprache im Kontext*, ed. Ruth Wodak and Martin Stegu (Frankfurt am Main: Peter Lang, 2014), 115–34.

102. European Commission, "A Political Agenda for Multilingualism" (memo/07/80, Brussels, Belgium, February 23, 2007), https://europa.eu/rapid/press-release_MEMO-07-80_en.htm.

103. European Commission, "Languages Mean Business: Companies Work Better with Languages" (report, Brussels, 2008), https://education.gov.mt/en/foreignlanguages/Documents/EC%202008%20Languages%20Mean%20Business.pdf.

104. CiLT: The National Center for Languages, "*ELAN*: Effects on the European Economy of Shortages of Foreign Language Skills" (research report, Luxembourg City, December 2006), https://ec.europa.eu/assets/eac/languages/policy/strategic-framework/documents/elan_en.pdf; European Commission, "Political Agenda for Multilingualism" (memo /07/08, Luxembourg City, February 23, 2007), https://ec.europa.eu/commission/presscorner/detail/en/MEMO_07_80.

105. Group of Intellectuals for Intercultural Dialogue, "A Rewarding Challenge: How the Multiplicity of Languages Could Strengthen Europe" (Luxembourg City, 2008), 4–5, https://op.europa.eu/en/publication-detail/-/publication/7f987cdd-dba2-42e7-8cdf-3f4f14efe783/language-en.

106. Ibid., 7–9.

107. Teresa Küchler, "Multilingualism a 'Damned Nuisance' Says Dutch Academic," *Euobserver*, September 15, 2008, https://euobserver.com/news/26742.

108. "Orban: Multilingualism 'Cost of Democracy' in EU," *EURACTIV Media Network*, November 13, 2008, https://www.euractiv.com/section/languages-culture/interview/orban-multilingualism-cost-of-democracy-in-eu.

109. Peter Teffer, "E.U. Fights to Get Everyone Speaking Same Language on Education," *New York Times*, March 16, 2014, http://www.nytimes.com/2014/03/17/world/europe/eu-fights-to-get-everyone-speaking-same-language-on-education.html.

110. European Commission, "Multilingualism: An Asset for Europe and a Shared Commitment," Communication from the Commission to the European Parliament, the Council, the European Economic and Social Committee and the Committee of the Regions, Luxembourg, Luxembourg," September 18, 2008, 8, https://eur-lex.europa.eu/legal-content/EN/TXT/PDF/?uri=CELEX:52008DC0566&from=EN.

111. Androulla Vassiliou, "Why Languages Still Matter" (speech at the Conference on Multilingualism, Nicosia, Cyprus, September 27, 2012), http://europa.eu/rapid/press-release_SPEECH-12-649_en.htm; Androulla Vassiliou, "Linguistic Diversity: The Heart of Europe's DNA" (speech at the IAMLADP Meeting, Luxembourg City, June 24, 2014), http://europa.eu/rapid/press-release_SPEECH-14-492_en.htm.

112. Peter Teffer, "E.U. Fights to Get Everyone Speaking Same Language," *New York Times*, March 16, 2014, https://www.nytimes.com/2014/03/17/world/europe/eu-fights-to-get-everyone-speaking-same-language-on-education.html.

113. European Commission, "Communication from the Commission: Europe 2020" (Brussels: March 3, 2010), https://ec.europa.eu/eu2020/pdf/COMPLET%20EN%20BARROSO%20%20%20007%20-%20Europe%202020%20-%20EN%20version.pdf.

114. Thematic Working Group "Languages for Jobs" of the European Strategic Framework for Education and Training, "Providing Multilingual Communication for the Labor Market" (report, Brussels, Belgium, 2011), 15, https://ec.europa.eu/assets/eac/languages/policy/strategic-framework/documents/languages-for-jobs-report_en.pdf, quoting European Commission, "Recommendations from the Business Forum for Multilingualism" (press release, Luxembourg City, July 11, 2008), https://ec.europa.eu/commission/presscorner/detail/en/MEMO_08_497.

115. European Commission, "Lingua Franca: Chimera or Reality? Studies on Translation and Multilingualism" (report, Luxembourg City, January 1, 2011), 50–51, https://op.europa.eu/en/publication-detail/-/publication/ae3e3148-43af-41b6-9734-7a2fa57cafa5/language-en.

116. European Civil Society Platform on Multilingualism, "Policy Recommendations for the Promotion of Multilingualism in the European Union" (recommendation, Luxembourg City, June 9, 2011), 55, https://elen.ngo/wp-content/uploads/2016/05/report-civil-society_en.pdf.

117. Ibid.

118. European Commission, "Rethinking Education: Investing in Skills for Better Socio-Economic Outcomes" (communication from the Commission to the European Parliament,

The Council, The European Economic and Social Committee and the Committee of the Regions, Luxembourg City, November 20, 2012), http://eur-lex.europa.eu/legal-content/EN/TXT/PDF/?uri=CELEX:52012DC0669.

119. European Commission, "Language Competences for Employability, Mobility and Growth" (commission staff working document 3, Strasbourg, France, November 11, 2012), 21, http://eur-lex.europa.eu/legal-content/EN/TXT/PDF/?uri=CELEX:52012SC0372.

120. Bessie Dendrinos, "Is 'Multilingualism' Taking a Back Seat in the EU?: Time for Action" (paper, 2013), http://www.efnil.org/conferences/13th-annual-conference-helsinki/proceedings/24__Dendrinos.pdf.

121. European Parliament, MENON Network EEIG, "Multilingualism: Between Policy Objectives and Implementation" (study manuscript, Luxembourg City, September 2008), iii–iv, http://www.europarl.europa.eu/RegData/etudes/etudes/join/2008/408495/IPOL-CULT_ET%282008%29408495_EN.pdf.

122. European Parliament, "Resolution of 24 March 2009 on Multilingualism: An Asset for Europe and a Shared Commitment" (resolution, Strasbourg, France, December 2, 2009), F4, F6, http://www.europarl.europa.eu/sides/getDoc.do?type=TA&language=EN&reference=P6-TA-2009-0162.

123. Rosita Rindler Schjerve and Eva Vetter, *European Multilingualism* (Bristol, UK: Multilingual Matters, 2012), 5.

124. European Council, "Recommendation on a Comprehensive Approach to the Teaching and Learning of Languages" (1019/C 189/03, May 22, 2019), https://eur-lex.europa.eu/legal-content/EN/TXT/?uri=CELEX:32019H0605(02).

125. European Commission, "Education Begins with Language" (report, Brussels, 2020), 9–10, https://op.europa.eu/en/publication-detail/-/publication/6b7e2851-b5fb-11ea-bb7a-01aa75ed71a1/language-en/format-PDF/source-148560937.

126. Kraus and Sciortino, "The Diversities of Europe," 495.

127. Robert Phillipson, *English-Only Europe? Challenging Language Policy* (London: Routledge, 2001), 191–92.

128. Baaij, "The EU Policy on Institutional Multilingualism," 24.

129. European Commission, "First European Survey on Language Competences: Executive Summary" (survey, Luxembourg City, June 2012), https://ec.europa.eu/assets/eac/languages/library/studies/executive-summary-eslc_en.pdf.

130. Eurostat, *Foreign Language Learning Statistics* (data extracted in September 2020), https://ec.europa.eu/eurostat/statistics-explained/index.php?title=Foreign_language_learning_statistics.

131. European Commission, "Europeans and Their Languages," 5–7, https://ec.europa.eu/commfrontoffice/publicopinion/archives/ebs/ebs_386_en.pdf.

132. Suzanne Romaine, "Politics and Policies of Promoting Multilingualism in the European Union," *Language Policy* 12, no. 2 (2013): 115–37, 123.

133. Eurostat, *Foreign Language Learning Statistics* (data extracted in September 2020), https://ec.europa.eu/eurostat/statistics-explained/index.php?title=Foreign_language_learning_statistics.

134. Eurydice, "Key Data on Teaching Languages in School in Europe" (May 2017), 29–31, https://eacea.ec.europa.eu/national-policies/eurydice/content/key-data-teaching-languages-school-europe-%E2%80%93-2017-edition_en.

135. European Commission, Directorate-General For Education, Youth, Sports, and Culture, "Flash Eurobarometer 466: The European Education Area" (survey report, Luxembourg City, April 2018), 48, https://ec.europa.eu/commfrontoffice/publicopinion/index.cfm/ResultDoc/download/DocumentKy/83257.

136. Ibid., 60.

137. Ibid., 41–44.

138. Ibid., 45.

139. Ibid., 52.

140. Megan Bowler, *A Language Crisis?* (Higher Education Policy Institute, 2020), https://www.hepi.ac.uk/wp-content/uploads/2020/01/HEPI_A-Languages-Crisis_Report-123-FINAL.pdf.

141. Teresa Tinsley, *Language Trends 2019: Language Teaching in Primary and Secondary Schools in England, Survey Report* (London: British Council, May 2019), 3.

142. "Traditional Phrasebook Dying Out for Tech-Savvy Millennials Heading Abroad," *British Council*, August 7, 2018, https://www.britishcouncil.org/organisation/press/traditional-phrasebook-dying-out-tech-savvy-millennials-heading-abroad.

143. Tinsley, *Language Trends 2019*, 15.

144. "The Guardian View on Languages and the British: Brexit and an Anglosphere Prison," *Guardian*, November 3, 2017, https://www.theguardian.com/commentisfree/2017/nov/03/the-guardian-view-on-languages-and-the-british-brexit-and-an-anglosphere-prison.

145. British Academy, "Language in the UK: A Call for Action" (statement, London, February 2019), 4, https://www.thebritishacademy.ac.uk/sites/default/files/Languages-UK-2019-academies-statement.pdf.

146. University Council of Modern Languages, *Language Provision in UK Modern Foreign Languages (MFL) Departments 2019 Survey*, December 2019, https://university-council-modern-languages.org/2019/12/24/ucml-language-acts-report-2019.

147. Jean Coussins and Philip Harding-Esch, introduction to *Languages After Brexit: How the UK Speaks to the World*, ed. Michael Kelly (New York: Palgrave MacMillan, 2018), 3–5.

148. Jasone Cenoz, Fred Genesee, and Durk Gorter, "Critical Analysis of CLIL: Taking Stock and Looking Forward," *Applied Linguistics* 35, no. 3 (2014): 244–47.

149. Ibid., 247–54.

150. Julie Dearden, *English as a Medium of Instruction: A Growing Global Phenomenon* (London: British Council, 2015), 20–21.

151. Guus Extra and Durk Gorter, *Multilingual Europe: Facts and Policies* (Berlin: Mouton de Gruyter, 2008), 44.

152. Ofelia García, *Bilingual Education in the 21st Century: A Global Perspective* (Malden, MA: Wiley-Blackwell, 2009).

153. "Lingua Franca Learning: The Growth of EMI," *PIE Review* 12 (2016): 64.

154. Hans de Wit, *Internationalization of Higher Education in the United States of America and Europe* (Westport, CT: Greenwood, 2002), 6.

155. "Erasmus+ Supported Nearly 800,000 International Placements in 2017," *ICEF Monitor*, March 6, 2019, http://monitor.icef.com/2019/03/erasmus-supported-nearly-800000-international-placements-2017.

156. European Commission, Directorate-General For Education, Youth, Sports, and Culture, "Flash Eurobarometer 466: The European Education Area" (survey report, Luxembourg City, April 2018), 5–8.

157. European Commission, "Erasmus+: Another Record Year in 2017" (press release, Luxembourg City, January 24, 2019), http://europa.eu/rapid/press-release_IP-19-601_en.htm.

Chapter 3

1. Anna Kristina Hultgren, "The Drive towards EMI in Non-English-Dominant European HE: The Role of University Rankings," *Language Teaching* 52, no.2 (2019): 233–36.

2. Friedhelm Maiworm and Bernd Wächter, "The Big Picture," in *English-Taught Programmes in European Higher Education: The State of Play in 2014*, ed. Bernd Wächter and Friedhelm Maiworm (Bonn, Germany: Lemmens, 2014), 48–49, https://www.lemmens.de/dateien/medien/buecher-ebooks/aca/2014_english_taught.pdf.

3. Ibid.

4. Institute of International Education, "English-Taught Master's Programs in Europe: A 2013 Update" (briefing paper, New York, September 2013), 4–6, https://www.iie.org/Research-and-Insights/Publications/English-Language-Masters-Briefing-Paper-2013-Update.

5. Francesca Costa and James A. Coleman, "A Survey of English-Medium Instruction in Italian Higher Education," *International Journal of Bilingual Education and Bilingualism* 16, no. 1 (2013): 3–19.

6. Anna-Malin Sandström and Carmen Neghina, *English-Taught Bachelor's Programmes: Internationalising European Higher Education* (Amsterdam: European Association for International Education, 2017), 12–13, https://www.studyportals.com/wp-content/uploads/2017/09/EAIE-StudyPortals-English-taught-bachelor-programmes-Europe.pdf.

392

NOTES

7. Brendan O'Malley, "Challenges for 'European Universities' Revealed by Survey," *University World News*, May 1, 2020, https://www.universityworldnews.com/post.php?story= 20200501095005418.

8. "EU Students Will Lose Home Fee Status in England in 2021–22," *ICEF Monitor*, June 24, 2020, https://monitor.icef.com/2020/06/eu-students-will-lose-home-fee-status-in-england-in-2021-22.

9. Brendan O'Malley, "Most EU Students 'Will Not Study in UK' after Fees Decision," *University World News*, July 1, 2020, https://www.universityworldnews.com/post.php?story=2020070108154994.

10. Eleanor Busby, "Brexit: European Universities Increase English-Speaking Courses to Prepare for Influx of Students, Study Suggests," *Independent*, February 19, 2018, https://www.independent.co.uk/news/education/education-news/brexit-universities-studyeu-european-international-students-poland-a8218521.html.

11. Seb Murray, "Schools in Mainland Europe Expect an Increase in LL.M. Students, Academics and Job Opportunities," *LL.M. Guide*, May 28, 2020, https://llm-guide.com/articles/why-eu-law-schools-stand-to-gain-from-brexit.

12. VSNU, "Definitieve inschrijfcijfers: 8% studenten in 2020–2021," nieuwsberichten ["Final enrollment figures: 8% students in 2020–2021," news release], February 4, 2021, https://vsnu.nl/nl_NL/nieuwsbericht/nieuwsbericht/705-definitieve-inschrijfcijfers-8-meer-studenten-in-2020-2021.html.

13. Viggo Stacey, "'Five Year Recovery Period' Predicted for Global Student Mobility," *PIE News*, March 25, 2020, https://thepienews.com/news/five-year-recovery-period-predicted-for-global-student-mobility.

14. European Parliament, "Research for CULT Committee—Virtual Formats Versus Physical Mobility" (briefing paper, March 20, 2020), https://www.europarl.europa.eu/RegData/etudes/BRIE/2020/629217/IPOL_BRI(2020)629217_EN.pdf.

15. "Joint declaration on harmonization of the architecture of the European higher education system" (joint declaration, Paris, May 25, 1998), http://www.ehea.info/media.ehea.info/file/1998_Sorbonne/61/2/1998_Sorbonne_Declaration_English_552612.pdf; "The Bologna Declaration of 19 June 1999: Joint Declaration of the European Ministers of Education" (joint declaration, Luxembourg City, June 19, 1999) http://www.magna-charta.org/resources/files/BOLOGNA_DECLARATION.pdf.

16. "European Higher Education Area and Bologna Process," Bologna Process Secretariat, http://www.ehea.info.

17. "The Bologna Declaration," 4.

18. Clive W. Earls, *Evolving Agendas in European English-Medium Higher Education: Interculturality, Multilingualism and Language Policy* (New York: Palgrave, 2016), 68.

19. Robert Phillipson, "Figuring Out the Englishisation of Europe," in *Reconfiguring Europe: The Contribution of Applied Linguistics*, ed. Constant Leung and Jennifer Jenkins (London: Equinox, 2006), 72.

20. European Commission, "European Higher Education in the World" (communication from the Commission to the European Parliament, the Council, the European Economic and Social Committee and the Committee of the Regions, UK, July 11, 2013), 3, http://www.viaa.gov.lv/files/news/19791/erasmus_in_the_world_layouted.pdf.

21. Ibid., 10.

22. Ellen Hazelkorn, *Rankings and the Reshaping of Higher Education*, 2nd ed. (New York: Palgrave Macmillan, 2015), 94.

23. "World University Rankings 2021," *Times Higher Education*, September 2, 2020, https://www.timeshighereducation.com/world-university-rankings/2021/world-ranking#!/page/0/length/200/.

24. "QS World University Rankings 2021," Quacquarelli Symonds (QS), June 9, 2020, https://www.topuniversities.com/university-rankings/world-university-rankings/2021.

25. Ben McPartland, "'Lack of English Holding Back French Universities," *Local (France)*, October 2, 2014, https://www.thelocal.fr/20141002/language-holding-back-french-universities.

26. *Academic Ranking of World Universities 2020*, http://www.shanghairanking.com/ARWU2020.html.

27. Anna Kristina Hultgren, "The Drive towards EMI in Non-English-Dominant European HE: The Role of University Rankings," *Language Teaching* 52, no. 2 (2017): 233–36.
28. "Overall Outcomes of University Rankings Are 'Junk,'" *University World News*, October 13, 2017, https://www.universityworldnews.com/post.php?story=20171012083403751.
29. Andrée Sursock, *Trends 2015: Learning and Teaching in European Universities* (Brussels: European University Association, 2015), 65.
30. OECD, *Education at a Glance 2018: OECD Indicators* (Paris: OECD Publishing, 2018), 223–24, http://dx.doi.org/10.1787/eag-2018-en.
31. Vincent Doumayrou, "The Triumph of English," *Le Monde Diplomatique*, July 13, 2014, https://mondediplo.com/2014/07/13english.
32. Ulrich Ammon, "German as an International Language of the Sciences: Recent Past and Present," in *Globalization and the Future of German*, ed. Andreas Gardt and Bernd Hüppauf (Berlin: Mouton, De Gruyter, 2004), 157–72.
33. Ralph Mocikat, email to author, March 30, 2017.
34. Arbeitskreis Deutsch al Wissenschaftssprache (ADAWIS), "Bologna-Prozess Und Deutsch Als Wussenschaftssprache" ["Bologna Process and German as Science Language"] (open letter to all federal ministries dealing with higher education and/or science), February 2010, http://adawis.de/fileadmin/user_upload/Seiten/Archiv/Andere_Ereignisse/Brief_Minister_Bologna_2010.pdf.
35. ADAWIS, "Guidelines," http://adawis.de/fileadmin/user_upload/Leitlinien/Leitlinien_2015_englisch.pdf.
36. Rainer Enrique Hamel, "The Dominance of English in the International Scientific Periodical Literature and the Future of Language Use in Science," in "Linguistic Inequality in Scientific Communication Today," ed. Augusto Carli and Ulrich Ammon, special issue, *AILA Review* 20 (2007): 53–57.
37. "Manifesto en defensa del multilingüismo científico" [Manifesto in defense of scientific multilingualism] (April 2016), https://www.change.org/p/uni%C3%B3n-europea-manifiesto-en-defensa-del-multiling%C3%BCismo-cient%C3%ADfico.
38. Peter A. Kraus, "In Defense of a Multilingual Political Science," *European Political Science* 17 (2018), 343–46.
39. Anna Kristina Hultgren, "The Englishization of Nordic Universities," *European Journal of Language Policy* 10, no. 1 (2018): 79–80.
40. Abram de Swaan, "English in the Social Sciences," in *Critical Topics in Science and* Scholarship, ALLEA Biennial Yearbook 2004, ed. P. J. D. Drenth and J. J. F. Schroots (Amsterdam: KNAW/ALLEA, 2005), 137.
41. European Commission, "The Erasmus Impact Study: Effects of Mobility on the Skills and Employability of Students and the Internationalisation of Higher Education Institutions" (study, Luxembourg City, September 2014), 14, https://ec.europa.eu/programmes/erasmus-plus/resources/documents/erasmus-impact-study_en.
42. "The English Empire," *Economist*, February 15, 2014, https://www.economist.com/business/2014/02/15/the-english-empire.
43. Francis Hult, email to author, February 21, 2021.
44. Educational Testing Service, "Test and Score Data Summary for TOEFL iBT Tests and TOEFL PBT Test: January—December 2019" (data summary, Princeton, NJ, 2020), 22–23, https://www.ets.org/s/toefl/pdf/94227_unlweb.pdf.
45. EF Education First, "English Proficiency Index 2020" (Ranking Report of 100 Countries and Regions by English Skills, Signum International AG, 2020), 6, https://www.ef.com/__/~/media/centralefcom/epi/downloads/full-reports/v10/ef-epi-2020-english.pdf.
46. Mario Saraceni, *World Englishes: A Critical Analysis* (New York: Bloomsbury, 2015), 50–53.
47. Francis Hult, "English as a Transcultural Language in Swedish Policy and Practice," *TESOL Quarterly* 46, no. 2 (June 2012): 238.
48. Suresh Canagarajah, "Lingua Franca English, Multilingual Communities, and Language Acquisition," *Modern Language Journal* 91 (2007): 925.
49. Jennifer Jenkins, *English as a Lingua Franca in the International University* (London: Routledge, 2014), 124; Barbara Seidlhofer, *Understanding English as a Lingua Franca* (Oxford: Oxford University Press, 2011), 81.

50. Ernesto Macaro, *English Medium Instruction* (Oxford: Oxford University Press, 2018), 131.

51. Robert Philippson, "English as Threat or Opportunity in European Higher Education," in *English-Medium Instruction in European Higher Education*, ed. Slobodanka Dimova, Anna Kristina Hultgren, and Christian Jensen (Boston: Walter de Gruyter, 2015), 32–33.

52. Macaro, *English Medium Instruction*, 152.

53. Cyril Brosch and Sabine Fiedler, "How Can We Help Exchange Students Learn the Languages of Their Host Countries?," in *The MIME Vademecum: Mobility and Inclusion in Multilingual Europe*, ed. François Grin (June 2018), 130, https://www.mime-project.org/vademecum.

54. Scott L. Montgomery, *Does Science Need a Global Language?* (Chicago: University of Chicago Press, 2013), 74.

55. Ibid., 11.

56. Raoul Kamadjeu, "English: The Lingua Franca of Scientific Research," *Lancet Global Health* 7, no. 9 (September 2019): e1174.

57. Linus Salö, *The Sociolinguistics of Academic Publishing* (New York: Palgrave Macmillan, 2017), 23–24.

58. David Sapsted, "Dominance of English Resulting in 'Lost Scientific Knowledge,'" *Relocate Magazine*, February 2, 2016, https://www.relocatemagazine.com/news/david-sapsted-feb-2016-01-09-8519--dominance-of-english-resulting-in-lost-scientific-knowledge.

59. Montgomery, *Does Science Need a Global Language?*, 82.

60. Ulrich Ammon, "English as a Future Language at German Universities? A Question of Difficult Consequences, Posed by the Decline of German As a Language of Science," in *The Dominance of English as a Language of Science: Effects on Other Languages*, ed. Ulrich Ammon (Berlin: Mouton de Gruyter, 2001), 353.

61. Angel Calderon, "ARWU University Ranking Expands, Delivers Further Volatility," *University World News*, August 24, 2019, https://www.universityworldnews.com/post.php?story=20190823090723586.

62. Pat Strauss, "'It's Not the Way We Use English'—Can We Resist the Native Speaker Stranglehold on Academic Publications?" *Publications* 5, no. 27 (2017): 3.

63. Ismaeil Fazek and Joel Heng Hartse, "Reconsidering 'Predatory' Open Access Journals in an Age of Globalised English-Language Academic Publishing," in *Global Academic Publishing: Policies, Perspectives and Pedagogies*, ed. Mary Jane Curry and Theresa Lillis (Bristol, UK: Multilingual Matters, 2018), 202–3.

64. Adam Huttner-Koros, "The Hidden Bias of Science's Universal Language," *Atlantic*, August 21, 2015, https://www.theatlantic.com/science/archive/2015/08/english-universal-language-science-research/400919.

65. Manuel Célio Conceição, Elisa Caruso, and Neuza Costa, "What Is the Role for English in Multilingual and Multicultural Learning Spaces?" in Grin, *Mobility and Inclusion in Multilingual Europe*, 140, https://www.mime-project.org/vademecum.

66. Tatsuya Amano, Juan P. González-Varo, and William J. Sutherland, "Languages Are Still a Major Barrier to Global Science," *PLOS Biology* 14, no. 12 (December 29, 2016), https://journals.plos.org/plosbiology/article?id=10.1371/journal.pbio.2000933.

67. Yves Montenay and Damien Soupart, *La Langue Française* [The French Language] (Paris: Les Belles Lettres, 2105), 80.

68. Carmen Pérez-Llantada, Ramón Plo, and Gibson R. Ferguson, "'You Don't Say What You Know, Only What You Can': The Perceptions and Practices of Senior Spanish Academics Regarding Research Dissemination in English," *English for Specific Purposes* 30, no. 1 (2011): 28.

69. Eurostat, *Gross Domestic Expenditure on Research and Development, 2008–2018*, https://ec.europa.eu/eurostat/statistics-explained/index.php/R_%26_D_expenditure.

70. Juliane House and Magdalène Lévy-Tödter, "Linguistic Competence and Professional Identity in English Medium Instruction," in *Multilingualism at Work: From Policies to Practices in Public, Medical and Business Settings*, ed. Bernd Meyer and Birgit Apfelbaum (Amsterdam: John Benjamins, 2013), 13–45; Christian Jensen, Louise Denver, Inger M. Mees, and Charlotte Werther, "Students' Attitudes to Lecturers' English in English-Medium Higher Education in Denmark," *Nordic Journal of English Studies* 13, no. 1 (2013): 87–112.

71. Rosemary Salomone, "The End of French?" *Inside Higher Education*, June 7, 2013, https://www.insidehighered.com/views/2013/06/07/essay-debate-france-over-use-english-universities; Rosemary Salomone, "The Rise of English in Academe: A Cautionary Tale," *University World News*, July 20, 2013, https://www.universityworldnews.com/post.php?story=20130718115309353.

72. Queenie K. M. Lam and Friedhelm Maiworm, "English in the Classroom and Beyond," in Wächter and Maiworm, *English-Taught Programmes*, 103, https://www.lemmens.de/dateien/medien/buecher-ebooks/aca/2014_english_taught.pdf.

73. Annette Bradford, "Challenges for Adopting English-Taught Degree Programs," *International Higher Education* 69 (Fall 2012): 8–10; Robert Wilkinson, "English-Medium Instruction at a Dutch University: Challenges and Pitfalls," in *English-Medium Instruction at Universities: Global Challenges*, ed. Aintzane Doiz, David Lasagabaster, and Juan Manuel Sierra (Bristol, UK: Multilingual Matters, 2013), 20.

74. Ernesto Macaro, Samantha Curl, Jack Pun, Jiangshan, and Julie Dearden, "A Systematic Review of English Medium Instruction in Higher Education," *Language Teaching* 51, no. 1 (2018): 54.

75. Francis M. Hult and Marie Källkvist, "Global Flows in Local Language Planning: Articulating Parallel Language use in Swedish University Policies," *Current Issues in Language Planning* 17, no. 1 (2016): 56.

76. Nordiska Ministerrådet, "Deklaration om Nordisk Språkpolitik" ["Declaration on Nordic language policy"] (declaration, Copenhagen, November 1, 2006), 93, http://norden.diva-portal.org/smash/get/diva2:700895/FULLTEXT01.pdf.

77. Frans Gregersen et al., "More Parallel, Please! Best Practice of Parallel Language Use at Nordic Universities: 11 Recommendations" (pamphlet, Copenhagen: Nordic Council of Ministers, 2018), 9, https://norden.diva-portal.org/smash/get/diva2:1203291/FULLTEXT01.pdf; Anna Kristina Hultgren, *English in Nordic Universities: Ideologies and Practices*, ed. Frans Gregersen, and Jacob Thogersen (Amsterdam: Johns Benjamins, 2014).

78. Frans Gregersen, email to author, May 16, 2017.

79. Kingsley Bolton and Maria Kuteeva, "English as an Academic Language at a Swedish University: Parallel Language Use and the 'Threat' of English," *Journal of Multilingual and Multicultural Development* 33, no. 5 (2012), 429–47.

80. Swedish Code of Statutes no. 2009:600, https://www.eui.eu/Projects/International ArtHeritageLaw/Documents/NationalLegislation/Sweden/languageact.pdf.

81. Hult and Källkvist, "Global Flows in Local Language Planning," 59.

82. Anna Kristina Hultgren, "English Language Use at the Internationalised Universities of Northern Europe: Is there a Correlation between Englishisation and World Rank?" *Multilingua* 33 (2014), 3–4.

83. Ellie Bothwell, "Policy Shift Forces Danes to Close Degrees and Cut English Teaching," *Times Higher Education*, December 27, 2018, https://www.timeshighereducation.com/cn/news/policy-shift-forces-danes-close-degrees-and-cut-english-teaching.

84. Macaro et al., *English Medium Instruction*, 293.

Chapter 4

1. Loi 94–665 du 4 août 1994 rélative à l'emploi de la langue française [Law 94–665 of August 4, 1994 relating to the use of French language], *Journal Officiel de la République Française (JO)* , August 5, 1994, 11392, https://www.legifrance.gouv.fr/affichTexte.do?cidTexte=LEGITEXT000005616341.

2. European Commission, *European Higher Education in the World* (Brussels: Commission to the European Parliament, the Council, the European Economic and Social Committee, and the Committee of the Regions, 2013), 3, https://eur-lex.europa.eu/LexUriServ/LexUriServ.do?uri=COM:2013:0499:FIN:en:PDF;; European Commission, *Report to the European Commission on Improving the Quality and Learning in Europe's Higher Education Institutions* (Luxembourg City: Publication Office of the European Union, 2013), 50, http://hdl.voced.edu.au/10707/293965; ; Rosemary Salomone, "The End of French?," *Inside*

Higher Education, June 7, 2013, https://www.insidehighered.com/views/2013/06/07/essay-debate-france-over-use-english-universities.

3. Louise Nordstrom, "French Presidential Hopeful Macron Shocks by Speaking English," *France 24*, January 12, 2017, http://www.france24.com/en/20170112-france-presidential-candidate-emmanuel-macron-elections-le-pen-far-right-english; Darko Janjevic, "French Presidential Candidate Macron under Fire for Speaking English," *DM.com*, January 11, 2017, https://www.dw.com/en/french-presidential-candidate-macron-under-fire-for-speaking-english/a-37092723.

4. Maryline Baumard, "Luc Chatel nuance ses propos sur l'"enseignement précoce' de l'anglais" [Luc Chantal qualifies his remarks on English], *Le Monde*, February 2, 2011, https://www.lemonde.fr/societe/article/2011/02/02/luc-chatel-nuance-ses-propos-sur-l-enseignement-precoce-de-l-anglais_1474173_3224.html.

5. Ministère de l'Education, "Les langues vivantes étrangères et régionales" [Modern foreign and regional languages], https://www.education.gouv.fr/les-langues-vivantes-etrangeres-et-regionales-11249; Ingri Bergo, "Explained: The Foreign Languages Children Learn in French Schools," *Local (France)*, January 22, 2020, https://www.thelocal.fr/20200122/explained-what-languages-kids-learn-in-french-schools.

6. Cnesco (Conseil National d'Évaluation du Système Scolaire) and Ifé-ENS de Lyon (Institut français de l'éducation), "La découverte à l'appropriation des langues vivantes étrangères: comment l'école peut-elle mieux accompagner les élèves?" [The discovery of the appropriation of modern foreign languages: How can the school better support students?] (report, Paris, 2019), 2–5, http://www.cnesco.fr/wp-content/uploads/2019/04/190410_Dossier_synthese_Langues_.pdf.

7. Loi 94–665 du 4 août 1994 rélative à l'emploi de la langue française.

8. Ordonnance de Villers-Cotterêts (no. 188 de 1539) (Fr.), https://www.axl.cefan.ulaval.ca/francophonie/Edit_Villers-Cotterets-complt.htm.

9. Marcel Machill, "Background to French Language Policy and Its Impact on the Media," *European Journal of Communication* 12, no. 4 (1997): 484.

10. Eugen Weber, *Peasants and Frenchmen* (Stanford, CA: Stanford University Press, 1976), 308–09.

11. Yves Montenay and Damien Soupart, *La langue française: une arme d'équilibre de la mondialisation* [The French language: A weapon of balance in globalization] (Paris: Les Belles Lettres, 2017), 340–44; Roger Pilhion and Marie-Laure Poletti, ... *Et Le Monde Parlera Français* (Paris: Iggybook, 2017), 340–43.

12. Conseil constitutionnel decision no. 92–554, June 25, 1992, *JO*, June 26, 1992, 8406 (Fr.), https://www.conseil-constitutionnel.fr/les-revisions-constitutionnelles/loi-constitutionnelle-n-92-554-du-25-juin-1992.

13. Leila Sada Wexler, "Official English, Nationalism and Linguistic Terror: A French Lesson," *Washington Law Review* 71, no. 2 (1996): 313–15.

14. "Appel—L'avenir de la language française" [The future of the French language], *Le Monde*, July 11, 1992, http://www.avenir-langue-francaise.fr/articles.php?lng=fr&pg=42; Peter Grigg, "Toubon or Not Toubon: The Influence of the English Language in Contemporary France," *English Studies* 78, no. 4 (1997): 373.

15. Code l'éducation, Art. L.121–3 (Fr.).

16. Charles Bremner, "Gaullists Draft Bill to Outlaw English Patois," *Times* (London), April 14, 1994, 12.

17. Declaration of the Rights of Man and of the Citizen (1789), https://avalon.law.yale.edu/18th_century/rightsof.asp.

18. Conseil constitutionnel decision no. 94–345, July 29, 1994, *JO* 106, 11240 (Fr.), https://www.conseil-constitutionnel.fr/decision/1994/94345DC.htm.

19. Marcel Machill, "Background to French Language Policy and Its Impact on the Media," *European Journal of Communication* 14, no. 4 (1997): 482.

20. Thierry Bréhier, "Un pouvoir qui n'appartiennent qu'à l'usage" [A power that belongs only to use], *Le Monde*, August 1, 1994, 7.

21. "Ability to Speak the National Language Viewed as Very Important across Europe," PEW Research Center, January 31, 2017, https://www.pewresearch.org/global/2017/02/01/language-the-cornerstone-of-national-identity/pg-02-01-17_national-identity-1-00.

22. Benoît Floc'h and Aurélie M'Bida, "L'anglais, talon d'Achille de l'enseignement supérieure" [English, Achilles heel of higher education], Le Monde, April 10, 2013, https://www.lemonde.fr/enseignement-superieur/article/2013/04/10/l-anglais-talon-d-achille-de-l-enseignement-superieur_3157240_1473692.html.

23. Véronique Soulé, "Réforme du supérieur: le projet fade fâche déjà" [Reform of higher education: The bland project is already causing anger], Libération, March 19, 2013, https://www.liberation.fr/societe/2013/03/19/reforme-du-superieur-le-projet-fade-fache-deja_889812.

24. Antoine Compagnon, "Un amour de Mme Fioraso," [A passion of Mrs. Fioraso], Libération, April 3, 2013, https://next.liberation.fr/culture/2013/04/03/un-amour-de-mme-fioraso_893423.

25. OECD, "Who Studies Abroad and Where? Trends in International Education Market Shares," Education at a Glance 2013: OECD Indicators, June 25, 2013, (Chart C4.3), https://www.oecd-ilibrary.org/education/education-at-a-glance-2013_eag-2013-en.

26. Ben McPartland, "Opposition to English at French Unis is 'Hypocrisy,'" Local (France), May 22, 2013, https://www.thelocal.fr/20130827/opponents-of-english-at-unis-are-hypocrites-minister.

27. "Anglais a l'université: Fioraso dénonce une 'formidable hypocrise'" [English at the university: Fioraso denounces a "formidible hypocrisy"], Le Monde, May 21, 2019, https://www.lemonde.fr/societe/article/2013/05/21/anglais-a-l-universite-fioraso-denonce-une-formidable-hypocrisie_3410228_3224.html.

28. Ben McPartland, "Plan for Degree Courses in English Is Deluded," Local (France), April 17, 2013, https://www.thelocal.fr/20130417/university-english-french-werst.

29. François Héran, "No English Please! Survey on the Languages Used for Research and Teaching in France," Population et Sociétés 501, no. 6 (June 2013): 5.

30. Charles Huckabee, "In France, a Bill to Allow More Instruction In English Ignites Passions," Chronicle of Higher Education, May 16, 2013, https://www.chronicle.com/blogs/ticker/in-france-a-bill-to-allow-more-instruction-in-english-ignites-passions.

31. "Déclaration de l'académie français du mars 2013," (declaration, Académie française, March 22, 2013), http://www.academie-francaise.fr/actualites/declaration-de-lacademie-francaise-du-21-mars-2013.

32. "Newsletter N° 49" (newsletter, Observatoire Européen du Plurilinguisme, April–May 2013), https://www.observatoireplurilinguisme.eu/images/Lettre_d_information/Lettre_49/lettre_49_en.pdf.

33. Benoît Floc'h, "Le développement des cours en anglais à l'université déchire le monde academique" [The expansion of courses in English in universities is tearing the academic world apart], Le Monde, May 9, 3013, https://www.lemonde.fr/enseignement-superieur/article/2013/05/09/le-developpement-des-cours-en-anglais-a-l-universite-dechire-le-monde-academique_3174101_1473692.html; "La guerre des langues est relancée" [The war of languages is relaunched], Gaïa Universitas, April 26, 2013, https://rachelgliese.wordpress.com/2013/04/26/la-guerre-des-langues-est-relancee.

34. Claude Hagège, " 'Refusons le sabordage du français, par Claude Hagège" [We refuse the scuttling of French, by Claude Hagège], Le Monde, April 25, 2013, https://www.lemonde.fr/idees/article/2013/04/25/refusons-le-sabordage-du-francais-par-claude-hagege_3166350_3232.html.

35. Claude Truchot, "Un Enseignement en anglais dans les universities françaises?" [Teaching in English in French universities], Mémoire des lutes, May 22, 2013, http://www.medelu.org/Un-enseignement-en-anglais-dans.

36. "Anglais à l'université [English at the university].

37. McPartland, "Plan for Degree Courses in English is Deluded."

38. Jacques Attali, "Enseigner en Français!" [Teach in French!], Jacques Attali (blog), April 22, 2013, http://www.attali.com/geopolitique/enseigner-en-francais.

39. Jacques Attali, *Pour un modèle européen d'enseignement supérieur* [For a European model of higher education], (Paris: Stock, 1998): 24–25.

40. Jean-François Graziani, "De la loi Toubon à la loi Fioraso: Quel cadre legal pour les formations en anglais dans les universities françaises?" [From the Toubon Law to the Fioraso Law: What framework for educating in English in French universities?], *European Journal of Language Policy* 6, no. 2 (2014): 160–61.

41. François-Xavier Grison, "CONTRE la loi ESR 'Fioraso', parce que POUR la langue française!" [AGAINST the ESR Fioraso, because FOR the French language!] (petition, Petitionenligne. com, July 4, 2013), https://www.petitionenligne.com/contre_la_loi_esr_fioraso_parce_ que_pour_la_langue_francaise.

42. "Project de loi Fioraso: un ultra libéral, un projet de précarisation, un projet de destruction de la langue français" [The Fioraso law project: An ultra liberal one, a project of insecurity, a project of destruction for the French language], *Le Grand Soir*, March 21, 2013, https://www.legrandsoir.info/projet-de-loi-fioraso-un-projet-ultra-liberal-un-projet-de-precarisation-un-projet-de-destruction-de-la-langue-francaise.html.

43. "Anglais à l'université [English at the university].

44. Ben McPartland, "Minister Backtracks on English Degree Courses," *Local (France)*, May 3, 2013, https://www.thelocal.fr/20130503/minister-backtracks-on-english-degree-courses-plan.

45. "Facultés: Les cours en anglais sont une chance et une réalité" [Faculties: Courses in English are an opportunity and a reality], *Le Monde*, May 15, 2013, https://www.lemonde.fr/idees/article/2013/05/07/facultes-les-cours-en-anglais-sont-une-chance-et-une-realite_3172657_3232.html?contributions.

46. Clea Caulcutt, "French Can't Block the English Signal," *Times Higher Education*, June 6, 2013, https://www.timeshighereducation.com/news/french-cant-block-the-english-signal/2004317.article.

47. "Sans anglais, point de salut" [Without English, no salvation], *Le Parisien*, May 22, 2013, http://www.leparisien.fr/archives/sans-anglais-22-05-2013-2823527.php.

48. Arnaud Gonzague, "Cours 100% en anglais à la fac: ça fait déjà, my dear" [Courses 100% in English in the universities: It's already done, my dear], *L'Observateur*, April 19, 2013, https://www.nouvelobs.com/education/20130402.OBS6433/cours-100-en-anglais-a-la-fac-ca-se-fait-deja-my-dear.html.

49. Henry Samuel, "*Libération* Newspaper Publishes Whole Front Page in English," *Telegraph*, May 21 2013, https://www.telegraph.co.uk/news/worldnews/europe/france/10071025/Liberation-newspaper-publishes-whole-front-page-in-English.html.

50. Andrew Gallix, "The French Protect Their Language Like the British Protect Their Currency," *Guardian*, May 23, 2013, https://www.theguardian.com/commentisfree/2013/may/23/language-french-identity.

51. Loi 2013–660 du 22 Juillet 2013 relative à l'enseignement supérieur et à la recherche [Law 2013–660 of July 22, 2013, relating to higher education and research], Legifrance, 2014, http://www.legifrance.gouv.fr/affichTexte.do?cidTexte=JORFTEXT000027735009; Code l'éducation, Art. L.121–3 (Fr.).

52. Marianne Blattès, "Policy Development for English-medium Instruction in French Universities" (interview), *European Journal of Language and Policy* 10, no. 1 (2018): 31–32.

53. "Geneviève Fioraso, laureate du Prix exceptionnel 2013 de La Carpetter anglaise" [Geneviève Fioraso, winner of the 2013 English Carpetter outstanding prize], *Mémoire des lutes*, June 3, 2013, http://medelu.org/Genevieve-Fioraso-laureate-du-Prix.

54. Marc Rousset, "Le scandale de la non-application de la loi Fioraso" [The scandal of the non-application of the Fioraso law], *Boulevard Voltaire*, September 17, 2017, https://www.bvoltaire.fr/scandale-de-non-application-de-loi-fioraso.

55. Campus France, "Campus France Offices around the World," https://www.campusfrance.org/en/Campus-France-offices-world.

56. Christian Tremblay and Anne Bui, "La lettre de l'OEP N° 69" (newsletter, Observatoire Européen du Plurilinguisme, March–April 2017), https://www.observatoireplurilinguisme.eu/images/Lettre_d_information/Lettre_69/Lettre_69.pdf.

57. CAA de Paris, N° 16PA02801 (March 21, 2017), https://www.legifrance.gouv.fr/affichJuriAdmin.do?oldAction=rechJuriAdmin&idTexte=CETATEXT000034454610.

58. Campus France, "Programs Taught in English," https://www.usa.campusfrance.org/programs-taught-in-english.

59. Amy Baker, "Campus France Tells International Students, 'We Need You,' " *PIE News*, May 6, 2020, https://thepienews.com/news/campus-france-tells-international-students-we-need-you.

60. "Discours du Premier ministre sur la 'Stratégie du Gouvernement en matière de commerce extérieur' " [Speech by the prime minister on the "government's foreign trade strategy"], Gouvernement.fr, February 23, 2018, https://www.gouvernement.fr/partage/9996-discours-du-premier-ministre-sur-la-strategie-du-gouvernement-en-matiere-de-commerce-exterieur.

61. Adam Sage, "Stop Using So Much English, Édouard Philippe Warns Macron," *Times* (London), July 12, 2018, https://www.thetimes.co.uk/article/stop-using-so-much-english-edouard-warns-macron-n3c8trdx8.

62. "Une ambition pour la langue française et le plurilinguisme" [An ambitious plan for the French language and plurilingualism] (press release, France Diplomatie, March 20, 2018), https://www.elysee.fr/emmanuel-macron/2019/03/20/une-ambition-pour-la-langue-francaise-et-le-plurilinguisme.

63. Alex Taylor and Chantal Manes-Bonnisseau, "Propositions pour une meilleure maîtrise des languages vivantes étrangères" [Proposals for a better mastery of modern foreign languages], Ministére de l'Éducation National et de la Jeunesse, September 12, 2018, https://cache.media.education.gouv.fr/file/Racine/33/4/propositions_meilleure_maitrise_langues_vivantes_998334.pdf.

64. "More English Must Be Taught in French Primary Schools, Government Says," *Local (France)*, September 11, 2018, https://www.the.fr/20180911/more-english-must-be-taught-in-french-schools-government-says.

65. Education First, *English Proficiency Index 2019* (Ranking Report of 100 Countries and Regions by English Skills, Signum International AG, 2019), 6, https://www.ef.com/__/~/media/centralefcom/epi/downloads/full-reports/v9/ef-epi-2019-english.pdf.

66. Henry Samuel, "France to Encourage Children to Watch Cartoons in English in Drive to Improve Poor Language Skills," *Telegraph*, September 11, 2018, https://www.telegraph.co.uk/news/2018/09/11/france-encourage-children-watch-cartoons-english-drive-improve.

67. Campus France, "A Strategy for Attracting International Students" (press release, Service de Presse de Matignon, 2018), https://www.indonesie.campusfrance.org/system/files/medias/documents/2018-12/Press_Release_Strategy_international_students.pdf.

68. L'Equipe des rédacteurs d'Académie, "Pendant le confinement, les affaires LPPR continuent: la privatisation des diplômes universitaires en marche" [During the lockdown, LPPR business continues: The privatization of university degrees on the move], April 7, 2020, https://academia.hypotheses.org/22196.

69. Collectif, "La recherche francophone en sciences de gestion n'a aucune raison d'accepter une soumission à un ordre anglo-saxon" [Francophone research in science has no reason to accept submitting to an anglo-saxon order], *Le Monde*, February 20, 2019, https://www.lemonde.fr/idees/article/2019/02/20/la-recherche-francophone-en-sciences-de-gestion-n-a-aucune-raison-d-accepter-une-soumission-a-un-ordre-anglo-saxon_5425600_3232.html.

70. "Le management n'est pas une science anglo-saxonne" [Management is not an anglo-saxon science] (petition of Collectif d'enseignants-chercheurs en gestion, Change.org, March 2018), https://www.change.org/p/fnege-le-management-n-est-pas-une-science-anglo-saxonne.

71. Elena Lionnet, "Quelle place pour la langue française dans le monde de la recherché?" [What place for the French language in the world of science?], *TV5Monde*, December 15, 2019, https://information.tv5monde.com/info/quelle-place-pour-la-langue-francaise-dans-le-monde-de-la-recherche-334264.

72. John J. Metzler, "View from Paris: American English, Powered by Free Market Forces, Wins Battle of the Languages," *World Tribune*, August 9, 2019, https://www.worldtribune.com/view-from-paris-american-english-powered-by-free-market-forces-wins-battle-of-the-languages.

73. "JO 2024: le slogan en anglais de la candidature de Paris fait rager les internautes" [Olympics 2024: The slogan in English for the candidacy of Paris angers internet users], *RT France*, February 3, 2017, https://francais.rt.com/france/33482-jo-2024-slogan-anglais-candidature-paris-fait-rager-les-internautes; Gilles Festor, "Teddy Riner défend le

slogan en anglais de Paris 2024" [Teddy Riner defends the English slogan of Paris 2024], *Le Figaro*, April 2, 2017, https://www.lefigaro.fr/le-scan-sport/2017/02/04/27001-20170204ARTFIG00075-teddy-riner-defend-le-slogan-en-anglais-de-paris-2024.php.

74. "Coronavirus, les mots pour le dire" [Coronavirus, the words to say], *Ministère de la Culture*, April 9, 2020, https://www.culture.gouv.fr/Actualites/Coronavirus-les-mots-pour-le-dire.

75. "Franck Riester, notre langue est essentielle à notre pacte républicain et à la cohésion sociale" [Franck Riester, our language is essential to our republican pact and social cohesion], *Le Monde*, February 12, 2019, https://www.lemonde.fr/idees/article/2019/02/12/franck-riester-notre-langue-est-essentielle-a-notre-pacte-republicain-et-a-la-cohesion-sociale_5422536_3232.html.

76. "Défense de la language française: 100 signatures pour refuser la dictature du tout-anglais" [Defense of the French language: 100 signatures to reject the all-English dictatorship], *Le Parisien*, June 16, 2019, http://www.leparisien.fr/societe/defense-de-la-langue-francaise-100-signatures-pour-refuser-la-dictature-du-tout-anglais-16-06-2019-8094285.php.

77. Emily Prescott, "Macron Launches Crackdown on English Language—English is 'Distressing'—Speak French!," *Express*, August 5, 2019, https://www.express.co.uk/news/world/1161952/emmanuel-macron-france-news-english-french-language.

78. Luke Hurst, "'Say Things in French!': Minister Reignites Debate over Language with Twitter Plea," *Euro News*, August 6, 2019, https://www.euronews.com/2019/08/05/say-things-in-french-minister-reignites-debate-over-language-with-twitter-plea.

79. "Communiqué de l'Académie française" (declaration, Académie française, November 21, 2019), http://www.academie-francaise.fr/actualites/communique-de-lacademie-francaise-1.

80. Bernard Spolsky, "A Modified and Enriched Theory of Language Policy and Management," *Language Policy* 18, no. 3 (2019): 324–27.

81. EF Education First, "English Proficiency Index 2020" (Ranking Report of 100 Countries and Regions by English Skills, Signum International AG, 2020), 6, https://www.ef.com/__/~/media/centralefcom/epi/downloads/full-reports/v10/ef-epi-2020-english.pdf.

82. Michel Arseneault, "Internet, nouvelle académie française" [Internet, new académie française], *Le Monde*, January 28, 1996, https://www.lemonde.fr/archives/article/1996/01/28/internet-nouvelle-academie-francaise_3706947_1819218.html.

83. "Language: The Cornerstone of National Identity," *PEW Research Center*, February 1, 2017, https://www.pewresearch.org/global/2017/02/01/language-the-cornerstone-of-national-identity.

84. Sean Coughlan, "Italian University Switches to English," *BBC News*, May 16, 2012, https://www.bbc.com/news/business-17958520.

85. Education First, *English Proficiency Index 2020*, 6.

86. Ibid., 9.

87. Bologna Declaration of June 19, 1999, http://ehea.info/Upload/document/ministerial_declarations/1999_Bologna_Declaration_English_553028.pdf.

88. Francesca Costa and James Coleman, "A Survey of English-Medium Instruction in Italian Higher Education," *International Journal of Bilingual Education and Bilingualism* 16, no. 1 (2003): 10–11.

89. Virginia Pulcini and Sandra Campana, "Internationalisation and the EMI Controversy in Italian Higher Education," in *English-Medium Instruction in European Higher Education*, eds. Slobodanka Dimova, Anna Kristina Hultgren, and Christian Jensen (Boston: de Gruyter Mouton, 2015), 81.

90. Legge 30 dicembre 2010, n. 240, Tit. I, Art. 2 (2) (l), in G.U. 14 gennaio 2011, n. 10 (It.), https://www.unito.it/sites/default/files/legge_240_2010_gelmini.pdf.

91. Lee Adendorff, "English-Only Postgraduate Courses at Milan Polytechnic Spark Protest," *University World News*, May 13, 2012, https://www.universityworldnews.com/post.php?story=20120509174302914.

92. D. D. Guttenplan, "Old Italian School to Switch Instruction to English," *New York Times*, June 11, 2012, https://www.nytimes.com/2012/06/11/world/europe/11iht-educside11.html.

93. Alessandra Molino and Sandra Campagna, "English-Mediated Instruction in Italian Universities: Conflicting Views," *Sociolinguistica: Internationales Jahrbuch für europäische Soziolinguistik* 28, no. 1 (2014): 162–63.

94. Megan Williams, "Elite Italian University Struggles with Shift to English," *Chronicle of Higher Education*, June 3, 2013, https://www.chronicle.com/article/elite-italian-university-struggles-with-shift-to-english/.

95. Adendorff, "English-Only Postgraduate Courses at Milan Polytechnic Spark Protest."

96. Tullio Gregory, "La retorica dell'inglese per tutti" [The rhetoric of English for everyone], *Corriere della Sera*, March 7, 2012, https://accademiadellacrusca.it/sites/www.accademiadellacrusca.it/files/page/2012/04/19/gregory.pdf.

97. Giovanni Azzone, "Inglese obbligatorio, vantaggio per l'Italia" [Mandatory English, advantage for Italy], *Corriere della Sera*, March 11, 2012, https://accademiadellacrusca.it/sites/www.accademiadellacrusca.it/files/page/2012/04/19/azzone.pdf.

98. Alessandra Mangiarotti, "Se le nostre università si convertono all'inglese" [If our universities convert to English], *Corriere della Sera*, April 13, 2013, https://www.corriere.it/cultura/12_aprile_13/mangiarotti-universita-convertono-inglese_4d019c2a-856e-11e1-8bd9-25a08dbe0046.shtml.

99. Adendorff, "English-Only Postgraduate Courses at Milan Polytechnic Spark Protest."

100. "Assemblea Studentesca: Lauree magistrali in inglese al Politecnico di Milano" [Student Assembly, master's in English at the Politecnico of Milano], May 21, 2012, La Terna Sinistrorsa, video, http://youtube.com/watch?v=C1CTPVIYc60.

101. Molino and Campagna, "English-Mediated Instruction in Italian Universities," 164.

102. Sean Coughlan, "Italian University Switches to English," *BBC News*, May 16, 2012, https://www.bbc.com/news/business-17958520.

103. Dianne R. Hales, *La Bella Lingua* (New York: Broadway, 2009), 113–21.

104. Nicoletta Maraschio and Domenico De Martino, *Fuori l'italiano dall'università* [Italian outside the university] (Lecce: Editori Laterza, 2013).

105. Ibid, v–xiv, viii.

106. Guttenplan, "Old Italian School to Switch Instruction to English."

107. Rosemary Salomone, "The Rise of English in Academe: A Cautionary Tale," *University World News*, July 20, 2013, https://www.universityworldnews.com/post.php?story=20130718115309353.

108. Art. 6 Costituzione (It.).

109. Regio Decreto 31 agosto 1933, n. 1592, in G.U. 7 dicembre 1933, n. 283 (It.), https://www.gazzettaufficiale.it/eli/gu/1933/12/07/283/so/283/sg/pdf.

110. L. n. 240, Tit. I, Art. 2 (2) (l)/2010 (It.).

111. Art. 33 Costituzione (It.).

112. Tribunale Amministrativo Regionale (TAR) per la Lombardia, Sezione Terza, 23 maggio 2013, no. 01348/2013 Reg. Prov. Coll. N.01998/2012 Reg. Ric, https://ilsensodellamisura.files.wordpress.com/2013/12/tar-lombardia1.pdf.

113. Federica Cavadini, "No all'inglese come lingua esclusiva: Il TAR ferma il Politecnico" [No to English as an exclusive language: The TAR stops the Politecnico], *Corriere della Sera*, May 24, 2013, https://milano.corriere.it/milano/notizie/cronaca/13_maggio_24/no-all-inglese-come-lingua-esclusiva-il-tar-ferma-il-politecnico-di-milano-federica-cavadini-2221294413971.shtml.

114. Manuela Di Paola, "Politecnico di Milano, il ministro Carrozza favorevole all'inglese. Senato accademico convocato il 3 Giugno" [Politecnico of Milano, Minister Carrozza in favor of English. Academic senate convened on June 3rd], statement of Maria Chiara Carrozza, Minister of Instruction, Universities, and Research, *Universita.it*, May 28, 2013, https://www.universita.it/politecnico-milano-ministro-carrozza-corsi-inglese.

115. Luca De Vito, "Il ministro sta con il rettore: 'Politecnico, sì all'inglese'" [The minister is with the rector: "Politecnico, yes to English"], *La Repubblica Milano*, May 25, 2013, http://milano.repubblica.it/cronaca/2013/05/25/news/il_ministro_sta_con_il_rettore_politecnico_s_all_inglese-59594044.

116. Consiglio di Stato, 11 aprile 2014, n. 01779, 2014 Reg. Prov. Coll. n. 05151/2013 Reg. Ric., https://www.giustizia-amministrativa.it/portale/pages/istituzionale/visualizza/?nodeRef=&schema=cds&nrg=201305151&nomeFile=201401779_18.html&subDir=Provvedimenti.

117. Consiglio di Stato, 22 gennaio 2015, n. 00242/2015 Reg. Prov. Coll. n. 05151/2013 Reg. Ric., https://www.giustizia-amministrativa.it/portale/pages/istituzionale/visualizza/?nod eRef=&schema=cds&nrg=201305151&nomeFile=201500242_18.html&subDir=Provve dimenti.

118. Beppe Severgnini, "Italy's New Lingua Franca," *New York Times*, February 26, 2015, https://www.nytimes.com/2015/02/27/opinion/italys-new-lingua-franca.html.

119. Art. 34, Costituzione (It.).

120. Corte Cost., 21 febbraio 2017, n. 42/2017, Racc. uff. corte cost., https://www.cortecostituzionale.it/actionSchedaPronuncia.do?anno=2017&numero=42 (It.).

121. Rosemary Salomone, "Linguistic Battle Sparks Revolt Against Globalisation," *University World News*, March 10, 2017, https://www.universityworldnews.com/post.php?story=20170307132621476.

122. "'L'italiano siamo noi': lettera aperta a Mattarella e Gentiloni sui corsi in lingua inglese" [We are Italian: An open letter to Mattarella and Gentiloni on courses in the English language], *ROARS*, March 12, 2017, https://www.roars.it/online/litaliano-siamo-noi-lettera-aperta-a-mattarella-e-gentiloni-sui-corsi-in-lingua-inglese/.

123. Cons. Stato, sez. sesta, 1 febbraio 2018, n. 00617/2018, Reg. Prov. Coll. (It.), https://www.giustizia-amministrativa.it/portale/pages/istituzionale/visualizza/?nodeRef=&schema=cds&nrg=201305151&nomeFile=201800617_11.html&subDir=Provvedimenti.

124. Chiara Baldi, "Rettore del Politecnico dopo sentenza Consiglio de Stato: 'A rischio l'internazionale'" [Rector of the Politecnico after the Council of State ruling: "International at risk"], *La Stampa*, February 1, 2018, https://www.lastampa.it/milano/2018/02/01/news/rettore-del-politecnico-dopo-sentenza-consiglio-di-stato-a-rischio-l-internazionalizzazione-1.33974750.

125. Federica Cavadini, "Milano, stop alla linea internazionale del Politecnico: «L'inglese non può sostuire l'italiano»" [Milan, stop to the Politecnico's international direction: English cannot replace Italian], *Corriere della Sera*, January 31, 2018, https://milano.corriere.it/notizie/cronaca/18_gennaio_31/milano-stop-linea-internazionale-politecnico-l-inglese-non-puo-mai-sostituire-l-italiano-19baf2b0-064d-11e8-8b64-d2626c604009.shtml.

126. Federica Cavadini, "Milano, il ministro Fedeli: «Alt al Politecnico in inglese, la sentenza cambia i piani»" [Milan, Minister Fedeli: "Stop to the Politecnico in English, the ruling changes plans"], *Corriere della Sera*, February 2, 2018, https://milano.corriere.it/notizie/cronaca/18_febbraio_02/milano-ministro-fedeli-alt-politecnico-inglese-sentenza-39b07586-07e2-11e8-bfab-d44c18e4815f.shtml.

127. Valentina Romei, "Youth Unemployment in Italy Rises to Second Highest in Eurozone," *Financial Times*, March 1, 2019, https://www.ft.com/content/49ebe172-3c0e-11e9-b72b-2c7f526ca5d0.

128. Roger Abravanel, "Vietare l'insegnamento in inglese e contro l'interesse degli studenti" [Banning teaching in English is against the interests of students], *Corriere della Sera*, February 27, 2018, http://meritocrazia.corriere.it/2018/02/27/vietare-linsegnamento-in-inglese-e-contro-linteresse-degli-studenti.

129. "Milano, Politecnico: lo stop alle lingue lede il diritto al lavoro" [Milano, Politecnico: The stop to languages affects the right to work], *Corriere della Sera*, April 6, 2018, https://milano.corriere.it/notizie/cronaca/18_aprile_06/milano-politecnico-stop-lingue-lede-diritto-lavoro-6155ee18-395b-11e8-8e49-98826bd21e1a.shtml.

130. Giacomo Valtolina, "Milano e lo stop all'inglese al Politecnico: «Provinciali e sciovinisti: I professori contro l'inglese sono baroni senza futuro»" [Milan and the stop to English at the Politecnico: "Provincial and chauvinist: The professors against English are chiefs without a future"], *Corriere della Sera*, April 6, 2018, https://milano.corriere.it/notizie/cronaca/18_aprile_06/milano-provinciali-sciovinisti-professori-contro-l-inglese-sono-baroni-senza-futuro-fc13289c-38fe-11e8-88e7-5b815ecb2975.shtml.

131. Maria Gabriella Mulas, "Politecnico, l'inglese e i «barons», L'Intervento" [Politecnico, English, and "chiefs," the intervention], letter to the editor, *Corriere della Sera*, April 24, 2018, 13 (on file with author).

132. "Politecnico: vinci il ricorsi? A raddrizzarti la schiena ci pensa l'Advisory Board (e il Corriere)" [Will the Politecnico win the appeals? The advisory board (and the Corriere)

will make sure backs are kept straight], *ROARS*, May 6, 2018, https://www.roars.it/online/politecnico-vinci-il-ricorso-a-raddrizzarti-la-schiena-ci-pensa-ladvisory-board-e-il-corriere/.

133. Gaetano Manfredi, "Nota di 9 luglio 2018 a Maria Letizia Melina" (on file with author).

134. Maria Letizia Melina, "Offerta formativa in lingua inglese: Riscontro nota prot. 1630 del 9 luglio 2018" [Training offered in the English language: Response], https://www2.crui.it/crui/laboratorio_didattica/internazionalizzazione_offerta_formativa/4Corsi_erogati_in_lingua_inglese/2Note_MIUR/2Nota_MIUR_11_07_2018/NotaMIUR_11_07_2018.pdf.

135. Cons. Stato, sez. sesta, 11 novembre 2019, n. 07694.2019, Reg. Prov. Coll. (It.), https://www.giustizia-amministrativa.it/portale/pages/istituzionale/visualizza/?nodeRef=&schema=cds&nrg=201901886&nomeFile=201907694_11.html&subDir=Provvedimenti.

136. Politecnico di Milano website, https://www.polimi.it/en/the-politecnico/about-polimi/politecnico-di-milano-figures.

137. YouGov and Wall Street English, *Global English Language Report*, 2019, 21, https://cdn2.hubspot.net/hubfs/1982228/reports/Global%20English%20Language%20Report%202018.pdf.

138. National Agency for the Evaluation of Universities and Research Institutes, *Rapporto Biennale sullo Stato del Sistema Universitario e della Ricerca 2018*, (2018), http://www.anvur.it/download/rapporto-2018/ANVUR_Rapporto_Biennale_2018_Introduzione.pdf.

139. Confederazione deli Rettori della Università Italiano (CRUI), *L'Internazionalizzazione della Formazione Superiore in Italia. Le Università* [The internationalization of higher education in Italy. The universities] (December 2019), 33, https://www.crui.it/images/crui-rapporto-inter-digitale.pdf.

140. *TOELF iTB: Test Score and Data Summary 2019* (ETS, 2020), 19-20, https://www.ets.org/s/toefl/pdf/94227_unlweb.pdf.

141. Gisela Langé, video interview with author, June 8, 2015.

142. Letizia Cinganotto, "CLIL in Italy: A General Overview," *Latin American Journal of Content and Language Integrated Learning 9*, no. 2 (2016): 373–400.

143. Alessandro Carlucci, "Language, Education and European Unification: Perceptions and Reality of Global English in Europe," in *Antonio Gramsci: A Pedagogy to Change the World*, ed. Nicola Pizzolato and John D. Holst (Cham, Switzerland: Springer, 2017), 137.

Chapter 5

1. "Ability to Speak the National Language Viewed as Very Important Across Europe," PEW Research Center, January 31, 2017, https://www.pewresearch.org/global/2017/02/01/language-the-cornerstone-of-national-identity/pg-02-01-17_national-identity-1-00.

2. "English Is No Longer a Foreign Language in NL, But It Has a Unique Character Here," *DutchNews.nl*, January 17, 2018, https://www.dutchnews.nl/features/2018/01/english-is-no-longer-a-foreign-language-in-the-netherlands-but-it-has-a-unique-character-here.

3. Alison Edwards, *English in the Netherlands: Functions, Forms and Attitudes* (Amsterdam: John Benjamins, 2016), 36–52.

4. Jan Willem de Groot, "The Netherlands Commercial Court," accessed April 6, 2020, https://netherlands-commercial-court.com.

5. Tax Justice Network, *Corporate Tax Haven Index—2019 Results*, https://corporatetaxhavenindex.org/introduction/cthi-2019-results.

6. "Annual Survey Finds Continued Growth in International Schools," *ICEF Monitor*, September 5, 2018, http://monitor.icef.com/2018/09/annual-survey-finds-continued-growth-in-international-schools; "Total Population by Country 2018," World Population Review, http://worldpopulationreview.com/countries.

7. Eurostat, *Foreign Language Learning Statistics* (data extracted in September 2020), https://ec.europa.eu/eurostat/statistics-explained/index.php?title=Foreign_language_learning_statistics.

8. Ute Limacher-Riebold, "Bilingual Schools in the Netherlands," *Ute's International Lounge* (blog), http://www.utesinternationallounge.com/bilingual-schools-in-the-netherlands.

9. European Platform, *Bilingual Education in Dutch Schools: A Success Story* (brochure, Haarlem, May 25, 2016), 5–6, https://www.nuffic.nl/en/publications/bilingual-education-dutch-schools-success-story.

10. European Platform, "A Sustainable Advantage: The Findings of a Study into Bilingual Education," June 1, 2010, https://www.nuffic.nl/en/publications/sustainable-advantage-findings-study-bilingual-education.

11. Education First, *English Proficiency Index 2020* (Ranking Report of 100 Countries and Regions by English Skills, Signum International AG, 2020), 6 https://www.ef.com/__/~/media/centralefcom/epi/downloads/full-reports/v10/ef-epi-2020-english.pdf.

12. John Morgan, "Can the Netherlands' Old Masters Brush Off Populist Attacks?," *Times Higher Education*, May 9, 2019, https://www.timeshighereducation.com/features/can-netherlands-old-masters-brush-populist-attacks.

13. "World University Rankings 2021," *Times Higher Education*, https://www.timeshighereducation.com/world-university-rankings/2021/world-ranking.

14. "Statistics," European Research Council, https://erc.europa.eu/projects-figures/statistics.

15. "Tuition Fees," Study in Holland, https://www.studyinholland.nl/finances/tuition-fees; "Tuition Fees Halved for First Year of Higher Education," Government of the Netherlands, https://www.government.nl/topics/secondary-vocational-education-mbo-and-higher-education/plan-to-halve-higher-education-tuition-fees.

16. "Tuition Fees," Study in Holland; Farran Powell and Emma Kerr, "See the Average College Tuition in 2020–2021," *US News*, September 14, 2020, https://www.usnews.com/education/best-colleges/paying-for-college/articles/paying-for-college-infographic; "The Cost of Studying at a University in the UK," *Student*, May 4, 2020, https://www.timeshighereducation.com/student/advice/cost-studying-university-uk.

17. "Netherlands Attracts Record Number of International Students," *SI News*, March 9, 2018, https://www.studyinternational.com/news/netherlands-attracts-record-number-international-students.

18. Claudia Civinini, "The Lure of Work Rights for Int'l Students—Act 1: Policies," *PIE News*, September 14, 2018, https://thepienews.com/analysis/the-lure-of-work-rights-international-students-act-1-policies.

19. *Incoming Student Mobility in Dutch Higher Education—2018–2019* (Amsterdam, Netherlands: Nuffic, 2018), 8–11, https://www.nuffic.nl/en/publications/incoming-degree-student-mobility-dutch-higher-education-2018-2019.

20. Hans de Wit, *Internationalization of Higher Education in the United States of America and Europe* (Westport, CT: Greenwood, 2002), 187–88.

21. "Why One Academic Went Dutch," *Times Higher Education*, November 11, 1994, https://www.timeshighereducation.com/news/why-one-academic-went-dutch/154376.article.

22. Gretha Pama, "Wel of Geen, That's the Question," *NRC Handelsblad*, December 13, 1989, 2.

23. De Wit, *Internationalization of Higher Education*, 186.

24. "Nederlandse wettelijke voertaal aan universiteit" [Dutch legal language at the university], *NRC.nl*, February 14, 1992, https://www.nrc.nl/nieuws/1992/02/14/nederlandse-wettelijke-voertaal-aan-universiteit-7132879-a1036634.

25. Peter Kwikkers, video interview and email to author, September 6, 2018.

26. Wet op het hoger onderwijs en wetenschappelijk onderzoek [Higher education and research act] of June 7, 2017, Stb. 2017, 306 (Neth.), https://wetten.overheid.nl/BWBR0005682/2021-01-01.

27. Peter Kwikkers, testimony at court hearing of BON Appeal, June 2018 (on file with author).

28. Alison Edwards, "Language Policy and the Law: How Dutch Universities Legally Justify English-medium Instruction," *Dutch Journal of Applied Linguistics* 9 (2020), 15.

29. de Wit, *Internationalization of Higher Education*, 197; Ministerie van Onderwijs, Cultuur en Wetenschappen, *Talenten onbeperkt De internationalisering van het hoger onderwijs* [Unlimited talents: Internationalization of higher education] (1998), 17–19.

30. de Wit, *Internationalization of Higher Education*, 189–90.

31. Edwards, "Language Policy and the Law," 3.

32. Ibid., 9.

33. "De universiteit moet het Nederlands niet verkwanselen" [The university should not squander Dutch], *AdValvas*, October 28, 2014, https://www.advalvas.vu.nl/opinie/de-universiteit-moet-het-nederlands-niet-verkwanselen.

34. Hans de Wit, "Teaching in English: A Contentious Debate," *Inside Higher Education*, July 8, 2015, https://www.insidehighered.com/blogs/world-view/teaching-english-contentious-debate.

35. Elle van Baardewijk et al., "Het Groot Manifest der Nederlandse taal" [The great manifesto of the Dutch language] (manifesto, Beter Onderwijs Nederland, June 27, 2015), https://www.beteronderwijsnederland.nl/wp-content/uploads/2015/07/Groot%20Manifest%20de%20Nederlandse%20Taal_NRC_Handelsblad_20150627_2_04_1.pdf.

36. Wammes Bos, "Jasper van Dijk (SP): 'Too Much English in Higher Education,'" *Observant*, December 3, 2015, https://www.observantonline.nl/English/Home/Articles/articleType/ArticleView/articleId/10150/Jasper-van-Dijk-SP-Too-much-English-in-higher-education.

37. Arianne Mantel, "Inhoud colleges onduidelijk door steenkolenengels" [Course content unclear due to poor English], *De Telegraaf*, December 8, 2015, https://www.telegraaf.nl/nieuws/470622/inhoud-colleges-onduidelijk-door-steenkolenengels.

38. Kaya Bouma, "Geklaag over Gebrekkig Engels in Collegezaal neemt toe" [Complaints about poor English in college classes are increasing], *de Volkskrant*, September 27, 2016, https://www.volkskrant.nl/nieuws-achtergrond/geklaag-over-gebrekkig-engels-in-collegezaal-neemt-toe~bf244322.

39. "English Takes Over at Dutch Universities, Just 40% of Courses Still in Dutch," *DutchNews.nl*, August 26, 2016, https://www.dutchnews.nl/news/2016/08/english-takes-over-at-dutch-universities-just-40-of-courses-still-in-dutch/.

40. Raad voor de Nederlands Taal en Letteren, "Nederlands als taal van wetenschap en hoger onderwijs" [Dutch as a language of science and higher education] (brochure, The Hague, the Netherlands, September 2016), http://taalunieversum.org/sites/tuv/files/downloads/NTU16P302%20-%20Rapport%20Nederlands%20als%20taal%20van%20wetenschap%20en%20wetenschappelijk%20onderwijs_4_web.pdf.

41. Karl Dittrich, "Do International Students in the Netherlands Really Need Lectures in Perfect English?" *Times Higher Education*, October 25 2016, https://www.timeshighereducation.com/blog/do-international-students-netherlands-really-need-teaching-perfect-english.

42. Janneke H. Gerards, email to author, May 17, 2017.

43. "Dutch Universities Again Under Fire Over English: Court Case Looms," *DutchNews.nl*, May 26, 2017, https://www.dutchnews.nl/news/2017/05/dutch-universities-again-under-fire-over-english-court-case-looms.

44. Felix Huygen, "Engels als voertaal vernielt het hoger onderwijs" [English as language of instruction destroys higher education], June 28, 2017, https://www.volkskrant.nl/columns-opinie/opinie-engels-als-voertaal-vernielt-het-hoger-onderwijs~b7fd8359.

45. Marc van Oostendorp, "Niet minder maar meer Engels in het onderwijs" [Not less but more English in education], *NRC.nl*, July 5, 2017, https://www.nrc.nl/nieuws/2017/07/05/voer-de-verengelsing-nog-maar-wat-door-11652484-a1565650.

46. "Nederlands en/of Engels? Taalkeuze met beleid in het Nederlands hoger onderwijs" [Dutch and/or English? Language choice with policy in dutch higher education] (Koninklijke Nederlandse Akademie Van Wetenschappen (KNAW), July 11, 2017), https://www.knaw.nl/nl/actueel/publicaties/nederlands-en-of-engels.

47. Hans de Wit, "The Complex Politics of Teaching in English in HE," *University World News*, September 1, 2017, https://www.universityworldnews.com/post.php?story=20170829100757301.

48. "Talen Voor Nederland" [Languages for the Netherlands] (Koninklijke Nederlandse Academie Van Wetenschappen (KNAW), February 3, 2018), https://www.knaw.nl/nl/actueel/publicaties/talen-voor-nederland.

49. "Scheefgroei inkomsten en prestaties universiteiten" [Unbalanced growth of income and universities' performance], Rathenau Instituut, September 1, 2017, https://www.rathenau.nl/nl/kennisecosysteem/scheefgroei-inkomsten-en-prestaties-universiteiten; "Dutch Universities Have More Students But Government Funding Fails to Keep

Pace," *DutchNews.nl*, September 4, 2017, https://www.dutchnews.nl/news/2017/09/dutch-universities-have-more-students-but-government-funding-fails-to-keep-pace.

50. Anna-Malin Sandström and Carmen Neghina, "English-Taught Bachelor's Programs: Internationalising European Higher Education" (report, European Association for International Education and Studyportals, September 2017), https://www.studyportals.com/intelligence/english-taught-bachelor-programmes-in-europe.

51. Ellie Bothwell, "Fifty-Fold Growth in English-Taught Bachelor's Courses in Europe," *Times Higher Education*, September 24, 2017, https://www.timeshighereducation.com/news/fifty-fold-growth-english-taught-bachelors-courses-europe.

52. Annette de Groot, "Nederlands Moet: Over meertaligheid en de verengelsing van het universitaire onderwijs" [Dutch is a must: On multilingualism and the anglicization of university education], (valedictory presentation, University of Amsterdam, September 27, 2017), http://www.annettedegroot.com/content/4-publications/de-groot-2020-translation-of-valedictory-lecture-vertaling-afscheidscollege.pdf; Annette de Groot, email to author, September 2, 2018.

53. Frank Hermans, "Hoogleraar deelt zorg protesterende studenten over onderwijs in Engels" [Professor shares concerns of protesting students about education in English], *De Gelderlander*, October 17, 2017, https://www.gelderlander.nl/nijmegen/hoogleraar-deelt-zorg-protesterende-studenten-over-onderwijs-in-engels~a4897143/.

54. Lara Maassen, "Petitie tegen Engelstalige colleges bij psychologie" [Petition against English language lectures in psychology], *Vox*, October 10, 2017, https://www.voxweb.nl/nieuws/psychologiestudenten-starten-petitie-engelstalige-colleges; "Nederlandstalig Onderwijs" [Dutch education], Dutch Psychology Students, Petities.com, last modified October 13, 2017, https://www.petities24.com/nederlandstalig_onderwijs.

55. Martine Zuidweg, "Psychologiestudenten teleurgesteld: 'Geen stap verder'" [Psychology students disappointed: 'No further progress at all'], *Vox*, October 12, 2016, https://www.voxweb.nl/nieuws/psychologiestudenten-teleurgesteld-geen-stap.

56. "Confidence in the Future: 2017–2121 Coalition Agreement" (coalition agreement, Government of the Netherlands, October 10, 2017), 4, 15–16, https://www.government.nl/documents/publications/2017/10/10/coalition-agreement-confidence-in-the-future.

57. "Wet op taalbeleid écht handhaven: Volgens WHW-kenner Peter Kwikkers houden we ons al jaren niet meer aan Artikel 7.2 van de WHW" [Really enforcing the language policy law: According to WHW expert Peter Kwikkers, we have not adhered to Article 7.2 of the WHW for years], *ScienceGuide*, October 11, 2017, https://www.scienceguide.nl/2017/10/wet-op-taalbeleid-echt-handhaven.

58. "Echt taalbeleid hebben we nooit gehad" [We have never had a real language policy], *ScienceGuide*, October 9, 2017, https://www.scienceguide.nl/2017/10/echt-taalbeleid-hebben-we-nooit-gehad.

59. Interparlementaire Commissie van de Nederlandse Taalunie, *Vastgesteld verslag van de openbare vergadering van de raadsbrede commissie van 12 april 2018* (*Adopted Report of the Public Meeting of the Council-Wide Committee of 12 April 2018*), 4 December 2017, 16 (statement of Ad Verbrugge).

60. Ibid., 25 (statement of Hans Bennis, General Secretary Dutch Language Union).

61. Lotte Jensen, "Studie Nederlandse taal en cultuur kan niet meer op het hoogste niveau beoefend worden" [The study of Dutch language and culture can no longer be practiced at the highest level], *de Volkskrant*, December 15, 2017, https://www.volkskrant.nl/columns-opinie/studie-nederlandse-taal-en-cultuur-kan-niet-meer-op-het-hoogste-niveau-beoefend-worden~bed75608.

62. Bas Belleman, "Waarom geen Vondel in het Engels"? [Why not Vondel in English?], *Delta*, December 19, 2017, https://www.delta.tudelft.nl/article/waarom-geen-vondel-het-engels.

63. Karen I. J. Maex, "The International Paradox: Speech on the Occasion of the 386th Dies Natalis of the University of Amsterdam, January 8, 2018, https://www.dutchnews.nl/wpcms/wp-content/uploads/2018/01/UVA-speech-The-International-Paradox.pdf.

64. "De studie van de Nederlandse taal en cultuur kan niet meer op het hoogste niveau beoefend worden—Opinie" [The study of the Dutch language and culture can no longer be practiced at the highest level—opinion], Reddit thread, December 15, 2017, https://www.reddit.com/

r/thenetherlands/comments/7jy09d/de_studie_van_de_nederlandse_taal_en_cultuur_kan.

65. Hans de Witt, "Shifting Views on International Students and Teaching in English in the Netherlands," *The World View* (blog), Inside Higher Education, January 27, 2018, https://www.insidehighered.com/blogs/world-view/shifting-views-international-students-and-teaching-english-netherlands.

66. Ellie Bothwell, "Amsterdam Head Sparks Debate on Limits of Internationalisation," *Times Higher Education,* February 1, 2018, https://www.timeshighereducation.com/news/amsterdam-head-sparks-debate-limits-internationalisation.

67. "Hoezo verengelsing in het onderwijs? In België doen ze dat heel anders" [Why Anglicization in education? In Belgium they do it very differently], *NOS,* January 27, 2018, https://nos.nl/nieuwsuur/artikel/2214048-hoezo-verengelsing-in-het-onderwijs-in-belgie-doen-ze-dat-heel-anders.html.

68. "Kamer: treuzel niet met aanpak wildgroei Engels in hoger onderwijs" [House of Representatives: Do not linger tackling the proliferation of English in higher education], *NOS,* January 22, 2018, https://nos.nl/artikel/2213218-kamer-treuzel-niet-met-aanpak-wildgroei-engels-in-hoger-onderwijs.html.

69. Eelco Runia, "Waarom ik ontslag neem bij de universiteit" [Why I am resigning from the university], *NRC.nl,* January 19, 2018, https://www.nrc.nl/nieuws/2018/01/19/waarom-ik-ontslag-neem-bij-de-universiteit-a1589052.

70. Arianne Mantel, "Stop Engelse gekte!" [Stop English madness!], *De Telegraaf,* January 26, 2018, https://www.telegraaf.nl/nieuws/1589425/stop-engelse-gekte.

71. "Dutch Student Hopefuls Are Being Disadvantaged by 'English Madness,'" *DutchNews.nl,* January 26, 2018, https://www.dutchnews.nl/news/2018/01/dutch-student-hopefuls-are-being-disadvantaged-by-english-madness.

72. LSVb, "Amount of International Students Reaches Record High," press release, March 12, 2018, https://dutchstudentunion.nl/2018/03/12/amount-of-international-students-reaches-record-high.

73. "Official Language UT from 1 January 2020," August 28, 2019, https://www.utwente.nl/en/news/2019/8/494873/official-language-ut-from-1-january-2020.

74. Rik Visschedijk, "Language Policy: 'No Longer an Issue in Three Years' Time,'" *U-Today,* January 1, 2018, https://www.utoday.nl/news/65160/language-policy-no-longer-an-issue-in-three-years-time; Michaela Nesvarova, "UT Language Policy: What Does It Mean for You?," *U-Today,* March 3, 2018, https://www.utoday.nl/news/65163/ut-language-policy-what-does-it-mean-for-you.

75. Rik Visschedijk, "English is Also the Informal Language at Computer Science," *U-Today,* May 14, 2019, https://www.utoday.nl/news/66955/english-is-also-the-informal-language-at-computer-science.

76. Rik Visschedijk, "'More Support to Learn Dutch,'" *U-Today,* June 11, 2019, https://www.utoday.nl/news/67069/more-support-to-learn-dutch.

77. "Hoger Onderwijs -, Onderzoek- en Wetenschapsbeleid: Verslag van een Algemeen Overleg" [Higher education, research and science policy: Report of a general consultation], Tweede Kamer der Staten-Generaal 31 288, no. 626 (2017–2018), https://www.scienceguide.nl/wp-content/uploads/2018/05/an_een_algemeen_overleg_gehouden_op_3_april_2018_over_Nederlands-Engels_in_het_hoger_onderwijs.pdf.

78. Annette de Groot, "Bijdrage van Annette de Groot aan ons symposium" [Contribution of Annette de Groot to our symposium], Beter Onderwijs Nederland, April 26, 2018, https://www.beteronderwijsnederland.nl/nieuws/2018/04/bijdrage-van-annette-de-groot-aan-ons-symposium.

79. VSNU, *Internationalization Agenda for Higher Education* (The Hague: The Netherlands Association of Universities of Applied Sciences and the Association of Universities in The Netherlands, May 14, 2018), http://www.vsnu.nl/files/documents/Internationalisation%20Agenda%20for%20Higher%20Education.pdf.

80. Kaya Bouma, "Universiteiten voor rechter gedaagd vanwege Engels" [Universities taken to court over English], *de Volkskrant,* May 17, 2018, https://www.volkskrant.nl/nieuws-achtergrond/universiteiten-voor-rechter-gedaagd-vanwege-engels~befca20b.

81. Charlotte Van Ouwerkerk, "Shakespeare in Trouble: Dutch Fret about English on Campus," *Dawn*, June 4, 2018, https://www.dawn.com/news/1411955.

82. Beter Onderwijs Nederland, "Persbericht: BON sleep universiteiten voor rechter" [Press release: BON drags universities to court], May 18, 2018, https://www.beteronderwijsnederland.nl/nieuws/2018/05/persbericht-bon-sleept-universiteiten-voor-rechter.

83. "Verengelsing hoger onderwijs: steun onze rechtszaak" [The Anglicisation of higher education: Support our lawsuit], *Beter Onderwijs Nederland*, May 18, 2018, https://www.beteronderwijsnederland.nl/nieuws/2018/05/rechtszaak.

84. Ministerie van Onderwijs, Cultuur en Wetenschap, *Internationalisering in evenwicht* (*Internationalization in Balance*), no. 1362992 (The Hague: June 4, 2018), https://www.rijksoverheid.nl/regering/bewindspersonen/ingrid-van-engelshoven/documenten/kamerstukken/2018/06/04/kamerbrief-over-internationalisering-mbo-en-ho.

85. Claudia Civinini, "Dutch Minister Tells HEIs to Ensure Accessibility for Country's Own," *PIE News*, June 13, 2018, https://thepienews.com/news/dutch-minister-tells-heis-to-ensure-accessibility-in-letter.

86. Ibid.

87. LSVb, "Studentenbond teleurgesteld in aanmoediging internationalisering onderwijs" [Student union disappointed in encouragement to internationalize education], press release, June 4, 2018, https://lsvb.nl/2018/06/04/studentenbond-teleurgesteld-in-aanmoediging-internationalisering-onderwijs.

88. "Vonnis in kort geding van 6 juli 2018" [Interlocutory judgment of 6 July 2018], C/16/460210/KG ZA 18–278, Rechtbank Midden-Nederland, de Rechtspraak, last modified July 6, 2018, https://uitspraken.rechtspraak.nl/inziendocument?id=ECLI:NL:RBMNE:2018:3117.

89. Peter Kwikkers, email to author, September 6, 2018.

90. Rosemary Salomone, "Dutch Court Defers Decision on English in Universities," *University World News*, July 27, 2018, http://www.universityworldnews.com/article.php?story=20180724140627526.

91. Inspectie van het Onderwijs, Ministerie van Onderwijs, Cultuur en Wetenschap, *Nederlands of niet: gedragscodes en taalbeleid in het hoger onderwijs* [Dutch or not: Conduct codes and language policy in higher education] (Utrecht: Inspectie van het Onderwijs, November 2018), https://www.onderwijsinspectie.nl/documenten/rapporten/2018/12/21/nederlands-of-niet-gedragscodes-en-taalbeleid-in-het-hoger-onderwijs.

92. Janene Pieters, "Amsterdam University Drops Bachelor's Degree in Dutch," *NLTimes.nl*, February 25, 2019, https://nltimes.nl/2019/02/25/amsterdam-university-drops-bachelors-degree-dutch.

93. Annette De Groot, Eric Jurgens, Ad Verbrugge, et al. "Oproep aan de Tweede Kamer van 194 prominenten: volledige tekst" [Appeal to the House of Representatives of 194 prominent figures: full text], Beter Onderwijs Nederland, last modified March 29, 2019, https://www.beteronderwijsnederland.nl/nieuws/2019/03/oproep-tk-nederlands-volledig/.

94. Inspectie van het Onderwijs, Ministerie van Onderwijs, Cultuur en Wetenschap, *Rapport Uitkomst van Themaonderzoek naar Ontwikkeling van Aantal Internationale Studenten en Effecten daarvan voor de Financiele Positie van de Instellingen?* [Report Results from the thematic study on the development in the number of international students and its effects on the financial position of the institutions] (Utrecht,: Inspectie van het Onderwijs, June 2019), https://www.rijksoverheid.nl/documenten/publicaties/2019/06/30/inspectierapport-themaonderzoek-naar-ontwikkeling-van-aantal-internationale-studenten-en-effecten-daarvan-voor-de-financiele-positie-van-de-instellingen.

95. Rijksoverheid, *IBO Internationalisering van het (hoger) onderwijs* [IBO internationalization of (higher) education] (The Hague: Ministerie van Financiën, Inspectie der Rijksfinanciën/Bureau Strategische Analyse, July 2, 2019), https://www.rijksoverheid.nl/documenten/rapporten/2019/07/02/ibo-internationalisering-van-het-hoger-onderwijs.

96. Ministerie van Onderwijs, Cultuur en Wetenschap, *Kamerbrief met kabinetsreactie op het interdepartementaal beleidsonderzoek internationalisering van het (hoger) onderwijs* [Chamber letter with cabinet response to the interdepartmental policy research on the internationalization of (higher) education] (The Hague: Studiefinanciering, September 6, 2019),

https://www.rijksoverheid.nl/documenten/kamerstukken/2019/09/06/kamerbrief-met-kabinetsreactie-op-het-interdepartementaal-beleidsonderzoek-internationalisering-van-het-hoger-onderwijs.

97. Ministerie van Onderwijs, Cultuur en Wetenschap, "More Balanced Internationalisation in Higher Education," press release, *Rijksoverheid*, September 6, 2019, https://www.government.nl/ministries/ministry-of-education-culture-and-science/news/2019/09/06/more-balanced-internationalisation-in-higher-education.

98. Edwards, "Language Policy and the Law," 19–20.

99. Niek Pas, Daniël Rovers, Koen van Gulik, and Lotte Jensen, eds., *Against English: A Plea for Dutch* (Amsterdam: Wereldbibliotheek, 2019).

100. "Kamer behandelt de Wet taal en toegankelijkheid" [House of Representatives discusses the language and accessibility act], Tweede Kamer der Staten Generaal, December 11, 2019, https://www.tweedekamer.nl/kamerstukken/plenaire_verslagen/kamer_in_het_kort/kamer-behandelt-de-wet-taal-en-toegankelijkheid; "Bijdrage Eppo Bruins aan het plenair debat Wet taal en toegankelijkheid" [Eppo Bruins' contribution to the language and accessibility law plenary debate], contribution by Eppo Bruins, ChristenUnie, last modified December 11, 2019, https://www.christenunie.nl/k/n41733/news/view/1282585/963903/bijdrage-eppo-bruins-aan-het-plenair-debat-wet-taal-en-toegankelijkheid.html.

101. "University of Twente Goes English, MPs Question Minister About 'Bizarre' Plan," *DutchNews.nl*, December 16, 2019, https://www.dutchnews.nl/news/2019/12/university-of-twente-goes-english-mps-question-minister-about-bizarre-plan.

102. "The University of Twente Is an International University in The Netherlands Welcoming Everyone," University of Twente, https://www.utwente.nl/en/news/2019/12/181277/the-university-of-twente-is-an-international-university-in-the-netherlands-welcoming-everyone.

103. Lotte Jensen, "Universiteit Twente wil alleen nog Engels horen" [The University of Twente only wants to hear English from now on], *NRC.nl*, January 9, 2020, https://www.nrc.nl/nieuws/2020/01/09/universiteit-wil-alleen-nog-engels-horen-a3986236.

104. Eerste Kamer der Staten-General, Vergaderjaar 2019–2020, 35 282, E, https://www.raadvanstate.nl/@120564/w05-20-0046-vo.

Chapter 6

1. William Safran, "Politics and Language in Contemporary France: Facing Supranational and International Challenges," *International Journal of the Sociology of Language* 137, no. 1 (1999): 62.

2. "The New Scramble for Africa," *Economist*, March 9, 2019, https://www.economist.com/leaders/2019/03/07/the-new-scramble-for-africa.

3. Jean-Benoît Nadeau and Julie Barlow, *The Story of French* (New York: St. Martin's, 2006), 340.

4. Aaron Timms, "Macron Wants a French Empire Built on Language," *Foreign Policy*, December 31, 2020, https://foreignpolicy.com/2020/12/31/macron-wants-a-french-empire-built-on-language.

5. Onésime Reclus, *France, Algérie et colonies* [France, Algeria, and colonies] (Paris: Hachette Livre, 1886).

6. Louis-Jean Calvet, "Les politiques de diffusion des languages en Afrique francophone" [The poltics of language dissemination in French-speaking Africa], *International Journal of the Sociology of Language* 107, no. 1 (1994): 67.

7. Timms, "Macron Wants a French Empire Built on Language."

8. Nadeau and Barlow, *The Story of French*, 350–51.

9. "Message from Ms. Irina Bokova, Director-General of UNESCO, on the Occasion of International Francophonie Day," UNESCO, March 20, 2017, https://unesdoc.unesco.org/ark:/48223/pf0000247554.

10. Nadeau and Barlow, *The Story of French*, 341.

11. Thomas Hale, "The *Manifeste des Quarante-Quatre*, la *Françafrique* and Africa: From the Politics of Culture to the Culture of Politics" [The manifesto of the forty-four, Françafrique and Africa], *International Journal of Francophonie Studies* 12, no. 2–3 (2009): 196.

12. Organisation Internationale de la Francophonie, "La langue française dans le monde 2018: synthèse" [The French language in the world 2018: synthesis] (Paris: Gallimard, 2018), observatoire.francophonie.org/2018/synthèse.pdf.

13. Ibid.

14. "Francophonie: Discours de François Hollande à Kinshasa" [Francophonie: Speech by François Hollande in Kinshasa], Diaspora Katangaise, October 13, 2012, video, https://www.youtube.com/watch?v=INkbxXxLPSc.

15. Catherine Cullen, "Trudeau Promotes Women's, LGBT Rights at la Francophonie Summit of French-Speaking Nations," CBC News, November 26, 2016, http://www.cbc.ca/news/politics/trudeau-la-francophonie-1.3869268/.

16. Yohan Blavignat, "Les dessous de la francophonie en RD Congo, une arme au service de la France" [Beneath the francophonie in the Republic of the Congo, a weapon in the service of France], Le Figaro, November 11, 2016, http://www.lefigaro.fr/international/2016/11/26/01003-20161126ARTFIG00086-les-dessous-de-la-francophonie-en-rd-congo-une-arme-au-service-de-la-france.php.

17. Organisation Internationale de la Francophonie, France Diplomatie, "Repères," https://www.francophonie.org/qui-sommes-nous-5.

18. Organisation Internationale de la Francophonie, "La langue française dans le monde" [The French language in the world], 2019 ed. (Paris: Gallimard, 2019), 275, http://observatoire.francophonie.org/wp-content/uploads/2020/02/Edition-2019-La-langue-francaise-dans-le-monde_VF-2020-.pdf.

19. Blavignat, "Les dessous de la francophonie en RD Congo, une arme au service de la France [Beneath the francophonie in the Republic of the Congo, a weapon in the service of France]."

20. "Key Figures," Campus French (February 2020), 1, 42, https://ressources.campusfrance.org/publications/chiffres_cles/en/chiffres_cles_2020_en.pdf.

21. Ibid., 32.

22. Ibid., 33.

23. Matthew Reisz, "France Eyes Vast Student Market in Africa as It Strengthens Ties," Times Higher Education, November 27, 2016, https://www.timeshighereducation.com/news/france-eyes-vast-student-market-in-africa-as-it-strengthens-ties.

24. Chloe Kerr, "'France Is Back' Macron Vows French Success with a Closer Europe in Davos," Express, January 24, 2018, https://www.express.co.uk/news/world/909441/emanuel-macron-davos-conference-2018-speech-globalisation-forum.

25. Gérard Prunier, The Rwanda Crisis: History of Genocide (New York: Columbia University Press, 1995), 103.

26. "Emmanuel Macron's Speech at the University of Ouagadougou," Élysée, November 28, 2017, https://www.elysee.fr/emmanuel-macron/2017/11/28/emmanuel-macrons-speech-at-the-university-of-ouagadougou.en.

27. Organisation Internationale de la Francophonie, "La langue française dans le monde 2018: synthèse" [The French language in the world: synthesis], 7.

28. Ibid., 11.

29. "France and the Promotion of French Worldwide," Directorate for Communication and Press, Ministère des Affaires Étrangères et Européennes, 2012, http://www.diplomatie.gouv.fr/en/IMG/pdf/FR_promotion_du_francais_version_anglaise_cle4df411.pdf.

30. Michel Guerrin, "Sur la francophonie, des mots à la réalité, il y a un gouffre" [On the francophonie, from words to reality, there is a chasm], Le Monde, January 26, 2018, http://www.lemonde.fr/idees/article/2018/01/26/sur-la-francophonie-des-mots-a-la-realite-il-y-a-un-gouffre_5247526_3232.html.

31. Alain Mabanckou, "Francophonie, langue française: lettre ouverte à Emmanuel Macron" [Francophonie, French language: Open letter to Emmanuel Macron], Bibliobs, January 15, 2018, https://bibliobs.nouvelobs.com/actualites/20180115.OBS0631/francophonie-langue-francaise-lettre-ouverte-a-emmanuel-macron.html.

32. Abdourahman Waberi, "Emmanuel Macron a-t-il vraiment un projet francophone?" [Does Emmanuel Macron really have a francophone project?], Le Monde, January 25, 2018, http://www.lemonde.fr/afrique/article/2018/01/25/emmanuel-macron-a-t-il-vraiment-un-projet-francophone_5247163_3212.html.

33. Achille Mbembe, "Plaidoyer pour une langue-monde" [Advocacy for a world language], *Politis*, February 14, 2018, https://www.politis.fr/articles/2018/02/achille-mbembe-plaidoyer-pour-une-langue-monde-3837.

34. "Pour une 'littérature-monde' en français" [For a "world literature" in French], *Le Monde*, March 15, 2015, https://www.lemonde.fr/livres/article/2007/03/15/des-ecrivains-plaident-pour-un-roman-en-francais-ouvert-sur-le-monde_883572_3260.html.

35. Pierre Astier, "La francophonie est un grand désert éditorial" [Francophonie is a large editorial desert], *Le Monde*, February 14, 2018, http://www.lemonde.fr/idees/article/2018/02/13/la-francophonie-est-un-grand-desert-editorial_5256188_3232.html.

36. Pouria Amirshahi, "Le français en liberté" [French in freedom], *Politis*, February 14, 2018, 21.

37. Yann Gwet, "La vocation de la francophonie est essentiellement géopolitique" [The vocation of the francophonie is essentially geopolitical], *Le Monde*, February 20, 2018, http://www.lemonde.fr/afrique/article/2018/02/20/la-vocation-de-la-francophonie-est-essentiellement-geopolitique_5259749_3212.html.

38. Charles Bremner, "Macron's French Language Drive 'Is Imperialist,'" *Times* (London), March 19, 2018, https://www.thetimes.co.uk/article/macron-s-french-language-drive-is-imperialist-g9dlnmxql.

39. Bertrand Olivier, "Monsieur Mabanckou, vous détournez l'objet de la francophonie pour un combat personnel" [Mr. Mabanckou, you divert the purpose of the francophonie for a personal fight], *Le Monde*, January 30, 2018, http://www.lemonde.fr/afrique/article/2018/01/30/monsieur-mabanckou-vous-detournez-l-objet-de-la-francophonie-pour-un-combat-personnel_5249397_3212.html.

40. "Macron veut soutenir l'essor du français, 'langue monde'" [Macron wants to support the rise of French, 'language of the world'], *L'Obs*, March 20, 2018, https://www.nouvelobs.com/politique/20180320.AFP7892/macron-veut-soutenir-l-essor-du-francais-langue-monde.html.

41. "Journée internationale de la Francophonie: visite de Monsieur Emmanuel Macron, Président de la République (mise en ligne des discours)" [International Day of the Francophonie: Visit of Mr. Emmanuel Macron, president of the Republic (online speeches)], Académie française, March 20, 2018, http://www.academie-francaise.fr/actualites/journee-internationale-de-la-francophonie-visite-de-monsieur-emmanuel-macron-president-de.

42. "Une ambition pour la langue française et le plurilinguisme" [An ambitious plan for the French language and plurilingualism] (dossier de presse, Campus France, March 20, 2018), https://www.campusfrance.org/en/system/files/medias/documents/2018-03/20180322_Langue-francaise-plurilinguisme-et-plan-francophonie-toutes-les-mesures.pdf.

43. "European Business School Rankings 2020," *Financial Times*, December 2020, http://rankings.ft.com/exportranking/european-business-school-rankings-2020/pdf.

44. Emmanuel Macron, "REPLAY—Discours d'Emmanuel Macron lors de la Journée de la francophonie" [Speech by Emmanuel Macron during the Day of the francophonie], *France 24*, March 20, 2018, video, https://www.youtube.com/watch?v=CUuRwXkzJ10.

45. Véronique Tadjo, "Le français ne doit pas faire barrage aux languages nationales des pays dits francophones" [French should not stand in the way of the national languages of so-called francophone countries], *Le Monde*, March 22, 2018, http://www.lemonde.fr/idees/article/2018/03/21/le-francais-ne-doit-plus-faire-barrage-aux-langues-nationales-des-pays-dits-francophones_5274379_3232.html.

46. Gaël Faye, *Small Country: A Novel* (New York: Hogarth, 2018).

47. David Chazan, "English-speaking Macron Campaigns for French to Be a Global language," *Telegraph*, March 20, 2018, https://www.telegraph.co.uk/news/2018/03/20/english-speaking-macron-campaigns-french-global-language.

48. "Where Do All the Foreign Students in France Come From?," *Local* (France), October 9, 2019, https://www.thelocal.fr/20191009/where-do-all-the-foreign-students-in-france-come-from.

49. "Knowing English Will Not Be Enough for Students: French," *Business Standard*, July 19, 2018, https://www.business-standard.com/article/pti-stories/knowing-english-will-not-be-enough-for-students-french-118071900981_1.html.

50. Jagruthi Maddela, "The Embassy of France to Begin the Pre-Departure Sessions in Indian Cities," *Hans India*, July 6, 2018, https://www.thehansindia.com/posts/index/National/2018-07-06/The-Embassy-of-France-to-begin-the-pre-departure-sessions-in-Indian-cities/395711.

51. "'Choose France Tour' Roadshow to Hit Five Cities," *Hindu*, January 31, 2019, https://www.thehindu.com/news/cities/puducherry/choose-france-tour-roadshow-to-hit-five-cities/article26132396.ece.

52. "Multilingualism: Why and How to Promote It?," OIF Francophonie, December 12, 2016, video, https://www.youtube.com/watch?v=c7txbrB9OT8.

53. James Kanter and Michael Wolgelenter, "E.U. Leader Says (in English) That English is Waning," *New York Times*, May 5, 2017, https://www.nytimes.com/2017/05/05/world/europe/jean-claude-juncker-eu-english.html.

54. Ingrid Melander, "Macron Says Too Much English Spoken in Pre-Brexit Brussels," *Reuters*, March 20, 2018, https://www.reuters.com/article/us-france-politics-macron-french/macron-says-too-much-english-spoken-in-pre-brexit-brussels-idUSKBN1GW2JP.

55. Lise Verbeke, "Les francophones souffrent d'un déficit de légitimité par rapport aux Français de l'Hexagone" [Francophones suffer from a lack of legitimacy compared to French people in France], *France Culture*, March 20, 2018, https://www.franceculture.fr/sciences-du-langage/les-francophones-souffrent-dun-deficit-de-legitimite-par-rapport-aux-francais-de-lhexagone.

56. Ludovic Marin, "English-Speaking Macron Campaigns for French to be Global Language," *Telegraph*, March 20, 2018, https://www.telegraph.co.uk/news/2018/03/20/english-speaking-macron-campaigns-french-global-language.

57. Michel Feltin-Palas, "Francophonie: les contradictions de Macron sur la langue française" [Francophonie: The contradictions of Macron on the French language], *L'Express*, March 17, 2018, video, https://www.lexpress.fr/culture/francophonie-les-contradictions-de-macron-sur-la-langue-francaise_1988241.html.

58. Gilles Djéyaramane, "La francophonie, tellement que le simple partage d'une langue" [Francophonie: So much as the simple sharing of a language], *Les Echos*, March 28, 2018, https://www.lesechos.fr/idees-debats/cercle/cercle-180927-la-francophonie-tellement-plus-que-le-simple-partage-dune-langue-2164886.php.

59. "Discours au Sommet de la francophonie à Érevan" [Speech at the francophonie summit in Erevan], *Élysée*, October 12, 2018, https://www.elysee.fr/emmanuel-macron/2018/10/12/discours-au-sommet-de-la-francophonie-a-erevan.

60. Jody Neathery-Castro and Mark O. Rousseau, "Does French Matter? France and Francophonie in the Age of Globalization," *French Review* 78, no. 4 (March 2005): 688–89.

61. Louis-Jean Calvet, *La Guerre des Langues et Les Politiques Linguistiques* [The war of languages and linguistic politics] (Paris: Hachette, 1999), 262–70.

62. Alison R. Holmes and J. Simon Rofe, *Global Diplomacy: Theories, Types, and Models* (Boulder, CO: Westview, 2016), 272.

63. Irene Yuan Sun, Kartik Jayaram, and Omid Kassiri, "Dance of the Lions and Dragons: How Are Africa and China Engaging, and How Will the Partnership Evolve?" (report, McKinsey & Company, June 2017), https://www.mckinsey.com/featured-insights/middle-east-and-africa/the-closest-look-yet-at-chinese-economic-engagement-in-africa#.

64. Joseph S. Nye, Jr., *Soft Power: The Means to Success in World Politics* (New York: PublicAffairs, 2005).

65. Robin Brown, "Alternatives to Soft Power: Influence in French and German External Cultural Action," in *The Routledge Handbook of Soft Power*, ed. Naren Chitty, Li Ji, Gary D. Rawnsley, and Craig Hayden (London: Routledge, 2017), 43–44.

66. "China Is Spending Billions to Make the World Love It," *Economist*, March 23, 2017, https://www.economist.com/news/china/21719508-can-money-buy-sort-thing-china-spending-billions-make-world-love-it; Joseph P. Nye Jr., "Get Smart: Combining Hard and Soft Power," *Foreign Affairs*, July/August 2009, https://www.foreignaffairs.com/articles/2009-07-01/get-smart.

67. "Morocco, France Agree to Strengthen Bilateral Partnership," *Xinhuanet*, November 17, 2017, http://news.xinhuanet.com/english/2017-11/17/c_136758709.htm.

68. "China Will Continue Helping Africa with No Political Strings Attached–Li," *Lusaka Times*, September 29, 2018, https://www.lusakatimes.com/2018/09/29/china-will-continue-helping-africa-with-no-political-strings-attached-li.

69. Arvind Subramanian and Josh Felman, "R.I.P. Chinese Exceptionalism?," *Project Syndicate*, September 6, 2018, https://www.project-syndicate.org/commentary/china-economic-headwinds-by-arvind-subramanian-and-josh-felman-2018-09?utm_source=Project+Syndicate+Newsletter.

70. Yu-Shan Wu, "How Media and Film Can Help China Grow Its Soft Power in Africa," *Conversation*, June 7, 2018, https://theconversation.com/how-media-and-film-can-help-china-grow-its-soft-power-in-africa-97401; Richard King, "The Growing Influence of Chinese Media," *China Daily*, June 23, 2017, http://www.chinadaily.com.cn/a/201706/23/WS5a291255a310fcb6fafd35be.html.

71. Victoria Breeze and Nathan Moore, "China Has Overtaken the US and UK as the Top Destination for Anglophone African Students," *Quartz*, June 30, 2017, https://qz.com/1017926/china-has-overtaken-the-us-and-uk-as-the-top-destination-for-anglophone-african-students.

72. " 'Africa Is the Place to Be,' ADB President Tells Chinese Business Leaders at the China-Africa Forum," *Lusaka Times*, September 6, 2018, https://www.lusakatimes.com/2018/09/06/africa-is-the-place-to-be-adb-president-tells-chinese-business-leaders-at-the-china-africa-forum.

73. "Forum on China-Africa Cooperation Beijing Action Plan (2019–2021)" (report, Ministry of Foreign Affairs of the People's Republic of China, September 5, 2018), https://www.fmprc.gov.cn/mfa_eng/zxxx_662805/t1593683.shtml.

74. Brendan O'Malley, "Chinese Universities Hit New Heights in Global Ranking," *University World News*, September 17, 2017, http://www.universityworldnews.com/article.php?story=20170905140031381.

75. Ministry of Education, the People's Republic of China, *Statistical Report on International Students in China for 2018*, April 17, 2019, http://en.moe.gov.cn/documents/reports/201904/t20190418_378692.html; Wachira Kigotho, "Educational Superhighway from Africa to China Speeds Up Mobility," *University World News*, November 19, 2020, https://www.universityworldnews.com/post.php?story=20201118132655210.

76. Ross Anthony, "Is China the New Lodestar for Africa's Students?" *University World News*, April 7, 2017, http://www.universityworldnews.com/article.php?story=20170403173146423.

77. Howard W. French, *China's Second Continent: How a Million Migrants Are Building a New Empire in Africa* (New York: Vintage, 2015), 1–8.

78. Jeffrey Gil, *Soft Power and the Worldwide Promotion of Chinese Language Learning: The Confucius Institute Project* (Bristol, UK: Multilingual Matters, 2017), 32–33.

79. Moonhawk Kim, Amy H. Liu, Kim-Lee Tuxhorn, David Brown, and David Leblang, "Lingua Mercatoria: Language and Foreign Direct Investment," *International Studies Quarterly* 59, no. 2 (2015): 336–39.

80. "Confucius Institute Annual Development Report 2018" (report, Confucius Institute Headquarters [Hanban], 2018), http://www.hanban.org/report/2018.pdf.

81. Falk Hartig, "China's Institutes Aren't Perfect but Have Much to Offer Africa," *Conversation*, December 2, 2015, https://theconversation.com/chinas-confucius-institutes-arent-perfect-but-have-much-to-offer-africa-51596; Marshall Sahlins, *Confucius Institutes: Academic Malware* (Chicago: Prickly Paradigm, 2015).

82. "On Partnerships with Foreign Governments: The Case of Confucius Institutes" (report prepared by the Association's Committee on Academic Freedom and Tenure, American Association of University Professors, June 2014), https://www.aaup.org/report/confucius-institutes.

83. Rachelle Peterson, *Outsourced to China: Confucius Institutes and Soft Power in American Higher Education* (Washington, DC: National Association of Scholars, June 2017), https://www.nas.org/storage/app/media/images/documents/NAS_outsourcedToChinaMediaPacket.pdf.

84. *Chinese Influence and American Interests: Promoting Constructive Vigilance* (Stanford, CA: Hoover Institution Press, 2018), https://www.hoover.org/sites/default/files/research/docs/00_diamond-schell_fullreport_2ndprinting_web-compressed.pdf.

85. "Resisting Chinese Efforts to Undermine Academic Freedom Worldwide: A Code of Conduct for Colleges, Universities, and Academic Institutions Worldwide," (code of conduct, Human Rights Watch, March 21, 2019), https://www.hrw.org/sites/default/files/supporting_resources/190321_china_academic_freedom_coc_0.pdf.

86. Elizabeth Redden, "The Chinese Student Threat?," *Inside Higher Ed*, February 15, 2018, https://www.insidehighered.com/news/2018/02/15/fbi-director-testifies-chinese-students-and-intelligence-threats.

87. "US Proves to Be Such a Narrow-Minded Country," *Global Times*, February 24, 2018, http://www.globaltimes.cn/content/1090430.shtml.

88. *China's Impact on the U.S. Education System: Hearing before the Permanent Subcommittee of Investigations of the Committee on Homeland Security and Governmental Affairs United States Senate*, 116th Cong. 1 (2019), https://www.govinfo.gov/content/pkg/CHRG-116shrg36158/html/CHRG-116shrg36158.htm.

89. "Agreements Establishing Confucius Institutes at U.S. Universities Are Similar, but Institute Operations Vary" (report to Congressional Requesters, US Government Accountability Office, February 2019), https://www.gao.gov/assets/700/696859.pdf.

90. Anton Crace, "Australia: Belt and Road Disruption Warning," *PIE News*, March 25, 2019, https://thepienews.com/news/australia-belt-and-road-education-disruption-warning.

91. Elizabeth Redden, "Closing Confucius Institutes," *Inside Higher Ed*, January 9, 2019, https://www.insidehighered.com/news/2019/01/09/colleges-move-close-chinese-government-funded-confucius-institutes-amid-increasing.

92. Tara Francis Chan, "Pentagon to End Language Funding for Universities that Host Chinese Party-Funded Confucius Institutes," *Newsweek*, April 30, 2019, https://www.newsweek.com/confucius-institute-pentagon-communist-chinese-1406772.

93. Elizabeth Redden, "Closing a Confucius Institute, at Congressmen's Request," *Inside Higher Ed*, April 9, 2018, https://www.insidehighered.com/news/2018/04/09/texas-am-cuts-ties-confucius-institutes-response-congressmens-concerns.

94. Matthew Pennington, "China Institutes on US Campus: Fount of Learning or Threat?," *News-Herald*, June 6, 2018, https://www.news-herald.com/news/china-institutes-on-us-campus-fount-of-learning-or-threat/article_95255f7b-d1b6-5069-893f-c507be8ea2c4.html.

95. Heather Schmidt, "Reorientalism/Reorientality/Re-Orientality: Confucius Institutes' Engagement with Western Audiences," in *Spotlight on China: Chinese Education in the Globalized World*, ed. Shibao Guo and Yan Guo (Rotterdam, the Netherlands: Sense, 2016), 70.

96. Rodrigue Rwirahira, "High Student Interest Spurs New Advanced Chinese Course," *University World News*, May 4, 2018, http://www.universityworldnews.com/article.php?story=2018050311000291.

97. Jean d'Amour Mbonyinshuti, "Local African Language to Be Taught in Beijing University," *University World News*, November 14, 2019, https://www.universityworldnews.com/post.php?story=201911110758557.

98. Ismail Einashe, "How Mandarin is Conquering Africa via Confucius Institutes and Giving China a Soft-Power Advantage," *South China Morning Post*, May 16, 2018, http://www.scmp.com/lifestyle/article/2146368/how-mandarin-conquering-africa-confucius-institutes-and-giving-china-soft.

99. Wagdy Sawahel, "Arab-Chinese HE Cooperation on the Rise," *University World News*, September 8, 2018, http://www.universityworldnews.com/article.php?story=2018090806594431; "China's Arab Policy Paper" (paper, Ministry of Foreign Affairs of The People's Republic of China, January 13, 2016), https://www.fmprc.gov.cn/mfa_eng/zxxx_662805/t1331683.shtml.

100. "Transcription de la conférence de presse du Président de la République au Grand Palais en Chine" [Transcription of the press conference of the President of the Republic at the Grand Palace in China] (transcription, Ambassade de France à Pekin, January 9, 2018), https://cn.ambafrance.org/Transcription-de-la-conference-de-presse-du-President-de-la.

101. "Interview: Leading French Sinologist Says Language Key to Closer China-France Relation," *Xinhuanet*, March 22, 2019, http://www.xinhuanet.com/english/2019-03/22/c_137916086.htm.

102. "Foreign Secretary Jeremy Hunt: UK Wants to Be Partner of Choice Across Africa" (press release, *GOV.UK*, April 29, 2019), https://www.gov.uk/government/news/foreign-secretary-jeremy-hunt-uk-wants-to-be-partner-of-choice-across-africa.

Chapter 7

1. Nkonko M. Kamwangamalu, *Language Policy and Economics: The Language Question in Africa* (London: Palgrave MacMillan, 2016), 45.
2. Bernard Spolsky, *Educational Linguistics: An Introduction* (Rowley, MA: Newbury House, 1978), 30–31.
3. Ibrahima Diallo, *Geopolitics of French in Francophone Sub-Saharan Africa* (Newcastle upon Tyne, UK: Cambridge Scholars, 2018), 15.
4. Nicholas Ostler, *Empires of the Word: A Language History of the World* (New York: Harper Perennial, 2005), 418.
5. Einar Haugen, "The Language of Imperialism: Unity or Pluralism," in *Language and Inequality*, ed. Nessa Wolfson and Joan Manes (New York: Mouton, 1985), 11.
6. Mohamed Benrabah, *Language Conflict in Algeria: From Colonialism to Post-Independence* (Bristol, UK: Multilingual Matters, 2013), 114–15.
7. Elizabeth S. Buckner, "The Growth of English Language Learning in Morocco: Culture, Class, and Status Competition," in *Global English: Issues of Language, Culture, and Identity in the Arab World*, ed. Ahmad Al-Issa and Laila S. Dahan (New York: Peter Lang, 2011), 242.
8. Ilyes Zouari, "La Tunisie réaffirme son choix du français" [Tunisia reaffirms its choice of French], Association des Professeurs d'Histoire et de Géographie, March 6, 2017, https://www.aphg.fr/La-Tunisie-reaffirme-son-choix-du-francais.
9. Borzou Daragahi, "Revolution Leads Tunisians to Speak Less French," *Financial Times*, January 26, 2012, https://www.ft.com/content/da017290-483c-11e1-a4e5-00144feabdc0.
10. Palash Ghosh, "Sacre Bleu! After More Than 120 Years of French Domination, Gabon Adopts English as Official Language," *International Business Times*, October 12, 2012, http://www.ibtimes.com/sacre-bleu-after-more-120-years-french-domination-gabon-adopts-english-official-language-845629.
11. Diallo, *Geopolitics of French in Francophone Sub-Saharan Africa*, 38–39.
12. RFIPubliée, "Algeria: Towards More English in Universities at the Expense of French—RFI," *Teller Report*, July 24, 2019, https://www.tellerreport.com/news/2019-07-24---algeria--towards-more-english-in-universities-at-the-expense-of-french---rfi-.rJWOHsDrGr.html; "Algeria Seeks to Replace French with English at University, Sparks 'Language War,'" *Your Middle East*, August 3, 2019, https://yourmiddleeast.com/2019/08/03/algeria-seeks-to-replace-french-with-english-at-university-sparks-language-war.
13. "Algeria: 94,000 Say 'Yes' in Survey to English Accreditation at Universities," *Echoroukonline*, August 8, 2019, https://www.echoroukonline.com/algeria-94000-say-yes-in-survey-to-english-accreditation-at-universities.
14. Tayeb Bouzid (@ministre.mesrs.dz), "Following the results of the National Symposium of universities held in 2019: the inauguration of a sector thinking group on the implementation of the effort to promote the use of English in higher education and scientific research," Facebook post, August 20, 2019, https://www.facebook.com/ministre.mesrs.dz/posts/360448381548244.
15. Kamal Louadj, "Vers la fin du français en Algérie? L'anglais à l'Université et à la formation professionnelle" [Toward the end of French in Algeria? English at universities and in professional education], *Sputnik News*, August 21, 2019, https://fr.sputniknews.com/afrique/201908211041961268-vers-la-fin-du-francais-en-algerie-anglais-universite-et-a-la-formation-professionnelle.
16. Hugo Black, dir., *Black Earth Rising*, BBC Two and Netflix (2018).
17. Emmanuel Sibomana, "The Acquisition of English as a Second Language in Rwanda's Linguistic Landscape: Challenges and Promises," *Rwandan Journal of Education* 2, no. 2 (2014): 27.
18. Timothy P. Williams, "Oriented towards Action: The Political Economy of Primary Education in Rwanda," (working paper, Effective States and Inclusive Development

Research Centre, University of Manchester, Manchester, UK, August 2016), 7, http://www.effective-states.org/wp-content/uploads/working_papers/final-pdfs/esid_wp_64_williams.pdf.

19. Gaël Faye, *Small Country: A Novel*, trans. Sarah Ardizzone (New York: Hogarth, 2018), 1.

20. Gérard Prunier, *The Rwanda Crisis: History of a Genocide* (New York: Columbia University Press, 1996), 106–07.

21. Helen Epstein, "The Mass Murder We Don't Talk About," review of *In Praise of Blood: The Crimes of the Rwandan Patriotic Front*, by Judi Rever, *New York Review of Books*, June 7, 2018, https://www.nybooks.com/articles/2018/06/07/rwanda-mass-murder-we-dont-talk-about/.

22. Chigbo Arthur Anyaduba, "Portraying Rwanda's Genocide as an Encounter with Hell," *Conversation*, April 4, 2019, https://theconversation.com/portraying-rwandas-genocide-as-an-encounter-with-hell-114305.

23. Judi Rever, *In Praise of Blood: The Crimes of the Rwandan Patriotic Front* (Toronto: Random House Canada, 2018), 55–56.

24. Alison Des Forges, *Leave None to Tell the Story: Genocide in Rwanda* (New York: Human Rights Watch, March 1999), http://www.hrw.org/reports/1999/rwanda.

25. United Nations, *Convention on the Prevention and Punishment of the Crime of Genocide* (1948), http://www.hrweb.org/legal/genocide.html; Samantha Power, *A Problem from Hell: America in the Age of Genocide* (New York: Basic Books, 2013), 355, 359.

26. Kaj Hasselriis, "French Is Out of Fashion in Rwanda," *Macleans*, April 22, 2010, http://www.macleans.ca/news/world/french-is-out-of-fashion-in-rwanda.

27. *Rwanda: The Preventable Genocide*, International Panel of Eminent Personalities (July 7, 2008), http://www.refworld.org/pdfid/4d1da8752.pdf.

28. Cunningham Levy Muse LLP, *Report and Recommendation to the Government of Rwanda on the Role of French Officials in the Genocide Against the Tutsi*, December 11, 2017, http://www.cunninghamlevy.com/wp-content/uploads/2017/12/Cunningham-Levy-Muse-Report-To-GOR-2017-12-11.pdf.

29. Michele Schweisfurth, "Global and Cross-National Influences on Education in Post-Genocide Rwanda," *Oxford Review of Education* 32, no. 5 (2006): 698.

30. Constitution of the Republic of Rwanda, Title I, Article 5, http://www.cjcr.gov.rw/eng/constitution_eng.doc.

31. Paul Kagame, "Pourquoi la France nous hait" [Why France hates us], interview by François Soudan, *Jeune Afrique/L'intelligent*, February 20–26, 2005, https://www.jeuneafrique.com/86863/politique/pourquoi-la-france-nous-hait/.

32. Richard Wyatt, interview with author, December 3, 2019.

33. Chris McGreal, "Rwanda to Switch from French to English in Schools," *Guardian*, October 13, 2008, https://www.theguardian.com/world/2008/oct/14/rwanda-france.

34. Stephanie McCrummen, "Rwandans Say Adieu to Français," *Washington Post*, October 28, 2008, http://www.washingtonpost.com/wp-dyn/content/article/2008/10/27/AR2008102703165.html.

35. Emmanuel Sibomana, "Unpeeling the Language Policy and Planning Onion in Rwanda," *International Journal of Social Sciences and Humanities* 2, no. 2 (August 2018): 104.

36. Joseph A. Olzacki, "Why Rwanda's Move to English?," *New Times*, November 11, 2015, http://www.newtimes.co.rw/section/read/194295.

37. World Bank, *Doing Business 2010: Reforming through Difficult Times*, 2009, 2, https://www.doingbusiness.org/content/dam/doingBusiness/media/Annual-Reports/English/DB10-FullReport.pdf.

38. Euromonitor International, *The Benefits of the English Language for Individuals and Societies: Quantitative Indicators from Cameroon, Nigeria, Rwanda, Bangladesh and Pakistan*, December 10, 2010, 10, http://www.teachingenglish.org.uk/sites/teacheng/files/Euromonitor%20Report%20A4.pdf.

39. "Rwanda Attracts $3 Billion in Investments after Joining the Commonwealth, Reports KT Press," *PR Newswire*, December 1, 2015, http://www.prnewswire.com/news-releases/rwanda-attracts-3-billion-in-investments-after-joining-the-commonwealth-reports-kt-press-300185397.html.

40. "MasterCard Foundation Launches New Rwf85 Billion-Project to Support Youth, Education," *IGIHE*, March 23, 2018, http://en.igihe.com/news/mastercard-foundation-launches-new-rwf85-billion.html.

41. Kimiko de Freytas-Tamura, "Paul Kagame Appears Set for Victory in Rwanda Vote," *New York Times*, August 4, 2017, https://www.nytimes.com/2017/08/04/world/africa/rwanda-president-election-paul-kagame.html.

42. Amnesty International, *World Report 2018: Rwanda Events of 2017* (2018), https://www.hrw.org/world-report/2018/country-chapters/rwanda.

43. Thomas Kelley, "Maintaining Power by Manipulating Memory in Rwanda," *Fordham International Law Journal* 41, no. 1 (2017): 79–134; "Rwanda's Paul Kagame—Visionary or Tyrant?" *BBC News*, August 3, 2017, http://www.bbc.com/news/10479882.

44. "The Devil in the Details: Has Rwanda Been Fiddling Its Numbers?," *Economist*, August 17, 2019, https://www.economist.com/middle-east-and-africa/2019/08/15/has-rwanda-been-fiddling-its-numbers.

45. Republic of Rwanda Ministry of Education, *Education Sector Strategic Plan 2010–2015* (July 2010), 14, http://planipolis.iiep.unesco.org/en/2010/education-sector-strategic-plan-2010-2015-5152.

46. Beniamin Knutsson and Jonas Lindberg, "The Post-Politics of Aid to Education: Rwanda Ten Years after Hayman," *International Journal of Educational Development* 65 (2019): 148.

47. Ibid., 148.

48. Izabela Steflja, "The High Costs and Consequences of Rwanda's Shift in Language Policy from French to English," *AfricaPortal*, Backgrounder no. 30 (May 2012), https://media.africaportal.org/documents/Backgrounder_No__30_-_The_High_Costs_and_Consequences_of_Rwandas_Shift_in_Lang_QgWzM13.pdf.

49. Chris McGreal, "Why Rwanda Said Adieu to French," *Guardian*, January 16, 2009, https://www.theguardian.com/education/2009/jan/16/rwanda-english-genocide.

50. Beth Lewis Samuelson and Sarah Warshauer Freedman, "Language Policy, Multilingual Education, and Power in Rwanda," *Language Policy* 9 (2010): 195.

51. Emmanuel Sibomana, "Unpeeling the Language Policy and Planning Onion in Rwanda: Layer Roles," *International Journal of Social Sciences and Humanities* 2, no. 2 (August 2018): 107.

52. Magnus Mazimpaka, "Francophone v. Commonwealth: How Rwanda Bagged $3 Billion When It Said 'Au Revoir,'" *KT Press*, November 29, 2015, https://www.ktpress.rw/2015/11/francophonie-vs-commonwealth-how-rwanda-bagged-3-billion-when-it-said-au-revoir/.

53. Daniel Plaut, "Rwanda: Speaking the Language of the World?" *Think Africa Press*, December 11, 2012, https://allafrica.com/stories/201212120112.html.

54. "Rwanda English Action Programme," British Council, https://www.britishcouncil.org/partner/track-record/rwanda-english-action-programme.

55. Institute of Policy Analysis and Research, Rwanda, *Evaluation of Results Based on Aid in Rwandan Education—Year Two* (May 2015), 33, https://www.gov.uk/government/uploads/system/uploads/attachment_data/file/494809/Results-Based-Aid-Rwandan-Education-Year2-2014.pdf.

56. Jenny Clover, "Jury Out on Language-Switch Trend," *Guardian*, November 13, 2012, https://www.theguardian.com/education/2012/nov/13/rwanda-english-language-lessons.

57. Cyprien Tabaro, "Rwandans' Motivation to Learn and Use English as a Medium of Instruction," *International Journal of Humanities and Social Science* 5, no. 2 (February 2015): 78–85.

58. Ibid.

59. Republic of Rwanda Ministry of Education, *Education Sector Strategic Plan 2010–2015* (July 2010), 1, http://planipolis.iiep.unesco.org/en/2010/education-sector-strategic-plan-2010-2015-5152; Kate Spowage, "English and Marx's 'General Intellect': The Construction of an English-Speaking Élite in Rwanda," *Language Sciences* 70 (November 2018): 3.

60. USAID, *Task Order 7: Early Grade Reading and Mathematics in Rwanda: Final Report* (February 2012), 8, http://pdf.usaid.gov/pdf_docs/pdact621.pdf.

61. Pamela Pearson, "Policy without a Plan: English as a Medium of Instruction in Rwanda," *Current Issues in Language Planning* 15, no. 1 (2014): 52–53.

62. Knutsson and Lindberg, "The Post-Politics of Aid to Education," 148.

63. Timothy P. Williams, "The Political Economy of Primary Education: Lessons from Rwanda," *World Development* 96 (August 2017): 559.

64. Rwanda Education Board, "REB to Test and Improve English Language Proficiency of 40,000 Teachers in February 2014" (press release, February 11, 2014), https://www.newtimes.co.rw/section/advertorial/378.

65. Claudien Nzitabakuze, "A Longitudinal Study of the Impact of the English Mentoring Programme on Rwandan Primary and Lower Secondary School Teachers' Fluency in English," in *The Abuja Regional Hornby School: Language Lessons from Africa*, ed. Hamish McIlwraith (London: British Council, 2016), 95–106.

66. British Council, *Endline Assessment of English Language Proficiency of School Teachers in Rwanda* (2015), 13.

67. Diane Mushimiyimana, "School-Based Mentors to Undergo Intensive English Course," *New Times*, August 30, 2018, https://www.newtimes.co.rw/news/school-english-course.

68. World Bank, *Schooling for Learning: Strengthening Resilience of Education in Rwanda* (Rwanda Economic Update, December 2018), iv, https://openknowledge.worldbank.org/bitstream/handle/10986/30978/132832.pdf?sequence=1&isAllowed=y.

69. Timothy P. Williams, Pamela Abbott, and Alfred Mupenzi, "'Education at Our School Is Not Free': The Hidden Costs of Fee-Free Schooling in Rwanda," *Compare: A Journal of Comparative and International Education* 45, no. 6 (2015): 931–52.

70. World Bank, *Schooling for Learning*, iv-v.

71. Andrew Green, Wang Fangqing, Paul Cochrane, Jonathan Dyson, and Carmen Paun, "English Spreads as Teaching Language in Universities Worldwide," *University World News*, July 8, 2012, http://www.universityworldnews.com/article.php?story=20120621131543827.

72. Frank Tanganika, "Proficiency in English by College Graduates is Tenable," *New Times*, October 3, 2018, https://www.newtimes.co.rw/opinions/proficiency-english-college-graduates-tenable.

73. Ferdinand Maniraguha, "Lecturers Failing English Test Could Be Fired from Universities," *Taarifa*, August 27, 2018, https://taarifa.rw/lecturers-failing-english-test-could-be-fired-from-universities/.

74. Educational Testing Service, "Test and Score Data Summary for TOEFL iBT Tests and TOEFL PBT Test: January—December 2019" (data summary, Princeton, NJ, 2020), 21, https://www.ets.org/s/toefl/pdf/94227_unlweb.pdf.

75. Jean d'Amour Mbonyinshuti, "French to English—An 'Imperfect' Transition for Universities," *University World News*, March 12, 2020, https://www.universityworldnews.com/post.php?story=20200311085157484.

76. Pamela Abbott, Roger Sapsford, and John Rwirahira, "Rwanda's Potential to Achieve the Millennium Development Goals for Education," *International Journal of Educational Development*, 40 (2015): 123.

77. Education First, *English Proficiency Index 2020* (Ranking Report of 100 Countries and Regions by English Skills, Signum International AG, 2020), 7, https://www.ef.com/__/~/media/centralefcom/epi/downloads/full-reports/v10/ef-epi-2020-english.pdf.

78. Henry Samuel, "France to Throw Open Archives on Rwanda Genocide to Clarify Its Role 25 Years after the Massacre," *Telegraph*, April 5, 2019, https://www.telegraph.co.uk/news/2019/04/05/france-throw-open-archives-rwanda-genocide-clarify-role-25-years.

79. "Rwanda Reconsiders Role of Snubbed French Language," *France 24*, August 10, 2018, https://www.france24.com/en/20180810-rwanda-reconsiders-role-snubbed-french-language.

80. Vincent Hugeux, "Francophonie: le diktat d'Emmanuel Macron" [Francophonie: The diktat of Emmanuel Maron], *L'Express*, July 12, 2018, https://www.lexpress.fr/actualite/monde/afrique/guerre-sans-merci-pour-la-francophonie_2024881.html.

81. Marc Perelman, "Rwanda's Kagame: Macron Has Brought 'Freshness' to World Politics," *France 24*, October 12, 2018, https://www.france24.com/en/f24-interview/20181012-rwanda-kagame-france-macron-oif.

82. "Choice of Rwandan Minister as Francophonie Chief Makes Waves in Africa," *France 24*, October 12, 2018, https://www.france24.com/en/20181012-rwanda-francophonie-summit-choice-chief-mushikiwabo-makes-waves-africa-jean-armenia.

83. Commission de Recherche sur les Archives Françaises Relatives au Rwanda et au Génocide des Tutsi, *La France, le Rwanda et le genocide des Tutsi (1990–1994)*, Rapport remis au Président de la République le 26 mars 2021 [France, Rwanda, and the genocide of the Tutsi (1990–1994), report submitted to the president of the republic March 26, 2021], 980–89, https://www.vie-publique.fr/sites/default/files/rapport/pdf/279186_0.pdf.

84. Ignatius Ssuuna and Rodney Muhumuza, "Rwanda Recalls Genocide as France Seeks to Reset Relations," *ABC News*, April 7, 2021, https://abcnews.go.com/International/wireStory/rwanda-recalls-genocide-france-seeks-reset-relations-76919545.

85. Edith Wharton, *In Morocco* (Oxford: John Beaufoy, 2015), 108.

86. Fouad Laroui, "A Case of 'Fake Monolingualism': Morocco, Diglossa and the Writer," in *Challenging the Myth of Monolingualism*, ed. Liesbeth Minnaard and Till Dembeck (Amsterdam: Rodopi, 2014), 43.

87. Fouad Bouali, *The Language Debate and the Constitution Amendment in Morocco* (Arab Center for Research & Policy Studies, February 2, 2011), https://www.dohainstitute.org/en/lists/ACRPS-PDFDocumentLibrary/The_Language_Debate_and_the_Constitution_Amendment_in_Morocco.pdf.

88. Kaoutar Ghilani, "'The Legitimate' after the Uprisings: Justice, Equity, and Language Politics in Morocco," *British Journal of Middle Eastern Studies*, 2020, 6, https://doi.org/10.1080/13530194.2020.1863772.

89. Alf Andrew Heggoy and Paul J. Zingg, "French Education in Revolutionary North Africa," *International Journal of Middle East Studies* 7 (1976): 573.

90. Moha Ennaji, *Multilingualism, Cultural Identity, and Education in Morocco* (New York: Springer, 2005), 36–37.

91. Vicente Llorent-Bedmar, "Educational Reforms in Morocco: Evolution and Current Status," *International Education Studies* 7, no. 12 (2014).

92. *Charte d'Agadir relative aux droits linguistiques et culturels* [Agadir charter on linguistic and cultural rights], August 5, 1991, http://www.axl.cefan.ulaval.ca/afrique/maroc-charte_agadir-1991.htm.

93. "Human Development Index," http://hdr.undp.org/en/content/human-development-index-hdi.

94. Ali Alalou, "The Question of Languages and the Medium of Instruction in Morocco," *Current Issues in Language Planning* 19, no. 1 (July 2017): 14, https://www.tandfonline.com/doi/full/10.1080/14664208.2017.1353329.

95. Kamal Salhi, "The Colonial Legacy of French and Subsequent Postcolonial Policy," *European Journal of Language Policy* 5, no. 2 (2013): 205; Ahmed Kabel, "There Is No Such Thing as 'Keeping Out of Politics,'" in *Multilingual Education and Sustainable Diversity Work: From Periphery to Center*, ed. Tove Skutnabb-Kangas and Kathleen Heugh (New York: Routledge, 2012), 220–23.

96. Wally Bordas, "Les grandes écoles françaises à la conquête de l'Afrique" [French grandes écoles in the conquest of Africa], *Le Figaro*, February 26, 2018, http://premium.lefigaro.fr/actualite-france/2018/02/26/01016-20180226ARTFIG00251-l-afrique-nouvel-eldorado-des-grandes-ecoles-francaises.php.

97. Taha Mebtoul, "Minister: 140,000 Students in Morocco Left Private Schools in 2020," *Morocco World News*, November 10, 2020, https://www.moroccoworldnews.com/2020/11/325451/minister-140000-students-in-morocco-left-private-schools-in-2020.

98. Charis Boutieri, *Learning in Morocco: Language Politics and the Abandoned Educational Dream* (Bloomington: University of Indiana Press, 2016), 14.

99. Sylvain Aubry, "The UN Expresses Concern About 'Privatisation' of Education in Morocco," *European Union Education and Development*, April 21, 2015, https://europa.eu/capacity4dev/education-and-development/blog/un-expresses-concern-about-%C2%AB-privatisation-%C2%BB-education-morocco.

100. *Parallel Report Submitted by the Coalition Moracaine pour l'Education Pour Tous, et al. to the United Nations Pre-sessional Working Group of the Committee on Economic, Social and*

Cultural Rights on the Occasion of the Consideration of the List of Issues for Morocco during the Committee's 55th Session (2014), 7–10.

101. Nora Fakim, "English Speaking in Morocco on the Increase," *BBC News*, September 9, 2013, http://www.bbc.com/news/business-24017596.

102. Frantz Fanon, *Peau Noire, Masques Blancs* [Black skin, white masks] (Paris: Éditions du Seuil, 1952), 16.

103. Mohammed Errihani, "English Education Policy and Practice in Morocco," in *English Language Education Policy in the Middle East and North Africa*, ed. Robert Kirkpatrick (Cham, Switzerland: Springer, 2017), 119.

104. Ursula Lindsey, "How Teaching in English Divides the Arab World," *Chronicle of Higher Education*, June 8, 2015, https://www.chronicle.com/article/how-teaching-in-english-divides-the-arab-world/.

105. "Morocco Facing a Major Rebuild of Education Systems," *ICEF Monitor*, October 2, 2014, https://monitor.icef.com/2014/10/morocco-facing-major-rebuild-education-systems/.

106. Larbi Arbaoui, "Benkirane Calls for Adopting English as First Foreign Language in Morocco," *Morocco World News*, February 15, 2015, https://www.moroccoworldnews.com/2015/02/152524/benkirane-calls-adopting-english-first-foreign-language-morocco.

107. Larbi Arbaoui, "Moroccan Think Tank Calls for English to Replace French in Schools," *Morocco World News*, May 28, 2015, https://www.moroccoworldnews.com/2015/05/159494/moroccan-think-tank-calls-for-english-to-replace-french-in-schools.doc.

108. "Morocco and the English Language Debate," *View from Fez* (blog), July 31, 2018, http://riadzany.blogspot.com/2018/07/morocco-and-english-language-debate.html.

109. "85% of Moroccans Want English as First Foreign Language," *Moroccan World News*, March 15, 2015, https://www.moroccoworldnews.com/2015/03/153952/85-moroccans-want-english-first-foreign-language.

110. Abdellatif Zaki, "At What Costs the New Language Policy Will Be Delivered in Morocco?" *Morocco World News*, March 17, 2016, https://www.moroccoworldnews.com/2016/03/182297/at-what-costs-the-new-language-policy-will-be-delivered-in-morocco.

111. Ahlam Ben Saga, "Education Minister: English Will Not Replace French," *Morocco World News*, January 18, 2019, https://www.moroccoworldnews.com/2019/01/263726/education-minister-english-french-morocco.

112. Ahmed Eljechtimi, "Morocco Looks to French as Language of Economic Success," *Reuters*, February 18, 2019, https://www.reuters.com/article/us-morocco-education/morocco-looks-to-french-as-language-of-economic-success-idUSKCN1Q70YF.

113. Tarek Bazza, "Education Minister Disregards English in Morocco, Not in London," *Morocco World News*, January 24, 2019, https://www.moroccoworldnews.com/2019/01/264264/education-minister-english-morocco-london.

114. Safaa Kasraoui, "French vs. English: How Morocco Is Debating Foreign Languages in Schools," *Morocco World News*, March 1, 2019, https://www.moroccoworldnews.com/2019/03/266978/french-english-morocco-languages-schools.

115. Safaa Kasraoui, "Abdelilah Benkirane Slams PJD's Stance on French Teaching Law, Calls on El Othmani to Resign," *Morocco World News*, April 1, 2019, https://www.moroccoworldnews.com/2019/04/269420/abdelilah-benkirane-pjd-french-teaching-law-el-othmani.

116. Safaa Kasraoui, "Muslim Scholars Union President Rebukes Morocco for Putting French First," *Morocco World News*, April 2, 2019, https://www.moroccoworldnews.com/2019/04/269524/muslim-scholars-union-president-rebukes-morocco-for-putting-french-first.

117. Zakaria Oudrhiri, "Morocco's Benkirane Defends Teaching in Arabic, English," *Morocco World News*, March 19, 2019, https://www.moroccoworldnews.com/2019/03/268390/moroccos-benkirane-teaching-arabic-english; Mohammed Amine Benabou, "Modernity, Democracy Forum to Discuss Language in Moroccan Schools," *Morocco World News*, April 4, 2019, https://www.moroccoworldnews.com/2019/04/269730/modernity-democracy-language-morocco-schools.

118. Mohammed Amine Benabou, "150 Moroccan Activists Endorse Arabic in Schools over French," *Morocco World News*, April 10, 2019, https://www.moroccoworldnews.com/2019/04/270272/150-moroccan-activists-endorse-arabic-in-schools-over-french.

119. Mohammed Amine Benabou, "Moroccan Amazigh Associations Endorse Use of French in Schools," *Morocco World News*, April 6, 2019, https://www.moroccoworldnews.com/2019/04/269886/moroccan-amazigh-associations-endorse-use-of-french-in-schools.

120. Safaa Kasraoui, "Moroccan University Presidents: Science Is 'Produced' in French and English," *Morocco World News*, March 11, 2019, https://www.moroccoworldnews.com/2019/03/267734/moroccan-university-presidents-science-french-english.

121. Associated Press, "Enseigner les maths en français? Au Maroc, la question divise" [Teaching math in French" In Morocco the question divides], *Challenges*, April 4, 2019, https://www.challenges.fr/societe/enseigner-les-maths-en-francais-au-maroc-la-question-divise_652114.

122. Tamba François Koundouno, "Education Minister: Moroccan Schools Need French for Social Equality," *Morocco World News*, April 23, 2019, https://www.moroccoworldnews.com/2019/04/271284/education-minister-moroccan-schools-french-social-equality.

123. Ghilani, "'The Legitimate' after the Uprisings," 13.

124. "Moroccan Parliament Votes to Bolster French Language," MEMO, July 25, 2019, video, https://www.youtube.com/watch?v=0c-tuLpnQrQ.

125. "Morocco Activists, Politicians Oppose 'Frenchification' of Education System," *Middle East Monitor*, August 10, 2019, https://www.middleeastmonitor.com/20190810-morocco-activists-politicians-oppose-frenchification-of-education-system/.

126. Tamba François Koundouno, "Morocco, France Sign French Language Learning Agreement," *Morocco World News*, December 13, 2018, https://www.moroccoworldnews.com/2018/12/260350/morocco-france-french-language-agreement.

127. Wagdy Sawahel, "Broader Horizons—Universities Switch to Bachelor Degree," *University World News*, January 13, 2020, https://www.universityworldnews.com/post.php?story=20200113100149303.

128. Imru Al Qays Talha Jebril, "English and Personnel Exchange—Economic Policy Strategies for Economic Growth and Greater Moroccan Socio-Political Integration in ECOWAS," in *Morocco's Socio-Economic Challenges*, ed. Dina Fakoussa and Laura Lale Kabis-Kechrid (Berlin: Forschungsinstitut der Deutschen Gesellschaft für Aswärtige Politik, 2020), 20–22, https://www.ssoar.info/ssoar/bitstream/handle/document/67081/ssoar-2020-fakoussa_et_al-Moroccos_Socio-Economic_Challenges_Employment_Education.pdf.

129. EF Education First, *English Proficiency Index* 2020, 7.

Chapter 8

1. Lauren Said-Moorhouse and Simon Cullen, "South Africa's New President Invokes Mandela, Promises 'A New Dawn,'" *CNN*, February 16, 2018, https://www.cnn.com/2018/02/16/africa/south-africa-politics-intl/index.html.

2. "1950. Population Registration Act no. 30," O'Malley Archives, Nelson Mandela Centre of Memory, https://omalley.nelsonmandela.org/omalley/index.php/site/q/03lv01538/04lv01828/05lv01829/06lv01838.htm; Republic of South Africa, Department of Statistics, Statistical Release P0302, "Mid-Year Population Estimates, 2019," vi, http://www.statssa.gov.za/publications/P0302/P03022019.pdf.

3. Thiven Reddy, "The Politics of Naming: The Constitution of Coloured Subjects in South Africa," in *Coloured by History, Shaped by Place*, ed. Zimitri Erasmus (Cape Town: Kwela, 2001), 76–78.

4. Hermann Giliomee, *The Afrikaners: Biography of a People* (Charlottesville: University of Virginia Press, 2009), 53.

5. William W. Bostock, "South Africa's Evolving Language Policy: Educational Implications," *Journal of Curriculum and Teaching* 7, no. 2 (May 2018): 27.

6. Kathleen Heugh, "Can Authoritarian Separatism Give Way to Linguistic Rights? A South African Case Study," *Current Issues in Language Planning* 4, no. 2 (April 2003): 128–29.

7. Giliomee, *The Afrikaners*, 376–78.

8. Ibid., 401.

9. Timothy G. Reagan, *Linguistic Legitimacy and Social Justice* (Cambridge: Cambridge University Press, 2019), 243.

10. Amaka E. Ideh and John O. Onu, "Multilingualism and the New Language Policy in South Africa: Innovation and Challenges," *Covenant Journal of Language Studies* 5, no. 2 (December 2017): 67.

11. Neville Alexander, "The Politics of Language Planning in Post-Apartheid South Africa," *Language Problems and Language Planning* 28, no. 2 (November 2004): 120–21.

12. Universal Declaration of Human Rights (1948), https://www.ohchr.org/EN/UDHR/Documents/UDHR_Translations/eng.pdf.

13. Timothy G. Reagan, "The Politics of Linguistic Apartheid: Language Policies in Black Education in South Africa," *Journal of Negro Education* 56, no. 3 (Summer 1987): 302.

14. Selma K. Sonntag, *The Local Politics of Global English* (Lanham, MD: Lexington, 2003), 81.

15. "South Africa Has One of the World's Worst Education Systems," *Economist,* January 7, 2017, https://www.economist.com/middle-east-and-africa/2017/01/07/south-africa-has-one-of-the-worlds-worst-education-systems.

16. *The Use of Vernacular Languages in Education,* Monographs on Foundations of Education no. 8 (Paris: UNESCO, 1953), http://www.tolerancia.org/upimages/Manifiestos/unesco_1953_english.pdf.

17. Albert Luthuli, *Let My People Go* (London: Fount Paperbacks, 1962), 48–49.

18. Kathleen Heugh, "Languages, Development and Reconstructing Education in South Africa," *International Journal of Educational Development* 19, nos. 4–5, no. 19 (1999): 303.

19. Jim Cummins, "BICS and CALP: Empirical and Theoretical Status of the Distinction," in *Encyclopedia of Language and Education,* vol. 2: *Literacy,* ed. Brian Street and Nancy H. Hornberger (New York: Springer, 2010), 71–83.

20. Nkonko M. Kamwangamalu, "One Language, Multilayered Identities: English in Society in Transition, South Africa," *World Englishes* 26, no. 3 (July 2007): 267.

21. Giliomee, *The Afrikaners,* 579.

22. Heugh, "Languages, Development and Reconstructing Education," 303.

23. Sandra Land, "English Language as Siren Song: Hope and Hazard in Post-Apartheid South Africa," in *English Language as Hydra: Its Impact on Non-English Language Cultures,* ed. Vaughan Rapatahana and Pauline Bunce (Bristol, UK: Multilingual Matters, 2012), 191.

24. Cass R. Sunstein, *Designing Democracy: What Constitutions Do* (New York: Oxford University Press, 2001), 261; Penelope Andrews, "Incorporating International Human Rights Law in National Constitutions: The South African Experience," in *Progress in International Law,* ed. Russell Miller and Rebecca Bratspies (Leiden, Netherlands: Martinus Nijhoff, 2008), 839.

25. S. Afr. Const., 1996 Preamble, https://www.gov.za/documents/constitution-republic-south-africa-1996-preamble.

26. Grundgesetz (FRG Const.); Can. Const. (Constitutional Act, 1982), pt. 1 (Canadian Charter of Rights and Freedoms), https://laws-lois.justice.gc.ca/eng/Const/page-15.html.

27. United Nations, "Universal Declaration of Human Rights" (declaration, Paris, France, December 10, 1948), https://www.ohchr.org/EN/UDHR/Documents/UDHR_Translations/eng.pdf.

28. S. Afr. Const., 1996, ch. 2, §9, https://www.gov.za/documents/constitution/chapter-2-bill-rights.

29. Mark S. Kende, *Constitutional Rights in Two Worlds: South Africa and the United States* (New York: Cambridge University Press, 2009), 294; Anton Kok, email to author, July 28, 2021.

30. Neville Alexander, "Linguistic Rights, Language Planning and Democracy in Post-Apartheid South Africa," in *Language Policy: Lessons from Global Models* (Monterey, CA: Monterey Institute of International Studies, 2002), 117.

31. S. Afr. Const., 1996, ch. 2, §29, https://www.gov.za/documents/constitution/chapter-2-bill-rights.

32. Ibid., ch. 2, § 31; Gerrit Brand, "The Role of 'Europe' in the South African Language Debate, with Special Reference to Political Traditions," in *Language Ideologies, Policies and Practices: Language and the Future of Europe,* ed. Clare Mar-Molinero and Patrick Stevenson (New York: Palgrave Macmillan, 2006), 68–69.

33. S. Afr. Const., 1996, ch. 1, § 6, https://www.gov.za/documents/constitution/chapter-1-founding-provisions.

34. Abram de Swaan, *Words of the World* (Cambridge: Polity, 2001), 135–36.
35. Suzanne Romaine, "The Impact of Language Policy on Endangered Languages," *International Journal of Multicultural Societies* 4, no. 2 (2002): 204.
36. Kathleen Heugh, "Harmonisation and South African Languages: Twentieth Century Debates of Homogeneity and Heterogeneity," *Language Policy* 15, no. 3 (August 2016): 247.
37. Mahmood Mamdani, "The African University," *London Review of Books* 40, no. 14 (July 2018): 29–32.
38. Edward Fagan, "The Constitutional Entrenchment of Memory," in *Negotiating the Past: The Making of Memory in South Africa*, ed. Sarah Nuttall and Carli Coetzee (New York: Oxford University Press, 1998), 254.
39. Hermann Giliomee, "Cyril Ramaphosa and the Language Challenge," Address Prepared for the Centennial Festival Dinner of the Afrikanerbond, *Politics Web*, June 10, 2018, http://www.politicsweb.co.za/opinion/cyril-ramaphosa-and-the-language-challenge.
40. S. Afr. Const., 1996, ch. 1, § 6, https://www.gov.za/documents/constitution/chapter-1-founding-provisions.
41. Marianne Thamm, "Multilingualism: Pan South African Language Board Going Nowhere Slowly, Hemorrhaging Millions," *Daily Maverick*, February 25, 2016, https://www.dailymaverick.co.za/article/2016-02-25-multilingualism-pan-south-african-language-board-going-nowhere-slowly-haemorrhaging-millions/.
42. *Madiba and Others v. Minister of Arts and Culture and Others* 2017 (4) SA 111 (GP) (S. Afr.), www.saflii.org/za/cases/ZAGPPHC/2017/502/html; "South Africa: Court Affirms Decision on PanSALB Board," *AllAfrica*, August 23, 2017, https://allafrica.com/stories/201708230815.html.
43. "Pan South African Language Board (PanSALB)," Constitutional Bodies, Central Government Administration (CGA), National Government of South Africa, https://nationalgovernment.co.za/units/view/58/pan-south-african-language-board-pansalb.
44. "Language in Education Policy," Department of Basic Education, Republic of South Africa, July 14, 1997, https://www.education.gov.za/Portals/0/Documents/Policies/GET/LanguageEducationPolicy1997.pdf.
45. Alexander, "The Politics of Language Planning in Post-Apartheid South Africa," 120.
46. Ibid.
47. *Census 2011: Census in Brief*, fig. 2.8: Population by First Language and Population Group (Percentage) (Pretoria: Statistics South Africa, 2012), 27, http://www.statssa.gov.za/census/census_2011/census_products/Census_2011_Census_in_brief.pdf.
48. Liesel Hibbert, *The Linguistic Landscape of Post-Apartheid South Africa: Politics and Discourse* (Clevedon, UK: Multilingual Matters, 2016), 72.
49. "Tongues under Threat: English is Dangerously Dominant," *Economist*, January 20, 2011, http://www.economist.com/node/17963285.
50. Amnesty International, *Broken and Unequal: The State of Education in South Africa* (report, May 2020), 32, https://www.justice.gov/eoir/page/file/1247956/download.
51. Marius Roodt, *The South African Education Crisis: Giving Power Back to Parents* (Johannesburg: South African Institute of Race Relations, 2018), 10, https://irr.org.za/reports/occasional-reports/files/the-south-african-education-crisis-31-05-2018.pdf/.
52. Centre for Development and Enterprise, *Low-Fee Private Schools: International Experience and South African Realities* (Johannesburg: Centre for Development and Enterprise, 2015), 10, https://www.cde.org.za/low-fee-private-schools-international-experience-and-south-african-realities.
53. Thabile Vilakazi, "South African Students Protest against School's Alleged Racist Hair Policy," *CNN*, September 2, 2016, https://www.cnn.com/2016/08/31/africa/south-africa-school-racism/index.html.
54. Alan Greenblatt, "Decrying Hair Rule, South African Students Demand to Be 'Naturally Who We Are,'" NPR, September 6, 2016, https://www.npr.org/sections/goatsandsoda/2016/09/06/492417635/a-ban-on-black-hairstyles-raises-deeper-issues-about-race.
55. Carolyn McKinney, *Language and Power in Post-Colonial Schooling* (New York: Routledge, 2017), 80–81.

56. Kathleen Heugh, "Contesting the Monolingual Practices of a Bilingual to Multilingual Policy," *English Teaching: Practice and Critique* 8, no. 2 (September 2009): 96–113.

57. Neville Alexander, "Schooling in and for the New South Africa," *Focus* 56 (February 2010): 7–13, 12, https://hsf.org.za/publications/focus/focus-56-february-2010-on-learning-and-teaching/schooling-in-and-for-the-new-south-africa.

58. Neville Alexander, *Language Policy and National Unity in South Africa/Azania* (Cape Town: Buchu, 2013), 64.

59. Reagan, "The Politics of Linguistic Apartheid," 304.

60. *The Incremental Introduction of African Languages in South African Schools: Draft Policy* (Pretoria: Department of Basic Education, Republic of South Africa, September 2013), https://www.education.gov.za/Portals/0/Documents/Reports/IIAL%20Policy%20September%202013.pdf.

61. Laurence Wright, "Why English Dominates the Central Economy: An Economic Perspective on 'Elite Closure' and South African Policy," in *Language Policy and Political Economy: English in a Global Context*, ed. Thomas Ricento (New York: Oxford University Press, 2015), 200.

62. Bulelwa Dayimani, "African Language Policy to Be Introduced Next Year," *Destinyconnect.com*, June 17, 2015, http://www.destinyconnect.com/2015/06/17/african-language-policy-improve-learning.

63. EFA Global Education Monitoring Report Team, *Teaching and Learning: Achieving Quality for All* (Paris: UNESCO, 2014), http://unesdoc.unesco.org/images/0022/002256/225660e.pdf.

64. Paul Herman, "Target Schools to Offer African Language from Grade 1 in 2018," *News24*, June 29, 2017, https://allafrica.com/stories/201706300312.html.

65. Rinelle Evans and Ailie Cleghorn, "Parental Perceptions: A Case Study of School Choice Amidst Language Waves," *South African Journal of Education* 34, no. 2 (May 2014): 7.

66. Birgit Brock-Utne and Halla B. Holmarsdottir, "Language Policies and Practices in Tanzania and South Africa: Problems and Challenges," *International Journal of Educational Development* 24, no. 1 (January 2004): 67–83; Heugh, "Languages, Development and Reconstructing Education," 301–13; Margie Probyn, S. Murray, L. Botha, Paula Botya, M. Brookes, and Vivian Westphal, "Minding the Gaps—An Investigation into Language Policy and Practice in Four Eastern Cape Districts," *Perspectives in Education* 20, no. 1 (January 2002): 669–86.

67. Kathleen Heugh, email to author, April 19, 2019.

68. Ina Mullis et al., *PIRLS 2016: International Results in Reading* (Chestnut Hill, MA: International Association for the Evaluation of Educational Achievement, 2017), 20, 55, https://files.eric.ed.gov/fulltext/ED580353.pdf.

69. Equal Education, "Media Statement: Children Who Cannot Read, Cannot Participate in Democracy," January 10, 2017, https://equaleducation.org.za/2018/01/10/media-statement-children-who-cannot-read-cannot-participate-in-democracy.

70. *Head of Dep't, Mpumalanga Dep't of Educ. & Another v. Hoërskool Ermelo*, [2009] ZACC 32 (S.Afr.), https://collections.concourt.org.za/handle/20.500.12144/3584.

71. Ibid., 52, para. 103.

72. Ibid., 53, para. 106.

73. Erika M. Serfontein and Elda de Waal, "The Effectiveness of Legal Remedies in Education: A School Governing Body Perspective," *De Jure* 46, no. 1 (June 2013): 61.

74. *Mpumalanga Dep't of Educ.*, 2010 (2) SA 415, 2, para. 2.

75. South African Schools Act 84 of 1996 Preamble (S. Afr.), https://www.education.gov.za/LinkClick.aspx?fileticket=aIolZ6UsZ5U%3D.

76. S. Afr. Const., 1996, http://www.gov.za/documents/constitution/chapter-2-bill-rights#9.

77. Ibid.

78. Neville Alexander, *Language Education Policy, National and Sub-National Identities in South Africa* (Strasbourg, France: Council of Europe, 2003), 18, http://citeseerx.ist.psu.edu/viewdoc/download?doi=10.1.1.476.2445&rep=rep1&type=pdf.

79. Alexander, "Linguistic Rights, Language Planning and Democracy," 119.

80. Use of Official Languages Act of 2012 (S. Afr.), http://www.dhet.gov.za/Management%20Support/Language%20Policy%20for%20Higher%20Education.pdf, citing Nelson Mandela, "Address by President Nelson Mandela on the Occasion of his Acceptance of an Honorary

Doctorate of the University of Stellenbosch" (address, University of Stellenbosch, October, 25, 1996), http://www.mandela.gov.za/mandela_speeches/1996/961025_stellenbosch.htm.

81. South Africa Ministry of Education, *Language Policy for Higher Education*, November 2002, ¶ 15.4, 11, http://www.dhet.gov.za/Management%20Support/Language%20Policy%20for%20Higher%20Education.pdf.

82. Karen MacGregor, "Higher Education in the 20th Year of Democracy," *University World News*, April 27, 2014, http://www.universityworldnews.com/article.php?story=20140425131554856.

83. Theodorus Du Plessis, "From Monolingual to Bilingual Higher Education: The Repositioning of Historically Afrikaans-Medium Universities in South Africa," *Language Policy* 5 (2006): 99.

84. Open Stellenbosch Memorandum of Demands, May 13, 2015, http://www.sun.ac.za/english/management/wim-de-villiers/Documents/Open%20Stellenbosch%20Memo%2020150513.pdf.

85. Bassey E. Antia and Chanel van der Merwe, "Speaking with a Forked Tongue about Multilingualism in the Language Policy of a South African University," *Language Policy* 18, no. 2 (November 2018): 407–29.

86. "Luister," video, August 20, 2015, https://www.youtube.com/watch?v=sF3rTBQTQk4.

87. Wim de Villiers, "Our Response to the 'Luister' Video—Stellenbosch University," *Politicsweb*, August 25, 2015, http://www.politicsweb.co.za/politics/our-response-to-the-luister-video--stellenbosch-un.

88. Jonathan Jansen, "As by Fire—The End of the South African University," *University World News*, August 24, 2017, http://www.universityworldnews.com/article.php?story=2017082408304974.

89. Munene Mwaniki, "South African Higher Education Language Politics Post #RhodesMustFall: The Terrain of Advanced Language Politics," *Southern African Linguistics and Applied Language* 36, no. 1 (May 2018): 28.

90. Du Plessis, "From Monolingual to Bilingual Higher Education," 96–97.

91. Ibid., 108–9.

92. Richard Mamabolo, "The ConCourt vs Afrikaners: A Reply to Ernst Roets," *PoliticsWeb*, January 15, 2018, http://www.politicsweb.co.za/opinion/the-concourt-vs-afrikaners-a-reply-to-ernst-roets.

93. Max du Preez, "AfriForum 'Hijacking the Afrikaner Mainstream,'" *News24*, July 26, 2016, https://www.news24.com/Columnists/MaxduPreez/afriforum-hijacking-the-afrikaner-mainstream-20160726.

94. Eve Fairbanks, "The Last White Africans," *Foreign Policy*, January 16, 2017, https://foreignpolicy.com/2017/01/16/the-last-white-africans.

95. "About Us: Vision & Mission," AfriForum, accessed February 16, 2020, https://www.afriforum.co.za/en/about-us.

96. Danie Rossouw, attorney at West & Rossouw, video interview with author, January 10, 2018; Danie Rossouw, email to author, January 11, 2018.

97. Jonathan Jansen, "The Big Read: The 'bittereinders' of taal," *Sunday Times*, March 16, 2017, https://www.timeslive.co.za/news/south-africa/2017-03-16-the-big-read-the-bittereinders-of-taal/.

98. Nancy Hornberger and Viniti Vaish, "Multilingual Language Policy and School Linguistic Practice: Globalization and English-Language Teaching in India, Singapore and South Africa," *Compare* 39, no. 3 (May 2009): 312.

99. Eve Fairbanks, "A House Divided," *Slate*, June 24, 2013, http://www.slate.com/articles/news_and_politics/foreigners/2013/06/university_of_the_free_state_in_bloemfontein_s_segregation_how_the_legacy.html.

100. South Africa Ministry of Education, *Language Policy for Higher Education*, ¶ 2.

101. *AfriForum and Another v. U. of the Free State*, [2017] ZACC 48 at 8-9 (S. Afr), https://collections.concourt.org.za/handle/20.500.12144/34583.

102. Higher Education Quality Committee (HEQC), *Executive Summary: Audit Report of the University of the Free State: Report of the Higher Education Quality Committee to the University of the Free State* (Pretoria: HEQC, March 2008).

103. Eve Fairbanks, "The Healer," *New Republic*, June 15, 2010, https://newrepublic.com/article/75261/the-healer.

104. Jonathan Jansen, "Not Even Colonial Born: England, the English and the Problem of Education in South Africa," Percy Baneshik Memorial Lecture, the English Academy of South Africa, University of the Free State, September 13, 2013, reprinted in *Ingesluit LitNet Akademies*, October 10, 2013, http://www.litnet.co.za/percy-maneshik-memorial-lecture-2013.

105. Russell H. Kaschula, "A Response to Jonathan Jansen's Percy Baneshik Memorial Lecture to the English Academy of South Africa," *Ingesluit LitNet Akademies*, October 8, 2013, http://www.litnet.co.za/a-response-to-jonathan-jansens-percy-baneshik-memorial-lecture-to-the-english-academy-of-s.

106. South African Press Association, "Jansen Is Wrong about English as Primary Tuition Language, Says FF Plus," *Mail & Guardian*, October 2, 2013, https://mg.co.za/article/2013-10-02-jansen-speech-on-language-in-education-was-distorted/.

107. Ibid.

108. Jonathan Jansen, "The Best Universities Know That Talent Can't Be Contained within Borders," *Conversation*, May 11, 2015, https://theconversation.com/the-best-universities-know-that-talent-cant-be-contained-within-borders-40986.

109. Theodorus du Plessis, "Language Policy Evaluation and Review at the University of the Free State," *Language Matters* 48, no. 3 (September 2017): 1–21.

110. *AfriForum and Another v. U. of the Free State* at 2–3.

111. Ibid., 26 para. 62.

112. Ibid., 28–30 paras. 67–72.

113. Ibid., 35 para. 88 (Froneman, J., dissenting).

114. Ibid., 37 para. 93.

115. Ibid., 34–35 para. 88, quoting J. R. R. Tolkien, "English and Welsh," in *The Monsters and the Critics, and Other Essays*, ed. Christopher Tolkien (London: Harper Collins, 2013), 178–79.

116. Ibid., 21 para. 52.

117. Ibid., 42.

118. Ibid., 33 para. 83.

119. "UFS Says Court Ruling 'Not a Victory Against Afrikaans," *Times Live*, December 30, 2017, https://www.timeslive.co.za/news/south-africa/2017-12-30-ufs-says-court-ruling-not-a-victory-against-afrikaans.

120. "SA Civics Organisation Hails ConCourt Judgment on University Language Policy," *Citizen*, December 30, 2017, https://citizen.co.za/news/south-africa/1770314/sa-civics-organisation-hails-concourt-judgment-on-university-language-policy.

121. James de Villiers, "Minorities Were Lied to in 1994—AfriForum on UFS Court Ruling," *News24*, December 29, 2017, https://www.news24.com/SouthAfrica/News/minorities-were-lied-to-in-1994-afriforum-on-ufs-concourt-ruling-20171229.

122. Josca Human, "'New#UFS Language Policy is Punishment for Afrikaans Speaking Students'—CDP," *Bloemfontein Courant*, January 2, 2018, http://www.bloemfonteincourant.co.za/new-ufs-language-policy-punishment-afrikaans-speaking-students-cdp.

123. "Constitutional Court Ruling on UFS Language Policy Proves Minorities Were Deceived about Language Rights," *AfriForum*, December 29, 2017, https://www.afriforum.co.za/constitutional-court-ruling-ufs-language-policy-proves-minorities-deceived-language-rights.

124. Alana Bailey, email to author, January 3, 2018.

125. Hein Willemse, "More Than an Oppressor's Language: Reclaiming the Hidden History of Afrikaans," *Conversation*, April 27, 2017, https://theconversation.com/more-than-an-oppressors-language-reclaiming-the-hidden-history-of-afrikaans-71838.

126. S. Afr. Const., 1996, ch. 1, Art. 6 (2), http://www.justice.gov.za/legislation/constitution/SAConstitution-web-eng.pdf.

127. Dumisile Mkhize, "The Language Question at a Historically Afrikaans University: Access and Social Justice Issues," *Southern African Linguistics and Applied Language* 36, no. 1 (March 2018): 22.

128. Russell Kaschula, Zakeera Docrat, and Monwabisi Ralarala, "Languages Aren't Racist, People Are," *News24*, January 28, 2018, https://www.news24.com/Columnists/GuestColumn/languages-arent-racist-people-are-20180128-2.

129. Zakeera Docrat and Russell Kaschula, "Litigating Multilingualism," *Ingesluit LitNet Akademies*, April 4, 2018, http://www.litnet.co.za/litigating-multilingualism.

130. A. S. Coetzee-Van Rooy, "Discrepancies between Perceptions of English Proficiency and Scores on English Tests: Implications for Teaching English in South Africa, *Journal of Language Teaching* 45, no. 2 (December 2011): 151–81.

131. Department of Higher Education and Training, Republic of South Africa, "Language Policy for Higher Education (draft)," *Government Gazette* 632, no. 41463 (February 23, 2018): 17, https://www.gpwonline.co.za/Gazettes/Gazettes/41463_23-2_HighEduTraining.pdf.

132. Sharon Dell, "University Language Policy Exposes Societal Fractures," *University World News*, February 8, 2019, https://www.universityworldnews.com/post.php?story=20190201152805780.

133. *Gelyke Kanse v. U. of Stellenbosch and Others*, [2019] ZACC 38 (S. Afr.), https://collections.concourt.org.za/handle/20.500.12144/34621.

134. Howard Phillips, *The University of Cape Town, 1918–1948: The Formative Years* (Cape Town: UCT Press, 1993), 18.

135. "Statistical Profile: Overview 2018," Stellenbosch University, http://www.sun.ac.za/english/statistical-profile-2014-test, accessed June 11, 2019.

136. Mercy Kannemeyer, *Die Ander Kant = The Other Side*, YouTube, February 22, 2017, video, https://www.youtube.com/watch?v=_oRfpixLl9g.

137. *Gelyke Kanse v. U. of Stellenbosch and Others* at 15 para. 33.

138. Ibid., 13 para. 28 (Froneman, J. concurring).

139. Ibid., 21 para. 49.

140. Ibid., 27–28, para. 64, 65.

141. Ibid., 35–37, para. 76,77, 79.

142. Ibid., 46, para. 89.

143. Yoliswa Sobuwa, "Nzimande Welcomes Court's Ruling on University Language Policy," *Sowetan Live*, October 14, 2019, https://www.sowetanlive.co.za/news/south-africa/2019-10-14-nzimande-welcomes-courts-ruling-on-university-language-policy.

144. Stephen Coan, "Reclaiming the Past to Create a Decolonized Future," *University World News*, January 26, 2018, http://www.universityworldnews.com/article.php?story=20180124125355129.

145. Munyaradzi Makoni, "Universities Play an Active Role in Mandela Day," *University World News*, July 20, 2018, http://www.universityworldnews.com/article.php?story=20180720134912872.

146. Ngũgĩ wa Thiong'o, *Decolonising the Mind: The Politics of Language in African Literature* (Oxford: James Currey, 1986), 9.

147. Wanjiku Maina, "Kenya: We Have Normalised Negativity towards African Languages - Ngugi wa Thiong'o," *Daily Nation*, February 8, 2019, https://allafrica.com/stories/201902080531.html.

148. H. Ekkehard Wolff, "How the Continent's Languages Can Unlock the Potential of Young Africans," *The* Conversation, February 7, 2018, https://theconversation.com/how-the-continents-languages-can-unlock-the-potential-of-young-africans-90322.

149. Russell H. Kaschula and Zakeera Docrat, "Multilingualism Must Be Celebrated as a Resource, Not a Problem," *Conversation*, February 15, 2019, https://theconversation.com/multilingualism-must-be-celebrated-as-a-resource-not-a-problem-90397.

150. Lesley Le Grange, "Decolonising the University Curriculum," *South African Journal of Higher Education* 30, no. 2 (July 2016): 1–12..

151. Wolff, "How the Continent's Languages Can Unlock the Potential of Young Africans."

152. Omar Mohammed, "Tanzania Dumps English as Its Official Language in Schools, Opts for Kiswahili," *Quartz*, March 5, 2015, https://qz.com/355444/tanzania-dumps-english-as-its-official-language-in-schools-opts-for-kiswahili.

153. Matome Sebelebele, "Teaching Swahili in SA Schools a Major Triumph," *Sowetan Live*, September 23, 2018, https://www.sowetanlive.co.za/sundayworld/lifestyle/talk/2018-09-23-teaching-swahili-in-sa-schools-a-major-triumph.

154. Quentin Williams, video interview with author, June 19, 2019.

155. Quentin Williams, "AfriKaaps Is an Act of Reclamation," *Mail and Guardian*, December 15, 2016, https://mg.co.za/article/2016-12-15-00-afrikaaps-is-an-act-of-reclamation.

156. Giliomee, "Cyril Ramaphosa and the Language Challenge."

157. Campus France, "The International Mobility of African Students," special edition, *Campus France Notes* 16 (October 2016), 4, https://ressources.campusfrance.org/publications/notes/en/note_16_hs_en.pdf.

158. Hermann Giliomee, "The Rise and Fall of the Afrikaans Universities" (paper presentation, "The Internationalisation of Universities and the National Language" Symposium, Leuven University, May 4, 2018), 37.

159. Yaroslav Lissovolik, "BRICS-Plus: Alternative Globalization in the Making?," Valdai Papers 69, Valdai Discussion Club, July 12, 2017, https://valdaiclub.com/a/valdai-papers/valdai-paper-69.

160. Rosemary Salomone, "Court Moves Beyond the Past in Favouring English," *University World News*, October 19, 2019, https://www.universityworldnews.com/post.php?story=20191017160303180.

Chapter 9

1. Naz Rassool, *Global Issues in Language, Education and Development: Perspectives from Postcolonial Countries* (Clevedon, UK: Multilingual Matters, 2007), 143.

2. Gauri Shinde, dir., *English Vinglish*, (Mumbai: Eros International, 2012), DVD.

3. Saket Chaudhary, dir., *Hindi Medium* (Mumbai: Maddox Films and T-Series, 2017), DVD.

4. National Statistical Consumption Office, Ministry of Statistics and Programme Implementation, Government of India, *Household Social Consumption on Education in India* (2020), http://mospi.nic.in/sites/default/files/publication_reports/KI_Education_75th_Final.pdf; Atul Thakur, "Literacy Rate for Muslims Worse than SC/STs," *Times of India*, August 13, 2020, https://timesofindia.indiatimes.com/india/literacy-rate-for-muslims-worse-than-sc/sts/articleshow/77514868.cms.

5. Geeta Pandey, "An 'English Goddess' for India's Down-Trodden," *BBC News*, February 15, 2011, http://www.bbc.com/news/world-south-asia-12355740.

6. "Indian Languages Carry the Legacy of Caste," *Rediff*, March 5, 2007, https://www.rediff.com/news/2007/mar/05inter.htm.

7. Selma K. Sonntag, "Ideology and Policy in the Politics of the English Language in North India," in *Ideology, Politics and Language Policies: Focus on English*, ed. Thomas Ricento (Amsterdam: John Benjamins, 2000), 135.

8. Salman Rushdie, "The Empire Writes Back with a Vengeance," *London Times*, July 3, 1982, 8; Bill Ashcroft, Gareth Griffiths, and Helen Tiffin, *The Empire Writes Back: Theory and Practice in Post-Colonial Literatures* (London: Routledge, 2002).

9. Roxana-Elisabeta Marinescu, "Control and Empowerment through English in Salman Rushdie's Writings," *Dialogos* 36 (2019): 289–90.

10. Annie Montaut, "But Why Do You Write in Hindi?," *Études anglaises* 62, no. 3 (July 2009): 334.

11. Office of the Registrar General, *Census of India 2011: Language*, 2011, 5–18, http://censusindia.gov.in/2011Census/C-16_25062018_NEW.pdf.

12. Shiv Sahay Singh, "Language Survey Reveals Diversity," *The Hindu*, July 22, 2013, https://www.thehindu.com/news/national/language-survey-reveals-diversity/article4938865.ece.

13. Education First, *English Proficiency Index 2020* (Ranking Report of 100 Countries and Regions by English Skills, Signum International AG, 2020), 7 https://www.ef.com/__/~/media/centralefcom/epi/downloads/full-reports/v10/ef-epi-2020-english.pdf.

14. E. Annamalai, *Managing Multilingual India: Political and Linguistic Manifestations* (New Delhi: Sage, 2001), 94–98.

15. Bureau of Education, "Minute by Hon'ble T. B. Macaulay, Dated 2nd February 1835," in *Selections from Educational Records*, ed. Henry Sharp (Delhi: National Archives of India, 1965), 107–17, http://www.columbia.edu/itc/mealac/pritchett/00generallinks/macaulay/txt_minute_education_1835.html.

16. Ibid., 30.

17. Stephen Evans, "Macaulay's Minute Revisited: Colonial Language Policy in Nineteenth-Century India," *Journal of Multilingual and Multicultural Development* 23, no. 4 (2002): 260–81; Vaidehi Ramanathan, *The English-Vernacular Divide: Postcolonial Language and Politics and Practice* (Clevedon, UK: Multilingual Matters, 2005): 32–33.

18. Minglang Zhou, "Language Ideology and Language Order: Conflicts and Compromises in Colonial and Postcolonial Asia," *International Journal of the Sociology of Language* 243 (2017): 105.

19. Ramachandra Guha, "The Question of English—Worldwide, English Remains the Choice for Communication," *Telegraph* (Calcutta), November 5, 2011, https://www.telegraphindia.com/opinion/the-question-of-english-worldwide-english-remains-the-choice-for-communication/cid/330254.

20. Mahatma K. Gandhi, *India of My Dreams* (Ahmedabad, India: Jitendra T. Desai, 1947), https://www.mkgandhi.org/indiadreams/chap44.htm.

21. Keki N. Daruwalla, "The Decolonized Muse," in *Creative Aspects of Indian English*, ed. Shantinath K. Desai (Delhi: Sahitya Akademi, 1995), 30.

22. Sonntag, "Ideology and Policy," 136–37.

23. *Report of the University Education Committee* (New Delhi: Government of India Press, 1949), 316.

24. India Const., arts. 349–51, https://legislative.gov.in/sites/default/files/COI_1.pdf.

25. Selma K. Sonntag, *The Local Politics of Global English* (Lanham, MD: Lexington, 2003), 61–62.

26. Asha Sarangi, "India's Language Regime: The Eighth Schedule," in *State Traditions and Language Regimes*, ed. Linda Cardinal and Selma K. Sonntag (Montreal: McGill-Queens' University Press, 2015), 206–10.

27. Rama Kant Agnihotri, "Constituent Assembly Debates on Language," *Economic and Political Weekly* 1, no. 8 (February 21, 2015): 48.

28. India Const., art. 348.

29. Ajay Singh, "The Brahminisation of Justice or Why Our English-Only Supreme Court Needs a Taste of Linguistic Democracy," *Firstpost*, November 16, 2018, https://www.firstpost.com/india/the-brahminisation-of-justice-or-why-our-english-only-supreme-court-needs-a-taste-of-linguistic-democracy-5560311.html.

30. India Const., art. 30.

31. India Const., art. 350A.

32. Usree Bhattacharya and Lei Jiang, "The Right to Education Act (2009): Instructional Medium and Dis-Citizenship," *International Journal of the Sociology of Language* 253 (2018): 149–68.

33. Taylor C. Sherman, "Education in Early Postcolonial India: Expansion, Experimentation and Planned Self-Help," *History of Education* 47, no. 4 (July 2018), 508.

34. Norman Berdichevsky, *Nations, Language and Citizenship* (Jefferson, NC: McFarland, 2004), 126.

35. Duncan B. Forrester, "The Madras Anti-Hindi Agitation," *Pacific Affairs* 39, no. 1/2 (1966): 22.

36. Harold F. Shiffman, "Bilingualism in South Asia: Friend or Foe?," *Proceedings of the 4th International Symposium on Bilingualism* (Somerville, MA: Cascadilla, 2003).

37. The Education Commission 1964–1966, *Education and National Development* (New Delhi: Ministry of Education, Government of India, June 1966), https://archive.org/details/ReportOfTheEducationCommission1964-66D.S.KothariReport/page/n267/mode/2up.

38. Jeffrey Gettleman, Kai Schultz, Suhasini Raj, and Hari Kumar, "Under Modi, a Hindu Nationalist Surge Has Further Divided India," *New York Times*, April 11, 2019, https://www.nytimes.com/2019/04/11/world/asia/modi-india-elections.html; Gurcharan Das, "The Modi Mirage," *Foreign Affairs*, April 11, 2019, https://www.foreignaffairs.com/articles/india/2019-04-11/modi-mirage.

39. Aatish Taseer, "Can the World's Largest Democracy Endure Another Five Years of a Modi Government?," *Time Asia*, May 20, 2019, https://time.com/5586415/india-election-narendra-modi-2019.

40. Ananya Vajpeyi, "Minorities and Populism in Modi's India: The Mirror Effect," in *Minorities and Populism: Critical Perspectives from South Asia and Europe*, ed. Volker Kaul and Ananya Vajpeyi (Cham, Switzerland: Springer, 2020), 20–21.

41. NDTV, "The Big Fight over Language," YouTube video, June 14, 2014, https://www.youtube.com/watch?v=Rc-kwHE2ZGo.

42. Mandakini Gahlot, "India's 'Business Friendly' Prime Minister Rejects English," *Global Post PRI*, August 4, 2014, https://www.pri.org/stories/2014-08-04/india-s-business-friendly-prime-minister-rejects-english.

43. Express News Service, "Focus More on Hindi, Then Learn English," *The Indian Express*, June 25, 2017, https://indianexpress.com/article/cities/ahmedabad/focus-more-on-hindi-then-learn-english-naidu-4720688.

44. Dipankar De Sarkar, "Mr. Venkaiah Naidu and India's 'English Mind,'" *Live Mint*, June 30, 2017, https://www.livemint.com/Opinion/8ap2t2rAaOTsp9nKNBaspK/Mr-Venkaiah-Naidu-and-Indias-English-mind.html.

45. "Hindi Speakers Asked for Cooperation," *Language Magazine*, October 10, 2017, https://www.languagemagazine.com/2017/10/hindi-speakers-asked-cooperation.

46. Sanjay Kumar, "Indian Government's Bid to Make Hindi Official UN Language Lacks Local Support," *Arab News*, January 8, 2018, http://www.arabnews.com/node/1220966/world.

47. Rejimon Kuttappan, "Hindi as Official UN Language: Experts Divided on Centre's Move and Spending of RS 5 cr," *News Minute*, March 15, 2018, https://www.thenewsminute.com/article/hindi-official-un-language-experts-divided-centres-move-and-spending-rs-5-cr-78002.

48. Express News Service, "Hindi Symbol of Socio-Political, Linguistic Unity, Says Venkaiah," *Indian Express*, September 15, 2018, https://indianexpress.com/article/india/hindi-symbol-of-socio-political-linguistic-unity-says-venkaiah-naidu-5357349.

49. Shemin Joy, "English an Illness Inflicted by British: Venkaiah," *Deccan Herald*, September 14, 2018, https://www.deccanherald.com/national/preference-eng-illness-692619.html.

50. Sadanand Dhume, "For India, English Is a Cure, Not a 'Sickness,'" *Wall Street Journal*, September 20, 2018, https://www.wsj.com/articles/for-india-english-is-a-cure-not-a-sickness-1537481134.

51. Rajni Pandey, "Not Making Hindi Language Compulsory in NEP: Prakash Javadekar," *Times of India*, January 10, 2019, https://timesofindia.indiatimes.com/home/education/news/not-making-hindi-language-compulsory-in-nep-hrd-minister/articleshow/67470366.cms.

52. Jatin Verma, "Quantum Leap in Students Heading to France," *Times of India*, June 17, 2017, http://timesofindia.indiatimes.com/city/chandigarh/quantum-leap-in-students-heading-to-france/articleshow/59626758.cms.

53. Ambassade de France en Inde, "France in India," https://in.ambafrance.org/Study-in-France-12461.

54. Chandrashekar Srinivasan, "'Our Reliance on English . . .': PM Modi's Pitch to Foreign Firms," *NDTV*, September 25, 2019, https://www.ndtv.com/india-news/our-reliance-on-english-pm-modi-pitch-to-foreign-firms-2107174.

55. Akhilesh Pillalamarri, "Language and Basic Rights in India: Beyond English," *The Diplomat*, July 16, 2014, http://thediplomat.com/2014/07/language-and-basic-rights-in-india-beyond-english.

56. NDTV, "The Language Debate—Hindi Hain Hum," YouTube video, July 20, 2014, https://www.youtube.com/watch?v=DtMVHlI8J_I.

57. D. Shyam Babu, "The Perilous March of Hindistan," *The Hindu*, March 24, 2018, http://www.thehindu.com/opinion/op-ed/the-perilous-march-of-hindistan/article22492143.ece.

58. *Chennai Declaration of Language Rights* (Chennai, India: Language Rights Conference, September 19–20, 2015), https://www.academia.edu/17518341/Chennai_Declaration_on_Language_Equality_and_Rights.

59. Campaign for Language Equality and Rights (CLEAR), *International Mother Language Day* (February 21, 2017), http://clearindia.org/wp-content/uploads/2017/02/PR-Language-Rights-Feb-21-2017-final.pdf.

60. Deepa Balakrishnan, "Activists from Non-Hindi States Unite, Plan Seminar to Take Language Battle Forward," *News18.com*, July 10, 2017, http://www.news18.com/news/india/activists-from-non-hindi-states-unite-plan-seminar-to-take-language-battle-forward-1456995.html.

61. Samanth Subramanian, "India after English?," *New York Review of Books*, June 9, 2014, http://www.nybooks.com/daily/2014/06/09/india-newspapers-after-english.

62. Selma K. Sonntag, "Linguistic Diversity in India's Polity and Economy," in *The Economics of Language Policy*, ed. Michele Gazzola and Bengt-Arne Wickström (Cambridge, MA: MIT Press, 2016), 482–83.

63. Pratham, *Annual Status of Education Report 2018* (January 15, 2019), http://img.asercentre.org/docs/ASER%202018/Release%20Material/enrollmentandlearningenglish.pdf.

64. India Const., art. 45, https://www.mea.gov.in/Images/pdf1/Part4.pdf.

65. Pavan K. Varma, *Being Indian: The Truth about Why the 21ˢᵗ Century Will Be India's* (New York: Penguin, 2005), 114–15.

66. Nancy Hornberger and Viniti Vaish, "Multilingual Language Policy and School Linguistic Practice: Globalization and English-Language Teaching in India, Singapore and South Africa," *Compare* 39, no. 3 (May 2009): 310.

67. Amy Kazmin, "India: Learning a Hard Lesson," *Financial Times*, May 7, 2015, https://www.ft.com/content/96c189a4-ef58-11e4-a6d2-00144feab7de.

68. Open Doors Report on International Educational Exchange, "International Students in the United States, 2019–20," https://opendoorsdata.org/annual-release.

69. Nalini Cook, "India All Set for International Education Expansion," *International Schools Magazine* 2018 (June 6, 2017): https://www.iscresearch.com/uploaded/images/Publicity/IS_magazine_-_India_all_set_for_international_education_expansion_-_2018.pdf.

70. Hemali Chhapia, "Int'l Schools Double, India at Second Spot," *Times of India*, November 18, 2019, https://timesofindia.indiatimes.com/india/intl-schools-double-india-at-second-spot/articleshow/72101112.cms.

71. "Cambridge International in India," Cambridge Assessment International Education, https://www.cambridgeinternational.org/cambridge-international-in-india; "India," the IB by Country, International Baccalaureate, https://www.ibo.org/about-the-ib/the-ib-by-country/i/india.

72. "Different Tongues, Diverse Avenues," *The Hindu*, March 3, 2018, https://www.thehindu.com/todays-paper/tp-in-school/different-tongues-diverse-avenues/article22913972.ece.

73. Sreedeep Bhattacharya, "The Branding of Indian Education," *The Wire*, March 14, 2019, https://thewire.in/education/indian-education-images.

74. Geetha B. Nambissan, "The Indian Middle Classes and Educational Advantage: Family Strategies and Practices," in *The Routledge Handbook of the Sociology of Education*, ed. Michael W. Apple, Stephen J. Ball, and Luis Armando Gandin (New York: Routledge, 2009), 285–95.

75. Ross Baird, *Private Schools for the Poor: Development, Provision, and Choice in India, A Report for Gray Matters Capital* (May 2009), http://dise.in/downloads/use%20of%20dise%20data/ross%20baird.pdf.

76. Dean Nelson, "India's 'Untouchables' to Build Temple to 'Goddess of the English Language,'" *Telegraph*, October 27, 2010, http://www.telegraph.co.uk/news/worldnews/asia/india/8090491/Indias-untouchables-to-build-temple-to-Goddess-of-the-English-language.html.

77. Ramachandra Guha, "The Question of English—Worldwide, English Remains the Choice for Communication," *Telegraph*, November 5, 2011, https://www.telegraphindia.com/opinion/the-question-of-english-worldwide-english-remains-the-choice-for-communication/cid/330254.

78. Maseeh Rahman, "India's Outcasts Put Faith in English," *Guardian*, January 11, 2011, https://www.theguardian.com/education/2011/jan/11/learning-english-india-dalits-rahman.

79. Rita Kothari, "Caste in a Casteless Language? English as a Language of 'Dalit' Expression," *Economic and Political Weekly* 48, no. 39 (September 28, 2013): 65–67.

80. A. Giridhar Rao, "The (Illusory) Promise of English in India," in *Why English? Confronting the Hydra*, ed. Pauline Bunce et al. (Bristol, UK: Multilingual Matters, 2016), 199.

81. "The War on Private Schools," *Economist*, October 13, 2018, https://www.economist.com/asia/2018/10/13/indian-states-are-struggling-to-lift-public-school-attendance.

82. Pratham, *Annual Status of Education Report 2020 Wave 1 (Rural) Findings—India* (October 2020), http://img.asercentre.org/docs/ASER%202020/ASER%202020%20REPORT/nationalfindings.pdf.

83. James Tooley, Pauline Dixon, and S. V. Gomathi, "Private Schools and the Millennium Development Goal of Universal Primary Education: A Census and Comparative Survey in Hyderabad, India," *Oxford Review of Education* 33, no. 5 (2007).

84. Padma M. Sarangapani and Christopher Winch, "Tooley, Dixon and Gomathi on Private Education in Hyderabad: A Reply," *Oxford Review of Education* 36, no. 4 (2010); Geetha B. Nambissan, "Private Schools for the Poor: Business as Usual?," *Economic and Political Weekly* 47, no. 41 (October 2012): 51–58.

85. Sukanya Bose, Priyanta Ghosh, and Arvind Sardana, *Exit at the Bottom of the Pyramid: Empirical Explorations in the Context of Elementary Schooling in Delhi* (New Delhi: National Institute of Public Finance and Policy, May 27, 2020), 7, https://www.nipfp.org.in/media/medialibrary/2020/05/WP_306_2020.pdf.

86. Nupur Garg, "Low Cost Private Education in India: Challenges and Way Forward" (master's thesis, Massachusetts Institute of Technology, 2011), 14, https://dspace.mit.edu/handle/1721.1/65779.

87. Mohanty, *The Multilingual Reality*, 200.

88. Ajit Mohanty, "Multilingualism, Education, English and Development: Whose Development?" in *Multilingualism and Development*, ed. Hywel Coleman (London: British Council, 2017), 273–74.

89. Human Rights Watch, *They Say We're Dirty: Denying an Education to India's Marginalized Children* (April 2009), https://www.hrw.org/sites/default/files/reports/india0414_ForUpload_1.pdf.

90. Right of Children to Free and Compulsory Education Act, 2009, No. 35, Acts of Parliament, 2009 (India), https://indiacode.nic.in/bitstream/123456789/2086/1/200935.pdf; India Const., art. 21A, amended by the Constitution (Eighty-Sixth Amendment) Act, 2002, https://www.india.gov.in/my-government/constitution-india/amendments/constitution-india-eighty-sixth-amendment-act-2002.

91. Rebecca M. Klenk, "Accessing Justice? India's Right to Education Act," in *Accessing and Implementing Human Rights and Justice*, ed. Kurt Mills and Melissa Labonte (New York: Routledge, 2018), 88.

92. *Soc'y for Un-aided Private Schs. of Rajasthan v. Union of India* (2012), 6 SCC 1 (India), 161, https://main.sci.gov.in/judgment/judis/39251.pdf; India Const., arts. 29–30.

93. *Pramati Educ. & Cultural Tr. v. Union of India* (2014), 8 SCC 1 (India), https://main.sci.gov.in/judgment/judis/41505.pdf.

94. Thomas Benedikter, *Minority Languages in India* (Bozen, Italy: March 2013), 80, http://sgindia.org.in/pdf/download/research-analysis001.pdf.

95. Geeta Gandhi Kingdon, "The Private Schooling Phenomenon in India: A Review" (working paper no. 17–06, Department of Quantitative Social Science, Institute of Education, University College of London, London, April 2017), 35, https://www.documentcloud.org/documents/4374730-IndiaPrivateSchools.html.

96. Kanika Verma, Aakriti Kalra, and Cecil Philip John, eds. *The Bright Spots: Status of Social Inclusion through RTE Section 12(1)(c)* (New Delhi: Indus Action, December 2018), 54–57, https://issuu.com/indusaction/docs/indusactionreportissue.

97. Geetha B. Nambissan and Stephen J. Ball, "Advocacy Networks, Choice and Private Schooling of the Poor in India," *Global Networks* 10, no. 3 (August 2010): 326.

98. Geetha B. Nambissan, "Poverty, Markets and Elementary Education in India" (working paper, Transnational Research Group: Poverty and Education in India, German Historical Institute London, 2014), 10–14, https://perspectivia.net/rsc/viewer/ploneimport_derivate_00011899/nambissan_poverty.doc.pdf.

99. Nupur Garg, "Low Cost Private Education in India," 35.

100. Ibid.

101. "Bridge Academies Battles Its Enemies," *Economist*, June 21, 2018, https://www.economist.com/middle-east-and-africa/2018/06/21/bridge-academies-battles-its-enemies.

102. Bridge International Academies, website, "Impact: Kenya," https://www.bridgeinternationalacademies.com/impact.

103. Curtis Riep, *What Do We Really Know about Bridge International Academies?* (Brussels: Education International Research, February 2019), 11, https://issuu.com/educationinternational/docs/2019_ei_research_gr_bia.

104. K. Sujatha, "Private Tuition in India: Trends and Issues," *Revue international d'éducation de Sèvres,* June 2014, 4, https://journals.openedition.org/ries/3913.

105. Manabi Majumdar, "The Shadow School System and New Class Divisions in India," (working paper, Max Weber Foundation, Transnational Research Group: Poverty and Education in India, Centre for Studies in Social Sciences, Calcutta, 2014), 5, https://www.ghil.ac.uk/fileadmin/redaktion/dokumente/trg_india/Paper_2_Manabi_Majumbar.pdf.

106. Shalini Bhorkar and Mark Bray, "The Expansion and Roles of Private Tutoring in India: From Supplementation to Supplantation," *International Journal of Educational Development* 62 (December 2018): 149.

107. Arundhati Roy, "Election Season in a Dangerous Democracy," *New York Review of Books,* September 3, 2018, https://www.nybooks.com/daily/2018/09/03/election-season-in-a-dangerous-democracy.

108. Anjali Mody, "India's Obsession with English Is Depriving Many Children of a Real Education," *Quartz,* September 3, 2015, https://qz.com/india/494396/indias-obsession-for-english-is-depriving-many-children-of-a-real-education.

109. "The War on Private Schools," *Economist,* October 11, 2018, https://www.economist.com/asia/2018/10/11/indian-states-are-struggling-to-lift-public-school-attendance.

110. S. Bageshree, "Language: The Challenge Is in Ensuring Quality Delivery," *The Hindu,* April 29, 2011, http://www.thehindu.com/todays-paper/tp-national/tp-karnataka/Language-the-challenge-is-in-ensuring-quality-delivery/article14903229.ece.

111. *Karnataka v. Associated Mgmt. of English Medium Primary & Secondary Schs.* (2014), 9 SCC 485 (India), https://main.sci.gov.in/judgment/judis/41504.pdf.

112. Meyer v. Nebraska, 262 U.S. 390 (1923), https://supreme.justia.com/cases/federal/us/262/390/#tab-opinion-1930013; Pierce v. Society of Sisters, 268 U.S. 510 (1925), https://supreme.justia.com/cases/federal/us/268/510/#tab-opinion-1930961; Rosemary C. Salomone, *Visions of Schooling: Conscience, Community, and Common Education* (New Haven, CT: Yale University Press, 2000), 78–85.

113. Sonntag, "Linguistic Diversity in India's Polity and Economy," 470.

114. "English Medium Schools Almost Double in 5 Years," *Times of India,* July 7, 2013, https://timesofindia.indiatimes.com/city/bengaluru/English-medium-schools-almost-double-in-5-years/articleshow/20950892.cms.

115. Ralph Alex Arakal, "English Medium Classes Back in Karnataka Government Schools after 25 Years," *Indian Express,* April 20, 2019, https://indianexpress.com/article/cities/bangalore/english-medium-classes-back-in-karnataka-government-schools-after-25-years-kannada-outfit-kumaraswamy-1994-education-5685870.

116. Sharan Poovanna, "Karnataka: English Medium Government Schools Face Criticism at Kannada Literary Meet," *Live Mint,* January 5, 2019, https://www.livemint.com/Politics/9YrAS8wS0UDc6WULAbzvHN/Karnataka-English-medium-government-schools-face-criticism.html.

117. G. Parameshwara, "English Medium in Govt. Schools Is Our Policy Decision: Deputy CM," *The Hindu,* January 8, 2019, https://www.thehindu.com/news/national/karnataka/english-medium-in-govt-schools-is-our-policy-decision-deputy-cm/article25934946.ece.

118. Manash Pratim Gohain, "After Backlash, Education Policy Panel Drops Hindi as Must Language," *Times of India,* June 4, 2019, https://timesofindia.indiatimes.com/india/after-backlash-education-policy-panel-drops-hindi-as-must-language/articleshow/69641151.cms.

119. "Tongue Twisted," *Indian Express,* June 6, 2019, https://indianexpress.com/article/opinion/editorials/national-education-policy-hindi-language-south-india-5763281.

120. Ministry of Human Resource Development, Government of India, *National Education Policy 2020* (2020), 13–15, https://www.education.gov.in/sites/upload_files/mhrd/files/NEP_Final_English_0.pdf.

121. Selma K. Sonntag, "Linguistic Globalization and the Call Center Industry: Imperialism, Hegemony or Cosmopolitanism?" *Language Policy* 8 (2009): 11.

122. Amy Baker, "New ELT Player in India Reports Big Demand," *PIE News*, December 5, 2014, https://thepienews.com/news/new-elt-player-india-reports-big-demand.

123. Sazana Jayadeva, "'Below English Line': An Ethnographic Exploration of Class and the English Language in Post-Liberalization India," *Modern Asian Studies* 52, no. 2 (March 2018): 592, 594.

124. Subramanian, "India After English?"

125. S. Anandhi and M. Vijayabaskar, "Making Sense of Tamil Nadu's Anti-Hindi Protests," *The Wire*, July 11, 2017, https://thewire.in/politics/tamil-nadu-anti-hindi-protests.

126. Garga Chatterjee, "A Bridge Too Far: Why Imposing Hindi on All Threatens More Than Just India's Diversity," *Scroll.in*, April 26, 2017, https://scroll.in/article/835626.

127. "English Edge: Those Who Speak the Language Fluently 'Earn 34% More than Others,'" *Times of India*, January 5, 2014, https://timesofindia.indiatimes.com/india/English-edge-Those-who-speak-the-language-fluently-earn-34-more-than-others/articleshowprint/28414991.cms.

128. Imtiaz Ali, dir., *Jab We Met* (Mumbai: Shemaroo Entertainment, 2007), DVD.

129. Rana D. Parshad et al., "What Is India Speaking: Exploring the 'Hinglish' Invasion," *Physica A: Statistical Mechanics and its Applications* 449 (May 2016): 378.

130. Zareer Masani, "English or Hinglish—Which Will India Choose?," *BBC Magazine*, November 27, 2012, http://www.bbc.com/news/magazine-20500312.

131. Varma, *Being Indian*, 124.

132. E. Annamalai, "India's Economic Restructuring with English: Benefits versus Costs," in *Language Policies in Education: Critical Issues*, ed. James W. Tollefson (New York: Routledge, 2013), 194–95.

133. Education First, *EF English Proficiency Index 2017*, 5, https://www.ef.edu/assetscdn/WIBIwq6RdJvcD9bc8RMd/legacy/___/~/media/centralefcom/epi/downloads/full-reports/v7/ef-epi-2017-english.pdf.

134. Papiya Sengupta, *Language as Identity in Colonial India* (Singapore: Palgrave Pivot, 2018), 113.

Chapter 10

1. Fernanda Santos, "Bilingual Invitation to Arizona Mayor Draws an Angry Reply, in English," *New York Times*, August 13, 2016, https://www.nytimes.com/2016/08/14/us/ken-taylor-arizona-mayor-bilingual-invitation.html.

2. Emma G. Fitzsimmons, "Know English? For New York Cabdrivers, That's No Longer Required," *New York Times*, August 19, 2016, http://www.nytimes.com/2016/08/20/nyregion/new-york-taxi-drivers-english-exam.html.

3. "Arizona Mayor Exposes Language Silliness," *El Paso Times*, August 15, 2016, http://www.elpasotimes.com/story/opinion/editorials/2016/08/16/editorial-arizona-mayor-exposes-language-silliness/88806944.

4. Janell Ross, "What That Cruz-Rubio 'He Doesn't Speak Spanish' Thing Was About," *Washington Post*, February 14, 2016, https://www.washingtonpost.com/news/the-fix/wp/2016/02/14/what-that-cruz-rubio-he-doesnt-speak-spanish-thing-was-about/.

5. Amy Zerba, "Should English Be a Requirement for a Taxi License? Cabbies Tell Us," *New York Times*, August 30, 2016, http://www.nytimes.com/interactive/2016/08/29/nyregion/new-york-taxi-drivers-english-exam.html.

6. Liz Robbins, "Man Threatens Spanish-Speaking Workers: 'My Next Call Will Be to ICE,'" *New York Times*, May 16, 2018, https://www.nytimes.com/2018/05/16/nyregion/man-threatens-spanish-language-video.html.

7. Johnson, "Foreign Languages Ought to Be an Asset for Politicians—Not a Liability," *Economist*, April 27, 2019, https://www.economist.com/books-and-arts/2019/04/27/foreign-languages-ought-to-be-an-asset-for-politicians-not-a-liability.

8. Noah Webster, *Dissertations on the English Language* (Gainesville, FL: Scholars' Facsimiles & Reprints, 1951).

9. Rosemary C. Salomone, *True American: Language, Identity, and the Education of Immigrant Children* (Cambridge, MA: Harvard University Press, 2010), 17.

10. N. C. Dougherty, "Recent Legislation upon Compulsory Education in Illinois and Wisconsin," in *Proceedings of Superintendence of the National Education Association Meeting in Philadelphia, February 24th, 25th, 26th 1891* (New York: J. J. Little, 1891), 20.

11. William J. Olson and Alan Woll, *An Historical Examination of the English Literacy Requirement in the Naturalization of Aliens* (Sterling, VA: One National Indivisible, February 2002), 5–6, http://www.lawandfreedom.com/site/special/English.pdf.

12. "Abolish Hyphen, Roosevelt's Last Words to Public," *Chicago Daily Tribune*, January 7, 1919, 4.

13. Department of the Interior, Bureau of Education, *Proceedings, Americanization Conference* (Washington, DC: US Government Printing Office, 1919), 27–30.

14. *Meyer v. Nebraska*, 262 U.S. 390 (1923), https://supreme.justia.com/cases/federal/us/262/390/#tab-opinion-1930013.

15. Salomone, *True American*, 35–36.

16. "Americans Strongly Favor English as Official Language," *Rasmussen Reports*, March 7, 2019, http://www.rasmussenreports.com/public_content/lifestyle/general_lifestyle/april_2018/americans_strongly_favor_english_as_official_language.

17. Salomone, *True American*, 5–6.

18. Michael Schneider, "With 100 Foreign-Language Series, Netflix Will Take Binge-Watching Global," *Indie Wire*, November 15, 2018, https://www.indiewire.com/2018/11/netflix-international-casa-de-papel-dark-sacred-games-erik-barmack-interview-1202020918.

19. Jill Goldsmith, "Netflix Wants to Make Its Dubbed Foreign Shows Less Dubby," *New York Times*, July 19, 2019, https://www.nytimes.com/2019/07/19/arts/television/netflix-money-heist.html.

20. Sandra E. Garcia, "After 'Parasite,' Are Subtitles Still a One-Inch Barrier for Americans?," *New York Times*, February 12, 2020, https://www.nytimes.com/2020/02/12/movies/movies-subtitles-parasite.html.

21. The President's Commission on Foreign Language and International Studies, *Strength through Wisdom: A Critique of U.S. Capability* (November 1979), 5–10, https://babel.hathitrust.org/cgi/pt?id=mdp.39015005504900.

22. Paul Simon, *The Tongue-Tied American: Confronting the Foreign Language Crisis* (New York: Continuum, 1980), 1–2.

23. Commission on Language Learning, *The State of Languages in the United States: A Statistical Portrait* (Cambridge, MA: American Academy of Arts and Sciences, 2016), 4, 8, https://www.amacad.org/sites/default/files/academy/multimedia/pdfs/publications/researchpapersmonographs/State-of-Languages-in-US.pdf.

24. American Councils for International Education, *The National K–12 Foreign Language Enrollment Survey Report* (June 2017), 7, https://www.americancouncils.org/sites/default/files/FLE-report-June17.pdf.

25. Niall McCarthy, "The Transatlantic Divide in Language Learning," *Forbes*, August 14, 2018, https://www.forbes.com/sites/niallmccarthy/2018/08/14/the-transatlantic-divide-in-language-learning-infographic.

26. American Councils for International Education, *National K–12 Foreign Language Enrollment Survey Report*, 8.

27. Ibid., 7.

28. Ibid., 28.

29. Ibid., 11.

30. Ibid., 21.

31. Ibid., 6.

32. Jennifer Palmer, "World Language Classes Vanish from Many Oklahoma High Schools," *Oklahoma Watch*, December 31, 2017, http://oklahomawatch.org/2017/12/31/world-language-classes-vanish-from-many-oklahoma-high-schools.

33. Scott Jaschik, "Computer Science as (Foreign Language) Admissions Requirement," *Inside Higher Ed*, November 27, 2017, https://www.insidehighered.com/admissions/article/2017/11/27/should-computer-science-fulfill-foreign-language-admissions.

34. Pew Research Center, *The State of American Jobs* (October 6, 2016), https://www.pewresearch.org/social-trends/2016/10/06/the-state-of-american-jobs.

35. *Mapping Internationalization on U.S. Campuses, 2017 Edition* (Washington, DC: American Council on Education, 2017), 5, https://www.acenet.edu/Documents/Mapping-Internationalization-2017.pdf.

36. Natalia Lusin, *The MLA Survey of Postsecondary Entrance and Degree Requirements for Languages Other Than English* (New York: Modern Language Association, 2012), 2, https://www.mla.org/content/download/3316/81618/requirements_survey_200910.pdf; College Transitions Dataverse, "Foreign Language Requirements for College," August 30, 2020, https://www.collegetransitions.com/dataverse/foreign-language-requirements.

37. Asaf Shalev, "Declining Enrollment Leads the Middlebury Institute to Soften Its Language Requirements," *Monterey County Weekly*, June 5, 2019, http://www.montereycountyweekly.com/news/local_news/declining-enrollment-leads-the-middlebury-institute-to-soften-its-language/article_7649b506-87f3-11e9-a4ad-ebc325a34d8a.html.

38. Dennis Looney and Natalia Lusin, *Enrollments in Languages Other Than English in United States Institutions of Higher Education, Summer 2016 and Fall 2016: Final Report* (New York: Modern Language Association, June 2019), 3, https://www.mla.org/content/download/110154/2406932/2016-Enrollments-Final-Report.pdf.

39. Ibid., 31.

40. Ibid., 40.

41. Ibid., 21.

42. Scott Jaschik, "Study Finds Sharp Decline in Foreign Language Enrollments," *Inside Higher Education*, March 7, 2018, https://www.insidehighered.com/news/2018/03/07/study-finds-sharp-decline-foreign-language-enrollments.

43. Steven Johnson, "Colleges Lose 'Stunning' 651 Foreign-Language Programs in 3 Years," *Chronicle of Higher Education*, January 22, 2019, https://www.chronicle.com/article/Colleges-Lose-a-Stunning-/245526.

44. Looney and Lusin, *Enrollments in Languages Other Than English*, 59.

45. Matt Pickles, "K-Pop Drives Boom in Korean Language Lessons," *BBC News*, July 11, 2018, https://www.bbc.co.uk/news/business-44770777.

46. Maxwell Williams, "Korean Wave Makes a Splash Worldwide," *Financial Times*, August 23, 2017, https://www.ft.com/content/06a541aa-8725-11e7-8bb1-5ba57d47eff7.

47. Kang Hyun-kyung, "K-Pop Craze Stirs Fan Migration," *Korea Times*, April 12, 2018, https://www.koreatimes.co.kr/www/art/2018/04/682_247183.html; Joan MacDonald, "How K-Pop and K-Drama Made Learning Korean Cool," *Forbes*, September 1, 2019, https://www.forbes.com/sites/joanmacdonald/2019/09/01/how-k-pop-and-k-drama-made-learning-korean-cool.

48. Joe Coscarelli, "Why Obsessive K-Pop Fans Are Turning toward Political Activism," *New York Times*, June 23, 2020, https://www.nytimes.com/2020/06/22/arts/music/k-pop-fans-trump-politics.html.

49. Cindy Blanco, "2020 Duolingo Language Report: Global Overview," *Duolingo Blog*, December 15, 2020, 15, https://blog.duolingo.com/global-language-report-2020.

50. Looney and Lusin, *Enrollments in Languages Other Than English*, 50.

51. Freddie Cross, *Teacher Shortage Areas: Nationwide Listing, 1990–1991 through 2017–2018* (Washington, DC: US Department of Education, May 2017), https://www2.ed.gov/about/offices/list/ope/pol/teacheshortageareasreport2017.pdf.

52. James B. Conant, *Slums and Suburbs* (New York: McGraw-Hill, 1961), 22.

53. Louise J. Hubbard, "The Minority Student in Foreign Languages," *Modern Language Journal* 64, no. 1 (Spring 1980): 76.

54. Nancy C. Rhodes and Ingrid Pufahl, *Foreign Language Teaching in U.S. Schools: Results of a National Survey* (Washington, DC: Center for Applied Linguistics, November 2009).

55. Rosemary Salomone, "Educating English Learners: Reconciling Bilingualism and Accountability," *Harvard Law and Policy Review* 6, no. 1 (Winter 2012): 129–30.

56. The Education Trust, *Inequities in Advanced Coursework* (January 2020), 5, https://edtrustmain.s3.us-east-2.amazonaws.com/wp-content/uploads/2014/09/08183916/

Inequities-in-Advanced-Coursework-Whats-Driving-Them-and-What-Leaders-Can-Do-January-2019.pdf.

57. College Board, *AP Program Participation and Performance Data 2020: National Report* (College Board, 2020), https://research.collegeboard.org/programs/ap/data/participation/ap-2020.

58. Jürgen Gerhards and Silke Hans, "Transnational Human Capital, Education, and Social Inequality: Analyses of International Student Exchange," *Zeitschrift für Soziologie* 42, no. 2 (April 2013); Pierre Bourdieu and Jean-Claude Passeron, *Reproduction in Education, Society, and Culture* (Beverly Hills, CA: Sage, 1977).

59. National Center for Education Statistics, *Digest of Education Statistics*, Total Fall Enrollment in Degree-Granting Postsecondary Institutions, table 306.10 (2019), https://nces.ed.gov/programs/digest/d19/tables/dt19_306.10.asp; Institute for International Education, *Open Doors*, Profile of U.S. Study Abroad Students (November 2020), https://opendoorsdata.org/data/us-study-abroad/student-profile.

60. Mark H. Salisbury, Paul D. Umbach, Michael B. Paulsen, and Ernest T. Pascarella, "Going Global: Understanding the Choice Process of the Intent to Study Abroad," *Research in Higher Education* 50 (2009): 119–43.

61. "Senator Paul Simon Study Abroad Program Act," NAFSA, http://www.nafsa.org/Policy_and_Advocacy/What_We_Stand_For/Education_Policy/Senator_Paul_Simon_Study_Abroad_Program_Act.

62. Ofelia García, Zeena Zakharia, and Bahar Otcu, *Bilingual Education and Multilingualism: Beyond Heritage Languages in a Global City* (Bristol, UK: Multilingual Matters, 2013).

63. Huaxia Chinese School website, http://www.hxcs.org/Home.aspx.

64. Maria Carreira and Olga Kagan, "Heritage Language Education: A Proposal for the Next 50 Years," *Foreign Language Annals* 51 (2018): 160.

65. US House of Representatives, Committee on Armed Services, *Building Language Skills and Cultural Competencies in the Military: DOD's Challenge in Today's Educational Environment* (November 2008), 5, https://armedservices.house.gov/_cache/files/3/7/3737c7c1-efeb-4672-bc99-74b340faf0ba/540DE3C82A9F532C584E402C683E8439.language-and-culture-report-11-08-vf.pdf.

66. Statement of Daniel Akaka, Chairman, Subcommittee on Oversight of Government Management, the Federal Workforce, and the District of Columbia, in *A National Security Crisis: Foreign Language Capabilities in the Federal Government: Hearing Before the S. Comm. on Homeland Security and Governmental Affairs*, 112th Cong. 1 (2012); *Education for Global Leadership: The Importance of International Studies and Foreign Language Education for U.S. Economic and National Security* (Washington, DC: Committee for Economic Development, 2006), 1–2, https://www.ced.org/pdf/Education-for-Global-Leadership.pdf.

67. "CIA Director Calls for National Commitment to Language Proficiency at Foreign Language Summit," Central Intelligence Agency press release, December 8, 2010, https://www.cia.gov/news-information/press-releases-statements/press-release-2010/foreign-language-summit.html.

68. "Education and the Language Gap: Secretary Arne Duncan's Remarks at the Foreign Language Summit," *US Department of Education*, December 8, 2010, https://www.ed.gov/news/speeches/education-and-language-gap-secretary-arne-duncans-remarks-foreign-language-summit.

69. Rosemary C. Salomone, "The Foreign Language Deficit: A Problem in Search of an Obvious Solution," *Teachers College Record*, January 28, 2011, http://www.tcrecord.org/PrintContent.asp?ContentID=16317.

70. Statista, "Number of College and University Students from the United States Studying in China between 2006/07 and 2017/18," *Education in China—Statistics and Facts*, November 19, 2019, https://www.statista.com/statistics/374169/china-number-of-students-from-the-us.

71. Looney and Lusin, *Enrollments in Languages Other Than English*, 32.

72. American Councils for International Education, *The National K–12 Foreign Language Enrollment Survey Report*, 8.

73. Timothy Reagan, *Linguistic Legitimacy and Social Justice* (Cham, Switzerland: Palgrave Macmillan, 2019), 345.

74. Department of State, *Foreign Language Proficiency Has Improved, but Efforts to Reduce Gaps Need Evaluation* (Washington, DC: US Government Accountability Office, March 2017), https://www.gao.gov/assets/690/683533.pdf.

75. Ryan Scoville, "Troubling Trends in Ambassadorial Appointments: 1980 to Present," *Lawfare*, February 20, 2019, https://www.lawfareblog.com/troubling-trends-ambassadorial-appointments-1980-present.

76. Alexander Traub-Goik, "Lost in Translation: How Language Impacts Diplomacy," *Market Mogul*, July 3, 2018, https://themarketmogul.com/lost-translation-language-diplomacy.

77. Karl McDonald, "The Government's Brexit White Paper Was Translated into German So Badly It Barely Makes Sense in Parts," *Independent*, July 19, 2018, https://inews.co.uk/news/brexit/brexit-white-paper-badly-translated-languages.

78. James Blitz, "May's Brexit Plan Lost in Translation," *Financial Times*, July 20, 2018, https://www.ft.com/content/bc3153b0-8c10-11e8-b18d-0181731a0340.

79. American Councils for International Education, *The National K–12 Foreign Language Enrollment Survey Report*, 11.

80. Looney and Lusin, *Enrollments in Languages Other Than English*, 32.

81. American Councils for International Education, *The National K–12 Foreign Language Enrollment Survey Report*, 11.

82. Rebecca Rubin Damari, William P. Rivers, Richard D. Brecht, Philip Gardner, Catherine Pulupa, and John Robinson, "The Demand for Multilingual Human Capital in the U.S. Labor Market," *Foreign Language Annals* 50, no. 1 (2018): 32.

83. Pamela Druckerman, "Parlez-Vous Anglais? Yes, of Course," *New York Times*, August 10, 2019, https://www.nytimes.com/2019/08/10/opinion/sunday/europeans-speak-english.html.

84. United States Census Bureau, *Language Spoken at Home*, 2019, https://data.census.gov/cedsci/table?q=S1601&tid=ACSST1Y2019.S1601.

85. National Center for Education Statistics, "English Language Learners in Public Schools," *Condition of Education*, May 2020, https://nces.ed.gov/programs/coe/indicator_cgf.asp.

86. Rubén G. Rumbaut, "A Language Graveyard? The Evolution of Language Competencies, Preferences and Use among Young Adult Children of Immigrants," in *The Education of Language Minority Immigrants in the United States*, ed. Terence G. Wiley, Jin Sook Lee, and Russell Rumberger (Clevedon, UK: Multilingual Matters, 2009), 35–71.

87. Pew Research Center, *Topline: 2015 National Survey of Latinos, October 21–November 30, 2015* (2015), http://assets.pewresearch.org/wp-content/uploads/var/www/vhosts/cms.pewresearch.org/htdocs/wp-content/blogs.dir/12/files/2018/04/02163256/PewResearchCenter_040218_NSL_Topline_FINAL-1.pdf.

88. François Grosjean, *Bilingual: Life and Reality* (Cambridge, MA: Harvard University Press, 2010), 107.

Chapter 11

1. Denis Villeneuve, dir., *Arrival* (Hollywood: Paramount Pictures, 2006), DVD.

2. Ted Chiang, "Story of Your Life," in *Stories of Your Life and Others* (New York: Vintage, 2002), 91–145; Jessica Coon, "The Linguistics of *Arrival*: Heptapods, Field Linguistics, and Universal Grammar," in *Language Invention for Linguistics Pedagogy*, ed. Jeffrey Punske, Amy Fountain, and Nathan Sanders (New York: Oxford University Press, 2020).

3. Benjamin Lee Whorf, *Language, Thought, and Reality: Selected Writings of Benjamin Lee Whorf*, ed. John B. Carroll (Cambridge, MA: MIT Press, 1956), 25–30; Chris Swoyer, "The Linguistic Relativity Hypothesis," *Stanford Encyclopedia of Philosophy Archive* (Spring 2015 ed.), https://stanford.library.sydney.edu.au/archives/spr2015/entries/relativism/supplement2.html.

4. Aneta Pavlenko, *The Bilingual Mind and What It Tells Us about Language and Thought* (Cambridge: Cambridge University Press, 2014), 14–16.

5. Ben Panko, "Does the Linguistic Theory at the Center of the Film 'Arrival' have Any Merit?," *Smithsonian Magazine*, December 2, 2016, https://www.smithsonianmag.com/science-nature/does-century-old-linguistic-hypothesis-center-film-arrival-have-any-merit-180961284/; Marissa Martinelli, "How Realistic Is the Way Amy Adams' Character Hacks

the Alien Language in *Arrival*? We Asked a Linguist," *Slate*, November 22, 2016, https://slate.com/culture/2016/11/a-linguist-on-arrival-s-alien-language.html.

6. Guillaume Thierry, "Neurolinguistic Relativity: How Language Flexes Human Perception and Cognition," *Language Learning* 66, no. 3 (September 2016): 690–713.

7. Delaney Michael Skerrett, "Can the Sapir-Whorf Hypothesis Save the Planet? Lessons from Cross-Cultural Psychology for Critical Language Policy," *Current Issues in Language Planning* 11, no. 4 (November 2010): 338–39; Rosemary C. Salomone, *True American: Language, Identity, and the Education of Immigrant Children* (Cambridge, MA: Harvard University Press, 2010), 71.

8. S.S. Laurie, *Lectures on Language and Linguistic Method in School*, 2nd, ed. (London: Simpkin, Marshall & Co., 1893), 18, https://archive.org/details/lecturesonlangua00laurrich/page/n7/mode/2up.

9. Otto Jespersen, *Language, Its Nature, Development, and Origin* (New York: Henry Holt, 1922), 148.

10. Seth Arsenian, *Bilingualism and Mental Development: A Study of the Intelligence and the Social Background of Bilingual Children in New York City* (New York: Teachers College, Columbia University, 1937), 134.

11. Florence L. Goodenough, "Racial Differences in the Intelligence of School Children," *Journal of Experimental Psychology* 9, no. 5 (October 1926): 392–93.

12. Rafael M. Diaz, "Thought and Two Languages: The Impact on Cognitive Development," *Review of Research in Education* 10 (1983): 24–27.

13. Elizabeth Peal and Wallace E. Lambert, "The Relation of Bilingualism to Intelligence," *Psychological Monographs: General and Applied* 76, no. 26 (1962): 1–23.

14. Colin Baker, *Foundations of Bilingual Education and Bilingualism*, 5th ed. (Bristol, UK: Multilingual Matters, 2011), 144–45.

15. Wallace E. Lambert, "The Effects of Bilingualism on the Individual: Cognitive and Sociocultural Consequences," in *Bilingualism: Psychological, Social, and Educational Implications*, ed. Peter A. Hornby (New York: Academic Press, 1977), 15–27, 16.

16. Yudhijit Bhattacharjee, "Why Bilingual Are Smarter," *New York Times*, March 17, 2012, https://www.nytimes.com/2012/03/18/opinion/sunday/the-benefits-of-bilingualism.html; Tobias Jones, "The Joys and Benefits of Bilingualism," *Guardian*, January 20, 2018, https://www.theguardian.com/commentisfree/2018/jan/21/the-joys-and-benefits-of-bilingualism; Gaia Vince, "The Amazing Benefits of Bilingualism," *BBC*, August 12, 2016, https://www.bbc.com/future/article/20160811-the-amazing-benefits-of-being-bilingual.

17. Judith F. Kroll and Paola E. Dussias, "The Benefits of Multilingualism to the Personal and Professional Development of Residents of the US," *Foreign Language Annals* 50, no. 2 (Summer 2017): 249.

18. Baker, *Foundations of Bilingual Education*, 141.

19. Albert Costa, Sayuri Hayakawa, Melina Aperici, Jose Apesteguia, Joy Heafner, and Boaz Keysar, "Your Morals Depend on Language", *PLOS One* 9, no. 4 (April 2014): 1–7.

20. Jean-Marc Dewaele and Li Wei, "Multilingualism, Empathy and Multicompetence," *International Journal of Multilingualism* 9, no. 4 (September 10, 2012): 352–66.

21. Salomone, *True American*, 185–86.

22. Samantha P. Fan, Zoe Liberman, Boaz Keysar, and Katherine D. Kinzler, "The Exposure Advantage: Early Exposure to a Multilingual Environment Promotes Effective Communication," *Psychological Science* 26, no. 7 (May 8, 2015): 1090–97; see also Katherine Kinzler, "The Superior Social Skills of Bilinguals," *New York Times*, March 11, 2016, http://www.nytimes.com/2016/03/13/opinion/sunday/the-superior-social-skills-of-bilinguals.html.

23. Olusola O. Adesope, Tracy Lavin, Terri Thompson, and Charles Ungerleider, "A Systematic Review and Meta-Analysis of the Cognitive Correlates of Bilingualism," *Review of Educational Research* 80, no. 2 (June 2010): 207–45; Maurits van den Noort, Esli Struys, and Peggy Bosch, "Individual Variation and the Bilingual Advantage: Factors that Modulate the Effect of Bilingualism on Cognitive Control and Cognitive Reserve," *Behavioral Sciences* 9, no. 12 (December 2019): 120.

24. Heather McLeay, "The Relationship between Bilingualism and the Performance of Spatial Tasks," *International Journal of Bilingual Education and Bilingualism* 6, no. 6 (2003): 435–43.

25. Anatoliy V. Kharkhurin, "The Effect of Linguistic Proficiency, Age of Second Language Acquisition, and Length of Exposure to a New Cultural Environment on Bilinguals' Divergent Thinking," *Bilingualism: Language and Cognition* 11, no. 2 (July 2008): 238; Anatoliy V. Kharkhurin, "Bilingual Verbal and Nonverbal Creative Behavior," *International Journal of Bilingualism* 14, no. 2 (May 6, 2010): 211–26.

26. Boaz Keysar, Sayuri L. Hayakawa, and Sun Gyu An, "The Foreign-Language Effect: Thinking in a Foreign Tongue Reduces Decision Biases," *Psychological Science* 23, no. 6 (April 18, 2012): 661–68.

27. Sarah Grey, Cristina Sanz, Kara Morgan-Short and Michael T. Ullman, "Bilingual and Monolingual Adults Learning an Additional Language: ERPs Reveal Differences in Syntactic Processing," *Bilingualism: Language and Cognition* 21, no. 5 (November 2018): 970–94.

28. James Bartolotti and Viorica Marian, "Language Learning and Control in Monolinguals and Bilinguals," *Cognitive Science* 36, no. 6 (August 2012): 1129–47.

29. Christos Pliatsikas, Elisavet Moschopoulou, and James Douglas Saddy, "The Effects of Bilingualism on the White Matter Structure of the Brain," *PNAS* 112, no. 5 (February 3, 2015): 1334–37.

30. Ana Maria Gonzalez-Barrero and Aparna S. Nadig, "Can Bilingualism Mitigate Set-Shifting Difficulties in Children with Autism Spectrum Disorders?" *Child Development* 90, no. 3 (November 2017): 1043–60.

31. Ellen Bialystok, "Cognitive Complexity and Attentional Control in the Bilingual Mind," *Child Development* 70, no. 3 (May/June 1999): 636–44.

32. Kyle J. Comishen, Ellen Bialystok, and Scott A. Adler, "The Impact of Bilingual Environments on Selective Attention in Infancy," *Developmental Science* 22, no. 4 (July 2019): https://onlinelibrary.wiley.com/doi/abs/10.1111/desc.12797.

33. Ellen Bialystok, "Consequences of Bilingualism for Cognitive Development," in *Handbook of Bilingualism: Psychololinguistic Approaches*, ed. Judith F. Kroll and Annette M. B. De Groot (Oxford: Oxford University Press, 2005), 428.

34. Pascale M. J. Engel de Abreu, Anabela Cruz-Santos, Carlos J. Tourinho, Romain Martin, and Ellen Bialystok, "Bilingualism Enriches the Poor: Enhanced Cognitive Control in Low-Income Minority Children," *Psychological Science* 23, no. 11 (November 2012): 1364–71.

35. Danielle Thomas-Sunesson, Kenji Hakuta, and Ellen Bialystok, "Degree of Bilingualism Modifies Executive Control in Hispanic Children in the USA," *International Journal of Bilingual Education and Bilingualism* 21, no. 2 (2018): 197–206.

36. Ramesh Kumar Mishra, "Cognitive Advantages of Bilingualism and Its Criticisms," in *Bilingualism and Cognitive Control*, ed. Ramesh Kumar Mishra (New York: Springer International, 2018), 67–89.

37. Tiziana Metitieri, "Bilingualism and Cognitive Advantage: Bialystok versus de Bruin," *PsicoLab*, June 2, 2015, http://neuropsicolab.blogspot.com/2015/06/bilingualism-and-cognitive-advantage.html.

38. Kenneth R. Paap, Hunter A. Johnson, and Oliver Sawi, "Bilingual Advantages in Executive Functioning Either Do Not Exist or Are Restricted to Very Specific and Undetermined Circumstances," *Cortex* 69 (August 2015): 265–68; Kenneth R. Paap and Zachary I. Greenberg, "There Is No Coherent Evidence for a Bilingual Advantage in Executive Processing," *Cognitive Psychology* 66, no. 2 (March 2013): 232–58; Raymond M. Klein, "On the Belief That the Cognitive Exercise Associated with the Acquisition of a Second Language Enhances Extra-Linguistic Cognitive Functions: Is 'Type-I Incompetence' at Work Here?" *Cortex* 73 (December 2015): 340–41; Angela de Bruin, Barbara Treccani, and Sergio Della Sala, "Cognitive Advantage in Bilingualism: An Example of Publication Bias?" *Psychological Science* 26, no. 1 (December 4, 2014): 99–107.

39. Ellen Bialystok, "The Bilingual Adaptation: How Minds Accommodate Experience," *Psychological Bulletin* 143, no. 3 (March 2017): 253.

40. Thomas H. Bak, Jack J. Nissan, Michael M. Allerhand, and Ian J. Deary, "Does Bilingualism Influence Cognitive Aging?" *Annals of Neurology* 75, no. 6 (June 2, 2014): 962.

41. Guillermo Albán-González and Teresa Ortega-Campoverde, "Relationship between Bilingualism and Alzheimer's," *Suma de Negocios* 5, no. 11 (December 2014): 126–33.
42. Thomas H. Bak, "Beyond a Simple 'Yes' or 'No,'" *Cortex*, 73 (August 15, 2015): 332–33.
43. Ellen Bialystok, *Bilingualism in Development: Language, Literacy, and Cognition* (Cambridge: Cambridge University Press, 2001), 248.
44. Bialystok, "The Bilingual Adaptation," 253.
45. Ellen Bialystok and Raluca Barac, "Cognitive Effects," in *The Psycholinguistics of Bilingualism*, ed. François Grosjean and Ping Li (Malden, MA: Wiley-Blackwell, 2013), 205.
46. Ed Yong, "The Bitter Fight Over the Benefits of Bilingualism," *Atlantic*, February 10, 2016, http://www.theatlantic.com/science/archive/2016/02/the-battle-over-bilingualism/462114.
47. Matthias Berkes, Ellen Bialystok, Fergus I. M. Craik, Angela Troyer, and Morris Freedman, "Conversion of Mild Cognitive Impairment to Alzheimer Disease in Monolingual and Bilingual Patients," *Alzheimer Disease and Associated Disorders* 34 (2020): 225–30, https://journals.lww.com/alzheimerjournal/Abstract/2020/07000/Conversion_of_Mild_Cognitive_Impairment_to.6.aspx.
48. Bialystok and Barac, "Cognitive Effects," 209–10.
49. Vincent DeLuca, Jason Rothman, Ellen Bialystok, and Christos Pliatsikas, "Redefining Bilingualism as a Spectrum of Experiences That Differentially Affects Brain Structure and Function," *PNAS* 116, no. 5 (April 9, 2019): 7571–73.
50. See Peter Bright and Roberto Filippi, "Editorial: Perspectives on the 'Bilingual Advantage': Challenges and Opportunities," *Frontiers in Psychology* 10 (June 6, 2009), https://www.frontiersin.org/articles/10.3389/fpsyg.2019.01346/full.
51. Rebecca Fox, Olga Corretjer, Kelley Webb, and Jie Tian, "Benefits of Foreign Language Learning and Bilingualism: An Analysis of Published Empirical Research 2005–2011," *Foreign Language Annals* 52, no. 3 (Fall 2019): 470–90; Rebecca Fox, Olga Corretjer, and Kelley Webb, "Benefits of Foreign Language Learning and Bilingualism: An Analysis of Published Empirical Research 2012–2019," *Foreign Language Annals* 52, no. 4 (Winter 2019): 699–726.
52. Aneta Pavlenko, "Whorf's Lost Argument: Multilingual Awareness," *Language Learning* 66, no. 3 (September 2016): 599.
53. Robert Slater, email to author, February 24, 2021.
54. Corey Mitchell, "Nearly Half of U.S. States Offer Special Recognition for Bilingual Graduates," *Education Week, Learning the Language Blog*, September 28, 2016, http://blogs.edweek.org/edweek/learning-the-language/2016/09/nearly_half_of_us_states_recog.html.
55. US Department of Health and Human Services and US Department of Education, "Policy Statement on Supporting the Development of Children Who are Dual Language Learners in Early Childhood Programs" (ERIC: Institute of Education Services, June 2, 2016), https://files.eric.ed.gov/fulltext/ED566723.pdf.
56. Ibid., 1.
57. Mike Gonzalez, *New White House Policy Promotes Ethnic Separation–Congress Should Reject It*, Issue Brief no. 4572 (Heritage Foundation, June 8, 2016), https://www.heritage.org/education/report/new-white-house-policy-promotes-ethnic-separation-congress-should-reject-it.
58. William P. Rivers and Richard D. Brecht, "America's Languages: The Future of Language Advocacy," *Foreign Language Annals* 51, no. 1 (Spring 2018): 26.
59. American Academy of Arts and Sciences, "American Academy of Arts & Sciences to Conduct First National Study on Foreign Language Learning in More Than 30 Years," press release, July 30, 2015, https://www.amacad.org/news/american-academy-arts-sciences-conduct-first-national-study-foreign-language-learning-more-30.
60. Tammy Baldwin (D-Wisconsin), Orin G. Hatch (R-Utah), Mark Kirk (R-Illinois), and Brian Schatz (D-Hawaii), Senators; and Rush Holt (D-New Jersey), Leonard Lance (R-New Jersey), David E. Price (D-North Carolina), and Don Young (R-Alaska), members of Congress, letters to Dr. Don M. Randel, Chair of the Board, Academy of Arts and Sciences and Dr. Jonathan F. Fanton, President, Academy of Arts and Sciences, November 20, 2014, https://www.amacad.org/content/Research/researchproject.aspx?i=21896.

61. Leon Panetta, "Americans Are Losing Out Because So Few Speak a Second Language," *San Francisco Chronicle*, August 6, 2018, https://www.sfchronicle.com/opinion/openforum/article/Americans-are-losing-out-because-so-few-speak-a-13135901.php.

62. Commission on Language Learning, *America's Languages: Investing in Language Education for the 21st Century* (Cambridge, MA: American Academy of Arts and Sciences, 2017), https://www.amacad.org/sites/default/files/publication/downloads/Commission-on-Language-Learning_Americas-Languages.pdf.

63. National Academies of Sciences, Engineering, and Medicine, *Promoting the Educational Success of Children and Youth Learning English: Promising Futures*, ed. Ruby Takanishi and Suzanne Le Menestrel (Washington, DC: National Academies Press, 2017), 2.

64. *The National K–12 Foreign Language Enrollment Report* (Washington, DC: American Councils for International Education, June 2017), https://www.americancouncils.org/sites/default/files/FLE-report-June17.pdf.

65. "Not Lost in Translation: The Growing Importance of Foreign Language Skills in the U.S. Job Market" (New American Economy Research Fund, March 1, 2017), https://research.newamericaneconomy.org/report/not-lost-in-translation-the-growing-importance-of-foreign-language-skills-in-the-u-s-job-market.

66. "The Link between Foreign Language and U.S. National Security," (transcript of meeting, Council of Foreign Relations, June 14, 2017), https://www.cfr.org/event/link-between-foreign-languages-and-us-national-security.

67. Teri West, "Experts, Educators Say Benefits of Bilingualism Are Brushed Aside in U.S. Schools," *Washington Diplomat*, September 29, 2017, https://washdiplomat.com/experts-educators-say-benefits-of-bilingualism-are-brushed-aside-in-us-schools/.

68. Lead with Languages website, http://www.leadwithlanguages.org.

69. John Tessitore, "Bridging America's Language Gap: A Call to Action" (American Academy of Arts and Sciences, November 12, 2019), https://www.amacad.org/news/bridging-americas-language-gap-call-action.

70. America's Languages Working Group, "Language Education in the Time of COVID-19," https://www.change.org/p/language-educators-language-education-in-the-time-of-covid-19.

71. American Academy of Arts and Sciences et al., *The Importance of Languages in Global Context: An International Call to Action* (report, 2020), https://www.amacad.org/sites/default/files/media/document/2020-11/Joint-Statement-on-Languages.pdf.

72. Commission on the Humanities and Social Sciences, *The Heart of the Matter: The Humanities and Social Sciences for a Vibrant, Competitive, and Secure Nation* (Cambridge, MA: American Academy of Arts and Sciences, 2013), http://www.humanitiescommission.org/_pdf/hss_report.pdf.

73. Corey Mitchell, "Is Congress Lagging in Nationwide Push for Language Learning?" *Learning the Language* (*Education Week* blog), July 26, 2019, http://blogs.edweek.org/edweek/learning-the-language/2019/07/is_language_learning_a_national_priority.html.

74. World Language Advancement and Readiness Act of 2019, H.R. 1094, 116th Cong. (2019), https://www.govtrack.us/congress/bills/116/hr1094.

75. "America's Languages Caucus is Born," *Language Magazine*, December 2, 2019, 9, https://www.languagemagazine.com/2019/12/02/americas-languages-caucus-is-born/.

76. Senator Paul Simon Study Abroad Program Act of 2019, S. 1198, 116th Cong. (2019), https://www.govtrack.us/congress/bills/116/s1198.

77. World Language Advancement and Readiness Act of 2019, H.R. 1094, 116th Cong. (2019).

78. *Preparing Our Youth for an Inclusive and Sustainable World: The OECD PISA Global Competence Framework* (Paris: OECD, 2018), 12–13, https://www.oecd.org/pisa/aboutpisa/Global-competency-for-an-inclusive-world.pdf.

79. Amy J. Heineke and Kristin J. Davin, "Prioritizing Multilingualism in U.S. Schools: States' Policy Journeys to Enact the Seal of Biliteracy," *Educational Policy* 34, no. 4 (September 27, 2018), https://doi.org/10.1177/0895904818802099.

80. Salomone, *True American*, 152–56.

81. TESOL International Association, "Guidelines for Implementing the Seal of Biliteracy" (March 10, 2015), http://www.tesol.org/docs/default-source/advocacy/seal-of-biliteracy-approved-guidelines---final-3-10-2015.pdf.

82. Ashley Aguirre, "The California Seal of Biliteracy: Summary for the 2019–20 School Year" (Californians Together, July 6, 2021), https://www.californianstogether.org/the-california-state-seal-of-biliteracy-summary-for-the-2019-20-school-year.

83. Diana A. Porras, Jongyeon Ee, and Patricia Gándara, "Do Bilingual Applicants and Employees Experience an Advantage?" in *The Bilingual Advantage: Language, Literacy and the U.S. Labor Market*, ed. Rebecca M. Callahan and Patricia C. Gándara (Bristol, UK: Multilingual Matters, 2014), 250.

84. CertiLingua website, https://www.certilingua.net.

85. Kristin J. Davin and Amy J. Heineke, "The Seal of Biliteracy: Variations in Policy and Outcomes," *Foreign Language Annals* 50, no. 3 (Fall 2017): 486–99.

86. Maria C. Schwedhelm and Kendall A. King, "The Neoliberal Logic of State Seals of Biliteracy," *Foreign Language Annals* 53, no. 1 (Spring 2020): 20.

87. Amy J. Heineke, Kristin J. Davin, and Amy Bedford, "The Seal of Biliteracy: Considering Equity and Access for English Learners," *Education Policy Analysis Archives* 26, no. 99, (August 2018): 5–6.

88. Candace R. Black, "The New York State Seal of Biliteracy: 2018–2019 Report" (New York State Department of Education, Office of Bilingual Education and World Languages, February 4, 2020), 18, http://www.nysed.gov/common/nysed/files/programs/world-languages/nyssb-annual-report-2018-19.pdf.

89. Nicholas Close Subtirelu, Margaret Borowczyk, Rachel Thorson Hernández, and Francesca Venezia, "Recognizing Whose Bilingualism? A Critical Policy Analysis of the Seal of Biliteracy," *Modern Language Journal* 103, no. 2 (Summer 2019): 371–90; Schwedhelm and King, "Neoliberal Logic," 19–20; Verónica E. Valdez, Juan A. Freire, and M. Garrett Delavan, "The Gentrification of Dual Language Education," *Urban Review* 48, no. 4 (November 2016): 601–27.

90. American Council of Teachers of Foreign Languages et al., *2020 Guidelines for Implementing the Seal of Biliteracy* (report, 2020), https://sealofbiliteracy.org/doc/sobl-updated-guidelines-final-october-2020.pdf.

Chapter 12

1. Elizabeth Weise, "The State of Mandarin Immersion in the United States: June 2019" (blogpost), Mandarin Immersion Parents Council, June 16, 2019, https://miparentscouncil.org/2019/06/16/the-state-of-mandarin-immersion-in-the-united-states-june-2019.

2. Elizabeth R. Howard et al., *Guiding Principles for Dual Language Education*, 3rd ed. (Washington, DC: Center for Applied Linguistics, 2017), 10–11.

3. "French Immersion in Louisiana," Office of Cultural Development: CODOFIL—Agence des Affaires Francophone, Louisiana Department of Culture, Recreation and Tourism, https://crt.state.la.us/cultural-development/codofil/programs/french-immersion/index.

4. "Delaware Immersion Program," Delaware Department of Education website, https://www.joindelawareschools.org/delaware-immersion-program.

5. Ariel G. Ruiz Soto, Sarah Hooker, and Jeanna Batalova, "Top Languages Spoken by English Language Learners Nationally and by State," Migration Policy Institute, Fact Sheet Series no. 4 (June 2015), http://www.migrationpolicy.org/research/top-languages-spoken-english-language-learners-nationally-and-state.

6. Corey Mitchell, "Critics Protest Opening of Houston Immersion Elementary School," *Learning the Language* (*Education Week* blog), August 24, 2015, http://blogs.edweek.org/edweek/learning-the-language/2015/08/critics_protest_opening_of_hou.html.

7. Dylan Baddour and Ericka Mellon, "Protesters at Houston's Arabic Immersion Magnet School on First Day of Class," *Houston Chronicle*, August 24, 2015, http://www.chron.com/news/education/article/Protesters-at-Houston-s-Arabic-Immersion-Magnet-6461817.php.

8. Corey Mitchell, "Dual-Language: How Schools Can Invest in Cultural and Linguistic Diversity," *Learning the Language* (*Education Week* blog), September 19, 2018, http://blogs.edweek.org/edweek/learning-the-language.

9. Verónica E. Valdez, Juan A. Freire, and M. Garrett Delavan, "The Gentrification of Dual Language Education," *Urban Review* 48 (2016): 620–21.

10. Nelson Flores and Ofelia García, "A Critical Review of Bilingual Education in the United States: From Basements and Pride to Boutiques and Profit," *Annual Review of Applied Linguistics*, 37 (2017): 26.

11. Nelson Flores, Amelia Tseng, and Nicholas Subtirelu, "Bilingualism for All or Just for the Rich and White? Introducing a Raciolinguistic Perspective to Dual Language Education," in *Bilingualism for All?: Raciolinguistic Perspectives on Dual Language Education in the United States*, ed. Nelson Flores, Amelia Tseng, and Nicholas Subtirelu (Bristol, UK: Multilingual Matters, 2021), 6.

12. Thomas Ricento, "Problems with the 'Language-as-Resource' Discourse in the Promotion of Heritage Languages in the U.S.A.," *Journal of Sociolinguistics*, 9, no. 3 (2005): 15.

13. "Oyster-Adams Bilingual School: Enrollment by Race/Ethnicity," *D.C. School Report Card*, https://www.dcschoolreportcard.org/schools/1-0292.

14. Sean F. Reardon, Ilana Umansky, Rachel Valentino, Ritu Khanna, and Christina Wong, "Differences among Instructional Models in English Learners' Academic and English Proficiency Trajectories: Findings from the SFUSD/Stanford Research Partnership," Policy Analysis for California Education (PACE), February 18, 2014, http://www.edpolicyinca.org/sites/default/files/PACE%20slides%20feb2014.pdf.

15. Virginia P. Collier and Wayne P. Thomas, "Validating the Power of Bilingual Schooling: Thirty-Two Years of Large-Scale, Longitudinal Research," *Annual Review of Applied Linguistics* 37 (September 2017): 213.

16. Ibid., 207.

17. Jennifer L. Steele, Robert O. Slater, Gema Zamarro, Trey Miller, Jennifer Li, Susan Burkhauser, and Michael Bacon, "Effect of Dual-Language Immersion Programs on Student Achievement: Evidence from Lottery Data," *American Educational Research Journal* 54, no. 1 (April 11, 2017): 302S–304S.

18. Shelly Spiegel-Coleman, telephone interview with author, August 17, 2017.

19. Corey Mitchell, "Bilingual Education Poised for a Comeback in Schools," *Education Week* 36, no. 8 (October 12, 2016): 1–20.

20. Jazmine Ulloa, "'Yes on Prop 58' Radio Ads Tout Importance of Speaking More Than One Language," *Baltimore Sun*, October 9, 2016, https://www.baltimoresun.com/la-pol-sac-essential-politics-updates-yes-on-prop-58-radio-ad-touts-1475792699-htmlstory.html.

21. Jazmine Ulloa, "Bilingual Education Has Been Absent from California Public Schools for Almost 20 Years. But That May Soon Change," *Los Angeles Times*, October 12, 2016, https://www.latimes.com/politics/la-pol-ca-proposition-58-bilingual-education-20161012-snap-story.html.

22. "CalChamber Takes Position on Proposition 58; Recaps Positions on All Ballot Measures" (CalChamber Advocacy, California Chamber of Commerce, September 15, 2016), http://advocacy.calchamber.com/2016/09/15/calchamber-takes-position-on-proposition-58-recaps-positions-on-all-ballot-measures-2/#.V9q29FMleY8.twitter.

23. Mitchell, "Bilingual Education Poised for a Comeback."

24. Héctor Tobar, "The Spanish Lesson I Never Got at School," *New York Times*, November 15, 2016, http://www.nytimes.com/2016/11/15/opinion/the-spanish-lesson-i-never-got-at-school.html.

25. Senate Bill No. 1174 (Chapter 753) (2014), https://leginfo.legislature.ca.gov/faces/billNavClient.xhtml?bill_id=201320140SB1174; Noah Katznelson and Katie A. Bernstein, "Rebranding Bilingualism: The Shifting Discourses of Language Education Policy in California's 2016 Election," *Linguistics and Education* 40 (August 2017): 11–26.

26. Shelly Spiegel-Coleman, telephone interview with author, August 17, 2017.

27. Californians Together: Championing the Success of English Learners website, https://www.californianstogether.org.

28. Van Ou, "California State Board of Education Adopts an English Learner Roadmap—Historical Day: From English Only to Bilingualism and Biliteracy" (Californians Together, July 13, 2017), https://www.californianstogether.org/1802-2.

29. California Department of Education, "Global California 2030" (2019), https://www.cde.ca.gov/sp/el/er/documents/globalca2030.pdf; Shelly Spiegel-Coleman, email to author, June 13, 2018.

30. California Department of Education, "State Superintendent Torlakson Launches 'Global California 2030,'" news release no. 18–42, May 30, 3018, https://www.cde.ca.gov/nr/ne/yr18/yr18rel42.asp.

31. James Vaznis, "New Law Clears Way for Bilingual Teaching in Mass. Public Schools," *Boston Globe*, November 22, 2017, https://www.bostonglobe.com/metro/2017/11/22/baker-signs-bilingual-education-bill/XtYnsI3vW7ZQEXBpUxN0VN/story.html.

32. Brigham Young University, Center for Language Studies website, http://cls.byu.edu.

33. Utah State Office of Education, "Utah's Portuguese Dual Language Immersion Program," http://www.utahportuguesedli.org/wp-content/uploads/2019/03/portuguese-immersion-brochure-08-16.pdf.

34. Nina Porzucki, "Utah Bets Big on Foreign Language Learning, But Not Everyone Is on Board," *World from PRX*, May 18, 2015, https://www.pri.org/stories/2015-03-18/utah-bets-big-foreign-language-learning-not-everyone-board.

35. Gaétan Mathieu, "Aux États-Unis, l'avenir de la langue française passe par le bilinguisme" [In the United States, the future of the French language depends on bilingualism], *France-Amérique*, November 6, 2014, https://france-amerique.com/aux-etats-unis-lavenir-de-la-langue-francaise-passe-par-le-bilinguisme/.

36. Jamie Leite and Raquel Cook, "Utah: Making Immersion Mainstream," in *Building Bilingual Education Systems: Forces, Mechanisms and Counterweights*, ed. Peeter Mehisto and Fred Genesee (Cambridge: Cambridge University Press, 2015), 86.

37. Susan Eaton, "Utah's Bilingual Boon," *One Nation Indivisible*, March 2014, http://www.onenationindivisible.org/wp-content/uploads/2014/03/ONIstoryNo.13UtahV3.pdf; Samara Freemark and Stephen Smith, "This Is Your Brain on Language," *American Radio Works*, August 18, 2014, http://www.americanradioworks.org/segments/this-is-your-brain-on-language.

38. Leite and Cook, "Utah: Making Immersion Mainstream," 86.

39. Utah Dual Language Immersion, "Why Immersion?" http://utahdli.org/whyimmersion.html.

40. Gregg Roberts, email to author, February 12, 2021.

41. "What to Look for When Hiring DLI Teachers" (DLI Advisory Council, Utah Dual Language Immersion, Utah State Office of Education, March 23, 2015), http://utahdli.org/images/March%2023%202015%20DLI%20Advisory.pdf.

42. "Delegation from Confucius Institute at University of Utah Visits Members of Congress in Washington, D.C.," *Hanban News*, May 15, 2018, http://english.hanban.org/article/2018-05/15/content_731490.htm.

43. "Utah Parliament Confers Letter of Commendation to Confucius Institutes," *Hanban News*, May 31, 2018, http://english.hanban.org/article/2018-05/31/content_734344.htm.

44. "U.S. State of Utah Aims to Better Connect with China via Language," *China.org.cn*, May 14, 2019, http://www.china.org.cn/arts/2019-05/14/content_74781574.htm.

45. Gregg Roberts, email to author, February 12, 2021.

46. Gregg Roberts, email to author, February 13, 2021.

47. Alan Hall, "Why Utah is Forbes Best State for Business (and 10 Tips to Help You Gain These Advantages Too)," *Forbes*, January 5, 2013, http://www.forbes.com/sites/alanhall/2013/01/05/why-utah-is-forbes-best-state-for-business-and-10-tips-to-help-you-gain-these-advantages-too/#46488dd93786.

48. Elizabeth A. Harris, "Dual-Language Programs Are on the Rise, Even for Native English Speakers," *New York Times*, October 8, 2015, http://www.nytimes.com/2015/10/09/nyregion/dual-language-programs-are-on-the-rise-even-for-native-english-speakers.html.

49. "The French Quarter of New York," *Scribner's Monthly*, November 1879, 1.

50. *State of Our Immigrant City: Mayor's Office of Immigrant Affairs (MOIA) Annual Report for Calendar Year 2019* (New York, New York: Mayor's Office of Immigrant Affairs, April 2020), 18, https://www1.nyc.gov/assets/immigrants/downloads/pdf/MOIA-Annual-Report-for-2019.pdf.

51. *Rapport du Gouvernement sur la Situation des Français Établis Hors de France: 2019* [Government report on the situation of French people living outside of France: 2019] (Paris: Ministère de l'Europe et des Affaires étrangères, 2019), 10, https://www.diplomatie.gouv.fr/fr/services-aux-francais/voter-a-l-etranger/quelle-representation-

politique-pour-les-francais-residant-a-l-etranger/actualites/article/rapport-du-gouvernement-sur-la-situation-des-francais-etablis-hors-de-france.

52. Agence pour l'enseignement français à l'étranger (AEFE) [Agency for French education abroad] website, https://www.aefe.fr.

53. Jane Flatau Ross, *Two Centuries of French Education in New York* (New York: TBR, 2020), 159.

54. "New York City and France Partner to Fuel International Tech Expansions, Job Creation" (press release, New York City Economic Development Corporation, April 20, 2018), https://nycedc.com.

55. New York in French website, https://newyorkinfrench.net.

56. Fabrice Jaumont, email to author, February 13, 2021.

57. Fabrice Jaumont, "L'essor des filières bilingues à New York: L'histoire de Giselle McGee" [The rise of bilingual programs in New York: The story of Giselle McGee], *France-Amérique*, September 20, 2018, https://france-amerique.com/en/the-boom-in-dual-language-classes-in-new-york-1-3-the-story-of-giselle-mcgee.

58. "Destination Francophonie #115—Brooklyn," DailyMotion, uploaded by *TV5Monde*, June 13, 2015, https://www.dailymotion.com/video/x2u0thr.

59. *France & the United States: 2018 Economic Report* (Washington, DC: Embassy of France in the United States, Economic Department, 2018), 8, https://frenchtreasuryintheus.org/wp-content/uploads/2018/08/2018_France-US_economic_report.pdf.

60. Jérôme Brisson, "New York, laboratoire du français" [New York, laboratory of French], *France-Amérique*, September 16, 2010, https://france-amerique.com/new-york-laboratoire-du-francais.

61. Olivia Ramsey, telephone interview with author, December 12, 2019.

62. Fabrice Jaumont, *The Bilingual Revolution: The Future of Education is in Two Languages* (New York: TBR, 2017).

63. French Morning Staff, "According to Fabrice Jaumont, 'The Future of Education Is Bilingual,'" *Frenchly.us*, September 1, 2017, https://frenchly.us/according-fabrice-jaumont-future-education-bilingual.

64. Alexis Buisson, "Les programmes bilingues à la recherche de leur Bill Gates" [Bilingual programs seeking their Bill Gates], *French Morning*, March 21, 2016, http://frenchmorning.com/progrmmes-bilingues-a-recherche-de-bill-gates.

65. Décret n°2012-40 du 12 janvier 2012 portant creation du label «LabelFrancEducation» [Decree n°2012-40 of January 12, 2012 regarding the creation of the label "LabelFrancEducation"], Journal Officiel de la République Française, January 14, 2012, p. 706, https://www.legifrance.gouv.fr/affichTexte.do?cidTexte=JORFTEXT000025145183&dateTexte=&categorieLien=id.

66. Ministère des Affaires Étrangères et Europeennes, "The FrancEducation Label, A Linguistic and Diplomatic Asset," *Actualité en France* 16 (April 2012), https://cm.ambafrance.org/The-FrancEducation-Label-a.

67. "LabelFrancÉducation: A Seal of Quality for Bilingual Education in French and Another Language," LabelFrancÉducation, https://www.labelfranceducation.fr/en.

68. *Guide de l'Éducation Bilingue: Grandir et vivre en plusieurs langues* [Bilingual education guide: Growing up and living in multiple languages] (New York: French Morning Editions, 2014).

69. Emmanuel Saint-Martine, telephone interview with author, October 27, 2016.

70. "Internationals Network: Transforming Education for Multilingual Learners," Internationals Network for Public Schools website, http://internationalsnps.org.

71. "French Heritage Language Program," GovServ, https://www.govserv.org/US/New-York/117834618325858/French-Heritage-Language-Program.

72. Fabrice Jaumont, Benoît Le Dévédec, and Jane F. Ross, "Institutionalization of French Heritage Language Education in U.S. School Systems," in *The Routledge Handbook of Heritage Language Education: From Innovation to Program Building*, ed. Olga E. Kagan, Maria M. Carreira, and Claire Hitchins Chik (New York: Routledge, 2017), 245–46.

73. "French Dual Language in the United States," FrenchDLI.org website, https://sites.google.com/face-foundation.org/frenchdli.

74. Cultural Services of the French Embassy, *French Dual Language and Immersion Programs in the U.S.: 2017 Trends and Supports* (2017), 11, https://frenchlanguagek12.org/4669-french-dual-language-and-immersion-programs-us.

75. French Morning Staff, "Emmanuel Macron Tells French People in NY to 'Come Back,'" *Frenchly*, September 20, 2017, https://frenchly.us/emmanuel-macron-tells-french-people-ny-come-back.

76. Alexis Buisson, "Fonds bilingue: 58 programmes et écoles bilingues se partagent 150.000 dollars," *French Morning*, January 23, 2018, https://frenchmorning.com/fonds-bilingue-58-programmes-ecoles-bilingues-se-partagent-150-000-dollars.

Chapter 13

1. Nikhil Sonnad and Richard Macauley, "Mark Zuckerberg's 20-Minute Speech in Clumsy Mandarin Is His Latest Attempt to Woo China," *Quartz*, October 26, 2015, https://qz.com/532834/mark-zuckerbergs-20-minute-speech-in-clumsy-mandarin-is-his-latest-attempt-to-woo-china.

2. KiniTV, "Mark Zuckerberg speaks fluent Mandarin during Q&A in Beijing," YouTube video, October 23, 2014, https://www.youtube.com/watch?v=HTmHtOSqHTk.

3. Michael LaForgia and Gabriel J. X. Dance, "Facebook Gave Data to Chinese Firm Flagged by U.S. Intelligence," *New York Times*, June 5, 2018, https://www.nytimes.com/2018/06/05/technology/facebook-device-partnerships-china.html; Paul Mozur and Lin Qiqing, "How Facebook's Tiny China Sales Floor Helps Generate Big Ad Money," *New York Times*, February 7, 2019, https://www.nytimes.com/2019/02/07/technology/facebook-china-internet.html.

4. Vindu Goel, Austin Ramzy, and Paul Mozur, "Mark Zuckerberg, Speaking Mandarin, Tries to Win Over China for Facebook," *Bits Blog* (*New York Times* blog), October 23, 2014, https://bits.blogs.nytimes.com/2014/10/23/zuckerberg-speaking-chinese-shows-up-at-beijing-forum/.

5. Benny Lewis, *Fluent in 3 Months: How Anyone at Any Age Can Learn to Speak Any Language from Anywhere in the World* (New York: HarperOne, 2014).

6. Cheryl Conner, "How Learning an Additional Language Could Influence Your Business," *Forbes*, April 17, 2014, https://www.forbes.com/sites/cherylsnappconner/2014/04/17/how-learning-an-additional-language-could-influence-your-business.

7. Monica Heller, "The Commodification of Language," *Annual Review of Anthropology* 39 (2010): 102–3.

8. François Vaillancourt, "Language and Socioeconomic Status in Quebec: Measurement, Findings, Determinants, and Policy Costs," *International Journal of the Sociology of Language* 121, no. 1 (1996): 81.

9. Jacob Marschak, "The Economics of Language," *Behavioral Science* 10, no. 2 (1965): 136.

10. François Vaillancourt, *"Difference in Earnings by Language Groups in Quebec, 1970: An Economic Analysis"* (PhD thesis, Laval University, 1980), 20, https://files.eric.ed.gov/fulltext/ED196262.pdf.

11. François Grin, "Economic Considerations in Language Policy," in *An Introduction to Language Policy: Theory and Method*, ed. Thomas Ricento (Malden, MA: Blackwell, 2006), 77–94.

12. François Grin, "The Economic Approach to Minority Languages," *Journal of Multilingual and Multicultural Development* 11, nos. 1–2 (1990): 155

13. Pierre Bourdieu, *Language and Symbolic Power*, trans. Gino Raymond and Matthew Adamson (Cambridge: Polity, 1991), 18.

14. Heller, "The Commodification of Language," 106–7.

15. François Grin, "English as Economic Value: Facts and Fallacies," *World Englishes* 20, no. 1 (2001): 67.

16. François Grin, Claudio Sfreddo, and François Vaillancourt, *The Economics of the Multilingual Workplace* (New York: Routledge, 2010), 123–34.

17. Ibid., 49.

18. François Grin, "Economic Considerations in Language Policy," in *An Introduction to Language Policy: Theory and Method* (Oxford: Blackwell, 2006), 89.

19. A. T. Kearney, *2016 Global Services Location Index: On the Eve of Disruption* (January 2016), https://www.kearney.com/digital/article?/a/2016-global-services-location-index-

20. Education First, *English Proficiency Index 2020* (Ranking Report of 100 Countries and Regions by English Skills, Signum International AG, 2020), 7 https://www.ef.com/assetscdn/WIBIwq6RdJvcD9bc8RMd/legacy/___/~/media/centralefcom/epi/downloads/full-reports/v10/ef-epi-2020-english.pdf.

21. Don Lee, "The Philippines Has Become the Call-Center Capital of the World," *LA Times*, February 1, 2015, http://www.latimes.com/business/la-fi-philippines-economy-20150202-story.html.

22. Monica Heller, "The Commodification of Language," *Annual Review of Anthropology* 39 (2010): 109.

23. Shruti Saxena, *Stilettos in the Boardroom* (New Delhi: Zubaan, 2009).

24. Brinda S. Narayan, *Bangalore Calling* (Gurgaon, India: Hachette India, 2011).

25. Chetan Bhagat, *One Night @ the Call Center* (New Delhi: Rupa, 2005).

26. Anna Michal Guttman, "Call Center Cosmopolitanism: Global Capitalism and Local Identity in Indian Fiction," *Postcolonial Text* 12, no. 1 (2017): 11–12.

27. Shehzad Nadeem, "Macauley's (Cyber) Children: The Cultural Politics of Outsourcing in India," *Cultural Sociology* 3, no. 1 (2009): 112.

28. Mehdi Boussebaa, Shuchi Sinha, and Yiannis Gabriel, "Englishization in Offshore Call Centers: A Postcolonial Perspective," *Journal of International Business Studies* 45, no. 9 (2014): 1158–59.

29. A. Aneesh, *Neutral Accent: How Language, Labor, and Life Become Global* (Durham, NC: Duke University Press, 2015), 57.

30. Jan Blommaert, *The Sociolinguistics of Globalization* (Cambridge: Cambridge University Press, 2010), 55–61.

31. Morgan Hartley and Chris Walker, "The Culture Shock of India's Call Centers," *Forbes*, December 12, 2012, http://www.forbes.com/sites/morganhartley/2012/12/16/the-culture-shock-of-indias-call-centers.

32. Datamark, "Why Call Centers Once Outsourced Overseas Are Coming Back to the U.S.," November 20, 2016, https://insights.datamark.net/why-call-centers-once-outsourced-overseas-are-coming-back-to-the-u-s/.

33. Kunal Talgeri and Shelley Singh, "BPO Firms with Indian Operations Have a 3-Step Plan to Manage Anti-Offshoring Wave," *Economic Times*, April 5, 2018, https://economictimes.indiatimes.com/tech/ites/bpos-with-indian-operations-have-a-3-step-plan-to-manage-anti-offshoring/printarticle/63621206.cms.

34. Steve Lohr, "Hello, India? I Need Help with My Math," *New York Times*, October 31, 2007, http://www.nytimes.com/2007/10/31/business/worldbusiness/31butler.html.

35. "How It Works," TutorVista, May 4, 2019, https://web.archive.org/web/20190504082242/http://www.tutorvista.com/howitworks.php.

36. Naz Rassool, *Global Issues in Language, Education, and Development: Perspectives from Postcolonial Countries* (Clevedon, UK: Multilingual Matters, 2007), 133–34.

37. Blommaert, *The Sociolinguistics of Globalization*, 49.

38. Ibid., 56–57.

39. Judy Ravin, "Accent Reduction: Giving Up or Taking On?," Accents International, March 5, 2018, https://www.lessaccent.com/blog/accent-reduction-giving-taking/.

40. Accents International website, https://www.lessaccent.com/about-accents-international/testimonials.

41. Wall Street English website, https://www.wallstreetenglish.com.

42. YouGov and Wall Street English, *Global English Language Report* (2019), 3–5, https://cdn2.hubspot.net/hubfs/1982228/reports/Global%20English%20Language%20Report%202018.pdf.

43. Education First, *English Proficiency Index 2018* (Ranking Report of 100 Countries and Regions by English Skills, Signum International AG, 2018), 14, https://www.ef.com/assetscdn/WIBIwq6RdJvcD9bc8RMd/legacy/___/~/media/centralefcom/epi/downloads/full-reports/v8/ef-epi-2018-english.pdf.

44. Miroslav Beblavý, Brian Fabo, and Karolien Lenaerts, *The Importance of Foreign Language Skills in the Labour Markets of Central and Eastern Europe: An Assessment Based on Data from Online Job Portals*, CEPS Special Report 129 (January 2016), https://wageindicator.org/documents/

publicationslist/publications-2016/beblavy-m-fabo-b-lenaerts-k-2016-the-importance-of-foreign-language-skills-in-the-labour-markets-of-central-and-eastern-europe-an-assessment-based-on-data-from-online-job-portals-ceps-special-report-no-129-janaury-2016-en.

45. "French Workers Fear Their Poor English Is Harming Their Career Chances," *Local (France)*, April 28, 2017, https://www.thelocal.fr/20170428/french-workers-fear-their-poor-english-is-leaving-them-behind.

46. Sara Custer, "British Council: English Vital for MENA," *PIE News*, May 29, 2012, http://thepienews.com/news/british-council-english-vital-for-mena; Elizabeth J. Erling, *The Relationship between English and Employability in the Middle East and North Africa* (British Council, 2015), http://oro.open.ac.uk/44825/1/MENA%20Publication%20Erling%20 Final.pdf.

47. Education First, *English Proficiency Index 2020*, 36.

48. TOEFL, "Table 15," in *TOEFL iBT Test and Score Data Summary 2019* (Princeton, NJ: Educational Testing Service, 2020), 19, https://www.ets.org/s/toefl/pdf/94227_ unlweb.pdf.

49. "First Language," Test Taker Performance 2019, IELTS, https://www.ielts.org/en-us/for-researchers/test-statistics/test-taker-performance

50. "English Language Skills a Key for Mobility and Employment in the Middle East and North Africa," *ICEF Monitor*, April 21, 2015, http://monitor.icef.com/2015/04/english-skills-a-key-for-mobility-and-employment-in-the-middle-east-and-north-africa/.

51. British Council, *English in Mexico: An Examination of Policy, Perceptions, and Influencing Factors* (May 2015), 32, 46, https://www.teachingenglish.org.uk/sites/teacheng/files/English%20in%20Mexico.pdf; British Council, *English in Argentina: An Examination of Policy, Perceptions, and Influencing Factors* (May 2015), 29, 41, https://www.teachingenglish.org.uk/sites/teacheng/files/English%20in%20Argentina.pdf.

52. British Council, *English in Peru: An Examination of Policy, Perceptions, and Influencing Factors* (May 2015), 55, https://www.teachingenglish.org.uk/sites/teacheng/files/English%20 in%20Peru.pdf.

53. Daniela Casale and Dorrit Posel, "English Language Proficiency and Earnings in a Developing Country: The Case of South Africa," *Journal of Socio-Economics* 40 (2011): 392.

54. Pearson, *The Global Learner Survey* (September 2019), 28, https://www.pearson.com/content/dam/global-store/global/resources/Pearson_Global_Learner_Survey_2019.pdf.

55. O. C. S. Wilson, S. Premagowrie, A. H. Baharom, and Muzafar Shah Habibullah, "Impact of Language Augmented Human Capital on Foreign Direct Investment: A Study of Developing Countries," *Academicia: An International Multidisciplinary Research Journal* 6, no. 2 (February 2016): 81–93, http://www.indianjournals.com/ijor.aspx?target= ijor:aca&volume=6&issue=2&article=007.

56. Education First, *English Proficiency Index 2017* (Ranking Report of 100 Countries and Regions by English Skills, Signum International AG, 2017), 5, https://www.ef.edu/assetscdn/WIBIwq6RdJvcD9bc8RMd/legacy/___/~/media/centralefcom/epi/downloads/full-reports/v7/ef-epi-2017-english.pdf.

57. English First, *The English Margin: What Language Means to a Business' Bottom Line* (January 6, 2016), https://www.ef.com/wwen/epi/downloads.

58. Education First, *Global Fluency: How Better Communication Improves Business Performance* (2018), https://www.ef.edu/corporate-lp/global-fluency.

59. Andrew Hill, "Rise of the Multilingual Boss Creates a 'Monoglot Ceiling,'" *Financial Times*, December 2, 2015, https://www.ft.com/content/0dbf22c2-9824-11e5-95c7-d47aa298f769.

60. Schumpeter, "The English Empire," *Economist*, February 15, 2014, https://www.ef.com/wwen/epi/downloads.

61. "The Great English Divide: In Europe, Speaking the Lingua Franca Separates the Haves and the Have-Nots," *Bloomberg Businessweek*, August 12, 2001, https://www.bloomberg.com/news/articles/2001-08-12/the-great-english-divide.

62. Ephrat Livni, "Volkswagen Is Changing Its Official Language from German to English," *Quartz*, December 30, 2016, https://qz.com/875425/volkswagen-is-changing-its-official-language-from-german-to-english.

63. "The Great English Divide," *Bloomberg Businessweek*.

64. Dionino Zappacosta, "Embauche et Compétences Linguistique: Le Point de Vue de L'Entreprise," *Repères-Dorif*, December 2013, 6, https://www.dorif.it/ezine/ezine_articles.php?art_id=148.

65. Steven J. Sacco, "Multilingual Franca: Workplace Language Use within Multilingual Corporations in French West Africa," *Global Advances in Business and Communications Conference and Journal* 7, no. 1, art. 5 (2018): 6, https://commons.emich.edu/cgi/viewcontent.cgi?article=1076&context=gabc.

66. "Rakuten Forges Ahead," editorial, *Japan Times*, May 23, 2015, https://www.japantimes.co.jp/opinion/2015/05/23/editorials/rakuten-forges-ahead-english/.

67. Tsedal Neeley, *The Language of Global Success: How a Common Tongue Transforms Multinational Organizations* (Princeton, NJ: Princeton University Press, 2017); Tsedal Neeley, "Global Business Speaks English," *Harvard Business Review* 90, no. 5 (May 2012): 116-24.

68. Education First, *English Proficiency Index 2018*, 12.

69. Economist Intelligence Unit, *Competing Across Borders: How Cultural and Communication Barriers Affect Business* (2012), 15, https://eiuperspectives.economist.com/economic-development/competing-across-borders.

70. Cambridge English, *English at Work: Global Analysis of Language Skills in the Workplace* (November 2016), 12–13, http://cambridgeenglish.org/images/english-at-work-full-report.pdf.

71. Ibid., 31.

72. Ibid., 19.

73. Anne-Wil Harzing and Markus Pudelko, "Languages Competencies, Policies and Practices in Multinational Corporations: A Comprehensive Review and Comparison of Anglophone, Asian, Continental European and Nordic MNCs," *Journal of World Business* 48, no. 1 (January 2012): 87–97.

74. Andrew Hill, "Rise of the Multilingual Boss Creates a 'Monoglot Ceiling,'" statement of Richard Hardie, chair of UBS Financial Services London), *Financial Times*, December 2, 2015, https://www.ft.com/content/0dbf22c2-9824-11e5-95c7-d47aa298f769.

75. Susanne Ehrenreich, "English as a Business Lingua Franca in a German Multilingual Corporation," *Journal of Business Communication* 47, no. 4 (2010): 420.

76. Terrence G. Wiley, Sarah Catherine K. Moore, and Margaret S. Fee, "Renewing America," Policy Innovation Memorandum no. 24 (Council on Foreign Relations, June 26, 2012), https://www.cfr.org/sites/default/files/pdf/2012/05/Policy_Innovation_Memo24_ForeignLanguage.pdf.

77. "Usage Statistics of Content Languages for Websites," Web Technology Surveys, https://w3techs.com/technologies/overview/content_language; "Internet World Users by Language: Top Ten Languages," Internet World Stats, https://internetworldstats.com/stats7.htm

78. "World Internet Users and Population Statistic 2021 Year-Q1 Estimates," Internet World Stats, https://www.internetworldstats.com/stats.htm.

79. Jochelle Mendonca, "As Non-English Speaking Markets Beckon, IT Firms Boost Language Training," *India Times*, October 10, 2019, https://tech.economictimes.indiatimes.com/news/corporate/as-non-english-speaking-markets-beckon-it-firms-boost-language-training/71510265.

80. Asia Society, "Jobs Tied to International Trade," http://asiasociety.org/files/uploads/127files/JobsFinal.png.

81. Lisa Chau, "Why You Should Learn Another Language," *Economic Intelligence* (*U.S. News* blog), January 29, 2014, http://www.usnews.com/opinion/blogs/economic-intelligence/2014/01/29/the-business-benefits-of-learning-a-foreign-language.

82. Alan J. Feely and Anne-Wil Harzing, "Language Management in Multilingual Companies," *Cross Cultural Management: An International Journal* 10, no. 2 (2003): 43

83. Linda Cohen and Jane Kassis-Henderson, "Revisiting Culture and Language in Global Management Teams: Toward a Multilingual Turn," *International Journal of Cross-Cultural Management* 17, no. 1 (January 2017): 7–22.

84. S. Tamer Cavusgil and Gary Knight, "The Born Global Firm: An Entrepreneurial and Capabilities Perspective on Early and Rapid Internationalization," *Journal of International Business Studies* 46, no. 1 (January 2015): 3–16.

85. Forbes Insights, *Reducing the Impact of Language Barriers* (September 2011), http://www.forbes.com/forbesinsights/language_study_reg.

86. Hans Fenstermacher, "Language Drives Economic Growth, Creates Jobs, and Fosters Competitiveness for U.S. Businesses," written testimony submitted to the U.S. Senate Committee on Homeland Security and Governmental Affairs, Subcommittee on Oversight of Government Management, the Federal Workforce, and the District of Columbia, May 21, 2012, 5, https://www.hsgac.senate.gov/imo/media/doc/Andrew%20Lawless%20Testimony2.pdf.

87. Language Flagship, *What Business Wants: Language Needs in the 21st Century* (2010), 4, https://www.thelanguageflagship.org/media/docs/reports/what_business_wants_report_final_7_09.pdf.

88. Ibid., 6.

89. Ibid., 4.

90. Danielle Duran Baron, "21st Century Global Competitiveness Depends on Foreign Language Master," PRWeb, March 5, 2010, http://www.prweb.com/releases/2010/03/prweb3689604.htm.

91. Forbes Insights, "Reducing the Impact of Language Barriers."

92. Rosetta Stone, *Bilingualism, The Newest Competitive Advantage for Companies* (2011), http://resources.rosettastone.com/CDN/us/pdfs/Biz-Public-Sec/Bilingualism-The-Newest-Competitive-Advantage-for-Companies.pdf.

93. American Council on the Teaching of Foreign Languages, *Making Languages Our Business: Addressing Foreign Language Demand among U.S. Employers* (2019), 4, https://www.leadwithlanguages.org/wp-content/uploads/MakingLanguagesOurBusiness_FullReport.pdf.

94. Cushing Anderson and John F. Gantz, "Skills Requirements for Tomorrow's Best Jobs" (International Data Corporation, October 2013), https://news.microsoft.com/download/presskits/education/docs/IDC_101513.pdf.

95. "Survey of Employers in APEC Economies: U.S. Survey Results," Asia-Pacific Economic Cooperation, April 12, 2017, https://www.apecglobalcompetencies.com/single-post/2016/12/30/Phase-I-Survey-of-Employers-in-APEC-Economies.

96. Rebecca Rubin Damari, William P. Rivers, Richard D. Brecht, Philip Gardner, Catherine Pulupa, and John Robinson, "The Demand for Multilingual Human Capital in the U.S. Labor Market," *Foreign Language Annals* 50, no. 1 (February 28, 2017): 27–28.

97. New American Economy, *Not Lost in Translation: The Growing Importance of Foreign Language Skills in the U.S. Job Market* (March 2017), 4–5, 12–13, 25, http://research.newamericaneconomy.org/wp-content/uploads/2017/03/NAE_Bilingual_V9.pdf.

98. Katie Johnson, "Which Job Seekers Are in Hot Demand? Bilingual Workers," *Boston Globe*, March 13, 2017, https://www.bostonglobe.com/business/2017/03/12/wanted-bilingual-workers/t8C9txqPmwCtIGDHX1jSTI/story.html.

99. American Management Association, *Developing Successful Global Leaders: The Third Annual Study of Challenges and Opportunities 2012* (2012), 17, https://www.shrm.org/ResourcesAndTools/hr-topics/organizational-and-employee-development/Documents/developing-successful-global-leaders.pdf.

100. Shirley J. Daniel, Fujiao Xie, and Ben L. Kedia, "2014 U.S. Business Needs for Employees with International Expertise," *Future of International and Foreign Language Studies*, April 11–13, 2014, https://www.wm.edu/offices/revescenter/globalengagement/internationalization/papers%20and%20presentations/davidsonkediaexec.pdf.

101. CIEP, *Langues et Employabilité (LEMP), Analysis of the Foreign Language Skills Requirements of French Employers* (September 2015), https://www.ecml.at/Portals/1/National%20Contact%20Points/France/FR_CIEP_bibliographie-langues-et-employabilite.pdf.

102. "These Are the Most Important Foreign Languages for the French Jobs Market," *Local (France)*, February 14, 2018, https://www.thelocal.fr/20180214/these-are-the-most-important-languages-for-the-french-jobs-market/#:~:text=After%20Italian%20the%20Arabic%20language,%2C%20Portuguese%2C%20Russian%20and%20Japanese.

103. "El 31% de las ofertas de trabajo requieren saber una lengua extranjera" [31% of job offers require knowing a foreign language], *El Imparcial*, October 3, 2013, https://www.elimparcial.es/noticia/129004/sociedad/el-31-de-las-ofertas-de-trabajo-requieren-saber-una-lengua-extranjera.html.

104. British Council, *Culture at Work: The Value of Intercultural Skills in the Workplace* (2014), https://www.britishcouncil.org/sites/default/files/culture-at-work-report-v2.pdf.

105. Economist Intelligence Unit, *Competing across Borders: How Cultural and Communication Barriers Affect Business* (2012), https://eiuperspectives.economist.com/economic-development/competing-across-borders.

106. Eva Lavric, "Stratégies et identities plurilingues des entreprises et des individus dans les entreprises" [Plurilingual strategies and identities of companies and individuals in companies], *WU Online Papers in International Business Communication, Series One: Intercultural Communication and Language Learning* 7 (2009), 12, http://epub.wu.ac.at/1990.

107. Luisa Araújo, et al., *Languages and Employability* (European Commission, 2015), http://publications.jrc.ec.europa.eu/repository/bitstream/JRC97544/languages%20and%20employabilityonline.pdf.

108. Alejandro Donado, "Foreign Languages and Their Impact on Income and Unemployment," *Beiträge zur Jahrestagung des Vereins für Socialpolitik* 2014, https://www.econstor.eu/bitstream/10419/100288/1/VfS_2014_pid_123.pdf.

109. Grin, Sfreddo, and Vaillancourt, *Economics of the Multilingual Workplace*, 68.

110. Johnson. "What Is a Foreign Language Worth?" *Economist*, March 11, 2014, https://www.economist.com/prospero/2014/03/11/johnson-what-is-a-foreign-language-worth; Albert Saiz and Elena Zoido, *The Returns of Speaking a Second language*, Working Paper 02–16 (Philadelphia: Federal Reserve Bank of Philadelphia, October 2002), https://ideas.repec.org/p/fip/fedpwp/02-16.html.

111. Michele Gazzola and Daniele Mazzacani, "Foreign Language Skills and Employment Status of European Natives: Evidence from Germany, Italy, and Spain," *Empirica* 46 (2019), 733.

112. National Center for Languages, *ELAN: Effects on the European Economy of Shortages of Foreign Language Skills in Enterprise* (December 2006), 5, https://ec.europa.eu/assets/eac/languages/policy/strategic-framework/documents/elan_en.pdf.

113. Grin, Sfreddo, and Vaillancourt, *The Economics of the Multilingual Workplace*, 48–49.

114. European Commission, *Report on Language Management Strategies and Best Practice in European SMEs: The PIMLICO Project* (April 2011), 4, https://op.europa.eu/en/publication-detail/-/publication/7837c78d-445f-49c2-b3c5-2968dd533604.

115. CELAN, *Report on Language Needs in Business: Companies' Linguistic and Language Related Needs in Europe* (European Commission, August 2011), http://www.celan-platform.eu/assets/files/D1.3-Business_Needs_Report-Final.pdf.

116. European Commission, *Eurobarometer Survey: Employers' Perception of Graduate Employability* (December 2010), http://europa.eu/rapid/press-release_MEMO-10-638_en.htm.

117. Ingela Bel Habib, *Multilingual Skills Export Benefits and Better Access to New Emerging Markets* (Sens Public, 2011), http://www.sens-public.org/IMG/pdf/SensPublic_Ingela_Bel_Habib_Report_Multilingual_Skills.pdf.

118. European Commission, "Study on Foreign Language Proficiency and Employability: Executive Summary," *European Journal of Language Policy* 8, no. 2 (2015): 243–53.

119. Imane Khaouja, Ibrahim Rahhal, Mehdi Elouali, Ghita Mezzour, Ismail Kassou, and Kathleen M. Carley, "Analyzing the Needs of the Offshore Sector in Morocco by Mining Job Ads" (paper presented at the IEEE Global Engineering Conference (EDUCON), April 2018), https://ieeexplore.ieee.org/document/8363390.

120. Cambridge Public Policy Strategic Research Initiative, *The Value of Languages* (University of Cambridge, May 2016), https://www.publicpolicy.cam.ac.uk/pdf/value-of-languages.

121. CBI, *The Right Combination: CBI/Pearson Education and Skills Survey 2016* (July 2016), 35, https://epale.ec.europa.eu/sites/default/files/cbi-education-and-skills-survey2016.pdf.

122. James Foreman-Peck and Yi Wang, *The Costs to the UK of Language Deficiencies as Barrier to UK Engagement in Exporting: A Report to UK Trade and Investment* (Cardiff Business School, 2004), 35–36, https://www.gov.uk/government/uploads/system/uploads/

attachment_data/file/309899/Costs_to_UK_of_language_deficiencies_as_barrier_to_
UK_engagement_in_exporting.pdf.

123. CBI, *Educating for the Modern World*, November 2018, 31, https://www.cbi.org.uk/media/
1171/cbi-educating-for-the-modern-world.pdf.

124. Becky Barr, "The Highest Paid Languages of 2017," *Adzuna*, June 22, 2017, https://
www.adzuna.co.uk/blog/2017/06/22/the-highest-paid-languages-of-2017.

125. Teresa Tinsley and Kathryn Board, *Language Trends 2015/16: The State of Language
Learning in Primary and Secondary Schools in England* (British Council, 2016), https://
www.britishcouncil.org/sites/default/files/language_trends_survey_2016_0.pdf.

126. Lucy Pawle, "Language Skills Deficit Costs the UK £48bn a Year," *Guardian*, December
10, 2013, https://www.theguardian.com/education/2013/dec/10/language-skills-
deficit-costs-uk-economy.

127. All-Party Parliamentary Group on Modern Languages, *Manifesto for Languages*
(British Council), https://www.britishcouncil.org/sites/default/files/manifesto_for_
languages.pdf.

128. Baroness Coussins, "UK Withdrawal from the EU and Potential Withdrawal for
the Single Market," *House of Lords*, motion, 11:37 a.m., January 26, 2017, https://
hansard.parliament.uk/Lords/2017-01-26/debates/59755AA8-ED1B-4215-B3AE-
C334CCE167D0/UKWithdrawalFromTheEUAndPotentialWithdrawalFromTheSingleMarket.

129. Teresa Tinsley and Kathryn Board, *Languages for the Future* (British Council, November
2017), https://www.britishcouncil.org/sites/default/files/languages_for_the_future_
2017.pdf.

130. Gino Diño, "How the Public Sector and Regulations Shaped Language Services Demand
in 2018," *Slator*, January 8, 2019, https://slator.com/features/how-the-public-sector-
and-regulations-shaped-language-services-demand-in-2018.

131. Bureau of Labor Statistics, "Interpreters and Translators," September 1, 2020, https://
www.bls.gov/ooh/media-and-communication/interpreters-and-translators.htm.

132. United States Census Bureau, *Language Spoken at Home*, 2019, https://data.census.gov/
cedsci/table?q+S1601&tid=ACSST1Y2019.S1601.

133. United States Census Bureau, "Census Bureau Reports at Least 350 Languages Spoken in
U.S. Homes," press release, November 3, 2015, http://www.census.gov/newsroom/press-
releases/2015/cb15-185.html.

134. Eden Estopace, "How the Public Sector and Regulations Shaped Language Services,"
Slator, December 27, 2017, https://slator.com/demand-drivers/public-sector-regulations-
shaped-language-services-demand-2017.

135. Doximity, "First-Ever National Study to Examine Different Languages Spoken by U.S.
Doctors," press release, October 17, 2017, https://www.doximity.com/press_releases/
first_ever_national_study_to_examine_different_languages_spoken_by_us_doctors.

136. Esther Bond, "Why This Texas Hospital System Is Doubling Down on Hiring In-
House Interpreters," *Slator*, May 23, 2018, https://slator.com/demand-drivers/
why-this-texas-hospital-system-is-doubling-down-on-hiring-in-house-interpreters.

137. Katie Johnson, "Bilingual Workers," *Boston Globe*, March 13, 2017, https://
www.bostonglobe.com/business/2017/03/12/wanted-bilingual-workers/
t8C9txqPmwCtIGDHX1jSTI/story.html.

138. Jennifer Medina, "Anyone Speak K'iche' or Mam? Immigration Courts Overwhelmed by
Indigenous Languages," *New York Times*, March 19, 2019, https://www.nytimes.com/
2019/03/19/us/translators-border-wall-immigration.html.

139. Tom Jawetz and Scott Shuchart, "Language Access Has Life-or-Death Consequences
for Migrants," *Center for American Progress*, February 20, 2019, https://
www.americanprogress.org/issues/immigration/reports/2019/02/20/466144/language-access-
life-death-consequences-migrants.

140. Laura K. Abel, *Language Access in the Federal Courts* (New York: National Center for Access
to Justice at Cardozo Law School, 2013), https://www.migrationpolicy.org/sites/default/
files/language_portal/Language%20Access%20in%20the%20Federal%20Courts_0.pdf;
US Department of Justice, *Language Access in State Courts* (September 2016), https://
www.justice.gov/crt/file/892036/download.

141. Angelo Franco, "Lack of Language Access Is a Nationwide Crisis," *Highbrow Magazine*, February 19, 2018, https://www.highbrowmagazine.com/8892-lack-language-access-nationwide-crisis.

142. Partnership for a New American Economy, *Language Diversity and the Workforce: The Growing Need for Bilingual Workers in Massachusetts' Economy* (2016), http://www.newamericaneconomy.org/wp-content/uploads/2016/06/MA-Biliteracy-Brief.pdf.

143. World Tourism Council, *Travel and Tourism: Economic Impact 2019* (2019), 1, https://www.slovenia.info/uploads/dokumenti/raziskave/raziskave/world2019.pdf.

144. "Translate for TWB," Translators without Borders, https://web.archive.org/web/20200410012307/https://translatorswithoutborders.org/covid-19.

145. California Coronavirus (COVID-19) Response, https://covid19.ca.gov/translate.

146. Lionbridge Technologies, Inc., "Lionbridge Named Largest Language Services Provider in the World," *Cision PR Newswire*, July 11, 2017, https://www.prnewswire.com/news-releases/lionbridge-named-largest-language-services-provider-in-the-world-300485941.html.

147. International Association of Language Centres website, https://www.ialc.org/destinations.

148. "Global Language Games Worth $2.5 Billion by 2026," *Language Magazine*, November 2, 2018, https://www.languagemagazine.com/2018/11/02/global-language-games-worth-2-5-billion-by-2026.

149. Alec Ross, "The Language Barrier Is About to Fall," *Wall Street Journal*, January 29, 2016, https://www.wsj.com/articles/the-language-barrier-is-about-to-fall-1454077968.

150. Jesus Rodriguez, "Latino Outreach or Google Translate? 2020 Dems Bungle Spanish Websites," *Politico*, March 31, 2019, https://www.politico.com/interactives/2019/2020-democrats-spanish-translation.

151. Carol N., "Language AI Won't Replace Human Translators Just Yet—Here's Why," *Tarjama*, December 8, 2020, https://www.tarjama.com/language-ai-wont-replace-human-translators-just-yet-heres-why.

152. George Lakoff and Mark Johnson, *Metaphors We Live By* (1980; repr. Chicago: University of Chicago Press, 2003).

153. Carina Doyle, "Why You Shouldn't Use an Online Translator for Learning French," *Frenchly*, December 28, 2018, https://frenchly.us/online-translators-bad-language-learning.

154. Tatiana Nersessian, "Knowledge Base Is Power: Quick Tips for a Multilingual Help Center," *Unbabel*, July 18, 2019, https://unbabel.com/blog/multilingual-knowledge-base-faqs.

155. Sumant Patil and Patrick Davies, "Use of Google to Translate in Medical Communication: Evaluation of Accuracy," *BMJ* 2014 (December 15, 2014): 349–51, https://www.bmj.com/content/349/bmj.g7392.

156. Sidney Fussell, "Palestinian Man Arrested after Facebook Auto-Translates 'Good Morning' as 'Attack Them.'" *Gizmodo*, October 23, 2017, https://gizmodo.com/palestinian-man-arrested-after-facebook-auto-translates-1819782902.

157. Tanasia Kenney, "Freudian Slip? Translation Gaffe at Major China-Africa Event Describes Relationship as 'Exploitation,'" *Atlanta Black Star*, February 12, 2019, https://atlantablackstar.com/2019/02/12/freudian-slip-translation-gaffe-at-major-china-africa-event-describes-relationship-as-exploitation.

158. Yeganeh Torbati, "Google Says Google Translate Can't Replace Human Translators. Immigration Officials Have Used It to Vet Refugees," *Alternet*, September 26, 2019, https://www.alternet.org/2019/09/google-says-google-translate-cant-replace-human-translators-immigration-officials-have-used-it-to-vet-refugees.

159. "Cloud Translation: Attribution Requirements," Google, https://cloud.google.com/translate/attribution.

Conclusion

1. Hans de Wit, "Dutch Cuts to Internationalization Send the Wrong Message," *Inside Higher Ed*, July 22, 2019, https://www.insidehighered.com/blogs/world-view/dutch-cuts-internationalization-send-wrong-message.

2. Stephanie Rudwick, "Englishes and Cosmopolitanisms in South Africa," *Human Affairs* 28 (2018): 426.

3. Neville Alexander, *Language Education Policy, National and Subnational Identities in South Africa* (Strasbourg, France: Council of Europe, 2003), 19, https://citeseerx.ist.psu.edu/viewdoc/download?doi=10.1.1.476.2445&rep=rep1&type=pdf.

4. Nelson Flores, "The Unexamined Relationship Between Neoliberalism and Plurilingualism: A Cautionary Tale," *TESOL Quarterly* 47, no. 3 (September 2013): 500–520.

5. Alexandre Duchêne and Monica Heller, eds., *Language in Late Capitalism: Pride and Profit* (New York: Routledge, 2012), 6–14.

6. Will Kymlicka, *Politics in the Vernacular* (Oxford: Oxford University Press, 2001), 216.

7. American Academy of Arts and Sciences, *The Importance of Languages in Global Context: An International Call to Action* (statement, 2020), https://www.amacad.org/sites/default/files/media/document/2020-11/Joint-Statement-on-Languages.pdf.

INDEX

For the benefit of digital users, indexed terms that span two pages (e.g., 52–53) may, on occasion, appear on only one of those pages.